THE COMPLETE
RHYMING
DICTIONARY
AND
POET'S CRAFT BOOK

THE COMPLETE
RHYMING
DICTIONARY
AND
POET'S CRAFT BOOK

Edited by

CLEMENT WOOD

GARDEN CITY PUBLISHING CO., INC.
Garden City, New York

TO GLORIA GODDARD

ACKNOWLEDGMENTS

ACKNOWLEDGMENT is gratefully made to the following publishers and poets, for the portions of their work used as illustrations herein:

Publisher	Author	Poem Source
Boni & Liveright	Samuel Hoffenstein	Poems in Praise of Practically Nothing
The Century Company	Brander Matthews	En Route
Dodd Mead & Company	Austin Dobson	July; The Ballade of Prose and Rhyme
Dodd Mead & Company	Carolyn Wells	Four Limericks
Doubleday, Doran & Company	Rudyard Kipling	The Sons of Martha
Henry Holt & Company	Walter de la Mare	The Listeners
Henry Holt & Company	Robert Frost	The Death of the Hired Man; The Black Cottage; "Out, Out—"
Henry Holt & Company	Carl Sandburg	Cahoots; Cool Tombs; Fog
Houghton, Mifflin & Company	Guy Wetmore Carryll	How the Helpmate of Bluebeard Made Free with a Door
Alfred A. Knopf, Inc.	John V. A. Weaver	Sonnet
The Macmillan Company	Edwin Arlington Robinson	Merlin; Roman Bartholow
Manas Press	Adelaide Crapsey	Triad
	Samuel Minturn Peck	"Before the Dawn"
The Poets Press	Clement Wood	Canopus; The Flight of the Eagle
Charles Scribner's Sons	Henry Cuyler Bunner	A Pitcher of Mignonette; Behold the Deeds!
Charles Scribner's Sons	William Ernest Henley	Ballade of Dead Actors
Charles Scribner's Sons	Edwin Arlington Robinson	The House on the Hill
Small, Maynard & Company	Charlotte Perkins Gilman	Homes; A Man Must Live
Frederick A. Stokes Company	Alfred Noyes	Marchaunt Adventurers

FOREWORD

THE desire to write poetry, or at least acceptable verse, is almost universal. The achievement of this desire may be gained by anyone, without excessive effort. Almost everyone, at some stage of his or her life, has yielded to the seductive siren, and has done his or her best to write poetry. An adequate craftbook on versification is a necessity, when the urge becomes unconquerable.

When the versifier's problem is narrowed down to rhyme, the need for a convenient and logically arranged rhyming dictionary soon becames self-evident. Rhyme is exclusively a matter of sound: what the scientists call phonetics. The logically arranged rhyming dictionary must be arranged scientifically by sound; arranged phonetically, to use the scientific word. The arrangement of rhyming sounds in the present volume is wholly phonetic.

The introductory study of versification is so complete, that the book will answer almost every question on technique that any would-be poet or versifier desires to have answered. Moreover, it provides models for the most intricate forms of poetry and versification that English-speaking poets use. Following a model is at best finger-exercises. But finger-exercises must precede mastery of the keyboard.

The phonetic devices in the volume are simplified from the leading standard dictionaries, by eliminating in general all phonetic signs except those placed above the accented or rhyming syllable. Once these simple phonetic devices are understood and absorbed, poets and versifiers will begin to think accurately, scientifically and phonetically about rhymes and rhyming. The technique of rhyming will become as automatic as the technique of walking: and the poetic energy will be proportionately released for the more effective creation of poetry.

CLEMENT WOOD.

Bozenkill.

vii

CONTENTS

THE POET'S CRAFT BOOK

ix

THE POET'S CRAFT BOOK

POETRY AND VERSIFICATION

Poetry and Verse

THE word *poetry* is often used loosely to mean whatever embodies the products of imagination and fancy, the finer emotions and the sense of ideal beauty. In this lax usage, men speak of "the poetry of motion," the poetry of Rodin or Wagner, the poetry of dahlia-raising. In accurate usage, poetry is a specific fine art, defined as follows:

> Poetry is the expression of thoughts which awake the higher and nobler emotions or their opposites, in words arranged according to some accepted convention.

This definition includes, for instance, Oriental forms of poetry, where the sole convention is the number of syllables to the line. Limiting it to usual Occidental poetry the following definition applies:

> Occidental poetry, in its usual form, is the expression of thoughts which awake the higher and nobler emotions or their opposites, in words whose rhythm tends toward uniformity or regularity, rather than toward variety.

Both prose and poetry have rhythm. But the rhythm of prose tends toward variety; and that of poetry toward regularity. There is no definite dividing line; each poet, each reader and appreciator of poetry, must arrive at his own dividing line. To some, the borderline of poetry includes only the strict regularity of Pope or Dryden, or—

> Baby in the caldron fell,—
> See the grief on mother's brow!
> Mother loved her darling well.
> Darling's quite hard-boiled by now.
> *Baby,* Harry Graham.

No one can quarrel with this, if it is an honest boundary. To others, the magnificent wilder rhythms of Walt Whitman and

Lincoln's *Gettysburg Address* are definitely poetry. No one can quarrel with this either.

The test as to subject-matter is subjective: does the alleged poem awake in the reader the higher and nobler emotions or their opposites? Each reader, appreciator, or poet is final arbiter in this test, as in the test of technique. The expression of thoughts which fail to register emotionally with a reader as poetry is called *verse*. Thus, divided by technique, there are the two classifications, poetry and prose; divided by subject-matter and its emotional effect, there are the two classifications, poetry and verse.

Poetry in Human Affairs

Poetry preceded prose, as a persisting form of literary expression. Writing was unknown to early man; and poetry was far better adapted to be retained in the mind than its more plodding relative, prose. The conventions of poetry formed memory devices which prose lacked. In the beginning, lyric cries, folk wisdom, tales of tribal heroes, formal odes of jubilation or lamentation, religious teachings, philosophies, pseudo-sciences, histories of men, men-gods, gods and peoples, developed first in the form of poetry.

Insofar as the conventions of poetry were artificial and un natural, poetry tended constantly to rigidify and petrify. It became artificial and unnatural, whereas prose continued natural. Man learned to write, and to preserve his writing in stone, papyrus, sheepskin, and paper. At first it was the poetry which was so preserved; at length the art patterns were broken, and humbler and more natural prose began to replace poetry. Today, we look to prose for folk wisdom, actual and fictional narratives, religious teachings, philosophies, scientific writings, and histories. Poetry, as the most concentrated and emotional expression of the soul of man, still should have its place in the lyric outbursts, the songs, of man. But poets, bound by fossilized conventions, have become a tepid social group, their words largely unimportant; and in the large prose tends today to replace poetry entirely. Many of the poets today and tomorrow seek and will to restore poetry to something of its original wide popularity, as a natural and unartificial expression of concentrated emotional speech.

Kings, rulers, statesmen, generals, philosophers, scientists, were once of necessity poets: it was their sole socially acceptable form of expression. This is so no longer. Poets were once doers; they are now at best sayers, increasingly unheard. This is one price of man's extreme specialization. The price paid may be more than the human gain, in this particular.

The Poet's Equipment

The poet, like all artists, is one of the race's sensitives: one of those more finely attuned to phrase the past and the present acceptably, and sense and phrase the future. The first necessary equipment is sincerity. This demands that commonplace phrasings must be avoided, in favor of fresh original expression of individual or group concentrated emotions. If the race recognizes these as its own, to that extent the poet will be hailed as poetically great.

Another essential is technical mastery: adeptness in the craft of poetry, skill in handling all the tools of the trade. Familiarity with all the conventions will enable you to break them and make new ones when your fresh subject-matter demands it. Technical mastery is as easy, and no easier, than learning how to raise better peas than your neighbor, or how to build better bridges and skyscrapers than anyone else. Having learned the craft, anyone with an ear for word-music can improvise flawless heroic blank verse or any other form of blank verse by the hour, or improvise elaborately rhymed sonnets with no appreciable hesitation. This is not poetry. But the familiarity with the craft makes the coming of poetry easier, in the rare hours when the poet has a concentrated word that must be said.

Poetic Greatness

One can become great poetically, either in his own sight alone or in the opinions of others, without knowledge of the craft. Homer, Sappho, Villon, Burns, made their own patterns, or poured their burning emotional beauty into ready-made patterns followed without being comprehended. The definitions of patterns were made afterwards, from a scholastic study of poetry widely recognized as great. Such greatness may be achieved by anyone today—the entirely satisfactory expression of one's soul's yearnings. But the recognition of such greatness today will ordinarily be limited to the poet and his immediate circle of admirers within or without his family.

With a complete technical mastery of the craft of poetry, any poet today can achieve complete greatness in his own sight. Whether he is hailed by others as great, and especially whether or not his name is hailed by his own and subsequent generations as great, depends largely on the extent to which his own concentrated heart-utterances express the desires of the race, in a new, fresh and original form. Given such recognition by the race, and enduring poetic greatness has been achieved. The poet can no more control this than Cnut could act as dictator over the tide.

How Poems Come

Verse upon any theme, and in treatment ranging from the most ponderously serious to the most frivolously flippant, can be manufactured at any time. Its technique is comparatively simple. Its devices, metre, rhyme, alliteration, assonance, consonance, stanza arrangement, may be mastered as easily as multiplication tables.

Poetry comes differently. It is primarily the intellect that manufactures verse; but the intellect plays only a secondary part in creating poetry. The desire that seeks expression, which it finds in the poem, springs from a deeper basic source than thinking. Man, indeed all forms of life, are compact of desires. The fulfilment of one desire causes others to spring hydra-like from its invisible corpse. Psychologists tell us that dreams are likewise expressions of desire, in the form of desires fulfilled: that is, wish-fulfilments. Much thinking is likewise wish-fulfilment; there is truth in Wordsworth's dictum, "The wish is father to the thought." There must be, also, an obstacle to the immediate fulfilment of the wish; otherwise, the poet would proceed to achieve his wish, and have no need for a poem to express it. As one poet has it:

> Singing is sweet; but be sure of this,
> Lips only sing when they cannot kiss.
> *Art,* James Thomson.

Because of the obstacle, a tremendous inner compulsion comes upon the sensitive poet to seek relief by creating his wish-fulfilment in words : and so it is that poems are born. This inner compulsion has, as one of its names, inspiration. Inspiration blows from no outer sky, but from the universe of desires within. The woman's insistent inner compulsion to deliver her child at the appointed hour is hardly more shatteringly imperative than the true poet's insistent inner commandment to write.

At times the whole poem forms itself within the mind, before the first word is written down. At times a couplet, a single line— perhaps the first, but more often the last—or even a phrase or a mood comes first, with the dominant insistence that it be given the intermittent immortality of writing. The wise procedure for the poet is to write down what comes, as it comes, even if only a single line or less is the result. As far as possible, write out the poem without delay, to prevent another visitor from Porlock's silencing part of your poem forever, as Coleridge's *Kubla Khan* was silenced forever.

When the poem or poetic fragment is written down, the critical intellect comes into play. If technical mastery has become habitual, the intellect may have no changes to suggest. The poet who fails to be a critic as well is usually his own self-slayer. More extended poems, of course, require more preparation and slower writing and criticism. In all cases the danger is rather in the overuse of the intellect, than in the use of inspiration.

Originality in Poetry

The easiest way, in poetry, is to rephrase your own emotional reactions in the words and phrases created by the favorite poets of the past: so that a thing is "white as the driven snow," or "red as a June rose." When these similes were first invented, they were creations; their repetition, unless in slightly altered form, is plagiarism or borrowing. Second-rate poets distrust their own vision, which differs in every case from that of every other person in the world; and hence sag into such uncreative repetitions. It is wisest to be true to your own differing vision, and seek to expand the boundaries of poetry by stating your own desires in your own terms.

The weakness of much verse and some poetry of the past is partly traceable to unoriginal teachers of English or versification, who advised their pupils to saturate themselves in this or that poet, and then write. Keats, saturated in Spenser, took a long time to overcome this echoey quality, and emerge into the glorious highland of his *Hyperion*. Many lesser souls never emerge. It is valuable to know the poetry of the past, and love it. But the critical brain should carefully root out every echo, every imitation—unless some alteration in phrasing or meaning makes the altered phrase your own creation.

The present double decade has splendidly altered the technique of versification in poetry, by the addition of freer rhythms, consonance, and other devices in the direction of natural speech. It has altered the themes and subjects of poetry as much, until the *Verboten* sign is unknown to the present generations of poets, as far as themes are concerned. If the speech is natural and conversational; the treatment sincere and original; the craftsmanship matured,—there is no reason in the poet's effort to withhold him from a seat among the immortals.

II

THE TECHNIQUE OF VERSIFICATION: RHYTHM

Accent and Rhythm

RHYTHM is the emphasis structure of successive sounds. It is easy to understand, and not easy to define. In prose and poetry, it means the flow of accented and unaccented syllables. It may be defined as:

The successive rise and fall of sounds, in pitch, stress, or speed; when used of words, depending on accents, pauses, or durational quantities.

In classical Greek and Latin poetry, rhythm was not based on accent, but on the conventionalized time it took to pronounce syllables. Syllables were not accented or unaccented, as in modern poetry, from a standpoint of versification; but were long or short. Since two consonants occurring together made a syllable long, and a short vowel made a syllable short when followed by one consonant, the word *honest* was scanned as short-long: the rhythmic stress occurring on the second syllable, not on the first, as with us. *Honest,* pronounced in the classical Greek or Roman way, would be ta-TUM; with us, it is pronounced rhythmically TUM-ta, the accent falling on the first syllable.

This one example will show why verse written in English according to classical rules of scansion, based upon long and short syllables instead of accent, is unnatural and only slightly pleasing to the ear. It is no more at home among modern poets writing in English than Greek clothing or the Greek language would be.

Modern poetry written in English must be in words whose rhythm, based upon accent, tends toward uniformity, rather than toward variety. Both prose and poetry have rhythm, the stream or flow of accented and unaccented syllables; in prose, the pattern constantly varies, while in poetry it approaches some sort of regularity. This is clearly poetry:

7

Music, when soft voices die,
Vibrates in the memory—
Odours, when sweet violets sicken,
Live within the sense they quicken.

Rose leaves, when the rose is dead,
Are heap'd for the beloved's bed;
And so thy thoughts, when Thou art gone,
Love itself shall slumber on.
"Music, when Soft Voices Die,"
Percy Bysshe Shelley.

It would be no less poetry if it were set up:

Music, when soft voices die, vibrates in the memory. Odours, when sweet violets sicken, live within the sense they quicken. Rose leaves, when the rose is dead, are heap'd for the beloved's bed.

And so thy thoughts, when Thou art gone, Love itself shall slumber on.

It did not take the line-division to make this poetry. Technically, the tendency toward regularity in the rhythm made it definitely verse, and not prose; while its emotional appeal, to most people, makes it poetry. It is equally poetic in either typographic form. Set up the opening of the first chapter of this book in the same line division:

The word poetry is often used
Loosely to mean whatever embodies
The products of imagination
And fancy, the finer emotions

And the sense of ideal beauty.
In this lax usage, men speak of
"The poetry of motion," the poetry
Of Rodin or Wagner, the poetry

This is prose. No magic worked by the line division can bring it any closer to poetry. Only a comparative regularity in the alternation of accented and unaccented syllables can make it acceptable verse; this, plus the proper emotional appeal, alone can make it poetry.

Metre and Metric Feet

Metre is a comparatively regular rhythm in verse or poetry. There are four common metric feet used in English verse. Their names are taken over from classic durational or quantity metres. In the examples below, the accented syllable is marked thus (′), and the unaccented syllables thus (˘). These feet are:

Name of Foot	Scansion	Description	Example	Example scanned	Accent pronunciation
Iamb	˘ ′	Unaccent—accent	Delight	De-light	ta-TUM
Trochee	′ ˘	Accent—unaccent	Going	Go-ing	TUM-ta
Anapest	˘ ˘ ′	Unaccent—unaccent—accent	Appertain	Ap-per-tain	ta-ta-TUM
Dactyl	′ ˘ ˘	Accent—unaccent—unaccent	Merrily	Mer-ri-ly	TUM-ta-ta

The first two feet listed below are occasionally encountered in English verse; the third rarely or never.

Spondee	′ ′	Accent—accent	Headlong	Head-long	TUM-TUM
Amphibrach	˘ ′ ˘	Unaccent—accent—unaccent	Believing	Be-liev-ing	ta-TUM-ta
Pyrrhic	˘ ˘	Unaccent—unaccent	with a	with a	ta-ta

In practice, the spondee may be used as an iamb or as a trochee; in combination, we may have—

$$\text{In head} \mid \text{-long flight}$$

in which the word is used as a trochee;

$$\text{He plunged} \mid \text{head-long}$$

in which the word is used as an iamb.

In actual verse and poetry, never forget that the actual rhythm of the words, as normally uttered in a conversational tone, differs from the artificial scansion pattern adopted. Take one of the most regular five-foot iambic lines in the language:

> The curfew tolls the knell of parting day.
> *Elegy Written in a Country Churchyard,*
> Thomas Gray.

Scanned normally, as this would be spoken, we have the following natural scansion:

> The curfew | tolls | the knell | of parting | day.

Here we have one iamb, two feet consisting of mere accented syllables for which we have no name, and two feet of three syllables each (unaccent—accent—unaccent, or amphibrachs). Yet this is described as an ideal iambic line, because the pattern indubitably is:

> ta TUM   ta TUM   ta TUM   ta TUM   ta TUM

To make the actual line fit the planned iambic pattern, we have to divide words as follows:

> The cur- | few tolls | the knell | of part- | ing day.

Absolutely natural iambic lines are rare:

> And dwell | upon | your grave | when you | are dead.
> *The Comedy of Errors,* William Shakespeare.

A repetition of such lines would be monotonous, unnatural and intrinsically unpoetic.

To show a still further group of variations, the opening of Hamlet's most famous soliloquy, commencing "To be or not to be," is theoretically in the same iambic five-foot pattern: three lines, each consisting theoretically of five ta-TUM's. The actual scansion brings in strange and unusual feet, or groups of unaccents with one accent; and shows that these three lines have only four actual feet apiece (a foot being, in English, normally grouped around one accent), where the pattern called for five in each line:

> To be | or not to be. | That | is the question.
> Whether | 'tis nobler | in the mind | to suffer
> The slings | and arrows | of outrageous | fortune . . .
> *Hamlet,* William Shakespeare.

Here are four feet of two syllables each (two iambs and two trochees) ; four of three syllables each (three amphibrachs and one anapest) ; one of one syllable ; and three of four syllables each (two of one type, one of another). And only four natural feet to each line.

This is acceptable five-foot iambic verse, in the hands of the world's greatest master. In later plays, his variations became more extreme, until at times his rhythms were less regular than Whitman's typical free verse or polyrhythmic poetry.

What is desired, in metric poetry, is a regular pattern, with restrained freedom and variety in its use. The poet should learn to scan his poetry—that is, to mark the accented and unaccented syllables as above, and then to divide it both into the natural speech rhythm and into the artificial pattern rhythm. There is no need for pride, if the poetry is excessively regular. As a rule, that means that it is strained and unnatural in phrasing, and to that extent falls below true greatness in technique.

In reading poetry aloud or to oneself, avoid most of all an unnatural singsong. Never read the lines from Hamlet as if they had been printed :

> to *BE* or *NOT* to *BE* that *IS* the *QUES*tion.
> whe*THER* 'tis *NO*bler *IN* the *MIND* to *SUF*fer
> the *SLINGS* and *AR*rows *OF* out*RA*geous *FOR*tune . . .

Instead, read this and all other poetry as naturally as if it were unpatterned prose. The pattern is there, and will make itself felt. Excellence in reading depends upon naturalness in expression.

Iambic Verse

The commonest line-pattern in English verse is based upon the iamb ($\smile\diagup$). Many more words in English are trochees than iambs. Iambic is the preferred pattern, because such trochaic words are normally introduced by a one-syllabled unaccented article, preposition, or the like. Normally lines do not open with the trochee *hoping,* but rather with such a phrase as *in hoping, for hoping, and hoping, this hoping, if hoping,* and so on.

Lines name the metric pattern ; and are described by the type of foot, and the number of feet to the line. Thus a one-foot iambic line could be written:

>   All hail!

A two-foot iambic line would be:

>   All hail to you!

A three-foot iambic line would be:

>   All hail to you, my friends!

A four-foot iambic line would be:

>   All hail to you, my worthy friends!

A five-foot iambic line would be:

>   All hail to you, my wholly worthy friends!

Note how naturally trochaic words like *wholly* and *worthy* fit into this iambic pattern. This line might have been:

>   In hailing friendship's wholly worthy sons,

in which case four words (hailing, friendship's, wholly, worthy) are complete trochees in themselves: yet are transformed into word-split units in the iambic pattern, by the introductory unaccented word *in* and the concluding accented word *sons*. This is an entirely legitimate following of the iambic pattern, which can be most easily remembered as:

>   ta TUM   ta TUM   ta TUM   ta TUM   ta TUM.

A word ending on an accented syllable is said to have a *masculine* ending; one ending on an unaccented syllable, a *feminine* ending. The iambic pattern may be used with a feminine ending: that is, with the addition of an unaccented syllable to the last foot. A stanza of five lines, successively one-, two-, three-, four-, and five-foot iambic lines with feminine endings, could be manufactured easily:

>   Good morning,
>   Benignant April,
>   With all your rainbow blossoms,
>   With birds all carolling their rapture,
>   With love alive within the hearts of maidens.

The scansion for this would be:

> Good morn- | ing,
> Benig- | nant A- | pril,
> With all | your rain- | bow blos- | soms,
> With birds | all car- | olling | their rap- | ture,
> With love | alive | within | the hearts | of maid- | ens.

This is often described as if the first line, for instance, were a two-foot line, with one syllable missing: and is called catalectic verse. The reality is that of an iambic foot, followed by a loose or unattached unaccented syllable.

Writing iambic verse is as easy as writing any form of verse. Get the metrical pattern firmly in mind:

> ta TUM   ta TUM   ta TUM   ta TUM

and then proceed to let the words flow into this pattern.

Iambic verse may be altered into trochaic at any time, by *adding* an accented syllable to each line's beginning; or by *removing* the opening unaccented syllable. The process may be reversed as easily, thus changing trochaic verse into iambic. Start with this iambic version:

> And then the little Hiawatha
> Remarked unto the old Nokomis,
> I know that hills are edged with valleys.

By adding an accented syllable at the beginning of each line, this becomes trochaic:

> Now and then the little Hiawatha
> Said aloud unto the old Nokomis,
> Well I know that hills are edged with valleys.

By removing the opening unaccented syllable in each iambic line above, the lines are four-foot trochaic:

> Then the little Hiawatha
> Said unto the old Nokomis,
> All the hills are edged with valleys.

This is the regular metre of Longfellow's *Hiawatha,* and is as easy to write as iambic verse.

Trochaic Verse

Trochaic verse is less usual in English than iambic, because the custom of the language is to introduce most remarks with an unaccented syllable or word. Based upon the trochee ($\diagup\ \smile$), the pattern is, in the case of four-foot trochees,

TUM-ta   TUM-ta   TUM-ta   TUM-ta

Hiawatha opens upon this pattern:

> Should you ask me, whence these stories,
> Whence these legends and traditions,
> With the odours of the forest,
> With the dew and damp of meadows.
>   *Hiawatha,* Henry Wadsworth Longfellow.

In natural accent, the first three of the lines quoted have only two accents apiece, and not four: so that the natural scansion, as of the third line, is

> With the odours | of the forest.

Shakespeare commences a witches' incantation with the abrupt staccato natural accent:

> Round about the cauldron go;
> In the poisoned entrails throw.
> Toad, that under cold stone
> Days and nights has thirty-one
> Sweltered venom sleeping got,
> Boil thou first i' the charmed pot.
>   *Macbeth,* William Shakespeare.

An interesting variation here is the use of *cold* as a dissyllable, as if it were pronounced *có-ŏld*. It may be regarded as the one-syllabled *cold,* followed by a pause consuming the length of time it would take to pronounce an unaccented syllable. In any case, it is an effective variant device.

Trochaic verse might certainly be described with propriety as iambic verse, with the introductory unaccented syllable omitted in each line. The description is unimportant; the important thing is to choose, understand, and use adequately the pattern, whatever it is called.

Again, in the sixth line quoted above from *Macbeth,* there is an extra unaccented syllable, a sort of grace-note, added : making the second foot in reality a dactyl :

Boíl thŏu | fírst ĭ' thĕ | chármĕd | pót.

If preferred, though it is less usual, this could be scanned slightly differently :

Boíl thŏu | fírst ĭ' | thĕ chármĕd | pót,

in which case there is an amphibrach in the third foot ; or it might be scanned :

Boíl thŏu | fírst ĭ' | thĕ chár- | mĕd pót,

regarding it as two trochees followed by two iambs. But the accepted pattern is trochaic four-foot, and the custom is to prefer the first scansion given. At any time, within reason dictated by the poet's own inner ear and sense of music, the substitution of an anapest or a dactyl for an iamb or a trochee is permitted. Or the substitution of a spondee (′ ′), and any of the other feet (iamb, trochee, dactyl or spondee, as well as amphibrach etc.) may be substituted for a foot in anapestic verse. Similar substitutions may take place in dactylic verse. The best poetry contains variety within uniformity.

Notice that in the trochaic lines from *Macbeth* the last unaccented syllable is omitted in every line. This again gives an example of catalectic verse. The name is unimportant : a trochaic line may end on a masculine ending, as easily as an iambic line ends on a feminine ending. A dactylic line may end on a trochee or an accented syllable ; an anapestic line may have an extra unaccented syllable, or even two of them, without losing its anapestic character. Variety in uniformity. . . .

Anapestic Verse

The anapest (�’ �’ ′) is a foot of three syllables, the first two unaccented, the last accented. It may be described as an iamb with an extra unaccented syllable added before it. It may be indicated ta ta TUM, so that a three-foot anapestic pattern would be :

ta ta TUM   ta ta TUM   ta ta TUM.

A typical line following this pattern would be:

> To the end of the world in the dawn.

The English language has more accented syllables than many others, and a succession of two unaccented syllables is comparatively infrequent. Constantly the anapestic pattern is broken by a foot called the *amphimacer* ($/ \smile /$), accent—unaccent—accent, giving us a result such as:

> Let me go anywhere I can find,

scanned as anapestic thus:

> Lĕt mĕ gó | ănў̆whére | Ĭ căn fínd,

but having a natural scansion consisting of three amphimacers:

> Lét mĕ gó | ánў̆whére | Í căn fínd.

There are so few natural anapests in the language, that this is usual and permitted. The same thing applies to dactylic verse. Even more unusual three-syllabled feet appear, each with two accents: the antibacchius, ($/ / \smile$), the bacchius, ($\smile / /$), the tribrach ($\smile \smile \smile$), the molossus ($/ / /$). In anapestic and dactylic verse, a fourth syllable, usually unaccented, again like a gracenote, may appear in any foot. So long as such variations please the inner ear, the inner sense of word music, they are aids.

The natural poet will always make his own patterns, knowing that poetry is self-created, and not devised by rigid rules.

Dactylic Verse

The dactyl ($/ \smile \smile$) is a foot of three syllables, the first accented, the next two unaccented. It may be described as a trochee with an extra unaccented syllable added after it. Here is an illustration:

> Cannon to right of them,
> Cannon to left of them,
> Cannon in front of them
>   Volleyed and thundered;
> Stormed at with shot and shell,
> Boldly they fought, and well. . . .
> *The Charge of the Light Brigade,* Alfred Tennyson.

Scanned as dactylic verse, this would appear:

> Cánnŏn tŏ | ríght ŏf thĕm,
> Cánnŏn tŏ | léft ŏf thĕm,
> Cánnŏn ĭn | frónt ŏf thĕm
> Vólleÿĕd ănd | thúndĕrĕd;
> Stórmĕd ăt wĭth | shót ănd shĕll,
> Bóldlÿ thĕy | fóught, ănd wĕll.

As a matter of fact, these last two lines would have a different natural scansion, including amphimacers:

> Stórmĕd ăt wĭth | shót ănd shéll,
> Bóldlÿ thĕy | fóught, ănd wéll.

Once the technique of scansion is mastered, the poet must be his own court of last appeal upon it.

Dactylic verse is not wholly at home in English; and amphibrachic verse (using as its norm the amphibrach, ˘ ⁄ ˘) is as much of an alien. These feet become excessively monotonous in long poems, though they may be used with advantage in brief lyrics.

Variations in Metric Verse

The use of variations in metric verse is widespread. The development of every poet of importance, whose technique did not begin and remain rigid and crystallized, has been in the direction of more and more variety. This is displayed impressively by the development of Shakespeare and of Keats. Little such development is shown in the technique of more rigid minor poets. A few examples must suffice. Shakespeare in his final peak period wrote lines whose natural scansion was as loose as:

A malady

> Mŏst ín- | cídĕnt | tŏ maíds; | bŏld óxlĭps ănd
> The crown imperial; lilies of all kinds,
> Thĕ flów- | ĕr-dĕ-lúce | bĕiŋ óne! | Ŏ, thése | Ĭ láck. . . .
>   *The Winter's Tale,* William Shakespeare.

The most unusual usage is the ending of the second line in the extraordinary foot which seems a spondee followed by a pyrrhic, (´ ´ ⌣ ⌣). The reverse foot opens a line in one of his sonnets,

> Of the wide world | dreaming | on things | to come.
> *Sonnet CVII,* William Shakespeare.

One of the most praised lines in Keats is:

> Robs not | one light | seed from | the feath- | er'd grass.
> *Hyperion,* John Keats.

Here two spondees introduce the rest of the line; the scansion being as if his pattern were—

TUM TUM   TUM TUM   TUM ta   ta TUM   ta TUM

Keats has at least one line, in the same pattern, consisting of five trochees:

> Thea! | Thea! | Thea! | Where is | Saturn?
> *Hyperion,* John Keats.

Robert Frost has such masterly lines as the following, in the same five foot iambic pattern:

> And spread her apron to it. She put out her hand. . . .
> *The Death of the Hired Man,* Robert Frost.
> Strange how such innocence gets its own way.
> *The Black Cottage,* Robert Frost.
> And the saw snarled and rattled, snarled and rattled.
> *"Out, Out—",* Robert Frost.
> So. But the hand was gone already.
> *"Out, Out—",* Robert Frost.

In this last line the monosyllable *So* is followed by a pause that takes the place of a foot and a half. One of Frost's most triumphant variations is:

> Little—less—nothing! And that ended it.
> *"Out, Out—",* Robert Frost.

In natural scansion, this would be:

> Little— | less— | nothing! | And that ended it.

A common variation is an alternation of iamb and anapest, as in this old English ballad:

> Ŏ Ăl- | īsŏn Gróss, | thăt líves | ĭn yŏn tówĕr.
> *Alison Gross*, Old English Ballad.

We find the reverse of this order in a Browning lyric,

> Whĕre thĕ chaf- | finch sings | ŏn thĕ or- | chărd bóugh. . . .
> *Home-Thoughts, from Abroad*, Robert Browning.

So numerous are the variations to which the metric pattern in English can be adapted, to the greater naturalness of the poetry.

Accent Pattern Instead of Metric

Coleridge, in one poem, abandoned the formal metric foot altogether, in favor of a rediscovered old English method of letting the line pattern consist of a definite number of accents, with any number of unaccented syllables, occurring in any order. Here are the opening lines:

> 'Tĭs thĕ mid- | dlĕ ŏf níght | bў thĕ cás- | tlĕ clóck,
> Ănd thĕ owls | hăve awak- | ĕned thĕ crow- | ĭng cóck.
> Tu- | whit! | Tu- | whoo!
> Ănd hark, | agáin; | thĕ crow- | ĭng cóck
> Hŏw drow- | sĭly | ĭt crew.
> *Christabel*, Samuel Taylor Coleridge.

Thomas Hood uses lines consisting of only three accented syllables,

> Stítch! | Stítch! | Stítch!
> Ĭn pov- | ĕrtў, hung- | ĕr ănd dírt. . . .
> *The Song of the Shirt*, Thomas Hood.

This follows the same method of accent versification. Walter de la Mare's most famous poem is built around a pattern of three accents to the line, as the second and fourth line below indicate; he uses unaccented syllables where he pleases:

But on- | ly a host | of phantom listeners
That dwelt | in the lone | house then,
Stood lis- | tening in the qui- | et of the moonlight |
To that voice | from the world | of men.
The Listeners, Walter de la Mare.

Other modern poets have done as much, or more. Variety within uniformity. . . .

Blank Verse and Free Verse

Blank verse means simply unrhymed verse. Any line pattern, if unrhymed, is blank verse. *Heroic blank verse* is unrhymed five foot iambic poetry or verse. Most of Shakespeare is written in heroic blank verse. *Heroic couplets,* beloved of Dryden and Pope, are pairs of five foot iambic lines rhymed with each other.

Free verse may be rhymed or unrhymed, although it is usually unrhymed, since rhyming is an even more unnatural convention of poetry than metre; and the poet who has abandoned formal metre will hardly, as a rule, still use the device of rhyming. Free verse is verse without a metric pattern, but with a wider pattern than metre allows. It still tends toward regularity, rather than variety: and the final court of appeals as to whether any example should be classified as poetry or prose from a standpoint of content, or as verse or prose from a standpoint of technique, is the individual poet or reader himself. To many readers, the following are all poetry:

Lord, thou hast been our dwelling-place in all generations. Before the mountains were brought forth, or ever thou hadst formed the earth and the world, even from everlasting to everlasting, thou art God. Thou turnest man to destruction; and sayest, return, ye children of men. . . . 　　　　　　　　*The Ninetieth Psalm.*

But, in a larger sense, we cannot dedicate—we cannot consecrate—we cannot hallow—this ground. The brave men, living and dead, who struggled here, have consecrated it far above our poor power to add or to detract. The world will little note, nor long remember, what we say here; but it can never forget what they did here. . . .
The Gettsburg Address, Abraham Lincoln.

Out of the cradle endlessly rocking, out of the mockingbird's throat, the musical shuttle, out of the Ninth-month midnight, over the sterile sands, and the fields beyond, where the child leaving his bed wandered alone, bareheaded, barefoot, down from the showered halo, up from the mystic play of shadows twining and twisting as if they were alive. . . .

Out of the Cradle, Endlessly Rocking,
Walt Whitman.

Walt Whitman used the artificial line-division of poetry to present the third of these selections; the King James version of the Bible and Lincoln used the natural line-division so familiar in the printing of prose. Little or nothing is added by the artificial line division:

> Out of the cradle endlessly rocking,
> Out of the mocking-bird's throat, the musical shuttle,
> Out of the Ninth-month midnight,
> Over the sterile sands, and the fields beyond, where the
> child leaving his bed wandered alone, bareheaded,
> barefoot,
> Down from the showered halo,
> Up from the mystic play of shadows twining and
> twisting as if they were alive. . . .

It is poetry, to many, in either form; and the first form is the more natural and readable. Scan the Whitman selection, or any of the others, and the tendency toward regularity of rhythm becomes apparent: a wider regularity, perhaps only an up-rhythm or a down-rhythm; but still inevitably there. This distinguishes free verse from prose, from the technical point of view.

At times writers of free verse let their lines reach surprising lengths, no matter how lovely the music is: thus Sandburg,

> Pocahontas' body, lovely as a poplar, sweet as a
> red haw in November or a pawpaw in May,
> did she wonder? does she remember? in the dust,
> in the cool tombs. . . .

Cool Tombs, Carl Sandburg.

Again, the lines can be extremely brief:

> It sits looking
> over harbor and city

> on silent haunches
> and then moves on.
>
> *Fog,* Carl Sandburg.

The free verse writer devises his own line-division pattern. This form, eliminating the devices of metre and rhyme, calls on the poet to avoid the inconsequential and the trivial, and to write down only his important utterances. If rhyme is a shelter for mediocrity, as Shelley wrote in his preface to *The Revolt of Islam,* free verse is a test of the best that the poet has in him.

Line Length in Verse

Oliver Wendell Holmes, himself a doctor, advanced the theory that line length in verse marked physiologically the normal breathing of the poet. In other words, a breath should be taken at the end of each line; and the line should be no longer than the poet's ability to hold his breath. No artificial line division is used in prose, to indicate where a breath should be taken. There is no greater reason for artificial line division in poetry. It still remains true that the long Greek lines, each consisting of six feet, called for huge-breasted warrior-bards to chant them; that the norm of English verse, the five-foot iambic line, indicates a lesser chest-expansion in the typical English poet; and that the briefer modern tendency shows a further deterioration in the chest-expansion of poets.

Where poetry consists in *end-stopped* lines—lines with a natural pause at the end of each line—there is more reason for an artificial line division. Shakespeare began so; many poets never get beyond this, in the main. But when we come to poetry like—

> We are such stuff
> As dreams are made on, and our little life
> Is rounded with a sleep,
>
> *The Tempest,* William Shakespeare.

the break comes after *on,* and not after *stuff* or *life;* and the last reason for the artificial line division has vanished.

A sonnet set up in this manner appears:

O bitter moon, O cold and bitter moon, climbing your midnight hillside of bleak sky, the earth, as you, once knew a blazing noon.

Night brings the silver hour when she will die. We shall be cold as
you are, and as bitter, icily circling toward a tepid fire, playing at
life with our deceitful glitter, past joy, past hope, forever past desire.

Yet still the forest lifts its leafy wings to flutter for a while before
the chill. And still the careless heart is gay, and sings in the green
temple on the dusty hill. And the gulls tumble, and the homing ships
peer for the harbor. . . .

And the sand drips.

The Flight of the Eagle, v, Clement Wood.

In an earlier volume, this had appeared with the usual line-division
of poetry as ordinarily printed. Rhyme can occur of course in
ordinary prose, although this usage is extremely rare. Where the
rhythm of verse is used, as in the sonnet quoted, it is possible for
poets to use the line and paragraph division usual to prose, if this
is desired.

IMPORTANT CLASSICAL TERMS FOR POETIC DEVICES

VERSES AND GROUPS OF VERSES

Classical Name	Common Name, or Explanation
Monometer	A verse containing one metrical foot.
Dimeter	A verse containing two metrical feet.
Dipody	A measure consisting of two metrical feet; a ditrochee.
Trimeter	A verse containing three metrical feet.
Tetrameter	A verse containing four metrical feet.
Pentameter	A verse containing five metrical feet.
Hexameter	A verse containing six metrical feet.
Heptameter	A verse containing seven metrical feet.
Octometer	A verse containing eight metrical feet.
Distich	A strophic verse of two lines, usually called a couplet today.

UNUSUAL METRIC FEET

Tribrach	Three unaccented syllables	⌣ ⌣ ⌣
Molossus	Three accented syllables	/ / /
Amphimacer	Accent, unaccent, accent	/ ⌣ /
Bacchius	Unaccent, accent, accent	⌣ / /
Antibacchius	Accent, accent, unaccent	/ / ⌣

Ditrochee	Two trochees regarded as a compound foot	/ ◡ / ◡
Paeon	Accent, unaccent, unaccent, unaccent	/ ◡ ◡ ◡
Choriamb	Accent, unaccent, unaccent, accent	/ ◡ ◡ /
Epitrite	Three accents and one unaccent: of the 1st, 2nd, 3rd or fourth class, depending on the location of the unaccented syllable	◡ / / / / ◡ / / / / ◡ / / / / ◡

OTHER TERMS

Classical Name	*Explanation*
Acatalectic Verse	Verse not defective in the last foot; verse complete in its number of syllables.
Arsis	The lighter or unstressed part of a foot, especially in quantitative verse; later, the accented syllable of a foot.
Caesura	A break in a verse caused by the ending of a word within a foot. A *masculine caesura* follows the thesis, or stressed part of a foot. A *feminine caesura* follows the arsis or unstressed part. A *trithemimeral caesura* comes after the third half foot, which means in the second foot; a *penthemimeral caesura,* after the fifth half foot; a *hepthemimeral caesura,* after the seventh half foot; and so on. A *bucolic caesura,* in dactylic hexameter, is a caesura occurring in the fourth foot, especially in pastoral poetry.
Catalectic Verse	Verse lacking a syllable at the beginning, or terminating in an imperfect foot.
Diaeresis, Dieresis	The break caused by the coincidence of the end of a foot with the end of a word. *Bucolic diaeresis,* a diaeresis occurring in the fourth foot, especially in pastoral poetry.
Enjambement	The extension of the sentence beyond the limitations of the distich.
Ictus	Metrical stress.
Thesis	The heavier or stressed part of a foot in classical prosody, especially in quantitative verse; later, the unaccented syllable or syllables of a verse.

III

THE TECHNIQUE OF VERSIFICATION: RHYME

Correct and Incorrect Rhyme

RHYME is as simple to define as rhythm is difficult.

Rhyme is the identity in sound of an accented vowel in a word,
usually the last one accented, and of all consonantal and
vowel sounds following it; with a difference in the sound
of the consonant immediately preceding the accented vowel.
Rhyme deals exclusively with sounds, and has nothing to do with
spelling. The rhyming dictionary terminating this book is strictly
phonetic, and therefore logical and useful.

Correct rhymes may be spelled alike:

<blockquote>ate, plate, mate, abate, syncopate.</blockquote>

They may be spelled differently:

<blockquote>ate, bait, straight, freight.</blockquote>

In this case the spelling is immaterial.

So called "eye rhymes,"—that is, words spelt alike that look
alike but are pronounced differently—are not rhymes at all; they
slip into versification, if at all, as *consonance,* which will be dis-
cussed later. That is, the incorrect rhyme

<blockquote>earth, hearth,</blockquote>

so popular among English versifiers, is no more a rhyme than
the following sets of words identically spelled, but pronounced
differently:

<blockquote>
cow, blow
climber, timber
finger, ginger, singer
cough, enough, plough, though, through.
</blockquote>

Identities do not rhyme, no matter what the spelling is; since
the preceding consonantal sounds must differ. The following are
identities, and not rhymes:

> bay, obey
> bare, bear, forbear
> laying, overlaying
> ability, possibility, probability.

Sounds *almost* alike, after the identical accented vowel sounds, do not rhyme. These are properly called assonance, and have not succeeded as a versification device in English. Examples are:

> main, game, reins, lamed
> hate, shape, played
> feed, sleet, creep
> sandwich, orange, lozenge
> childhood, wildwood
> Norfolk, war talk
> anguish, Flatbush
> silver, deliver

You can find examples of incorrect rhymes in poems by many accepted poets, and in a much higher percentage of popular songs and newspaper versification. Two of the above examples were taken directly out of songs nationally popular. Slovenly rhyming is one of the sure signs of mediocrity in versification. Learn correct rhyming first; then, if you wish to break the rule you understand, that is your privilege.

The language's poverty in rhyming has caused the following almost-rhymes to become widely accepted:

> given, Heaven; bosom, blossom; shadow, meadow;
> God, road; war, more; bliss, is; was, grass.

Among widely used "eye rhymes," which are not rhymes at all, but mere identities in spelling, are:

> earth, hearth; bare, are; north, forth; real, steal.

Bosom-blossom, was-grass, are combinations of consonance and assonance; *bliss-is* is assonance; the others in the first list are consonance. The first three pairs in the second set are acceptable consonance; *real, steal* is an attempt to rhyme a two-syllabled word with a one-syllabled one, and has no justification from any standpoint. Use consonance or assonance purposely, if desired; but always know that this is not correct rhyming.

If the poet is tone-deaf as to sounds, it is best to rely upon the phonetic symbols above each group of rhyming words in the rhyming dictionary that terminates this book, or upon dictionary markings. Many people can not distinguish the obvious difference in sounds between this pair of words, which do not rhyme :

north, forth.

Take away the *th* sound, and many people still hear no difference between this pair of words, which do not rhyme :

nor, fore.

Take away the *r* sound, and some people still hear no difference between this pair of words, which do not rhyme :

gnaw, foe.

Gnaw plus *r* plus *th* can not rhyme with *foe* plus *r* plus *th*. If in doubt as to such off-rhymes, follow the phonetic markings.

A third common error in rhyming comes from such mispronunciations as dropping a terminal -*g*. These do not rhyme :

martin, parting.
herding, burden.

They may be rhymed colloquially, that is, in quoted words, as follows :

martin, partin',
herdin', burden,

the latter being not quite a rhyme, at that. But unless writing colloquially, do not use such incorrect rhymes as those given first above. A similar error comes from ignoring the *r* sounds, which causes such off-rhymes as :

court (pronounced *cou't,* like *coat*), boat
Lord (pronounced *Lawd*), gaud.

Rhymes can be made of two or more words. Here are examples of perfect rhymes :

satin, flat in.
Quentin, went in.
pray tin, hate in.

Such couplings are more appropriate to light and humorous verse than to serious poetry. Rhyming must always give the effect of unobtrusive *naturalness,* or it fails of its proper effect.

Robert Browning is in a class by himself in fantastic many-word rhymings and near-rhymings, often in serious verse:

> The wolf, fox, bear and monkey
> By piping advice in one key. . . .
> *Pacchiarotto, and How He Worked*
> *in Distemper, et cetera,*
>   Robert Browning.

This is not a rhyme, because *monkey* is, phonetically, a rhyme sound for *ŭngki,* or at best *ŭngke;* and *one key* is, phonetically, a rhyme sound for *ŭnkē:* the unguessed *g* sound in the first spoiling it as a rhyme. Again, in the same poem, he uses this fantastic coupling:

> While, treading down rose and ranunculus,
> You *Tommy-make-room-for-your-uncle-us!*

Ranunculus has as its rhyme sound *ungk'ū-lus;* the next line, *ŭngk'ool-us:* a minor difference, but enough to spoil the rhyme. Much closer is Byron's celebrated couplet:

> O ye lords of ladies intel*lectual,*
> Inform us truly, have they not hen*pecked you all?*
>   *Don Juan,* I, xxii, Lord Byron.

The unaccented last syllable of the first line differs from the unaccented last syllable of the second with the difference of *ă* and *ô.* Barham furnishes many perfect many-worded rhymes, such as:

> Should it even set fire to one's castle and *burn it, you're*
> Amply insured for both building and *furniture.* . . .
>   *Sir Rupert the Fearless,*
>   Richard Harris Barham (Thomas Ingoldsby).

Samuel Hoffenstein furnishes a splendid example:

> You haven't the nerve to take bi*chloride;*
> You lie up nights till you're gaunt and *sore-eyed,*
>   *Poems in Praise of Practically Nothing,*
>   Samuel Hoffenstein.

In using such rhyme combinations, it is wise to put the combination with the inevitable sound first: *bichloride;* following this with the combination of words to rhyme with it. Thus W. S. Gilbert, a master rhymester, uses in this order:

> monotony, got any.
> cerebellum too, tell 'em to.

In light and humorous verse, such rhyming cleverness is a crown; in serious verse, if used sparingly, it is permitted.

Function and Types of Rhyme

In serious verse, since obvious cleverness defeats the appeal to the serious emotions, rhyming should be unobtrusive. To have your rhyme words merely conveniences demanded by your rhyming pattern is one of the chief faults of rhymed verse.

Rhyme is a potent shaper. Once you have written down a line of verse or poetry, and intend to have the next line or the next line but one rhyme with it, your choice of terminal words for the rhyming line is limited by the limited rhyming resources of the language. If a poet commences,

> October is the wildest month,

he has estopped himself from any rhyme; since *month* has no rhyme in English.

Assuming that the first line's rhyming word has certain rhyming mates, the choice of terminal rhyme words for the rhyming line is limited to these; and the direction of the poet's thought and its expression must be deflected into some natural use of one of these rhyming mate words. Rhyming is a brain-stimulant, and may even spur on the poetic imagination. The meaning of the planned poem may have been clear in the mind; but its expression, if rhyme is used, must work in limited fields, and only the master achieves in these that finality of natural utterance which is one of the charms of great poetry.

To the authentic poet, especially the living poet, there is no such thing as *poetic license:* the right to warp and twist the language out of its natural order or grammar, to suit the exigencies of rhyme. Mr. Browning continued his *Tommy-make-room-for-your-uncle-us* couplet with this:

> Quick march! for Xanthippe, my housemaid,
> If once on your pates she a souse made. . . .
> I would not for worlds be your place in,
> Recipient of slops from the basin!

What Browning meant, in the direct natural order, was:

> Quick march! for Xanthippe, my housemaid,
> If once she made a souse on your pates,
> I would not for worlds be in your place,
> Recipient of slops from the basin!

Even this is unnatural; the real order would be, "Quick march! for if once Xanthippe, my housemaid, made . . ." etc. Let us suppose that inspiration worked with him in the erratic fashion quoted above. Then would be the time for the critical sense to come in, and rigorously to eliminate all such evidences of poetic license—inversions, ungrammatical constructions, and the like. Not one has a place in poetry, more than in speech.

This is a rigid rule to lay down. It is not any individual's rule. It is the rule that Shakespeare followed, when he wrote:

> Tomorrow, and tomorrow, and tomorrow,
> Creeps in this petty pace from day to day
> To the last syllable of recorded time,
> And all our yesterdays have lighted fools
> The way to dusty death. Out, out, brief candle!
> Life's but a walking shadow, a poor player
> That struts and frets his hour upon the stage
> And then is heard no more; it is a tale
> Told by an idiot, full of sound and fury,
> Signifying nothing.
>
> *Macbeth,* William Shakespeare.

This was written some three hundred years ago. There is not an obsolete or even archaic word in it, not a strained construction, not an inversion or instance of ungrammatical poetic license. The quotation given in fragmentary form from Browning, which includes *ranunculus, homunculus, skoramis,* and countless inversions, was outdated long ago: the words of Shakespeare live. The best of Burns, of Shelley, of the Keats of *Hyperion,* of the best among the modern poets, always follows this rule: no inversions, no archaisms, no poetic license. This is the price of a chance for wide poetic greatness.

To return to the strict technique of rhyming, one-syllabled rhymes are called single or masculine rhymes. Examples are:

> we, flee, sea, apostrophe, harmony.
> disk, tamarisk, odalisque.
> fling, sing, carolling.

In the last pair of the first grouping, and the third rhymes in the others, note that only a secondary accent falls on the rhyming syllable. This is enough. A rhyme may be more smothered, if read naturally,—a modern variation in which it may be said that an accented syllable is rhymed with an unaccented one: such as *anguish, wish; ring, wedding.* Used sparingly, this is effective.

Two-syllabled rhymes are called double or feminine rhymes. Examples are:

> ocean, motion, devotion.
> traded, aided, play did.
> see us, flee us.

Three-syllabled rhymes are called triple rhymes. Examples:

> saleable, mailable.
> lyrical, miracle, empirical, satirical.
> going now, blowing now.
> rest of it, best of it, palimpsest of it.

There may be rhymes, especially in light verse, of four or even more syllables. A rhyme like the one last given shows little cleverness, since it is merely "rest, best, palimpsest" with the phrase "of it" added. The lack of cleverness makes it more suitable for serious poetry than for light verse.

End rhyme is used at the end of the lines. Here is an example, the rhyming words being italicized, and the rhyme scheme indicated by the corresponding numerals:

> Gather ye rose-buds while ye *may,*   1
>   Old Time is still *a-flying;*   2
> And this same flower that smiles *today,*   1
>   Tomorrow will be *dying.*   2
>   *Counsel to Girls,* Robert Herrick.

Rhyme 1 is a single or masculine rhyme; rhyme 2 is a double or feminine rhyme.

Internal rhyme is rhyme used within the line, to give added effectiveness by a closer repetition of the rhyming sounds.

"Each day, all day," these poor folk say,
"In the same old *year-long, drear-long* way,
We *weave* in the *mills* and *heave* in the *kilns,*
We *sieve* mine-meshes under the hills,
And *thieve* much gold from the Devil's bank tills,
To *relieve,* O God, what manner of ills?"

The Symphony, Sidney Lanier.

Here *year-long* rhymes internally with *drear-long; weave, heave, sieve, thieve* and *relieve* are further internal rhymes; and *mills* is an internal rhyme to *kilns* and the three next end rhymes.

Undesirable Rhymes

Incorrect rhymes, or rhymes constructed by straining the natural expression into inversions and grammatical perversions, excused on the outworn plea of poetic license, are always undesirable. Quite as undesirable are rhymes which are hackneyed and overworked, such as:

kiss, bliss.
yearn, burn; yearning, burning.
love, dove, above.
fire, desire.
trees, breeze.

These are unobjectionable technically. But they have been so used and overused by other poets, that the only excuse for them today is use in an entirely new manner.

It is the fact that most rhymes have been comparatively overworked that has caused the tendency toward consonance, which is such a marked feature of modern poetry, from Emily Dickinson onward.

Alliteration

Alliteration, like rhyme, is a repetition of sounds. But the sound repeated is only the initial consonant of syllables or words. This was one of the major devices of Anglo-Saxon poetry, which did not use rhyme. Langland's *Piers Plowman* opens:

In a *s*ummer *s*eason, when *s*oft was the *s*un,
I *sh*ope me in *sh*roudes, as I a *sh*eep were.
The Vision of Piers Plowman, William Langland.

Alliteration is used effectively by later poets in connection with rhyme, as this example illustrates :

> Whether *t*empter sent, or whether *t*empest *t*ossed thee here ashore,
> *D*esolate yet all un*d*aunted, on this *d*esert land enchanted,
> In this *h*ome by *H*orror *h*aunted, tell me truly, I implore.
> > *The Raven,* Edgar Allan Poe.

If not overused, this is highly effective. Swinburne was one of the masters of alliteration, tending to overuse it, as in—

> The *l*ilies and *l*anguors of *v*irtue
> For the *r*oses and *r*apture of *v*ice.
> > *Dolores,* Algernon Charles Swinburne.

Where there is no sense of unnaturalness in the repetition of allitrative sounds, it may be successfully employed.

Assonance

Assonance, called also *vowel rhyme,* consists in the identity of the final accented vowel sound, with dissimilarity in the subsequent consonantal and vowel sounds. It was used in Provencal and Old French poetry, and is still used in Spanish. George Eliot tried unsuccessfully to introduce it into English, the assonances being italicized :

> Maiden crowned with glossy *blackness,*
> Lithe as panther forest-*roaming,*
> Long-armed naead, when she *dances,*
> On the stream of ether *floating,*
> Bright, O bright Fedalma !
> > *Song of Joan,* in *The Spanish Gipsy,*
> > > George Eliot.

The repetition here is not sufficiently marked to make this device popular in English versification. Typical groups of assonantal masculine or single-rhymed endings are :

> grab, crack, had, tan, sham, hang, fat
> face, shade, hate, pain, claim, male
> led, wreck, hem, then, set, step
> bide, kine, fight, pipe, wise, advice

In feminine endings, we would have:

> aiming, faded, scraping, hailing, painter, lateness
> roaming, floated, coping, goader, golden
> coming, dumbness, stubborn, rustle

Unpopular so far, at any time assonance may achieve a popularity in English versification.

Consonance

Consonance, also loosely called *off rhymes, sour rhymes,* and *analyzed rhymes,* consists in an identity of all consonantal and vowel sounds after the accented vowel; and a difference in the accented vowels. An improvised model would be:

> There's a golden willow
>   Underneath a hill,
> By a babbling shallow
>   Brook and waterfall;
>
> And a mill-wheel turning
>   Under moon and sun,
> As if gently scorning
>   Time and tide and man.

There can be any combination of end and internal consonance with end or internal rhyme in the same poem, according to the best modern practice: the poet himself being the judge of what form is most pleasing to his inner sense of music, and that of his prospective readers.

Edna St. Vincent Millay, in *The Poet and His Book,* uses these pairs of words in consonance:

> worry, bury; withered, gathered; cluttered, spattered;
>   quarrel, laurel; hunters, winter's; valleys, bellies.

She also twice uses assonance:

> cupboard, upward; only, homely.

Elinor Wylie uses such instances of consonance as:

> bloody, body; people, ripple; mourner, corner;
>   primer, dreamer; standard, pondered; noble,
>   trouble; music, physic; Circe, hearsay; Vulcan,

falcon; languish, distinguish; lost, ghost;
sword, lord; suns, bronze;

and many more. Emily Dickinson is more lavish in her use of consonance than any of these.

The reason has been hinted before: the limited field of rhymes in the language, in spite of the impressive length of any rhyming dictionary. One advantage of a phonetic rhyming dictionary is that it makes the use of precise and accurate consonance possible. Words are arranged by rhyme, and not by consonance; and yet the phonetic arrangement gives a start toward arriving at accurate consonance. If the following method is used, consonance can be achieved by little more effort than is required for rhyme.

There are five *a* sounds that occur in accented syllables; three *e*'s; two *i*'s; six *o*'s; and three *u*'s, or a total of nineteen vowel sounds appearing in accented syllables. Most of these sets are grouped together: most of the *a*'s; two of the *e*'s (omitting the *e* followed by *r,* which appears only when *er* is reached); both of the *i*'s, and so on. Thus *ĀD* is followed by *ĂD* and this by *ÄD:* so that we may proceed directly from rhyming sounds like *aid* to *sad* and then to *charade.* In double rhymes, *Ō'li, ÔL'i* and *ŎL'i* follow in regular sequence; thus *holy, Macaulay,* and *folly* are near neighbors.

Suppose it is desired to locate all the consonance sounds possible for a line ending with *holy.* Turn under the *a*'s to all the phonetic symbols similar to *Ō'li—Ā'li* (as, *daily*) *ĂL'i* (as, *alley*); under *e,* to *Ē'li* (as, *freely*), *ĔL'i* (as, *jelly*); under *i,* to *Ī'li* (as, *drily*) and *ĬL'i* (as, *hilly*); also under *o* to *ŎOL'i* (as, *woolly*), *OIL'i* (as, *oily*); under *u,* to *Ū'li* (as, *truly*) and *ŬL'i* (as, *dully*). Look up also *OUL'i* and other possible vowel combinations, to make sure there are no rhyme sounds under them. And now the poet has an accurate test to see which words are in precise consonance with *holy,* and which are not.

Thus this most modern of all sound-repetition devices in English versification can be achieved most perfectly through the use of a phonetic rhyming dictionary. The phonetic symbols, of course, must be in precise alphabetical order. Turn, under each of the five vowels (not forgetting that the vowel sounds OI, OO and OU come alphabetically also), to the vowel followed by the identical consonant and vowel sounds following the accented vowel in the rhymed syllable you wish consonances for; and all consonances that the lists of words affords will be found.

There is small adventure in rhyming, except in the made rhymes of two or more words more common to light verse. Compilers of rhyming dictionaries have completed the adventure, long ago. There is great adventure in the use of consonance, which expands the sound-repetition resources of the language. It is possible to write a poem where not one of the consonance couplets has been used before. The adventurous will not overlook this.

Your Mental Rhyming Dictionary

At times it is inconvenient or impossible to have a rhyming dictionary available. Especially where the poet desires to write such a piece of formal verse as a ballade, requiring fourteen rhymes on one sound, no two of which could be identical, it is advisable to be able to improvise your own temporary rhyming dictionary.

The method is simple. First write down all the single, double and triple consonantal sounds you can remember. It is not necessary to write down all of them, although for your convenience the list on opposite page is approximately complete.

Having jotted down as many of these as you remember, test the rhyme sound desired against this table, and write out the results. Thus, if the rhymes to *aye*, the long *Ā* sound, are desired, the poet would get, to begin with, of the single consonantal sounds:

> aye, bay, day, fay, gay, hay, jay, kay or cay, lay, may, nay or neigh, pay, ray, say, decolleté for the *t* sound, survey for the *v* sound, way, yea.

Be careful, when a one-syllabled rhyme in such an instance is missing, to use ingenuity to find longer words with the desired rhyme, as *decolleté, survey*.

Then, for the double consonantal sound rhymes, the following could be added:

> redoublé for the *bl* sound, bray, dray, flay, fray, gray, clay, McCrae for the *cr* sound, play, pray or prey, shay, risqué

Single (Vowel)	*Double*	*Triple*	*Rare*
B	BL		BW
	BR		
—	CH		
D	DR		DW
F	FL		
	FR		
G	GL		GW
	GR		
H			
J			
K (C)	KL (CL)		
	KR (CR)		
L			
M			
N			
P	PL		PW
	PR		
Q (KW)			
R			
S	SH	SHR	
	SK (SC)	SKR (SCR)	
	SL		
	SM		
	SN		
	SP	SPL	
		SPR	
	SQ (SKW)		
	ST	STR	
	SV		
	SW		
T	TH		
	th	thR	
	TR		
	TW		
V			VL
W			
Y			
Z			ZH
			ZL

> for the *sk* sound, slay, dismay perhaps for the *sm* sound,
> stay, sway, they, tray, tway.

In addition, the triple consonantal sounds would give:

> splay, spray, stray.

Altogether, this has furnished thirty-nine rhymes for *aye*: and
this is more than enough to satisfy the requirements of any formal
verse.

Suppose only four rhymes for the purposes of the rhyming
pattern are needed, and the poet decides to use *huge* as one of them.
Using the above rhyming dictionary, only a group of *f* rhymes
are discovered:—*febrifuge, subterfuge, vermifuge* and so on; and
perhaps, if the poet is expert in pronunciation, *gamboge,* which
also rhymes with it. But no fourth rhyming sound. The *huge*
rhyme-sound would then have to be discarded, and some other
sound tried.

Try a double rhyme, *ended*. Using this mental rhyming dictionary, the poet discovers:

> ended, bended, fended or defended, Jen did, Len did, mended
> or amended, depended, rended, tended or attended,
> vended, wended;

and, using double and triple consonantal initial sounds,

> blended, friended and befriended, expended for *sp,* extended
> for *st,* trended, then did, splendid,

and this can be supplemented with *men did* and many other two
word rhymes. Here are at least eighteen rhyming mates, which
can be used as the 2 rhyme in a ballade, which requires fourteen
rhyming mates.

So, even if the rhyming dictionary is left behind, a mental
rhyming dictionary can always be improvised, once the mechanism
is learned.

IV

STANZA PATTERNS

The Couplet

A SINGLE line of poetry is called, technically, a *verse* of poetry.
A series of lines arranged formally as a part of a poem is called
a *stanza*. Stanza forms may be rigid, with a fixed order of
sequence as to line length, metre, or rhyme; or they may be mere
divisions of a poem, corresponding to the paragraphs of prose.

The simplest stanza is one of two lines, called a couplet. The
word *couplet* is used to mean either a two-line poem, or a two
line stanza—that is, a part of a poem: and this is equally true of
triplets or tercets, quatrains, and so on. It may be rhymed:

> "Where are you going, my pretty maid?"   1
> "I'm going a milking, sir," she said.   1
> > *Mother Goose's Nursery Rhymes.*

Naturally, if our stanza has only two lines, it can be rhymed in
only one way: each line followed immediately by its rhyming
mate. This is called rhyming in couplets, and is indicated by 1, 1.
The second rhyme sound used in the poem would be designated by
2, the third by 3, and so on. Thus a series of couplet stanzas, if
rhymed, would be rhymed 1, 1; 2, 2; 3, 3, and so on. This is called
couplet rhyming,—a term used of any lines rhymed in this
fashion, even when not divided into separate couplet stanzas.

Five-foot iambic lines rhymed couplet fashion are called *heroic
couplets*. This was the favorite measure employed by Dryden and
Pope, who enriched the language with many polished quotations:

> Vice is a monster of so frightful mien   1
> As, to be hated, needs but to be seen;   1
> Yet seen too oft, familiar with her face,   2
> We first endure, then pity, then embrace.   2
> > *An Essay on Man,* Alexander **Pope.**

These pairs of lines are not stanzas, much less complete two-line poems. Thus *couplet* is used with the third meaning of a method of rhyming—the 1, 1; 2, 2 method.

A couplet need not be rhymed: it may be an unrhymed two line poem, or two line stanza. It may be in any rhythm or combination of rhythms.

The Triplet or Tercet

A group of three lines, whether a complete poem or a stanza, is called a triplet, or tercet. This is not as common a form as the couplet or the four-line form, the quatrain. An example is:

A still small voice spake unto me,	1
"Life is so full of misery,	1
Were it not better not to be?"	1

The Two Voices, Alfred Tennyson.

It is clear, that with three lines to work from, the lines in such a group might be rhymed 1, 1, 2, in which the third line rhymes with nothing in the triplet; or 1, 2, 2; or 1, 2, 1. In the case of groups of triplet stanzas, the rhymes may be interlocked:

Make me thy lyre, even as the forest is:	1
What if my leaves are falling like its own!	2
The tumult of thy mighty harmonies	1
Will take from both a deep autumnal tone,	2
Sweet though in sadness. Be thou, Spirit fierce,	3
My spirit! Be thou me, impetuous one!	2
Drive my dead thoughts over the universe	3
Like withered leaves to quicken a new birth!	4
And, by the incantation of this verse,	3
Scatter, as from an unextinguished hearth	4
Ashes and sparks, my words among mankind!	5
Be through my lips to unawakened earth	4
The trumpet of a prophecy! O wind,	5
If Winter comes, can Spring be far behind?	5

Ode to the West Wind, Percy Bysshe Shelley.

This interlocked rhyming, where the unrhymed middle line of one triplet becomes the rhymed first and third lines of the next, the

whole ending with a thirteenth and fourteenth line rhyming with
the unrhymed central line of the preceding triplet, is a special
Italian verse stanza form, called *terza rima*. As Shelley used it, it
might be regarded as an apt variation of the Shakespearean
sonnet. It may be constituted of less or more triplets, always followed by such a concluding couplet.

Notice, in the hands of this master, the rhyming devices. *Is-har-
monies* illustrates rhyming a primary accent with a secondary one:
and the secondary one is an indeterminate sound, more often
rhymed with *seas* than with *is,* which gives it the effect of partial
consonance. *Fierce-universe* is consonance, not rhyme, as is *birth-
hearth-earth,* long defended as an "eye rhyme," but admissible
as consonance. The same is true of *mankind-wind-behind*. It is
incorrect to pronounce the noun *wind* as if it were the verb *to
wind; wind* here rhymed with *thinned,* and is in consonance with
behind.

Triplets may be in any rhythm, including free verse or polyrhythm. And they may be unrhymed:

> I have had playmates, I have had companions,
> In my days of childhood, in my joyful school-days;
> All, all are gone, the old familiar faces.
>
> I have been laughing, I have been carousing,
> Drinking late, sitting late, with my bosom cronies;
> All, all are gone, the old familiar faces.
> *The Old Familiar Faces,* Charles Lamb.

In this poem Lamb invented his own pattern—unrhymed six foot
trochaic in the main, with seven feet in the fifth line; and with
the terminal line of each triplet a refrain, repeated without
alteration. Any poet may make his own pattern for any poem he
wishes; and, if it finds favor, it may become a standard pattern.

The Quatrain

A quatrain is a stanza or poem of four lines. This is the most
popular brief stanza in English versification, and has a variety
of familiar rhyme schemes. Ordinary *ballad metre* was originally
seven-foot iambic rhymed couplets:

As Robin Hood in the forest strayed, all under the greenwood tree, 1
He was aware of a brave young man, as fine as fine might be.   1

> *Old English Ballad.*

As normally printed today, this becomes a quatrain, with the first
and third lines unrhymed, and only the second and fourth rhyming
—a rhyme scheme that may be used with other metres as well,
and with any number of feet to each line:

> As Robin Hood in the forest strayed,   1
> All under the greenwood tree,   2
> He was aware of a brave young man,   3
> As fine as fine might be.   2

Almost as popular is the quatrain rhymed on alternate lines:

> A violet by a mossy stone   1
> Half-hidden from the eye!   2
> —Fair as a star, when only one   1
> Is shining in the sky.   2
>
> *The Lost Love,* **William Wordsworth.**

Quatrains may be rhymed couplet-wise:

> Tiger, tiger, burning bright   1
> In the forests of the night,   1
> What immortal hand or eye   2
> Framed thy fearful symmetry?   2
>
> *The Tiger,* **William Blake.**

Note that this is not indented: that is, that line two is set directly
under line one. The purpose of *indentation* is primarily to show
the rhyme scheme: lines rhyming with each other may be normally
set beneath each other, as in the two previous examples. Indentation is used either to show identities of rhyme, or to center
briefer lines in a stanza or poem.

The *In Memoriam* stanza is built upon a four-foot iambic
pattern, rhymed as follows:

> Ring out old shapes of foul disease;   1
> Ring out the narrowing lust of gold;   2
> Ring out the thousand wars of old,   2
> Ring in the thousand years of peace.   1
>
> *In Memoriam,* **Alfred Tennyson.**

Edward Fitzgerald's translation or recreation of the quatrains or
Rubaiyat of Omar Khayyam has one of the most famous quatrain
rhyme patterns in the language, using five-foot iambic lines :

> The Moving Finger writes; and, having writ,   1
> Moves on: nor all your Piety nor Wit   1
>   Shall lure it back to cancel half a Line   2
> Nor all your Tears wash out a Word of it.   1
> > *The Rubaiyat of Omar Khayyam,*
> > translated by Edward Fitzgerald.

Other possible quatrain rhyme arrangements are: 1, 1, 1, 1;
1, 1, 1, 2; 2, 2, 2, 2; 1, 2, 1, 1; 1, 2, 3, 1; 1, 1, 2, 3; 1, 2, 3, 3; 1, 2,
2, 3; and no doubt others. Hereafter, no additional rhyming patterns will be listed, since by now it should be understood that none
is forbidden.

As for the number of feet to the line in these quatrains, the
number for the better known patterns is as follows:

> Ballad metre, 4, 3, 4, 3. Called also Long Metre in hymns.
> *In Memoriam,* 4, 4, 4, 4.
> *Rubaiyat,* 5, 5, 5, 5.
> Short metre (in hymns), 3, 3, 4, 3.

This last was popular in the sixteenth century as *Poulter's
measure.* These four are all in iambic lines. Of course, any metric
foot or combination of feet may be employed. It need not be
repeated again that the quatrain, as any other stanza, may be
unrhymed, or may be in polyrhythm.

Stanzas of More Than Four Lines

A five-line stanza or poem is called a cinquain. Adelaide Crapsey
invented one containing 1, 2, 3, 4, and 1 iambic feet respectively
in the lines:

> These be
> Three silent things:
> The falling snow . . . . the hour
> Before the dawn . . . . the mouth of one
> Just dead.
> > *Triad,* by Adelaide Crapsey.

A rhymed cinquain is used in one of Shelley's best known odes:

Hail to thee, blithe Spirit!	1
Bird thou never wert,	2
That from heaven, or near it,	1
Pourest thy full heart	2
In profuse strains of unpremeditated art.	2

To a Skylark, by Percy Bysshe Shelley.

Notice how the indentation centers the briefer lines, as well as indicating, in the first four, rhyming mates. The number of feet here is 3, 3, 3, 3, 6. A terminal six-foot iambic line is called an *Alexandrine;* this was constantly used with iambic five-foot lines as a terminal.

Shelley uses this pattern throughout his poem *To a Skylark.* Poe, another master craftsman, altered his rhyme and metre pattern from stanza to stanza in his greatest lyrics. The familiar love song *To Helen* ("Helen, thy beauty is to me——") has, in his three cinquains or five-line stanzas, these three different rhyme arrangements: 1, 2, 1, 2, 2; 3, 4, 3, 4, 3; 5, 6, 6, 5, 6. To his inner musical ear, these changes were more musical than regularity could have been.

A six-line stanza is called a sextet or sestet. Here is an example:

Fear no more the heat o' the sun	1
Nor the furious winter's rages;	2
Thou thy worldly task hast done,	1
Home art gone and ta'en thy wages:	2
Golden lads and girls all must,	3
As chimney-sweepers, come to dust.	3

Dirge from *Cymbeline,* William Shakespeare.

The trochaic pattern here is four-foot lines. One of the favorite stanzas of Robert Burns has the iambic pattern of 4, 4, 4, 2, 4, 2; as in his *To a Field-Mouse:*

Wee, sleekit, cow'rin', tim'rous beastie,	1
O what a panic's in thy breastie!	1
Thou need na start awa sae hasty,	1
Wi' bickering brattle!	2
I wad be laith to rin and chase thee	1
Wi' murd'ring pattle!	2

To a Field-Mouse, Robert Burns.

The consonance, *beastie, breastie, hasty, chase thee* was to be expected, in the hands of a master. A popular pattern (using an unusual trochaic 4, 4, 2, 4, 4, 2 measure) was used by Whittier:

And if I should live to be	1
The last leaf upon the tree	1
In the spring,	2
Let them laugh, as I do now,	3
At the old, forsaken bough	3
Where I cling.	2

The Last Leaf, Oliver Wendell Holmes.

This may be used in longer stanzas, with a scheme such as 1, 1, 1, 2, 3, 3, 3, 2, a variant of this being popularized by Tennyson:

Willows whiten, aspens quiver,	1
Little breezes dusk and shiver	1
Through the wave that runs for ever	1
By the island in the river	1
Flowing down to Camelot.	2
Four gray walls, and four gray towers,	3
Overlook a space of flowers,	3
And the silent isle embowers	3
The Lady of Shalott.	2

The Lady of Shalott, by Alfred Tennyson.

This stanza is called *tail rhyme* stanza, and is a mere elaboration of the pattern of *The Last Leaf.*

Certain Other Stanzas

It may seem like profanation to some, to subject to the critical scalpel such a masterpiece as Keats's *Ode to a Grecian Urn.* But the poem suffers no loss from the process, for the reader returns to it to find it all uninjured in the end; and no other method will permit an understanding of the technical achievement involved in such lasting beauty. Here are five ten-line stanzas. Each opens with a 1, 2, 1, 2 sequence. Thereafter, there are differences. The first and last have the next six lines 3, 4, 5, 4, 3, 5; the fourth and fifth use instead 3, 4, 5, 3, 4, 5; while the second has 3, 4, 5, 3, 5, 4.

A famous seven-lined stanza is called *Rhyme Royal.* This was

used by James I of Scotland in his *The Kinges Quhair,* and repeatedly by Chaucer and others. Here is a typical use by Chaucer:

To you, my purse, and to none other wight	1
Complain I, for ye be my lady dear.	2
I am full sorry, now that ye be light,	1
For, certes, ye now make me heavy cheer.	2
Me were as lief-y laid upon my bier	2
For which unto your mercy thus I cry,	3
Be heavy again, or elles mote I die.	3

The Complaint to His Empty Purse, Geoffrey Chaucer.

This has a terminal couplet rhyming, 3, 3, which breaks the flow
of the narrative somewhat. To avoid this, the *Canopus* stanza
points a way out:

The night's mysterious wings pulsed thru the dark,	1
The night's mysterious noises cracked and shivered,	2
And where their fingers met a visible spark	1
Seemed to leap forth at them, and pulsed and quivered	2
Throughout them both. Their thickened tongues were dumb,	3
The pretty words of star-lore undelivered,	2
The pretty words that found no breath would come.	3

Canopus, Clement Wood.

Note here also that the use of some feminine or double rhymes
with single or masculine rhymes is effective. This is especially
effective in a Shakespearean sonnet.

Ottava Rima is an Italian stanza adopted in English by many
poets. It is an eight-line stanza, composed of a sestet rhymed
alternately, followed by a terminal rhyming couplet. The Italians
use their heroic metre, eleven syllables to the line, in it; the
English prefer iambic five-foot measure. Spenser, Milton, and
Keats used it, and Byron preferred it, as in his *Don Juan:*

But " why then publish?"—There are no rewards	1
Of fame or profit when the world grows weary.	2
I ask in turn,—Why do you play at cards?	1
Why drink? Why read?—To make some hour less dreary.	2
It occupies me to turn back regards	1
On what I've seen or pondered, sad or cheery;	2
And what I write I cast upon the stream	3
To sink or swim—I have had at least my dream.	3

Don Juan, Lord Byron.

Again note the use of double and single rhymes in the same
stanza, quite often effective.

The *Spenserian Stanza* was invented by Edmund Spenser, and
has long been used in serious dignified verse. The eight opening
five-foot iambic lines are terminated by an Alexandrine, or six-
foot iambic line; the pattern may be seen in this opening of
Keats's poem, which uses the stanza throughout:

St. Agnes' Eve—ah, bitter cold it was!	1
The owl, for all his feathers, was acold.	2
The hare limped trembling through the frozen grass,	1
And silent was the flock in woolly fold.	2
Numb were the Beadsman's fingers while he told	2
His rosary, and while his frosted breath	3
Like pious incense from a censer old,	2
Seemed taking flight for heaven without a death,	3
Past the sweet Virgin's picture, while his prayer he saith.	3

The Eve of St. Agnes, John Keats.

Terza Rima is an iambic rhythm, usually of five feet to the line.
It is usually written continuously, and not in stanzas. It consists
of groups of three lines, rhymed 1, 2, 1; but the rhyming sound
of the middle line, 2, becomes the first and third line of the next
group; and so on. The end of the canto or poem is a couplet, tieing
up the rhyme sound left loose as the central line terminal sound
in the preceding triplet. Thus it is a sort of chain verse, its rhyme
scheme proceeding: 1, 2, 1; 2, 3, 2; 3, 4, 3; 4, 5, 4;......n-l, n,
n-l; n, n. Shelley, in his *Ode to the West Wind,* used this in fourteen line groups, separating the triplets and concluding couplet as if
they were separate stanzas.

It is advisable for the poet or versifier to spend some time in
the pleasant chore of analyzing the favorite poems of the great
poets—the odes of Keats, the sonnets of Shakespeare, the greater
lyrics of Poe, and so on. Scansion will indicate the metre employed; and the numeral system 1, 1, 2, 2 will mark for you the
rhyming pattern. Let your especial attention be directed to
ingenious devices for securing variety within a formal pattern.

The sonnet, which will be reached in the study of lyric poetry,
has been used often and successfully as a stanza.

In polyrhythmic or free verse, the stanza division follows the poet's inner mandate of where each group of lines should end, as if it were a paragraph in prose.

Sapphics and Other Classic Forms

Elegiac verse, according to the classical models, consists of lines alternately dactylic hexameter and dactylic pentameter; and then this difference is explained away by saying that the shorter lines have six accents, but omit the unaccented syllables in the third and sixth feet. Coleridge indicates the method:

> In the hexameter rises the fountain's all-silvery radiance;
> In the pentameter aye falling in melody back.
> *Translation from Schiller,* Samuel Taylor Coleridge.

It is significant that none of the five greatest examples of elegiac poetry—that based upon death, or reflections upon death—in the English language, use this form. These five poems are Milton's *Lycidas,* Shelley's *Adonais,* Tennyson's *In Memoriam,* Gray's famous elegy, and Whitman's *When Lilacs Last in the Dooryards Bloomed,* a tribute to Lincoln.

The Greek *dactylic hexameter,* the classic model as the iambic five-foot line is in English, is far more complicated, according to the prosodists, than it sounds. There are six feet. The first four are dactyls or spondees. The fifth must be a dactyl: otherwise, if a spondee appears here, the verse is called spondaic. The last is a spondee or a trochee. A diagram makes this clearer.

```
 / ⌣ ⌣  |  / ⌣ ⌣  |  / ⌣ ⌣  |  / ⌣ ⌣  |          |   / /
  or    |   or    |   or    |   or    |  / ⌣ ⌣   |   or
 / /    |  / /    |  / /    |  / /    |          |   / ⌣
```

This may be written in English, with an accent basis instead of a quantity basis (that is, long and short syllables).

Hendecasyllabics were 11-syllabled lines composed of a spondee, a dactyl, and trochees. Thus:

```
/ / | / ⌣ ⌣ | / ⌣ | / ⌣ | / ⌣
```

This metre has never been successfully naturalized into English.

Alcaics, named from the lyric poet Alcaeus, a contemporary of Sappho, are of several kinds. The first variety has a five-foot line, consisting of a spondee or iamb, an iamb, a long syllable, and two dactyls. Here is the pattern:

or   / / | ⌣ / | / | / ⌣ ⌣ | / ⌣ ⌣
       ⌣ /

The second variety has two dactyls and two trochees to the line:

/ ⌣ ⌣ | / ⌣ ⌣ | / ⌣ | / ⌣

And, for the third, the line is composed:

(I)   ⌣ / / /

or

(II)   / ⌣ / /

or   / ⌣ ⌣ /   / ⌣ ⌣ /

(III) / / ⌣ /   (stress on   (stress on   ⌣ / /

or   1st or 4th   1st or 4th   (Stress on first

(IV) / / / ⌣   syllable)   syllable)   long syllable)

What are the names of these feet? The first is an epitrite (first, second, third, or fourth epitrite, depending upon the location of the short syllable); two choriambi or choriambs as above; and a bacchius. This technique does not often produce poetry in English; more often, it produces prosody or verse.

For an *Alcaic ode,* each strophe consists of four lines. The first two are eleven-syllabled Alcaics of the first kind; the third an especial form of iambic two-foot of nine syllables, described as hypercatalectic; and the fourth a ten-syllabled Alcaic of the second kind. Tennyson tried to catch it in:

> O mighty-mouthed inventor of harmonies,
> O skilled to sing of time or eternity,
> God-gifted organ-voice of England,
> Milton, a name to resound for ages.
>
> *Milton,* Alfred Tennyson.

Sapphics are named after the poet Sappho, who is said to have used the form with high skill. A sapphic line consists of five equal beats, its central one of three syllables, and the rest of two each. The original Greek sapphic stanza consisted of three of these lines, followed by a shorter line called an *adonic,* the whole following this pattern:

/ ⌣ | / / or / ⌣ | / ⌣ ⌣ | / ⌣ | / / or / ⌣

/ ⌣ | / / or / ⌣ | / ⌣ ⌣ | / ⌣ | / / or / ⌣

Certain English poets have essayed this metre. In the examples given, the accent sign ($\diagup$) means a syllable described as long; the other symbol ($\smile$) one described as short. Here is Swinburne's use of the form:

Saw the | white im- | placable | Aphro- | dite,
Saw the | hair un- | bound and the | feet un- | sandalled
Shine as | fire of | sunset on | western | waters;
        Saw the re- | luctant

Feet, the straining plumes of the doves that drew her,
Looking, always looking with necks reverted,
Back to Lesbos, back to the hills whereunder
        Shone Mitylene;
                Sapphics, Algernon Charles Swinburne.

and so on to the end. A *choriambic line* consists of a spondee, three choriambi, and an iamb. A *galliambic line* is composed of iambs, one of which drops its final syllable: the next foot to the last being an anapest.

Indentation

The purpose of indentation is primarily to indicate the rhyme scheme. Indenting a line means sinking it inward by an increased blank space in the left hand margin. Every paragraph in prose is indented, at its beginning. An early indentation of poetry was similar to this, and consisted in indenting only the first line of each stanza. Where the poet desires to impress the reader with his rhyme scheme, indenting of lines similarly rhymed is proper:

        Yet this inconstancy is such
            As you too shall adore:
        I could not love thee, Dear, so much,
            Loved I not Honour more.
    To Lucasta, on Going to the Wars, Richard Lovelace.

The following indentation is improper and essentially illiterate:

> That which her slender waist confined
> Shall now my joyful temples bind:
> No monarch but would give his crown
> His arms might do what this has done.
>
> *On a Girdle,* Edmund **Waller.**

Needless to say, the poet set this up without indentation. The motive for such misindentation seems to be the following foggy thinking on the part of the versifier:

(a) Some poems by great poets are indented.
(b) Therefore I must indent my poem, to make sure it is regarded as great.

Once let the motive for indentation be learned—to show the similarity of rhyme-sounds terminating lines indented to the same point—and this error will be avoided.

A second purpose of indentation is to center short lines in the central portion of the poem, instead of leaving them dangling off to the left. One of Guy Wetmore Carryll's eight verse poems proceeds:

> A maiden from the Bosphorus,
> With eyes as bright as phosphorus,
> Once wed the wealthy bailiff
> Of the caliph
> Of Kelat.
> Though diligent and zealous, he
> Became a slave to jealousy.
> (Considering her beauty,
> 'Twas his duty
> To be that!)
>
> *How the Helpmate of Bluebeard Made Free with a Door,*
> Guy **Wetmore.**

Here the first, third, fourth, and sixth indentations indicate rhyming changes; the second and fifth are to center briefer rhyming lines. The object is to make the poem appear as presentable as possible, considering rhyme scheme and length of line. Recall the indentation of Shelley's *To a Skylark,* already given.

As to sonnets, there are only two proper ways to present them: indenting for rhyme, and omitting indentation. The Italian and

Shakespearean form would then have the following indentation, if this is used to indicate the rhyme scheme:

Italian Sonnet				Shakespearean Sonnet			
1				1			
	2				2		
	2			1			
1					2		
1				3			
	2				4		
	2			3			
1					4		
	3			5			
		4			6		
			5	5			
	3				6		
		4		7			
			5	7			

It is more usual to set up sonnets without indentation. The original method of indenting the Shakespearean sonnet consisted of twelve lines without indentation, and an indentation for the concluding couplet.

All this assumes that the poet wishes to impress on the reader the rhyming scheme, and the poet's fidelity in following it. But this is initiating the reader into the irrelevant laboratory work of the poet, and has its many disadvantages, since the reader primarily wishes to know what the poet has to say,—not the devices by which he increases his effectiveness. The modern tendency is to eliminate indentation in all poems. If poems are printed similar to prose, the indentation will be the same as prose, to indicate paragraph openings, or to inset a quotation.

V

DIVISIONS OF POETRY

Narrative Poetry

POETRY is commonly divided, from the point of view of the poet's presentation of his material, into narrative, dramatic, and lyric poetry. The distinction is simple :

> In *narrative poetry,* the poet tells a story as if he had been a spectator, but not a participant, in the events.
>
> In *dramatic poetry,* the poet lets the characters of the story speak their own words.
>
> In *lyric poetry,* the poet speaks his own moods, thoughts and aspirations.

These, like all definitions, define from the centers, not from the boundaries. A long-winded narrative in the first person, telling the poet's own adventures, might be classed with reason as any of the three : narrative poetry because it tells a story; dramatic, like a long dramatic monologue; and lyric, because the poet himself is speaking. This attitude classification is not of primary importance.

A fourth division, *didactic poetry,* that which teaches or points a moral, was once popular and is still encountered. It is regarded at best as a low flight of poetry.

Epic, Metrical Romance, Tale

An epic is——

> a long narrative poem, dealing with heroic events, usually with supernatural guidance and participation in the action.

Epics are divided into natural or folk epics, and literary epics. There is a suggested theory that folk epics are preceded by and composed of folk ballads. The earliest known epics exhibit little or no trace of any welding or amalgamating process.

The earliest literary remains in Greece are of the epic type, of three varieties. Epics of personal romance and war center around

53

the semi-mythical blind bard Homer, with his *Iliad*—the story of the flight of Helen of Sparta with her Trojan lover, Paris; the war of Greeks against Trojans to avenge this; the anger of Greek Achilles and its effects; the defeat of Troy—and the *Odyssey,* telling the world-wanderings of Grecian Odysseus after the sack of Troy, and of his return to his native Ithaca. Parts of these long poems are essentially prosy; but they have never been equalled for long poetic flight in narrative form. Epics dealing with the mysteries of religion center around the mythical singer Orpheus. Epics of a didactic nature center around the name of Hesiod. Scholars state that many lost epics in all three fields preceded the epics now remaining.

The *Mahabharata* and the *Ramayana* in Sanskrit, the *Shah-nameh* in Persian, the *Niebelungenlied* in Middle German, *Beowulf* in Anglo-Saxon, the fragmentary *Elder Edda* from Iceland, the *Poem of the Cid* from Spain, the *Song of Roland* in medieval France, the *Kalevala* from Finland, are all folk epics. They originated before the invention of writing, and were transmitted orally, with inevitable changes and additions from time to time. Literary epics are a later attempt to catch the charm of the ancient epics; and as a rule they are a lower flight. Virgil's *Æneid,* Tasso's *Jerusalem Delivered,* Ariosto's *Orlando Furioso,* Dante's didactic *Commedia,* are the most outstanding among these. The *Lusiads* of Camoens gave form to the Portuguese language, much as Dante did to modern Italian, Chaucer to English, and Luther to German. Spenser's *Faerie Queene* has lost most of its charm for many modern English readers; even Milton's *Paradise Lost,* which sought to express English Puritanism as Dante had sought to express medieval Catholicism, is largely dull to modern readers.

Stories in verse preceded stories in prose. Chaucer's *Canterbury Tales,* the narrative metrical romances and tales of Scott, Byron, and others, preceded the novel and the short story in English. But prose has become the popular medium, as it is the more natural one: and the long poetic narrative today usually seems artificial.

The Ballad

The ballad, the brief story in verse, alone retains some general popularity. The name meant first a folk song-and-dance, like the surviving *London Bridge Is Falling Down* or *Oats, Peas, Beans and Barley Grow.* It came to mean the folksong that tells a brief story—at first to be sung, later to be said or read. The Germanic bards or scalds, the gleemen, harpers, minstrels, troubadours, minnesingers, were a distinguished lot—the oral literature (and music) of races in the pre-bookish age. The chief figures in the ballads at first were noble, since nobles were the patrons of the singers. Later on, the lower classes became vocal—the oppressed Saxons in the Robin Hood ballads, and many early ballads in which a commoner ends by marrying one of noble lineage. The technique at first was simple, often with a simple refrain that the hearers might chorus. In English, the first *ballad metre* was seven-foot iambic lines, rhymed in couplets. A variant of this is the Scottish ballad *Edward, Edward,* with a pause between the invoked names taking the place of a foot in alternate lines:

"Quhy does zour brand sae drop wi' bluid, Edward, Edward?
 Quhy does zour brand sae drop wi' bluid, and quhy sae sad
                                        gang zee, O?"
"O, I hae kill-ed my hauke sae guid, Mither, Mither,
 O, I hae kill-ed my hauke sae guid; and I had nae mair but he, O."

Like the majority of the older ballads, this is a gory thing, full of blood and stark universal passions. If modern poetry gave us more of such red meat instead of caviar canapes, it would hold a wider popularity than it now has.

The rhythm is much freer than centuries of later iambic versification. The modern versifier can learn much of the way to sprinkle anapests in an iambic pattern, and of more important devices in versification, from old English folk ballads, as from that other depository of English folk verse, *Mother Goose.* Folk ballads originate among people largely pre-bookish; certain American mountaineers and certain Negroes still commemorate thrilling events with folk ballads, like the one within our memory on *The Sinking of the Titantic.*

Literary ballads are more successful than literary epics. Ballads by Heine and Housman, Coleridge's *Rime of the Ancient Mariner,* have been taken to the heart of the race. The stanza form is almost invariably simple. Yet it is worth while to study the slight elaborations of the ballad metre that Coleridge employed—with stanzas ranging from four to nine ballad half-lines. There are many more successful literary ballads.

Dramatic Poetry

Like story-telling, drama is largely a lost field to poetry, purely because of the unnaturalness of poetic drama as usually written. There is a field for drama in natural free verse, which may yet be widely used. Classic drama was divided into *tragedy,* a play ending in death, and *comedy,* a play not ending in death. This division was unworkable, and has been abandoned today.

Thespis, reputed father of Grecian drama, never permitted more than one actor on the stage at one time, with a chorus to interpret the action to the audience. This rigid convention was shattered by Aeschylus, who added a second actor. Sophocles added a third; but classic Greek drama never permitted a fourth. The typical Shakespearean play had five acts, the climax occurring during the third act, the solution at the end. This usually meant a dragging fourth act, which only *Othello* among the great tragedies avoided. Shakespeare and most other English verse dramatists used a five-foot iambic line, most often in blank or unrhymed verse. None of these conventions are more sacred than the one actor convention of Thespis.

The *dramatic monolog* or *dramatic lyric,* sprung from the speeches of Thespis's actor and the unnatural soliloquy of classic and English drama, is the one form of drama in verse which preserves considerable popularity. Robert Browning made this field peculiarly his own, with such magnificent dramatic vignettes as *My Last Duchess, Andrea del Sarto, Caliban upon Setebos,* and so many more. His tremendous *The Ring and the Book* is, within a brief framework, ten immense dramatic monologs: the same group of facts, as seen through the eyes of ten differing personalities. Such dramatic monologs may be in any rhythm, any line length, and with or without rhyme. Success comes in proportion to the naturalness of the speech, the universality and depth of the emotion displayed, and the accuracy in character-drawing.

Lyric Poetry: Ode, Elegy, Pastoral

Perhaps the earliest, and certainly the most enduringly popular type of poetry, is the lyric. As the name indicates, it meant originally poetry to be sung to the lyre,—a dance at first accompanying this.

The *ode,* the most exalted form of lyric poetry, had strict rules in classic times. The Greek Pindaric ode had three movements: a strophe, in which the chorus moved from a given spot toward the right; the antistrophe, following the same versification pattern, and to the same tune, in which the chorus moved correspondingly to the left; and the concluding epode, different in structure, sung to a different tune, and with the chorus standing still. Efforts to revive this form in English have not succeeded. In English, the ode is a dignified lyric on some high theme, with constant progress in its stanzas toward its conclusion. Familiar odes in English include Wordsworth's:

> Our birth is but a sleep and a forgetting;
> The Soul that rises with us, our life's Star,
> Hath elsewhere its setting
> And cometh from afar;
> Not in entire forgetfulness,
> And not in utter nakedness,
> But trailing clouds of glory do we come
> From God, who is our home.
> Heaven lies about us in our infancy!
> *Ode on the Intimations of Immortality from*
> *Recollections of Early Childhood,*
> William Wordsworth.

and also the great odes by Shelley and Keats already referred to.

An *elegy* is a formal expression of the poet's grief at death, whether general or centered about the death of an individual. It has no more definite a pattern in English than the ode. Milton, in *Lycidas,* uses an iambic measure, with lines of differing lengths, and a fluidic rhyme scheme. Shelley, in *Adonais,* chose the Spenserian stanza. Tennyson, in *In Memoriam,* selected the quatrain pattern already encountered. Whitman, in his major Lincoln threnody, *When Lilacs Last in the Dooryard Bloomed,* wrote in magnificent polyrhythmic verse. Gray's familiar *Elegy Written in a*

Country Churchyard, alone among these a meditation upon death in general, used alternate-rhymed five-foot iambic lines. There are many familiar short elegies in the language.

The *pastoral* is a reflective lyric upon some aspect of nature. formerly concerned with shepherd life, whence its name. Milton's shapely *L'Allegro* and *Il Penseroso,* and Whittier's *Snowbound,* are examples in this genre. As city living increasingly replaces country living, some form of city lyric may supplant the pastoral, if it does not die without offspring.

The Simple Lyric: The Song

The word *song* is loosely used for any simple lyric, on the theory that it may always be set to music. It is best to reserve the word for a lyric intended to be set to music. This calls for a knowledge, on the part of the poet, of the human voice in music, and the ease or difficulty with which the various sounds are produced. Certain consonants and combinations of consonants are sinagable only with great difficulty. A line like:

The gross-sized much-touched scratch will itch

is not easily singable. The terminal consonants *m, n, l, r* are sung with ease; *s, z, ch, sh,* as terminals, with difficulty. Of the vowels, broad *a,* long *o,* long *a, ou,* are easiest to sing, though no vowel is really difficult. The words chosen should always end, and as far as possible include, only sounds which open the mouth, instead of closing it. Simple words are to be preferred to complicated ones; definite precise words to indefinite abstract ones; emotion-evoking words to intellectualized ones.

The lyric canon in English is one of the glories of its literature. After the dawn-hour lyrics before the Elizabethan age, the golden song of Campion—

Shall I come, sweet Love, to thee,
    When the evening beams are set?
Shall I not excluded be,
    Will you find no feigned let?
Let me not, for pity, more
Tell the long hours at your door;
    Shall I Come, Sweet Love? Thomas Campion.

the equally melodious singable lyrics of Shakespeare and his con-
temporaries, the lyrics of Shelley, Keats, Byron, Burns, Housman,
and so many more in England, and of Poe, Emily Dickinson,
Sidney Lanier, and a few later singers, together make up a body
of song that the race continues to treasure.

The themes and treatments of the lyric may vary as widely as
the desires and visions of the poets. A lyric may have any chosen
form of rhythm, with or without rhyme. It is often natural and
effective in free verse or polyrhythmic poetry, since in this form
the precise emotion-moving thoughts and images may be written
down, without the warping often demanded by such devices of
versification as rhyme, assonance, consonance, and formal metre
and stanza arrangement. Here is an example from the chief American user of the form, in a lyric called *Reconciliation:*

> Word over all, beautiful as the sky,
> Beautiful that war and all its deeds of carnage must
>   in time be utterly lost,
> That the hands of the sisters Death and Night
>   incessantly softly wash again, and ever again,
>   this soil'd world;
> For my enemy is dead, a man divine as myself is dead,
> I look where he lies white-faced and still in the
>   coffin—I draw near,
> Bend down and touch lightly with my lips the white
>   face in the coffin.
>   *Reconciliation,* Walt Whitman.

Modern users of polyrhythmic poetry as a rule use less eloquence
than Whitman, and less of the expansive cosmic note; and tend
instead toward the tense and gripping emotional appeal usual in
rhymed and metric lyrics. Much shorter line-division is also common.

The Sonnet

The sonnet is the most popular fixed form in English. It is a
lyric of fourteen iambic five-foot lines, with a defined and definite
rhyme scheme. There are two forms of it widely used in English,
the Italian or Petrarchian sonnet, and the Shakespearean sonnet.

The rhyme-scheme of the Italian sonnet appears from the
following example:

The world is too much with us; late and soon,	1
Getting and spending, we lay waste our powers:	2
Little we see in Nature that is ours;	2
We have given our hearts away, a sordid boon!	1
This sea that bares her bosom to the moon,	1
The winds that will be howling at all hours,	2
And are up-gathered now like sleeping flowers;	2
For this, for everything, we are out of tune;	1
It moves us not.—Great God! I'd rather be	3
A Pagan suckled in a creed outworn;	4
So might I, standing on this pleasant lea,	3
Have glimpses that would make me less forlorn;	4
Have sight of Proteus rising from the sea;	3
Or hear old Triton blow his wreathéd horn.	4

Sonnet, William Wordsworth.

The first eight lines of any sonnet are called the *octave*. In the Italian sonnet, the rhyme-scheme is rigid, and may not be departed from. The octave consists of two quatrains rhymed 1, 2, 2, 1, the *In Memoriam* rhyming pattern made familiar by Tennyson's use of it. The entire octave then rhymes 1, 2, 2, 1; 1, 2, 2, 1. It is not permitted to vary the rhymes in the second half of the octave, by using 1, 2, 2, 1; 3, 2, 2, 3, or a form too commonly encountered, 1, 2, 2, 1; 3, 4, 4, 3.

The concluding six lines of any sonnet are called the sestet. The two permissible rhyme-schemes for the sestet of an Italian sonnet are 3, 4, 3, 4, 3, 4, and 3, 4, 5, 3, 4, 5. It will be noted that the sonnet by Wordsworth, quoted above, uses the proper octave rhyme-scheme and the first of these two sestet arrangements.

As to treatment, the octave must be end-stopped—that is, the eighth line must mark the termination of a sentence. Even the halves of the octave should be end-stopped. The first quatrain should introduce the theme, and develop it in a certain direction; the second should continue this development in the same direction. The sestet introduces a new development in a different direction, with the first tercet carrying this new direction to a definite point; and the final tercet bringing the theme to a conclusion. The actual movement of the strict Italian sonnet may be expressed as a flow in the octave, and an ebb in the sestet—so Theodore Watts-

Dunton phrased it in his sonnet, *The Sonnet's Voice.* This does not mean, of course, that the inspiration or the emotional effect should ebb.

Wordsworth's sonnet, emotionally effective as it is, violates several of these strict rules. The octave movement does not end with the eighth line, but trespasses into the ninth. There is no break in thought between the two tercets that together comprise the sestet. We will find constantly among the masters violations of the rules, at times in the nature of experiments; none of these has as yet established its popularity in English poetry. In his sonnet *On the Extinction of the Venetian Republic,* Wordsworth's octave rhymes 1, 2, 2, 1; 1, 3, 3, 1,—another variation.

One authority examined 6,283 Italian sonnets in English, and found these variations for the terminal sestet rhymes:

3, 4, 5, 3, 4, 5	3, 3, 4, 5, 5, 4
3, 4, 3, 4, 5, 5	3, 4, 5, 5, 3, 4
3, 4, 4, 3, 5, 5	3, 4, 5, 5, 4, 3
3, 4, 5, 4, 3, 5	3, 4, 4, 5, 3, 5
3, 4, 3, 5, 4, 5	3, 4, 5, 4, 5, 3
3, 4, 5, 3, 5, 4	3, 4, 3, 5, 5, 4

Two of these have terminal couplets, the most regrettable variation of the Italian sonnet. Six others include a couplet somewhere within the sestet. In addition to the above, the following two-rhyme variants are found:

3, 4, 3, 4, 3, 4	3, 4, 3, 4, 4, 3
3, 4, 4, 3, 3, 4	3, 4, 3, 3, 4, 4
3, 4, 4, 3, 4, 3	3, 4, 3, 3, 4, 3

Only the first excludes any couplet rhyming. Shelley's poem *Ozymandias* had the rhyme scheme: 1, 2, 1, 2; 1, 3, 4, 3; 5, 4, 5, 6, 5, 6. Milton led the way in failing to separate clearly the octave and sestet, so much so that his type of sonnet is sometimes called the Miltonic—Italian in rhyme-pattern, but without the characteristic Italian flow and ebb of theme, broken after the eighth line.

The Shakespearean sonnet is simpler and more natural in rhyming, and is in wider favor among English-using poets. An example is:

When, in disgrace with fortune and men's eyes,	1
I all alone beweep my outcast state,	2
And trouble deaf heaven with my bootless cries,	1
And look upon myself and curse my fate,	2
Wishing me like to one more rich in hope,	3
Featur'd like him, like him with friends possess'd,	4
Desiring this man's art and that man's scope,	3
With what I most enjoy contented least;	4
Yet in these thoughts myself almost despising,	5
Haply I think on thee, and then my state,	6
Like to the lark at break of day arising	5
From sullen earth, sings hymns at heaven's gate;	6
For thy sweet love remember'd such wealth brings	7
That then I scorn to change my state with kings.	7

Sonnet XXIX, William Shakespeare.

This is the accepted Shakespearean indentation for this form: though it may be indented to show rhyming mates, as the Italian also may be. Both types of the sonnet at times are printed with octave and sestet separated, making a poem of two stanzas; or octave divided into two quatrains, and at times the sestet similarly divided.

The rhyming scheme of the Shakespearean sonnet is three quatrains, 1, 2, 1, 2; 3, 4, 3, 4; 5, 6, 5, 6; with a concluding couplet, 7, 7. A shrewd interspering of double or feminine rhymes aids. Many variations have been tried on this simple rhyming basis. Sir Philip Sidney repeated the rhymes of the first quatrain in the second, giving him a pattern of 1, 2, 1, 2; 1, 2, 1, 2; 3, 4, 3, 4; 5, 5. Spenser, in his hundred and twenty sonnets, used a chain-verse device of interlocking rhymes throughout each sonnet, so that his pattern was: 1, 2, 1, 2,; 2, 3, 2, 3; 3, 4, 3, 4; 5, 5. Keats, in his second sonnet on *Fame*, wedded the Shakespearean octave to the Italian sestet, with his rhyme scheme 1, 2, 1, 2; 3, 4, 3, 4; 5, 6, 5, 7, 7, 6. Rupert Brooke, in the first and fifth of his soldier sonnets, used the Shakespearean octave, and a straight Italian sestet: 5, 6, 7, 5, 6, 7. The third and fourth of the same series also wander from any strict pattern.

The sonnet was invented in Italy in the 13th century, probably by Pier delle Vigne, secretary of state in the Sicilian court of Frederick. His sonnet *Però ch' amore* is the earliest known. His rhyme form, 1, 2, 1, 2; 1, 2, 1, 2; 3, 4, 5, 3, 4, 5, has never become popular in English. The French sonnet prefers the strict Italian octave, with a sestet of three rhymes commencing with a couplet. This also has not become naturalized in English. There are occasional variations in English poetry, such as 1, 2, 1, 2; 2, 1, 2, 1; 3, 4, 3, 4, 5, 5; Italian sonnets with sestet 3, 4, 3, 4, 5, 5; and so on. Watts-Dunton points out, in his article on the sonnet in the 11th edition of *The Encyclopedia Brittanica,* that the charm of this and other fixed forms comes from familiarity in advance with the rhyme-scheme to be followed; and that this charm is dissipated, when any break in the expected rhyme-scheme occurs. We feel somewhat as if we listened to a limerick with an extra foot or an extra line: a sense of surprise, its pleasure being doubtful. In spite of this, poets continue to vary the rigid forms from time to time, and will continue to do so.

The sonnet, of either form, is used by many poets as a fourteen-line stanza. Many of the Elizabethan sonnet sequences illustrate this; and there are many more recent examples. In writing the sonnet, it will aid to write down the rhyme scheme to the right of the space where your lines are to be written, and thereafter to mark across from each numbered rhyme the initial consonantal sounds used: giving a check against repeating a rhyming sound (that is, identity), which is inexcusable false rhyming. We would then have a notebook page like:

		Rhyme Sounds			
		ŌLD	ĒN	ĪZ	ĔN
Much have I travell'd in the realms of gold	1	G			
And many goodly states and kingdoms seen;	2		S		
Round many western islands have I been	2		B		
Which bards in fealty to Apollo hold.	1	H			
Oft of one wide expanse had I been told	1	T			
That deep-browed Homer ruled as his demesne:	2		M		
Yet never did I breathe its pure serene	2		R		
Till I heard Chapman speak out loud and bold.	1	B			
—Then felt I like some watcher of the skies	3			SK	
When a new planet swims into his ken;	4				K
Or like stout Cortez—when with eagle eyes	3			Vowel	
He stared at the Pacific—and all his men	4				M
Look'd at each other with a wild surmise—	3			M	
Silent, upon a peak in Darien.	4				Vowel

On First Looking into Chapman's Homer, John Keats.

Thus, by this check, it appears that the poet used, for rhyme 1, ŌLD, these consonantal sounds: g, h, t, b; for rhyme 2, ĒN, s, b, m, r; for rhyme 3, ĪZ, sk, the unconsonanted vowel sound, and m; for rhyme 4, ĔN, k, m, and the unconsonanted vowel sound. No identities; rhyme throughout. The sonnet, from a technical rhyming standpoint, has no flaws. When this method is followed during the writing of the sonnet—the first group of columns, that containing the numerals, properly indented, being written down first—this gives a check as the writing of the sonnet proceeds, and saves much rewriting.

VI

THE FRENCH FORMS. LIGHT AND HUMOROUS VERSE

Into Formal and Light Verse

ANY poetic form may be used either to arouse the great serious emotions, or the lighter and more frivolous ones. Nor is there any reason for holding the serious poet higher than the comic poet. Surely Aristophanes, the great Athenian comic dramatist, ranked as high, and was doubtless more popular and influential, than any of the great serious triad, Aeschylus, Sophocles and Euripides. Shakespeare the comic dramatist, the author of *Merry Wives of Windsor, Midsummer Night's Dream, The Taming of the Shrew,* is as impressive a figure as the Shakespeare who let the melancholy Dane live and die in Elsinore, the Shakespeare who was the chronicler of Othello's jealousy and Lear's senility. Cervantes, who jeered knighthood to death, is greater as a writer than any other Spaniard; Racine, Moliere, Voltaire, Anatole France, were greatest as satirists; and so the roll continues. Serious writers and poets are more popular, and are taken more seriously; but this may be because it is more civilized and difficult to laugh than to weep. Animals can suffer agonies; but they cannot chuckle. And yet the race would not willingly exchange Robert Burn's *Tam o' Shanter* and W. S. Gilbert's *The Bab Ballads* for any number of closet dramas, ponderous versified essays and odes, or a whole trainload of lyrics to spring and young love.

Fixed forms of poetry tend to become outgrown, like a child's shirt too small to close over a man's heart. They then become relegated to minor versifiers, to light verse writers, and to college and high school exercises. Prose ages more quickly than poetry: witness such masterpieces, written for adults, as the world's great fairy stories, Aesop's fables, the *Arabian Nights, Robinson Crusoe, Gulliver's Travels* in the nursery; and the essays and novels of yesterday encountered in school or college. Poetry itself ages:

Shakespeare, Milton, Virgil, Horace, are more used in the class-
room than in the living room today, and so of the rest of them.
In spite of constant insistence that nothing changes under the
sun, the nature of man is stretched outward by his expanding environment, and coiled more tensely into molecules and atoms and
complexes and other inner things: and the poetry, the concentrated
heart's expression, of yesterday cannot forever be the poetry of
today. Prose, in the large, must be rephrased every fifty years, or
less, to be enjoyable to living men; poetry survives longer, but the
hour will come when the most enduring poem of a Shakespeare
or a Sappho will seem ancient, and must be restated or recreated
by a living poet, to speak again for the maturing soul of man. If
this is true of the poetry itself, it is truer of the patterns in which
poetry has been uttered, and especially of the fixed forms.

The sonnet, an emigrant from Italy that became naturalized in
English literature, still holds its own as a major method of expressing serious poetry, in the eyes of many poets and readers.
Even at that, it is now regarded as puerile by the extreme advo-
cates of free verse or polyrhythmic poetry, especially since Whitman and the Imagist movement. Numerous other alien verse
forms did not fare so well, and have established themselves primarily as mediums for light and humorous verse. These include
the ballade, the rondeau, the villanelle, the triolet, and so on. This
may be because of their rigid rules and formal repetitions, which
were not acceptable to the living poet. And yet, they started as
seriously as Sapphics, heroic blank verse, or polyrhythms. . . .

Of all the forms of verse originating in medieval Provence,
among those that failed to acclimatize themselves in English are
the *vers, canzo, sirvente, tenso, alba, serena, pastorella, breu-doble,*
and the *retroensa.* Only the most elaborate of the lot, the intricate
sestina, has survived in English. When religious crusades wiped
out this culture, the germs of formalized verse took root in north-
ern France, especially under Charles d'Orleans and François
Villon. The *ballade* appeared. Spenser used 3,848 of his nine-line
Spenserian stanzas in one poem: across the Channel, Eustache
Deschamps, a friend of Chaucer's, left no less than 1,175 complete ballades. Froissart the chronicler wrote many. Charles
d'Orleans is hailed as the early master of the roundel, as Villon is
lauded as the prince of ballade-makers. Jean Passerat gave the

villanelle its present form, in the sixteenth century; Voiture, a century later, perfected the rondeau. In the seventeenth century, after the forms had been known for two hundred years in English, Patrick Carey published a series of dignified religious triolets; and the over-artificialized forms have repeatedly been revived since.

Rules of the Fixed Verse Forms

In English verse, the rules for the fixed forms are stricter than in French:

I. No syllable once used as a rhyme can be used again in the same poem as a rhyme, not even if it be spelled differently; nor if the whole word is altered by a prefix.

This bars such identities as *Ruth*, a girl's name, and *ruth*, pity; *bear*, an animal, *bear*, to support, *bare*, *forbear*, and so on; *sale* and *sail; claim, reclaim*, and *disclaim; facility, imbecility;* and, if this be taken as a single rhyme, not a triple one, it forbids the use of more than one from this group: *tea, manatee, imbecility, impossibility, lenity*, and so on.

As to the *refrain*, an important element in many of these forms:

II. The refrain must not be a meaningless repetition of sounds as in many English ballads; it must aid in the progress of the thought; come in naturally; and be repeated in all its sounds, without any change of sound.

Slipshod versifiers alter the refrain by changing the introductory word, as by using an *and* for a *but*, a *then* for an *if*. This is unforgiveable. But the requirement goes no further than the repetition of all *sounds*. Punctuation may be changed, spelling may be changed, meaning may be changed: permitting the following—

> It's meet, this sale; Its meat, this sail.
> Gray day; Grade aye; Grade A.

The Ballade Family

There are two standard forms of the *ballade*. The more usual one consists of three stanzas of eight lines each; followed by a concluding quatrain. known as the *envoy*. It is thus a poem of twenty-eight lines, or twice the length of a sonnet. Each stanza, and the envoy, terminate with a line repeated sound by sound, and called the *refrain*. The rhyme scheme is 1, 2, 1, 2, 2, 3, 2, 3R for each stanza, 3R being the refrain; and 2, 3, 2, 3R for the envoy. The rules of the ballade may be stated as follows:

I. The same set of rhyme-sounds used in the first stanza, in the same order, must be used in each stanza; and the last half of this scheme must be used in the envoy.

II. No rhyme-sound once used as a rhyme may be used again for that purpose anywhere in the poem.

III. Each stanza and the envoy must close with the refrain line, repeated without any alteration of sound; though its punctuation, meaning and spelling may be altered.

IV. The sense of the refrain must be supreme throughout the ballade, the culminating refrain line being always brought in without strain or effort as the natural close of the stanza or envoy.

Formerly, the length of the refrain governed the length of the stanza. Thus an eight-syllabled refrain dictated an eight-line stanza, and a ten-syllabled refrain a ten-line stanza. This rule is followed no longer.

V. The stanza should carry an unbroken sense throughout, and not be split in meaning into two quatrains, or any other division. The needful pauses for punctuation are allowed, but the sense is not to be finished midway of the stanza.

VI. The envoy, as used in ballades and the chant royal, was at first addressed to the patron of the poet. It is thus usual to commence it with some such invocation as *Prince! Princess! Sire!* or by some mythical or symbolic person so introduced. This is at times omitted. The envoy is properly both a dedication and a culmination, and should be richer in wording and meaning and more stately in imagery than the preceding lines.

Here is a well-wrought ballade, in four-foot iambic verse. The rhyme-scheme is indicated by the numerals 1, 2, and 3, the refrain line being designated 3R. To the right appear the checking col-

umns for the three rhyming sounds, to make sure that there are
no repetitions,—unforgivable, in strict formal verse of this type.

		AD	Ō	ŌL
			Rhyme Sounds	
Where are the passions they essayed,	1	S		
And where the tears they made to flow?	2			FL
Where the wild humours they portrayed	1		TR	
For laughing worlds to see and know?	2		N	
Othello's wrath and Juliet's woe?	2		W	
Sir Peter's whims and Timon's gall?	3			G
And Millamant and Romeo?	2		Vowel	
Into the night go one and all.	3R			Vowel
Where are the braveries, fresh or frayed?	1	FR		
The plumes, the armours—friend and foe?	2		F	
The cloth of gold, the rare brocade,	1	K		
The mantles glittering to and fro?	2		FR	
The pomp, the pride, the royal show?	2		SH	
The cries of youth and festival?	3			V
The youth, the grace, the charm, the glow?	2		GL	
Into the night go one and all.	3R			Vowel
The curtain falls, the play is played:	1	PL		
The Beggar packs beside the Beau;	2		B	
The Monarch troops, and troops the Maid;	1	M		
The Thunder huddles with the Snow.	2		SN	
Where are the revellers high and low?	2		L	
The clashing swords? The lover's call?	3			K
The dancers gleaming row on row?	2		R	
Into the night go one and all.	3R			Vowel

Envoy.

Prince, in one common overthrow	2		THR	
The Hero tumbles with the Thrall;	3			THR
As dust that drives, as straws that blow,	2		BL	
Into the night go one and all.	3R			Vowel

Ballade of Dead Actors, William Ernest Henley.

As to the two requirements about rhyming, a ballade requires
six 1 rhymes. Here the six consonantal sounds, as the checking column establishes, are *s, tr, fr, k, pl,* and *m.*

A ballade requires fourteen 2 rhymes. Here the fourteen consonantal sounds, as the checking column establishes, are *fl, n, w,*
the unconsonanted vowel, *f, fr, sh, gl, b, sn, l, r, thr,* and *bl.*

A ballade requires five 3 rhymes, one of which reappears
three times as the refrain. The five sound used here are *g,* the

unconsonanted vowel, *v, k,* and *thr.* The rhyming is correct throughout.

The refrain line is used without any alteration of any kind throughout, satisfying the third requirement. It is used throughout as a natural climax of each stanza. Each stanza has its own climactic rise to the refrain. The envoy meets the requirements wholly.

This ballade, then may be used as a model.

The meter of a ballade need not be four-foot iambic, as in this example. Andrew Lang's *Ballade of Primitive Man* has a three-foot anapestic movement, with the refrain, " 'Twas the manner of Primitive Man." Dactyls may be used, or anapests. A recent newspaper ballade had only two trochees to the line, its refrain being "Life is gay." Another had merely one iambic foot to each line, with the refrain "I love." No doubt someone has written a ballade with only one syllable to each line.

The most famous of all ballades is François Villon's ballade *Des Dames du Temps Jadis, (Ballade of Bygone Ladies).* There are many familiar translations of this, Rossetti's with the refrain "But where are the snows of yester-year?" John Payne's with "But what is become of last year's snow?" and others. None of these are authentic recreations in living poetry; not even of the refrain *Mais ou sont les neiges d'antan?* (But where are the last year's snows?) In technique, Rossetti has entirely different rhyming sounds in each stanza, and another in the envoy. Payne is accurate, though he repeats some rhyme-sounds, and uses words as unliving as *vade* (that is, *go*), *marish, whilere, dole;* and surely "Virgin debonair" is an unfortunate mistranslation of Villon's stately *Vierge souvraine.* At least, none of this is as archaic as two words in this line of Rossetti's version:

(From love he won such dule and teen!)

Examining the Villon original, we find that he uses the terminal sound *-maine* seven times, and rhymes it with *moyne* and other apparent consonances; rhymes *lis* and *Allis;* and otherwise is as lax as French rules allow, rather than following the strict and at that time unpromulgated English rules. An acceptable version in English may take advantages of the practices in the original; although it will have to be an authentic poetic recreation.

The second standard form of the ballade consists of stanzas of
ten lines, usually of ten syllables each, as in the five-foot iambic
pattern; followed by an envoy of five lines. The regular rhyme
scheme for each stanza is 1, 2, 1, 2, 2, 3, 3, 4, 3, 4R, 4R being
the refrain line. For the envoy, the rhyme scheme is 3, 3, 4, 3, 4R.
This is much rarer in English than the foregoing.

The *ballade with double refrain* uses two refrains, one occurring at the fourth line of every stanza, and one at the eighth;
while, in the envoy, the refrains are the second and fourth lines
respectively, the envoy being rhymed couplet-wise. The rhyme
scheme for each stanza is 1, 2, 1, 2R; 2, 3, 2, 3R, 2R being the
first refrain line, and 3R the second. The rhyme scheme for the
envoy is 2, 2R, 3, 3R. The best technique selects two antithetical
refrains, and develops each stanza upon the refrain used to close
it. Here is an excellent example:

When the roads are heavy with mire and rut,	1
In November fogs, in December snows,	2
When the North Wind howls, and the doors are shut,	1
There is place and enough for the pains of prose;—	2R
But whenever a scent from the whitethorn blows,	2
And the jasmine-stars to the casement climb,	3
And a Rosalind-face at the lattic shows,	3
Then hey!—for the ripple of laughing rhyme!	3R

When the brain gets dry as an empty nut,	
When the reason stands on its squarest toes,	
When the mind (like a beard) has a "formal cut,"	
There is place and enough for the pains of prose;—	2R
But whenever the May-blood stirs and glows,	
And the young year draws to the "golden prime,"—	
And Sir Romeo sticks in his ears a rose,	
Then hey!—for the ripple of laughing rhyme!	3R

In a theme where the thoughts have a pedant strut,	
In a changing quarrel of "Ayes" and "Noes,"	
In a starched procession of "If" and "But",	
There is place and enough for the pains of prose;—	2R
But whenever a soft glance softer glows,	
And the light hours dance to the trysting-time,	
And the secret is told "that no one knows,"	
Then hey!—for the ripple of laughing rhyme!	3R

Envoy

In a work-a-day world,—for its needs and woes,	2
There is place and enough for the pains of prose;	2R
But whenever the May-bells clash and chime, . . .	3
They hey!—for the ripple of laughing rhyme!	3R

The Ballade of Prose and Rhyme, Austin Dobson.

The position of the two refrains is indicated throughout by 2R and 3R; and the couplet rhyming of the envoy is also indicated.

The *double ballade* consists of six stanzas of eight or ten lines each, rhymed as in the ballades already given. Thus this may be six stanzas rhymed 1, 2, 1, 2, 2, 3, 2, 3R; or 1, 2, 1, 2, 2, 3, 3, 4, 3, 4R. Usually the envoy is omitted. Henley, who liked the form, always used an envoy. His *Double Ballade of the Nothingness of Things* goes beyond these schemes, and has eleven lines to each stanza, rhymed 1, 2, 1, 2, 2, 3, 3, 4, 5, 4, 5R; with an envoy rhymed 3, 3, 4, 5, 4, 5R. And he has stranger varieties. Swinburne's *Ballade of Swimming* has ten lines to the stanza, and seven anapests to each line—a long interval between rhymes.

The *chant royal* is the longest and most dignified offspring of the ballade. It has five stanzas of eleven lines each, usually rhymed 1, 2, 1, 2, 3, 3, 4, 4, 5, 4, 5R. The envoy has five lines, rhymed 4, 4, 5, 4, 5R. Sixty lines, in all. . . . Seven (5) rhymes, ten each of (1), (2), and (3), and eighteen separate rhymes for (4). . . . Here is an amusing example:

> I would that all men my hard case might know;
>> How grievously I suffer for no sin;
> I, Adolphe Culpepper Ferguson, for lo!
>> I, of my landlady am locked in,
>>> For being short on this sad Saturday,
>>> Nor having shekels of silver wherewith to pay;
> She has turned and is departed with my key;
> Wherefore, not even as other boarders free,
>> I sing (as prisoners to their dungeon stones
> When for ten days they expiate a spree):
>> Behold the deeds that are done of Mrs. Jones!

> One night and one day I have wept my woe;
>> Nor wot I when the morrow doth begin,
> If I shall have to write to Briggs & Co.,
>> To pray them to advance the requisite tin

For ransom of their salesman, that he may
  Go forth as other boarders go alway—
As those I hear now flocking from their tea,
Led by the daughter of my landlady
  Piano-ward. This day, for all my moans,
Dry bread and water have been servéd me.
  Behold the deeds that are done of Mrs. Jones!

Miss Amabel Jones is musical, and so
  The heart of the young he-boardér doth win,
Playing "The Maiden's Prayer," *adagio*—
  That fetcheth him, as fetcheth the banco skin
    The innocent rustic. For my part, I pray:
    That Badarjewska maid may wait for aye
Ere she sits with a lover, as did we
Once sit together, Amabel! Can it be
  That all that arduous wooing not atones
For Saturday shortness of trade dollars three?
  Behold the deeds that are done of Mrs. Jones!

Yea! she forgets the arm was wont to go
  Around her waist. She wears a buckle whose pin
Galleth the crook of the young man's elbów;
  I forget not, for I that youth have been.
    Smith was aforetime the Lothario gay.
    Yet once, I mind me, Smith was forced to stay
Close in his room. Not calm, as I, was he:
But his noise brought no pleasaunce, verily.
  Small ease he gat of playing on the bones,
Or hammering on the stove-pipe, that I see.
  Behold the deeds that are done of Mrs. Jones!

Thou, for whose fear the figurative crow
  I eat, accursed be thou and all thy kin!
Thee will I shew up—yea, up will I shew
  Thy too thick buckwheats, and thy tea too thin.
    Ay! here I dare thee, ready for the fray!
    Thou dost *not* "keep a first-class house," I say!
It does not with the advertisements agree.
Thou lodgest a Briton with a puggaree,
  And thou hast harboured Jacobses and Cohns,
Also a Mulligan. Thus denounce I thee!
  Behold the deeds that are done of Mrs. Jones!

Envoy

Boarders; the worst I have not told to ye:
She hath stolen my trousers, that I may not flee
    Privily by the window. Hence these groans,
There is no fleeing in a *robe de nuit*.
    Behold the deeds that are done of Mrs. Jones!

> *Behold the Deeds! (Being the Plaint of Adolphe
> Culpepper Ferguson, Salesman of Fancy Notions,
> held in durance of his Landlady for a failure to
> connect on Saturday night,)* Henry Cuyler Bunner.

The stanza rhyme-scheme is 1, 2, 1, 2, 3, 3, 4, 4, 5, 4, 5R, 5R being the refrain; with the envoy 4, 4, 5, 3, 5R. The rhyming throughout is accurate, and the result is a perfect chant royal. The form is intricate, and the method of checking the various rhyme sounds as they are put down should be followed, to be sure that no rhyming sound is repeated. A great deal of reworking is often necessary to perfect such a form as this. In order to make the envoy the culmination of the verses, it is often necessary to shift the strongest and most vigorous rhyming sounds to it, and substitute other words in the earlier stanzas.

It is wise, for rhyme 4, which must be repeated eighteen times, and similar others repeated constantly in the fixed forms, to choose a comparatively simple rhyming sound, such as the Ē here, to prevent a lack of rhyming words.

Chain Verse

We have already noted that form of chain verse used in *terza rima*, where the triplets rhyme 1, 2, 1; 2, 3, 2; 3, 4, 3; 4, 5, 4, and so on. Any repetition of a rhyme, word, phrase, line or group of lines, to tie up a section of the poem with the succeeding section, constitutes chain verse. John Byrom lets line four of each quatrain become line one of the next:

> My spirit longeth for thee
> Within my troubled breast,
> Although I be unworthy
> Of so divine a Guest.

Of so divine a Guest
Unworthy though I be,
Yet has my heart no rest,
Unless it comes from thee.

Unless it comes from thee,
In vain I look around,
    The Desponding Soul's Wish, John Byrom.

and so on. Chain verse can rise to the elaborateness of a chain of sonnets or more, with the final line in each repeated as the opening line of the next, or even the final word or rhyme-sound so used.

The Kyrielle

The kyrielle, strictly described, consists of quatrains with eight syllables to the line, each stanza terminating with the same line,— a simple use of the refrain. Here is an example from a poem by John Payne:

A little pain, a little pleasure,
A little heaping up of treasure,
Then no more gazing upon the sun.
All things must end that have begun.

Where is the time for hope or doubt?
A puff of the wind, and life is out;
A turn of the wheel, and the rest is won.
All things must end that have begun.

Golden morning and purple night,
Life that fails with the failing light;
Death is the only deathless one.
All things must end that have begun.
    Kyrielle, John Payne.

Here the eight-syllabled pattern is intermittently broken. There is of course no sacredness in any pattern. Such a simple form must compensate by climactic development from stanza to stanza, to justify itself in poetry.

The Pantoum

Ernest Fouinet introduced the Malayan pantoum into French versification, and Victor Hugo popularized it in the *Orientales*. It is written in four-line stanzas; and the second and fourth line of each stanza become the first and third of the succeeding stanza. In the last stanza, the second and fourth lines are the third and first of the first stanza; so that the opening and closing lines of the pantoum are identical. The rhyme scheme would then be: 1, 2, 1, 2; 2, 3, 2, 3; 3, 4, 3, 4; . . . n, 1, n, 1.

Brander Matthews gives an example of one in English:

Here we are riding the rail,
   Gliding from out of the station;
Man though I am, I am pale,
   Certain of heat and vexation.

Gliding from out of the station,
   Out from the city we thrust;
Certain of heat and vexation,
   Sure to be covered with dust.

Out from the city we thrust:
   Rattling we run o'er the bridges:
Sure to be covered with dust,
   Stung by a thousand of midges. . . .
      En Route, Brander Matthews.

to the final stanza, ending as the verses began:

Ears are on edge at the rattle,
   Man though I am, I am pale,
Sounds like the noise of a battle,
   Here we are riding the rail.

The Triolet

The triolet was the first of the rondeau family to appear. The first ones known appeared in the *Cléomadés* of Adenèz-le-Roi, who wrote in the latter part of the thirteenth century. At first, with ten syllables to each line, the triolet dealt with serious subjects. Today the form is usually eight syllables to the line, or even six; and the themes have grown appreciably and constantly lighter.

It has eight lines, with only two rhymes. The first line is repeated as the fourth line; the first two lines reappear as the seventh and eighth. The rhyme scheme is 1R, 2R, 1, 1R, 1, 2, 1R, 2R, the repeated lines appearing as 1R and 2R.

Suppose you decide to write a brief triolet, opening with the couplet:

> Drink deep—the glass
> Is full—and near!

You can at once fill out your fourth, seventh and eighth lines from this, making your pattern now appear as:

> Drink deep—the glass   1R
>   Is full—and near!   2R
> ——————————   1
> Drink deep! The glass   1R
> ——————————   1
> ——————————   2
> Drink deep—the glass   1R
>   Is full—and near!   2R

Only three lines, then, remain to be filled in. Once this is done, you have the triolet complete:

> Drink deep—the glass
>   Is full—and near!
> Come, lad and lass,
> Drink deep! The glass
> Too soon will pass
>   And disappear.
> Drink deep—the glass
>   Is full—and near!

At times a more serious mood rules the use of the form. Thus H. C. Bunner wrote:

> A pitcher of mignonette
>   In a tenement's highest casement;
> Queer sort of a flower-pot—yet
> That pitcher of mignonette
> Is a garden of heaven set
>   To the little sick child in the basement,
> The pitcher of mignonette
>   In the tenement's highest casement.
> > *Triolet,* Henry Cuyler Bunner.

Here we have no progress in thought in the use of the reiterated refrain or repetend. Worse than that, the refrain line alters from *A pitcher* to *That pitcher* and *The pitcher,* a vital fault in the use of refrains in the French forms.

A transition to the rondeau form is furnished by this eight-line verse by Leigh Hunt:

> Jenny kissed me when we met,
>   Running to the chair I sat in.
> Time, you thief, who love to get
>   Sweets upon your list, put *that* in!
> Say I'm weary, say I'm sad,
>   Say that health and wealth have missed me;
> Say I'm growing old, but add—
>   Jenny kissed me.
>   *"Jenny Kissed Me,"* Leigh Hunt.

The opening half of line one, reappearing as the refrain in line eight, prophesies the rondeau and similar forms. This brilliant little pattern has never become accepted and named.

The Rondel, Rondeau and Roundel Family

The triolet is the seed of the rondeau family. The *rondel* (the word is an old form of the later word *rondeau*) arose in all probability in Provence, and appeared later in the fourteenth century writings of north France, in the verse of Froissart, Deschamps and others. It began as a lyric of two stanzas, each stanza having four or five lines only, and rhyming triolet-wise upon two sounds. . . . Either a triolet, or a ten-line variant of the triolet.

With Charles d'Orleans, the rondel took the distinct form now assigned to it, of fourteen lines on two rhymes. The first two lines reappear as the seventh and eighth, and as the final couplet. —A mere variation of the triolet. This double repetition of the two-lined refrain made the form unwieldy. Later French poets shortened the form to thirteen lines, omitting the second line of the original refrain at the end.

The form as Charles d'Orleans used it appears in this rondel:

Paper, inviolate, white,	1R
Shall it be joy or pain?	2R
Shall I of fate complain,	2
Or shall I laugh tonight?	1

Shall it be hopes that are bright?	1
Shall it be hopes that are vain?	2
Paper, inviolate, white,	1R
Shall it be joy or pain?	2R

A dear little hand so light,	1
A moment in mine hath lain;	2
Kind was its pressure again—	2
Ah, but it was so slight!	1

Paper, inviolate, white,	1R
Shall it be joy or pain?	2R

To a Blank Sheet of Paper, Cosmo Monkhouse.

The following rondel, by Samuel Minturn Peck, is in the preferred modern pattern:

Before the dawn begins to glow,	1R
A ghostly company I keep;	2R
Across the silent room they creep,	2
The buried forms of friend and foe.	1
Amid the throng that come and go,	1
There are two eyes that make me weep;	2
Before the dawn begins to glow,	1R
A ghostly company I keep.	2R

Two dear dead eyes. I love them so!	1
They shine like starlight on the deep,	2
And often when I am asleep	2
They stoop and kiss me, being low,	1
Before the dawn begins to glow.	1R

"Before the Dawn," Samuel Minturn Peck.

The *rondeau* is, next to the ballade, the French form most popular in English. It is written, like triolet and rondel, on two rhymes throughout: thirteen full-length lines, and two briefer unrhymed refrains. The refrain may consist of the first half of the first line, but may consist merely of the first word. The fifteen lines are

THE COMPLETE RHYMING DICTIONARY
3grouped in three stanzas, the first of five lines, the second of three
lines and refrain, the third of five lines and refrain. The rhyme
scheme then is: 1, 1, 2, 2, 1; 1, 1, 2, R; 1, 1, 2, 2, 1, R. Here is a
rondeau that is a poem as well:

A man must live. We justify	1
Low shift and trick to treason high,	1
A little vote for a little gold	2
To a whole senate bought and sold	2
By that self-evident reply.	1
But is it so? Pray tell me why	1
Life at such cost you have to buy?	1
In what religion were you told	2
A man must live?	R
There are times when a man must die.	1
Imagine, for a battle-cry,	1
From soldiers, with a sword to hold,—	2
From soldiers, with the flag unrolled,	2
This coward's whine, this liar's lie,—	1
A man must live!	R

A Man Must Live, Charlotte Perkins Gilman.

The *roundel,* based upon occasional early French variants, is
today associated with the name of Swinburne, because of his
volume *A Century of Roundels.* As used by Swinburne, the
roundel was eleven lines long, two of which were the brief refrain
lines. The refrain either consisted of the opening word of line one,
or of a portion or a half of that line. If it consisted of more than
one word, it usually rhymed with the (2) sound rhyme. The
rhyming pattern then would be 1, 2, 1, R; 2, 1, 2; 1, 2, 1, R; or
1, 2, 1, 2R; 2, 1, 2; 1, 2, 1, 2R. Here is an example:

A Roundel is wrought as a ring or a starbright sphere,
With craft of delight and with cunning of sound unsought,
That the heart of the hearer may smile if to pleasure his ear
A roundel is wrought.

Its jewel of music is carven of all or of aught—
Love, laughter, or mourning—remembrance of rapture or fear—
That fancy may fashion to hang in the ear of thought.

As a bird's quick song runs round, and the hearts in us hear—
Pause answers to pause, and again the same strain caught,
So moves the device whence, round as a pearl or tear,
    A roundel is wrought.
    The Roundel, Algernon Charles Swinburne.

The *rondelet* is a seven-line fixed form, normally of four eight-syllabled lines, and three, the refrain lines, with four syllables each. The rhyme and rhythm scheme is: 1R, 2, 1R, 1, 2, 2, 1R—1R standing for the refrain line, and 1 for the line rhyming with it. Here is an example by May Probyn:

"Which way he went?"	1R
I know not—how should I go spy	2
Which way he went?	1R
I only know him gone. "Relent?"	1
He never will—unless I die!	2
And then, what will it signify	2
Which way he went?	1R

    Rondelet, May Probyn.

The *rondeau redoublé,* a remote relative of the rondeau, is in reality a formalized Theme With Variations treatment. It starts with a quatrain as a theme. This is followed by four additional quatrains, in each of which successively lines one, two, three, and four of the theme quatrain appear as the terminal lines. A concluding stanza has four lines of regular length, and a refrain (the first half of line one of the theme) to terminate.
An example will make this clearer:

My soul is sick of nightingale and rose,	1-a
The perfume and the darkness of the grove;	2-b
I weary of the fevers and the throes,	1-c
And all the enervating dreams of love.	2-d
At morn I love to hear the lark, and rove	2
The meadows, where the simple daisy shows	1
Her guiltless bosom to the skies above—	2
My soul is sick of nightingale and rose.	1-a
The afternoon is sweet, and sweet repose,	1
But let me lie where breeze-blown branches move.	2
I hate the stillness where the sunbeams doze,	1
The perfume and the darkness of the grove.	2-b

I love to hear at eve the gentle dove   2
Contented coo the day's delightful close.   1
   She sings of love and all the calm thereof,—   2
I weary of the fevers and the throes.   1-c

I love the night, who like a mother throws   1
   Her arms round hearts that throbbed and limbs that strove,   2
As kind as Death, that puts an end to woes   1
   And all the enervating dreams of love.   2-d

   Because my soul is sick of fancies wove   2
Of fervid ecstasies and crimson glows;   1
   Because the taste of cinnamon and clove   2
Palls on my palate—let no man suppose   1
            My soul is sick.   R
            Rondeau Redoublé, Cosmo Monkhouse.

As far as strict rhyming goes, *repose—suppose* and *throes—throws* are identities, and not rhymes.

The *glose,* which is superficially a freer variant of the foregoing pattern, derives apparently from a different source, and is found more often in Spanish and Portuguese verse than in French. It begins, like the rondeau redoublé, with a quatrain, here called the *texte,* which may be a quotation. This texte the glose proceeds to develop, in four stanzas of ten lines each, closing each stanza, as in the rondeau redoublé, with the successive four lines of the texte. The concluding stanza and refrain of the preceding form are omitted here. In the rhyme scheme, lines six, nine and the tenth or texte line in each stanza rhyme; the rest of the rhyme scheme differs with different users of the form.

Gleeson White, author of a definitive book on the French forms, was unable to discover at the time he wrote any example of the form in English. There are not many examples available. The texte in the following is from Graham R. Tomson's *Ballade of Asphodel.*

      "Queen Prosperpine, at whose white feet   1-a
         In life my love I may not tell,   2-b
      Wilt give me welcome when we meet   1-c
         Along the mead of Asphodel?"   2-d

Your Majesty, permit me to   3
   Indite, as one would say, this bit   4
Of verse respectfully to you;   3
Of course admitting *entre nous*   3
   You may not really fancy it;   4
Although it will be rather neat.   1
   And yet the dedication 's fit;   4
   I want assistance from your wit: 4
I should permit my heart to beat,   1
Queen Proserpine, at *whose* white feet?   1-a

Remember, Proserpine, I know   5
   That quite discriminatingly   6
You made your mind up long ago;   5
You did not like your Stygian beau;   5
   He smacked a bit of deviltry,—   6
And you were not designed for hell.   2
   This shows you're quite a clever she;   6
   Ergo, you ought to counsel me.   6
I *must* make up my mind, or,—well,   2
In life my love I may not tell.   2-b

Should I ask Venus, she would vote
   (That surely is a goddess' right)
For some dame with "a quivering throat
And bosom of desire"—I quote
   From memory the line tonight.
Minerva would choose some discreet
   Young woman, staid and erudite;
   But only she could give delight
Who would, though life's young roses sweet
Wilt, give me welcome when we meet.   1-c

Come, choose her for me! Let her be
   Stately or dumpy, brown or fair,
If only she'll agree that we
Should learn to dwell in harmony,
   Giving a gay good-bye to care,—
A beatific way to dwell!
   Come, Queen, be gracious to my prayer!
   But, no! Such maidens here are rare;
You'd scarce find such a demoiselle
Along the mead of Asphodel!   2-d
             The Quest, Clement Wood.

Naturally, the rhyming scheme of the texte (which is 1, 2, 1, 2 here), dictates the rhyming of the sixth, ninth and tenth lines of each main stanza. In other examples, the quatrain that forms the texte may have any quatrain rhyming, and so a similar extent dictates similar rhymes in each stanza. It is permissible to use the same rhymes in each stanza, except where the rhyme-sound of the texte line ordains differently. In other words, the four stanzas might be:

1-a, 2-b, 1-c, 2-d
3, 4, 3, 3, 4, 1, 3, 3, 1, 1-a
3, 4, 3, 3, 4, 2, 3, 3, 2, 2-b
3, 4, 3, 3, 4, 1, 3, 3, 1, 1-c
3, 4, 3, 3, 4, 2, 3, 3, 2, 2-d

This is not required by the strict rules.

The Sestina

Arnaut Daniel, a Provençal troubadour, invented the sestina at the end of the thirteenth century. In France it has been slightly popular. Dante and Petrarch liked to use it. Here are the rules, as drawn up by Daniel and his followers in Italy, Spain and Portugal:

1. The sestina has six stanzas, each of six lines, of the same length; and a concluding three-line stanza.
2. The lines of the six stanzas end with the same six words, not rhyming with each other; these end words are chosen exclusively from two-syllabled nouns.
3. The arrangement of these six terminal words follows a regular law, very complex in ancient times, and altered toward simplicity later, as appears hereafter.
4. The closing three-line stanza uses the six terminal words, three at the centers of the lines, three at their ends.

Modern usage permits the variation of allowing the terminating words to rhyme, either on two rhyming sounds, as Swinburne uses it, or on three. In every case, the six terminal words must be repeated, with no change in sound or spelling, through each succeeding stanza. The order for the six terminal words in the six successive stanzas is as follows:

1st stanza	1, 2, 3, 4, 5, 6
2nd stanza	6, 1, 5, 2, 4, 3
3rd stanza	3, 6, 4, 1, 2, 5
4th stanza	5, 3, 2, 6, 1, 4
5th stanza	4, 5, 1, 3, 6, 2
6th stanza	2, 4, 6, 5, 3, 1

The concluding half stanza ends with 2, 4, and 6; and uses 1, 3, and 5 at the beginning—not necessarily as the first word—of the lines; or at the half-line, in rhymes that permit their introduction there.

Here is an example: The numerals refer to terminal words, and not rhyme sounds.

We are the smiling comfortable homes,	1
With happy families enthroned therein,	2
Where baby souls are brought to meet the world,	3
Where women end their duties and desires,	4
For which men labor as the goal of life,	5
That people worship now instead of God.	6
Do we not teach the child to worship God?—	6
Whose soul's young range is bounded by the homes	1
Of those he loves, and where he learns that life	5
Is all constrained to serve the wants therein,	2
Domestic needs and personal desires,—	4
These are the early limits of his world.	3
And are we not the woman's perfect world,	3
Prescribed by nature and ordained of God,	6
Beyond which she can have no right desires,	4
No need for service other than in homes?	1
For doth she not bring up her young therein?	2
And is not rearing young the end of life?	5
And man? What other need hath he in life	5
Than to go forth and labor in the world,	3
And struggle sore with other men therein?	2
Not to serve other men, nor yet his God,	6
But to maintain these comfortable homes,—	1
The end of all a normal man's desires.	4

Shall not the soul's most measureless desires   4
Learn that the very flower and fruit of life   5
Lies all attained in comfortable homes,   1
With which life's purpose is to dot the world   3
And consummate the utmost will of God,   6
By sitting down to eat and drink therein.   2

Yea, in the processes that work therein—   2
Fulfilment of our natural desires—   4
Surely man finds the proof that mighty God   6
For to maintain and reproduce his life   5
Created him and set him in the world;   3
And this high end is best attained in homes.   1

Are we not homes? And is not all therein?   1, 2
Wring dry the world to meet our wide desires!   3, 4
We crown all life! We are the aim of God!   5, 6

Homes, Charlotte Perkins Gilman.

Here the lines end on accented syllables, and by no means on two-syllabled nouns exclusively. There is no sestina in any of the collections in English which follows this convention; it may be dismissed, with the reflection that the French, Spanish and Italian languages have more double rhymes than English.

The movements of each terminal word follow a definite pattern, as a graph of the numbered terminal words will show. The order of position is successively 1, 2, 4, 5, 3, 6, 1, 2, 4, 5, 3, etc. By this means the last word of one stanza terminates the first line of the next; and meanwhile the last line of next has been shifted from third position to last, to terminate line one of the ensuing stanza.

Swinburne uses, as terminal words in one of his rhymed sestinas, *day, night, way, light, may, delight,* as 1, 2, 3, 4, 5, 6; and thereafter achieves alternate rhymes throughout, by creating his own sequence pattern, as follows: 6, 1, 4, 3, 2, 5; 5, 6, 1, 4, 3, 2; 2, 5, 6, 1, 4, 3; 3, 2, 1, 6, 5, 4; 4, 3, 2, 5, 6, 1, with the terminals of the concluding triplet *light, way, delight* (4, 3, 6), and the internal rhymes here *day, night, may* (1, 2, 5). He has worked out even more intricately his rhymed double sestina, *The Complaint of Lisa*—twelve stanzas of twelve lines each, with a concluding sestet, of one hundred and fifty lines in all. Charles W. Coleman, in his sestina *Love's Going,* used three rhyme sounds, *sing, rose, heart, thing, goes, apart;* but he retains the unrhymed sequence formula, and thus has rhyming couplets in four of his stanzas. Swinburne's variation is to be preferred to this.

Clearly, in writing the sestina, after the first stanza has been completed, the next task is to write down the terminals for all the lines of the next five stanzas, and the terminals and center words of the brief concluding stanza. Then proceed to write. . . . The form is more suitable to clever light verse, than to poetry.

The Villanelle

The villanelle lends itself to seriousness, as well as to frivolity. It consists of nineteen lines: five three-lined stanzas, concluding with a quatrain. The refrain couplet, which terminates the form, consists of lines one and three of the first triplet. Moreover, line one (the first half of the refrain) terminates stanzas two and four, and line three (the other half of the refrain) stanzas three and five. Only two rhyming sounds are used. The following villanelle follows the pattern strictly:

O Singer of Persephone!	1-a
In the dim meadows desolate,	2
Dost thou remember Sicily?	1-b
Still through the ivy flits the bee	1
Where Amaryllis lies in state,	2
O Singer of Persephone!	1-a
Simaetha calls on Hecate,	1
And hears the wild dogs at the gate;	2
Dost thou remember Sicily?	1-b
Still by the light and laughing sea	1
Poor Polypheme bemoans his fate,	2
O Singer of Persephone!	1-a
And still in boyish rivalry	1
Young Daphnis challenges his mate:	2
Dost thou remember Sicily?	1-b
Slim Lacon keeps a goat for thee;	1
For thee the jocund shepherds wait,	2
O Singer of Persephone!	1-a
Dost thou remember Sicily?	1-b

Theocritus, Oscar Wilde.

Edwin Arlington Robinson pours poetry into the form, in a villanelle concluding:

> There is ruin and decay
>   In the House on the Hill:
> They are all gone away,
> There is nothing more to say.
> *The House on the Hill,* Edwin Arlington Robinson.

The Lai and the Virelai

The ancient French lai was composed of couplets of five-syllabled lines, all on the same rhyme, separated by single lines of two syllables each, which rhymed with one another. The number of lines in each stanzas was not fixed, nor the number of stanzas in the complete poem. An improvised example would be:

Summer heat today	1
In its torrid way,	1
I see,	2
With its awful ray	1
Sears till it must slay	1
Poor me,	2
Tree and grass and clay.	1
It's the bay—the spray	1
And glee!	2

A curious old tradition connected with the form is that the indentation of the shorter lines is forbidden. This detail was called *arbre fourchu,* a forked tree, from the fancied resemblance of the poem on paper to a tree with branches projecting. Where lais have more than one stanza, the two rhymes in each stanza have no reference to the rhymes in any other.

The *virelai* or *virelai ancien* grew out of this, with a sequence of rhymes throughout. Thus, in a twelve-line stanza, the rhymes would be 1, 1, 2, 1, 1, 2, 1, 1, 2, 1, 1, 2. The next stanza would be 2, 2, 3, 2, 2, 3, 2, 2, 3, 2, 2, 3; and so on, until the last stanza appeared as n, n, 1, n, n, 1, n, n, 1, n, n, 1. Thus each rhyme sound would appear once in the longer lines, and once in the shorter. The form is too simple to need illustration.

The *virelai nouveau* is written throughout on two rhymes. Its initial rhymed couplet serves as a refrain for the later stanzas; and the two lines close each stanza alternately until the last, when they both appear together, but in inverse order. Here is an example which begins with the couplet as its first stanza,

> Good-bye to the Town!—good-bye!   1 a
> Hurrah for the sea and the sky!   1-b
>
> *July,* Austin Dobson.

The second stanza is rhymed, 1, 1, 1, 2, 1, 1-a. Its third stanza is 1, 2, 1, 2, 1, 2, 2, 1, 1-b. The succeeding stanzas are as irregular, but each is confined to the two rhymed sounds, and the refrains occur in the prescribed order. And here is the concluding stanza, showing the refrain reversed:

> So Phyllis, the fawn-footed, hie   1
> For a hansom! Ere close of the day   2
> Between us a "world" must lie,—   1
> Hurrah! for the sea and the sky!   1-b
> Good-bye to the Town! GOOD-BYE!   1-a

The *Sicilian octave* at times is used as a fixed form. It consists in eight iambic five-foot lines, rhymed 1, 2, 1, 2, 1, 2, 1, 2. No difficulty will be found in writing in this pattern.

The *rispetto* is an Italian form, with inter-rhyming lines ranging from six to ten in number, though not usually exceeding eight. Used rarely in English, it is usually divided into two stanzas, rhymed 1, 2, 1, 2; 3, 3, 4, 4.

A brief American fixed form, called the *sonnette,* was originated by Sherman Ripley, and had a vogue for a time. It consisted of seven five-foot iambic lines, rhymed: 1, 2, 2, 1; 3, 2, 3. It differed only slightly from the *Canopus* stanza, already described, which also used seven five-foot iambic lines, but rhymed them 1, 2, 1, 2, 3, 2, 3. Both avoid the terminal couplet, and hence have an uninterrupted flow for narrative verse.

Another recent form is the *Douzet,* its origin unknown. It consists of twelve five-foot iambic lines, rhymed as follows: 1, 2, 2, 1; 3, 4, 4, 3; 1, 2, 3, 4. This introduces a novelty in the repetition of rhyme not encountered so far elsewhere: the concluding quatrain's rhyme-scheme amounting to a summary of the rhyme-sounds gone before.

There is no limit to the patterns that ingenuity in versification can produce. Only the rare few among these achieve enduring popularity.

The Japanese form, the *hokku,* follows Japanese poetry *(tanka or uta)* in having alternate verses of five and seven syllables. The hokku or *haikai* consists of only three lines, of 5, 7, and 5 syllables, or 17 in all. An improvised example is:

> More fleeting than the
> Flash of withered windblown leaf,
> This thing men call life.

The Japanese *tanka* ordinarily has 31 syllables, consisting of five lines, with respectively 5, 7, 5, 7, and 7 syllables. An improvised example is:

> The rippling sea-swell,
> Curling upon the gold sand,
> And, curving over,
> A bough of cherry blossoms,—
> Youth shielding eternal age.

Longer Japanese poems may be constructed in the tanka form, with the invariable alternation of 5 and 7 syllables to the line, and the addition of a terminal 7-syllabled line. The rhythm in Japanese poetry is not regarded. The only convention is the number of syllables to the line.

The Limerick

The limerick is the only fixed form indigenous to the English language. It first appeared in *Songs for the Nursery, or, Mother Goose's Melodies for Children,* published by Elizabeth Goose, (formerly Vertigoose, married to Thomas Fleet, a Boston printer,) in 1719. Moreover, in this collection it appeared in all three of its successive forms. The first stage opened and closed the five-line form with a nonsense line:

> Hickory, dickory, dock!
> The mouse ran up the clock.
> The clock struck one—
> The mouse ran down,
> Hickory, dickory, dock!
> *Nursery Rhymes,* Mother Goose.

The second form, the one used by Edward Lear throughout, ended the first and fifth line with a geographical name, at times these lines being identical :

> As I was going to Bonner,
> Upon my word of honor,
>   I met a pig
>   Without a wig,
> As I was going to Bonner.
>> *Nursery Rhymes,* Mother Goose.

The third and culminating form has a new rhyme sound in the fifth line—as this example :

> There was an old soldier of Bister
> Went walking one day with his sister,
>   When a cow at one poke
>   Tossed her into an oak,
> Before the old gentleman missed her.
>> *Nursery Rhymes,* Mother Goose.

A classic model to follow is the famous limerick—

> There was a young lady from Niger,
> Who smiled as she rode on a tiger.
>   They came back from the ride
>   With the lady inside,
> And the smile on the face of the tiger.
>> *More Limericks,* Cosmo Monkhouse.

The identity instead of rhyme in lines 2 and 5 cannot spoil the charm of this, although the pure pattern would avoid it. This would be—remembering that an extra unaccented syllable can be added either to the 1, 2, 5 rhyme group, or to the 3, 4 group, or to both :

> ta TUM—ta ta TUM—ta ta TUM
> ta TUM—ta ta TUM—ta ta TUM,
>   ta ta TUM—ta ta TUM
>   ta ta TUM—ta ta TUM
> ta ta TUM—ta ta TUM—ta ta TUM.

In other words, an anapestic pattern, 5, 5, 3, 3, 5 feet to the lines respectively, rhymed 1, 1, 2, 2, 1; usually with an iamb opening lines 1 and 2. Any trick rhyming device is permissible, as :

An amorous M. A.
Says that Cupid, that C. D.,
    Doesn't cast for his health,
    But is rolling in wealth—
He's the John Jaco-B. H.
                                    Anonymous.

This must be read by pronouncing *M. A.* "master of arts," and by
rhyming lines two and five properly to it,—"caster of darts" and
"Jacob Astor of hearts." Here is one of the tongue-twister variety:

A tutor who tooted the flute
Tried to teach two young tooters to toot.
    Said the two to the tutor,
    "Is it harder to toot, or
To tutor two tooters to toot?"
                        Four Limericks, Carolyn Wells.

Among other possible variations is:

There was a young lady of Diss,
Who said, "Now I think skating bliss!"
    This no more will she state,
    For a wheel off her skate
¡sᴉɥʇ ǝʞᴉl ƃuᴉɥʇǝɯos dn ɥsᴉuᴉɟ ɹǝɥ ǝpɐW
                                    Anonymous.

The writing of limericks at times becomes extremely popular.

Little Willies

Any form may become, almost overnight, a favorite with poets
and especially light verse writers. Some college student wrote and
published in his college paper a rhyme proceeding approximately
like this:

Tobacco is a filthy weed.
    I like it.
It satisfies no normal need.
    I like it.
It makes you thin, it makes you lean,
It takes the hair right off your bean;
It's the worst darned stuff I've ever seen.
    I like it.
                                    Anonymous.

At once this form was copied by newspaper and other light versifiers the breadth and length of the land, and is still intermittently alive.

Another form assumed wide popularity, arising from one of Col. D. Streamer's (Harry Graham's) *Ruthless Rhymes for Heartless Homes:*

> Billy, in one of his nice new sashes,
> Fell in the fire and was burned to ashes.
> Now, although the room grows chilly,
> I haven't the heart to poke poor Billy.
> *Tender-Heartedness,* Harry Graham.

The quatrain here consists of two couplets, rhymed 1, 1, 2, 2. The metre combines trochees and dactyls; it might be iambs and anapests, of course, or any of the four. Somehow Billy became rechristened Willie, and at least one anonymous volume has appeared since, dealing in this or other simple quatrains with the adventures of Willie and his family. Among famous ones are:

> Willie and two other brats
> Licked up all the Rough-on-Rats.
> Father said, when mother cried,
> "Never mind, they'll die outside."
> Anonymous.

> Father heard his children scream,
> So he threw them in the stream,
> Saying, as he drowned the third,
> "Children should be seen, *not* heard!"
> *The Stern Parent,* Harry Graham.

> Late last night I slew my wife
> Stretched her on the parquet flooring.
> I was loath to take her life,
> But I *had* to stop her snoring.
> *Necessity,* Harry Graham.

> Willie poisoned father's tea;
> Father died in agony.
> Mother looked extremely vexed:
> "Really, Will," she said, "what next?"
> Anonymous.

The model for a Little Willie, with its trick last line and its sadistic content, can be taken from any of these.

Light Verse in English

Light verse, including its elegant form called *vers de société,* demand a technical dexterity greater than that of poetry; for the obviousness and cleverness of the rhyme are a charm here, where they usually interfere with the emotional effect of poetry. The student of versification will benefit by studying Tom Hood, for the use of puns in light verse; *Mother Goose,* for inspired use of rhythm; Edward Lear and Lewis Carroll, for shapely nonsense verse; Charles Stuart Calverley for mastery of every trick of rhyming, and great dexterity in stanza-devising; W. S. Gilbert, for mastery of the whole field. The long finale of his *Iolanthe* is his peak in rhyming, and almost the peak of light verse in English. Split words are a constant device: as in Carroll's—

> Who would not give all else for two p-
> Ennyworth of beautiful soup?
> *Soup of the Evening*, Lewis Carroll.

or another surprise rhyming sung by Canning:

> Sun, moon, and thou vain world, adieu,
>   That kings and priests are plotting in;
> Here doomed to starve on water-gru-
> -El, never shall I see the U-
>   -Niversity of Gottingen,
>   -Niversity of Gottingen!
> *Song by Rogero,* George Canning.

Humorous verse need not be clever. A poem like Ernest Lawrence Thayer's *Casey at the Bat* is a perpetual favorite because the theme invokes deep laughter, not because it is trickily versified. Dialect verse is in a class by itself. In writing dialect verse, be careful

(1) To use dialect spelling only where required.

(2) Not to overuse it, or the reader will not understand it. Such an improvised quatrain as—

Sum niggers iz peculyer,
I reitteratez agen,
They mus' come f'um Atlanta
An' not from Bummin'ham

is full of bad writing. *Sum* is the correct pronunciation of *some,*
not a dialect pronunciation; the same is true of *iz, reitteratez,* and
agen. The same is probably true of *peculyer.* And why *f'um* and
from in the same poem? This is as inept as using *you* and *thou*
(in any form) in the same poem, to refer to the same person.
F'um, mus' and *an'* are accurate dialect speech.

Among other forms of light verse are *parody,* aping the versifying mannerisms of another; *nonsense verse; whimsical verse* of
many kinds; *mosaic* or *composite verse,* each line taken from some
other poet; *macaronic verse,* where two or more languages are
hashed together; *shaped whimsies,* where the typography pictures
the theme, as in the *Song of the Decanter,* on page 96.

Various forms of *typographical oddities* may be devised, in
which certain of the lines (as the terminals of each quatrain)
represent the way a person walks, sober, or intoxicated, or the
way he falls down.

Acrostics are verses where the opening letters of the lines, or
the closing letters, or letters arrived at by some other system, name
a person, or convey a special message. Here is an example:

*F*rom your bright sparkling Eyes I was undone;
*R*ays, you have; more transparent than the Sun,
*A*midst its glory in the rising Day
*N*one can you equal in your bright array;
*C*onstant in your calm and unspotted mind,
*E*qual to all, but will to none Prove kind,
*S*o knowing, seldome one so Young, you'll Find,
*A*h! woe's me, that I should Love and conceal
*L*ong have I wished, but never dared reveal,
*E*ven though severely Love's Pains I feel;
*X*erxes that great, wasn't free from Cupid's Dart,
*A*nd all the great Heroes, felt the smart.
                    Acrostic, George Washington.

The words conveyed by the acrostic are revealed by reading downward the first or italicized letters of each line.

The actual writing of light verse calls upon the versifier for every resource and device within the technique of versification. The rhymes should be natural and not rhyme-induced, and the entire treatment natural and adapted to please and amuse.

There was an old decanter
and its mouth was gaping
wide; the rosy wine had
ebbed away and left
its crystal side;
and the wind
went humming
—humming up
and down: the
wind it flew, and
through the reed-
like hollow neck the
wildest notes it blew.
I placed it in the window,
where the blast was blow-
ing free, and fancied that its
pale mouth sang the queerest
strains to me. "They tell me—puny
conquerors! the Plague has slain his ten,
and war his hundred thousand of the very
best of men; but I"—'twas thus the Bottle spake—
"but I have conquered more than all your famous
conquerors, so feared and famed of yore. Then come,
ye youths and maidens all, come drink from out my cup,
the beverage that dulls the brain, and burns the spirits up;
that puts to shame your conquerors that slay their scores
below; for this has deluged millions with the lava
tide of woe. Tho' in the path of battle darkest
streams of blood may roll, yet while I killed the
body, I have damned the very soul. The
cholera, the plague, the sword such ruin
never wrought, as I in mirth or
malice on the innocent have
brought. And still I breathe
upon them, and they shrink before
my breath, while year by year my
thousands go my dusty way of death."

Song of the Decanter, Warfield Creath Richardson.

POETRY AND TECHNIQUE

The Vocabulary of Poetry

THE vocabulary used by a poet in his poetry should be the vocabulary that he uses in his living speech. Prose uses this, or else it becomes stilted and affected. If an orator commences,

O Mississippi, Father of Waters, thou wast engendered in the hills of Minnehaha; thou hast meandered through meadows green and valleys dappled for more miles than man computeth,

his hearers feel that there is something strained and unnatural in his words. The same thought occurs, when poetry, especially modern poetry, contain words no longer in the living vocabulary of man, because they have become archaic; or else unknown to the living vocabulary, because they are artificially constructed to meet the exigencies of rhyme or metre: such words as—

Thou, thee, thy, ye, mineself.

Art (verb form), *wast, wert, dost, wilt* (verb form), *hast, hadst, wouldst, shouldst, shalt,* and all verb forms ending in *-est, -st* and the like.

'Tis, 'gainst, 'gin, 'tween, 'neath, e'er, and other contractions not in living speech; as opposed to *it's* and other contractions used in living speech.

Wroth, bethink, reft, reaving, athwart, welkin, rathe, fardel, burthen, murther, nave, chaps, gins, sooth, Norweyan, proof (for *armor*), *composition* (for *terms of peace*), *ronyon,* and all other archaic, obsolescent or obsolete words.

Except for "unless," *memorize* for "make memorable," and other outworn usages of words.

All unnatural and elliptical expressions, improper in living speech, such as *as to* for "as if to," *bethink me* for "recall," *for to that* for "for to that end," and the like.

All inversions and strained expressions improper in living speech, such as *the soldier brave, have I seen, I battles fought,* and the like. These are common, because rhyme-induced.

Poetry that speaks a dead language is dead from its birth; poetry that speaks a warped and distorted language is warped and distorted from its birth. For when real poetry from real poets is encountered, its speech is as direct, forthright and living as:

> Our revels now are ended. These our actors,
> As I foretold you, were all spirits, and
> Are melted into air, into thin air;
> And, like the baseless fabric of this vision,
> The cloud-capp'd towers, the gorgeous palaces,
> The solemn temples, the great globe itself,
> Yea, all which it *inherit*, shall dissolve,
> And, like this insubstantial pageant *faded*,
> Leave not a *rack* behind. We are such stuff
> As dreams are made *on*, and our little life
> Is rounded with a sleep.
> > *The Tempest*, William Shakespeare.

The captious might suggest *inherits* for *inherit*; might point out that *faded* is out of place; that "made *of*" is preferable to "made *on*"; we might query the *rack*. At that, *rack* is still used in "rack and ruin," a "cloud-rack," "the rack of a storm": and *rack*, used here in the sense of a vestige, is intelligible and may be regarded as living. And this poetry was written more than three hundred years ago, by William Shakespeare, who knew too much, even then, to stud his verse with *thee's* and *thou's* and their outmoded verb forms, *welkin, athwart, amaranthine,* and so on.

The test for the phrasing of poetry is: could you have said the same thing, or its equivalent, to your maid or your butcher, and not been regarded as eccentric? If your poetry speaks your own living language, its vocabulary is acceptable. If it is marred with word-fossils no longer acceptable in living speech, to that extent it falls below its possible flight.

No word acceptable in acceptable prose is out of place in poetry. Any word may be so ineptly or awkwardly used in poetry, that it becomes a blemish. When Shakespeare wrote:

> It is a tale
> Told by an idiot, full of sound and fury,
> Signifying nothing,
> > *Macbeth,* William Shakespeare.

he used *idiot* magnificently and poetically; when Wordsworth
wrote:

> Why bustle thus about your door?
> What means this bustle, Betty Foy?
> Why are you in this mighty fret?
> And why on horseback have you set
> Him whom you love, your Idiot Boy?
>> *The Idiot Boy*, William Wordsworth.

the word *idiot* is as unpoetic as the rest of the passage. The living
speech, the colloquial, can be magical, poetic, as in this sonnet
sestet:

> It is some lie that under a windswept tree,
>   Touching your lips, I touched my vanished youth,
> And found again a young, new ecstasy.
>   It is a lie, I say. This—this is Truth!
> Now—I shall rest. For youth and you are gone.
> Tomorrow I shall put my flannels on.
>> *Sonnet*, John V. A. Weaver.

Edwin Arlington Robinson will be remembered for lines as
colloquially magical as:

> The man who had made other men
> As ordinary as arithmetic . . .

> I'll have to tell you, Brother Bedivere,
> That crowns and orders, and high palaces, . . .
> Will not go rolling down to hell just yet
> Because a pretty woman is a fool.
>> *Merlin*, Edwin Arlington Robinson.

He will have to be forgiven for verse as bookish as:

> Born with a face
> That on a bullfrog would ensure for life
> The lucubrations of a celibate . . .

> Less to remembering an obscure monition
> Than to confessing an assured renascence—
>> *Roman Barthalow*, Edwin Arlington Robinson.

though both of these are not so much archaic as morbidly pedantic.
Frost rarely departs from living speech; he has enriched the

language by phrases immortally and colloquially true, including the familiar:

> The trial by market everything must come to.

Even slang has its place: did not Shakespeare have Hamlet say—

> So I do still, by these pickers and stealers . . .
> > *Hamlet,* William Shakespeare.

Nor is Sandburg more unpoetic, when he writes:

> Play it across the table.
> What if we steal this city blind?
> If they want anything let 'em nail it down.
> > *Cahoots,* Carl Sandburg.

John Livingston Lowes, in *Convention and Revolt in Poetry,* phrases words of gold for poets to remember:

> The very greatest effects of poetry are often produced without the use of a single word which might not be employed in ordinary speech.

Thomas Gray wrote, in one of his letters:

> The language of the age is never the language of poetry. . . . Our poetry . . . has a language peculiar to itself.

This attitude explains the common idea permitting dead speech in verse; it can not resurrect poets following it from the graves their practice of this dug. Such poets live only insofar as they violate this statement.

Wordsworth followed this, when he preluded his *The Force of Prayer* with the double archaism:

> What is good for a bootless bene?

Witty Mary Lamb flashed back, when her brother Charles read this to her, "A shoeless pea," and punned this absurd line into immortality. And there is Rossetti's phrase from his rendition of the Villon ballade,

> From Love he won such dule and teen!

Poetry does not gain by using such mummified speech.

Kipling was more successful than any previous poet so far in using the language of the machine age in poetry:

It is their care, in all the ages, to take the buffet and cushion the
  shock;
It is their care that the gear engages; it is their care that the switches
  lock;
It is their care that the wheels run truly; it is their care to embark
  and entrain,
Tally, transport, and deliver duly the sons of Mary by land and main.
                         The Sons of Martha, Rudyard Kipling.

In a memorandum dealing with the writing of *Leaves of Grass,*
Walt Whitman wrote:

> I had great trouble in leaving out the stock
> "poetical" touches, but succeeded at last.

Even this great plain-speaking master slipped back, as he aged,
into stock poeticisms such as:

> 'mid, unrecked, know I, yield we, ye valleys grand.

But in the main he avoided this blemish. And he has made the
task easier for those who followed him.

Sidney Lanier lays stress upon *phonetic syzygy,* that extension
of alliteration which includes all related consonants, as *t, d, th,* and
TH; g, k, ch, and other gutturals, and so on. Other authorities deal
extensively with *onomatopoeia,* the language device in which
words reproduce the sounds they are intended to convey, as in—

> With lisp of leaves and ripple of rain.
> *Chorus from Atalanta in Calydon,* Algernon Charles Swinburne.

With any inner sense of music, we will avoid lines as awkward,
inept and unsingable as Browning's familiar:

> Irks care the crop-full bird, frets doubt the maw-crammed beast?
>   *Rabbi Ben Ezra,* Robert Browning.

Let your poetic speech be your own living speech at its best, dictated by an innate sense of music, and the result will satisfy.

On Translating Poetry

Poetry can not be translated; it can only be recreated in the
new language. We are dealing with the ingredients of verse, not
of poetry, in this book: a study of the essence of poetry would

not deal with iambs and cinquains and sestinas, it would deal with the stimuli that most deeply affect the human emotions. The emotion-arousing quality in words can not be stated otherwise even in the same language, much less in another one. There is no translation in English for emotion-arousing words such as *home, mother, love,* and so on; not *house* or *domicile,* not *mamma* or *maternal ancestor* or *Moms* or *ma,* not *affection* or *devotion* or *lust* or *rut.* How can *night* be expressed in another word, or *moon* or *sun,* or *May,* or *December?* Each of these words—to some extent each word in the language—has a tone-color, a history, a personality, an effectiveness of its own. With many of the words in the language, each person has strange and personal associations, naturally untranslatable. There are emotions which are not translatable from country to country, but which can only be recreated by some remote equivalent. When Noyes climaxes a poem with the glorious invocation,

> Englande!—Englande!—Englande!—Englande!
> *Marchaunt Adventurers,* Alfred Noyes.

he utters a battle-cry that only an Englishman could thrill to. Its word music is lost the moment it reappears as *Angleterre! Angleterre! Angleterre! Angleterre!* "Finland! Finland! Finland! Finland!" would not thrill similarly, though the rhythm and word tune are the same. A fourfold repetition of *Switzerland,* or *Czechoslovakia,* or, queerly enough, even of *United States,* would not evoke a similar thrill. Moreover, Shelley could have used the same repetition of *England,* in a poem in the bitter mood of *The Masque of Anarchy,* and it would have evoked utter detestation: so intangible are the elements in sounds that uplift or break the heart, that send a Cardigan or a Pickett with a whole brigade of men to death at the monosyllable "Charge!," that spell heaven in a girl's whispered "Yes," and a lifetime's dearth in her even briefer "No."

In Keats's *Ode to a Nightingale* we have two lines of peak magic:

> Charmed magic casements, opening on the foam
> Of perilous seas, in faery lands forlorn.

These two lines can not be said differently in English, without wrecking the magic. Accurately paraphrased, they would give:

> Enchanted supernatural windows, unclosing on the bubbles
> Of dangerous oceans, in unreal romantic countries dejected.

There is no poetry here, now. Translate it with absolute fidelity into another language, and the poetry is as dead. It must be re-created by a poet of like emotional power in the other language, if it is to survive there as poetry.

Fitzgerald did such magic, when he took a literal translation of the poetic *Rubaiyat* of Omar Khayyam, such as these two groups of lines:

> Everywhere that there has been a rose or tulip-bed,
> It has come from the redness of the blood of a king;
> Every violet shoot that grows from the earth
> Is a mole that was once on the cheek of a beauty.
>
>   *Quatrains,* Omar Khayyam.

This is inaccurate botanically, and only whimsically effective as an idea. It is certainly not poetry. Nor is:

> Hell is a spark from my useless worries,
> Paradise is a moment of time when I am tranquil.
>
>   *Quatrains,* Omar Khayyam.

But out of this material Fitzgerald wrought—created, recreated—what thousands hail as poetry:

> I sometimes think that never blows so red
> The Rose, as where some buried Caesar bled;
>   That every Hyacinth the Garden wears
> Dropt in her Lap from some once lovely Head. . . .

> Heav'n but the Vision of fulfilled Desire,
> And Hell the Shadow from a Soul on fire,
>   Cast on the Darkness into which Ourselves,
> So late emerged from, shall so soon expire.
>
>   *Rubaiyat of Omar Khayyam,* Edward Fitzgerald.

This is no longer Omar Khayyam; it is far more Fitzgerald, inspired by Omar Khayyam. The reflection about the rose is acceptable now; the whimsey about the hyacinth is more pleasing to us than the more fleshly Oriental passion of the mole on the cheek of a beauty. The definitions of heaven and hell no longer resemble the original at all. Oriental impassivity and superiority to things

earthly have been replaced by a viewpoint accurate enough to have
come out of Freud, and acceptable as concentrated truth to many
of us. All of this is expressed with the most effective devices of
versification, a language in which poetry must speak, if it speak at
all.

Something like this must be done, each time you seek to make a
translation. A literal translation can give the idea, but never the
poetry.

For a last example, here is an accurate translation of the first
five verses of the first chapter of *Genesis,* by Fagnani:

> At the beginning of Elohim's forming the heavens and the earth,
> when darkness was upon the face of the abyss, Elohim said, "Let
> there be light," and there was light.
> Elohim saw that the light was excellent.
> And Elohim separated the light from the darkness and he called
> the light Day and the darkness he called Night.
> Evening came, and Morning came.
>> *The Beginning of History, According to the Jews,*
>>   Charles Prosper Fagnani.

This is near to poetry, so magnificent is the primitive conception.
But it is not mere familiarity that makes us recognize, from the
hands of greater poets writing in English, the magnificent poetry
of the same verses, as they appear in the King James' Bible:

> In the beginning God created the heavens and the earth.
> And the earth was without form, and void; and darkness was
> upon the face of the deep. And the Spirit of God moved upon the
> face of the waters.
> And God said, Let there be light: and there was light.
> And God saw the light, that it was good; and God divided the
> light from the darkness.
> And God called the light Day, and the darkness he called Night.
> And the evening and the morning were the first day.
>> *Genesis,* King James's Translation.

The most accurate translation of a poem is no more than rude
notes for a poem to be built upon. There is always need for accurate renditions of the poetry of other lands and tongues. But,
unless the English versifier re-issue the product as his own re-cre-
ation, it remains mere verse, a museum curiosity rather than impassioned song.

Exercises in Versification

To give the book its greatest value, the reader, having reached this point, should start over again, and write exercises in each poetic device treated. Practice iambic lines, each number of feet to the line, rhymed and unrhymed. The same with trochaic, anapestic, and dactylic lines. At times seek to pour poetry into these molds; at times find the relief of light verse in them.

Essay the stanzas, from the couplet up to such involved arrangements as the Spencerian stanza and *terza rima*. Work on sonnets of both kinds: aiming at technical mastery, rather than poetic excellence, at first. Get the patterns etched on your mind, and then you can write in them accurately without consciously remembering them. Try the solace of concentrated and poetic free verse. And then, if you care to, go at the fixed forms one after another, preferably in light verse, and among all these attempts you will startle yourself by achieving at times a veritable poem or gem of light verse when you merely intended finger-exercises.

And at all times, when the poetic mood comes, write what comes, from a phrase, a line, a couplet, to an epic fragment: and preserve it, on the chance that, sooner or later, the rest of the poem will come.

VIII

THE COMPLETE RHYMING DICTIONARY

What Rhyme Is

RHYME is the identity in sound of an accented vowel in a word, usually the last one accented, and of all consonantal and vowel sounds following it; with a difference in the sound of the consonant immediately preceding the accented vowel.

Rhyme thus deals exclusively with sound. Sound is indicated in all dictionaries by phonetic markings. In this rhyming dictionary, each group of words that rhyme is preceded by a heading consisting of the accented vowel, marked phonetically, and followed by all the consonantal and vowel sounds following it. The unaccented vowels are not marked phonetically, since they are relatively unimportant: except to distinguish between rhyme sounds like *pasture* (ĂS'tŭr) and *faster* (ĂS'tŭr).

The one-syllabled rhymes are given first, with the rhyme-sound headings arranged alphabetically, from the first A sound to the last U sound. Then follow the two-syllabled rhymes, similarly arranged; and, last of all, the three-syllabled rhymes.

The Vowel Sounds

In this phonetic arrangement, the vowel sounds used are indicated as follows. After each is given the various ways in which the sound appears in spelling in English.

A

Ā as in ale; heard also in pain, day, break, veil, obey, gaol, gauge, eh.
Â as in care; heard also in there, pear, air, heir, prayer, e'er.
Ă as in add; heard also in plaid, bade.
Ä as in arm, father; heard also in hearth, sergeant, memoir.
Å as in ask. Strictly, authorities say that A should be so pronounced
    (midway between the A in *father* and the A in *add*) when fol-

lowed by *s, th, f,* or *m* or *n* plus a consonant. In practice, this sound is usually pronounced like the A in *add*. The rule becomes absurd, when we try to pronounce *pan* with the A sound in *add,* and *pans* with a different A sound.

E

Ē as in me; heard also in eve, feet, beam, deceive, people, key, Caesar, machine, field, quay, phoebe.

Ẹ̄ as in here; heard also in fear, dreary, weird.

Ĕ as in end; heard also in heifer, leopard, friends, Aetna, feather, asafoetida, bury, any, Thames, said, says.

I

Ī as in ice; heard also in vie, rye, height, eye, aisle, aye meaning *yes,* sky, buy, choir.

Ĭ as in ill; heard also in sieve, English, pretty, been, breeches, women, busy, build, nymph, hymnal.

O

Ō   as in old; heard also in note, oh, roam, foe, shoulder, grow, owe, sew, yeoman, beau, hautboy, brooch.

Ô   as in or; heard also in all, talk, swarm, haul, caught, law, fought, broad, memoir.

Ŏ   as in odd; heard also in want, wash, shone.

OI   as in oil; heard also in boy.

OŎ   as in foot; heard also in full, wolf, could.

OU   as in out; heard also in cow, sauerkraut.

U

Ū as in use; heard also in beauty, feud, pew, queue, lieu, view, cue, suit, yule, you, do, rule, true, food, group, drew, fruit, canoe, rheum, maneuvre, blue. (The difference in sound between *dew* and *do* is that *dew* is properly dyŪ, with a consonantal *y* sound preceding the long U. This difference does not affect rhyming, except as it concerns preceding consonants. For the sake of convenience, the yŪ group ordinarily precedes the Ū group.)

Û as in urn; heard also in fern, err, heard, sir, word, journal, myrrh, colonel.

Ŭ as in up; heard also in won, one, does, flood, double.

The Consonant Sounds

The consonant sounds used in English, and in most instances spelt phonetically in the headings preceding all groups of words rhyming together, are as follows:

B   as in baby.

CH   as in chair; heard also in match, question, righteous.

D   as in did; heard also in robbed.

F   as in fill; heard also in philosophy, laugh.

G   as in go, anger; heard also in guard, plague, ghost.

GZ   as the sound represented by *x* in exist.

H   as in hat.

HW   as the sound represented by *wh* in what.

J   as in joke; heard also in gem, religion, pigeon, soldier, edge.

K   as in keep; heard also in chorus, epoch, cube, pack, conquer, pique.

KS   as the sound represented by *x* in vex.

KW   as the sound represented by *qu* in queen.

L   as in late.

M   as in man.

N   as in no.

N   The French nasal sound, not natural in English.

NG   as in sing; heard also in tongue, bank, junction, linger, canker.

P   as in papa.

R   as in red; heard also in rhombus.

S   as in so, this; heard also in cell, scene, hiss.

SH   as in she; heard also in machine, ocean, social, conscious, sure, nauseous, pension, issue, passion, nation.

T   as in time.

TH   as in then.

th   as in thin.

TU   as in nature. This sound is more accurately TY consonantal.

V   as in van.

W   as in want; heard also in persuade, choir.

Y   as in yet; heard also in union.

Z   as in zone; heard also in is, lives, Xenophon.

ZH   as the sound represented by *z* in azure; heard also in glazier, pleasure, vision, abscission, rouge, genre.

A few warnings are important.

C is not a separate sound. Words spelt with *c* appear under K or S

Q is not a separate sound. Words spelt with *qu* or *q* appear under KW.

X is not a separate sound. Words spelt with *x* appear under GZ or KS; initial *x* appears as Z.

NK, in words like *rank,* is properly NGK, and so appears. *Hankow* would appear under ĂN′kow; hanker, under ĂNGK′ur.

To form plurals and other inflections, F, K, P and T are followed by the sound S; the plain vowel, G, D, B, M, N, S, V, J, CH, L, R, KS (X) and Z are followed by the sound Z.

To form past tenses and other inflections, CH, S, F, K and P are followed by the sound T; the plain vowel, G, D, B, M, N, S, V, J, L, R and Z are followed by the sound D.

Sound Does Not Depend on Spelling

Sound does not depend on spelling. "Eye-rhymes," or words matched as rhymes only because they are spelled alike, need not be rhymes at all. For instance, here are five different sounds spelled alike, *ough:*

cough, enough, plough, though, through.

It is as logical to rhyme these together as to rhyme *earth-hearth, bare-are, north-forth, real-steal.*

Again, note that *timber* and *climber* are spelled alike; but the first rhymes with limber (ĬM′bur) and the second with rhymer (ĪM′ur). Three more words spelled alike but rhymed very differently are *ginger* (ĬNJ′ur); *singer* (ĬNG′ur); and *finger* (ĬNG′gur). Until *cow* rhymes with *blow* it is well to avoid all these words spelled alike but pronounced differently.

This Dictionary Makes Consonance Accurate

Consonance consists in the identity of all consonantal and vowel sounds after the accented vowel; and a difference in the accented vowel. This dictionary, classified according to strict phonetic pronunciation, for the first time makes consonance easy and accurate. Alphabetically arranged by the headings preceding each group of rhyme words, the following three rhyme sounds appear together: Ō′li (wholly), Ô′li (Raleigh), ŎL′i (folly). Naturally these three groups are in consonance with each other.

To get the other groups of rhyming words which may be used in consonance with these three, look up successively Ā′li, ĂL′i, Ē′li, ĔL′i, OIL′i, OŎl′i, OUL′i, Ū′li, ŬL′i; and you have all the possible sounds in consonance with the three sounds given. You may stretch a point and add ÂR′li, ĂR′li, ĒR′li and ŪR′li if you wish, and now nothing conceivable is omitted.

Consonance, always used by the best poets, is growing so increasingly in favor, that this use of the present *Complete Rhyming Dictionary* may become very important.

Why This is Called Complete

This volume contains hundreds of rhyming words omitted from former collections. Many of these omissions are inexplicable, unless by oversight. Others consist of words recently added to the vocabulary, especially in the fields of general science, pure and applied; inventions and popular applications of them, such as moving pictures, aviation, and radio; and the vivid field of recent slang words generally acceptable. The effort has been to include all words that are a proper part of the living vocabulary of man: for it is in this language that living poetry must speak.

Archaic and obsolete words, and many words used only in an artificial solemn or poetic style, have not been omitted. Instead, as a rule these have been italicized. They are still available to the seeker who wishes to use them, each in its proper niche. But this feature both includes them for convenience, and badges them with the suggestion that, since they are not a part of man's living vocabulary, they may well be avoided.

In addition to this, the present volume contains more proper names than were ever listed in a rhyming dictionary before. This includes especially:

The familiar first names of boys and girls, men and women.

The familiar and easily rhymable geographical names.

The more familiar surnames, family names or last names.

In listing proper names, the name is not repeated when it differs only from a common word by the use of a capital. Thus, since *wood* is included, *Wood* is not. Where the spelling differs, the rhyming proper name is usually added. Thus, to *main* is added

Maine. Moreover, unnecessary duplication of words is generally avoided throughout the book. A large number of words ending in *-y* is given as rhymes for the long E sound; but, at the end of this large list, the reader is referred to other words ending in *-y,* to be found in such three-syllabled rhyme groups as the words rhyming with *ability;* which is to be consulted, if the seeker desires more rhymes for long *E.* Moreover, at the end of the rhyming words listed to rhyme with 'fade,' the reader is referred to the list of words rhyming on the long A sound, to which *-ed* is to be added, to make further rhymes for 'fade'; and this is to be consulted, if the seeker desires more rhymes for 'fade.' There is as little such cross-reference as possible, and it is never perplexing.

The dictionary is not wholly complete, and probably none will ever be. Rare and unusual scientific and geographic terms and names, for instance, as a rule have been omitted. It will add to the value of your copy of the book if you add, at the appropriate place, all omitted words that you discover.

In the lists of words rhyming on the last syllable and on the syllable before the last, certain words are included, which have no rhyming mates. The monosyllables or words accented on the last syllable which appear to be rhymeless are:

aitch, H	lounge	recumb
avenge, revenge	mauve	rouge
avenged, revenged	month	sauce
bilge	morgue	scarce
bourne	mourned, bemourned,	spoilt
bourse	unmourned	swoln
bulb	mouthe	sylph
coif	of, hereof, thereof,	torsk
culm	whereof	twelfth
cusp	peart	plagued, unplagued
doth	porch	warmth
film	pork	wasp
forge	poulp	wharves
fugue	prestige	wolf
gulf, engulf	puss	wolves

In addition to these forty-three rhymeless sounds, there is a group which has no rhyme in the living vocabulary:

amongst	forth, fourth
breadth	ninth
depth	sixth
eighth	tenth
fifth	width

These can all be rhymed by using permissible contractions of archaic or obsolete forms, such as: *clung'st, shed'th, step'th, hate'th, sniff'th, pour'th, pine'th, mix'th, pen'th* and *skid'th*. There is a limited group of words which find their rhyming mates only in proper names, including:

alb (De Kalb)   hemp (Kemp)   oblige (Lije)

There are other words which have no proper rhyming mates, but have words so close in sound that they are used as rhyming mates by many poets:

blague (vague)	en masse (class)
raj (dodge)	basque (mask, masque)
wand (pond)	else (belts)
melange (blanc mange)	grilse (wilts)
swap (top)	Welsh (belch)

THE DICTIONARY
OF RHYMING WORDS

Section I

MONOSYLLABLES, AND WORDS ACCENTED ON THE LAST SYLLABLE:

MASCULINE RHYMES; SINGLE RHYMES

A

These words include the following accented vowel sounds:

Ā as in ale; heard also in pain, day, break, veil, obey, gaol, gauge, eh.

Â as in care; heard also in there, pear, air, heir, prayer, e'er.

Ă as in add; heard also in plaid, bade.

Ä as in arm, father; heard also in hearth, sergeant, memoir.

Å as in ask. In practice, this is usually pronounced like the A sound in *add*.

For the vowel sound heard in all, talk, swarm, haul, caught, law, see under Ô.

For the vowel sound heard in want and wash, see under Ŏ.

Ā	astay	belay	Bordelais
affray	astray	bepray	bouquet
agley	au fait	betray	brae
allay	auto-da-fé	*bewray*	bray
alackaday	away	birthday	bridle-way
array	aweigh	Biscay	byway
Ascension-day	*aye*	bobsleigh	cabriolet
assay	bay	bobstay	Calais
assagai	bey	Bombay	caraway

In compound words—words consisting of two or more words united—the parts of the words may be joined without a hyphen, may be joined with a hyphen, or may be written separately. In some words usage is fixed; in others it varies. No standard rule is followed; though the hyphen today is less used than formerly. In this book, the usual practice of the best prose-writers and poets is followed, modified in instances by the editor's own preference. In general, poets and versifiers make such decisions for themselves in each instance.

ōld, ôr, ŏdd, oil, foŏt, out; ūse, ûrn, ŭp; THis, thin

113

castaway | fairway | interlay | overlay
causeway | fair-play | interplay | overpay
Chevalier | fay | inveigh | overstay
Chevrolet | feather-spray | irongray | papier mâché
Christmas-day | fey | jay | passée
clay | fireclay | judgment-day | Passion-play
Cloisonné | first-day | Kay | pathway
convey | flay | lack-a-day | pay
corvée | footway | Lady-day | payday
coryphée | foray | leaden-gray | play
coupé | forelay | lay | playday
crossway | foresay | leeway | popinjay
dapple-bay | forestay | Leigh | portray
dapple-gray | forlay | Lord's-day | pray
day | fray | mainstay | prepay
dead-pay | gainsay | Malay | prey
decay | gala-day | Mandalay | protegé
defray | galloway | market-day | protegée
dejeuner | gangway | matinée | purvey
delay | gay | May | qua
dey | get-away | mid-day | quarter-day
disarray | good-day | mid-way | railway
dismay | gourmet | Milky Way | raisonné
disobey | gray | mislay | ray
display | grey | missay | relay
distingué | habitué | Monterey | repay
distrait | Haigh | Monterrey | résumé
doomsday | halfway | nay | reveillé
Doré | hay | née | ricochet
dragonné | hearsay | negligêe | Roget
dray | hey | neigh | roturier
Dupré | heyday | noonday | roundelay
Easter-day | *highday* | nosegay | runaway
eh | highway | obey | sachet
émigré | hodden-gray | O'Day | Salomé
employé | hogmanay | Okay | San Jose
employée | holiday | O'Shay | Santa Fé
entremets | Honoré | outlay | Saturday
essay | hooray | outstay | say
estray | horseplay | outré | scray
exposé | inlay | outweigh | settling-day

seventh-day
shay
silver-gray
slay
sleigh
sley
sobriquet
soiree
soothsay
soufflé
spay
splay
spray
stageplay
stay
steerage-way
stowaway
strathspey
stray
subway
survey
sway
thereaway
they
to-day
Tokay
toupet
tourniquet
tramway
tray
trey
trysting-day
tway
underlay
underpay
underplay
undersay
unlay
unpray
unsay
uplay

upstay
virelay
visé
water-way
way
waylay
wedding-day
weekday
weigh
welladay
wellaway
wey
whey
workaday
working-day
Wray
yea
yesterday

Ä

Aceldama
ah
aha
algebra
alumina
amphibia
anathema
Andromeda
anglophobia
animalcula
Apocrypha
Aquila
automata
baa
baccarat
bacteria
bah
basilica
blah
bourgeois
camera

carnivora
chapeau bras
cholera
cinema
clepsydra
cupola
éclat
Egeria
ephemera
et cetera
fa
faux-pas
formula
genera
Golgotha
gondola
grandmamma
ha
hah
ha-ha
Hegira
holla
hurrah
huzza
hydrophobia
hypochondria
incognita
insomnia
Jah
la
ma
mamma
majolica
mandragora
nebula
opera
orchestra
pa
padishah
pah
papa

parabola
pariah
pas
pasha
peninsula
phantasma-
 goria
phenomena
plethora
prolegomena
Pthah
quadrigesima
quadrumana
quinquagesima
replica
retina
septuagesima
sexagesima
Shah
silica
spa
spatula
tarantula
tonic sol-fa
Utopia
uvula
vertebra
viola

ĀB

Abe
astrolabe
babe
cosmolabe
foster-babe

ĂB

abb
bab
Babb
baobab

ōld, ôr, ŏdd, oil. fŏŏt, out; ūse, ûrn, ŭp; THis, thin

bedab
blab
cab
Cantab
confab
crab
dab
drab
frab
gab
grab
jab
knab
lab
mab
McNabb
nab
rab
scab
shab
slab
stab
tab
taxi-cab

ĂB

squab
swab, etc.
(See blob, etc.,
  ŎB)

ĀCH

aitch
H

ĂCH

attach
batch
brach
catch
cratch

detach
dispatch
hatch
latch
match
overmatch
patch
percussion-
  match
ratch
scatch
scratch
slatch
smatch
snatch
tache
thatch
unlatch

ĂCH

watch
(see blotch,
  ŎCH)

ĂCHT

hatched
semi-detached
attached, etc.

ĀD

abrade
abraid
accolade
Ade
Adelaide
afraid
aid
alcaide
ambassade
ambuscade
arcade

bade
balustrade
barricade
bæstinade
bejade
Belgrade
blade
blockade
braid
brigade
brocade
cade
camerade
camisade
cannonade
carronade
cascade
cassonade
cavalcade
centigrade
charade
co-aid
cockade
colonnade
corrade
croupade
crusade
dade
dairy-maid
Damascus-
  blade
decade
deep-laid
defilade
degrade
dissuade
dragonnade
enfilade
escalade
escapade
esplanade

estacade
estrapade
evade
fade
falcade
fanfaronade
fire-brigade
flanconnade
free-trade
fusillade
gabionnade
gallopade
gambade
gasconade
glade
glissade
grade
grass-blade
grenade
grillade
hade
handmaid
harlequinade
harquebusade
inlaid
interlaid
invade
jade
lade
laid
lancepesade
lemonade
made
maid
make the grade
marinade
marmalade
masquerade
McDade
mermaid
milkmaid

new-made
nightshade
old-maid
orangeade
overlaid
overpaid
overstayed
over-persuade
overshade
paid
palisade
panade
parade
pasquinade
passade
persuade
pervade
pesade
pistolade
plaid
plantigrade
pomade
postpaid
prepaid
promenade
raid
rayed
ready-made
renegade
retrograde
rodomontade
saccade
scalade
sea-maid
self-made
serenade
serving-maid
shade
slade
spade
stade

staid
stockade
storm-stayed
suade
suède
tirade
trade
unafraid
unarrayed
unassayed
unbraid
underaid
underlaid
undismayed
unessayed
unlade
unlaid
unmade
unmaid
unpaid
unprayed
unrepaid
unstaid
unweighed
upbraid
wade
(see Ā + ed)

ÅD

ad
add
bad
bedad
begad
bade
brad
cad
Chad
chiliad
clad
dad

egad
englad
fad
footpad
forbade
gad
glad
grad
had
heath-clad
hebdomad
iron-clad
ivy-clad
lad
Leningrad
mad
moss-clad
myriad
Olympiad
pad
Petrograd
pine-clad
plaid
rad
sad
scad
shad
superadd
tonguepad
Trinidad
unclad
undergrad
unforbade
unsad
winter-clad
yclad

ÄD

baa'd
chamade
charade

couvade
estrade
façade
glissade
ha-ha'd
hurrahed
hussa'd
lancepesade
noyade
pomade
promenade
psha'd
roulade
wad
(see *cod,* etc.)

ÄDZ

ads
adze
scads
adds, etc.

ĀF

chafe
enchafe
safe
strafe
unsafe
vouchsafe
waif

ÅF

actinograph
agraffe
anagraph
autograph
behalf
belly-laugh
betterhalf
calf
calligraph

ōld, ôr, ŏdd, oil, fŏŏt, out; ūse, ûrn, ŭp; THis, thin

carafe
cenotaph
chaff
chronograph
cinematograph
cross-staff
cryptograph
diagraph
dictagraph
distaff
draff
eidograph
epigraph
epitaph
flagstaff
gaff
giraffe
graff
hagiograph
half
half-and-half
halfstaff
heliograph
holograph
ideograph
idiograph
laugh
lithograph
monograph
mooncalf
palaeograph
pantograph
paragraph
penny-gaff
phonograph
photograph
polygraph
quaff
quarter-staff
raff
riff-raff

shandy-gaff
staff
stenograph
stereograph
telegraph
tipstaff
whipstaff

ĂF

behalf
belly-laugh
betterhalf
calf
graf
haaf
half
half-and-half
laugh
mooncalf
strafe

ĂFT

abaft
aft
craft
daft
draft
draught
engraft
fellow-craft
graft
haft
handicraft
ingraft
overdraft
priestcraft
raft
river-craft
sea-craft
shaft
waft

witchcraft
chaffed, etc.

ĀG

Hague
plague
Prague
vague

ĂG

bag
battle-flag
brag
Bragg
bullyrag
cag
chew the rag
crag
drag
fag
fishfag
flag
gag
hag
jag
knag
lag
mag
nag
nighthag
quag
rag
ragtag
saddle-bag
sag
ᵒcallawag
scrag
shag
shrag
slag
snag

sprag
stag
swag
tag
wag
Wragg
zigzag

ĂG

blague

ĀGD

unplagued

ĂGD

betagged
bagged, etc.

ĀJ

acreage
age
alienage
anchorage
appanage
arbitrage
armitage
assuage
average
baronage
beverage
brigandage
brokerage
cage
cartilage
chaperonage
compage
concubinage
cooperage
discage
disengage
encage

---

engage
enrage
equipage
espionage
flowerage
foliage
foot-page
fortilage
gage
gauge
harborage
hemorrhage
heritage
hermitage
hospitage
leverage
lineage
mage
matronage
mid-age
mucilage
outrage
page
parentage
parsonage
pastorage
pasturage
patronage
peonage
personage
pilgrimage
pilotage
plunderage
porterage
pre-engage
presage
pupilage
quarterage
rage
rampage
ramgauge

sage
saxifrage
seignorage
stage
surplusage
swage
tutelage
tutorage
uncage
unsage
vassalage
verbiage
vicarage
vicinage
villanage
villenage
wage
weather-gauge

ĂJ

badge
cadge
fadge
hadj

ÄJ

raj
(Cf. badge, ĂJ)

ĀK

ache
after-rake
aslake
awake
backache
bake
barley-brake
bellyache
betake
blacksnake
Blake

brake
break
cake
crake
day-break
drake
earache
earthquake
fake
flake
forespake
forsake
garter-snake
hake
hard-bake
heartache
heart-break
jake
johnny-cake
lake
make
mandrake
milk-snake
mistake
namesake
opaque
outbreak
overtake
partake
quake
rake
rattlesnake
robin-wake
sake
seed-cake
shake
sheik
sheldrake
slake
snake
snow-flake

spake
stake
steak
stomachache
strake
sweepstake
take
toothache
undertake
unmake
upbreak
uptake
wake
wapentake
water-break
water-crake
water-snake
wedding-cake

ĂK

aback
alack
almanac
ammoniac
attack
bac
back
bareback
bivouac
black
blackjack
bootjack
brach
bric-a-brac
cardiac
chack
clack
claque
crack
cul-de-sac
demoniac

dipsomaniac
Dyak
egomaniac
elegiac
Fond du Lac
good-lack
gripsack
hack
Hackensack
hackmatack
haversack
haystack
horseback
huckaback
humpback
hunchback
hypochondriac
jack
jimcrack
kayak
kleptomaniac
knack
knicknack
kodak
lac
lack
ladybrach
lakh
leather-jack
macaque
maniac
monomaniac
natterjack
pack
pickaback
plack
Pontiac
pyromaniac
quack
rack

ransack
rucksack
sac
sack
sacque
sal ammoniac
seawrack
shack
skipjack
slack
slapjack
Slovak
smack
snack
stack
stickleback
symposiac
tack
tamarack
thrack
thunder-crack
thwack
tick-tack
track
umiak
Union-jack
unpack
whack
woolpack
woolsack
wrack
yak
yashmak
yellow-jack
zodiac
zwieback

ĂK

plaque
Sarawak

ĀKS

Jakes
(see ĀK + s)

ĂKS

Analax
anticlimax
Astyanax
ax
battle-ax
flax
Halifax
income-tax
lax
parallax
pax
relax
Sachs
Saxe
slacks
tax
wax
zax
(see ĂK + s.)

ĂKT

abstract
act
attacked
attract
bract
cataract
compact
contract
counteract
detract
diffract
distract
enact
entr' acte
exact

extract
fact
impact
infract
intact
matter-of-fact
overact
pact
protract
react
redact
re-enact
refract
retract
retroact
saddle-backed
subtract
tact
tract
transact
underact
untracked
backed, etc.

ĀL

Abigail
ail
ale
all-hail
assail
avail
aventail
bail
bale
bepale
betail
bewail
blackmail
Bloomingdale
bobtail
brail

Braille
camail
canaille
cocktail
countervail
curtail
dale
dead-pale
death-pale
derail
detail
disentail
dovetail
draggle-tail
dwale
empale
engaol
engrail
enjail
enscale
entail
entrail
exhale
fail
fairy-tale
farthingale
flail
foresail, etc.
frail
Gael
Gail
gale
gaol
grail
grisaille
hail
hale
handrail
hobnail
impale
inhale

interpale
inveil
jail
kail
kale
mail
male
martingale
monorail
nail
nightingale
outsail
overveil
pail
pale
paravail
pigtail
prevail
quail
rail
regale
retail
sail
sale
scale
shale
sliding-scale
snail
spale
stale
swale
tael
tail
tale
tenaille
they'll
trail
travail
trundle-tail
unveil
vail

vale
veil
wail
wale
whale
wholesale

ĂL
aboriginal
academical
accentual
admiral
aërial
aesthetical
affectional
agricultural
Al
alchemical
alchemistical
alexipharmical
alexiterical
algebraical
alkalimetrical
allegorical
allodial
alluvial
alphabetical
amatorial
analogical
analytical
anarchical
anatomical
angelical
animal
annual
antediluvial
anthological
antiphonal
antipodal
antithetical
apochryphal

apologetical
apostolical
arboreal
arboricultural
archeological
architectural
arithmetical
arsenal
arsenical
ascetical
asthmatical
astrological
atmospherical
Babylonical
bacchanal
bacchical
bacteriological
bal
balsamical
banal
barometrical
baronial
basilical
beatifical
biblical
bibliographical
bibliomaniacal
bibliopolical
biographical
biological
boreal
botanical
Brahmanical
bureaucratical
cabal
cacophonical
Cal
Calvinistical
canal
cannibal
canonical

capital
caracal
cardinal
carnival
cartographical
casual
casuistical
categorical
catholical
cervical
chaparral
characteristical
chemical
cherubical
chimerical
chronological
circumlocu-
　tional
classical
clerical
climatical
clinical
collateral
colloquial
comical
communal
complexional
conclusional
conditional
confessional
congressional
conical
conjectural
conjugal
connubial
consanguineal
consistorial
constitutional
continual
contradictional
conventical

conventional
conventual
conversational
corporal
corral
cortical
cosmetical
cosmical
coxcombical
criminal
critical
cryptical
cubical
cyclical
cylindrical
cynical
dal
decanal
decimal
deistical
democratical
demoniacal
demonological
denominational
descensional
destinal
devotional
diabolical
diaconal
diacritical
diagonal
diagraphical
dialectical
dialogical
dialogistical
diametrical
diaphonical
dictatorial
didactical
dietetical
digital

digressional
diluvial
diplomatical
dipsomaniacal
discretional
divisional
doctrinal
dogmatical
dolorifical
dominical
dramatical
dropsical
Druidical
dynamical
eccentrical
ecclesiastical
economical
ecstatical
ecumenical
educational
effectual
egoistical
egotistical
electrical
elegiacal
elliptical
emblematical
emotional
emphatical
empirical
empyreal
encomiastical
encyclical
encyclopedical
endemical
energetical
energical
enigmatical
enthusiastical
ephemeral
epical

epidemical
epigrammati-
　cal
Episcopal
episodical
epithetical
equivocal
erotical
esoterical
ethereal
ethical
ethnical
ethnological
etymological
Eucharistical
eulogistical
euphemistical
euphonical
evangelical
eventual
evolutional
exceptional
exegetical
exoterical
exotical
expurgatorial
extemporal
extrinsical
falderal
fanatical
fantastical
farcical
federal
festival
fictional
finical
forensical
fractional
functional
funeral
funereal

gal
galvanical
geminal
genealogical
general
generical
genial
geographical
geological
geometrical
germinal
gradual
grammatical
graphical
habitual
Hal
harmonical
Hebraical
heliacal
hemispherical
herbal
heretical
heroical
hexagonal
hierarchical
historical
horticultural
hospital
hygienical
hymeneal
hyperbolical
hypercritical
hypochondria-
    cal
hypocritical
hysterical
identical
idiotical
illogical
imaginal
imitational

immaterial
immechanical
immemorial
imperial
impersonal
inaugural
incorporeal
individual
industrial
ineffectual
infinitesimal
infusorial
inimical
initial
inquisitorial
inspirational
institutional
instructional
insurrectional
intellectual
intentional
intercessional
interjectional
international
interval
iridal
ironical
jesuitical
jovial
juridical
lachrymal
lackadaisical
laical
lethargical
Levitical
liberal
literal
littoral
liturgical
logical
longitudinal

lyrical
madrigal
magical
magnifical
majestical
mall
maniacal
mareschal
marginal
marital
mathematical
matinal
matronal
mechanical
medical
medicinal
memorial
mercurial
meridional
metaphorical
metaphysical
methodical
Methodistical
metrical
microscopical
mineral
ministerial
misanthropical
monarchical
municipal
musical
mutual
mystical
mythical
mythological
national
natural
nautical
nectareal
nominal
nonsensical

notional
numerical
occasional
octagonal
optical
optional
oratorical
original
pal
paradisaical
parabolical
parenthetical
passional
pastoral
pathetical
pathological
patrimonial
patronal
patronymical
pedagogical
pedantical
pedestal
pedestrial
penological
pentagonal
perennial
periodical
peripheral
periphrastical
perpetual
personal
phantasma-
    gorial
Pharisaical
pharmaceutical
phenomenal
philanthropi-
    cal
philological
philosophical
photographical

ōld, ôr, ŏdd, oil, fŏŏt, out; ūse, ûrn, ŭp; THis, thin

phrenological
phthisical
physical
physiological
pictorial
pictural
pietistical
piratical
pivotal
platonical
pneumatolog-
ical
poetical
polemical
political
pontifical
post-prandial
practical
pragmatical
precautional
preternatural
primordial
principal
probational
problematical
processional
prodigal
professional
professorial
progressional
prophetical
proportional
proverbial
provisional
psychiatrical
psychical
psychological
punctual
puritanical
purpureal
pyramidal

pyramidical
pyrotechnical
quadrennial
quadrigesimal
quadrilateral
quadrupedal
quizzical
radical
rational
recessional
reciprocal
remedial
residual
retinal
rhapsodical
rhetorical
rheumatical
rhythmical
ritual
sabbatical
sal
sartorial
satanical
satirical
scenical
skeptical
schismatical
scholastical
scriptural
sculptural
seigneurial
seigniorial
seneschal
sensational
seraphical
several
shall
sideral
sidereal
sociological
Socratical

sophistical
spasmodical
spherical
sporadical
stoical
strategical
supernatural
sybaritical
symbolical
symmetrical
synchronal
synchronical
synodical
synonymal
synonymical
synoptical
synthetical
systematical
tactical
technical
technicological
temporal
terminal
terrestrial
territorial
testimonial
theatrical
theological
theoretical
theosophical
topical
topographical
traditional
tragical
trivial
tropical
typical
typographical
tyrannical
umbilical
uncanonical

usual
uxorial
vatical
vegetal
ventriloquial
vertebral
vertical
vesperal
vicarial
victorial
viminal
virginal
virtual
visional
visual
volitional
vortical
whimsical
zodiacal
zoological

ĂL
kraal
Lasalle
morale

ĂLB
alb
De Kalb

ĀLD
bobtailed
unbewailed
unhaled
unassailed
ailed, etc.

ĂLD
caballed
corralled

āle,   câre,   ădd,   ärm,   åsk;   mē,   hĕre,   ĕnd;   īce,   ĭll;

emerald

palled

ĂLF

Alf

Ralph

ĂLK

catafalque

talc

ĂLKS

calx

catafalques

ĂLP

alp

palp

scalp

ĂLPS

Alps

palps, etc.

ĂLT

shalt

ĂLV

bivalve

priming-valve

safety-valve

salve

valve

ĀLZ

Marseilles

Wales

(see ĀL + s)

ĂM

acclaim

aflame

aim

ashame

became

blame

came

claim

counterclaim

crème de la

crème

dame

declaim

defame

disclaim

disfame

entame

exclaim

fame

flame

frame

game

hame

inflame

lame

maim

Mame

melodrame

misname

name

nickname

overcame

proclaim

reclaim

same

self-same

shame

surname

tame

ĂM

Abraham

ad nauseam

am

Amsterdam

anagram

battering-ram

Birmingham

cablegram

cam

Cham

clam

cofferdam

cram

cryptogam

cryptogram

Cunningham

dam

damn

diagram

diaphragm

dithyramb

drachm

dram

epigram

flimflam

gam

gram

ham

jam

jamb

lam

lamb

ma'am

madame

Mam

marjoram

McAdam

monogram

Nizam

Nottingham

oriflamme

parallelogram

Petersham

pram

ram

Rotterdam

salaam

Schiedam

scram

sham

shram

slam

stereogram

swam

telegram

tram

whim-wham

yam

ĂM

balm

becalm

calm

embalm

Guam

imam

impalm

Islam

ma'am

malm

palm

psalm

qualm

salaam

ĂMB

dithyramb

gamb

ĀMD

unblamed

unclaimed

unframed

unnamed	**ĀMZ**	champaign	frangipane
unreclaimed	Ames	Champlain	gain
unshamed	James	Charles's Wain	germane
untamed	acclaims, etc.	chatelaine	grain
acclaimed, etc.		chicane	henbane
	ĂMZ	chilblain	humane
ĂMP	alms	chow mein	hurricane
after-damp	balms, etc.	cocaine	hydrophane
camp		Cockaigne	hydroplane
champ	**ĀN**	complain	immane
clamp	abstain	constrain	inane
cramp	aerophane	contain	ingrain
damp	aeroplane	co-ordain	insane
Davy lamp	again	counterpane	interchain
death-damp	Aisne	coxswain	interreign
decamp	allophane	crane	inurbane
encamp	amain	Dane	jain
enstamp	appertain	deign	Jane
firedamp	aquaplane	delaine	Jayne
gamp	arraign	demesne	jean
guimpe	ascertain	deraign	lain
lamp	attain	detain	lane
minedamp	*atwain*	detrain	legerdemain
ramp	bane	diaphane	lithophane
revamp	battering-**train**	disdain	Lorraine
safety-lamp	Bayne	distrain	main
samp	bearing-rein	domain	Maine
scamp	bestain	drain	maintain
signal-lamp	blain	Duchesne	mane
stamp	boatswain	Duquesne	Mayne
tamp	bower-thane	elecampane	McLain
tramp	brain	enchain	McLean
vamp	bridle-rein	engrain	*mediterrane*
	Cain	entertain	misfeign
ĂMP	Caine	entrain	moraine
swamp	campaign	explain	mortmain
(see ŎMP)	campane	fain	obtain
	cane	fane	ordain
ĂMPT	chain	feign	pain
undamped	chamberlain	fleabane	Paine
camped, etc.	champagne	foreordain	pane

Payne
pertain
plain
plane
pleasure-train
porcelain
preordain
profane
pursuit plane
quatrain
rain
refrain
regain
reign
rein
remain
restrain
retain
sane
scatterbrain
Seine
sextain
skein
slain
soutane
Spain
sprain
stain
strain
subterrane
sugarcane
sustain
suzerain
swain
ta'en
tain
terrain
thane
thegn
train
twain

unchain
unrein
uptrain
urbane
vain
vane
vein
vervain
wain
water-crane
wane
weather-vane

ĂN

Acadian
African
alabastrian
Alcoran
Aldebaran
alderman
Alexandrian
Algerian
also ran
amatorian
Amazonian
American
amphibian
an
Anglican
Ann
Anne
antediluvian
artisan
Baconian
ban
Barbadian
barbarian
barbican
barracan
bartizan
basilican

Batavian
Bavarian
began
Bezonian
Bohemian
bran
Briarean
Bulgarian
caducean
Caledonian
Cambrian
can
Canadian
caravan
castellan
Catalan
catamaran
charlatan
Cimmerian
clan
clergyman
Columbian
comedian
Copernican
corban
Corinthian
cosmopolitan
countryman
courtesan
cran
custodian
Cyprian
Dan
Delphian
diluvian
divan
Dominican
echinidan
Englishman
equestrian
Ethiopian

fan
firman
fisherman
flan
foo young dan
foremast-man
foreran
frying-pan
fugleman
Gallican
gargantuan
gentleman
hard-pan
harridan
Hesperian
historian
husbandman
Indian
inspan
Isfahan
Isle of Man
Japan
journeyman
juryman
khan
latitudinarian
librarian
lighterman
liveryman
luggage-van
man
Marianne
Matapan
medicine-man
merchantman
meridian
merman
metropolitan
Mexican
Michigan
midshipman

Milan
minute-man
Mohammedan
Mussulman
nectarean
nobleman
octogenarian
Olympian
oppidan
orang-utan
ortolan
ottoman
outran
outspan
overman
overran
pan
Parmesan
partisan
pavane
pecan
pedestrian
pelican
pemmican
Peruvian
plan
platitudinarian
postmeridan
praetorian
predestinarian
Presbyterian
prison-van
procrustean
proletarian
Promethean
publican
puritan
quarry-man
quotidian
Ramadhan
ran

rattan
redan
Republican
Sabbatarian
Sacramenta-
  rian
sacristan
Samaritan
scan
Sedan
serving-man
shandrydan
signal-man
span
spick-and-span
Stygian
subterranean
suffragan
superman
talisman
tally-man
tan
than
Thespian
tragedian
trepan
unman
utilitarian
Utopian
valerian
valetudinarian
Valkyrian
van
Vatican
vegetarian
Vesuvian
veteran
veterinarian
vulgarian
warming-pan
waterman

wherryman
Zoroastrian

ÄN
corban
swan
wan, etc.
(see ÖN)

ANCH
avalanche
blanch
branch
carte-blanche
flanch
ganch
ranch
scranch
stanch

ÄNCH
Blanche
haunch
launch
manche
paunch
stanch
staunch

ÄNCHD
unstanched
launched, etc.

ĀND
bloodstained
constrained
diaphaned
disdained
feather-
  brained
hare-brained

hot-brained
interveined
maned
muddy-brained
rattle-brained
scatter-brained
self-restrained
shallow-
  brained
shatter-brained
travel-stained
unascertained
unconstrained
unplained
unprofaned
unreined
unrestrained
unstained
unstrained
unsustained
untrained
abstained, etc.

ĂND
aband
abbey-land
ampersand
and
band
bland
brand
bridle-hand
command
contraband
countermand
demand
deodand
disband
expand
fairy-land
fatherland

ăle, câre, ădd, ärm, åsk; mē, hẹre, ĕnd; īce, ĭll;

firebrand
first-hand
four-in-hand
full-manned
gland
grand
hand
ill-manned
imband
land
lotus-land
manned
master-hand
minute-hand
multiplicand
overhand
overland
rand
remand
reprimand
Rio Grande
Samarcand
sand
saraband
second-hand
self-command
stand
strand
underhand
understand
unhand
unland
unmanned
unscanned
upper-hand
washstand
withstand
wonderland
(see ĂN + ed)

ĂND
wand
(see ŎND)

ĂNG
bang
bhang
boomerang
clang
fang
gang
gobang
hang
harangue
meringue
mustang
orang-outang
overhang
pang
Penang
rang
sang
sea-tang
serang
shebang
slang
slap-bang
spang
sprang
stang
swang
tang
trepang
twang
uphang
vang
whang

ĂNGD
langued

unpanged
banged, etc.

ĂNGK
bank
Blanc
blank
brank
chank
clank
crank
dank
drank
embank
enrank
flank
franc
frank
hank
lank
mountebank
outflank
outrank
plank
point-blank
prank
rank
sank
savings-bank
shank
shrank
slank
spank
stank
tank
thank
twank
water-tank
Yank

ĂNGKS
Manx
(see
 ĂNGK + s)

ĂNGKT
sacrosanct
spindle-
 shanked
unspanked
(see
 ĂNGK + ed)

ĀNJ
arrange
change
counter-change
derange
disarrange
enrange
estrange
exchange
grange
interchange
mange
range
rearrange
seachange
strange

ĂNJ
flange
phalange

ĀNS
advance
ambulance
appurtenance
arrogance
askance

ōld, ôr, ŏdd, oil, fŏŏt, out;   ūse, ûrn, ŭp;   THis, thin

bechance
chance
circumstance
complaisance
concomitance
consonance
continuance
conversance
countenance
country-dance
dance
death-dance
deliverance
demi-lance
discountenance
dissonance
dominance
elance
elegance
enhance
entrance
expanse
extravagance
exuberance
finance
France
furtherance
glance
heritance
ignorance
impuissance
incogitance
incognisance

inconsonance
inhabitance
inheritance
intemperance
intolerance
irrelevance
lance
luxuriance
manse
mischance
Nance
ordinance
penetrance
perchance
petulance
prance
precipitance
predominance
preponderance
protuberance
puissance
radiance
recognizance
reconnaissance
relevance
resonance
romance
sibilance
significance
stance
sufferance
suppliance
tolerance

trance
utterance
variance
vigilance
(Cf. ĂNT + s)

ĂNS

fer-de-lance
insouciance

ĂNT

acquaint
ain't
attaint
bepaint
besaint
complaint
constraint
daint
depaint
distraint
faint
feint
Geraint
liver-complaint
mayn't
paint
plaint
quaint
restraint
saint
self-restraint
straint

taint
'taint
teint
unconstraint
unsaint

ĂNT or ÅNT

abdicant
adamant
adjutant
adulterant
agglutinant
altitonant
altivolant
ambulant
annuitant
ant
anticipant
applicant
appurtenant
arrogant
askant
aslant
aunt
brant
cant
can't
chant
combatant
commandant
communicant
complaisant
concomitant

Throughout this rhyming dictionary, sounds as close alike as *ant, chant,* and *abdicant* are listed together as perfect rhymes. Strictly, these three words differ slightly in the pronunciation of the *a* sound: they are properly pronounced as

ănt   chănt   abdicănt

Similarly, words like *age* and *acreage* are listed together as perfect rhymes: for this is the immemorial practice of poets. Their strict pronunciation, as used in conversation or prose, differs: *age* rhyming with *stage,* and *acreage* with *ridge.* The poetic pronunciation might be regarded as an eye-rhyme universally accepted in versification.

confidant
confidante
congratulant
consonant
conversant
cormorant
corposant
corroborant
Corybant
courant
covenant
decant
deplant
descant
determinant
dilettant
disenchant
disputant
dissonant
dominant
elegant
elephant
emigrant
enchant
excommunicant
executant
exorbitant
extant
extravagant
exuberant
fabricant
figurant
figurante
flagellant
fulminant
gallant
gallivant
Gant
germinant
grant
gratulant

habitant
hesitant
hierophant
ignorant
illuminant
imaginant
immigrant
implant
impuissant
incogitant
incognisant
inconsonant
inhabitant
insignificant
intolerant
intoxicant
irradiant
irrelevant
irritant
itinerant
jubilant
Kant
Levant
litigant
luminant
luxuriant
mendicant
militant
miscreant
nonchalant
occupant
odorant
pant
penetrant
petulant
plant
postulant
precipitant
predominant
preponderant
procreant

Protestant
protuberant
puissant
pursuivant
quant
rant
recalcitrant
recant
recreant
recusant
refrigerant
reiterant
relevant
resonant
resuscitant
reverberant
ruminant
sacrificant
scant
scintillant
sensitive-plant
shan't
sibilant
significant
slant
stimulant
suffragant
supplant
suppliant
supplicant
sycophant
tant
termagant
tintinnabulant
tolerant
toxicant
transplant
undulant
variant
vigilant

visitant
vociferant

ĂNT

aunt
can't
debutante
shan't

ĂNTH

amaranth
amianth
tragacanth

ĂNTS

pants
(see ĂNT + s)

ĀNZ

Raines
Raynes
(see ĀN + s)

ĂNZ

banns
(see ĂN + s)

ĂNZH

melange

ĀP

agape
ape
cape
chape
crape
crèpe
drape
escape
fire-escape
gape

grape
jape
landscape
Lape
nape
pape
rape
red-tape
scape
scrape
seascape
shape
ship-shape
tape
transshape
trape
uncape
unshape

ĂP

after-clap
agape
bestrap
cap
chap
clap
claptrap
dap
entrap
enwrap
flap
flip-flap
foolscap
forage-cap
frap
gap
gape
genapp
genappe
handicap
hap

heel-tap
Jap
knap
lagniappe
lap
Lapp
map
mayhap
mishap
nap
night-cap
overlap
pap
percussion-cap
rap
rattle-trap
sap
scrap
shoulder-strap
slap
snap
stopgap
strap
tap
thunder-clap
trap
unlap
unwrap
wapp
water-tap
wishing-cap
wrap
yap

ÄP

gape
swap
(see ŎP)

ĀPS

jackanapes

Mapes
traipse
apes, etc.

ĂPS

apse
collapse
craps
elapse
illapse
interlapse
lapse
perhaps
relapse
schnapps
after-claps, etc.

ĀPT

aped
(see ĀP + ed)

ĂPT

adapt
apt
enrapt
inapt
moss-**capped**
rapt
snow-**capped**
wrapt
bestrapped,
   etc.

ÂR

Adair
affair
affaire
air
aire
anywhere
armchair

arrière
aware
Ayr
ayre
backstair
bare
bear
bêche-de-mer
bedare
beglare
beware
billionaire
blare
capillaire
care
chair
chare
chargé
   d'affaires
claire
clare
cockle-stair
commissionaire
compare
concessionnaire
dare
debonair
declare
Delaware
despair
devil-may-care
disrepair
doctrinaire
earthenware
eclair
e'er
elsewhere
ensnare
ere
etagère
everywhere

eyre	prayer	vin-ordinaire	debar
fair	prepare	vivandière	deodar
fare	prickly-pear	ware	disbar
flair	proletaire	wear	dissimilar
flare	*quair*	whate'er	embar
forbear	rare	whatsoe'er	evening-star
forswear	repair	whene'er	Excalibar
gare	scare	where	falling-star
glair	sedan-chair	where'er	far
glare	share	wheresoe'er	Farr
Gruyère	Sinclair	yare	feldspar
hair	snare		funicular
hare	solitaire	**ÄR**	gar
heir	somewhere	afar	globular
howe'er	spare	ajar	gnar
impair	square	angular	guitar
jardinière	stair	animalcular	hospodar
lair	stare	annular	hussar
laissez-faire	stere	are	instar
maidenhair	*sware*	avatar	insular
mal de mer	swear	axle-bar	irregular
mare	tare	bar	jaguar
McNair	tear	bazaar	jar
McNare	their	binocular	jaunting-car
mid-air	there	bizarre	jemadar
millionaire	thoroughfare	boulevard	jocular
misfare	threadbare	calendar	jugular
mohair	trouvère	canard	knar
ne'er	tuyère	car	Lascar
otherwhere	unaware	catarrh	lodestar
outdare	*unbeware*	caviar	Loire
outstare	underbear	char	Malabar
outswear	underwear	cigar	mar
outwear	unfair	cinnabar	modular
overbear	unswear	circular	molecular
pair	*unware*	consular	morning-star
pare	upbear	crepuscular	night-jar
parterre	upstare	cymar	north-star
pear	uptear	czar	ocular
Pierre	vair	dar	par
portiere	vare	daystar	parr

particular
peninsular
perpendicular
pilot-star
popular
quadrangular
registrar
regular
saddle-bar
scapular
scar
scimitar
sea-star
secular
shackle-bar
shooting-star
similar
singular
somnambular
spar
spectacular
star
stellular
subahdar
tabernacular
tabular
tar
tintamarre
tintinnabular
titular
triangular
tsar
tutelar
unbar
unspar
upbar
uvular
valvular
vehicular
vermicular
vernacular

versicular
vinegar
Zanzibar
zamindar

ÄRB

barb
garb
yarb

ÄRCH

arch
countermarch
dead march
inarch
larch
march
outmarch
overarch
overmarch
parch
starch

ÂRD

Baird
golden-haired
laird
silver-haired
uncared
unheired
unimpaired
unpaired
unprepared
unshared
unspared
aired, etc.

ÄRD

after-guard
avant-garde
bard

Bernard
blackguard
body-guard
bombard
boulevard
camelopard
canard
card
chard
closebarred
discard
disregard
dynamitard
enguard
evil-starred
fard
foulard
Girard
guard
hard
interlard
lard
life-guard
milliard
nard
pard
petard
placard
poultry-yard
regard
retard
sard
shard
spikenard
starred
under-sparred
unguard
unmarred
wedding-card
yard
(see ÄR + ed)

ÄRF

'arf and 'arf
larf
scarf

ÄRJ

barge
charge
discharge
embarge
encharge
enlarge
Farge
La Farge
large
litharge
marge
overcharge
sea-marge
sparge
surcharge
targe
uncharge
undercharge

ÄRJD

undischarged
barged, etc.

ÄRK

aardvark
arc
ark
Asiarch
bark
barque
bedark
cark
Clark
Clarke
clerk

dark	**ÄRL**	unalarmed	**ÄRS**
debark	Albemarle	alarmed, etc.	farce
disembark	carl	**ÄRMZ**	parse
dispark	ensnarl	Armes	sarse
easy mark	gnarl	assault-at-arms	sparse
ecclesiarch	harl	gentleman-at-	**ÄRSH**
embark	imparl	arms	harsh
endark	jarl	king-at-arms	marsh
flood-mark	Karl	man-at-arms	**ÄRT**
foot-mark	marl	alarms, etc.	apart
hark	snarl		art
hierarch		**ÄRN**	cart
impark	**ÄRLZ**	bairn	carte
iremarch	Charles	cairn	chart
knark	(see ÄRL + s)	tairn	counterpart
lark			dart
marc	**ÄRM**	**ÄRN**	depart
mark	alarm	barn	dispart
marque	arm	darn	flint-heart
meadow-lark	axle-arm	*imbarn*	hart
oligarch	barm	incarn	heart
park	becharm	Marne	impart
patriarch	charm	tarn	indart
remark	counter-charm	yarn	lion-heart
sark	decharm		mart
sea-lark	disarm	**ÄRNZ**	part
shark	disencharm	Barnes	quarte
sky-lark	farm	(see ÄRN + s)	sart
snark	fire-alarm		smart
spark	firearm	**ÄRP**	start
stark	forearm	carp	sweetheart
Starke	gendarme	epicarp	tart
water-mark	harm	escarp	uncart
	love-charm	harp	unheart
ÄRKS	unarm	monocarp	upstart
Marx	uncharm	pericarp	water-cart
(see ÄRK + s)	unharm	scarp	
		sharp	
ÄRKT	**ÄRMD**	**ARS**	**ÄRTH**
unmarked	forearmed	scarce	Applegarth
barked, etc.			

garth
hearth
swarth

ÄRV
carve
larve
starve

ÄRTS
Harz
(see ÄRT + s)

ÂRZ
backstairs
stairs
theirs
unawares
unbewares
unwares
airs, etc.

ÄRZ
Mars
(see ÄR + s)

ÄS
abase
ace
aface
anelace
apace
base
bass
begrace
belace
birthplace
boniface
brace
breathing-
   space

carapace
case
chariot-race
chase
commonplace
dace
debase
deface
disgrace
displace
efface
embrace
encase
enchase
enlace
erase
face
footpace
footrace
grace
grimace
hiding-place
horse-race
idocrase
interlace
interspace
lace
mace
misplace
outface
outpace
pace
place
plaice
populace
race
replace
resting-place
retrace
scapegrace
space

steeple-chase
thorough-bass
Thrace
trace
trysting-place
ukase
unbrace
uncase
underbrace
unlace
vase

ÅS
after-grass
alas
All-hallowmas
amass
ass
bass
bonnilass
brass
Candlemas
class
crass
crevasse
cuirass
declass
demi-tasse
en masse
first-class
flint-glass
galloglass
gas
glass
grass
Hallowmas
hippocras
hour-glass
isinglass
kavass
Khyber Pass

kvass
lass
looking-glass
mass
Michaelmas
middle-class
minute-glass
morass
object-glass
overpass
paillasse
pass
paterfamilias
rubasse
sassafras
sparrow-grass
strass
surpass
tarantass
tass
weather-glass
working-class

ÄS
en masse

ÄSH
crèche

ÄSH
abash
ash
balderdash
bash
bedash
brache
brash
cache
calabash
calash
calipash

cash
clash
crash
dash
fash
flash
gash
gnash
hash
interdash
lâche
lash
mash
mountain-ash
moustache
Nash
pash
patache
plash
rash
rehash
sabretache
sash
slap-dash
slash
smash
splash
splatter-dash
squabash
thrash
trash
unlash
weeping-ash

ĂSH

quash
wash, etc.
(see ŎSH)

ĂSHT

undashed

unlashed
unthrashed
abashed, etc.

ĂSK

antimask
ask
bask
basque
bemask
Bergamask
cask
casque
flask
immask
mask
masque
overtask
Pasch
powder-flask
task
unmask
water-cask

ĂSKT

unasked
unmasked
basked, etc.

ĂSP

asp
clasp
enclasp
engrasp
gasp
grasp
hasp
rasp
unclasp

ĂSP

wasp

ĀST

after-taste
apple-faced
barefaced
baste
brazen-faced
chaste
distaste
double-faced
dough-faced
fair-faced
foretaste
freckle-faced
furrow-faced
hard-faced
haste
hatchet-faced
horse-faced
impaste
Janus-faced
laced
lambaste
leaden-paced
lean-faced
lily-faced
mottle-faced
pale-faced
paper-faced
paste
pippin-faced
platter-faced
plump-faced
poste-haste
pudding-faced
pug-faced
retraced
sad-faced
self-abased
shame-faced
sheep-faced
slow-paced

smock-faced
smooth-faced
smug-faced
snail-paced
strait-laced
tallow-faced
taste
thorough-
    paced
two-faced
traced
unbraced
unchaste
undefaced
undisgraced
ungraced
unshamefaced
untraced
waist
waste
weasel-faced
well-graced
whey-faced
wizen-faced
abased, etc.

ĂST

aghast
avast
bast
blast
bombast
cast
caste
contrast
devast
downcast
ecclesiast
elegiast
ember-fast
encomiast

enthusiast
fast
flabbergast
forecast
ghast
handfast
hast
high-caste
iconoclast
idoloclast
jury-mast
last
mast
metaphrast
metaplast
outlast
overcast
paraphrast
past
protoplast
recast
repast
scholiast
steadfast
storm-blast
symposiast
unfast
unsurpassed
vast
amassed, etc.
wast

ĀT

abalienate
abate
abacinate
abbreviate
abdicate
ablocate
abnegate
abnodate

abominate
abrogate
absinthiate
absquatulate
accelerate
accentuate
acclamate
acclimate
accommodate
accumulate
accurate
acidulate
actuate
acuminate
adequate
adjudicate
adulate
adulterate
advocate
aërate
affectionate
affiliate
affreight
agglomerate
agglutinate
aggravate
aggregate
agitate
alienate
alleviate
allocate
altercate
alternate
alveolate
amalgamate
ambulate
ameliorate
ampliate
amputate
angulate
animate

annihilate
annotate
annulate
annumerate
annunciate
antedate
antepenulti-
    mate
anticipate
antiquate
apostolate
applicate
appreciate
approbate
appropriate
approximate
arbitrate
armour-plate
arrogate
articulate
asphyxiate
aspirate
assassinate
asseverate
assimilate
assimulate
associate
ate
attenuate
augurate
aureate
auspicate
authenticate
aviate
await
baccalaureate
bait
bate
belate
berate
Billingsgate

bimaculate
binoculate
cachinnate
calculate
caliphate
calumniate
campanulate
camphorate
cancellate
candidate
capacitate
capitate
capitulate
captivate
carbonate
cardinalate
casemate
castigate
cate
celebrate
celibate
certificate
chalybeate
checkmate
chocolate
circulate
circumstantiate
classmate
coagulate
cogitate
collaborate
collate
collegiate
collocate
commemorate
commensurate
comminate
commiserate
communicate
compassionate
compensate

complicate
concatenate
concentrate
conciliate
conditionate
confabulate
confederate
confiscate
conflate
conglomerate
congratulate
congregate
conjugate
consecrate
considerate
consolidate
constipate
consulate
consummate
contaminate
contemplate
co-operate
co-ordinate
copper-plate
copulate
coronate
corporate
correlate
corroborate
corrugate
crate
create
cremate
crenellate
crepitate
criminate
culminate
cultivate
date
dead-weight
death-rate

debate
debilitate
decapitate
decimate
decolorate
decorate
dedicate
degenerate
delate
delegate
deliberate
delicate
delineate
demonstrate
denominate
denunciate
deodate
depopulate
deprecate
depreciate
depredate
depucelate
derivate
derogate
desecrate
desiderate
designate
desolate
desperate
deteriorate
determinate
detonate
devastate
deviate
devirginate
diaconate
diagnosticate
dial-plate
dictate
differentiate
digitate

dilapidate
dilate
directorate
disconsolate
discriminate
disintegrate
dislocate
disseminate
dissimulate
dissipate
dissociate
doctorate
domesticate
dominate
donate
dunder-pate
duplicate
educate
effectuate
effeminate
efflate
eight
ejaculate
elaborate
elate
electorate
electro-plate
elevate
eliminate
elucidate
emaciate
emanate
emancipate
emasculate
emigrate
emolliate
emulate
enervate
enumerate
enunciate
episcopate

equate
equivocate
eradicate
estate
estimate
estivate
etiolate
evacuate
evaluate
evaporate
eventuate
exacerbate
exacinate
exaggerate
exasperate
excavate
excogitate
excommunicate
excoriate
excruciate
exculpate
execrate
exhilarate
exonerate
exorbitate
expatiate
expatriate
expectorate
expiate
expostulate
extenuate
exterminate
extirpate
extortionate
extravagate
extricate
fabricate
facilitate
fascinate
fate
feather-weight

federate
felicitate
fête
first-mate
first-rate
flagellate
floodgate
fluctuate
foliolate
foreordinate
formulate
fortunate
freight
fructuate
frustrate
fulminate
fumigate
funambulate
gait
gate
gelatinate
generate
germinate
gesticulate
glaciate
graduate
granulate
grate
gratulate
gravitate
great
habilitate
habituate
hate
heavy-weight
helpmate
hesitate
hibernate
humiliate
hypothecate
illiterate

illuminate
illustrate
imitate
immaculate
immarginate
immateriate
immediate
immensurate
immigrate
immoderate
immolate
impassionate
impersonate
impetrate
implicate
importunate
imprecate
impropriate
improvisate
inaccurate
inadequate
inanimate
inappropriate
inarticulate
inaugurate
incapacitate
incarcerate
incastellate
inchoate
incinerate
incommensur-
   ate
incompassion-
   ate
inconsiderate
incorporate
increate
incriminate
incubate
inculcate
indelicate

indeterminate
indevirginate
indicate
indiscriminate
individuate
indoctrinate
indurate
inebriate
infatuate
inflate
infuriate
ingerminate
ingrate
ingratiate
ingurgitate
initiate
innate
innovate
inoculate
inordinate
insatiate
inseminate
insinuate
instate
instigate
insubordinate
insulate
integrate
intenerate
intemperate
intercessionate
intermediate
interminate
interpolate
interrogate
intimate
intimidate
intonate
intoxicate
intricate
inundate

invalidate
investigate
invertebrate
inveterate
invigorate
inviolate
invocate
irate
irradiate
irrigate
irritate
isolate
iterate
itinerate
Kate
lacerate
lanceolate
late
laureate
legislate
legitimate
levigate
levirate
liberate
licentiate
liquidate
literate
litigate
lixiviate
locate
lubricate
lucubrate
luxuriate
macerate
machinate
magistrate
magnate
manipulate
marinate
marquisate
masticate

āle,   **oâ**re,   ădd,   ärm,   åsk;   mē,   hēre,   ĕnd;   īce,   ĭll;

mate	participate	promulgate	reprobate
matriculate	passionate	propagate	repudiate
mediate	pastorate	propitiate	restate
meditate	pate	proportionate	resuscitate
mess-mate	patronate	pro-rate	retaliate
migrate	peculate	prostrate	reticulate
militate	penetrate	protectorate	reverberate
mitigate	peninsulate	protuberate	roseate
moderate	pennyweight	provinciate	rotate
modulate	perambulate	proximate	ruminate
motivate	percolate	pulsate	runagate
mutilate	peregrinate	punctuate	rusticate
narrate	perforate	quadruplicate	salivate
Nate	permeate	radiate	sanitate
navigate	perorate	rate	sate
necessitate	perpetrate	ratiocinate	satiate
negociate	perpetuate	rattle-pate	saturate
nickle-plate	personate	rebate	scintillate
nominate	placate	recalcitrate	Sea Gate
novitiate	plait	recapitulate	second-rate
obdurate	plate	reciprocate	secretariate
obligate	playmate	recreate	sedate
obliterate	poet-laureate	recriminate	segregate
obstinate	pontificate	rectorate	separate
obviate	populate	recuperate	shipmate
officiate	postulate	refrigerate	sibilate
operate	potentate	regenerate	silicate
opiate	prate	regrate	silver-plate
orate	precipitate	regulate	simulate
orchestrate	predate	regurgitate	situate
originate	predestinate	rehabilitate	skate
ornate	predicate	reinstate	slate
oscillate	predominate	reiterate	somnambulate
osculate	premeditate	rejuvenate	sophisticate
over-rate	preponderate	relate	spate
overstate	prevaricate	relegate	speculate
overweight	procrastinate	remediate	spifflicate
oxygenate	procreate	remonstrate	spoliate
palliate	professoriate	remunerate	stalemate
palpitate	profligate	renovate	state
paper-weight	prognosticate	repatriate	stearate

ōld, ôr, ŏdd, oil, fŏŏt, out; ūse, ûrn, ŭp; THis, thin

stellulate
stimulate
stipulate
straight
strait
stridulate
stylobate
subjugate
sublimate
subordinate
subrogate
substantiate
sufflate
suffocate
superannuate
supererogate
supplicate
suppurate
syncopate
syndicate
tabulate
Tait
temperate
tergiversate
terminate
tête-à-tête
third-rate
titillate
titivate
tolerate
trait
translate
transliterate
transubstan-
   tiate
triangulate
triturate
triumvirate
ulcerate
ultimate
ululate

uncreate
underrate
understate
underweight
undulate
unfortunate
unstate
vacate
vaccinate
vacillate
validate
variate
variegate
vassalate
vaticinate
vegetate
venerate
ventilate
verberate
vermiculate
vertebrate
vertiginate
vicariate
vindicate
violate
vitiate
vituperate
vizierate
vociferate
wait
water-rate
weight

ĂT

acrobat
aflat
Ararat
aristocrat
assignat
at
autocrat

automat
bat
bepat
brat
brickbat
cat
caveat
chat
civet-cat
commissariat
cravat
dandiprat
democrat
diplomat
drat
fallow-chat
fat
flat
frat
forgat
gat
gnat
habitat
hat
heliostat
hellcat
hereat
high-hat
hydrostat
kittycat
lariat
Magnificat
marrow-fat
mat
matte
monocrat
pat
pitapat
plat
Platt
Platte

proletariat
plutocrat
polecat
rat
requiescat
rheostat
sat
scat
secretariat
slat
spat
sprat
Surat
tabby-cat
tat
that
theocrat
thereat
thermostat
unhat
vampire-bat
vat
water-rat
whereat

ÄT

Kalat
Khelat
squat
what, etc.
yacht
(see ŎT)

ĀTH

bathe
lathe
scathe
snathe
spathe
swathe
unswathe

Āth
faith
i'faith
misfaith
rathe
Snaith
unfaith
water-wraith
wraith

ĀTth
eighth
hate'th, etc.

ĂTH
aftermath
allopath
Gath
hath
homeopath
math
osteopath
philomath
physiopath
psychopath
snath

ĂTH
bath
bridle-path
footpath
lath
path
rath
wrath

ĀTS
Bates
Cates
Yates
Yeats
(see Ā**T** + **s**)

ĀV
angusticlave
architrave
behave
belave
beslave
brave
cave
concave
crave
Dave
deprave
drave
élève
encave
enclave
engrave
enslave
forgave
galley-slave
gave
glaive
grave
impave
knave
lave
misbehave
misgave
nave
outbrave
pave
rave
save
shave
slave
stave
suave
they've
thrave
trave
ungrave

waive
wave

ĂV
have
Slav

ĂV
calve
enclave
halve
salve
Slav
suave
zouave

ĀZ
ablaze
adaze
amaze
appraise
baize
Blaise
beacon-blaze
bepraise
blaze
braise
braze
chaise
chrysoprase
craze
daze
dispraise
emblaze
faze
fraise
gaze
glaze
graze
Haas

Hayes
haze
laze
maize
malaise
Marseillaise
Mays
Mayes
mayonnaise
maze
metaphrase
naze
nowadays
outblaze
outgaze
paraphrase
phase
phrase
polonaise
praise
raise
rase
raze
self-praise
then-a-days
underpraise
unpraise
upblaze
upgaze
upraise
vase
wonder-maze
(see Ā + **s**)

ĂZ
as
has
jazz
razz
whereas

ōld, ôr, ŏdd, oil, fŏŏt, out; ūse, ûrn, ŭp; THis, thin

ÄZ
Shiraz
vase
(see Ä + s)

ĀZD
adazed
bemazed
unamazed
unpraised
amazed, etc.

ĀZD
jazzed
razzed

ĀZH
cortegé

ĀZH
badinage
barrage
camouflage

entourage
garage
menage
mirage
persiflage

ĂZM
bioplasm
cataplasm
chasm
demoniasm

ectoplasm
enthusiasm
iconoclasm
metaplasm
miasm
phantasm
phasm
plasm
pleonasm
protoplasm
sarcasm
spasm

E

These words include the following accented vowel sounds:

Ē as in me; heard also in eve, feet, beam, deceive, people, key, Caesar, machine, field, quay, phoebe.

Ę as in here; heard also in fear, dreary, weird.

Ĕ as in end; heard also in heifer, leopard, friend, Aetna, feather, asafoetida, bury, any, Thames, said, says.

Ē
A.B.
abandonee
absentee
addressee
advowee
agape
Agapemone
agree
aknee
alee
allottee
anemone
Anglice
antistrophe
apogee
apostraphe

appellee
appointee
assignee
avowee
axle-tree
bailee
bain-marie
banshee
bargee
bawbee
be
bee
belee
bel-esprit
Benedicite
biographee
blea

bohea
bonhomie
bootee
bouilli
bourgeoisie
bumblebee
burgee
B.V.D.
C.O.D.
calipee
Calliope
calorie
cap-a-pie
catastrophe
Chaldee
chariotee
Cherokee

chickadee
chickeree
chimpanzee
Chinee
Christmas-tree
coatee
consignee
corroboree
coryphee
Cybele
D.D.
debauchee
debris
decree
dedicatee
Dee
degree

devisee	garnishee	McFee	pugaree
devotee	gee	McGee	Q.T.
diablerie	geegee	McKee	quay
disagree	Gethsemane	me	raki
divorcee	ghee	Melpomene	rani
dominie	glee	mestee	rapparee
donee	goatee	mortgagee	rappee
drawee	grandee	mustee	razee
dree	grantee	N.G.	recipe
Dundee	guarantee	nebulae	referee
dungaree	he	Niobe	refugee
Dupree	heart-free	nominee	releasee
eau de vie	honey-bee	O.G.	remittee
employee	humblebee	obligee	repartee
endorsee	hyperbole	ogee	rhe
enfree	interrogatee	on dit	Rosalie
ennui	jamboree	oversea	rupee
epopee	Japanee	oversee	Sadducee
esprit	jeu d'esprit	Ph.D.	sangaree
etui	jinnee	Parsee	Sault St. Marie
Eugenie	jubilee	passaree	scarabee
Eulalie	key	patentee	scree
examinee	killdee	Pawnee	sea
extempore	knee	payee	see
facetiae	langue d'oui	pea	selvagee
facsimile	lea	pedigree	sesame
fäerie	lee	Penelope	settee
fancy-free	legatee	perigee	she
fee	lessee	permittee	si
felo de se	levee	petitionee	simile
fiddle-de-dee	ley	Pharisee	skilligalee
filigree	li	picotee	snee
flea	licensee	plea	snickersnee
flee	litchi	pledgee	spree
fleur-de-lis	M.D.	point-d'appui	stingaree
foresee	manatee	poison-tree	suttee
free	Manichee	pongee	sycee
fricassee	Marie	pontee	synecdoche
fusee	marquee	pot-pourri	systole
Galilee	Marshalsea	presentee	tea
gallows-tree	master-key	promisee	tee

tehee	adversity	ascendancy	Calvary
Tennessee	advisability	asperity	canopy
Terpsichore	affability	assiduity	capability
the	affinity	astrology	capacity
thee	agency	astronomy	captivity
third degree	agility	atrocity	casualty
three	agony	atrophy	catholicity
topee	alacrity	audacity	causticity
toupee	alchemy	augury	cavalry
transferee	allopathy	austerity	cavity
tree	ambiguity	authenticity	celebrity
trustee	amenability	authority	celerity
Tweedledee	amenity	autonomy	century
unforesee	amicability	avidity	certainty
unfree	amity	bakery	changeability
vendee	amnesty	balcony	chancery
vertebrae	analogy	barbarity	charity
vis-a-vis	anarchy	barony	chastity
vouchee	anatomy	barratry	chivalry
warrantee	ancestry	bastardy	Christianity
we	animosity	battery	chronology
wee	anniversary	beggary	civility
weeping-tree	annuity	benignity	clemency
whiffletree	anomaly	bigamy	cogency
whippletree	anonymity	bigotry	colloquy
ye	antipathy	billowy	colony
	antiphony	biography	combustibility
Zuyder Zee	antiquity	biology	comedy
abbacy	anxiety	blasphemy	comity
ability	apathy	blossomy	commodity
absurdity	apology	botany	community
academy	apostasy	bravery	company
acclivity	applicability	brevity	compatability
accompany	archery	bribery	complacency
acerbity	argosy	brilliancy	complexity
acidity	aridity	brutality	complicity
acridity	aristocracy	bryony	complimentary
activity	armory	burglary	comprehensi-
actuality	arrowy	cadency	bility
adaptability	artillery	calamity	compulsory
adultery	artistry	calumny	conformity

āle,　câre,　ădd, 　ärm, 　åsk;　mē, 　hẹre, 　ĕnd; 　īce, 　ĭll;

connubiality
consanguinity
consistency
conspiracy
constancy
contiguity
contingency
contradictory
contrariety
conveniency
convention-
  ality
convexity
coquetry
courtesy
Coventry
credulity
criminality
crotchety
crudity
cruelty
cupidity
curacy
curiosity
custody
debauchery
debility
decency
declivity
deformity
deity
delivery
democracy
demonry
density
dependency
depravity
deputy
destiny
devilry
deviltry

dexterity
diary
dignity
dimity
diplomacy
directory
discordancy
discourtesy
discovery
discrepancy
dishonesty
disparity
dissatisfactory
dissimilarity
dissuasory
diversity
divinity
docility
domesticity
doxology
drapery
drudgery
dubiety
duplicity
dynasty
ebony
eccentricity
economy
ecstasy
efficiency
effigy
effrontery
elasticity
electricity
elegy
elementary
elusory
embassy
emergency
enemy
energy

enginery
enmity
enormity
entity
Epiphany
epitome
equality
equanimity
equity
errantry
eternity
eulogy
euphony
expectancy
expediency
extremity
facility
factory
faculty
fallacy
falsity
familiarity
family
fantasy
fatality
fatuity
feathery
fecundity
felicity
felony
fernery
ferocity
fertility
fervency
festivity
fidelity
fidgety
fiery
finery
fixity
flagrancy

flattery
flippancy
fluency
flummery
foppery
forestry
forgery
formality
fortuity
fragility
fragrancy
fraternity
frequency
frigidity
frivolity
frugality
futility
futurity
gaiety
galaxy
gallantry
gallery
garrulity
genealogy
generosity
geniality
gentility
geography
geology
geometry
Germany
gluttony
gratuity
gravity
harmony
harvestry
heathery
heraldry
heredity
heresy
hilarity

---

history	incongruity	jugglery	mediocrity
homeopathy	inconsistency	juvenility	melody
homily	inconstancy	knavery	memory
honesty	incredulity	knight-errantry	mendacity
hospitality	indignity	laity	mendicity
hostelry	individuality	larceny	merchantry
hostility	industry	laxity	mercury
humanity	inebriety	legacy	mimicry
humility	infallibility	legality	ministry
husbandry	infamy	leniency	minority
hypocrisy	infancy	lenity	misanthropy
identity	infantry	lethargy	misery
idiocy	infelicity	levity	mobility
idiosyncrasy	inferiority	liberality	mockery
idolatry	infertility	liberty	modesty
illiteracy	infidelity	limpidity	monarchy
illusory	infinity	litany	monody
imagery	infirmary	liturgy	monopoly
imbecility	infirmity	livery	monotony
immaturity	ingenuity	Lombardy	monstrosity
immensity	inhumanity	longevity	morality
immodesty	iniquity	loquacity	mortality
immorality	injury	lottery	multiplicity
immortality	insincerity	loyalty	mummery
immunity	insipidity	lubricity	municipality
imparity	insufficiency	lucidity	mutability
impassivity	insularity	lunacy	mutiny
impecuniosity	insurgency	luxuriancy	mystery
impetuosity	integrity	luxury	mythology
impiety	intensity	machinery	nationality
importunity	intestacy	magnanimity	nativity
impropriety	intrepidity	mahogany	necessity
impunity	irony	majesty	neutrality
impurity	Italy	majority	nobility
inability	ivory	malady	non-conformity
inadvertency	jealousy	malignancy	normalcy
incapacity	jeopardy	malignity	Normandy
inclemency	jewelry	masonry	notary
incompatibility	jocundity	mastery	notoriety
incomprehen-	jollity	maternity	novelty
sibility	joviality	maturity	nudity

nullity	piety	propinquity	robbery
nursery	pillory	propriety	rockery
obeisancy	pillowy	prosperity	roguery
obesity	piracy	provinciality	Romany
obliquity	pleasantry	proximity	rosary
obloquy	pliancy	prudery	rosemary
obscurity	poesy	psalmistry	rotundity
oddity	poetry	psalmody	royalty
Odyssey	poignancy	psychiatry	rubicundity
opportunity	policy	publicity	rudimentary
originality	polity	puerility	rusticity
pageantry	polygamy	pugnacity	sagacity
palmary	pomposity	punctuality	salary
panoply	ponderosity	pungency	salinity
papacy	popery	purity	salubrity
parity	popularity	pusillanimity	sanctity
parliamentary	pornography	putridity	sanity
parody	posterity	quackery	satiety
partiality	potency	quality	satisfactory
particularity	poverty	quandary	savagery
paternity	precocity	quantity	scarcity
peculiarity	precursory	quiescency	scenery
pedantry	prelacy	raillery	scrutiny
penalty	priority	rapacity	secrecy
penury	priory	rapidity	security
peppery	privacy	rarity	seigniory
perfidy	privity	rascality	senility
perfumery	probity	reality	sensibility
perfunctory	proclivity	reciprocity	sensuality
perjury	prodigality	recovery	sentimentality
perpetuity	prodigy	rectory	serenity
perplexity	profanity	refractory	servility
personality	professory	regency	severity
perspicuity	proficiency	regeneracy	shadowy
pertinacity	profundity	remedy	shivery
perversity	progeny	revelry	silvery
philanthropy	prolixity	rhapsody	similarity
philosophy	promiscuity	ribaldry	simony
phylactery	propensity	rickety	simplicity
physiognomy	property	rigidity	sincerity
Picardy	prophecy	rivalry	sinewy

ōld, ôr, ŏdd, oil, fŏŏt, out; ūse, ûrn, ŭp; THis, thin

singularity	tenantry	vagrancy	words ending
slavery	tendency	valedictory	in "y")
slippery	tenuity	valiancy	absorbingly
snuggery	testamentary	validity	abusively
sobriety	theocracy	vanity	accordingly
society	theology	vapidity	accurately
solemnity	theory	vapoury	acidly
solidity	theosophy	variety	affectedly
soliloquy	thievery	velocity	aimlessly
solvency	threnody	velvety	airily
sophistry	thundery	venality	alluringly
sorcery	timidity	verbosity	allusively
spontaneity	tonicity	verdancy	ambitiously
stability	topography	verity	amusingly
stagnancy	torpidity	versatility	anciently
sterility	totality	vicinity	appealingly
stolidity	tracery	victory	ardently
strategy	tragedy	villainy	assertively
stupidity	tranquillity	virginity	atrociously
suavity	travesty	viridity	auspiciously
subjectivity	treachery	virility	awfully
sublimity	treasury	virtuality	banefully
subsidy	trickery	virtuosity	becomingly
subtlety	trilogy	viscidity	befittingly
sufficiency	trinity	viscosity	beggarly
sugary	triviality	vivacity	bespottedly
summary	truancy	volatility	bewailingly
superficiality	trumpery	voracity	bitterly
superfluity	tyranny	votary	bloodlessly
superiority	ubiquity	vulgarity	bloomingly
supremacy	unanimity	waggery	bloomlessly
symmetry	uniformity	watery	blushingly
sympathy	unity	whimsicality	blushlessly
symphony	university	willowy	bodily
taciturnity	unsavoury	wintery	bootlessly
tapestry	urbanity	witchery	boundlessly
technicality	urgency	yeomanry	boyishly
telegraphy	usury	zoology	brainlessly
temerity	utility	(see ability, etc.,	breathlessly
tenacity	vacancy	part iii, for	broodingly
tenancy	vacuity	many more	brotherly

āle, câre, ădd, ärm, åsk; mē, hĕre, ĕnd; īce, ĭll;

brutally
bumptiously
carefully
carelessly
changelessly
chirpingly
chokingly
churlishly
civilly
clownishly
complainingly
concludingly
condescend-
　ingly
conducively
confoundedly
confusedly
consummately
convivially
countlessly
cousinly
cowardly
cravingly
crouchingly
crownlessly
cruelly
crushingly
cumbrously
dastardly
daughterly
decorously
deductively
defencelessly
deliciously
delusively
devotedly
disapprovingly
discerningly
disorderly
distastefully
distrustfully

divergently
divertingly
doggedly
dolefully
doubtfully
doubtingly
dreamingly
dreamlessly
drippingly
droopingly
dustily
easterly
elusively
enduringly
engagingly
engrossingly
eternally
exclusively
expansively
exultantly
exultingly
fadelessly
fairily
faithlessly
fatherly
feelingly
ferociously
fervidly
feudally
flippantly
floridly
flurriedly
flushingly
foolishly
foppishly
forebodingly
foreknowingly
forgivingly
formerly
forsakenly
fruitfully

fruitlessly
fulsomely
giddily
girlishly
gloomily
gloriously
gorgeously
gropingly
groundlessly
grudgingly
gruesomely
grumblingly
grumpily
guiltily
guiltlessly
gushingly
gustily
happily
harmfully
harmlessly
heartbrokenly
heart-rending-
　ly
heavenly
hereditarily
homelessly
hopefully
hopelessly
horridly
humanly
hungrily
hurriedly
illusively
immorally
immortally
imploringly
inclusively
indignantly
indulgently
infernally
inhumanly

insensately
instantly
instructively
insultingly
intermittently
inwardly
irksomely
iridescently
jokingly
joyfully
joyously
judiciously
juicily
laughingly
lavishly
legendarily
lightfootedly
loathingly
locally
lonesomely
loungingly
lovelessly
loverly
lovingly
loyally
lucidly
luckily
lucklessly
luridly
luringly
lustrously
maidenly
maliciously
mannerly
masterly
maternally
matronly
meltingly
merrily
misgivingly
mistrustingly

modestly
morally
morbidly
mortally
motherly
mournfully
mournsomely
musingly
nakedly
namelessly
necessarily
neighbourly
niggardly
noiselessly
normally
northerly
northwardly
obnoxiously
obstructively
obtrusively
officiously
onwardly
opposingly
oppressively
orderly
outrageously
overtoppingly
owlishly
painfully
painlessly
pallidly
pathetically
peculiarly
peerlessly
peevishly
pellucidly
pervertedly
piquantly
plaintfully
plaintlessly
playfully

pluckily
poetically
portentously
prayerfully
precociously
prepossess-
    ingly
pretendingly
productively
properly
propitiously
provokingly
publicly
pungently
pursuantly
quarterly
quiescently
rapidly
readily
ready-wittedly
recklessly
recurrently
refulgently
rejoicingly
relentlessly
reluctantly
remorsefully
remorselessly
responsively
revengefully
rippingly
ripplingly
roaringly
rovingly
royally
ruefully
ruffianly
ruggedly
savagely
scholarly
scornfully

scowlingly
secretively
secretly
seducively
seductively
seemingly
self-accusingly
self-consciously
shamefully
shamelessly
shapelessly
sharp-wittedly
shiftlessly
shrewishly
silently
sisterly
sleepily
sleeplessly
slouchingly
slovenly
sluggishly
smilingly
smokily
soakingly
soberly
solemnly
solidly
sombrely
sordidly
sorrily
sorrowfully
soulfully
soullessly
soundlessly
spirally
splendidly
spoonily
sportfully
sportively
spotlessly
stirringly

stolenly
stormfully
stormily
stormlessly
straightfor-
    wardly
stubbornly
studiedly
stupendously
stupidly
sturdily
stylishly
suddenly
sultrily
sunnily
superhumanly
superstitiously
surefootedly
suspiciously
swimmingly
swollenly
sylvanly
tauntingly
tediously
thanklessly
thornily
thoroughly
thumpingly
tonelessly
tranquilly
tremendously
trippingly
triumphally
triumphantly
troublously
trustfully
trustily
trustingly
truthfully
truthlessly
tunefully

tunelessly	worthily	*forespeech*	**ĒD**
unbecomingly	worthlessly	*foreteach*	accede
unbendingly	yearningly	impeach	aniseed
unbiddenly	yeomanly	keech	antecede
unblushingly		*leach*	bead
unboundedly	**ĒB**	leech	bleed
unceasingly	glebe	overreach	*brede*
unchangingly	grebe	peach	breed
uncloudedly		preach	cede
unerringly	**ĔB**	queach	centipede
unfailingly	cobweb	reach	concede
unfeelingly	deb	screech	creed
unfeignedly	ebb	sea-reach	deed
unflaggingly	keb	sleech	*dispeed*
unguardedly	neb	speech	Ead
unknowingly	Seb	teach	exceed
unlovingly	web	unbreech	feed
unmaidenly	Webb	unpreach	Ganymede
unmannerly			glede
unmotherly	**ĔBD**	**ĔCH**	gleed
unneighborly	ebbed	etch	god-speed
unresistingly	webbed	fetch	greed
unswervingly		fletch	heed
unweariedly	**ĒBZ**	Jack-Ketch	impede
unwittingly	Thebes	ketch	implead
unwontedly	(see ĒB + s)	letch	inbreed
unyieldingly		out-stretch	indeed
urgently	**ĔBZ**	retch	interbreed
usurpingly	Debs	sketch	intercede
utterly	ebbs	stretch	interplead
verily	plebs	vetch	invalid
vividly	webs, etc.	wretch	jereed
voluntarily			knead
wantonly	**ĒCH**	**ĒCHD**	knock-kneed
warningly	beach	unbleached	lead
wastefully	beseech	unimpeached	mead
waywardly	beech	beached, etc.	Meade
wearily	bleach		Mede
wholesomely	breach	**ĔCHD**	meed
wittingly	breech	far-fetched	millipede
wontedly	each	etched, etc.	misdeed
	forereach		

ōld, ôr, ŏdd, oil, fŏŏt, out: ūse. ûrn, ŭp; THis, thin

mislead
misread
need
off his feed
outspeed
overfeed
plead
precede
proceed
read
Reade
recede
rede
reed
Reid
retrocede
Runnymede
screed
sea-weed
secede
seed
speed
stampede
steed
succeed
supersede
swede
teed
treed
Tweed
undecreed
unfeed
unpedigreed
upbreed
uplead
velocipede
weed
we'd
(see Ē + d)

ĔD
abed
adread
ahead
arrow-head
bed
bedspread
bedstead
behead
bespread
bestead
billet-head
bled
blunder-head
bread
breviped
chuckle-head
co-ed
copper-head
dead
dead-head
death-bed
death's-head
dread
dunderhead
Ed
embed
feather-head
fed
figure-head
fissiped
fled
foresaid
fountain-head
Fred
full-fed
ginger-bread
go-ahead
head
highbred
homebred

inbred
instead
jolter-head
lead
led
loggerhead
lowlihead
maidenhead
mast-head
misled
Ned
negro-head
niggerhead
outspread
overfed
overhead
overspread
pilot-bread
pled
poppy-head
quadruped
read
red
redd
said
shed
shewbread
shred
sled
sped
spread
stead
surbed
ted
thorough-bred
thread
thunder-head
timber-head
tread
truckle-bed
truebred

trundle-bed
trundle-head
underbred
unhead
unread
unsaid
unsped
unthread
unwed
watershed
wed
well-sped
Winifred
woolly-head
zed
accustomed
anchored
answered
astonished
attributed
balanced
banished
barren-spirited
base-spirited
bediamonded
bewildered
bigoted
blemished
blistered
bold-spirited
bonneted
brandished
breakfasted
burnished
carpeted
clustered
conquered
continued
contributed
covered
coveted

crescented | *measured* | unprofited | fief
diamonded | merited | unrespited | grief
diminished | *murmured* | untenanted | interleaf
discomforted | *overpowered* | visited | leaf
discredited | *overtowered* | *wandered* | lief
dispirited | *pardoned* | weak-spirited | reef
disquieted | patented | *wearied* | relief
distributed | *perjured* | *winnowed* | sheaf
dowered | pirated | *witnessed* | shereef
embarrassed | poor-spirited | *wondered* | thief
emblazoned | prohibited | *worshipped* | unbelief
enamored | public-spirited | |
exhibited | *punished* | **ĔDST** | **ĔF**
faceted | quieted | *bespread'st* | F
famished | *ravaged* | *dread'st* | chef
fine-spirited | *recovered* | *fed'st* | clef
flowered | *relinquished* | *fled'st* | deaf
forfeited | *remembered* | *led'st* | enfeoff
furnished | ringleted | *overspread'st* | feoff
garlanded | *rivalled* | *said'st* |
gathered | *sanctioned* | *thread'st* | **ĔFT**
gay-spirited | shepherded | *tread'st* | aleft
glimmered | *shimmered* | *wed'st* | bereft
glistened | *showered* | | cleft
hearkened | *shuddered* | **ĔDTH** | deft
helmeted | signeted | breadth | eft
heralded | *slumbered* | hairbreadth | enfeoffed
high-spirited | soft-spirited | *bespread'th,* etc. | heft
hungered | *sorrowed* | | left
imprisoned | spirited | **ĒDZ** | reft
inhabited | *suffered* | Eades | theft
inherited | talented | Leeds | unbereft
inspirited | *tempered* | (see ĔD + s) | weft
jeoparded | tenanted | | wheft
languished | *thundered* | **ĔF** |
light-spirited | turreted | bas-relief | **ĒG**
limited | unballasted | beef | colleague
lingered | unbonneted | belief | enleague
low-spirited | uninhabited | brief | fatigue
marvelled | unlimited | chief | intrigue
mean-spirited | unmerited | disbelief |

ōld, ôr, ŏdd, oil, fŏŏt, out; ūse, ûrn, ŭp; THis, thin

league
renege

ĔG

beg
beglerbeg
egg
goose-egg
keg
leg
Meg
peg
philabeg
skeg
teg
unpeg
Winnipeg
yegg

ĒGD

overfatigued
fatigued, etc.

ĔGD

spindle-legged
begged, etc.

ĔGZ

dregs
Meggs
sea-legs
begs, etc.

ĒJ

besiege
liege
siege

ĔJ

allege
cledge

dredge
edge
enhedge
fledge
hedge
impledge
interpledge
kedge
ledge
pledge
privilege
sacrilege
sedge
sledge
tedge
unedge
wedge

ĔJD

double-edged
sedged
two-edged
unhedged
dredged, etc.

ĒK

after-peak
aleak
antique
apeak
areek
beak
bespeak
bezique
bleak
bubble and
    squeak
cacique
caique
cheek
Chesapeake

chic
cleek
clinique
clique
comique
creak
creek
critique
eke
forepeak
forespeak
freak
gleek
Greek
hide-and-seek
leak
leek
Martinique
meak
meek
Mozambique
oblique
Passion-week
peak
physique
pique
reek
relique
seek
sheik
shriek
Sikh
sleek
sneak
speak
squeak
streak
teak
tweak
unique
unspeak

upseek
weak
week
wreak

ĔK

beck
bedeck
bewreck
breakneck
by heck
check
cheque
Czech
deck
fleck
henpeck
Kennebec
leatherneck
neck
neck-and-neck
peck
quarter-deck
Quebec
reck
rubberneck
shipwreck
spec
speck
trek
undeck
wreck

ĒKS

breeks
sneaks
beaks, ĕtc.

ĔKS

annex
becks

bedecks
Celotex
circumflex
complex
convex
ex
Exe
flex
inflex
kex
lex
Middlesex
multiplex
perplex
prex
reflex
rex
sex
unsex
vex
(see ĔK + s)

ĔKST

next
pretext
sexed
sext
text
unperplexed
unsexed
unvexed
annexed, etc.

ĔKT

cherry-cheeked
peaked
rosy-cheeked
unwreaked
beaked, etc.

ĔKT

abject
adject
affect
analect
annect
architect
arrect
bisect
circumspect
collect
confect
conject
connect
correct
defect
deflect
deject
detect
dialect
direct
disaffect
disconnect
disinfect
disrespect
dissect
effect
eject
elect
erect
expect
exsect
genuflect
incorrect
indirect
infect
inflect
inject
inspect
intellect
interject

intersect
introspect
misdirect
neglect
non-elect
object
perfect
porrect
prefect
prelect
project
prospect
protect
recollect
refect
reflect
reject
respect
resurrect
retrospect
sect
select
self-respect
subject
suspect
traject
trisect
unchecked
undecked
unsuspect
bedecked, etc.

ĒL

alguazil
all heal
anneal
appeal
automobile
balance-wheel
barleymeal
bastille

Camille
Castile
chenille
cochineal
commonweal
conceal
congeal
creel
deal
deil
deshabille
dial-wheel
difficile
driving-wheel
eel
enseal
feel
fly-wheel
forefeel
genteel
heal
heel
he'll
imbecile
infantile
interdeal
keel
Kiel
kneel
leal
Lille
Lucille
meal
misdeal
Neal
Neil
Neill
ne'er-do-weel
O'Neal
O'Neill
O'Sheel

paddle-wheel
pastille
peal
peel
privy-seal
reel
repeal
reveal
seal
seel
shabby-genteel
sheal
she'll
speel
spiel
squeal
steal
steel
sweal
teal
thunder-peal
tweel
uncongeal
unseal
unseel
vakil
veal
weal
we'll
wheal
wheel
zeal

ĚL

Abarbanel
asphodel
Astrophel
A.W.O.L.
bagatelle
bechamel
befell

bel
bell
belle
bonnibel
brocatel
Canterbury bell
caramel
caravel
carrousel
cell
chanterelle
Chaumontel
citadel
clientele
claribel
cockerel
cockle-shell
compel
cordelle
coronel
Crannell
crenel
damoiselle
damoselle
deathbell
dell
demoiselle
dentelle
dinner-bell
dispel
diving-bell
doggerel
dwell
El
ell
Emmanuel
excel
expel
farewell
fell
foretell

fricandel
gabelle
gazelle
harebell
heather-bell
hell
hotel
hydromel
Immanuel
immortelle
impel
infidel
inshell
intermell
Isabel
jargonelle
jell
Jezebel
kell
knell
lapel
Lionel
love-spell
mackerel
mademoiselle
mangonel
minute-bell
Moselle
muscatel
Nell
nonpareil
pallmall
parallel
Parnell
passing-bell
pell
pell-mell
pennoncelle
personnel
petronel

Philomel
pimpernel
propel
pucelle
Purnell
quadrelle
quell
rebel
refel
repel
rondelle
sacring-bell
sanctus-bell
sea-shell
sell
sentinel
shell
smell
snell
spell
swell
tell
tourelle
undersell
unshell
unspell
upswell
vesper-bell
vielle
villanelle
well
yell
zel
Zell

ĚLCH

belch
squelch
Welch
Welsh

ĒLD
afield
battlefield
Chesterfield
Dangerfield
Delafield
enshield
field
harvest-field
shield
unaneled
unrepealed
weald
wield
yield
annealed, etc.

ĔLD
beheld
eld
geld
held
meld
seld
unbeheld
unknelled
unparalleled
unquelled
upheld
weld
withheld
belled, etc.

ĔLF
delf
elf
Guelph
herself
himself
itself
mantel-**shelf**

myself
oneself
ourself
pelf
self
shelf
thyself
yourself

ĔLFT
delft

ĔLFTH
twelfth

ĔLK
elk
whelk
yelk

ĔLM
dishelm
elm
helm
overwhelm
realm
unhelm
weather-helm
whelm

ĔLP
help
kelp
self-help
skelp
swelp
whelp
yelp

ĔLPS
Phelps
(see ĔLP + s)

ĔLS
else
(cf. belts, etc.)

ĔLSH
Welsh
(see—leh)

ĔLT
belt
celt
dealt
dwelt
felt
gelt
heart-felt
kelt
knelt
melt
misspelt
pelt
smelt
spelt
svelte
swelt
unbelt
unfelt
veldt
welt

ĔLTH
commonwealth
stealth
health
wealth
dwell'th, etc.

ĔLV
delve
helve

shelve
twelve

ĔLVZ
elves
ourselves
selves
themselves
yourselves
delves, etc.

ĔLZ
Dardanelles
Elles
Lascelles
Seychelles
Welles
Wells
(see ĔL + s)

ĒM
abeam
academe
anatheme
beam
beseem
blaspheme
bream
centime
cream
daydream
deem
disesteem
distream
dream
embeam
enseam
esteem
extreme
fleam
gleam

ice-cream
leam
misdeem
moon-beam
ream
redeem
reem
regime
riem
scheme
scream
seam
seem
self-esteem
steam
stream
supreme
team
teem
theme
unbeseem
unseam
unteam
weather-gleam

ĔM
ad hominem
ahem
anadem
apothegm
bediadem
begem
Bethlehem
Brummagem
clem
condemn
contemn
diadem
em
'em

gem
hem
mem
phlegm
pro tem
requiem
stem
stratagem
them
theorem

ĒMD
undreamed
unredeemed
beamed, etc.

ĔMD
uncondemned
undiademed
begemmed, etc.

ĔMP
hemp
Kemp

ĔMS
temse

ĔMT
adreamt
attempt.
contempt
dreamt
exempt
kempt
pre-empt
self-contempt
tempt
undreamt
unkempt

ĒMZ
meseems
beams, etc.

ĔMZ
temse
Thames
gems, etc.

ĒN
advene
Algerine
almandine
alpigene
aniline
anserine
aquamarine
argentine
atropine
atween
Augustine
baleen
bandoline
barkentine
bean
been
Beguine
benzene
benzine
bescreen
between
bombazine
bottine
bowling-green
brigantine
caffeine
canteen
Capuchin
careen
carotene
carrageen

chagrin
chorine
clean
codeine
coileen
come clean
Constantine
contravene
convene
crinoline
cuisine
damascene
dean
demean
demesne
dene
dudeen
duvetyn
ean
e'en
eighteen
Eocene
epicene
Ernestine
Eugene
Evangeline
evergreen
fairy-queen
fascine
fellahin
fifteen
fillipeen
Florentine
foreseen
fourteen
gabardine
galantine
gasoline
gazogene
gelatine
Geraldine

āle,   câre,   ădd,   ärm,   ȧsk;   mē,   hẹre,   ĕnd;   īce,   ĭll;

Ghibelline
glean
gleen
go-between
good-e'en
gradine
grass-green
green
guillotine
Hallow-e'en
harvest-queen
heterogene
impregn
incarnadine
indigene
intervene
Irene
Jean
Josephine
keen
kerosene
lateen
lean
lene
libertine
lien
long green
machine
magazine
Magdalene
margarine
margravine
marine
May-queen
mazarine
meadow-queen
mean
mesne
mezzanine
mien
Miocene

misdemean
moreen
nankeen
naphthalene
Nazarene
nectarine
Nicene
nicotine
nineteen
obscene
oleomargarine
opaline
overseen
overween
palanquin
Palmyrene
Pauline
pean
peen
Peregrine
pistareen
Pleistocene
Pliocene
poteen
praying-
   machine
preen
putting-green
quadragene
quarantine
quean
queen
quinine
ravine
routine
St. Augustine
sardine
sateen
scalene
scene
screen

sea-green
seen
seine
seltzogene
serene
serpentine
seventeen
shagreen
Shean
shebeen
sheen
sixteen
spalpeen
spleen
stein
submarine
subterrene
subvene
superterrene
supervene
tambourine
teen
terrene
thirteen
tourmaline
trephine
tureen
'tween
ultramarine
umfteen
unclean
unforeseen
unqueen
unseen
uplean
vaseline
velveteen
visne
wean
ween
winter-green

wolverine
yean
yestreen

ĚN

again
aldermen
amen
ben
brevipen
cayenne
Cheyenne
citizen
cyclamen
Darien
den
denizen
equestrienne
fen
fountain-pen
glen
halogen
hen
hydrogen
impen
ken
Magdalen
men
nitrogen
oxygen
Parisienne
pen
prairie-hen
regimen
Saracen
sen
sen-sen
specimen
ten
then
tragedienne

unpen
Valenciennes
varsovienne
water-hen
wen
when
wren
yen

ĔNCH

bedrench
bench
blench
clench
drench
flench
French
intrench
monkey-
    wrench
quench
retrench
squench
stench
tench
trench
unclench
wench
wrench

ĔNCHD

unblenched
bedrenched,
    etc.

ĒND

fiend
piend
teind
advened, etc.
cleaned, etc.

ĔND

amend
an-end
append
apprehend
ascend
attend
befriend
bend
blend
commend
comprehend
condescend
contend
defend
depend
descend
distend
dividend
emend
end
expend
extend
fend
forefend
forfend
friend
gable-end
godsend
hornblende
impend
intend
interblend
kenned
lend
mend
minuend
misapprehend
misspend
obtend
offend

Ostend
penned
perpend
pitch-blende
portend
prepend
pretend
recommend
rend
repetend
reprehend
reverend
send
South Bend
spend
subtend
subtrahend
superintend
suspend
tend
transcend
trend
unbend
unfriend
unkenned
unpenned
upend
upsend
vend
vilipend
weather-fend
wend
Zend

ĔNDZ

amends
ascends, etc.

ĔNGK

Schenck

ĔNGKS

Jenkes
Jenks

ĔNGTH

full-length
length
strength

ĔNJ

avenge
revenge
Stonehenge

ĔNJD

unavenged

ĔNS

abstinence
accidence
affluence
beneficence
benevolence
blandiloquence
breviloquence
circumference
coincidence
commence
commonsense
competence
concupiscence
condense
conference
confidence
confluence
consequence
continence
convenience
corpulence
defence
deference

dense
difference
diffidence
diligence
disobediencē
dispense
dissidence
eloquence
eminence
equivalence
evidence
excellence
exigence
expedience
expense
experience
fence
flatulence
flocculence
frankincense
fraudulence
grandiloquence
hence
immanence
immense
imminence
impenitence
impertinence
impotence
imprevalence
improvidence
impudence
incense
incidence
incipience
incoincidence
incompetence
incongruence
inconsequence
incontinence
inconvenience

indifference
indigence
indolence
inexpedience
inexperience
inference
influence
innocence
insipience
insolence
intelligence
intense
irreverence
magnificence
magniloquence
maleficence
malevolence
mellifluence
munificence
negligence
nescience
non-residence
obedience
offence
omnipotence
omiscience
opulence
pence
penitence
percipience
permanence
pertinence
pestilence
plenipotence
pre-eminence
preference
prepense
prescience
pretence
prevalence
prominence

propense
providence
prurience
quantivalence
recompense
redolence
reference
residence
resilience
reticence
reverence
salience
sapience
self-confidence
self-defence
sense
somnolence
spence
subservience
subsidence
subtense
succulence
supereminence
suspense
tense
thence
truculence
turbulence
vehemence
violence
virulence
whence
(Cf. ĔNTS)

ĔNST
against
anenst
commenced
condensed
dispensed
evidenced

experienced
fenced
fornenst
'gainst
incensed
inexperienced
influenced
reverenced
sensed

ĔNT
abandonment
abolishment
absent
abstinent
accent
accident
accipient
accompaniment
accomplish-
   ment
accoutrement
acknowledg-
   ment
admeasurement
admonishment
advertisement
affamishment
affluent
àffranchise-
   ment
aggrandize-
   ment
aliment
ambient
anent
aperient
apportionment
acquent
arbitrament
argument

ōld, ôr, ŏdd. oil, fŏŏt, out; ūse, ûrn, ŭp; THis, thin

armament
ascent
assent
astonishment
attent
augment
babblement
banishment
battlement
bedevilment
bedizenment
belligerent
beneficent
benevolent
bent
besprent
betterment
bewilderment
blandishment
blazonment
blemishment
blent
botherment
brabblement
brent
cement
cent
chastisement
cherishment
circumambient
circumfluent
circumvent
coincident
comment
competent
complement
compliment
condiment
confident
confluent
congruent

consent
consequent
constituent
content
continent
convenient
corpulent
dazzlement
decipherment
decrement
deferent
dement
demolishment
dent
descent
detent
detriment
development
devilment
different
diffident
diffluent
diligent
diminishment
dimplement
disablement
disarmament
discontent
discourage-
   ment
disfigurement
disfranchise-
   ment
disobedient
disparagement
dispiritment
dissent
dissident
distinguish-
   ment
divertisement

document
element
eloquent
embarrassment
embattlement
embellishment
embezzlement
embitterment
emblazonment
embodiment
eminent
emollient
emolument
empannelment
enablement
encompassment
encouragement
endangerment
endeavorment
enfeeblement
enfranchise-
   ment
enlightenment
ennoblement
enravishment
entanglement
envelopment
environment
envisagement
equivalent
esculent
establishment
esurient
event
evident
excellent
excrement
exigent
expedient
experiment
extent

extinguishment
famishment
fent
ferment
filament
firmament
flocculent
foment
foremeant
forespent
fornent
fosterment
franchisement
fraudulent
frequent
garnishment
gent
Ghent
government
gracilent
gradient
grandiloquent
habiliment
harassment
hereditament
ignipotent
ill-content
immanent
imminent
impediment
impenitent
imperilment
impertinent
implement
impotent
impoverish-
   ment
imprisonment
improvident
impudent
incident

āle, câre, ădd, ärm, åsk; mē, hẹre, ĕnd; īce, ĭll;

incipient
incoincident
incompetent
incongruent
inconsequent
incontinent
inconvenient
increment
indent
indifferent
indigent
indolent
inexpedient
influent
ingredient
innocent
insentient
insipient
insolent
instrument
integument
intelligent
intent
inveiglement
invent
irreverent
Kent
lament
languishment
lavishment
leant
lenient
lent
ligament
lineament
liniment
luculent
magnificent
magniloquent
malcontent
maleficent

malevolent
management
meant
measurement
medicament
mellifluent
merriment
miscontent
misrepresent
misspent
monument
munificent
muniment
negligent
nourishment
nutriment
obedient
occident
omnipotent
opulent
orient
ornament
ostent
overspent
parliament
pediment
penitent
pent
percipient
permanent
pertinent
pesterment
pestilent
plenipotent
portent
prattlement
precedent
predicament
pre-eminent
premonishment
prescient

present
presentiment
president
prevalent
prevent
prominent
provident
prurient
punishment
ravishment
recipient
redolent
refluent
regiment
relent
relinquishment
rent
repent
replenishment
represent
resent
resident
resilient
reticent
reverent
rudiment
sacrament
salient
sapient
scent
sediment
self-confident
sent
sentient
sentiment
settlement
somnolent
spent
sprent
stent
subsequent

subservient
succulent
supereminent
supplement
temperament
tenement
tent
testament
thereanent
torment
tournament
tremblement
Trent
truculent
turbulent
unbent
underwent
unkent
unmeant
unsent
unspent
untent
vanishment
vanquishment
vehement
vent
vinolent
violent
virulent
wanderment
well-content
well-meant
well-spent
went
wilderment
wonderment
worriment

ĒNTH

greenth
thirteenth

fourteenth, etc.
lean'th, etc.

ĒNTH

tenth
pen'th, etc.

ĔNTS

accoutrements
contents
cents, etc.
(Cf. ĔNS)

ĒNZ

Essenes
greens
smithereens
teens
advenes, etc.

ĔNZ

cleanse
ens
flense
gens
lens
Valenciennes
Vincennes
(see ĔN + s)

ĒP

adeep
aheap
asleep
beauty-sleep
beweep
bo-peep
cheap
cheep
clepe
chimney-sweep
chepe

creep
deep
ensweep
estrepe
forweep
heap
keep
leap
neap
outleap
outsleep
outweep
overleap
oversleep
peep
reap
seep
sheep
sleep
steep
sweep
swepe
threap
under-peep
upkeep
weep

ĔP

demi-rep
footstep
hep
overstep
pep
rep
skep
step
steppe

ĒPS

creeps
cheeps, etc.

ĔPS

steps, etc.

ĒPT

beneaped
neaped
unsteeped
upheaped
heaped, etc.

ĔPT

accept
adept
crept
except
inept
intercept
kept
leapt
outslept
overslept
overstepped
pepped
sept
slept
stepped
swept
unkept
unswept
unwept
wept
yclept

EPTH

depth
stepp'th, etc.

Ẹ̆R

adhere
äerosphere
affeer

amir
anear
appear
arrear
asmear
atmosphere
auctioneer
austere
bandoleer
bayadere
beer
belvedere
besmear
bevel-gear
bier
blear
bombardier
brevier
brigadier
buccaneer
canceleer
cannoneer
caravaneer
carbineer
career
cashier
cavalier
cere
chandelier
chanticleer
charioteer
cheer
chevalier
chiffonier
chimere
circuiteer
clear
cohere
commandeer
compeer
congé d'élire

crotcheteer
cuirassier
dear
deer
disappear
domineer
drear
ear
electioneer
emir
endear
engineer
ensear
ensphere
fakir
fallow-deer
fear
financier
fineer
fleer
friction-gear
frontier
fusileer
garreteer
gaselier
gazeteer
gear
ginger-beer
gondolier
gonfalonier
grand-vizier
grenadier
halberdier
hear
Heer
hemisphere
here
indear
Indianeer
inhere
insincere

insphere
interfere
jeer
killdeer
lear
leer
madrier
meer
mere
mir
mountaineer
muffineer
muleteer
musketeer
mutineer
near
overhear
overseer
pamphleteer
peer
persevere
petardeer
pier
pioneer
pistoleer
planisphere
privateer
pulpiteer
queer
racketeer
reappear
rear
reindeer
revere
scrutineer
sear
seer
sere
sermoneer
severe
shear

sheer
sincere
skeer
smear
sneer
sonneteer
souvenir
spear
specksioneer
sphere
steer
tabasheer
targeteer
tear
teer
tier
timberstere
timoneer
Tyr
undersphere
ungear
unnear
unsphere
upcheer
uprear
veer
veneer
vizier
volunteer
weir
year

ĒRD
beard
flap-eared
lop-eared
uneared
unfeared
unpeered
weird

adhered, etc.
feared, etc.

ĒRS
fierce
pierce
tierce
transpierce

ĒRT
peart

ĒRZ
Algiers
shears
sheers
adheres, etc.

ĒS
afterpiece
ambergris
apiece
battlepiece
Berenice
Bernice
cantatrice
caprice
cease
cerise
chimney-piece
Clarice
coulisse
crease
creese
decease
decrease
esquisse
Felice
fleece
fowling-piece
frontispiece

ōld, ôr, ŏdd, oil, fŏŏt, cut; ūse, ûrn, ŭp; THis, thin

geese
grease
grece
Greece
increase
lease
Lucrece
mantel-piece
master-piece
Maurice
Nice
niece
obese
peace
pelisse
piece
pocket-piece
police
popping-crease
predecease
Reese
release
semese
surcease
Therese
valise
verdigris

ĔS

accresce
acquiesce
address
aggress
ambassadress
ancestress
archeress
assess
baroness
Bess
blemishless
bless

bodiless
bottomless
canoness
caress
cess
chess
coalesce
color!ess
comfortless
comfortress
compress
confess
conqueress
conscienceless
convalesce
cress
cultureless
cumberless
dauphiness
deaconess
deliquesce
demoness
depress
digress
dinnerless
dispossess
distress
diving-dress
dress
duress
editress
effervesce
effloresce
effortless
egress
evanesce
excess
executress
express
fanciless
fatherless

fathomless
favorless
featureless
fess
fetterless
finesse
flavorless
flowerless
foreguess
fortuneless
frondesce
full-dress
gala-dress
gentilesse
giantess
governess
guess
harborless
head-dress
idolatress
impress
ingress
inheritress
intumesce
jess
Kress
less
limitless
marchioness
masterless
mayoress
meaningless
measureless
merciless
mess
ministress
moneyless
monitress
motherless
motionless
motiveless

nevertheless
noblesse
numberless
obsess
obsolesce
odorless
opalesce
oppress
overdress
pantheress
patroness
penniless
phosophoresce
pitiless
pleasureless
poetess
politesse
possess
powerless
power-press
prepossess
press
prioress
procuress
profess
progress
prophetess
proprietress
purposeless
pythoness
Quakeress
quiesce
ransomless
recess
redress
regress
repossess
repress
respiteless
retrogress
rudderless

S.O.S.
shadowless
shelterless
shepherdess
silverless
slumberless
sorceress
spiritless
stewardess
stress
success
sultaness
suppress
tailoress
temptationless
Tess
Titaness
transgress
tress
turgesce
unbless
underdress
undress
unless
valueless
virtueless
votaress
water-cress
weaponless
yes
abjectedness
abstractedness
abusiveness
accidentalness
adaptiveness
addictedness
adhesiveness
advantageous-
   ness
affectedness
affrontiveness

agedness
aggressiveness
agileness
agreeableness
airiness
alimentiveness
alliterativeness
allusiveness
almightiness
amazedness
ambitiousness
amiableness
amicableness
ampleness
ancientness
angelicalness
angriness
anonymousness
anticness
anxiousness
apishness
apparentness
appeasableness
appositeness
apprehensive-
   ness
approachable-
   ness
arbitrariness
ardentness
arduousness
aridness
artfulness
articulateness
artificialness
artlessness
assiduousness
atrociousness
attentiveness
attractiveness
auspiciousness

avariciousness
awfulness
awkwardness
backhanded-
   ness
backwardness
balefulness
banefulness
bareheadedness
barrenness
bashfulness
beastliness
beeriness
beseechingness
besottedness
bitterness
blamelessness
blessedness
blissfulness
blithesomeness
bloatedness
blockishness
blood-guiltiness
bloodiness
bloodthirsti-
   ness
bloomingness
bluntishness
boastfulness
boisterousness
bonniness
bookishness
boorishness
bootlessness
boundlessness
bounteousness
boyishness
brackishness
brassiness
brawniness
brazenness

breathlessness
brilliantness
brittleness
brokenness
brotherliness
brushiness
brutishness
bulkiness
bumptiousness
bunchiness
burliness
bushiness
buxomness
candidness
capaciousness
capriciousness
captiousness
carefulness
carelessness
cautiousness
ceaselessness
chalkiness
changefulness
chariness
charmingness
chattiness
cheerfulness
cheeriness
cheerlessness
childishness
childlessness
chilliness
chubbiness
churlishness
clandestine-
   ness
clannishness
cleanliness
clearsighted-
   ness
cleverness

cliquishness
cloddishness
cloudiness
clownishness
clumsiness
coldhearted-
 ness
collectedness
collusiveness
comeliness
commonness
composedness
comprehen-
 siveness
compulsiveness
conceitedness
conclusiveness
conduciveness
confusedness
conjunctive-
 ness
conscientious-
 ness
consciousness
consecutive-
 ness
conspicuous-
 ness
constructive-
 ness
contentedness
contentious-
 ness
contradictious-
 ness
contrariness
contumacious-
 ness
copiousness
cordialness
corrosiveness

costliness
courageousness
courtliness
covertness
covetousness
crabbedness
craftiness
craggedness
cragginess
cravingness
craziness
creaminess
credulousness
crookedness
cruelness
crustiness
cumbrousness
curiousness
curliness
customariness
daintiness
dampishness
daringness
dauntlessness
deadliness
deathfulness
deathiness
debauchedness
deceitfulness
deceptiveness
decisiveness
decorativeness
defectiveness
defenceless-
 ness
defiantness
definiteness
deformedness
degenerateness
dejectedness
deliciousness

delightfulness
delightsome-
 ness
deliriousness
delusiveness
dementedness
depressiveness
derisiveness
desirousness
despitefulness
destructiveness
desultoriness
detersiveness
detractiveness
devotedness
dewiness
diffusedness
diffusiveness
dilatoriness
dilutedness
dinginess
direfulness
disastrousness
discontented-
 ness
discursiveness
disdainfulness
disinterested-
 ness
dismalness
disposedness
disputatious-
 ness
distastefulness
distinctiveness
dizziness
doggedness
dolefulness
doubtfulness
doughtiness
downiness

dreadfulness
dreaminess
dreariness
droughtiness
drowsiness
drunkenness
dumpishness
duskiness
dustiness
dwarfishness
eagerness
earliness
earnestness
earthiness
earthliness
earthly-
 mindedness
easefulness
easiness
eeriness
effectiveness
efficaciousness
effusiveness
egregiousness
elatedness
emotiveness
emptiness
endearedness
endlessness
enduringness
engagingness
enormousness
entertaining-
 ness
equalness
essentialness
estrangedness
evasiveness
everlastingness
exaltedness
exceptiousness

excessiveness
exclusiveness
excursiveness
expansiveness
expeditiousness
expensiveness
explicitness
expressiveness
exquisiteness
extensiveness
facetiousness
factiousness
faithfulness
faithlessness
fallaciousness
false-hearted-
   ness
far-sightedness
fastidiousness
fatefulness
fatherliness
faultlessness
favoredness
fearfulness
fearlessness
feeble-
   mindedness
feebleness
feignedness
ferociousness
fervidness
fickleness
fictiousness
fiendishness
fieriness
filminess
fishiness
fitfulness
fixedness
flabbiness
flaccidness

flakiness
flashiness
fleshiness
fleshliness
flexibleness
flightiness
flimsiness
flippantness
floridness
floweriness
fluentness
fogginess
foolhardiness
foolishness
foppishness
forcedness
foreignness
forgetfulness
formlessness
forwardness
fractiousness
fragileness
frankhearted-
   ness
francticness
fraudlessness
freakishness
freckledness
freehearted-
   ness
fretfulness
friendlessness
friendliness
frightfulness
frigidness
friskiness
frivolousness
frostiness
frothiness
frowardness
frozenness

frugalness
fruitfulness
fruitlessness
frumpishness
fugaciousness
fulsomeness
fumishness
fundamental-
   ness
furiousness
fussiness
fustiness
gaddishness
gallantness
gamesomeness
garishness
garrulousness
gashliness
gaudiness
generousness
genialness
gentleness
ghastliness
ghostliness
giddiness
giftedness
girlishness
gladfulness
gladsomeness
glariness
glassiness
gloominess
gloriousness
glossiness
godlessness
godliness
goodliness
gorgeousness
gracefulness
gracelessness
graciousness

graphicness
grassiness
gratefulness
greasiness
greediness
greenishness
grievousness
griminess
grittiness
grogginess
groundlessness
guardedness
guidelessness
guilefulness
guiltiness
guiltlessness
gustfulness
hairiness
handiness
handsomeness
haplessness
happiness
hard-hearted-
   ness
hardiness
harmfulness
harmlessness
harmonious-
   ness
hastiness
hatefulness
haughtiness
haziness
headiness
healthfulness
healthiness
healthlessness
heartedness
heartiness
heartlessness
heathenness

heavenliness
heavenly-
   mindedness
heaviness
heedfulness
heedlessness
heinousness
hellishness
helpfulness
helplessness
heterogeneous-
   ness
hiddenness
hideousness
highminded-
   ness
hilliness
hoariness
hoggishness
holiness
hollowness
homelessness
homeliness
hopefulness
hopelessness
horridness
huffishness
humbleness
humidness
humorousness
hurtfulness
huskiness
iciness
idleness
ignobleness
illicitness
illiterateness
ill-naturedness
illusiveness
illustriousness

imaginative-
   ness
imitativeness
immaculate-
   ness
impartialness
impassiveness
imperfectness
imperiousness
imperviousness
impetuousness
impiousness
implicitness
imponderous-
   ness
imposingness
impressiveness
impulsiveness
inattentiveness
inauspicious-
   ness
incapaciousness
incautiousness
incidentalness
incoherentness
incomprehen-
   siveness
inconclusive-
   ness
incongruous-
   ness
inconsistent-
   ness
inconspicuous-
   ness
indebtedness
indecisiveness
indecorous-
   ness
inefficacious-
   ness

infectiousness
ingeniousness
ingenuousness
injuriousness
inkiness
innoxiousness
inobtrusive-
   ness
inoffensiveness
insidiousness
insipidness
instructiveness
intensiveness
intrusiveness
inventiveness
invidiousness
invincibleness
involuntariness
inwardness
irefulness
irksomeness
jaggedness
jauntiness
jealousness
jettiness
Jewishness
jolliness
jovialness
joyfulness
joylessness
joyousness
judiciousness
juiciness
jumpiness
kind-hearted-
   ness
kindliness
kingliness
knavishness
knightliness
knottiness

languidness
large-hearted-
   ness
lasciviousness
lawfulness
lawlessness
laziness
leafiness
leaflessness
leaviness
lengthiness
licentiousness
lifelessness
light-hearted-
   ness
lightsomeness
likeableness
likeliness
limberness
limpidness
liquidness
lissomeness
listlessness
literalness
litigiousness
littleness
liveliness
lividness
livingness
loathliness
loathsomeness
loftiness
loneliness
lonesomeness
longsomeness
loquaciousness
lordliness
loutishness
love-in-idleness
loveliness
lovingness

lowliness
loyalness
lucidness
luckiness
lugubriousness
luminousness
lumpishness
lusciousness
lustfulness
lustiness
maidenliness
maliciousness
manfulness
manliness
mannerliness
mannishness
many-sidedness
marshiness
massiness
massiveness
matchlessness
mawkishness
maziness
meagreness
mealiness
meatiness
meditativeness
mellowness
meltingness
meretorious-
   ness
meretricious-
   ness
merriness
mightiness
milkiness
mindfulness
miraculousness
miriness
mirthfulness
mirthlessness

miscellaneous-
   ness
mischievous-
   ness
misshapenness
missishness
mistiness
modernness
modishness
momentous-
   ness
monkishness
monotonous-
   ness
monstrousness
moodiness
mopishness
morbidness
mortalness
mossiness
motherliness
mouldiness
mournfulness
mulishness
multifarious-
   ness
mumpishness
murkiness
muskiness
mustiness
mutinousness
mysteriousness
mysticalness
nakedness
namelessness
narrow-mind-
   edness
narrowness
nastiness
nationalness
nativeness

nattiness
naturalness
naughtiness
near-sighted-
   ness
nebulousness
necessariness
necessitious-
   ness
nectareousness
needfulness
neediness
needlessness
nefariousness
neglectedness
neglectfulness
neighborliness
nervousness
niggardliness
nimbleness
nobleness
noiselessness
noisiness
noisomeness
notableness
notedness
notelessness
nothingness
notoriousness
noxiousness
numerousness
nutritiousness
objectiveness
obligatoriness
obligingness
obliviousness
obsequiousness
observableness
obstreperous-
   ness
obtrusiveness

obviousness
odiousness
odoriferous-
   ness
odorousness
offensiveness
officiousness
oiliness
oleaginousness
openhanded-
   ness
openhearted-
   ness
openness
oppressiveness
opprobrious-
   ness
orderliness
ostentatious-
   ness
outlandishness
outrageousness
outwardness
painfulness
painlessness
pallidness
paltriness
parlousness
parsimonious-
   ness
passiveness
pawkiness
peaceableness
peacefulness
pearliness
peerlessness
peevishness
pellucidness
penetrative-
   ness
pennilessness

pensileness
pensiveness
penuriousness
peremptoriness
perfectness
perfidiousness
perfunctoriness
perilousness
perniciousness
perplexedness
perplexiveness
perspicacious-
　ness
perspicuous-
　ness
persuasiveness
pertinacious-
　ness
pervicacious-
　ness
perviousness
pestilential-
　ness
pettiness
pettishness
piercingness
pig-headedness
pitchiness
piteousness
pithiness
pitiableness
pitilessness
placableness
placidness
plaintiveness
playfulness
playsomeness
pleasantness
pleasingness
plenteousness
pliantness

poachiness
pointedness
pompousness
ponderous-
　ness
poorliness
porousness
portliness
positiveness
powerfulness
powerlessness
practicalness
praiseworthi-
　ness
prayerfulness
prayerlessness
precariousness
preciousness
precipitous-
　ness
precociousness
prejudicialness
preposterous-
　ness
presumptu-
　ousness
pretentious-
　ness
prettiness
previousness
prickliness
pridefulness
priestliness
priggishness
primitiveness
princeliness
prodigiousness
productive-
　ness
progressive-
　ness

properness
propitiousness
prosiness
prospective-
　ness
protectiveness
prudishness
public-minded-
　ness
puffiness
pugnacious-
　ness
pulpiness
pulpousness
pulselessness
punctiliousness
puniness
pursiness
pusillanimous-
　ness
putridness
quakiness
qualmishness
queasiness
queenliness
quenchlessness
querulousness
quick-sighted-
　ness
quick-witted-
　ness
quietness
rabidness
raciness
raggedness
raininess
rakishness
rancidness
rapaciousness
rapidness
ravenousness

readiness
rebelliousness
recentness
receptiveness
recklessness
reddishness
reflectiveness
refractiveness
refractoriness
regardlessness
relativeness
relentlessness
remorsefulness
remorseless-
　ness
reproachful-
　ness
repulsiveness
resistlessness
resoluteness
respectfulness
responsiveness
restfulness
restiveness
restlessness
restrictiveness
retentiveness
revengefulness
rightfulness
right-handed-
　ness
right-minded-
　ness
rigidness
rigorousness
riotousness
robustiousness
rockiness
roguishness
rompishness
roominess

ropiness
rosiness
rottenness
ruddiness
ruefulness
ruggedness
ruthlessness
sacredness
sacrilegious-
ness
sagaciousness
saintliness
salaciousness
sallowness
salutariness
sanctimonious-
ness
sandiness
sanguineness
sappiness
satisfactoriness
sauciness
savageness
savingness
savoriness
scaliness
scantiness
scorchingness
scornfulness
scragginess
scurviness
sea-worthiness
secondariness
secretiveness
secretness
sedentariness
seditiousness
seediness
seemingness
seemliness
seldomness

self-conceited-
ness
self-conscious-
ness
selfishness
self-righteous-
ness
senselessness
sensitiveness
sensuousness
sententious-
ness
seriousness
shabbiness
shadiness
shadowiness
shagginess
shakiness
shallowness
shamefulness
shamelessness
shapelessness
shapeliness
sheepishness
shieldlessness
shiftiness
shiftlessness
shiningness
shoaliness
short-sighted-
ness
showeriness
showiness
shrewishness
shrubbiness
sickliness
sightlessness
silentness
silkiness
silliness

simplemind-
edness
simpleness
simultaneous-
ness
sinfulness
singleness
sinlessness
sketchiness
skilfulness
skittishness
slabbiness
slatiness
slavishness
sleaziness
sleepiness
sleeplessness
sleetiness
slenderness
sliminess
slipperiness
slothfulness
sluggishness
smilingness
smokiness
snappishness
sneakiness
snobbishness
sober-minded-
ness
soberness
sociableness
soft-hearted-
ness
solidness
solitariness
solubleness
sombreness
sombrousness
sonorousness
sordidness

sorriness
sorrowfulness
sottishness
spaciousness
sparklingness
speciousness
speckledness
speculativeness
speechlessness
speediness
spiciness
spitefulness
splendidness
sponginess
spontaneous-
ness
sportiveness
spotlessness
spottedness
spottiness
springiness
spriteliness
spuminess
spuriousness
squeamishness
starchiness
starriness
stateliness
steadfastness
steadiness
stealthfulness
stealthiness
steeliness
steepiness
stickiness
stinginess
stintedness
stolidness
stoniness
storminess

ōld, ôr, ŏdd, oil, fŏŏt, out; ūse, ûrn, ŭp; THis, thin

straightfor-
  wardness
strenuousness
stringentness
stringiness
stubbiness
stubbornness
studiousness
stuffiness
stuntedness
stupendousness
stupidness
sturdiness
stylishness
subjectiveness
submissiveness
subordinate-
  ness
substantialness
subtleness
successfulness
suddenness
sugariness
suggestiveness
suitableness
sulkiness
sulleness
sultriness
sumptuousness
sunniness
supercilious-
  ness
superstitious-
  ness
suppleness
suppliantness
surliness
surprisingness
susceptiveness
suspectedness
suspiciousness

swarthiness
sweatiness
sweetishness
talkativeness
tamelessness
tardiness
tastefulness
tastelessness
tawdriness
tawniness
tediousness
tempestuous-
  ness
temporariness
temptingness
tenaciousness
tender-hearted-
  ness
tepidness
testiness
thankfulness
thievishness
thirstiness
thoroughness
thoughtfulness
thoughtless-
  ness
threadiness
thriftiness
thriftlessness
thrivingness
ticklishness
tidiness
timeliness
timidness
timorousness
tipsiness
tiresomeness
toilsomeness
toothsomeness
torpidness

torridness
tortuousness
totalness
touchiness
toyishness
tracklessness
traitorousness
tranquilness
transcendent-
  ness
transientness
transitiveness
transitoriness
transparent-
  ness
trashiness
treacherous-
  ness
tremendous-
  ness
tremulousness
tributariness
trickiness
trickishness
tricksiness
true-hearted-
  ness
trustfulness
trustiness
trustlessness
trustworthi-
  ness
truthfulness
truthlessness
tunefulness
turfiness
turgidness
ugliness
umbrageous-
  ness

unanimous-
  ness
unbendingness
unblessedness
unbounded-
  ness
uncleanliness
uncloudedness
uncourtliness
undauntedness
uneasiness
unexpected-
  ness
unfeignedness
unfriendliness
ungainliness
ungentleness
ungodliness
ungrounded-
  ness
unholiness
universalness
unkindliness
unlikeliness
unloveliness
unmanliness
unprepared-
  ness
unquietness
unreadiness
unrighteous-
  ness
unruliness
unseaworthi-
  ness
unseemliness
unsightliness
unstableness
untowardness
untrustiness
unwieldiness

unwillingness
unwontedness
unworldliness
unworthiness
uppishness
usefulness
uselessness
uxoriousness
vacuousness
vagrantness
valetudinari-
  ness
valiantness
validness
vapidness
vexatiousness
viciousness
victoriousness
vigorousness
vindictiveness
viridness
virtuousness
viscousness
visionariness
vitreousness
vivaciousness
vividness
vociferousness
voluminous-
  ness
voluntariness
voluptuousness
voraciousness
vulgarness
waggishness
wakefulness
wantonness
warefulness
wariness
warm-hearted-
  ness

washiness
waspishness
wastefulness
watchfulness
waveringness
waviness
waxiness
waywardness
wealthiness
weariness
wearisomeness
weightiness
welcomeness
whimsicalness
whitishness
wholesome-
  ness
wickedness
wilderness
wilfulness
wiliness
willingness
winsomeness
wiriness
wishfulness
wistfulness
witheredness
witlessness
wittiness
woefulness
womanliness
wondrousness
wontedness
woodiness
woolliness
wordiness
wordishness
worldliness
worldy-mind-
  edness
worshipfulness

worthiness
worthlessness
wrathfulness
wretchedness
wretchlessness
wrongfulness
wrongheaded-
  ness
yeastiness
yellowishness
yellowness
yieldingness
youthfulness
zealousness

ĒSH
affiche
leash
McLeish
McNeish
schottische
unleash

ĔSH
afresh
crèche
enmesh
flesh
fresh
mesh
nesh
refresh
secesh
thresh

ĔSK
arabesque
barbaresque
burlesque
chivalresque
Dantesque

desk
gardensque
gigantesque
grotesque
Moresque
naturalesque
picaresque
picturesque
plateresque
reading-desk
Romanesque
sculpturesque
soldatesque
statuesque

ĒST
archpriest
artiste
batiste
beast
deceased
east
feast
harvest-feast
least
modiste
priest
queest
triste
underpoliced
unpriest
wedding-feast
yeast
pieced, etc.
ceased, etc.
fleeced, etc.

ĔST
abreast
acquest
alkahest

ōld, ôr, ŏdd, oil, fŏŏt, out; ūse, ûrn, ŭp; THis, thin

anapest	molest	*attributest*	dreamiest
arrest	nest	*banishest*	dreariest
attest	north-west	beamiest	drowsiest
behest	obsessed	beguilingest	dustiest
bequest	obtest	bleariest	earliest
best	over-dressed	blestfullest	easiest
blest	palimpsest	*blisterest*	eeriest
breast	pest	blithefulest	effectedest
Brest	predigest	blithesomest	*emblazonest*
Bucharest	protest	*blunderest*	emptiest
Budapest	quest	breeziest	*enviest*
cest	recessed	brilliantest	evenest
chest	request	briniest	*exhibitest*
congest	rest	burliest	filmiest
contest	second-best	cheerfullest	filthiest
crest	self-possessed	cheeriest	fleeciest
depressed	suggest	cheerliest	flimsiest
detest	test	chilliest	flightiest
devest	tressed	chokiest	flintiest
digest	Trieste	cleanliest	*flowerest*
distressed	unblest	*clusterest*	foamiest
divest	unbreast	*conquerest*	forcefullest
dressed	under-crest	*continuest*	*forfeitest*
Everest	underdressed	cosiest	*freshenest*
funest	undressed	costliest	friendliest
gest	unexpressed	courtliest	funniest
golden-tressed	unguessed	*coverest*	fussiest
guest	unprepossessed	creamiest	*gatherest*
hard-pressed	unpressed	creepiest	genialest
hest	unredressed	cruellest	giddiest
imprest	unrest	crustiest	*glimmerest*
increst	untressed	curliest	*glistenest*
infest	vest	daintiest	gloomiest
ingest	west	decisivest	glossiest
interest	wrest	derisivest	*glowerest*
invest	yessed	*determinest*	goutiest
jessed	zest	dingiest	grimiest
jest	(see ĔS + ed)	dizziest	guilefulest
Key West	*answerest*	doughtiest	guiltiest
lest	*astonishest*	dowdiest	gustiest
manifest	attentivest	*dowerest*	happiest

āle, câre, ădd, ärm, åsk; mē, hĕre, ĕnd; īce, ĭll;

haughtiest	mellowest	ruggedest	*sufferest*
healthiest	*meritest*	rustiest	*sunderest*
hearkenest	merriest	sacredest	sunniest
heartiest	mightiest	sedgiest	surliest
heaviest	moistiest	seemliest	tearfullest
holiest	morbidest	*severest*	*temperest*
homeliest	mossiest	*shimmerest*	thirstiest
hopefullest	mouldiest	shiniest	thriftiest
horridest	mournfullest	shoddiest	*thunderest*
huffiest	*murmurest*	showiest	timidest
hungerest	muskiest	*shudderest*	trustiest
hungriest	mustiest	sightliest	ugliest
huskiest	*narrowest*	silentest	unholiest
iciest	noisiest	silliest	unreadiest
incumberest	*nourishest*	sketchiest	veriest
inheritest	*offerest*	skilfullest	vindictivest
inkiest	*pardonest*	skinniest	vulgarest
inliest	patentest	sleepiest	*wanderest*
inspiritest	pearliest	slimiest	wealthiest
jolliest	pensivest	*slumberest*	weariest
juiciest	pleasantest	smokiest	wheeziest
kindliest	*pleasurest*	snuffiest	windiest
kingliest	portliest	soapiest	wilfulest
knightliest	preciousest	solidest	*winnowest*
labourest	*predestinest*	*sorrowest*	winsomest
languishest	princeliest	spiciest	wintriest
libellest	prosiest	spikiest	*witnessest*
likeliest	*punishest*	*spiritest*	*wonderest*
lingerest	*quarrellest*	splendidest	*worriest*
lissomest	*questionest*	spongiest	yeastiest
listenest	quietest	spooniest	
lithesomest	*recoverest*	springiest	**ĒT**
liveliest	*relinquishest*	spriteliest	accrete
livenest	*rememberest*	steadiest	afreet
loftiest	*rescuest*	stealthiest	athlete
loneliest	restfulest	stilliest	balance-sheet
loveliest	rightfulest	stingiest	beat
lowerest	*rivallest*	stormiest	beet
lowliest	rosiest	stuffiest	bitter-sweet
loyalest	rowdiest	stupidest	bleat
marvellest	royalest	sturdiest	carte-de-visite

cheat
cheet
cleat
cleet
compete
complete
conceit
concrete
country-seat
county-seat
Crete
dead-beat
dead-heat
dead-meat
deceit
defeat
delete
deplete
discreet
Dutch **treat**
eat
effete
elite
entreat
escheat
estreat
facete
feat
feet
fleet
geat
greet
heat
help-meet
honey-sweet
ill-treat
incomplete
indiscreet
judgment-seat
Lafitte
íeat

leet
lorikeet
maltreat
marguerite
meadow-sweet
meat
meet
mercy-seat
mete
neat
obsolete
overeat
parrakeet
peat
pleat
preconceit
receipt
repeat
replete
retreat
sea-beat
seat
secrete
self-conceit
self-deceit
sheet
skeet
sleet
street
suite
sunny-sweet
sweet
teat
terete
treat
unmeet
unseat
unsweet
vegete
weet

wheat
winding-sheet

ĔT
abet
aigrette
ailette
alette
allumette
all wet
alphabet
amourette
amulet
anchoret
angelet
anisette
Annette
Antoinette
backset
baguette
banneret
banquette
barbette
Barnett
baronet
bassinet
bayonet
beget
benet
beset
bet
bewet
blanquette
bobbinet
Brett
brevet
brochette
brunette
Burnett
cabinet
cadet

calumet
canzonet
carcanet
cassolette
castanet
cellaret
chansonette
chemisette
cigarette
clarinet
coquette
coronet
corvette
coverlet
croquette
crossette
crystal set
curvet
dancette
dead-set
debt
duet
epaulet
epithet
estafette
etiquette
facette
falconet
farmerette
flageolet
flet
floweret
forget
formeret
fossette
fourchette
fret
frett
fumette
gazette
genet

āle,   câre,   ădd,   ärm,   åsk;   mē,   hẹre,   ĕnd;   īce,   ĭll;

get
Gillette
globulet
grisette
Harriet
historiette
illset
inset
interset
jet
Jeanette
Joliet
judgment-debt
Juliet
Juliette
landaulet
leaderette
let
Lett
leveret
lorgnette
Lucette
luncheonette
lunette
Margaret
marionette
marmoset
martinet
medalet
met
mignonette
minaret
minionette
minuet
misbeget
motet
musette
Nanette
net
noisette
novelette

octet
off-set
Olivet
omelet
oubliette
overset
parapet
parroket
parquet
pet
pianette
pillaret
pipette
piquet
piquette
pirouette
planchette
poussette
quartet
quintet
regret
ret
revet
ricochet
rivulet
rosette
roulette
sarcenet
septet
serviette
sestet
set
sett
sextet
sharp-set
silhouette
somerset
soubrette
statuette
stet
suffragette

sunset
sweat
tabaret
tabinet
taboret
Thibet
thickset
threat
Tibet
toilette
tournette
tourniquet
tret
underset
unfret
unget
upset
vedette
vet
vignette
villanette
vinaigrette
violet
wagonette
well-met
wet
whet
yet
zonulet

ĒTH
bequeath
breathe
ensheath
enwreathe
inbreathe
insheathe
interwreathe
inwreathe
seethe
sheathe

sneathe
teethe
unsheathe
unwreathe
upbreathe
wreathe

Ēth
beneath
heath
Keith
Leith
'neath
sheath
sneath
teeth
underneath
wreath

Ĕth
Ashtoreth
breath
death
Elizabeth
Macbeth
saith
'sdeath
Seth
shibboleth
twentieth
thirtieth, etc.
answereth
astonisheth
attributeth
banisheth
blemisheth
blistereth
blundereth
busieth
clustereth
conquereth

continueth
covereth
determineth
dowereth
emblazoneth
enspiriteth
envieth
exhibiteth
flowereth
forfeiteth
gathereth
glisteneth
glowereth
hearkeneth
hungereth
incumbereth
inheriteth
inspiriteth
laboureth
languisheth
libelleth
lingereth
listeneth
liveneth
lowereth
marvelleth
measureth
meriteth
murmureth
nourisheth
offereth
overpowereth
overtowereth
pardoneth
pleasureth
predestineth
punisheth
quarrelleth
questioneth
quieteth
recovereth

relinquisheth
remembereth
rescueth
rivalleth
severeth
shimmereth
showereth
shuddereth
silvereth
slumbereth
sorroweth
spiriteth
suffereth
sundereth
tempereth
thundereth
ventureth
wandereth
wearieth
whispereth
winnoweth
witnesseth
wondereth
worrieth
worshippeth

ĒTHD

unbreathed
bequeathed,
   etc.

ĒTZ

Keats
beats, etc.

ĔTZ

Metz
bets, etc.

ĒV

achieve

aggrieve
beeve
believe
bereave
breve
Christmas-eve
cleave
conceive
deceive
deev
disbelieve
eave
engrieve
eve
greave
grieve
heave
interleave
interweave
inweave
keeve
khedive
leave
lieve
make-believe
misconceive
naive
New Year's
   eve
perceive
preconceive
qui vive
reave
receive
recitative
reeve
relieve
reprieve
retrieve
seave
sheave

shire-reeve
shrieve
sleave
sleeve
steeve
Steve
thieve
undeceive
unreave
unreeve
unweave
upheave
vive
weave
we've
yester-eve

ĒVD

self-deceived
unbelieved
unperceived
unrelieved
achieved, etc.

ĒVZ

eaves
achieves, etc.

ĒZ

aborigines
analyses
Annamese
antipodes
antitheses
appease
Arakanese
Aragonese
Assamese
bee's knees
Belize
Bengalese

āle,   câre,   ădd,   ärm,   åsk;   mē,   hĕre,   ĕnd;   īce,   ĭll;

bise	frieze	obsequies	Tyrolese
Bolognese	Genevese	parentheses	unease
breeze	grease	pease	unfreeze
Burmese	Havanese	periphrases	valise
B.V.D.s	heart's-ease	Pierides	Veronese
Carlylese	heeze	please	Viennese
Caryatides	Hesperides	Pleiades	vortices
cerise	hypotheses	*Polonese*	wheeze
Ceylonese	imprese	Portuguese	(see Ē + s)
cheese	indices	Pyrenees	
chemise	isosceles	rabies	**ĔZ**
chersonese	Japanese	remise	cortez
cheval-de-frise	Javanese	sea-breeze	fez
Chinese	Johnsonese	seize	says
congeries	journalese	Siamese	
D.T.'s	lees	Singhalese	**ĒZH**
Diogenes	Leonese	sneeze	prestige
disease	Louise	squeeze	tige
displease	Maltese	syntheses	
ease	Milanese	tease	**ĔZH**
enfreeze	mease	these	barège
Eumenides	Navarrese	trapeze	cortège
feaze	Nepaulese	tweeze	manège
freeze			

I

These words include the following accented vowel sounds:

Ī as in ice; heard also in vie, rye, height, eye, aisle, aye meaning *yes,* sky, buy, choir.

Ĭ as in ill; heard also in sieve, English, pretty, been, breeches, women, busy, build, nymph, hymnal.

Ī	alkalify	apply	bedye
acidify	ally	awry	belie
adry	amplify	ay	bespy
alacrify	angelify	aye	black eye
alibi	Anglify	beatify	brutify
alkali	apple-pie	beautify	butterfly

ōld, ôr. ŏdd, oil, fŏŏt, out; ūse, ûrn, ŭp; THis, thin

buy	falsify	lye	rye
by	fie	magnify	saccharify
bye	firefly	magpie	sanctify
bye-bye	fly	modify	satisfy
by-and-by	forby	mollify	scarify
by the by	fortify	mortify	scorify
candify	fossilify	multiply	scye
certify	Frenchify	my	sea-pie
clarify	fructify	my eye	sheep's-eye
classify	fry	mystify	shy
cockneyfy	gasify	nigh	sigh
codify	genii	notify	signify
comply	glorify	nullify	simplify
countrify	go-by	nye	sky
crucify	good-bye	occupy	Skye
cry	gratify	ossify	sky-high
damnify	gri	outcry	sly
dandify	guy	outfly	sny
decry	heigh	outvie	solidify
defy	hereby	pacify	specify
deify	hie	passer-by	spry
demi	high	personify	spy
demy	horrify	petrify	stander-by
deny	humanify	pi	stellify
descry	humble-pie	pie	stultify
die	hushaby	ply	stupefy
dignify	identify	preachify	sty
disqualify	imply	preoccupy	supply
dissatisfy	incubi	prophesy	tabefy
diversify	indemnify	pry	termini
dragon-fly	ineye	purify	terrify
dry	intensify	putrefy	testify
dye	July	qualify	thereby
edify	justify	quantify	thigh
electrify	labefy	ramify	thy
emulsify	lazuli	rarefy	tie
ensky	lenify	ratify	torpify
espy	lie	rectify	torrefy
eternify	lignify	rely	transmogrify
exemplify	liquefy	reply	try
eye	lullaby	revivify	typify

āle, câre, ădd, ärm, åsk; mē, hĕre, ĕnd; īce, ĭll;

umble-pie	**ĬB**	flitch	broadside
under-buy	ad lib	Gabrilowitsch	bromide
underlie	bib	hitch	chide
unify	Bibb	itch	Christmas-tide
unshy	crib	*lich*	Clyde
untie	dib	miche	cockeyed
verbify	drib	niche	coincide
verify	fib	pitch	collide
versify	gib	quitch	confide
vie	Gibb	rich	countrified
vilify	glib	scritch	countryside
vitrify	jib	stitch	decide
vivify	nib	switch	deicide
weather-eye	*quib*	twitch	deride
weather-spy	rib	which	dignified
well-nigh	sib	witch	dissatisfied
whereby	squib		diversified
why		**ĬCHT**	divide
wry	**ĪBD**	unbewitched	double-dyed
wye	uninscribed	unhitched	dove-eyed
	ascribed, etc.	unwitched	dull-eyed
ĪB		bewitched, etc.	eagle-eyed
ascribe	**ĬBD**		Eastertide
bribe	rock-ribbed	**ĪD**	ebb-tide
circumscribe	cribbed, etc.	abide	elide
describe		Allhallow-tide	Ember-tide
diatribe	**ĬBZ**	alongside	eventide
gibe	dibs	Argus-eyed	evil-eyed
imbibe	Gibbs	aside	excide
inscribe	his nibs	astride	fireside
interscribe	cribs, etc.	backslide	flood-tide
jibe		barmecide	foreside
kibe	**ĬCH**	Bartholomew-	fortified
prescribe	bewitch	tide	fratricide
proscribe	bitch	bedside	full-eyed
scribe	Cesarewitch	beside	glide
subscribe	*chich*	bestride	goggle-eyed
superscribe	czarevitch	betide	green-eyed
transcribe	ditch	bide	gride
tribe	enrich	bonafide	guide
	fitch	bride	Hallowtide

ōld, ôr, ŏdd, oil, fŏŏt, out; ūse, ûrn, ŭp; THis, thin

hawk-eyed | pop-eyed | unsanctified | pyramid
herpicide | preside | unsatisfied | quid
hide | pride | unspied | rid
high-tide | provide | untried | skid
hillside | purified | uxoricide | slid
homicide | qualified | vaticide | squid
Hyde | regicide | vermicide | thrid
I'd | reside | vitrified | unbid
infanticide | ride | vulpicide | underbid
insecticide | riverside | wall-eyed | undid
inside | sea-side | water-side | unforbid
iodide | self-pride | wayside
justified | self-satisfied | weather-side | **ĬDST**
Lammas-tide | Shrove-tide | weather-tide | amidst
landslide | side | Whitsuntide | *bid'st*
lapicide | slide | wide | *chid'st*
lee-tide | snide | Yule-tide | *did'st*
liberticide | soft-eyed | (see Ī + ed) | *forbid'st*
lynx-eyed | sororicide | | *hid'st*
matricide | spring-tide | **ĬD** | *kid'st*
meek-eyed | squint-eyed | amid | midst
misallied | state-wide | bid | *rid'st*
misguide | stillicide | *chid* | *slid'st*
morning-tide | stride | Cid
nation-wide | subdivide | did | **ĬDTH**
nide | subside | fid | width
noontide | suicide | forbid | *bid'th*, etc.
open-eyed | sulphide | *fordid*
outride | tide | gid | **ĪDZ**
outside | tyrannicide | grid | besides
outstride | unapplied | hid | ides
override | unbetide | invalid | abides, etc.
owl-eyed | underside | katydid
ox-eyed | undertide | kid | **ĪF**
pale-eyed | undescried | lid | after-life
parenticide | undignified | Madrid | bowie-knife
parricide | undried | mid | fife
Passion-tide | unespied | outbid | fishwife
patricide | ungratified | outdid | goodwife
pied | unpurified | overbid | housewife
pie-eyed | unqualified | overdid | knife

life
rife
still-life
strife
wife

ĪF
biff
cliff
diff
glyph
griff
handkerchief
hieroglyph
hippogriff
if
jiff
miff
neckerchief
skiff
sniff
stiff
Tenerife
Teneriffe
tiff
undercliff
whiff
wiff

ĪFT
adrift
drift
forelift
gift
lift
rift
shift
shrift
sift
snow-drift
spendthrift

spiffed
spindrift
swift
thrift
tift
topping-lift
unthrift
uplift
miffed, etc.

ĪFTH
fifth
miff'th, etc.

ĪG
big
brig
cig
dig
fig
gig
grig
guinea-pig
infra-dig
jig
nig
periwig
pig
prig
renege
rig
snig
sprig
swig
thimblerig
thingumajig
trig
twig
unrig
Whig

whirligig
wig

ĪGD
bewigged
full-rigged
jury-rigged
square-rigged
digged, etc.

ĪGZ
Biggs
Briggs
Higgs
Riggs
(see ĪG + s)

ĪJ
Lije
oblige

ĪJ
abridge
bridge
enridge
midge
nidge
ridge
upridge
(see also ÅJ)

ĪJD
unabridged
unbridged
abridged, etc.

ĪK
Alibi Ike
alike
assassin-like
belike

bike
boarding-pike
brotherlike
dislike
dyke
fairy-like
fyke
ghostlike
hike
kike
like
maidenlike
manlike
marlinspike
mike
mislike
oblique
peasantlike
pike
shrike
spike
starlike
strike
tyke
unlike
Vandyck
Vandyke
Van Wyck
womanlike
workmanlike
Wyke

ĪK
arithmetic
arsenic
bailiwick
Benedick
bestick
bishopric
brick
candlestick

ōld, ôr, ŏdd, oil, fŏŏt, out; ūse, ûrn, ŭp; THis, thin

candlewick
Catholic
chick
chivalric
choleric
click
crick
Dick
double-quick
fiddle-stick
flick
heart-sick
heretic
hick
impolitic
kick
kinnikinnick
lick
limerick
love-sick
lunatic
maverick
mick
nick
pick
plethoric
pogo-stick
politic
prick
quick
rhetoric
rick
sic
sick
single-stick
slick
snick
stich
stick
thick
tic

tick
trick
turmeric
walking stick
wick

ĪKS

Dykes
Rikes
Sykes
(see ĪK + s)

ĬKS

admix
affix
Beatrix
cicatrix
commix
crucifix
Dix
executrix
fiddlesticks
fix
Hicks
Hix
immix
inheritrix
intermix
mix
nix
Pnyx
politics
prefix
prolix
pyx
Ricks
Rix
six
Styx
transfix

Trix
(see ĬK + s)

ĬKST

atwixt
betwixt
click'st
kick'st
lick'st
pick'st
prick'st
stick'st
trick'st
'twixt
unfixed
unmixed
admixed, etc.

ĬKSTH

sixth
mix'th, etc.

ĬKT

addict
afflict
astrict
benedict
conflict
constrict
contradict
convict
delict
depict
derelict
evict
inflict
interdict
Pict
predict
relict
restrict

strict
unlicked
unpicked
bricked, etc.

ĪL

aisle
Anglophile
awhile
beguile
bibliophile
bile
camomile
chyle
compile
crocodile
defile
diastyle
enisle
ensile
erewhile
erstwhile
file
Francophile,
    etc.
guile
infantile
isle
juvenile
Kabyle
lisle
Lyle
meanwhile
mercantile
mile
Nile
otherwhile
paper-file
pentastyle
peristyle
pile

---

puerile
reconcile
resile
revile
rile
smile
somewhile
spile
stile
style
therewhile
tile
up-pile
versatile
vibratile
vile
voltaic pile
while
wile

ĪL
Amityville
Anglophile
befrill
bestill
bibliophile
bill
Bozenkill
Brazil
brill
chill
chlorophyle
chrysophyll
Cobleskill
codicil
daffodil
dill
distil
domicile
downhill
drill

enthrill
Evansville
espadrille
fill
Francophile,
    etc.
freewill
frill
fulfil
gill
good-will
grill
grille
hill
ill
ill-will
imbecile
infantile
instil
jill
juvenile
kill
kiln
Louisville
mercantile
mill
nil
pill
powder-mill
prill
puerile
quadrille
quill
rill
self-will
Seville
shrill
sill
skill
spadille
spill

squill
still
stock-still
swill
thill
thrill
till
trill
twill
'twill
until
unwill
uphill
versatile
vibratile
vill
volatile
water-mill
whip-poor-will
will

ĪLCH
filch
milch
pilch
Zilch

ĪLD
child
childe
enfiled
foster-child
love-child
mild
self-styled
unbeguiled
unchild
unmild
unreconciled
unwild
wild

Wilde
beguiled, etc.
aisled

ĪLD
befrilled
begild
build
gild
guild
rebuild
self-willed
unbuild
unchilled
unfulfilled
unskilled
untilled
unwilled
chilled, etc.

ĪLF
sylph

ĪLJ
bilge

ĪLK
bilk
ilk
milk
silk
spun-silk

ĪLKS
Wilkes
(see ĪLK + s)

ĪLM
film

ĪLN
kiln
Milne

ĬLS
grilse
(cf.—lts)

ĬLST
beguil'st
defil'st
whilst
whils't, etc.

ĬLT
atilt
basket-hilt
begilt
built
clinker-built
clipper-built
frigate-built
gilt
guilt
hilt
jilt
kilt
lilt
milt
quilt
rebuilt
silt
spilt
stilt
tilt
unbuilt
ungilt
Vanderbilt
wilt

ĬLTH
filth
spilth
tilth
till'th, etc.

ĬLTS
kilts
[cf. grilse]
basket-hilts,
    etc.

ĬLZ
Giles
Miles
otherwhiles
whiles
wiles
beguiles, etc.

ĪM
aftertime
bedtime
begrime
belime
berhyme
beslime
birdlime
breathing-time
chime
chyme
climb
clime
crime
daytime
dime
eaning-time
grime
Guggenheim
haying-time
I'm
lifetime
lime
Lyme
maritime
meantime
mime

overtime
pairing-time
pantomime
prime
quicklime
rhyme
Rosenheim
rime
seed-time
slime
sometime
spring-time
sublime
summer-time
thyme
time
upclimb

ĬM
antonym
bedim
betrim
brim
cherubim
dim
enlimn
gim
glim
grim
gym
him
hymn
interim
Jim
Kim
Klim
limb
limn
maritime
Nym
prelim

prim
pseudonym
rim
Sanhedrim
seraphim
shim
skim
slim
swim
synonym
Tim
trim
vim
whim
zimb

ĪMD
well-timed
begrimed, etc.

ĬMD
brimmed
untrimmed
bedimmed, etc.

ĬMF
lymph
nymph
sea-nymph

ĬMP
blimp
crimp
gimp
imp
jimp
limp
pimp
primp
scrimp
shrimp

simp
skimp
tymp

ĬMPS

glimpse
crimps, etc.

ĬMZ

betimes
oftentimes
ofttimes
sometimes
begrimes, etc.

ĬMZ

Simms
(see ĬM + s)

ĪN

Adaline
Adeline
adulterine
agatine
align
alkaline
aniline
anodyne
anserine
Apennine
apple-wine
aquiline
argentine
ashine
asinine
assign
Beckstein
benign
beshine
bine
brigantine

brine
Byzantine
caballine
caffeine
calcine
canine
Capitoline
carabine
Caroline
celandine
Celestine
chine
Clementine
Clyne
columbine
combine
concubine
condign
confine
consign
Constantine
coraline
countermine
countersign
crystalline
decline
define
design
dine
disincline
divine
dyne
eglantine
Esquiline
enshrine
ensign
entwine
Epstein
Esenwein
Esquiline
Evaline

Evangeline
eyne
Fescennine
fine
Florentine
Ghibelline
Goldstein
Hoffenstein
hyaline
incarnadine
incline
infantine
interline
intermine
intertwine
Jacqueline
kine
Klein
Kline
langsyne
leonine
libertine
Liechtenstein
life-line
line
load-line
Madeline
malign
matutine
mine
moonshine
nine
opaline
opine
outshine
overtwine
Palatine
pavonine
peregrine
petaline
Philistine

pine
porcupine
powder-mine
Proserpine
recline
refine
repine
resign
resupine
Rhine
Rubinstein
saline
sapphirine
saturnine
serpentine
shine
shrine
sibylline
sign
sine
snow-line
spine
spline
star-shine
stein
subdivine
subsign
sunshine
superfine
supine
swine
sycamine
syne
thine
tine
trephine
trine
Turn Verein
turpentine
twine
Tyne

ōld, ôr, ŏdd, oil, fŏŏt, out; ūse, ûrn, ŭp; THis, thin

unbenign	Berlin	herein	sin
underline	bin	heroine	skin
undermine	Boleyn	hyaline	spin
undersign	bulletin	in	sycamine
unline	Byzantine	incarnadine	take-in
untwine	caballine	infantine	tambourin
Ursuline	caffeine	inn	therein
valentine	cannikin	Jacobin	thick-and-thin
vespertine	Capuchin	javelin	thin
vine	carabine	jessamine	tigerkin
viperine	carotin	jinn	tiger-skin
vulturine	Catherine	Katherine	tin
water-line	Celestine	kilderkin	tourmaline
Weinstein	chagrin	kin	twin
whine	chin	libertine	underpin
wine	chinquapin	lin	Ursuline
wolverine	clavecin	Lynn	unpin
woodbine	codeine	mandarin	unsin
Zollverein	coraline	mandolin	vaseline
	crinoline	manikin	vespertine
IN	crystalline	masculine	violin
adulterine	culverin	mezzanine	viperine
agatine	din	minikin	vulturine
agrin	discipline	moccasin	wherein
akin	Evangeline	nectarine	whin
alizarin	feminine	nicotine	whipper-in
alkaline	Fescennine	opaline	win
all in	fin	origin	within
almandine	finikin	paladin	Zeppelin
aniline	Finn	pavonine	
anserine	Florentine	peregrine	**INCH**
aquiline	francolin	petaline	bepinch
argentine	gelatin	Philistine	cinch
aspirin	genuine	pin	chinch
atropine	Ghibelline	Quinn	clinch
baldachin	gin	saccharine	fallow-finch
bandoline	Glyn	sapphirine	finch
bearskin	Glynn	seal-skin	flinch
been	grin	shin	inch
begin	gyn	sibylline	linch
belaying-pin	harlequin	side-spin	lynch

āle, câre, ădd, ärm, åsk; mē, hẹre, ĕnd; īce, ĭll;

pinch
unclinch
winch

ÌND
behind
bind
blind
color-blind
crined
disinclined
find
gavelkind
grind
hind
humankind
inbind
interwind
intertwined
kind
mankind
master-mind
mind
overtwined
purblind
remind
rind
rynd
snow-blind
storm-wind
unbind
unblind
unconfined
undefined
underbind
undersigned
undesigned
unkind
unrefined
unshrined
unwind

upbind
upwind
vined
wind
womankind
combined, etc.

ÏND
abscind
disciplined
exscind
lind
Lynd
rescind
Rosalind
storm-wind
tamarind
thick-skinned
thin-skinned
undisciplined
wind
grinned, etc.

ÏNG
anything
atheling
besing
bewing
bing
bring
chitterling
cling
daughterling
dayspring
ding
driving-spring
easterling
enring
evening
everything
fairy-king

fling
full-swing
heart-string
king
lifespring
ling
Ming
outwing
ping
ring
sea-king
seal-ring
sea-wing
shuffle-wing
signet-ring
sing
sling
spring
starveling
sting
string
swing
Synge
thing
ting
underling
underwing
unking
unsling
unstring
wedding-ring
weeping-spring
wing
wring
abandoning
accomplishing
accrediting
accustoming
actioning
admonishing
afforesting

altering
angering
answering
apparelling
arguing
armouring
astonishing
attributing
auctioning
auditing
auguring
awakening
badgering
balancing
ballasting
bandying
banishing
bantering
barbering
bargaining
barracking
barrelling
bartering
battering
bedeviling
beflattering
beggaring
belaboring
beleaguering
belecturing
bellowing
bepattering
bepowdering
bepummelling
bescattering
beslabbering
bespattering
betokening
bevelling
bewildering
bickering

---

blackening
blandishing
blanketing
blarneying
blathering
blazoning
blemishing
blistering
blossoming
blubbering
blundering
blustering
bolstering
bonneting
brandishing
breakfasting
broadening
buffeting
bullying
burdening
burnishing
burying
busying
butchering
buttressing
cancelling
candying
cankering
cannoning
cantering
canvassing
capering
capturing
carolling
carpeting
carrying
cautioning
cavilling
challenging
channelling
chartering

chastening
chattering
chiselling
christening
Christmasing
ciphering
clambering
clamoring
clattering
clustering
cockering
coloring
compassioning
conjecturing
conquering
considering
continuing
contributing
conveyancing
covering
coveting
cowering
crediting
cudgelling
cumbering
dallying
damaging
darkening
deadening
deciphering
destining
determining
devilling
dickering
dieting
diminishing
discouraging
discrediting
disestablishing
disfavoring
dishallowing

dishonoring
disparaging
dispiriting
displeasuring
disquieting
dissevering
distinguishing
distributing
dowering
drivelling
duelling
embarrassing
embellishing
emblazoning
embodying
emboldening
embosoming
empitying
enameling
enamoring
encouraging
encumbering
enharboring
enheartening
enravishing
entering
entrammelling
envisaging
envying
establishing
examining
exhibiting
faltering
famishing
fancying
farrowing
fashioning
fathoming
favoring
feathering
festering

filtering
fingering
finicking
finishing
flattering
flavoring
flickering
flittering
flourishing
flowering
flurrying
flustering
fluttering
focussing
following
foregathering
foreshadowing
foretokening
forfeiting
forwarding
freshening
furnishing
furthering
galloping
gambolling
gammoning
gardening
garlanding
garnishing
gathering
gesturing
gladdening
glimmering
glittering
glowering
gravelling
grovelling
hallowing
hammering
hampering
hankering

happening	littering	overmastering	pilfering
harassing	livening	overpowering	pillaging
harboring	lobbying	overshadowing	placarding
hardening	long-suffering	overtowering	plastering
harrowing	lowering	paltering	pleasuring
harrying	lumbering	pampering	plundering
harvesting	maddening	polishing	racketing
hastening	managing	pommelling	rallying
hazarding	manufacturing	pondering	ransoming
hearkening	marketing	pottering	rapturing
heartening	marrying	powdering	ravaging
heralding	marshalling	practising	ravening
hovering	martyring	predestining	ravishing
humoring	marvelling	prohibiting	reasoning
hungering	meandering	promising	reckoning
imagining	measuring	prospering	recovering
imprisoning	menacing	publishing	remembering
incumbering	mentioning	punishing	rendering
indenturing	meriting	purposing	rescuing
inhabiting	mirroring	quarrelling	revelling
inheriting	modelling	quarrying	rivalling
inspiriting	monkeying	quartering	riveting
issuing	mothering	quavering	roystering
jabbering	motoring	querying	rubbering
jeoparding	murdering	questioning	rubbishing
jollying	murmuring	quieting	saddening
junketing	mustering	quivering	sallying
labelling	muttering	pandering	sanctioning
laboring	narrowing	panelling	sauntering
lacquering	neighboring	pardoning	savaging
languishing	nourishing	parrying	savoring
lathering	numbering	passioning	scaffolding
lavishing	offering	patenting	scampering
lazying	omening	pattering	scattering
lecturing	opening	pedalling	scavenging
lessening	ordering	pencilling	seasoning
levelling	outbalancing	pensioning	severing
libelling	outnumbering	peppering	shadowing
limiting	outrivalling	perishing	shattering
lingering	overbalancing	perjuring	shepherding
listening	overburdening	pestering	shimmering

ōld, ôr, ŏdd, oil, fŏŏt, out; ūse, ûrn, ŭp; THis, thin

shivering
shouldering
showering
shuddering
sickening
silvering
simmering
simpering
sistering
slackening
slandering
slaughtering
slobbering
slumbering
smartening
smattering
smouldering
snivelling
sorrowing
spattering
spiralling
spiriting
spluttering
stammering
stationing
stencilling
stuttering
suffering
sugaring
summering
sundering
sweetening
tallying
tampering
tapering
tarnishing
tarrying
tasselling
tempering
thundering
tinselling

tittering
toadying
tottering
towelling
towering
trafficing
travelling
tunnelling
undervaluing
unfaltering
unflattering
unmeriting
unmurmuring
unperishing
unpitying
unpromising
unravelling
unreasoning
unremember-
   ing
unslumbering
unwandering
unwavering
upholstering
uttering
valuing
vanishing
vanquishing
vaporing
varnishing
velveting
venturing
visioning
visiting
volleying
voyaging
wakening
walloping
wandering
wantoning
wassailling

watering
wavering
weakening
wearying
weathering
westering
whimpering
whinneying
whispering
winnowing
wintering
witnessing
wondering
worrying
worshipping

ĬNGD

bewinged
dinged
eagle-winged
ringed
stringed
winged, etc.

ĬNGK

bethink
blink
bobolink
brink
chink
cinque
clink
counter-sink
drink
enlink
Finck
Fink
forethink
gink
hoodwink
Humperdinck

ink
interlink
jink
kink
link
meadow-pink
mink
pink
prink
rink
shrink
sink
skink
slink
snow-blink
stink
think
tiddlywink
tink
trink
twink
unlink
unthink
wink
zinc

ĬNGKS

jinx
lynx
methinks
minx
sphinx
tiddledywinks
tiddlywinks
clinks, etc.

ĬNGKT

blinked
distinct
extinct
indistinct

instinct
procinct
succinct
tinct
clinked, etc.

ĬNGZ
awakenings
leading-strings
besings, etc.

ĬNJ
befringe
binge
constringe
cringe
dinge
fringe
hinge
impinge
infringe
perstringe
scringe
singe
springe
swinge
tinge
twinge
unhinge

ĬNJD
unhinged
unsinged
befringed, etc.

ĬNS
convince
evince
merchant-
  prince
mince

prince
quince
rinse
since
unprince
Vince
wince
(cf. flints,
  chintz)

ĬNSK
Dvinsk
Minsk
Pinsk

ĬNT
ahint
behint
pint

ĬNT
asquint
calamint
dint
flint
footprint
glint
hint
imprint
lint
mezzotint
mint
misprint
peppermint
print
quint
reprint
septuagint
sodamint
spearmint
splint

sprint
squint
stint
tint
vint

ĬNTH
ninth
pine'th, etc.

ĬNTH
colocynth
hyacinth
labyrinth
plinth
terebinth

ĬNTS
Heintz
pints

ĬNTS
aquatints
chintz
flints, etc.
(cf. convince,
  etc.)

ĬNZ
Appenines
Tynes
dines, etc.

ĬNZ
ods-bodikins
winze
withershins
(see ĬN + s)

ĪP
antitype
archetype

autotype
bagpipe
blowpipe
daguerreotype
dead-ripe
electrotype
graphotype
gripe
gutter-snipe
heliotype
hornpipe
hype
kipe
linotype
logotype
monotype
overripe
pipe
pitchpipe
prototype
ripe
snipe
stereotype
stipe
stripe
swipe
teletype
tintype
tripe
type
unripe
windpipe
wipe

ĬP
apple-pip
atrip
battleship
chip
clip
dip

drip
equip
flip
grip
grippe
gyp
hip
horsewhip
hyp
kip
landslip
lip
nip
outstrip
overtrip
pip
pleasure-**trip**
quip
rip
scrip
ship
sip
skip
slip
snip
strip
tip
training-**ship**
tranship
trip
underlip
unrip
unship
warship
weather-strip
whip
zip
acquaintance-
    ship
administra-
    torship

agentship
aldemanship
apprentice-
    ship
archonship
babyship
bachelorship
cardinalsip
censorship
chairmanship
championship
chancellorship
chaplainship
chieftainship
churchman-
    ship
churchmem-
    bership
citizenship
collectorship
commander-
    ship
companion-
    ship
consortship
consulship
controllership
co-partner-
    ship
cousinship
craftsmanship
creatorship
deaconship
demonship
draughtsman-
    ship
eldership
electorship
emperorship
ensignship
farmership

fathership
fellowship
generalship
good-fellow-
    ship
governorship
guardianship
horsemanship
huntsmanship
impostorship
inspectorship
jockeyship
justiceship
leadership
lectureship
legislatorship
librarianship
lordship
marksmanship
marshalship
mastership
membership
Messiahship
neighborship
noviceship
ownership
paintership
partnership
pastorship
penmanship
praetorship
preachership
prelateship
probationship
professorship
proprietorship
questorship
rajahship
rangership
readership
recordership

rectorship
regentship
relationship
scholarship
seamanship
secretaryship
senatorship
sextonship
sheriffship
sizarship
speakership
spectatorship
sponsorship
sportsmanship
statesmanship
stewardship
studentship
sultanship
suretyship
survivorship
swordsman-
    ship
treasurership
umpireship
viceroyship
virtuosoship
wardenship
workmanship
wranglership

ĪPS

pipes, etc.

ĬPS

Apocalypse
chips
eclipse
ellipse
Phipps
apple-pips

āle,   câre,   ădd,   ärm,   åsk;   mē,   hĕre,   ĕnd;   īce,   ĭll;

acquaintance-
  ships, etc.

ĬPST

chip'st
clip'st
dip'st
eclipsed
equip'st
grip'st
rip'st
ship'st
sip'st .
skip'st
slip'st
strip'st
tip'st
trip'st
uneclipsed
whip'st

ĬPT

hunger-griped
prison-striped
griped, etc.

ĬPT

apocalypt
crypt
frost-nipped
hipped
manuscript
script
subscript
superscript
tipt
chipped, etc.

ĪR

acquire
admire

afire
aspire
attire
beacon-fire
bemire
byre
choir
conspire
death-fire
desire
dire
enquire
entire
esquire
expire
fire
flat tire
galley-fire
grandsire
gyre
hell-fire
hire
inquire
inspire
ire
lyre
McIntyre
Meyer
mire
Molly Maguire
perspire
pyre
quire
require
respire
retire
shire
signal-fire
sire
spitfire
squire

spire
suspire
swire
tire
transpire
Tyre
unsquire
Untermyer
vire
wildfire
wire
(cf. crier, high-
  er, prior, fri-
  ar, etc.)

ĪRD

overtired
spired
unacquired
undesired
unexpired
uninspired
acquired, etc.

ĬS

advice
bespice
bice
concise
device
dice
entice
gneiss
grice
ice
lice
mice
nice
overnice
Paradise
precise

price
rice
sacrifice
self-sacrifice
sice
slice
spice
splice
suffice
syce
thrice
trice
twice
vice
vise
Weiss
Zeiss

ĬS

abiogenesis
abyss
acropolis
ambergris
amiss
anabasis
analysis
antithesis
apheresis
aphesis
armistice
artifice
avarice
Beatrice
benefice
biogenesis
bis
bliss
chrysalis
cicatrice
clematis
cockatrice

---

cowardice
cuisse
dehisce
dentifrice
diæresis
dialysis
diathesis
Dis
dismiss
edifice
ectogenesis
elephantiasis
emphasis
fortalice
genesis
hiss
hypostasis
hypothesis
kiss
liquorice
Liss
metabasis
metamorphosis
metastasis
metathesis
metropolis
miss
M'liss
necropolis
nemesis
orifice
paralysis
parenthesis
periphrasis
precipice
prejudice
remiss
Salamis
sis
siss
sui generis

Swiss
synthesis
this
verdigris
vis
wis
y-wis

ĬSH

cnish
dish
fish
gibberish
impoverish
McNish
pilot-fish
pish
slish
squish
swish
Tish
unwish
wish
babyish
bitterish
cleverish
Cockneyish
devilish
dowdyish
feverish
heathenish
kittenish
lickerish
mammonish
ogreish
quakerish
tigerish
vaporish
viperish
vixenish
vulturish

waterish
willowish
womanish
yellowish, etc.

ĬSK

asterisk
basilisk
bisque
brisk
disc
disk
fisc
Fiske
frisk
obelisk
odalisque
risk
tamarisk
whisk

ĬSP

crisp
encrisp
lisp
whisp
wisp

ĬST

antichrist
Christ
emparadised
enticed
tryst
bespiced, etc.

ĬST

agist
amethyst
assist
atwist

bekissed
bemist
beneficed
cist
coexist
consist
cyst
desist
dismissed
enlist
entwist
exist
fist
frist
gist
glist
grist
hissed
hist
insist
intertwist
kissed
list
missed
mist
persist
pre-exist
prejudiced
resist
schist
sissed
sist
subsist
trist
tryst
twist
unkissed
unmissed
untwist
unwist
whist

āle,   câre,   ădd,   ärm,   åsk;   mē,   hẹre,   ĕnd;   īce,   ĭll;

wist
wrist
xyst
abolitionist
absolutist
academist
accompanist
aerologist
agamist
agonist
agricolist
agriculturalist
agriculturist
alchemist
allegorist
allopathist
amorist
anagrammatist
analogist
analyst
anarchist
anatomist
animalculist
animist
annalist
annualist
antagonist
anthropologist
antinomist
antipathist
apathist
aphorist
apiarist
apologist
Arabist
arboriculturist
arborist
archaeologist
artillerist
atheist
atomist

augurist
balladist
biblicist
bibliophilist
bibliopolist
bicyclist
bigamist
bimetallist
biologist
Bolshevist
botanist
Bourbonist
Brahmanist
cabalist
Calvinist
campanologist
canonist
capitalist
casuist
catechist
centralist
chirographist
chiropodist
choralist
chronologist
circumlocu-
    tionist
classicalist
classicist
coalitionist
colloquist
colonist
colorist
communist
conchologist
Confucionist
congregation-
    alist
constitutional-
    ist
constitutionist

constructionist
contortionist
controversialist
conversationist
corruptionist
cremationist
culturist
dactylist
Darwinist
degenerationist
demonist
demonologist
despotist
destinist
destructionist
deuterogamist
devotionalist
devotionist
dialist
dialogist
diplomatist
dogmatist
dramatist
dualist
duellist
ecclesiologist
economist
educationalist
educationist
egoist
egotist
electro-
    biologist
elegist
elocutionist
empiricist
enamelist
enigmatist
entomologist
epigrammatist
epitomist

equilibrist
essayist
eternalist
ethicist
etymologist
Eucharist
eudemonist
eulogist
euphuist
evangelist
evolutionist
excursionist
exorcist
experimental-
    ist
externalist
fabulist
fatalist
federalist
feudalist
fictionist
financialist
floriculturist
formalist
fossilist
fossilogist
funambulist
futilist
galvanist
genealogist
geologist
glacialist
gymnosophist
harmonist
Hebraist
hedonist
Hellenist
herbalist
horticulturist
humanist
humorist

---

hyperbolist
hypnotist
idealist
illusionist
imitationist
immaterialist
immersionist
immortalist
imperialist
inspirationist
instrumentalist
insurrectionist
intellectualist
internationalist
journalist
Judaist
Latinist
legitimist
liberalist
literalist
lithologist
lobbyist
loyalist
magnetist
malthusianist
mammonist
mannerist
martyrologist
materialist
mechanist
medallist
melodist
melodramatist
memorialist
Menshevist
mesmerist
metalist
meteorologist
methodist
mineralogist
ministerialist

misanthropist
miscellanist
misogamist
misogynist
modernist
monogamist
monopolist
moralist
motorist
mythologist
Napoleonist
nationalist
naturalist
necrologist
neologist
Neoplatonist
nepotist
nihilist
nominalist
novelist
obstructionist
oculist
ontologist
opinionist
oppositionist
optimist
organist
Orientalist
ornithologist
pacifist
passionist
pathologist
penologist
perfectionist
pessimist
petrologist
pharmacist
pharmacologist
phenomenist
philanthropist
Philhellenist

philologist
philosophist
phlebotomist
photographist
phrenologist
philatelist
physicist
physiognomist
physiologist
pianist
pietist
plagiarist
platonist
pleasurist
pluralist
pneumatologist
polygamist
positivist
posturist
pragmatist
precisianist
prelatist
progressionist
prohibitionist
protagonist
protectionist
proverbialist
provincialist
psalmodist
psychologist
publicist
pugilist
pythonist
quietist
rabbinist
rapturist
rationalist
realist
religionist
repudiationist
resurrectionist

revivalist
revolutionist
rhapodist
rigorist
ritualist
Romanist
romanticist
royalist
ruralist
satanist
satirist
schematist
scientist
sciolist
scripturalist
scripturist
secessionist
secularist
seismologist
sensationalist
sensualist
sentimentalist
sexualist
sibyllist
socialist
sociologist
soloist
somnambulist
Sorbonist
specialist
spiritualist
steganograph-
ist
stenographist
strategist
subjectivist
suffragist
symbolist
sympathist
syncopist
syncretist

synodist
synonymist
synthesist
tautologist
technicist
technologist
telegraphist
teleologist
telephonist
terrorist
textualist
theologist
theophilan-
  thropist
theorist
theosophist
threnodist
tobacconist
topographist
toxicologist
trades-unionist
traditionalist
traditionist
transcenden-
  talist
unionist
universalist
vaccinist
vacuist
vaticanist
ventriloquist
verbalist
violist
visionist
vitalist
vocabulist
vocalist
volumist
votarist
zealotist
zoologist

zoophilist
zootomist

ĪT

Aaronite
acolyte
aconite
actinolite
Adamite
Adullamite
aerolite
affright
alight
aluminite
Ammonite
anchorite
anight
anthracite
appetite
aright
Baalite
Babylonite
bedight
bedlamite
behight
beknight
belemnite
benight
Bethlehemite
bight
bipartite
bite
blatherskite
blight
bright
Canaanite
Carmelite
chrysolite
cite
contrite
copyright

cosmopolite
crystallite
daylight
dead-light
delight
despite
dight
disunite
dolomite
downright
dynamite
Ebionite
ebonite
Elamite
electrolyte
entomolite
enwrite
eremite
erudite
excite
expedite
Fahrenheit
fight
Fite
flight
foresight
forthright
fright
good-night
Gothamite
grapholite
harbor-light
headlight
height
heteroclite
hight
ichnolite
ignite
impolite
incite
indict

indite
invite
Ishmaelite
Islamite
Israelite
Jacobite
kite
knight
light
malachite
mammonite
Maronite
McKnight
meteorite
midnight
midshipmite
might
mite
Moabite
moonlight
Mormonite
Muscovite
Nazarite
neophyte
night
outright
overdight
overnight
oversight
parasite
plebiscite
plight
polite
pre-Adamite
pre-Raphaelite
proselyte
Puseyite
quite
recite
recondite
requite

reunite
right
rite
satellite
sea-fight
sea-light
second-sight
siderolite
sight
signal-light
site
sleight
slight
smite
snow-white
spite
sprite
starlight
sunlight
sybarite
theodolite
tight
to-night
toxophilite
tripartite
trite
troglodyte
troth-plight
twilight
underwrite
undight
unite
unright
unsight
unwrite
upright
vulcanite
water-sprite
water-tight
white
wight

wright
write
yesternight
zoolite
zoophyte

ĬT

acquit
admit
after-wit
apposite
befit
beknit
benefit
bit
bitt
chit
cit
commit
counterfeit
definite
demit
DeWitt
emit
exquisite
favorite
fit
flit
frit
grit
hit
hypocrite
immit
indefinite
infinite
inknit
interknit
intermit
intromit
it
Jesuit

kit
knit
lit
manumit
McNitt
misfit
mitt
moon-lit
mother-wit
nit
omit
opposite
outfit
outsit
outwit
permit
perquisite
pit
Pitt
plebiscite
pretermit
preterite
prerequisite
quit
recommit
refit
remit
requisite
rifle-pit
Schmidt
sit
slit
smit
spit
split
sprit
submit
tit
tom-tit
to-wit
transmit

twit
unbit
unfit
unknit
unwit
whit
wit
Witt
writ

ĪTH

blithe
lithe
scythe
Smythe
tithe
withe
writhe

Ĭth

myth
stythe

ĬTH

forthwith
herewith
therewith
wherewith
with
withe

Ĭth

acrolith
aerolith
Arrowsmith
frith
kith
Ladysmith
lith
monolith
myth

---

palaeolith
pith
sith
smith
withe
forthwith
herewith
therewith
wherewith
with

ĪTS

anights
footlights
tights
acolytes, etc.

ĬTS

Fritz
quits
Schlitz
acquits, etc.

ĪV

alive
arrive
chive
Clive
connive
contrive
deprive
derive
dive
drive
five
gyve
hive
I've
live
power dive
revive

rive
shive
shrive
skive
stive
strive
survive
thrive
unhive
wive

ĬV

forgive
fugitive
give
live
misgive
narrative
negative
outlive
overlive
positive
relative
sieve
ablative
accusative
acquisitive
admonitive
affirmative
alternative
amative
argumentative
causative
coercitive
combative
comparative
compellative
compensative
competitive
complimenta-
tive

compulsative
confirmative
consecutive
conservative
contemplative
contributive
correlative
curative
declarative
definitive
demonstrative
derivative
derogative
desiccative
diminutive
dispensative
disputative
distributive
evocative
exclamative
executive
expletive
figurative
formative
fugitive
genitive
illustrative
impeditive
imperative
imputative
incarnative
inchoative
incrassative
indicative
infinitive
informative
inquisitive
insensitive
intensative
interrogative
intuitive

laudative
lenitive
lucrative
nominative
nutritive
premonitive
preparative
prerogative
preservative
primitive
prohibitive
provocative
pulsative
punitive
putative
quantitive
recitative
reformative
reparative
representative
restorative
retributive
sanative
sedative
semblative
sensitive
siccative
substantive
superlative
talkative
tentative
transitive
vibrative
vocative

ĪVD

long-lived
short-lived
unshrived
unwived
arrived, etc.

ĬVD

long-lived
negatived
outlived
short-lived
unlived

ĪVZ

fives
knives
lives
arrives, etc.

ĪZ

acclimatize
achromatize
actualize
adonize
advertise
advise
Africanize
after-wise
agatize
aggrandize
agonize
agrarianize
albumenize
alchemize
alcoholize
alkalize
allegorize
alphabetize
amalgamize
ambrosialize
Americanize
analyze
anathematize
anatomize
angelize
Anglicize
animalize

annalize
antagonize
anywise
aphorize
apologize
apostatize
apostrophize
apotheosize
appetize
apprise
arise
aromatize
artificialize
assize
astrologize
astronomize
atheize
atomize
atticize
attitudinize
augurize
authorize
balladize
baptize
barbarize
battologize
botanize
bowdlerize
brutalize
canonize
capitalize
capsize
catechize
cauterize
centralize
characterize
chastise
chimerize
Christianize
circularize
civilize

climatize
cognize
colonize
comprize
compromise
constitution-
  alize
contrariwise
conventionalize
corner-wise
crescent-wise
criticise
crystallize
dandyize
dastardize
decimalize
decolorize
dehumanize
demagnetize
demise
democratize
demonetize
demoralize
denarcotize
denaturalize
deodorize
deputize
despise
detonize
devilize
devise
devitalize
diabolize
dialogize
dialyze
disguise
disillusionize
disorganize
dogmatize
doxologize
dramatize

ebonize
economize
ecstasize
Edenize
effeminize
electrolyze
emblematicize
emblematize
emblemize
emphasize
emprize
energize
enigmatize
enterprise
epigrammatize
epitomize
equalize
eternalize
etherealize
etherize
etymologize
eulogize
euphemize
euphonize
euphuize
Europeanize
evangelize
excise
excursionize
exercise
exorcise
experimental-
  ize
extemporize
fabulize
familiarize
fanaticize
federalize
fertilize
feudalize
fluidize

āle, câre, ădd, ärm, ăsk; mē, hĕre, ĕnd; īce, ĭll;

focalize
formalize
formulize
fossilize
fraternize
galvanize
gelatinize
genealogize
generalize
gentilize
geologize
geometrize
gluttonize
gorgonize
gormandize
gospelize
guise
gutteralize
harmonize
heathenize
Hebraicize
Hebraize
Hellenize
Hibernicize
histrionize
humanize
hyperbolize
hypnotize
hypothesize
idealize
idiotize
idolatrize
idolize
immortalize
impatronize
imperialize
improvise
incise
individualize
internationalize
Italianize

italicize
jeopardize
journalize
Judaize
Latinize
legalize
legitimatize
lethargize
liberalize
likewise
lionize
liquidize
literalize
Lize
localize
Londonize
macadamize
magnetize
Mahomedanize
mammonize
manumize
martialize
martyrize
materialize
matronize
mechanize
mediatize
memorialize
memorize
mercerize
merchandise
mesmerize
methodize
mineralize
minimize
misanthropize
misprize
mobilize
modelize
modernize

Mohammedan-
  ize
monetize
monopolize
moonrise
moralize
mythologize
narcotize
nasalize
nationalize
naturalize
neutralize
novelize
organize
ostracize
otherguise
otherwise
overwise
oxidize
oxygenize
paganize
panegyrize
parallelize
paralyze
particularize
patronize
pauperize
pavonize
peculiarize
pedestrianize
penalize
penny-wise
personalize
personize
pessimize
philologize
philosophize
physiognomize
pilgrimize
plagiarize
platitudinize

Platonize
plebeianize
pluralize
poetize
polarize
pollenize
polygamize
popularize
prelatize
remise
revise
prize
proselytize
Protestantize
proverbialize
provincialize
psalmodize
pulverize
Puritanize
rapturize
rationalize
realize
recognize
rejuvenize
remise
remonetise
reprise
republicanize
resurrectionize
revise
revolutionize
rhapsodize
rhetorize
rise
Romanize
royalize
ruralize
saccharize
sacrifice
satirize
scandalize

___

öld, ôr, ŏdd, oil, fŏŏt, out; ūse, ûrn, ŭp; THis, thin

scepticize
schismatize
Scotticize
scrupulize
scrutinize
sectarianize
secularize
seigniorize
seniorize
sensualize
sentimentalize
sepulchralize
sermonize
sexualize
sice
signalize
silverize
singularize
size
soberize
socialize
Socinianize
solarize
solemnize
soliloquize
sonnetize
specialize
spiritualize
sterilize
stigmatize
subsidize
subtilize
summarize
sunrise
supervise
surmise
surprise
syllogize
symbolize
sympathize
symphonize

synchronize
syncopize
synonymize
synthesize
synthetize
systematize
systemize
tabularize
tantalize
tautologize
temporize
terrorize
Teutonize
theologize
theorize
theosophize
timonize
totalize
tranquillize
tyrannize
underprize
universalize
unwise
uprise
utilize
vagabondize
vaporize
ventriloquize
verbalize
victimize
villianize
visualize
vitalize
vocalize
volatilize
vulcanize
vulgarize
wantonize
weather-wise
wise
(see Ī + s)

ĬZ

Ariz.
befriz
biz
Cadiz
fizz
friz
his
is
Liz
phiz
quiz
riz
sizz
'tis
viz
whiz

ĪZD

ill-advised
unadvised
unapprised
unauthorized
unbaptized
uncanonized
uncivilized
undersized
undespised
undisguised
unprized
unsurmised
acclimatized,
etc.

ĬZM

abolitionism
absolutism
abysm
academism
accidentalism
achromatism

actinism
aestheticism
Africanism
agnosticism
agonism
agrarianism
agriculturism
alcoholism
alienism
altruism
Americanism
anachronism
anarchism
anathematism
anatomism
aneurism
Anglicanism
Anglicism
Anglo-
Saxonism
animalism
animism
anomalism
antagonism
antiquarianism
anti-Semitism
aphorism
archaism
asceticism
Asiaticism
asteism
asterism
astigmatism
atavism
atheism
atomism
Baalism
babyism
bacchanalian-
ism
bachelorism

---

barbarism
behaviorism
biblicism
bibliophilism
bibliopolism
bi-metallism
bloomerism
bluestocking-
  ism
bogeyism
Bohemianism
Bolshevism
boobyism
Bourbonism
braggardism
Brahmanism
brutalism
Buchmanism
cabalism
Calvinism
cataclysm
catechism
Catholicism
centralism
characterism
Chauvinism
chloralism
chrism
classicalism
classicism
clericalism
Cockneyism
colloquialism
colonialism
communalism
communism
Confucianism
congregational-
  ism
conservatism

constitutional-
  ism
cosmopolitan-
  ism
cretinism
criticism
cynicism
dandyism
Darwinism
demoniacism
demonianism
demonism
denomina-
  tionalism
despotism
determinism
devilism
diabolism
dialogism
diamagnetism
diplomatism
dogmatism
dualism
ecclesiasticism
eclecticism
egoism
egotism
electicism
embolism
emotionalism
empiricism
epicureanism
equestrianism
Erastianism
esotericism
etherealism
etherism
eudemonism
euphemism
euphonism
euphuism

evangelism
exorcism
exoticism
exquisitism
fairyism
fanaticism
fantasticism
fatalism
federalism
Fenianism
fetishism
feudalism
flunkeyism
fogeyism
foreignism
formalism
fossilism
Fourierism
frivolism
Gallicism
galvanism
gentilism
Germanism
Ghandiism
heathenism
Hebraism
hedonism
Hellenism
heroism
Hibernianism
Hibernicism
Hinduism
histrionicism
histrionism
Hitlerism
humanism
hyperbolism
hypercriticism
hypnotism
hypochondriac-
  ism

Ibsenism
idealism
ism
idiotism
immaterialism
imperialism
individualism
industrialism
intellectualism
international-
  ism
Irishism
Islamism
Italianism
Italicism
Jesuitism
jockeyism
journalism
Judaism
laconicism
laconism
ladyism
Latinism
latitudinarian-
  ism
legitimism
Leninism
liberalism
libertinism
literalism
localism
Lollardism
Londonism
loyalism
lyricism
magnetism
Mahometan-
  ism
mammonism
mannerism
materialism

mechanism
mediaevalism
Menshevism
mesmerism
metacism
methodism
modernism
Mohammedan-
   ism
monarchism
monasticism
monkeyism
Montanism
moralism
Mormonism
mysticism
nativism
naturalism
necessarianism
neologism
Neoplatonism
nepotism
nihilism
nominalism
occultism
ogreism
optimism
organism
orientalism
ostracism
pacifism
paganism
pantheism
parallelism
paroxysm
patricianism
patriotism
pauperism
peanism
pedantism
pedestrianism

peonism
peripateticism
personalism
pessimism
phalansterism
phenomenalism
phenomenism
philanthropic-
   ism
Philhellenism
Philistinism
philosophism
physicism
pietism
plagiarism
Platonism
plebeianism
pluralism
positivism
pragmatism
precisianism
predestinarian-
   ism
prelatism
pre-Raphaelism
Presbyterian-
   ism
prism
proletarianism
protectionism
Protestantism
proverbialism
provincialism
pugilism
puppyism
Puritanism
Puseyism
pythonism
Quakerism
quietism
Quixotism

rabbinism
radicalism
realism
religionism
Republicanism
rationalism
revivalism
rheumatism
rigorism
ritualism
Romanism
romanticism
royalism
ruffianism
ruralism
sabbatarianism
sacerdotalism
satanism
savagism
Saxonism
scepticism
schism
scholasticism
sciolism
Scotticism
scoundrelism
scripturalism
secessionism
sectarianism
secularism
Semitism
sensationalism
sensualism
sentimentalism
shamanism
Shavianism
Shintoism
socialism
Socinianism
solecism

somnambulism
somnolism
sovietism
Stalinism
stoicism
subjectivism
subtilism
supernatural-
   ism
syllogism
symbolism
synchronism
syncretism
Syrianism
terrorism
Teutonicism
theosophism
tigerism
Toryism
totemism
trades-union-
   ism
traditionalism
transcendental-
   ism
tribalism
unionism
Unitarianism
universalism
utilitarianism
Utopianism
valetudinarian-
   ism
vampirism
vandalism
Vaticanism
vegetarianism
ventriloquism
verbalism
vitalism

vocalism   vulpinism   Wesleyanism   Yankeeism
vulgarism   vulturism   witticism   zanyism

O

These words include the following accented vowel sounds:

Ō   as in old; heard also in note, oh, roam, foe, shoulder, grow,
     owe, sew, yeoman, beau, hautboy, brooch.

Ô   as in or; heard also in all, talk, swarm, haul, caught, law,
     fought, broad, memoir.

Ŏ   as in odd; heard also in want, wash, shone.

OI   as in oil; heard also in boy.

OO   as in foot; heard also in full, wolf, could.

OU   as in out; heard also in cow, sauerkraut.

For the vowel sound heard in *do,* see under Ū.

For the vowel sound heard in *one, flood,* see under Ŭ

Ō			
adagio	bravissimo	domino	furbelow
aglow	buffalo	dough	gazabo
ago	bummalo	duodecimo	generalissimo
alow	bungalow	eau	gigolo
although	bureau	*embow*	glow
apropos	cachalot	embroglio	go
archipelago	calico	embryo	grow
arow	cameo	entrepot	half-a-mo
banjo	chapeau	escrow	haricot
bateau	chateau	Eskimo	heigh-ho
beau	Co.	ex-officio	ho
below	comme il faut	Flo	hoe
besnow	crow	floe	how-so
bestow	curaçoa	flow	hullo
blow	death-blow	foe	ice-flow
bo	death-throe	folio	imbroglio
bon-mot	depot	forego	impresario
Bordeaux	de trop	foreknow	incognito
bow	Diderot	foreshow	indigo
braggadocio	do	fortissimo	inflow
	doe	fro	in statu quo

ōld,   ôr,   ŏdd,   oil,   fŏŏt,   out;   ūse,   ûrn,   ŭp;   THis,   thin

intaglio
jabot
Jo
Joe
know
little-go
lo
long-ago
long-bow
Lothario
low
Lowe
magnifico
malapropos
manito
Mexico
mistletoe
morceau
mot
mow
mustachio
no
nuncio
O
oboe
oh
olio
oratorio
outflow
outgo
outgrow
overcrow
overflow
overgrow
overthrow
owe
Papilio
pianissimo
pistachio
plateau
Po

Poe
portfolio
portico
portmanteau
pro
proximo
punctilio
quid-pro-quo
rainbow
raree-show
ratio
roe
rondeau
rouleau
Rousseau
row
Rowe
sabot
saddle-bow
seraglio
sew
shew
show
sloe
slow
snow
so
so-and-so
soho
sow
stow
strow
studio
tableau
tally ho
though
throe
throw
timber-toe
tiptoe
to-and-fro

toe
Tokio
touch-and-go
tow
tremolo
trousseau
trow
ultimo
undergo
under-tow
unknow
upgrow
upthrow
vertigo
Westward ho
woe

Ô

Arkansas
awe
begnaw
braw
brother-in-law
caw
chaw
claw
craw
daughter-in-
   law
dauw
daw
dawe
draw
father-in-law
faugh
flaw
foresaw
gnaw
guffaw
haw
heehaw

jackdaw
jaw
landau
law
macaw
maw
McGraw
mother-in-**law**
overawe
overdraw
oversaw
papaw
paw
pilau
pshaw
raw
saw
scaw
see-saw
Shaw
sister-in-**law**
slaw
son-in-law
spa
squaw
straw
tau
taw
thaw
thraw
underjaw
undraw
unlaw
usquebaugh
withdraw
yaw

ŌB
conglobe
disrobe
enrobe

āle, câre, ădd, ärm, åsk; mē, hẹre, ĕnd; īce, ĭll:

globe	**ŎBZ**	notch	rode
Job	Dobbs	outwatch	spode
lobe	Hobbes	Scotch	strode
Loeb	Hobbs	splotch	toad
probe	ods-bobs	swatch	unbestowed
robe	scobs	watch	unload
unrobe	blobs, etc.		unowed
		ŌCHD	woad
ÔB	**ŌCH**	unapproached	(see Ō + ed)
bedaub	abroach	unbroached	
daub	approach	approached,	**ÔD**
nawab	broach	etc.	abroad
	brooch		applaud
ŎB	coach	**ŌD**	bawd
athrob	cockroach	abode	belaud
blob	croche	a la mode	broad
bob	encoach	antipode	Claude
cabob	encroach	*arrode*	defraud
cob	loach	bestrode	fraud
Cobb	poach	bode	gaud
corncob	reproach	bridle-road	lantern-jawed
fob	roach	Clode	laud
gob	self-reproach	code	maraud
hob	slowcoach	commode	maud
hob-and-nob		corrode	overawed
hobnob	**ÔCH**	discommode	unawed
job	debauch	episode	whopper-jawed
knob	nautch	erode	awed, etc.
lob		explode	
mob	**ŎCH**	forebode	**ŎD**
nob	anchor-watch	goad	Aaron's-rod
quab	blotch	incommode	*begod*
rob	botch	load	clod
slob	crotch	lode	cod
snob	death-watch	lycopode	Codd
sob	gotch	mode	demi-god
squab	harbour-watch	node	divining-rod
stob	hotch	ode	Dodd
swab	hopscotch	overload	dry-shod
thingumbob	hotch-potch	pigeon-toed	Eisteddfod
throb	larboard-watch	road	God

golden-rod
hod
lycopod
nod
od
odd
piston-rod
platypod
plod
pod
prod
quad
quod
river-god
rod
rough-shod
sea-god
shod
slipshod
sod
squad
tod
trod
ungod
unshod
untrod
wad

ŌDZ
Rhoades
Rhodes
(see ŌD + s)

ŎDZ
emerods
odds
clods, etc.

ŌF
goaf
loaf

oaf
quartern-loaf

ŎF
cloff
cough
doff
golf
koff
long-field-off
off
pairing-off
philosophe
prof
scoff
shroff
sign off
soph
toff
toph
trough

ŎFT
aloft
croft
loft
oft
soft
toft
undercroft
doffed, etc.

ŌG
apologue
astrologue
brogue
collogue
embogue
Hogue
pirogue
prorogue

rogue
togue
trogue
vogue

ŎG
agog
analogue
apologue
befog
bog
bulldog
catalogue
clog
cog
Dannebrog
decalogue
demagogue
dialogue
dog
egg-nog
embog
epilogue
flog
fog
frog
Gog
grog
hedgehog
Herzog
hog
hot dog
incog
jog
log
monologue
mystagogue
nog
Patchogue
pedagogue
pettifog

philologue
Pokogue
polliwog
prairie-dog
prog
Quogue
scrog
shog
slog
synagogue
theologue
travelog
unclog

ŎGD
frogged
water-logged
befogged, etc.

ŎGZ
togs
befogs, etc.

OI
ahoy
alloy
annoy
boy
buoy
charity-boy
cloy
convoy
corduroy
coy
decoy
deploy
destroy
employ
enjoy
foy
goy

āle,   câre,   ădd,   ärm,   åsk;   mē,   hẹre,   ĕnd;   īce,   ĭll;

hobbledehoy
hoy
Illinois
joy
loblolly-boy
Loy
overjoy
paduasoy
Pomeroy
saveloy
Savoy
sepoy
soy
teapoy
toy
troy
viceroy
yellow-boy

OID

actinoid
albuminoid
alkaloid
aneroid
anthropoid
asteroid
avoid
"boid"
celluloid
coralloid
crystalloid
deltoid
dendroid
devoid
helicoid
hyaloid
metalloid
mongoloid
negroid
overjoyed
ovoid

pachyderma-
  toid
paraboloid
petaloid
pyramidoid
tabloid
trapezoid
unalloyed
unbuoyed
unemployed
varioloid
void
alloyed, etc.

OIDZ

Lloyd's
avoids, etc.

OIF

coif

OIL

aboil
assoil
boil
Boyle
broil
coil
counterfoil
Coyle
despoil
disembroil
Doyle
embroil
entoil
estoile
foil
langue d'oil
moil
noil
oil

overtoil
parboil
quatrefoil
recoil
roil
soil
spoil
toil
turmoil
uncoil
upcoil

OILD

hard boiled
unsoiled
unspoiled
boiled, etc.

OILT

spoilt

OILZ

noils
boils, etc.

OIN

adjoin
almoign
Boyne
coign
coin
conjoin
Des Moines
disjoin
eloign
enjoin
foin
frankalmoigne
groin
interjoin
join

loin
purloin
quoin
rejoin
sejoin
sirloin
subjoin
tenderloin

OIND

dead poind
poind
uncoined
adjoined, etc.

OINT

adjoint
anoint
appoint
aroint
conjoint
counterpoint
coverpoint
disappoint
disjoint
dowel-joint
dry-point
joint
point
reappoint
repoint

OIS

Boyce
choice
invoice
Joyce
outvoice
rejoice
voice

OIŜT
foist
hoist
joist
loud-voiced
moist
shrill-voiced
unrejoiced
unvoiced
voiced, etc.

OIT
adroit
dacoit
Detroit
doit
droit
exploit
maladroit
quoit
Voight

OIZ
avoirdupois
counterpoise
equipoise
erminois
froise
noise
Noyes
poise
(see OI + s)

ŌJ
doge
gamboge
horologe

ŎJ
dislodge
dodge

hodge
hodge-podge
horologe
lodge
splodge
stodge
unlodge

ŌK
artichoke
asoak
awoke
baroque
besmoke
bespoke
bloke
broke
choke
cloak
coak
coke
convoke
counterstroke
croak
death-stroke
equivoque
evoke
folk
forespoke
forspoke
gentlefolk
invoke
joke
Larocque
loke
master-stroke
moke
oak
outbroke
poke
provoke

revoke
scrub-oak
sloke
smoke
soak
spoke
stoke
stroke
thunder-stroke
toke
toque
unbroke
uncloak
understroke
unyoke
up-broke
woke
yoke
yolk

ÔK
auk
awk
balk
cakewalk
calk
chalk
dawk
Falk
gawk
hawk
mawk
Mohawk
outwalk
pawk
sidewalk
sparrow-hawk
squawk
stalk
talk

tomahawk
walk

ŎK
acock
alpenstock
amok
Antioch
Bach
Bankok
baroque
bedrock
belock
bemock
billycock
Bloch
block
bock
brock
chock
chockablock
clock
cock
crock
dead-lock
dock
fetlock
firelock
flintlock
flock
forelock
frock
half-cock
havelock
hoc
hock
hollyhock
interlock
jock
knock
lady's-smock

---

langue d'oc	**ŌKS**	**ŎKT**	feme-sole
laughing-	coax	concoct	foal
stock	hoax	decoct	foliole
Little Rock	Nokes	recoct	fumarole
loch	Oakes	unfrocked	furole
lock	Stokes	blocked, etc.	fusarole
love-lock	Vokes		girandole
Medoc	artichokes,	**ŌL**	girasole
mock	etc.	augur-hole	gloriole
Mohock		aureole	gloryhole
padlock	**ŎKS**	banderole	goal
Painted Rock	ballot-box	barcarolle	heart-whole
peacock	bandbox	bibliopole	hole
penstock	box	blowhole	inscroll
percussion-	chickenpox	bole	jowl
lock	Christmas-	boll	knoll
plock	box	borecole	kohl
pock	Cox	bowi	log-roll
poppycock	equinox	bunghole	loophole
Ragnarock	fox	buttonhole	Maypole
roc	hatbox	cajole	mole
rock	heterodox	camisole	oriole
shock	mailbox	capriole	parole
shuttle-cock	orthodox	caracole	patrol
smock	ox	carambole	peephole
soc	paddlebox	cariole	petiole
sock	paradox	carmagnole	pigeon-hole
spatch-cock	phlox	casserole	pinhole
stock	pillar-box	coal	pinole
stumbling-	powder-box	cole	pistole
block	signal-box	comptrol	pole
turkey-cock	smallpox	condol:	poll
turncock	vox	console	porthole
understock	alpenstocks,	control	rantipole
undock	etc.	curtainpole	rigmarole
unfrock		dhole	role
unlock	**ŌKT**	dole	roll
weathercock	unprovoked	droll	scroll
weepingrock	water-soaked	enbowl	scupper-hole
woodcock	evoked, etc.	enroll	segol
		extoll	self-control

Seminole	caterwaul	spall	**ŌLD**
shoal	caul	spawl	acold
shole	crawl	sprawl	afterhold
sole	disenthrall	spurgall	ahold
soul	drawl	squall	anchor-hold
stole	dwal	stall	behold
stroll	enthrall	tall	blindfold
tadpole	evenfall	therewithal	bold
thole	fall	thrall	bullet-mould
toll	fireball	trawl	clay-cold
tophole	football	trumpet-call	coaled
troll	footfall	wall	cold
unroll	forestall	waterfall	copyhold
unsoul	gall	wherewithal	enfold
unwhole	Gaul	windfall	fold
uproll	hall	withal	foothold
vacuole	haul	yawl	foretold
variole	install		fourfold
virole	judgment-hall	**ŌL**	freehold
vole	kraal	alcohol	gold
wassail-bowl	landfall	atoll	half-soled
whole	mall	baby doll	high-souled
	maul	capitol	hold
ŌL	McCall	consol	household
all	miscall	doll	ice-cold
all-in-all	nightfall	entresol	infold
appal	overfall	extol	interfold
awl	overhaul	folderol	leaf-mold
ball	pall	girasol	leasehold
banquet-hall	Paul	gun moll	Leopold
baseball	pawl	loll	manifold
basketball	pitfall	moll	marigold
bawl	rainfall	parasol	mold
befall	recall	poll	multifold
bemawl	Saul	protocol	old
Bengal	scall	Sol	overbold
bethrall	scrawl	vitriol	refold
blackball	sea-wall		retold
boxstall	shawl	**ŌLCH**	sable-stoled
brawl	small	Balch	scold
call	snowball	Walch	sold

---

spun-gold
stone-cold
stronghold
thousandfold
told
twice-told
twofold, etc.
uncontrolled
unfold
unsold
untold
uphold
withhold
wold
cajoled, etc.

ŌLD
Archibald
auld
blackballed
bald
scald
so called
unappalled
uncalled
unenthralled
ungalled
unrecalled
appalled, etc.

ŌLN
swoln

ÔLSH
Walsh

ŌLT
bolt
colt
demi-volt
dolt

holt
jolt
lavolt
molt
poult
revolt
shackle-bolt
smolt
thunderbolt
unbolt
volt

ÔLT
assault
basalt
cobalt
default
envault
exalt
fault
gault
halt
malt
salt
seasalt
smalt
somersault
spalt
vault

ÔLTS
false
salts
valse
waltz
assaults, etc.

ŎLV
absolve
circumvolve
convolve

devolve
dissolve
evolve
exolve
intervolve
involve
resolve
revolve
solve

ŎLVD
undissolved
unresolved
unsolved
absolved, etc.

ŌM
aerodrome
afoam
befoam
brome
catacomb
chrome
chromosome
clomb
comb
currycomb
dome
endome
foam
Frome
gastronome
gloam
gnome
harvest-home
heliochrome
hippodrome
holm
home
honey-comb

Jerome
loam
metallochrome
metronome
microsome
monochrome
nobody home
no'm
Nome
ohm
palindrome
polychrome
pome
roam
Rome
Salome
sea-foam
sea-holm
sloam
tome

ÔM
haum
imaum
maum
shawm

ŎM
aplomb
axiom
bomb
dom
from
hecatomb
om
pogrom
pompom
rhomb
swom
therefrom

ōld, ôr, ŏdd, oil, fŏŏt, out; ūse, ûrn, ŭp; THis, thin

ŎMP

comp
pomp
romp
swamp
trompe

ŎMPT

impromptī
prompt
romped, etc.

ŌMZ

Holmes
(see ŌM + s)

ŌN

alone
antiphone
Athlone
atone
audiphone
backbone
baritone
begroan
bemoan
bestrown
blown
bone
Boulogne
brimstone
chaperone
cicerone
clingstone
Cologne
condone
cone
corner-stone
crone
curbstone
depone

dethrone
dictaphone
disown
dispone
Dordogne
drone
eau-de-cologne
electrophone
enthrone
enzone
flagstone
flown
foreknown
foreshown
foundation-
  stone
fresh-blown
full-blown
full-grown
gramophone
graphophone
grass-grown
grindlestone
grindstone
groan
grown
hailstone
headstone
hearthstone
high-flown
holy stone
hone
impone
imposing-stone
interpone
intone
Joan
keystone
known
knucklebone
ladrone

limestone
loadstone
loan
lone
macrotone
marrow-bone
megaphone
microphone
milestone
millstone
moan
monotone
moonstone
moss-grown
mown
ochone
outblown
overgrown
overthrown
own
phone
pore
postpone
prone
propone
radiophone
Rhone
roan
saxophone
semitone
sewn
shewn
shown
soapstone
sown
stone
strown
telephone
throne
thrown
tone

trombone
unbeknown
unblown
undertone
unforeknown
ungrown
unknown
unsewn
unsown
unthrone
vitaphone
weather-blown
whalebone
whetstone
xylophone
zone

ŎN

awn
"bawn"
brawn
"cawn"
dawn
drawn
faun
fawn
impawn
indrawn
lawn
pawn
prawn
sawn
spawn
undrawn
withdrawn
yawn

ŎN

agone
amazon
anon

antiphon
automaton
Babylon
begone
Bellerophon
benison
bonbon
bonne
celadon
Ceylon
chiffon
colophon
con
cretonne
decagon
demijohn
dies non
don
Donne
echelon
encephalon
enchiridion
encomion
Euroclydon
glyptodon
gone
gonfalon
hanger-on
Helicon
hereon
hereupon
hexagon
hoot mon
Hyperion
iguanodon
irenicon
Jeanne
John
lexicon
long-field-on
Luzon

mastodon
Micklejohn
myrmidon
Oberon
octagon
on
Oregon
outshone
pantechnicon
paragon
Parthenon
pentagon
phaeton
phenomenon
polygon
prolegomenon
put upon
Rubicon
Saskatchewan
shone
silicon
sine quâ non
stereopticon
swan
tarragon
thereon
thereupon
undergone
upon
wan
whereon
whereupon
woebegone
yon
(cf. accordion,
   etc., under
   ŬN)
Yvonne

ŎNCH

craunch

haunch
launch
paunch

ŌND

high-toned
unatoned
unmoaned
unowned
unzoned
zoned
atoned, etc.

ŎND

beau monde
demi-monde
Fronde
Gironde
monde

ŎND

abscond
beau monde
beyond
blond
bond
correspond
demi-monde
despond
fond
frond
overfond
plafond
monde
pond
respond
unparagoned
vagabond
wand
yond
donned, etc.

ŎNG

all-along
along
battlesong
belong
daylong
ding dong
drinking-song
dugong
erelong
evensong
flong
gong
headlong
headstrong
Hong Kong
lifelong
livelong
long
mah-jongg
night-long
overlong
pingpong
prolong
prong
scuppernong
sing-song
song
souchong
strong
thong
throng
tong
undersong
wong
wrong

ŎNGD

unwronged
belonged, etc.

ŎNGK
conch
conk
honk
honky-tonk

ŎNGKS
Bronx
conchs, etc.

ŎNGST
alongst
belong'st
long'st
prolong'st
throng'st
wrong'st

ŎNGZ
tongs
belongs, etc.

ŎNS
ensconce
nonce
response
sconce

ŌNT
don't
won't

ÒNT
aflaunt
a-taunt
avaunt
daunt
flaunt
gaunt
haunt
jaunt

romaunt
taunt
vaunt
want

ŎNT
Dupont
font
Hellespont
want

ŎNTS
fonts
wants
(cf. nonce)

ŌNZ
Davy Jones
Jones
nones
atones, etc.

ŎNZ
bonze
bronze
by-gones
Johns
pons
(see ŎN+s)

OŎD
could
dead-wood
firewood
good
hood
misunderstood
plastic wood
purple-wood
sandal-wood
should

stood
understood
Underwood
unhood
wildwood
withstood
wood
would
angelhood
babyhood
brotherhood
deaconhood
fatherhood
foolhardihood
gentlemanhood
hardihood
kinglihood
kittenhood
ladyhood
likelihood
livelihood
lustihood
maidenhood
manhood
matronhood
monk's-hood
motherhood
neighbourhood
orphanhood
parenthood
sisterhood
spinsterhood
unlikelihood
widowerhood
widowhood
womanhood

OŎK
betook
book
brook

Chinook
cook
crook
forsook
hook
ingle-nook
look
minute-book
mistook
nook
outlook
overlook
overtook
partook
pastry-cook
pocket-book
rook
shook
took
unhook
undertook
uplook

OŎKS
Crookes
snooks
tenterhooks
crooks, etc.

OŎL
abb-wool
bull
cock-and-bull
full
lamb's-wool
pull
wool
beautiful
bountiful
dutiful
fanciful

masterful
merciful
pitiful
plentiful
powerful
sorrowful
thimbleful
unmerciful
weariful
wonderful
worshipful
acceptable
accessible
accountable
adorable
affable
amenable
amiable
attainable
audible
available
avoidable
believable
capable
changeable
combustible
commendable
compatible
constable
contemptible
corruptible
crucible
culpable
damnable
delectable
deplorable
desirable
detestable
flexible
forcible
horrible

illegible
immovable
immutable
impalpable
impassable
impeccable
imperturbable
implacable
impossible
impregnable
improbable
improvable
inaccessible
inadmissible
inaudible
incapable
incomparable
incompatible
incomprehen-
  sible
inconceivable
incontestable
incontrovert-
  ible
incorruptible
incredible
incurable
indelible
indescribable
indestructible
indispensable
ineffable
ineffaceable
inexcusable
inexhaustible
inexpressible
infallible
inflammable
inflexible
infrangible
inscrutable

insensible
insoluble
insupportable
insupposable
insuppressible
insurmountable
intangible
intelligible
interchange-
  able
intractible
invaluable
invincible
irascible
irrepressible
irreproachable
irresistible
irresponsible
irretrievable
justifiable
laudable
legible
Mehitable
mutable
notable
ostensible
palpable
passable
perceptible
permissible
placable
plausible
portable
possible
praisable
presentable
principle
probable
procurable
producible
pronounceable

ratable
redeemable
reliable
reprehensible
respectable
responsible
sensible
susceptible
syllable
tangible
tenable
terrible
tractable
unimpeachable
unmatchable
unquenchable
visible
voluble

OͦOLF

wolf

OͦOLVZ

wolves

OͦOS

puss

OͦOSH

bramble-bush
bush
push

OͦOSK

brusque

OͦOT

afoot
foot
forefoot
pussyfoot

---

put
underfoot

ŌP
agrope
antelope
anti-pope
aslope
astroscope
baroscope
bioscope
cantaloupe
Cape of Good
 Hope
cope
dispope
dope
electroscope
elope
envelope
foot-rope
galvanoscope
grope
gyroscope
helioscope
heliotrope
hope
horoscope
hydroscope
interlope
kaleidoscope
lope
microscope
misanthrope
mope
ope
polariscope
pope
rope
scope
seismoscope

slope
soap
spectroscope
stereoscope
stethoscope
stope
telescope
thermoscope
tope
trope
unpope

ÔP
gaup
scaup
whaup
yawp

ŎP
after-crop
atop
bedrop
chop
co-op
cop
crop
drop
eavesdrop
estop
flipflop
flippity-flop
flop
fop
foretop
galop
ginger-pop
hop
knop
lollipop
lop

overtop
mizzen top
mop
overtop
plop
pop
prop
shop
slop
snowdrop
soda pop
sop
stop
strop
swap
tiptop
top
underprop
unstop
whop
wop
workshop

ŎPS
copse
drops, etc.

ŌPT
unhoped
unsoaped
eloped, etc.

ŎPT
adopt
copped
Copt
outcropped
uncropped
unstopped
dropped, etc.

ŌR
adore
afore
albacore
ashore
back-door
Baltimore
battledore
before
boar
Boer
bore
chore
commodore
core
corps
crore
death's-door
deplore
door
encore
evermore
explore
first-floor
floor
folklore
foot-sore
forbore
fore
foreshore
forswore
four
fourscore
frore
furthermore
galore
gore
heartsore
heretofore
hoar
ignore

implore
inshore
Lahore
lore
matador
mirador
more
nevermore
oar
o'er
ore
outpour
outroar
outsoar
Parramore
picador
pinafore
pore
pour
restore
roar
sagamore
score
sea-shore
semaphore
shore
Singapore
snore
soar
sophomore
sore
spore
stevedore
store
swore
sycamore
Theodore
tore
troubadour
underscore
uproar

upsoar
weather-shore
whore
wore
yore

ÔR

abhor
ambassador
ancestor
anterior
apparitor
assignor
auditor
bachelor
chancellor
competitor
compositor
conqueror
conspirator
contributor
corridor
councillor
counsellor
creditor
depositor
dinosaur
dor
Dukhobor
Ecuador
editor
emperor
excelsior
executor
expositor
exterior
for
governor
guarantor
ichthyosaur
inferior

inheritor
inquisitor
interior
interlocutor
janitor
Labrador
legator
lessor
lor
louis d'or
man-of-war
matador
metaphor
meteor
minotaur
mirador
monitor
mortgagor
nominor
nor
or
orator
posterior
primogenitor
progenitor
proprietor
Salvador
scaur
senator
senor
servitor
solicitor
superior
therefor
Thor
tor
toreador
troubadour
ulterior
verderor
vice-chancellor

visitor
war

ÔRB

absorb
corb
orb
reabsorb
resorb

ÔRBD

full-orbed
absorbed, etc.

ŌRCH

porch

ÔRCH

bortsch
scorch
torch

ŌRD

aboard
afford
beaverboard
board
broadsword
ford
gourd
hoard
horde
ironing-board
oared
seaboard
shuffle-board
surfboard
sword
undeplored
unexplored
ungored

ōld, ôr, ŏdd, oil, fŏŏt, out; ūse, ûrn, ŭp; THis, thin

unhoard	**ŌRJ**	deiform	borne
unimplored	forge	dendriform	bourn
unrestored		diversiform	foot-worn
weather-board	**ÔRJ**	floriform	forborne
adored, etc.	disgorge	form	forsworn
	engorge	inform	mourn
ÔRD	George	misform	outworn
accord	gorge	misinform	overborne
award	regorge	multiform	sea-worn
belord		norm	shorn
bord	**ŌRK**	perform	sworn
chord	pork	reform	toil-worn
concord		snow-storm	torn
cord	**ÔRK**	stelliform	unshorn
disaccord	cork	storm	unsworn
fiord	fork	sunny-warm	water-worn
fjord	New York	swarm	wave-worn
harpsichord	"orch"	thunder-storm	way-worn
landlord	stork	transform	weather-worn
lord	torque	uniform	worn
lyrichord	uncork	unwarm	(cf. adorn, etc.)
master-chord	weeding-fork	upswarm	
McCord	York	vermiform	**ÔRN**
misericord		warm	adorn
Orde	**ÔRKD**		alpen-horn
overlord	storked	**ÔRMD**	barleycorn
polychord	corked, etc.	unformed	bescorn
record		uninformed	blackthorn
reward	**ÔRL**	unperformed	born
sward	orle	unreformed	buckthorn
unlord	schorl	unstormed	Cape Horn
ward	whorl	well-informed	Capricorn
abhorred, etc.		bestormed, etc.	cloudborn
	ÔRM		corn
ÔRF	aeriform	**ÔRMTH**	disadorn
corf	aquiform	warmth	dishorn
dwarf	bestorm	*storm'th,* etc.	drinking-horn
wharf	chloroform		first-born
	conform	**ŌRN**	fog-horn
ÔRG	cruciform	bemourn	forewarn
morgue	cuneiform	betorn	forlorn
	deform		

French-horn
greenhorn
hawthorn
heaven-born
high-born
horn
Horne
hunting-horn
inborn
Langhorne
longicorn
lorn
love-lorn
Matterhorn
morn
night-born
Norn
peppercorn
popcorn
powder-horn
priming-horn
readorn
scorn
sea-born
self-scorn
sky-born
still-born
suborn
thorn
tricorn
trueborn
unborn
unicorn
warn
yestermorn

ŌRND
bemourned
mourned
unmourned

ÔRND
unadorned
unforewarned
adorned, etc.

ÔRP
dorp
thorp
warp

ÔRPS
corpse
warps, etc.

ŌRS
coarse
course
discourse
divorce
enforce
force
hoarse
intercourse
perforce
recourse
reinforce
resource
source
water-course

ÔRS
corse
deadhorse
dextrorse
dorse
endorse
gorse
hobby-horse
horse
Morse
Norse

remorse
retrorse
sea-horse
stalking-horse
torse
unhorse

ÔRSK
torsk

ÔRST
addorsed
endorsed
horsed
Horst
unhorsed

ŌRT
comport
county court
court
davenport
decourt
deport
disport
export
fort
forte
import
misreport
passport
port
Porte
rapport
report
sally-port
seaport
sport
support
transport
(cf. ÔRT)

ÔRT
abort
amort
assort
athwart
bort
cavort
consort
contort
detort
distort
escort
exhort
extort
mort
ort
quart
resort
retort
short
snort
sort
swart
thwart
tort
wart
(cf. court, etc.)

ŌRTH
forth
fourth
henceforth
setter-forth
thenceforth
pour'th, etc.

ÔRTH
north
Orth
swarth
abhorr'th, etc.

ōld, ôr, ŏdd, oĭl, fŏŏt, out; ūse, ûrn, ŭp; THis, thin

ÔRTS
quartz
Schwartz
shorts
Swarz
aborts, etc.

ÔRVZ
wharves

ŌRZ
all-fours
Azores
indoors
outdoors
adores, etc.

ÔRZ
Louis-
  Quatorze
quatorze
(see ÔR + s)

ŌS
actuose
adipose
aggerose
albuminose
animose
annulose
bellicose
cellulose
close
comatose
cose
diagnose
dose
engross
floccose
foliose
gibbose

globose
glucose
grandiose
gross
jocose
metempsy-
  chose
morose
nodose
otiose
overdose
underdose
verbose

ÔS
applesauce
sauce

ŎS
across
albatross
Bos
boss
coloss
cross
doss
double cross
dross
emboss
fiery-cross
floss
fosse
gloss
joss
lacrosse
loss
moss
recross
rhinoceros
rosy-cross
sea-moss

Setebos
toss
weeping-cross

ŌSH
Foch
gauche
guilloche

ŎSH
awash
bellywash
bewash
bosch
bosh
debosh
frosh
galosh
gosh
hogwash
kibosh
josh
mackintosh
McIntosh
musquash
quash
slosh
squash
swash
splosh
tosh
wash

ŎSHT
caboshed
great unwashed
unwashed
squashed, etc.

ŎSK
bosk

imbosk
kiosk
mosque

ŎSP
wasp

ŌST
aftermost
bettermost
boast
bottommost
coast
dosed
engrossed
finger-post
foremost
furthermost
ghost
hindermost
hithermost
host
innermost
lowermost
most
nethermost
northernmost
oast
outermost
post
riposte
roast
sea-coast
southernmost
toast
undermost
uppermost
uttermost
westernmost
whipping-post

āle, câre, ădd, ärm, åsk; mē, hĕre, ĕnd; īce, ĭll;

ÔST
exhaust
holocaust

ŎST
accost
adossed
betossed
cabossed
cost
double crossed
embossed
enmossed
frost
geognost
hoar-frost
Lacoste
lost
Pentecost
sea-tossed
tempest-tost
uncrossed
unlost
wast
crossed, etc.

ŌT
afloat
anecdote
antidote
asymptote
bedote
bequote
bloat
boat
capote
coat
commote
connote
cote
creosote

denote
devote
dote
float
folkmote
footnote
garrote
gloat
goat
groat
life-boat
lote
misquote
moat
mote
note
oat
outvote
overcoat
petticoat
pilot-boat
promote
quote
redevote
redingote
remote
river-boat
rote
scote
sea-boat
shote
slote
smote
stoat
table d'hote
telephote
throat
tote
troat
underwrote
unsmote

vote
wrote
Witenagemot
wrote

ŎT
aeronaut
after-thought
argonaut
astraught
aught
besought
bestraught
bethought
bewrought
bought
brought
caught
dear-bought
distraught
dreadnought
forethought
fought
fraught
freethought
ghât
hard-fought
inwrought
Juggernaut
maut
merry-thought
methought
naught
nought
onslaught
ought
overwrought
selftaught
sought
taught
taut

thought
unbesought
unbought
unfraught
unfought
untaught
unthought
unwrought
upbrought
upcaught
wrought

ŎT
aliquot
allot
apricot
asquat
beauty-spot
begot
bergamot
besot
blot
bott
cachalot
calotte
Camelot
capot
clot
compatriot
cocotte
cot
counterplot
dogtrot
dot
dry-rot
eschalot
fiery-hot
first-begot
forget-me-not
forgot
gallipot

garrote
gavotte
got
grape-shot
grass-plot
grot
hard-got
hot
Hottentot
Huguenot
ill-got
ink-pot
jogtrot
jot
knot
kumquať
lot
love-knot
misbegot
not
overshot
patriot
plague-spot
plot
polyglot
pot
quot
rot
sans-culotte
Scot
Scott
shallot
shot
shoulder-knot
sighting-shot
slot
somewhat
sot
spot
squat
Stott

swat
tot
tommyrot
trot
unbegot
underplot
undershot
unforgot
ungot
unknot
wat
watt
what
witenagemot
wot
yacht

ŌTH
clothe
loathe

Ŏth
aftergrowth
behemoth
betroth
both
growth
loath
oath
overgrowth
quoth
sloth
Thoth
troth
undergrowth

Ôth
swath
wrath
wroth

Ŏth
Ashtaroth
barley-broth
behemoth
broadcloth
broth
cloth
Coth
froth
Goth
moth
Ostrogoth
pilot-cloth
saddle-cloth
troth
Visigoth
wroth

ŌTS
Coates
Oates
boats, etc.

ŎTS
Potts
(see ŎT + s)

OU
allow
anyhow
avow
bough
bow
bow-wow
brow
chow
cow
dhow
disallow
disavow
endow

enow
Foochow
frau
frow
Hankow
hoosegow
how
Howe
kow-tow
Kwangchow
landau
mow
now
overbrow
plough
plow
powwow
prow
row
scow
slough
snow-plough
somehow
Soochow
sow
Swatow
thou
upplow
vow
Wenchow
wow

OUCH
avouch
couch
crouch
grouch
ouch
pouch
scaramouch

slouch
vouch

OUD
aloud
becloud
beetle-browed
beshroud
cloud
crowd
disendowed
disenshroud
encloud
enshroud
intercloud
loud
overcloud
overcrowd
proud
shroud
thunder-cloud
unbowed
uncloud
unshroud
allowed, etc.

OUJ
gouge
scrouge

OUL
afoul
befoul
behowl
cowl
dowl
foul
fowl
growl
guinea-fowl

howl
jowl
owl
peafowl
prowl
scowl
screech-owl
sea-fowl
water-fowl

OULD
uncowled
befouled, etc.

OUN
adown
brown
clown
crown
decrown
discrown
down
downtown
drown
eider-down
embrown
frown
godown
gown
hand-me-down
noun
nut-brown
reach-me-down
renown
town
tumble-down
uncrown
ungown
upside-down
uptown

OUND
abound
aground
around
astound
back-ground
bloodhound
bound
boozehound
compound
confound
dumfound
expound
flower-crowned
found
ground
hell-bound
hidebound
home-bound
hound
icebound
impound
inbound
iron-bound
Mahound
merry-go-round
middle-ground
mound
outbound
outward-bound
pine-crowned
pleasure-
    ground
pound
profound
propound
rebound
redound
renowned
resound
round

smuthound
sound
spell-bound
superabound
surround
triple-crowned
unbound
underground
unground
unsound
vantage-ground
wound
browned, etc.

OUNDZ
zounds
abounds, etc.

OUNJ
lounge

OUNS
announce
bounce
denounce
enounce
flounce
frounce
ounce
pounce
pronounce
renounce
rounce
trounce
(cf. accounts,
    etc.)

OUNT
account
amount
catamount

count
discount
dismount
fount
miscount
mount
paramount
recount
remount
surmount
tantamount

OUNTS

accounts, etc.
(cf. announce,
    etc.)

OUR

bescour
besour
deflour
devour
flour
hour
our
scour
sour
sustaining hour
(cf. OU'ur.)

OURD

unsoured
bescoured, etc.

OUS

backhouse
blouse
chapterhouse
charnelhouse
charterhouse
chouse

customhouse
doghouse
douse
flindermouse
flittermouse
Gnauss
grouse
house
Kraus
louse
madhouse
Mickey Mouse
mouse
nous
outhouse
penthouse
pleasure-house
poorhouse
prison-house
public-house
slaughterhouse
souse
storehouse
warehouse
whorehouse
workhouse

OUST

browst
oust
roust
unhoused
choused, etc.

OUT

about
beshout
bespout
bout
clout
devout

diner-out
doubt
drinking-bout
drought
flout
gadabout
gout
grout
hereabout
hereout
holing-out
knockabout
knockout
knout
kraut
look-out
lout
mahout
out
out-and-out
pout
redoubt
right-about
roundabout
roustabout
rout
sauerkraut
scout
shout
snout
spout
sprout
stirabout
stout
thereabout
thereout
throughout
tout
trout
water-spout
whereabout

whereout
without

OUTH

mouthe

OUth

bemouth
drouth
mouth
south
allow'th, etc.

OUTS

hereabouts
outs
thereabouts
whereabouts
bouts, etc.

OUZ

arouse
blouse
blowze
bouse
browse
carouse
drowse
espouse
house
rouse
souse
spouse
touse
unhouse
uprouse
(see OU + s)

ŌV

clove
cove

āle,   câre,   ădd,   ärm,   åsk: mē,   hĕre,   ĕnd: īce,   ĭll;

dove
drove
grove
hove
interwove
inwove
Jove
mauve
rove
shrove
stove
strove
throve
treasure-trove
wove

ŎV

hereof
of
thereof
whereof

ŌZ

arose
bramble-rose
brose
chose

close
clothes
compose
couleur-de-rose
damask-rose
decompose
depose
disclose
discompose
dispose
doze
enclose
expose
foreclose
froze
gloze
hose
impose
inclose
indispose
interclose
interpose
moss-rose
nose
oppose
pose
predispose

presuppose
propose
prose
recompose
repose
rose
superpose
suppose
those
transpose
tuberose
unclose
unfroze
(see Ō + s)

ÔZ

applause
because
cause
clause
Dawes
gauze
Hawes
hawse
lantern-jaws
menopause
pause

taws
vase
yaws
(see Ô + s)

ŎZ

Boz
Oz
was

ŌZD

dozed
ill-disposed
indisposed
juxtaposed
predisposed
unopposed
well-disposed
closed, etc.

ŌZH

eloge
loge

ŎZM

macrocosm
microcosm

ōld, ôr ŏdd, oil, fŏŏt, out; ūse, ûrn, ŭp; THis, thin

U

These words include the following accented vowels sounds:

Ū as in use; heard also in beauty, feud, pew, queue, lieu, view, cue, suit, yule, you, do, rule, true, food, group, drew, fruit, canoe, rheum, maneuvre, blue. The difference between *dew* and *do* is that *dew* is properly dyŪ, with a consonantal *y* sound preceding the long U; while *do* is merely dŪ.

Û as in urn; heard also in fern, err, heard, sir, word, journal, myrrh, colonel.

Ŭ as in up; heard also in won, one, does, flood, double.

For the vowel sound in *full,* see under OŌ.

Ū			
acajou	brew	derring-do	Gentoo
accrue	bugaboo	dew	glue
adieu	cachou	do	gillaroo
ado	canoe	drew	gnu
anew	caribou	due	googoo
aperçu	cashew	Elihu	grew
askew	catechu	emu	halloo
avenue	chandoo	endew	haut-gout
baboo	chew	endue	hereinto
ballyhoo	clew	ensue	hereto
bamboo	clue	entre nous	hereunto
barbecue	cockatoo	eschew	hew
barley-broo	construe	ewe	Hindu
battue	coo	feu	hitherto
bayou	corkscrew	feverfew	honeydew
bedew	coup	few	hoodoo
beshrew	crew	fichu	hue
bestrew	cuckoo	firenew	Hugh
billet-doux	cue	Fitzhugh	hullabaloo
blew	curlew	flew	igloo
blue	Daibutsu	flu	imbrue
boo	Daikoku	flue	imbue
boohoo	debut	*fordo*	immew
	Depew	foreknew	impromptu

 āle, câre, ădd, ärm, ăsk; mē, hĕre, ĕnd; īce, ĭll;

indue	pursue	tew	yahoo
ingenue	queue	thereinto	yew
interview	ragout	thereto	yoohoo
in transitu	rendezvous	thereunto	you
I.O.U	renew	thew	zoo
Jew	residue	thitherto	Zulu
Kalamazoo	retinue	threw	
kangaroo	revenue	through	**ŪB**
karroo	review	Timbuktu	boob
Kew	rough hew	to	cube
kinkajou	roux	to-do	Rube
knew	rue	too	tube
lieu	screw	toodle-oo	
loo	sea-mew	to-whit-towhoo	**ŬB**
Manitou	set-to	true	battle-club
meadow-rue	shampoo	trueblue	Beelzebub
mew	shoe	two	blub
misconstrue	shoo	unclew	bub
misdo	shrew	underdo	chub
moo	Sioux	undo	Chubb
mountain-dew	skew	undue	club
napoo	skidoo	unglue	Clubb
new	sky-blue	unmew	cub
night-dew	slew	unscrew	drub
outdo	sloo	untrue	dub
overdo	slough	view	fub
overdue	slue	view-halloo	grub
overstrew	smew	virtu	hub
overthrew	sou	voodoo	hubbub
parvenu	spew	wahoo	nub
passe-partout	sprue	wallaroo	pub
peekaboo	stew	wanderoo	rub
perdu	strew	well-to-do	rub-a-dub
Peru	subdue	whew	scrub
pew	sue	whereinto	shrub
phew	sundew	whereto	sillabub
pooh	surtout	whereunto	slub
preview	*surview*	who	snub
prie-dieu	taboo	withdrew	stub
Pugh	tattoo	woo	sub
Purdue			tub

ōld, ôr, ŏdd, oil, fŏŏt, out; ūse, ûrn, ŭp; THis, thin

ŪCH

brooch
cooch
hooch
hoochy-cooch
mooch
pooch

ŬCH

clutch
crutch
cutch
Dutch
for-as-much
hutch
in-as-much
in-so-much
master-touch
much
mutch
overmuch
retouch
scutch
smutch
such
touch

ŬCHD

untouched
clutched, etc.

ŪD

abrood
abstrude
acerbitude
acritude
allude
altitude
amaritude
amplitude

aptitude
assuetude
attitude
beatitude
brood
certitude
claritude
collude
conclude
consuetude
crassitude
crude
decrepitude
definitude
delude
denude
desuetude
detrude
disquietude
dude
elude
exactitude
exclude
extrude
exude
feud
finitude
food
fortitude
gratitude
habitude
hebetude
home-brewed
illude
inaptitude
incertitude
include
ineptitude
infinitude
ingratitude

inquietude
insuetude
interclude
interlude
intrude
Jude
lassitude
latitude
lenitude
lewd
longitude
magnitude
mansuetude
mollitude
mood
multitude
necessitude
nude
obtrude
occlude
parvitude
platitude
plenitude
pood
preclude
prelude
promptitude
protrude
prude
pulchritude
quietude
rainbow-hued
reclude
rectitude
retrude
rood
rude
seclude
senectitude
serenitude

servitude
shrewd
similitude
slewed
snood
solicitude
solitude
stude
subnude
subtrude
thewed
torpitude
transude
turpitude
unglued
unpursued
unrenewed
unrude
unrued
unstrewed
unsubdued
unwooed
(see Ū+ed)
vastitude
verisimilitude
vicissitude
you'd

ŬD

bestud
blood
bud
Budd
cud
dud
flood
fud
Judd
life-blood
lud
mud

rudd
'sblood
scud
spud
stud
thud

ŬDZ

duds
suds
buds, etc.

ŪF

aloof
behoof
bullet-proof
disproof
fire-proof
foolproof
gable-roof
goof
hoof
loof
opera-bouffe
proof
reproof
roof
shadoof
spoof
Tartuffe
unroof
virtue-proof
waterproof
weather-proof
woof

ŬF

bepuff
besnuff
blindman's-buff
bluff

breadstuff
buff
chough
chuff
clough
counterbuff
cuff
duff
enough
fluff
garden-stuff
gruff
huff
luff
muff
powder-puff
puff
rebuff
rough
ruff
scruff
scuff
slough
snuff
sough
stuff
tough
tuff

ŬFS

fisticuffs
bepuffs, etc.

ŪFT

clovenhoofed
hoofed
roofed, etc.

ŬFT

candytuft
tuft

bepuffed, etc.
(cf. scuft)

ŪG

fugue

ŬG

bug
bunnyhug
doodlebug
drug
dug
fug
hug
jug
lug
mug
plug
pug
rug
shrug
slug
smug
snug
thug
trug
tug

ŬGZ

go bugs
drugs, etc.

ŪJ

demonifuge
febrifuge
gamboge
huge
insectifuge
Scrooge
scrouge
stooge

subterfuge
vermifuge

ŬJ

adjudge
begrudge
budge
drudge
forejudge
fudge
grudge
judge
misjudge
nudge
prejudge
rejudge
Rudge
sludge
smudge
trudge

ŬJD

ill-judged
unjudged
adjudged, etc.

ŪK

archduke
bashi-bazouk
beduke
chibouk
Chinook
duke
fluke
Heptateuch
Hexateuch
juke
Luke
mameluke
Marmaduke
Pentateuch

ōld, ôr, ŏdd, oil, fŏŏt, out; ūse, ûrn, ŭp; THis, thin

peruke
puke
rebuke
snook
spook
stook

ŬK
amuck
awestruck
beduck
buck
Canuck
chuck
cluck
Donald Duck
duck
horror-struck
ill-luck
Kalmuck
lame duck
laverock
luck
misluck
muck
pluck
pot-luck
puck
roebuck
ruck
rukh
shuck
struck
stuck
suck
terror-struck
thunder-struck
truck
tuck
waterbuck

woodchuck
wonderstruck

ŬKS
crux
dux
flux
lux
shucks
(see ŬK + s)

ŬKT
abduct
aqueduct
conduct
construct
deduct
duct
educt
eruct
good-plucked
induct
instruct
misconduct
misconstruct
obstruct
oviduct
product
reduct
reluct
subduct
substruct
superstruct
unplucked
usufruct
viaduct
beducked, etc.

ŬL
April-fool
befool

buhl
charity-school
cool
drool
ducking-stool
fool
footstool
ghoul
Istambul
Liverpool
mewl
misrule
molecule
mule
O'Toole
overrule
pool
pule
reticule
ridicule
rule
school
spool
stool
Sunday School
toadstool
tool
Toole
tulle
vermicule
vestibule
whirlpool
who'll
you'll
Yule

ŬL
ahull
annul
barnacle

chronicle
cull
disannul
dull
gull
hull
lull
miracle
Mogul
monocle
mull
null
numskull
obstacle
pinnacle
scull
sea-gull
skull
spectacle
stull
trull
vehicle
versicle

ŬLB
bulb

ŬLCH
gulch
mulch

ŬLD
unruled
unschooled
(see UL + d)

ŬLD
mulled
thick-skulled
annulled, etc.

ŬLF
engulf
gulf

ŬLJ
bulge
divulge
effulge
indulge
promulge

ŬLK
bulk
hulk
skulk
sulk

ŬLKT
bulked
mulct
hulked, etc.

ŬLM
culm

ŬLP
poulp

ŬLP
gulp
pulp
sculp

ŬLS
appulse
bulse
convulse
dulse
expulse
impulse
mulse

pulse
repulse
(cf. adult + s)

ŬLT
adult
catapult
consult
cult
difficult
exult
incult
indult
insult
occult
result

ŪLZ
gules
(see ŪL + s)

ŪM
abloom
addoom
anteroom
assume
begloom
beplume
bloom
boom
bridegroom
broom
brougham
brume
consume
coom
coomb
costume
disentomb
displume
doom

diningroom
drawing-room
dressing-room
elbow-room
embloom
engloom
entomb
enwomb
exhume
flume
foredoom
fume
gloom
groom
grume
heirloom
illume
inhume
jibboom
Khartoum
legume
livingroom
loom
lumber-room
perfume
plume
power-loom
predoom
presume
reading-room
reassume
relume
resume
rheum
room
sea-room
simoom
spoom
spume
subsume

unplume
tomb
untomb
whom
womb

ŬM
ad libitum
adventuresome
adytum
aquarium
auditorium
become
benumb
bum
Bumbledom
burdensome
cardamom
Christendom
chrysanthe-
mum
chum
Cockneydom
come
compendium
cranium
crematorium
crum
crumb
cumbersome
curriculum
delirium
drearisome
drum
dumb
emporium
encomium
epithalamium
equilibrium
exordium
fee-fi-fo-fum

flunkeydom
frolicsome
geranium
glum
grum
gum
gymnasium
halidom
heathendom
hum
humdrum
humorsome
intermeddle-
  some
kettle-drum
laudanum
Lum
martyrdom
maximum
meddlesome
medium
mettlesome
millennium
minimum
misbecome
modicum
moratorium
mum
natatorium
numb
odium
opium
opprobrium
overcome
pabulum
palladium
pandemonium
pelargonium
pendulum
pericardium
petroleum

platinum
plum
plumb
premium
prud'homme
quarrelsome
quietsome
radium
rascaldom
rebeldom
recumb
residuum
rhumb
rum
sanatorium
Saxondom
scrum
scum
sensorium
slum
some
speculum
strum
stum
succumb
sugar-plum
sum
swum
symposium
tedium
thrum
thumb
troublesome
tum
tum-tum
tweedledum
tympanum
unplumb
vacuum
venturesome
viaticum

wearisome
worrisome
wranglesome

ŪMD

assumed, etc.
full-bloomed
implumed
unfumed
ungloomed
unillumed
addoomed, etc.

ŬMD

begummed
bethumbed
unplumbed
benumbed, etc.

ŬMP

bethump
bump
chump
clump
crump
dump
frump
hump
jump
lump
mugwump
mump
plump
pump
rump
slump
stump
sump
thump
trump

tump
ump

ŬMPS

mumps
bethumps, etc.

ŪN

afternoon
aswoon
attune
baboon
balloon
barracoon
bassoon
batoon
bestrewn
boon
bridoon
Broun
buffoon
Calhoun
cartoon
cocoon
Colquoun
commune
coon
croon
Doon
doubloon
dragoon
dune
eftsoon
entune
excommune
expugn
festoon
forenoon
frigatoon
gadroon
galloon

gambroon
gazon
gossoon
harpoon
harvest-moon
hewn
honey-moon
immune
inopportune
importune
impugn
intercommune
jejune
June
lacune
lagoon
lampoon
loon
lune
macaroon
Mahoun
maroon
mid-noon
monsoon
moon
musketoon
noon
octoroon
opportune
oppugn
oversoon
overstrewn
pantaloon
patroon
picaroon
picayune
platoon
poltroon
pontoon
prune
quadroon

quintroon
racoon
Rangoon
ratoon
rigadoon
rough-hewn
rune
saloon
Schroon
seroon
shalloon
shoon
simoon
soon
spadroon
spittoon
spontoon
spoon
strewn
swoon
tune
Tycoon
typhoon
untune
walloon

ŬN
A 1
accordion
Albion
amazon
begun
benison
bun
Bunn
cardamon
caparison
cinnamon
colophon
comparison

Chesterton
done
dun
Dunn
foredone
forerun
foster-son
fun
galleon
Galveston
ganglion
garrison
gonfalon
gun
halcyon
hard-run
hard-won
Helicon
homespun
hon
Hun
jettison
Middleton
minute-gun
mon
myrmidon
none
nun
Number one
Oberon
oblivion
octagon
one
orison
outdone
outrun
orison
overdone
overrun
pantechnicon
paragon

Parthenon
pentagon
percussion-gun
phenomenon
polygon
prolegomenon
pun
quaternion
run
sally lunn
shun
simpleton
singleton
skeleton
son
spun
stun
sun
sunn
ton
tun
unbegun
underrun
undone
unison
unnun
venison
Whitsun
won

ŬNCH
brunch
bunch
clunch
crunch
hunch
lunch
munch
punch
scrunch

ōld, ôr, ŏdd. oil. fŏŏt, out; ūse, ûrn, ŭp; THis, thin

ŪND

disattuned
unattuned
untuned
wound
attuned, etc.
crooned, etc.

ŬND

bund
cummerbund
dunned
fund
immund
moribund
obrotund
orotund
punned
refund
retund
Rosamond
rotund
rubicund
shunned
stunned
unparagoned
unsunned
verecund
(cf. ŬN+ed)

ŬNG

among
behung
betongue
bung
clung
dung
flung
high-strung
hung
lung

mother-tongue
overhung
pung
rung
slung
sprung
strung
stung
sung
swung
tongue
underhung
Ung
unhung
unstrung
unsung
unwrung
upsprung
wither-wrung
wrung
young

ŬNGD

bunged
double-tongued
honey-tongued
leather-lunged
loud-lunged
pleasant-
  tongued
shrill-tongued
silver-tongued
tongued
trumpet-
  tongued

ŬNGK

bunk
chunk
drunk

flunk
funk
hunk
junk
monk
plunk
punk
quidnunc
shrunk
skunk
slunk
spunk
stunk
sunk
trunk
unk
wunk

ŬNGKT

bunked
compunct
conjunct
defunct
disjunct
funked
trunked

ŬNGST

amongst
clung'st, etc.

ŬNJ

allonge
blunge
dispunge
expunge
lunge
muskellunge
plunge
sponge

ŬNS

dunce
once
(cf. affront+s)

ŬNT

affront
afront
blunt
brunt
bunt
confront
exeunt
forefront
front
grunt
hunt
Lunt
punt
runt
shunt
sprunt
stunt
wont

ŬNTH

month
run'th, etc.

ŪNZ

Cameroons
eftsoons
croons, etc.

ŪP

adroop
aggroup
apple-scoop
cantaloupe

āle, câre, ădd, ärm. åsk; mē, hęre, ĕnd; īce, ĭll;

243

cock-a-hoop
coop
croup
droop
drupe
dupe
Guadeloupe
group
hoop
jupe
liripoop
loop
nincompoop
poop
recoup
roup
scoop
scroop
sloop
soup
stoop
stoup
supe
swoop
troop
troupe
unhoop
whoop

ŬP

blowing-up
buttercup
crup
cup
fed up
grace-cup
gup
hard-up
keyed-up
loving-cup
make-up

pup
scup
setter-up
slap-up
stirrup-cup
sup
tup
up
up-and-up
wassail-cup

ŬPT

abrupt
corrupt
cupped
disrupt
erupt
incorrupt
interrupt
supped

ŪR

abature
abbreviature
abjure
adjure
allure
amateur
amour
aperture
armature
assure
blackamoor
boor
breviature
brochure
calenture
candidature
caricature
cocksure
colure

comfiture
conjure
connoisseur
contour
coverture
cure
curvature
cynosure
demure
detour
discomfiture
divestiture
dure
endure
ensure
entablature
epicure
expenditure
forfeiture
furniture
garmenture
garniture
guipure
immature
immure
impure
insecure
insure
intermure
inure
investiture
judicature
Kohinoor
ligature
liqueur
literature
lure
manicure
manure
mature
miniature

moor
obscure
Ostermoor
overture
paramour
pedicure
perdure
perendure
poor
portraiture
premature
primogeniture
procure
pure
quadrature
reassure
reinsure
secure
sepulture
signature
sinecure
spoor
sure
tablature
temperature
tour
troubadour
unmoor
unsure
vestiture
water-cure
your
you're
(cf. Ū+er)

ŬR

aberr
astir
aver
befur

bestir
blur
burr
chirr
concur
confer
cur
defer
demur
deter
disinter
err
fir
fur
her
incur
infer
inter
Kerr
knur
liqueur
myrrh
occur
per
prefer
purr
recur
refer
shirr
sir
slur
spur
stir
transfer
were
whir

accoucheur
amateur
chasseur
chauffeur

coeur
colporteur
connoisseur
farceur
franc-tireur
friseur
frondeur
hauteur
litterateur
mitrailleur
persifleur
restaurateur
trouveur
voltigeur
voyageur

administer
admonisher
adulterer
adventurer
affiancer
almoner
amphitheatre
answerer
arbiter
archiater
armiger
armourer
artificer
astrologer
astronomer
autobiographer
baluster
banisher
banister
banqueter
banterer
bargainer
barometer
barrister
barterer

batterer
bibliographer
bickerer
biographer
blandisher
blazoner
blunderer
blusterer
borrower
botherer
brandisher
broiderer
burdener
burnisher
calender
caliper
canister
carpenter
caterer
cellarer
chafferer
challenger
character
chatterer
cherisher
chorister
chronicler
cofferer
comforter
commissioner
commoner
confectioner
conjurer
coroner
cottager
coverer
cricketer
customer
cylinder
decipherer
deliverer

demolisher
determiner
diameter
diaper
discoverer
disparager
distributer
dowager
driveller
embellisher
emblazoner
enameler
encourager
endeavourer
engenderer
enlightener
enlivener
establisher
examiner
Excalibur
executioner
fashioner
favorer
flatterer
flutterer
forager
foreigner
forester
forfeiter
furtherer
galloper
gardener
gatherer
gossamer
gossiper
harbinger
harborer
harvester
hexameter
idolater
imprisoner

interpreter
islander
jabberer
juniper
Jupiter
languisher
lavender
lavisher
lecturer
leveller
libeller
lingerer
lithographer
loiterer
Londoner
Lowlander
lucifer
malingerer
manager
manufacturer
mariner
marshaller
massacre
measurer
messenger
milliner
minister
miniver
modeller
murderer
murmurer
mutterer
nourisher
officer
palaverer
parishioner
passenger
pasturer
patterer
pensioner
pentameter

pepperer
perjurer
pesterer
petitioner
pewterer
philologer
philosopher
phonographer
photographer
pilferer
pillager
pitier
plasterer
plunderer
polisher
porringer
posturer
poulterer
practitioner
presbyter
prisoner
probationer
profferer
provender
publisher
punisher
purchaser
quarreller
quaverer
questioner
ransomer
ravager
ravisher
reasoner
register
relinquisher
reveller
reversioner
rioter
riveter
roisterer

saunterer
scavenger
scimiter
sepulchre
sinister
skirmisher
slanderer
slaughterer
slumberer
smatterer
sophister
sorcerer
splutterer
squanderer
stenographer
stutterer
succorer
sufferer
swaggerer
tamperer
terrier
tetrameter, etc.
theatre
thermometer
thunderer
topographer
torturer
totterer
traveller
treasurer
trespasser
trumpeter
typographer
upholsterer
usurer
utterer
valuer
vanquisher
vaporer
venturer
verderer

victualer
villager
vintager
visiter
voyager
wagerer
wagoner
wanderer
wassailer
waverer
whimperer
whisperer
widower
wonderer
worshipper

blearier
breezier
brinier
burlier
cheerfuller
cheerier
cheerlier
chillier
cleanlier
cosier
costlier
creamier
creepier
crueller
curlier
dingier
dizzier
doughtier
dowdier
drearier
drowsier
dustier
earlier
easier
eerier

emptier
evener
filmier
filthier
fleecier
flightier
flimsier
foamier
friendlier
funnier
fussier
giddier
gloomier
glossier
goutier
grimier
guiltier
happier
healthier
heavier
hillier
holier
homelier
horrider
huffier
hungrier
huskier
icier
inkier
jollier
juicier
kindlier
kinglier
knightlier
likelier
lissomer
lithesomer
livelier
loftier
lonelier
lonesomer

lovelier
lowlier
loyaler
merrier
mightier
moldier
mossier
mournfuller
muskier
mustier
narrower
noisier
pearlier
pleasanter
portlier
princelier
prosier
rosier
rowdier
ruggeder
seemlier
shinier
shoddier
showier
sightlier
silenter
sillier
skilfuller
skinnier
sleepier
slimier
soapier
solider
spicier
spikier
spongier
spoonier
springier
spritelier
steadier
stealthier

stingier
stormier
stuffier
stupider
sturdier
sunnier
surlier
thirstier
thriftier
timider
trustier
vivider
wealthier
wearier
wheezier
windier
winsomer
wintrier
(cf. ambassador
   and other ŎR
   words)

ŬRB

acerb
blurb
curb
disturb
gerb
herb
perturb
Serb
suburb
superb
verb

ŬRBD

imperturbed
uncurbed
undisturbed
unperturbed
curbed, etc.

ŬRCH

besmirch
birch
church
lurch
perch
research
search
smirch
weeping-birch

ŬRCHT

unsmirched
birched, etc.

ŪRD

gourd
reassured
self-assured
unassured
uninsured
unmatured
abjured, etc.
ensured, etc.

ŬRD

absurd
begird
bird
Cape Verde
curd
engird
frigate-bird
gallows-bird
gird
heard
hedge-bird
herd
humming-bird
Kurd

---

lady-bird
lovebird
mocking-bird
night-bird
overheard
pilot-bird
sea-bird
sherd
shirred
snow-bird
song-bird
storm-bird
surd
third
undergird
ungird
unsepulchred
verd
word
(see ÛR + ed)

ÛRF

scurf
serf
surf
turf

ÛRG

berg
burg
exergue
Goldberg
Heidelberg
iceberg

ÛRJ

converge
demiurge
deterge
dirge
diverge

dramaturge
emerge
gurge
immerge
merge
purge
scourge
serge
splurge
Spurge
submerge
surge
thaumaturge
urge
verge

ÛRJD

unurged
converged, etc.

ÛRK

O'Rourke

ÛRK

Burke
cirque
clerk
dirk
fancy-work
frostwork
handiwork
irk
jerk
jerque
kirk
lurk
master-work
murk
perk
quirk
shirk

smirk
stirk
Turk
underwork
water-work
wonderwork
work
yerk

ÛRKT

overworked
irked, etc.

ÛRL

becurl
bepearl
burl
charity-girl
churl
curl
earl
furl
girl
hurl
impearl
knurl
merle
mother-of-pearl
pearl
pirl
purl
querl
seed-pearl
skirl
swirl
thurl
twirl
uncurl
unfurl
upcurl
upwhirl

whirl
whorl

ÛRLD

impearled
new-world
old-world
pearled
uncurled
underworld
world
becurled, etc.

ÛRM

affirm
berm
confirm
derm
disaffirm
firm
germ
infirm
isotherm
misterm
pachyderm
reaffirm
sperm
squirm
term
worm

ÛRMD

unconfirmed
affirmed, etc.

ÛRN

bourn

ÛRN

adjourn
astern

attorn	urn	**ÛRS**	verse
Berne	yearn	accurse	worse
burn		adverse	
Byrne	**ÛRND**	amerce	**ÛRST**
churn	hard-earned	asperse	accurst
concern	unconcerned	averse	athirst
Dern	undiscerned	becurse	becurst
durn	unlearned	birse	burst
discern	unturned	burse	curst
earn	adjourned, etc.	coerce	double-first
erne		converse	durst
eterne	**ÛRNT**	curse	*erst*
externe	burnt	cutpurse	first
fern	earnt	disburse	Hearst
Hearn	learnt	disperse	Hurst
Hearne	unburnt	diverse	outburst
hern	unlearnt	Erse	thirst
intern	weren't	excurse	uncursed
interne		foster-nurse	unversed
inurn	**ÛRNZ**	hearse	versed
kern	Burns	herse	verst
learn	Kearns	imburse	worst
lucern	(see ÛRN + s)	immerse	accursed, etc.
lucerne		inhearse	
O'Byrne	**ÛRP**	intersperse	**ÛRT**
overturn	blurp	inverse	Adelbert
pirn	burp	nurse	advert
quern	chirp	perverse	alert
return	discerp	precurse	animadvert
secern	*extirp*	purse	assert
sojourn	twirp	rehearse	avert
spurn	usurp	reimburse	begirt
stern		reverse	Bert
subaltern	**ÛRPT**	sesterce	blurt
taciturn	chirped	submerse	cert
tern	excerpt	subverse	chert
turn	usurped	terce	concert
unconcern		terse	controvert
unlearn	**ÛRS**	transverse	convert
upturn	bourse	traverse	curt
		universe	desert

āle, câre, ădd, ärm, ȧsk; mē, hẽre, ĕnd; īce, ĭll;

dessert
dirt
disconcert
divert
engirt
Englebert
Ethelbert
evert
exert
expert
exsert
extrovert
flirt
girt
gurt
hurt
indesert
inert
inexpert
insert
intersert
intervert
introvert
invert
liverwort
malapert
obvert
pert
pervert
preconcert
retrovert
revert
sea-girt
shirt
skirt
spirt
spurt
squirt
subvert
syrt
transvert

ungirt
unhurt
vert
wert
Wirt
wort

ŪRTH

berth
birth
dearth
earth
firth
fuller's-earth
girth
inearth
mirth
penny-worth
Perth
unearth
unworth
worth

ŪRTZ

Wurtz
(see ŪRT + s)

ŪRV

conserve
curve
deserve
disserve
incurve
nerve
observe
outcurve
preserve
reserve
serve
subserve
swerve

unnerve
verve

ŪRVD

ill-deserved
undeserved
well-preserved
conserved, etc.

ŪRVZ

turves
conserves, etc.

ŪRZ

Tours
yours
amours, etc.

ŪRZ

furze
(see ŪR + s)

ŪS

abstruse
abuse
adduce
Bruce
burnoose
caboose
calaboose
Charlotte-**russe**
conduce
cruse
deduce
deuce
diffuse
disuse
douce
Druce
educe

excuse
flower-de-luce
goose
hypotenuse
induce
introduce
juice
loose
luce
misuse
moose
noose
nous
pappoose
obtuse
occluse
pertuse
produce
profuse
puce
recluse
reduce
reproduce
retuse
Roos
Russ
seduce
sluice
spruce
superinduce
Syracuse
Toulouse
traduce
transluce
truce
unloose
unsluice
use
vamoose
Zeus

ŬS

abaculus
abacus
acephalus
angelus
animus
blunderbuss
bus
buss
caduceus
Cerberus
convolvulus
cumulus
cuss
denarius
discuss
Erebus
esophagus
excuss
fuss
harquebus
Hesperus
hippopotamus
humerus
hydrocephalus
ignis fatuus
impetus
incubus
incuss
Leviticus
minimus
muss
nautilus
nonplus
nucleus
octopus
omnibus
overplus
Pegasus
percuss
phosphorus

platypus
plus
polypus
pus
radius
ranunculus
repercuss
rhus
Russ
sarcophagus
Sirius
stimulus
succubus
syllabus
tantalus
Tartarus
terminus
thus
truss
untruss
us

abstemious
acclivitous
acephalous
acidulous
adulterous
adventurous
agricolous
albuminous
aliferous
aligerous
alimonious
alkalous
alluvious
aluminous
amatorious
Americus
amorous
ambiguous
amphibolous

amphibious
analogous
androgenous
androphagous
anemophilous
anfractuous
angulous
anomalous
anonymous
anserous
antipathous
aqueous
arborous
arduous
armigerous
assiduous
augurous
balsamiferous
barbarous
beauteous
bibulous
bicephalous
bigamous
bipetalous
bituminous
blasphemous
blusterous
boisterous
bounteous
bulbiferous
burdenous
burglarious
cadaverous
calamitous
calcareous
calumnious
cancerous
cankerous
cantankerous
carboniferous
carnivorous

cautelous
cavernous
censorious
ceremonious
chivalrous
cinereous
circuitous
clamorous
commodious
congruous
compendious
consanguin-
    eous
conspicuous
contempora-
    neous
contemptuous
conterminous
contiguous
continuous
contrarious
contumelious
copious
courteous
covetous
crapulous
credulous
crepusculous
Cretaceous
criminous
curious
dangerous
deciduous
deleterious
delirious
devious
dexterous
diaphanous
diatomous
discourteous
disingenuous

āle,   câre,   ădd,   ärm,   åsk;   mē,   hẹre,   ĕnd;   īce,   ĭll;

doloriferous	gratuitous	inharmonious	multivious
dolorous	gregarious	iniquitous	murderous
dubious	harmonious	injurious	murmurous
dulcifluous	hazardous	innocuous	mutinous
duteous	herbaceous	inodorous	mysterious
emulous	heterogeneous	inquisitorious	nauseous
endogenous	hideous	insensuous	nebulous
envious	hilarious	insidious	necessitous
eponymous	homogeneous	instantaneous	nectareous
equilibrious	homologous	invidious	nefarious
erroneous	humorous	jeopardous	notorious
ethereous	idolatrous	laborious	numerous
exiduous	igneous	languorous	oblivious
expurgatorious	ignominious	lascivious	obsequious
extempora-	illustrious	lecherous	obstreperous
neous	*imaginous*	leguminous	obvious
extraneous	*immeritous*	libellous	odious
fabulous	impecunious	libidinous	odoriferous
farinaceous	imperious	ligneous	odorous
fastidious	impervious	litigious	oleaginous
fatuitous	impetuous	ludicrous	ominous
fatuous	impious	lugubrious	omnivorous
felicitous	imponderous	luminous	onerous
felonious	imposturous	luxurious	opprobrious
ferruginous	incendious	magnanimous	oviparous
fluminous	incestuous	marvelous	pachyderma-
fortitudinous	incommodious	mellifluous	tous
fortuitous	incongruous	melodious	parsimonious
fossiliferous	inconspicuous	membranous	pendulous
frivolous	incredulous	meretorious	penurious
fuliginous	incurious	metalliferous	perfidious
furious	indecorous	meticulous	periculous
garrulous	indigenous	miraculous	perilous
gelatinous	indubious	miscellaneous	perjurous
generous	industrious	mischievous	perspicuous
globulous	inebrious	monogamous	pervious
glorious	infamous	monotonous	pesterous
glutenous	infelicitous	mountainous	pestiferous
glutinous	ingenious	mucilaginous	petalous
gluttonous	ingenuous	multifarious	piteous
graminivorous	inglorious	multitudinous	platinous

ōld, ôr, ŏdd, oil, fŏŏt, out; ūse, ûrn, ŭp; THis, thin

platitudinous
plenteous
poisonous
polygamous
ponderous
populous
posthumous
precarious
precipitous
predaceous
preposterous
presumptuous
previous
promiscuous
prosperous
pseudony-
   mous
punctilious
pusillanimous
quarrelous
querulous
rancorous
rapturous
ravenous
rebellious
resinous
ridiculous
rigorous
riotous
roisterous
ruinous
sacchariferous
salacious
salubrious
sanctimonious
sanguineous
saponaceous
savorous
scandalous
scintillous
scrofulous

scrupulous
scrutinous
scurrilous
sedulous
sensuous
serious
setaceous
sibilous
simultaneous
sinuous
slanderous
slumberous
solicitous
somniferous
spontaneous
spurious
stentorious
strenuous
stridulous
studious
subterraneous
sulphurous
sumptuous
supercilious
superfluous
synchronous
synonymous
tautologous
tedious
temerarious
tempestuous
tenebrous
tenuous
thunderous
timidous
timorous
tintinnabulous
tortuous
torturous
traitorous
treacherous

treasonous
tremulous
tuberculous
tumultuous
tyrannous
ubiquitous
unanimous
unchivalrous
undulous
unscrupulous
uproarious
ungenerous
usurious
uxorious
vacuous
vagarious
vainglorious
valetudinarious
valetudinous
valorous
vaporous
various
vegetous
velutinous
venomous
ventriculous
venturous
verdurous
verisimilous
verminous
vernaculous
vertiginous
vicarious
vicissitudinous
victorious
vigorous
villainous
viperous
virtuous
vitreous
viviparous

vociferous
voluminous
voluptuous
voraginous
vortiginous
vulturous
zoophagous

ŪSH

barouche
bonne-bouche
bouche
cartouche
debouch
douche
gobemouche
Hindu Kush
Joosh
mouche
ruche
Scaramouch

ŬSH

blush
brush
crush
flush
gush
hush
lush
missel-thrush
mush
outblush
outrush
plush
rush
slush
thrush
tush
underbrush
uprush

āle,   câre,   ădd,   ärm,   åsk;   mē,   hẹre,   ĕnd;   īce,   ĭll;

ŬSK
adusk
brusque
busk
dehusk
dusk
fusc
husk
Lusk
musk
rusk
subfusk
tusk

ŬSP
cusp

ŬST
adduced
unproduced
deduced, etc.

boost
browst
joust
loosed
noosed
roost
spruced
unloosed
roust
vamoosed

ŬST
adjust
adust
angust
august
bedust
betrust
bust

coadjust
combust
crust
disgust
distrust
dost
dust
encrust
entrust
fust
gust
just
lust
mistrust
must
non-plussed
robust
rust
self-distrust
stardust
thrust
trust
unjust
untrussed
(see ŬS + ed)

ŪT
absolute
acute
argute
arrowroot
astute
attribute
baldicoot
beaut
birthday suit
boot
bruit
brute
Butte
cahoot

cheroot
chute
comminute
commute
compute
confute
constitute
coot
cornute
cute
deaf-mute
depute
destitute
dilute
dispute
disrepute
dissolute
electrocute
emeute
enroot
en route
execute
first-fruit
flute
forbidden-fruit
fruit
galoot
hirsute
hoot
imbrute
immute
impute
institute
involute
irresolute
jute
loot
lute
marabout
meute
minute

moot
mute
newt
outshoot
overshoot
parachute
permute
persecute
Piute
pollute
prosecute
prostitute
pursuit
Rajput
recruit
refute
repute
resolute
root
route
salute
scoot
scute
shoot
snoot
solute
soot
subacute
substitute
suit
suppute
toot
transmute
unboot
unroot
uproot
upshoot
Ute
versute
volute

ōld, ôr, ŏdd, oil, fŏŏt, out; ūse, ûrn, ŭp; THis, thin

ŬT
abut
astrut
besmut
betel-nut
but
butt
catgut
clear-cut
coconut
crut
cut
glut
gut
halibut
hut
jut
Lilliput
McNutt
mutt
nut
occiput
outshut
peanut
putt
rebut
rut
scut
scuttle-butt
shut
slut
smut
strut
surrebut
tut
uncut
waterbutt
woodcut

ŪTH
besmooth

booth
polling-booth
smooth
soothe

Ūth
booth
Duluth
forsooth
insooth
ruth
sleuth
sooth
tooth
truth
uncouth
untooth
untruth
youth

Ŭth
doth

ŪTHD
unsoothed
smoothed, etc.

ŪTS
cahoots
boots, etc.

ŬTS
smuts
(see ŬT + s)

ŪV
amove
approve
behoove
disapprove
disprove

groove
improve
ingroove
move
prove
remove
reprove
you've

ŬV
above
belove
dove
foxglove
glove
lady-love
light-o'-love
love
mourning-dove
self-love
shove
true-love
turtle-dove
unglove

ŪVD
unimproved
unmoved
unproved
unreproved
approved, etc.

ŬVD
unbeloved
unloved
beloved, etc.

ŪZ
abuse
accuse
amuse

bemuse
Betelgeuse
blues
booze
bruise
choose
circumfuse
confuse
contuse
cruise
cruse
diffuse
disabuse
disuse
effuse
enthuse
excuse
fuse
guze
Hughes
incuse
infuse
interfuse
lose
mews
misuse
muse
news
noose
ooze
percussion-fuse
perfuse
peruse
refuse
ruse
Santa Cruz
sea-ooze
snooze
suffuse
superinfuse

the blues	**ŪZ**	does	ill-used
transfuse	Chartreuse	doz.	misused
trews		fuzz	self-accused
use	**ŬZ**	Luz	abused, etc.
Vera Cruz		Uz	
who's	abuzz		**ŪZH**
whose	buzz	**ŪZD**	rouge
(see Ū + s)	coz	fused	Bruges

ōld, ôr, ŏdd, oil, fŏŏt, out; ūse, ûrn, ŭp; THis, thin

WORDS ACCENTED ON THE SYLLABLE BEFORE THE LAST: PENULTS; FEMININE RHYMES; DOUBLE RHYMES

A

For a discussion of words included under the accented vowels following, see the beginning of A rhymes in Section I.

Ā′ad
naiad

Ā′al
Baal
betrayal
defrayal
portrayal
surveyal

Ā′an
Biscayan

Ā′ans
abeyance
conveyance
purveyance
surveyance

Ā′ant
abeyant

Ā′ba
copaiba
Faba

Ă′ba
Kaaba

Ā′ban
Laban

ĂB′ard
(see ĂB′urd)

ĂB′as
Barabbas

ĂB′ath
Sabbath

Ā′be
Rabe

ĂB′er etc.
(see ĂB′ur, etc.)

ĂB′es
abbess

ĂB′est
blabbest
dabbest
drabbest
gabbest
grabbest

jabbest
stabbest

ĂB′eth
blabbeth
dabbeth
gabbeth
grabbeth
jabbeth
stabbeth

Ā′bez
Jabez
tabes
(cf. Ā′bi + s)

Ā′bi
Abey
baby
maybe

ĂB′i
abbey
Abbie
babby
cabby
crabby
dabby

drabby
flabby
gabby
grabby
rabbi
scabby
shabby
slabby
tabby

Ā′bi
kohl-rabi
tabi
Wahabi

ĂB′id
rabid
tabid

ĂB′ij
cabbage

ĂB′ik
decasyllabic
dissyllabic
hendecasylla-
bic
imparisyllabic

ale, câre, ădd, ärm, åsk; mē, hĕre, ĕnd; īce, ĭll;
256

monosyllabic
multisyllabic
octosyllabic
parisyllabic
polysyllabic
quadrisyllabic
syllabic
trisyllabic

ĀB'i!
labile
(cf. ĀB'l)

Ā'bin
Sabine

ĂB'ing
blabbing
cabbing
confabbing
dabbing
gabbing
jabbing
nabbing
slabbing
stabbing
taxicabbing

ĂB'it
cohabit
grab it
habit
inhabit
rabbet
rabbit
riding-habit

ĂB'jekt
abject

Ā'b'l
Abel

able
Abe'll
Babel
cable
disable
enable
fable
flabel
gable
label
Mabel
sable
stable
table
unable
unstable

ĂB"l
babble
bedabble
bedrabble
brabble
cabble
dabble
drabble
gabble
gibble-gabble
grabble
rabble
ribble-rabble
scabble
scrabble

Ā'blest
ablest
cablest, etc.

ĂB'lest
babblest
bedabblest
brabblest

dabblest
drabblest
gabblest
scrabblest

ĂB'let
tablet

ĂB'leth
cableth, etc.

ĂB'leth
babbleth
bedabbleth
brabbleth
dabbleth
drabbleth
gabbleth
grabbeth
scrabbleth

ĂB'li
babbly
dabbly
drably

ĂB'ling
babbling
bedabbling
bedrabbling
brabbling
cabbling
dabbling
drabbling
gabbling
grabbling
scrabbling

ĂB'lish
disestablish
establish

re-establish
stablish

Ā'blur
abler
disabler
enabler
fabler
stabler
tabler

ĂB'lur
babbler
bedrabbler
brabbler
cabbler
dabbler
drabbler
gabbler
grabbler
scabbler
scrabbler

Ā'bob
nabob

ĂB'ot
abbot
Abbott
Cabot
sabot

Ā'bra
candelabra

Ā'brak
day-break

ĂB'sens
absence

ĂB'sent
absent

Ā'bur
beggar-my-
 neighbor
belabor
caber
Gheber
labor
neighbor
saber
tabor

ĂB'ur
beslabber
blabber
bonny-clabber
dabber
grabber
jabber
knabber
nabber
slabber
stabber

ĀB'urd
unlabored
belabored, etc.

ĂB'urd
beslabbered
jabbered
scabbard
slabbered
tabard

ĂCH'el
Rachel
Vachel

ĂCH'el
hatchel
satchel

ĂCH'est
attachest
catchest
detachest
dispatchest
hatchest
latchest
matchest
patchest
scratchest
snatchest
thatchest
unlatchest

ĂCH'et
Bob Cratchet
hatchet
latchet
ratchet

ĂCH'eth
attacheth
batcheth
catcheth
detacheth
dispatcheth
hatcheth
latcheth
matcheth
patcheth
scratcheth
snatcheth
thatcheth
unlatched

ĂCH'ez
attaches
batches
catches
detaches
dispatches

hatches
latches
matches
Natchez
patches
scratches
snatches
thatches
unlatches

ĂCH'i
catchy
patchy
snatchy

ĂCH'ing
attaching
batching
catching
detaching
dispatching
hatching
latching
matching
patching
scratching
snatching
thatching
unlatching

ĂCH'les
matchless
patchless
scratchless
thatchless

ĂCH'ment
attachment
catchment
detachment
dispatchment

hatchment
ratchment

ĂCH'up
catchup

ĂCH'ur
attacher
back-scratcher
body-snatcher
catcher
cony-catcher
detacher
dispatcher
fly-catcher
hatcher
matcher
patcher
scratcher
snatcher
Thacher
thatcher
unlatcher

ĂCH'wa
hatchway

ĂCH'wurk
catchwork
patchwork

Ā'dā
hey-day
lay-day
May-day
pay-day
play-day

Ā'dȧ
Ada
armada

---

cicada	aided	heavy-laden	*madest*
Grenada	ambuscaded	laden	*over-persuadest*
Maida	barricaded	maiden	*persuadest*
Veda	bejaded	menhaden	*pervadest*
Zayda	blockaded	mermaiden	staidest
	braided	milkmaiden	*tradest*
ĂD'a	brocaded	overladen	*upbraidest*
dada	cannonaded	sea-maiden	*wadest*
	degraded	serving-maiden	
ĂD'a	dissuaded	underladen	**ĂD'est**
armada	evaded	unladen	*addest*
cicada	faded		baddest
Dada	graded	**ĂD'en**	*gaddest*
Granada	invaded	engladden	gladdest
Grenada	jaded	gladden	maddest
haggada	masqueraded	McFadden	*paddest*
Nevada	persuaded	madden	saddest
posada	pervaded	Macfadden	
Sierra Nevada	raided	sadden	**ĂD'eth**
	serenaded		*aideth*
ĂD'am	shaded	**ĂD'en**	*bejadeth*
Adam	traded	Aden	*braideth*
madam	unaided		*degradeth*
McAdam	unbraided	**ĀD'ens**	*dissuadeth*
	unfaded	cadence	*evadeth*
ĀD'ans, ĀD'ens	unshaded	(see ĀD'ans)	*fadeth*
aidance	upbraided		*invadeth*
cadence	waded	**ĀD'ent**	*madeth*
decadence		cadent	*over-per-*
	ĂD'ed	(see ĀD'ant)	*suadeth*
ĀD'ant, ĀD'ent	added		*persuadeth*
abradant	padded	**ĀD'est**	*pervadeth*
aidant	plaided	*abradest*	*raideth*
cadent	superadded	*aidest*	*serenadeth*
decadent		*bejadest*	*spadeth*
	ĀD'en	*braidest*	*tradeth*
ĂD'kap	Aden	*degradest*	*upbraideth*
madcap	Aidenn	*dissuadest*	*wadeth*
	bower-maiden	*evadest*	
ĀD'ed	dairy-maiden	*fadest*	**ĂD'eth**
abraded	handmaiden	*invadest*	*addeth*

ōld, ôr, ŏdd, oil, fŏŏt, out; ūse, ûrn, ŭp; THis, thin

gladdeth
paddeth

ĀD'ez
Hades
(cf. ĀD'its)

ĀD'ful
gladful
madful
sadful, etc.

Ā'di
belady
Brady
braidy
cadi
cascady
fady
glady
Grady
lady
landlady
Maidie
O'Grady
shady

ĂD'i
caddie
caddy
daddy
faddy
finnan haddie
laddie
paddy
plaidie
sugar daddy

Ă'di
cadi
irade

Mahdi
wadi

ĂD'ij
adage

ĂD'ik
decadic
dyadic
faradic
haggadic
monadic
nomadic
Sotadic
sporadic
tetradic
triadic
vanadic

ĀD'ing
abrading
aiding
ambuscading
barricading
bejading
blockading
braiding
brocading
cascading
co-aiding
crusading
degrading
dissuading
enfilading
evading
fading
free-trading
gasconading
grading
invading
jading

lading
masquerading
overlading
over-persuad-
    ing
parading
persuading
pervading
raiding
retrograding
serenading
shading
spading
trading
unbraiding
underaiding
unlading
upbraiding
wading

ĂD'ing
adding
gadding
gladding
madding
padding
superadding

ĂD'is
Addis
caddis

ĀD'ish
maidish
mermaidish
oldmaidish
staidish

ĂD'ish
baddish
caddish

faddish
gladdish
maddish
radish
saddish

ĂD'it
adit

ĀD'iz
ladies, etc.

ĂD'iz
caddies, etc.

ĂD'jet
gadget
Padgett

ĀD"l
cradle
encradle
ladle

ĂD"l
addle
astraddle
bestraddle
daddle
faddle
fiddle-faddle
paddle
raddle
saddle
skedaddle
spraddle
staddle
straddle
unsaddle

ĀD'les
aidless

barricadeless
bladeless
braidless
brigadeless
brocadeless
fadeless
gradeless
maidless
paradeless
serenadeless
shadeless
spadeless
tradeless

ĂD′li

gradely
retrogradely
staidly

ĂD′li

badly
Bradley
gladly
madly
sadly

ĀD′ling

cradling
encradling
ladling

ĂD′ling

addling
daddling
faddling
fiddle-faddling
paddling
raddling
saddling
skedaddling
straddling

spraddling
unsaddling

ĂD′lok

padlock

ĂD′lur

addler
daddler
faddler
fiddle-faddler
paddler
raddler
saddler
skedaddler
straddler

ĂD′man

Cadman

ĂD′mus

Cadmus

ĂD′ne

Ariadne

ĀD′nes

staidness
unstaidness

ĂD′nes

badness
gladness
madness
plaidness
sadness

Ā′do

ambuscado
barricado
bastinado

camisado
carbonado
crusado
dado
desperado
fumado
gambado
grenado
muscovado
renegado
scalado
stoccado
strappado
tornado

ĂD′o

foreshadow
overshadow
shadow

Ä′do

amontillado
amorado
avocado
bravado
Colorado
dado
desperado
El Dorado
imbrocado
Mikado
passado
pintado
stoccado
strappado
travado

ĂD′od

foreshadowed
overshadowed

shadowed
unshadowed

ĂD′ok

haddock
paddock
raddocke
shaddock

ĂD′on

Abaddon

ĀD′os

extrados
intrados

ĂD′pol

tadpole

ĂD′som

gladsome
madsome

ĀD′ur

aider
barricader
blockader
braider
crusader
degrader
dissuader
evader
free-trader
gasconader
grader
harquebusader
invader
nadir
over-persuader
parader
persuader

ōld, ôr, ŏdd, oil, fŏŏt, out; ūse, ûrn, ŭp; THis, thin

promenader	delayest	betrayeth	**Ā′far**
raider	dismayest	bewrayeth	Mayfair
serenader	disobeyest	brayeth	Playfair
trader	displayest	conveyeth	
unbraider	essayest	decayeth	**Ā′feld**
upbraider	flayest	defrayeth	Mayfield
wader	frayest	delayeth	Rayfield
	gainsayest	dismayeth	
ĂD′ur	gayest	disobeyeth	**ĂF′est**
adder	grayest	displayeth	chafest
bladder	greyest	essayeth	safest
gadder	inlayest	frayeth	vouchafest
gladder	inveighest	gainsayeth	
ladder	layest	inlayeth	**ĂF′eth**
madder	mislayest	inveigheth	chafeth
padder	missayest	layeth	Japheth
sadder	obeyest	mislayeth	vouchsafeth
step-ladder	overpayest	missayeth	
	overstayest	obeyeth	**ĂF′gan**
Ă′dur	payest	overpayeth	Afghan
cadre	playest	overstayeth	
	portrayest	payeth	**ĂF′i**
ĂD′us	prayest	playeth	baffy
gradus	preyest	portrayeth	chaffy
	purveyest	prayeth	daffy
ĂD′vent	repayest	preyeth	draffy
advent	sayest	purveyeth	taffy
	slayest	repayeth	
ĂD′vurb	sprayest	sayeth	**ĂF′ik**
adverb	stayest	slayeth	anaglypto-
	surveyest	stayeth	graphic
Ā′est	swayest	strayeth	autobiographic
allayest	underpayest	surveyeth	autographic
arrayest	uplayest	swayeth	bibliographic
assayest	waylayest	underpayeth	biographic
bayest	weighest	uplayeth	cacographic
betrayest		waylayeth	calligraphic
bewrayest	**Ā′eth**	weigheth	cartographic
brayest	allayeth		cinemato-
conveyest	arrayeth	**ĂF′a**	graphic
defrayest	assayeth	café	chirographic

choregraphic
chorographic
clinographic
cosmographic
cryptographic
crystallo-
  graphic
diagraphic
epigraphic
epitaphic
ethnographic
galvanographic
geographic
glyptographic
graphic
heliographic
heterographic
hierographic
historiographic
holographic
homolographic
horologio-
  graphic
hydrographic
hyetographic
ichnographic
ideographic
idiographic
lexicographic
lexigraphic
lichenographic
lithographic
logographic
maffick
monographic
orographic
orthographic
paleographic
pantographic
paragraphic
pasigraphic

petrographic
phonographic
photographic
polygraphic
pornographic
Sapphic
scenographic
sciagraphic
seismographic
selenographic
seraphic
siderographic
sphenographic
stenographic
stereographic
stratigraphic
stratographic
stylographic
tachygraphic
telegraphic
topographic
traffic
uranographic
xylographic
zincographic
zoographic

ĀF′ing
chafing
enchafing
vouchsafing

ĂF′ing
chaffing
gaffing
graffing
heliographing
lithographing
paragraphing
photographing

stenographing
telegraphing

ĂF′ing
laughing
quaffing
strafing

ĂF′ir
sapphire

ĂF′ish
raffish

ĂF″l
baffle
gaffle
haffle
raffle
scraffle
snaffle
yaffle

ĀF′li
safely
unsafely

ĂF′ling
baffling
haffling
raffling
scraffling
snaffling

ĂF′lur
baffler
haffler
raffler
scraffler

ĂF′ne
Daphne

ĂF′old
Saffold
scaffold
(cf. baffled,
  etc.)

ĂF′ral
taffrail

ĂF′rik
Afric

ĂF′ron
saffron

ĂF′som
laughsome

ĂF′ted
upwafted
wafted

ĂF′ted
drafted
engrafted
grafted
ingrafted
rafted
shafted
wafted

ĂF′test
daftest
draughtest
graftest
waftest

ĂF′teth
draughteth
grafteth
wafteth

ōld, ôr, ŏdd, oil, fŏŏt, out; ūse, ûrn, ŭp; THis, thin

ĂFT'hors
draft-horse
shaft-horse

ĀF'ti
safety

ĂF'ti
crafty
drafty
grafty

ĂF'tij
waftage

ĂF'ting
engrafting
drafting
grafting
hafting
rafting
shafting
wafting

ĂFT'les
craftless
draftless
graftless
raftless
shaftless

ĂF'ton
Afton
Grafton

ĂFTS'man
craftsman
draftsman
handicraftsman
raftsman

ĂF'tūr
wafture

ĂF'tŭr
after
dafter
drafter
grafter
hafter
hereafter
hereinafter
laughter
rafter
thereafter
wafter

Ā'ful
playful
trayful

Ā'fur
chafer
cockchafer
safer
wafer

ĂF'ur
Kaffir
zaffer

ĂF'ur
chaffer
gaffer
graffer
laugher
quaffer

ĂF'urd
Safford
Stafford
Trafford

ĀG'a
plaga
rutabaga
saga

ĂG'a
aga
quagga

Ä'ga
aga
saga

ĀG'al
plagal
vagal

ĀG'an
Hagan
pagan
O'Hagan
Regan

ĂG'ard
haggard
laggard
staggard
staggered
swaggered

ĂG'art
braggart
Taggart

ĂG'at
agate
moss-agate
(cf. faggot, etc.)

ĂG'ed
cragged

jagged
ragged
scragged

ĂG'end
fag-end
lagend

ĀG'est
plaguest
vaguest

ĂG'est
braggest
draggest
faggest
flaggest
gaggest
laggest
naggest
waggest

ĂG'eth
braggeth
draggeth
faggeth
flaggeth
gaggeth
laggeth
naggeth
raggeth
waggeth

ĂG'i
Aggie
baggy
braggy
craggy
faggy
flaggy
gaggy

jaggy
knaggy
laggy
Maggie
naggy
quaggy
raggy
saggy
scraggy
shaggy
slaggy
snaggy
swaggy
taggy
waggy

ĂG'ij

baggage

ĂG'ing

bagging
bragging
dragging
fagging
flagging
gagging
lagging
magging
nagging
ragging
sagging
tagging
unflagging
wagging

ĂG'is

haggis

ĂG'ish

haggish
iaggish

naggish
waggish

ĂG'l

bedaggle
bedraggle
daggle
draggle
gaggle
haggle
raggle
raggle-taggle
straggle
waggel
waggle

ĂG'ling

bedaggling
bedraggling
daggling
draggling
gaggling
haggling
raggling
straggling
waggling

ĂG'lur

bedraggler
daggler
draggler
haggler
straggler
waggler

ĂG'mag

cagmag

ĂG'man

bagman
dragman

flagman
ragman

ĂG'ment

fragment

ĂG'mir

quagmire

ĂG'mit

stalagmite

ĂG'nant

stagnant

ĂG'nat

agnate
magnate
stagnate

ĂG'nes

Agnes

ĂG'net

magnet

ĂG'num

magnum

Ā'go

farrago
imago
lumbago
plumbago
sago
San Diego
Terra del
  Fuego
Tobago
virago
vorago

Ă'go

farrago
Chicago
Santiago

ĂG'on

dragon
flagon
pendragon
snap-dragon
wagon

ĂG'ot

fagot
maggot
magot
(cf. agate)

ĂG'pi

magpie

ĂG'pip

bagpipe

ĂG'rans

flagrance
fragrance
(cf. vagrants)

ĂG'rant

flagrant
fragrant
infragrant
vagrant

ĂG'rik

chiragric
podagric

Ā'gu

ague

ĀG′ur
maigre
plaguer
vaguer

ĂG′ur
bagger
bragger
carpet-bagger
dagger
dragger
fagger
flagger
four-bagger
gagger
jagger
lagger
magger
nagger
one-bagger
ragger
sagger
stagger
swagger
tagger
three-bagger
two-bagger
wagger

Ā′gus
archimagus
choragus
magus

ĂGZ′man
cragsman
dragsman

Ă′hoo
wahoo
yahoo

Ā′i
clayey
sprayey
wheyey

Ă′ib
sahib

Ā′ij
drayage
weighage

Ā′ik
alcaic
algebraic
alhambraic
altaic
ante-Mosaic
Aramaic
archaic
Brahmaic
Chaldaic
Cyrenaic
deltaic
Eddaic
Hebraic
Jagataic
Judaic
laic
mosaic
paradisaic
pharisaic
prosaic
Ptolemaic
Passaic
Romaic
saddusaic
Sinaic
sodaic
spondaic
stanzaic

tesseraic
trochaic
voltaic

Ā′ing
allaying
amaying
arraying
assaying
baying
belaying
betraying
bewraying
braying
claying
conveying
decaying
defraying
delaying
disarraying
dismaying
disobeying
displaying
essaying
flaying
foresaying
fraying
gainsaying
haying
horseplaying
hurraying
inlaying
interlaying
interplaying
inveighing
laying
maying
mislaying
missaying
neighing
obeying

outlaying
outstaying
outweighing
overlaying
overpaying
overstaying
paying
playing
portraying
praying
prepaying
preying
purveying
relaying
repaying
saying
slaying
soothsaying
spraying
staying
surveying
swaying
undecaying
underpaying
underplaying
unsaying
unweighing
waylaying
weighing

Ā′is
dais
Lais

Ā′ish
clayish
gayish
grayish
greyish
silver-grayish

Ā′ist
algebraist
archaist
prosaist
Ptolemaist

Ā′izm
Chaldaism
Laism
Mosaism
prosaism

Ă′ja
maharajah
rajah

ĂJ′ant
pageant

ĀJ′ed
aged

Ā′jent
agent
reagent

ĀJ′est
agest
assuagest
engagest
enragest
gagest
gaugest
outragest
presagest
ragest
sagest
stagest
swagest
wagest

ĀJ′eth
ageth
assuageth
engageth
enrageth
gageth
gaugeth
outrageth
presageth
rageth
wageth

ĀJ′ez
ages
assuages
cages
disengages
encages
engages
enrages
gages
gauges
greengages
outrages
pages
pre-engages
presages
rages
sages
stages
wages
weather-gages

Ā′ji
cagey
ragy
sagy
stagy

ĂJ′i
cadgy

hadji
howadji

ĂJ′ik
archipelagic
ellagic
hemorrhagic
magic
omophagic
pelagic
tragic

ĂJ′il
agile
fragile

ĂJ′in
imagine

ĀJ′ind
imagined
unimagined

ĀJ′ing
aging
assuaging
caging
engaging
enraging
gaging
gauging
paging
presaging
raging
staging

ĂJ′ing
badging
cadging

ĀJ′les
ageless

cageless
gageless
gaugeless
pageless
rageless
sageless
stageless
wageless

ĀJ′li
sagely

ĀJ′ling
cageling

ĀJ′ment
assuagement
encagement
engagement
enragement
pre-engagement
presagement

ĀJ′nes
sageness

ĀJ′ur
assuager
cager
disengager
engager
enrager
gager
gauger
major
old-stager
pager
presager
sager
stager

trumpet-major
wager

ĂJ′ur
agger
badger
cadger

ĀJ′us
advantageous
ambagious
contagious
courageous
disadvanta-
  geous
oragious
outrageous
rampageous
umbrageous

Ä′ka
raca
Jamaica

ĂK′a
alpaca
Malacca
polacca

Ä′ka
jararaca

ĂK′al
jackal
pack-all

ĂK′ard
placard

ĂK′at
baccate

placate
saccate

ĂK′brand
crack-brained
slack-brained

ĂK′but
hackbut
sackbut

ĂK′daw
jackdaw

ĂK′doun
breakdown
shakedown

ĂK′ed
naked
(see ĀK + ed)

ĂK′en
awaken
bacon
forsaken
Jamaican
kraken
mistaken
overtaken
shaken
taken
undertaken
uptaken
waken
wind-shaken

ĂK′en
blacken
bracken
slacken

Ä′ken
kraken

ĂK′end
unawakened
awakened, etc.

ĀK′est
achest
awakest
bakest
betakest
breakest
fakest
forsakest
makest
mistakest
opaquest
overtakest
partakest
quakest
rakest
shakest
spakest
stakest
takest
undertakest
wakest

ĂK′est
attackest
backest
blackest
clackest
crackest
hackest
lackest
packest
quackest
rackest
ransackest

sackest
slackest
smackest
tackest
trackest
unpackest
whackest

ĂK′et
bracket
flacket
Hackett
jacket
packet
placket
racket
tacket

ĀK′eth
acheth
awaketh
baketh
betaketh
breaketh
faketh
forsaketh
maketh
mistaketh
overtaketh
partaketh
quaketh
raketh
shaketh
staketh
taketh
undertaketh
waketh

ĂK′eth
attacketh
backeth

blacketh
clacketh
cracketh
hacketh
lacketh
packeth
quacketh
racketh
ransacketh
sacketh
slacketh
smacketh
tacketh
tracketh
unpacketh
whacketh

ĀK'ful
wakeful

ĀK'i
achey
braky
caky
faky
flaky
quaky
shaky
snaky

ĂK'i
blackey
cracky
knacky
lackey

Ä'ki, Â'ki
sake
saki

ĀK'ij
breakage

ĂK'ij
package
sackage
stackage
trackage
wrackage

ĂK'ik
bacchic
stomachic

ĂK'sen
vaccine

ĀK'ing
aching
awaking
baking
betaking
braking
breaking
caking
faking
flaking
forsaking
heartbreaking
making
mistaking
overtaking
partaking
quaking
raking
shaking
slaking
spaking
staking
taking
undertaking
unmaking
upbreaking

uptaking
waking

ĂK'ing
attacking
backing
bivouacing
blacking
clacking
cracking
hacking
knacking
lacking
packing
quacking
racking
ransacking
sacking
slacking
smacking
tacking
thwacking
tracking
unpacking

ĀK'ish
rakish
snakish

ĂK'ish
blackish
brackish
knackish
quackish

ĂK'kloth
packcloth
sackcloth

ĂK''l
cackle

crackle
grackle
hackle
macle
quackle
ramshackle
shackle
tackle

ĂK''ld
unshackled
cackled, etc.

ĂK'les
knackless
sackless
trackless

ĀK'let
lakelet

ĂK'li
blackly
cackly
crackly
shackly
tackly

ĂK'ling
cackling
crackling
hackling
shackling
tackling

ĂK'log
backlog
hacklog

ĂK'lur
cackler

crackler
hackler
shackler
tackler

ĂK'man
blackman
jackman
packman

ĂK'me
acme

ĂK'nes
blackness
slackness

ĂK'ne
acne
hackney

ĀK'ning
wakening

Ā'ko
Saco
Waco

ĂK'o
goracco
shako
Sacco
tobacco

Ä'ko
guaco
guanaco
Gran Chaco

ĀK'of
take-off

Ā'kob
Jacob

ĀK'on
bacon
Lacon
Macon
(see ĀK'en)

Ā'korn
acorn

ĂP'pot
crackpot
jackpot

ĀK'red
sacred

ĂK'rid
acrid

ĀK'ring
sacring

ĀK'rist
sacrist

ĀK'rum
sacrum
simulacrum

ĂK'sent
accent

ĂK'ses
access

ĂK'shun
abstraction
action

arefaction
assuefaction
attraction
benefaction
calefaction
coaction
compaction
contaction
contraction
counteraction
counter-
  attraction
detraction
dissatisfaction
distraction
exaction
extraction
faction
fraction
inaction
infraction
interaction
labefaction
liquefaction
lubrifaction
madefaction
malefaction
paction
petrifaction
protraction
putrefaction
rarefaction
reaction
redaction
refraction
retraction
retroaction
rubefaction
satisfaction
stupefaction
subaction

subtraction
tabefaction
taction
tepefaction
torrefaction
traction
transaction
tumefaction

ĂK'shus
factious
fractious

ĂK'sez
axes
battle-axes
relaxes
taxes
waxes
Maxie's

ĂK'si
biotaxy
braxy
Cotopaxi
flaxy
heterotaxy
homotaxy
taxi
waxy

ĂK'sid
flaccid

ĂK'sim
maxim

ĂK'sis
axis
praxis

synaxis	contracted	*distracteth*	retractile
taxis	counteracted	*enacteth*	tactile
	detracted	*exacteth*	tractile
ĂK"sl	distracted	*extracteth*	
axle	enacted	*protracteth*	**ĂK'ting**
	exacted	*reacteth*	abstracting
ĂK'sman	extracted	*retracteth*	acting
cracksman	overacted	*subtracteth*	attracting
tacksman	protracted	*transacteth*	contracting
	reacted		counteracting
ĂK'son	refracted	**ĂKT'ful**	detracting
Anglo-Saxon	retracted	tactful	distracting
caxon	subtracted		double-acting
flaxen	transacted	**ĂK'tik**	enacting
Jackson	unacted	catallactic	exacting
klaxon	underacted	didactic	infracting
Saxon		emphractic	overacting
waxen	**ĂK'test**	eupractic	protracting
	abstractest	galactic	reacting
ĂK'sta	*actest*	lactic	refracting
backstay	*attractest*	parallactic	retracting
jack-stay	*contractest*	prophylactic	retroacting
	counteractest	protactic	self-acting
ĂK'ston	*detractest*	stalactic	subtracting
Braxton	*distractest*	syntactic	transacting
Caxton	*enactest*	tactic	underacting
Claxton	exactest		
	extractest	**ĂK'tiks**	**ĂK'tis**
ĂK'swell	*protractest*	catallactics	practice
Maxwell	*reactest*	tactics	
	retractest		**ĂK'tit**
ĂK'tat	*subtractest*	**ĂK'til**	stalactite
ablactate	*transactest*	attractile	
lactate		contractile	**ĂK'tiv**
tractate	**ĂK'teth**	dactyl	abstractive
	abstracteth	didactyl	active
ĂK'ted	*acteth*	heterodactyl	attractive
abstracted	*attracteth*	leptodactyl	calefactive
acted	*contracteth*	pachydactyl	coactive
attracted	*counteracteth*	protractile	contractive
compacted	*detracteth*	pterodactyl	counteractive

ōld, ôr, ŏdd, oil, fŏŏt, out; ūse, ûrn, ŭp; THis, thin

counter-
    attractive
detractive
diffractive
distractive
enactive
extractive
inactive
liquefactive
olfactive
petrifactive
protractive
putrefactive
radioactive
rarefactive
reactive
refractive
retractive
retroactive
satisfactive
stupefactive
subtractive
tractive

ĂKT′les

actless
bractless
factless
tactless
tractless

ĂKT′li

compactly
exactly
matter-of-factly

ĂKT′ment

enactment
extractment
reenactment

ĂKT′nes

compactness
exactness
intactness

ĂK′to

de facto
ex post facto

ĂK′tres

actress
benefactress
contractress
detractress
exactress
factress
malefactress

ĂK′tūr

facture
fracture
manufacture
vitrifacture

ĂK′tūr

abstracter
actor
attracter
benefactor
climacter
compacter
contractor
detractor
distracter
enactor
exacter
extractor
factor
infractor
malefactor
olfactor

phylacter
protractor
refractor
retractor
subtracter
tractor
transactor

ĂK′tus

cactus

ĀK′up

break-up
make-up
wake-up

ĀK′ur

acre
awaker
baker
ballad-maker
bookmaker
breaker
dressmaker
faker
fakir
forsaker
God's-acre
heart-breaker
image-breaker
maker
match-maker
mischief-maker
mistaker
nacre
painstaker
partəker
peacemaker
Quaker
raker

Sabbath-
    breaker
shaker
taker
truce-breaker
undertaker
watchmaker

ĂK′ur

attacker
backer
blacker
bushwhacker
clacker
cracker
hacker
hijacker
knacker
lacker
lacquer
nut-cracker
packer
racker
ransacker
sacker
slacker
smacker
tacker
tracker
unpacker
whacker

ĀK′urz

breakers
awakers, etc.

ĂK′us

Bacchus
Flaccus
jacchus

ĂK'wa
backway
pack-way
trackway

Ā'kwen
fay-queen
May-queen

ĂK'woodz
backwoods

Ā'la
gala
shillalah

ĂL'a
Allah
calla
galla
mashallah
Valhalla

Ā'la
gala

ĂL'ad
ballad
salad

ĂL'ans
balance
counter-
  balance
outbalance
overbalance
valance

ĂL'anst
balanced
outbalanced

overbalanced
unbalanced

ĀL'ant
assailant
exhalent
inhalent
intranscalent
transcalent

Ā'lanks
phalanx

ĂL'ard
Allard
Ballard
Callard
mallard

ĂL'as
balas
Dallas
palace
Pallas
(cf. chalice)

ĂL'ast
ballast

ĂL'bum
album

ĂL'burd
jailbird

ĂL'burt
Albert

ĂL'dik
heraldic

ĂL'din
Aldine

Ă'le
finale
kali
pastorale

Ā'leb
Caleb

ĂL'ek
Aleck
Halleck
smart Aleck
Talleck

ĂL'en
Alan
Allen

ĂL'enj
challenge

ĂL'enjd
challenged
unchallenged

ĀL'ens
valence

ĂL'ent
gallant
talent
ungallant

Ā'les
clayless
dayless
hayless
payless

playless
preyless
rayless
sprayless
wayless

ĀL'est
ailest
assailest
availest
bailest
balest
bewailest
curtailest
derailest
detailest
engaolest
entailest
exhalest
failest
frailest
hailest
halest
impalest
inhalest
mailest
nailest
outsailest
palest
prevailest
quailest
railest
regalest
retailest
sailest
scalest
trailest
unveilest
wailest

ōld, ôr, ŏdd, oil, fŏŏt, out; ūse, ûrn, ŭp; THis, thin

ĂL'et
gallet
mallet
palate
palette
pallet
sallet
valet

ĂL'eth
aileth
assaileth
availeth
baileth
baleth
bewaileth
curtaileth
deraileth
detaileth
engaoleth
entaileth
exhaleth
haileth
impaleth
inhaleth
naileth
outsaileth
paleth
prevaileth
quaileth
raileth
regaleth
retaileth
saileth
scaleth
traileth
unveileth
veileth
waileth

Ā'lez or Ă'lez
   or Ä'lez
Gonzales

ĂL'fa
alfalfa
alpha

ĂL'fred
Alfred

ĂL'ful
baleful
pailful
wailful

ĂL'gam
amalgam

Ā'li
Bailey
bailie
Braley
capercaillie
daily
Daly
gaily
Haley
kali
Mailly
Maley
rationale
shaly
shillaly
ukelele
vale
(cf. palely,
   etc.)

ĂL'i
alley
Allie

Aunt Sally
bally
dally
dilly-dally
galley
Hallie
kali
Lallie
O'Malley
rally
Sallie
sally
shilly-shally
tally
tomalley
valley
(see estatically,
   and all other
   -a l l y adjec-
   tives, ĂL +
   i)

ĂL'id
dallied
dilly-dallied
impallid
invalid
pallid
rallied
sallied
shilly-shallied
tallied
valid

ĂL'if
bailiff
Caliph

ĂL'ij
bailage
curtailage
retailage

ĂL'ik
Gaelic
malic
Salic

ĂL'ik
acrocephalic
bimetallic
brachisto-
   cephalic
brachycephalic
cephalic
dolichocephalic
encephalic
eurycephalic
Gallic
grallic
italic
macrencephalic
macrocephalic
malic
medallic
mesocephalic
metallic
microcephalic
monometallic
oxalic
phallic
platycephalic
salic
thallic
Uralic
Vandalic
vocalic

ĂL'ik
pashalik

ĂL'iks
calyx
Salix

ÄL'in or **ÄL'in**
Stalin

ĀL'ing
ailing
assailing
availing
bailing
baling
bewailing
blackmailing
countervailing
curtailing
derailing
detailing
empaling
entailing
exhaling
grayling
Greyling
hailing
haling
impaling
inhaling
jailing
mailing
nailing
outsailing
paling
prevailing
quailing
railing
regaling
retailing
sailing
scaling
Schmeling
tailing
trailing
unveiling

veiling
wailing
whaling
wholesaling

ÄL'ing
caballing
palling

ÄL'is
Alice
allice
chalice
Challis
malice
(cf. palace)

ÄL'is
Cornwallis

ĀL'ish
palish
shalish
stalish

ĂL'ji
cephalalgy
neuralgy
nostalgy
odontalgy

ĂL'jik
antalgic
cephalalgic
neuralgic
nostalgic
odontalgic

ĀL'kar
mailcar
railcar

ÄL'kat
defalcate
falcate

ĂL'kin
grimalkin

ÄL'ker
valkyr

ĀL'li
frailly
halely
palely
stalely
(cf. ĀL'i)

ĂL'ma
Alma
Thalma

ĂL'mat
palmate

ĀL'ment
ailment
assailment
availment
bailment
bewailment
curtailment
derailment
entailment
impalement
inhalement
prevailment
regalement
retailment

ĂL'mud
Talmud

ÄL'muk
Kalmuck

ĀL'nes
frailness
haleness
paleness
staleness

Ā'lo
halo

ĀL'o
All-hallow
aloe
callow
dishallow
fallow
hallow
mallow
marshmallow
sallow
shallow
summer-fallow
tallow
unhallow

ĂL'o
swallow
wallow
(see Ŏ'lo)

ĂL'on
gallon
talon

ÅL'on
salon

ĂL'op
gallop

jalap
scallop
shallop

ĂL'ot
ballot

ĂL'oz
gallows
hallows, etc.

ĂL'pin
Alpine
cisalpine
transalpine

ĂL'ping
scalping

ĀL'spin
tailspin

ĀL'ti
frailty

ĂL'to
alto
contralto

ĂL'to
rialto

ĂL'u
undervalue
value

ĂL'um
alum

ĀL'ūr
failure

ĀL'ŭr
assailer
bailer
baler
bewailer
curtailer
derailer
detailer
entailer
failer
frailer
gaoler
haler
impaler
inhaler
jailer
nailer
paler
prevailer
quailer
railer
regaler
retailer
sailer
sailor
Sayler
scaler
squalor
staler
tailor
Taylor
trailer
unveiler
wailer
whaler

ĂL'ur
caballer
pallor
valor

ĂL'us
callous
gallus

ĂL'va
Alva
Alvah
Halveh

ĂL'vij
salvage

ĂL'vin
Alvin
Calvin

ĂL'vo
salvo

ĂL'vur
quack-salver
salver
salvor

ĂL'vurt
Calvert

ĂL'win
Alwin

ĀL'ya
Bacchanalia
castalia
dahlia
mammalia
marginalia
paraphernalia
penetralia
regalia
saturnalia
terminalia
(cf. azalea)

ĂL'ya
dahlia

ĂL'ya
dahlia

ĀL'yan
alien
Australian
bacchanalian
Dædalian
episcopalian
Idalian
mammalian
marsupialian
Messalian
paralian
phantasmalian
Phigalian
Pygmalion
regalian
saturnalian
sesquipedalian
tenaillon
tobaccanalian
universalian

ĂL'yant
valiant

ĀL'yard
gaolyard
kailyard

ĂL'yo
intaglio
seraglio

ĂL'yon
battalion
Italian
medallion
rapscallion
rascallion
scallion
stallion

ĀLZ'man
dalesman
salesman
talesman
whalesman

ĂM'a
Bahama
krama

ĂM'a
Alabama
digamma
mamma

ĂM'a
Bahama
Brahma
cyclorama
cosmorama
Dalai Lama
diorama
drama
Fujiyama
georama
kaama
Kama
lama
llama
mamma
melodrama
neorama

panorama
pajama
pyjama
Rama
Teshu Lama
Yama
Yokohama

Ā'man
cayman
dayman
drayman
highwayman
layman

ĀM'ant
claimant
(cf. raiment, etc.)

ĂM'ant
clamant

ĂM'as
Lammas

ĂM'ask
damask

Ā'mat
day-mate
desquamate
hamate
playmate

ĂM'az
cat's pajamas
Brahmas, etc.

ĂM'ba
gamba

ĂM'bent
lambent

ĂM'bi
namby-pamby

ĂM'bik
choliambic
choriambic
dithyrambic
elegiambic
galliambic
iambic

ĂM'bist
cambist
gambist

ĂM'bit
ambit
gambit

ĂM'kin
lambkin

ĂM'b'l
amble
bramble
gamble
preamble
ramble
scamble
scramble
shamble
skimble-skamble

ĂM'blest
amblest
gamblest
ramblest

scramblest
shamblest

ĂM'bleth
ambleth
gambleth
rambleth
scrambleth
shambleth

ĂM'b'lz
ambles
gambles
rambles
scrambles
shambles

ĂM'bling
ambling
brambling
gambling
rambling
scambling
scrambling
shambling

ĂM'blur
ambler
gambler
rambler
scambler
scrambler
shambler

ĂM'bo
ambo
crambo
flambeau
sambo
zambo

ĂM′bol
gambol

ĂM′brik
cambric

ĂM′bur
ante-chamber
chamber

ĂM′būr
tambour

ĂM′bur
amber
camber
clamber

ĂM′bus
dithyrambus
iambus

ĂM′bush
ambush

ĂM′el
camel
Campbell
enamel
entrammel
Hamal
mammal
trammel

ĂM′eld
enamelled
untrammelled

Ā′men
amen
Bremen

examen
flamen
foramen
gravamen
Haman
Lehmann
stamen

Ä′men
amen

Ā′ment
allayment
betrayment
defrayment
payment
prepayment
raiment
(cf. claimant)

ĀM′est
acclaimest
aimest
blamest
claimest
declaimest
defamest
disclaimest
exclaimest
flamest
framest
gamest
inflamest
lamest
maimest
namest
proclaimest
reclaimest
shamest
tamest

ĂM′est
crammest
dammest
damnest
rammest
shammest
slammest

ÄM′est
calmest
embalmest
salaamest

ĀM′eth
acclaimeth
aimeth
blameth
claimeth
declaimeth
defameth
disclaimeth
exclaimeth
flameth
foreshameth
frameth
inflameth
lameth
maimeth
nameth
overcameth
proclaimeth
reclaimeth
shameth
tameth

ĂM′eth
crammeth
dammeth
damneth
rammeth

shammeth
slammeth

ÄM′eth
calmeth
embalmeth
salaameth

ĂM′fir
samphire

ĂM′flet
pamphlet

ĂM′for
camphor

ĀM′ful
blameful
flameful
shameful

ĀM′i
Amy
gamy
flamy
Mamie

ĂM′i
chamois
clammy
gammy
mammy
rammy
shammy
tammy

ÄM′i
balmy
calmy
Miami

palmy
pastrami
qualmy
salmi
swami

ÄM′ij
damage

ÄM′ik
Abrahamic
Adamic
adynamic
agamic
autodynamic
balsamic
biodynamic
ceramic
cinnamic
cosmoramic
cryptogamic
cycloramic
dioramic
dynamic
electro-
    dynamic
epithalamic
gamic
hydrodynamic
hyperdynamic
Islamic
isodynamic
keramic
monogamic
monogrammic
panoramic
parallelogram-
    mic
phanerogamic
polygamic
potamic

preadamic
telegrammic
trigrammic

ÄM′il
amyl
Tamil

ÄM′in
examine
famine
gamin

ĀM′ing
acclaiming
aiming
blaming
claiming
declaiming
defaming
disclaiming
exclaiming
flaming
framing
gaming
inflaming
laming
maiming
misnaming
naming
nicknaming
proclaiming
reclaiming
shaming
surnaming
taming

ÄM′ing
cramming
damming
damning

lambing
lamming
ramming
shamming
slamming
tramming

ÄM′ing
becalming
calming
embalming
qualming
salaaming

ÄM′is
amice
chlamys
tamis

ĀM′ish
lamish
tamish

ÄM′ish
affamish
enfamish
famish
Hamish
rammish

ÄM′ish
calmish
qualmish

ÄM′ist
embalmist
palmist
psalmist

ÄM′it
samite

ÄM′les
aimless
blameless
claimless
fameless
flameless
frameless
gameless
nameless
shameless
tameless

ÄM′les
balmless
palmless
psalmless
qualmless

ÄM′let
camlet
hamlet
samlet

ĀM′li
gamely
lamely
namely
tamely

ÄM′li
calmly

ÄM′ling
lambling

ÄM′ment
becalmment
embalmment

ĀM′nes
gameness

lameness
sameness
tameness

ĂM'nes
calmness

ĂM'ok
hammock
mammock

ĂM'on
Ammon
backgammon
daman
gammon
mammon
salmon
shaman

Ā'mond
Raymond

ĂM'ond
Hammond

Ā'mos
Amos
Shaemas

ĂM'oth
mammoth

ĂM'pan
jampan
sampan
tampan

ĂM'part
rampart

ĂM'paz
pampas

ĂM'pen
dampen

ĂM'per
ampere

ĂM'pest
campest
crampest
dampest
decampest
encampest
rampest
scampest
stampest
trampest
vampest

ĂM'peth
campeth
crampeth
dampeth
decampeth
encampeth
rampeth
scampeth
stampeth
trampeth
vampeth

ĂM'pi
crampy

ĂM'ping
camping
clamping
cramping
damping

decamping
encamping
lamping
ramping
scamping
stamping
tamping
tramping
vamping

ĂM'pir
vampire

ĂM'pish
dampish
scampish

ĂM'p'l
ample
ensample
example
sample
trample

ĂM'p'ld
untrampled
sampled, etc.

ĂMP'li
damply

ĂMP'ling
ensampling
sampling
trampling

ĂMP'lur
ampler
exampler
sampler
trampler

ĂMP'ment
decampment
encampment

ĂMP'nes
dampness

ĂM'pri
lamprey

ĂMP'son
Lampson
Sampson
(cf. Samson)

ĂMP'ton
Crampton
Hampton

ĂM'pur
camper
champer
clamper
cramper
damper
hamper
pamper
scamper
stamper
tamper
tramper
vamper

ĂM'purd
hampered
pampered
tampered
unhampered

ĂM'pus
campus
grampus

āle,   cåre,   ădd,   ärm,   åsk;   mē,   hĕre,   ĕnd;   īce,   ĭll;

ĂM'rod
ramrod

ĂM'rok
shamrock

ĀM'stur
gamester

ĂM'ond
almond
bitter-almond

ĀM'ur
acclaimer
aimer
blamer
claimer
declaimer
defamer
disclaimer
disfamer
exclaimer
framer
gamer
inflamer
Kramer
lamer
maimer
misnamer
namer
nicknamer
proclaimer
reclaimer
shamer
tamer
testamur

ĂM'ur
clamor
crammer

dammer
damner
enamor
gammer
glamor
grammar
hammer
ninnyhammer
rammer
shammer
slammer
sledge-hammer
stammer
yammer
yellow-hammer

ĂM'ur
Balmer
calmer
embalmer
palmer

ĂM'wa
tramway

ĀM'us
biramous
famous
hamous
ignoramus
mandamus
squamous

ĂM'ut
gamut

ĂM'zel
amsel
damsel

ĂM'zi
Malmsey

ĂM'zon
damson

Ā'na
Americana, etc
ana
anana
arcana
campana
Cartagena
Curtana
fistiana
Nicotiana
poinciana
scena
vox-humana

ĂN'a
Americana, etc.
anna
bandana
Christiana
Diana
fistiana
Georgiana
Hanna
Hannah
Havana
hosanna
Indiana
ipecacuanha
Joanna
Juliana
Louisiana
manna
Montana
Pollyanna
Roxana
savanna
Savannah
Stephana

Susanna
Susquehanna
sultana
Texarkana
Tia Juana
Urbana

Ăn'a
Americana, etc.
acqua tofana
anana
banana
Curtana
Fata Morgana
fistiana
Guiana
iguana
kerana
liana
Messana
Nirvana
purana
sultana
thana
zenana

Ā'nal
anal

ĂN'al
annal
cannel
channel
empanel
flannel
impanel
panel
pannel
scrannel
stannel
unpanel

ÄN'alz
annals
flannels, etc.

ÄN'ant
complainant

ÄN'at
impanate
lanate

ÄN'at
khanate
pomegranate
tannate

ÄN'at
khanate

ÄN'bo
rainbow

ÄN'chest
launchest
stanchest

ÄN'chest
blanchest
scranchest

ÄN'chet
manchet
planchet

ÄN'cheth
launcheth
stancheth

ÄN'cheth
blancheth
scrancheth

ÄN'chez
launches
paunches
stanches

ÄN'chez
avalanches
blanches
branches
ranches

ÄN'chi
paunchy

ÄN'chi
branchy

ÄN'ching
launching
stanching

ÄN'ching
blanching
branching
ranching

ÄN'chiz
affranchise
disfranchise
enfranchise
franchise

ÄNCH'les
launchless
paunchless

ÄNCH'les
branchless
ranchless
stanchless

ÄN'chur
launcher
stancher

ÄN'chur
brancher
rancher

ÄN'da
Amanda
jacaranda
Miranda
memoranda
propaganda
veranda

ÄN' dal
Randall
(cf. Randle)

ÄN'dant
commandant
demandant
mandant

ÄN'dat
mandate

ÄND'bag
handbag
sand-bag

ÄND'bal
hand-ball
sand-ball

ÄND'boi
band-boy
sand-boy

ÄND'boks
bandbox
sand-box

ÄND'child
grand-child

ÄN'de
Rio Grande

**ÄN'ded or
ÄN'ded**
backhanded
banded
blackhanded
branded
candid
clean-handed
close-handed
commanded
contrabanded
countermanded
demanded
deodanded
disbanded
empty-handed
even-handed
expanded
first-handed
forehanded
fourhanded
freehanded
full-handed
handed
hard-handed
heavy-handed
high-handed
landed
left-handed
light-handed
lily-handed
neat-handed
open-handed
over-handed
red-handed

āle,   câre,   ădd,   arm,   åsk;   mē,   hęre,   ĕnd;   īce,   ĭll;

remanded
reprimanded
right-handed
short-handed
single-handed
stranded
swift-handed
two-handed
unbranded
underhanded
unhanded
unlanded

ĂN′dent
candent
scandent

ĂN′der
reindeer

ĂN′dest or
  ÅN′dest
bandest
brandest
commandest
demandest
disbandest
expandest
grandest
handest
landest
remandest
reprimandest
standest
withstandest

ĂN′deth or
  ÅN′deth
bandeth
brandeth
commandeth
demandeth

disbandeth
expandeth
handeth
landeth
remandeth
reprimandeth
standeth
withstandeth

ĂN′dez
Andes
Hernandez

ĂND′fast
handfast

ĂN′di
Andy
bandy
brandy
candy
dandy
handy
jaborandi
jackadandy
Jim Dandy
Mandy
pandy
randy
Rio Grande
sandy
sugar-candy
unhandy

ĂN′did
bandied
brandied
candid
candied
uncandid
(cf. banded,
  p. 328)

ĂN′dij
bandage
glandage
standage

ĂN′ding or
  ÅN′ding
ampersanding
banding
branding
commanding
countermand-
  ing
demanding
disbanding
expanding
handing
landing
notwithstand-
  ing
outstanding
remanding
reprimanding
sanding
standing
stranding
understanding
withstanding

ĂN′dish
blandish
brandish
grandish
outlandish

ĂN′dist
contrabandist
propagandist

ĂN′dit
bandit

ĂN′d′l
candle
dandle
handle
sandal
scandal
vandal

ĂND′les or
  ÅND′les
bandless
brandless
commandless
glandless
handless
landless
sandless
strandless

ĂND′ling
brandling
handling

ĂND′lur
Candler
chandler
dandler
handler
tallow-chandler

ĂND′lord
landlord

ĂND′li
blandly
grandly

ĂND′mad
hand-made
handmaid

ĂND'mark
landmark

ĂND'ment or
ĂND'ment
commandment
disbandment
remandment

ĂND'nes
blandness
grandness

ĂN'do or
ÅN'do
commando
Ferdinando
Fernando
grando
Hernando
lentando
Orlando

ĂN'don
abandon
Landon
Shandon

ĂND'out
handout

ĂN'dra or
ÅN'dra
Alessandra
Alexandra
Cassandra

ĂN'drel
spandrel

ĂN'dres
pandress

ĂN'dres
laundress

ĂN'drik
polyandric
theandric

ĂN'dril
mandril

ĂN'drin
Alexandrine
salamandrine

ĂN'dri or
ÅN'dri
chandry
commandry
meandry
polyandry
shandry

ĂN'dri
laundry

ĂN'drus
meandrous
polyandrous

ĂND'sir
grandsire

ĂND'skap
landscape

ĂND'son
grandson

ĂND'stand
band-stand
grand-stand

ĂN'dum
ad captandum
avizandum
mandom
memorandum
random
tandem

ĀN'dur
attainder
remainder

ĂN'dūr
grandeur

ĂN'dur or
ÅN'dur
Africander
Alexander
back-hander
blander
bystander
brander
candor
commander
coriander
dander
demander
disbander
dittander
expander
gander
gerrymander
glander
goosey-gander
grander
hander
lander
Leander
meander
Menander

oleander
pander
philander
Pomander
remander
reprimander
right-hander
salamander
sander
slander
stander
understander
withstander

ĂN'dur
launder

ĂN'durd or
ÅN'durd
meandered
pandered
philandered
slandered
standard

ĂN'durz
Sanders
Saunders

ĂNDZ'man
bandsman
landsman

Ā'nes
gayness
greyness

ĀN'est
abstainest
appertainest

arraignest
ascertainest
attainest
canest
chainest
complainest
constrainest
containest
cranest
deignest
detainest
disdainest
enchainest
entertainest
explainest
feignest
humanest
inanest
maintainest
obtainest
ordainest
painest
plainest
profanest
rainest
refrainest
regainest
reignest
remainest
restrainest
retainest
sanest
stainest
strainest
sustainest
trainest
unchainest
urbanest
vainest
wanest

ĂN'est

bannest
fannest
mannest
plannest
scannest
spannest
tannest

ĂN'et

gannet
granite
Janet
planet
quannet
(cf. pomegran-
    ate)

ĀN'eth

abstaineth
appertaineth
arraigneth
ascertaineth
attaineth
caneth
chaineth
complaineth
constraineth
containeth
craneth
deigneth
detaineth
disdaineth
draineth
enchaineth
entertaineth
explaineth
feigneth
foreordaineth
gaineth
maintaineth

obtaineth
ordaineth
paineth
profaneth
raineth
refraineth
regaineth
reigneth
remaineth
restraineth
retaineth
staineth
straineth
sustaineth
traineth
unchaineth
waneth

ĂN'eth

banneth
fanneth
manneth
planneth
scanneth
spanneth
tanneth

ĂN'far

fanfare

ĂN'feld

Canfield

ĀN'ful

baneful
complainful
disdainful
painful

ĀN'gang

chain-gang
train-gang

ĂNG'gar

hangar

ĂNG'gor

languor

ĂNG'gur

anger
angor
clangor

ĂNG'gwid

languid

ĂNG'gwij

language

ĂNG'gwin

anguine
ensanguine
sanguine

ĂNG'gwish

anguish
languish

ĂNG'i

clangy
fangy
slangy

ĂNG'ing

banging
clanging
hanging
haranguing
overhanging
paper-hanging
slanging
slangwhanging
twanging

ĂNG'kest
blankest
clankest
dankest
embankest
flankest
frankest
lankest
outflankest
rankest
thankest
sankest
spankest

ĂNG'ket
banket
blanket

ĂNG'keth
clanketh
embanketh
flanketh
franketh
outflanketh
ranketh
sanketh
thanketh

ĂNGK'ful
prankful
thankful

ĂNG'ki
cranky
hanky
hanky-panky
lanky
planky
pranky
Yankee

ĂNG'king
banking
clanking
embanking
flanking
franking
outflanking
outranking
planking
ranking
spanking
thanking
yanking

ĂNG'kish
dankish
frankish
lankish
prankish

ĂNGK″1
ankle
crankle
hankle
rankle

ĂNGK'les
bankless
clankless
crankless
flankless
plankless
prankless
rankless
shankless
spankless
thankless

ĂNGK'let
anklet

ĂNGK'li
blankly
dankly
frankly
lankly
rankly

ĂNGK'ling
hankling
rankling

ĂNGK'ment
bankment
embankment
outflankment

ĂNGK'nes
blankness
crankness
dankness
frankness
lankness
rankness

ĂNG'ko
banco
calamanco

ĂNGK'shun
sanction

ĂNGK'shus
anxious

ĂNGK'tum
sanctum

ĂNGK'wet
banquet

ĂNGK'wil
tranquil

ĂNGK'wish
vanquish

ĂNG'kur
anchor
banker
blanker
canker
clanker
danker
encanker
flanker
franker
hanker
outflanker
planker
pranker
rancor
ranker
sheet-anchor
spanker
tanker
thanker
unanchor

ĂNG'kurd
brancard
cankered
tankard
unanchored
anchored, etc.

ĂNG″1
angle
bangle
bemangle
bespangle
brangle
dangle
disentangle
embrangle

entangle
interjangle
intertangle
jangle
mangle
mingle-mangle
phalangal
quadrangle
sea-tangle
spangle
strangle
tangle
triangle
twangle
untangle
Wrangel
wrangle

ĂNG″ld
new-fangled
star-spangled
angled, etc.

ĂNG′les
fangless
pangless

ĂNG′li
spangly
tangly

ĂNG′ling
angling
dangling, etc.

ĂNG′lur
angler
dangler, etc.

ĂNG′man
hangman

ĂNG′o
contango
fandango
mango
Pago Pago
tango

ĂNG′gri
angry

ĂN′grov
mangrove

ĂNG′stur
gangster

ĂNG′ur
banger
clangor
ganger
hangar
hanger
haranguer
paper-hanger
slang-whanger
straphanger

ĂN′hood
manhood

ĂN′i
Allegheny
brainy
Cheyney
Delaney
Eugenie
grainy
Rainey
rainy
veiny
zany

ĂN′i
Annie
branny
canny
cranny
Fannie
granny
mannie
Nannie
uncanny

ĂN′i
frangipani
Galvani
Hindustani
rani
soprani

ĂN′id
crannied

ĀN′ij
cranage
drainage

ĂN′ij
manage
pannage
tannage

ĂN′ik
Alcoranic
aldermanic
Alemannic
Aristophanic
botanic
Brahmanic
Britannic
charlatanic
diaphanic
ferricyanic

galvanic
Germanic
hydrocyanic
Indo-Germanic
interoceanic
lexiphanic
Magellanic
mechanic
Messianic
montanic
Mussulmanic
oceanic
organic
Ossianic
paganic
panic
Puranic
Puritanic
quercitannic
rhodanic
Romanic
satanic
stannic
sultanic
talismanic
tannic
tetanic
Theophanic
titanic
tympanic
tyrannic
Uranic
valerianic
volcanic
vulcanic

ĂN′iks
humanics
mechanics
panics

ōld, ôr, ŏdd, oil, fŏŏt, out; ūse, ûrn, ŭp; THis, thin

ĂN'ĭl

anil

ĂN'ĭl

anile

Ā'nim

paynim

ĀN'ing

abstaining
airplaning
appertaining
arraigning
ascertaining
attaining
bestaining
braining
campaigning
caning
chaining
complaining
constraining
containing
craning
deigning
deraigning
detaining
disdaining
draining
enchaining
entertaining
entraining
explaining
feigning
foreordaining
gaining
graining
hydroplaning
ingraining
maintaining

obtaining
ordaining
paining
pertaining
plaining
planing
preordaining
profaning
raining
refraining
regaining
reigning
reining
remaining
restraining
retaining
spraining
staining
straining
sustaining
training
unchaining
uncomplaining
unfeigning
uptraining
veining
waning

ĂN'ing

banning
canning
fanning
flanning
inspanning
japanning
manning
outspanning
panning
planning
scanning
spanning

tanning
trepanning
unmanning

ĂN'is

anise

ĀN'ish

Danish
sanish
urbanish
vainish

ĂN'ish

Alcoranish
banish
clannish
evanish
fannish
mannish
Mussulmanish
planish
Spanish
vanish

ĂN'ist

Alcoranist
pianist
tanist

ĀN'jel

angel

ĂN'jel

evangel

ĂN'jent

frangent
plangent
tangent

ĀN'jest

arrangest
changest
derangest
disarrangest
estrangest
exchangest
rangest
strangest

ĀN'jeth

arrangeth
changeth
derangeth
disarrangeth
estrangeth
exchangeth
interchangeth
rangeth

ĀN'jez

arranges
changes
deranges
disarranges
enranges
estranges
exchanges
granges
interchanges
ranges

ĂN'jez

flanges
Ganges
phalanges

ĀN'ji

mangy
rangy

ĀN'jing
arranging
changing
counter-
   changing
deranging
disarranging
estranging
exchanging
interchanging
ranging
unchanging

ĀNJ'ling
changling

ĀNJ'les
changeless
rangeless

ĀNJ'li
strangely

ĀNJ'ment
arrangement
derangement
disarrangement
estrangement
exchangement
interchange-
   ment

ĀNJ'nes
strangeness

ĀN'jur
arranger
bushranger
changer
danger
deranger

disarranger
endanger
estranger
exchanger
granger
interchanger
manger
money-changer
ranger
stranger

ĂN'ka or
   ÅN'ka
Bianca

ĂN'kin
Hankin
Rankin

ĂN'king
Nanking

ĂN'kinz
Hankins
Rankins

ĂN'kok
Hancock

ĀN'land
mainland

ĀN'les
brainless
caneless
chainless
craneless
domainless
drainless
gainless
grainless
maneless

painless
rainless
stainless
swainless
vaneless

ĂN'les
banless
clanless
fanless
manless
planless
spanless
tanless

ĀN'li
gainly
humanely
inanely
insanely
mainly
plainly
profanely
sanely
vainly

ĂN'li
Danley
Manley
manly
spick-and-
   spanly
Stanley
unmanly

ĂN'ling
manling
tanling

ĀN'ment
arraignment

ascertainment
attainment
obtainment
ordainment

ĀN'nes
humaneness
inaneness
insaneness
plainness
profaneness
saneness

Ā'no
volcano

ĂN'o
piano
Hanno
soprano

Ä'no
guano
Montesano
piano
soprano

ĂN'ok
bannock
jannock

ĂN'on
Balleyshannon
cannon
canon
fanon
Shannon

ĀN'sa
gainsay

ĀN'sal
mainsail

ĀN'sel
cancel
chancel
handsel

ĂN'sest
advancest
chancest
dancest
enhancest
entrancest
glancest
prancest
romancest

ĂN'set
lancet

ĂN'seth
advanceth
chanceth
danceth
enhanceth
entranceth
glanceth
pranceth
romanceth

ĂN'sez
advances
chances
dances
enhances
entrances
expanses
finances
glances
lances

mischances
prances
romances
trances

ĂNS'fur
transfer

ĂN'shal
circumstantial
financial
substantial
supersubstan-
  tial

ĂN'she
banshee

ĀN'shent
ancient

ĂN'shent
transient

ĂN'shun
expansion
mansion
scansion
stanchion

ĂN'si
aeromancy
aldermancy
alectoromancy
alectryomancy
aleuromancy
alphitomancy
anthropomancy
astragalo-
  mancy
austromancy

axinomancy
belomancy
bibliomancy
botanomancy
capnomancy
catoptromancy
ceromancy
chancy
chiromancy
cleromancy
consonancy
coscinomancy
crithomancy
crystallomancy
dactyliomancy
dancy
Delancey
enoptromancy
exorbitancy
extravagancy
exuberancy
fancy
gastromancy
geomancy
gyromancy
halomancy
hesitancy
hieromancy
hydromancy
ichthyomancy
lecanomancy
lithomancy
mendicancy
meteoromancy
mischancy
Miss Nancy
militancy
myomancy
Nancy
necromancy
occupancy

œnomancy
oneiromancy
onomancy
onychomancy
ophiomancy
ornithomancy
pedomancy
petulancy
precipitancy
pyromancy
psephomancy
psychomancy
sciomancy
sibilancy
sideromancy
significancy
spodomancy
stichomancy
supplicancy
sycophancy
tephramancy
termagancy
unchancy

ĂN'sid
fancied
rancid

ĂN'sing
advancing
chancing
dancing
enhancing
entrancing
fiancing
glancing
lancing
Lansing
necromancing
prancing
romancing

ĂN'sis
Frances
Francis

ĂN'sist
romancist

ĂN'siv
advancive
expansive

ĂNS'ment
advancement
enhancement
entrancement

ĂN'som
handsome
hansom
ransom
transom
unhandsome

ĂN'son
Anson
Hanson

ĀN'sta
main-stay

ĂN'sur
advancer
Anser
answer
cancer
chancer
chiromancer
dancer
enhancer
entrancer
geomancer

glancer
lancer
merganser
necromancer
prancer
romancer

ĂN'tā
infante

ĂN'ta
anta
Atalanta
Atlanta
infanta
Santa
Vedanta

ĂN'ta
Vedanta

ĀN'tal
consonantal
gigantal
quadrantal

ĂN'tam
bantam
phantom

ĀN'tans
acquaintance

ĂN'tazm
phantasm

ĂN'te
ante
Dante
dilettante

pococurante
zante

ĂN'te
andante
Dante
(cf. chianti)

ĀN'ted
acquainted
attainted
bepainted
besainted
depainted
fainted
feinted
painted
sainted
tainted
unacquainted
unattainted
unsainted
untainted

ĂN'ted, ĂN'ted
canted
chanted
decanted
enchanted
granted
implanted
panted
planted
ranted
recanted
slanted
supplanted

ĂN'test
acquaintest
faintest

feintest
paintest
quaintest
taintest

ĂN'test,
ÅN'test
cantest
chantest
decantest
enchantest
grantest
implantest
pantest
plantest
rantest
recantest
scantest
supplantest

ĀN'teth
acquainteth
feinteth
painteth
tainteth

ĂN'teth,
ÅN'teth
canteth
chanteth
decanteth
enchanteth
granteth
implanteth
panteth
planteth
recanteth
supplanteth

ĂN'tez
atlantes

corybantes
(cf. ĂN'ti + s)

ĂN'them
anthem

ĂNT'hood
sainthood

ĂN'thik
œnanthic
xanthic

ĂN'thin
acanthine
amaranthine
anthine
Rhadamanthine
tragacanthin
xanthin

ĂN'thur
anther
panther

ĂN'thus
acanthous
acanthus
Agapanthus
ailanthus
amianthus
anacanthous
ananthous
canthus
Chimonanthus
dianthus
epanthous
Galanthus
Hæmanthus
hysteranthous

polyanthus
synanthous

ĀN'ti
dainty

ĂN'ti
bacchante
canty
panty
scanty
shanty

ĂN'ti
aunty

ĀN'tif
plaintiff

ĂN'tij
advantage
disadvantage
plantage
vantage

ĂN'tik
antic
Atlantic
chiromantic
consonantic
corybantic
frantic
geomantic
gigantic
hierophantic
hydromantic
mantic
necromantic
onomantic
pedantic
pyromantic

romantic
spodomantic
sycophantic
transatlantic

ĂN'tik
Vedantic

ĂN'tin
adamantine
Brabantine
Byzantine
chrysele-
   phantine
Diophantine
elephantine
gigantine
Levantine

ĀN'ting
acquainting
attainting
fainting
feinting
painting
tainting
word-painting

ĂN'ting,
   ĀN'ting
Banting
canting
chanting
decanting
descanting
disenchanting
enchanting
granting
hanting
implanting

panting
planting
ranting
recanting
slanting
supplanting
transplanting

ĂN'tist
ignorantist
Kantist

ĂN'tist
Vedantist

ĂN'tiv
constraintive
plaintive

ĂN'tizm
dilettantism
ignorantism
Kantism
obscurantism
pococurantism
rantism

ĂN't'l
cantle
dismantle
immantle
mantel
mantle
scantle

ĂN't'ld
dismantled
ivy-mantled
mantled

ĂNT'let
cantlet

mantelet
plantlet

ÄNT'let
gauntlet

ÅNT'let
gantlet

ĀNT'li
quaintly
saintly
unsaintly

ÄNT'li
aslantly
scantly

ĀNT'lik
saintlike

ÄNT'ling
bantling
mantling
scantling

ÄNT'lur
antler
dismantler
mantler
pantler

ÄNT'ment
disenchantment
enchantment

ĀNT'nes
faintness
quaintness

ÄNT'nes
scantness

ÄN'to or ÅN'to
canto
coranto
portmanteau
pro tanto
quo warranto

ÄN'tom
(see ÄN'tam)

ÄN'ton
Canton
Clanton
Danton
Scranton
Stanton

ÄN'tor
cantor
grantor

ÅN'tres
chantress
enchantress

ÄN'tri
pantry

ÅN'tri
chantry

ÄN'tu
Bantu

ĀN'tur
acquainter
fainter
painter
quainter
tainter
word-painter

ÄN'tur or
ÅN'tur
banter
canter
chanter
decanter
descanter
enchanter
granter
implanter
instanter
Levanter
panter
planter
ranter
recanter
supplanter
transplanter
trochanter

ÅN'tur
chanter
disenchanter
enchanter

ÄN'turn
lantern

ĀN'ur
abstainer
appertainer
arraigner
ascertainer
attainer
bestainer
campaigner
complainer
constrainer
container
cordwainer
detainer

disdainer
drainer
enchainer
entertainer
explainer
feigner
gainer
grainer
inaner
maintainer
nonabstainer
obtainer
ordainer
plainer
profaner
refrainer
regainer
restrainer
retainer
saner
stainer
strainer
sustainer
trainer
unchainer
uptrainer
vainer

ÄN'ur
banner
canner
fanner
japanner
lanner
manner
manor
planner
scanner
spanner
tanner

ōld, ôr, ŏdd, oil, fŏŏt, out; ūse, ûrn, ŭp; THis, thin

trepanner
vanner

ĂN'urd
bannered
ill-mannered
mannered
unmannered
well-mannered

ĀN'us
heinous
incanous
Janus
Silvanus
veinous

ĂN'vas
canvas
canvass

ĂN'vil
anvil
Danville
Granville

ĀN'wurk
brainwork
chainwork
plain-work

ĂN'yan
banyan
canyon
companion

ĂN'yard
lanyard
Spaniard

ĂN'yel
Daniel

Nathaniel
spaniel
staniel
water-spaniel

ĂN'yur
pannier

ĂN'za
bonanza
extravaganza
ganza
stanza

ĂNZ'feld
Mansfield

ĂN'zi
chimpanzeee
pansy
tansy

ĂN'zvil
Janesville
Zanesville

Ä'o
cacao
tetrao

Ā'on
crayon

Ä'on
gaon

Ā'os
chaos

Ā'oth
Sabaoth

ĂP'en
happen

ĀP'est
apest
drapest
escapest
gapest
rapest
scrapest
shapest

ĂP'est
clappest
enwrappest
flappest
lappest
mappest
nappest
rappest
sappest
slappest
snappest
trappest
wrappest

ĂP'et
lappet
tappet

ĀP'eth
apeth
drapeth
escapeth
gapeth
rapeth
scrapeth
shapeth

ĂP'eth
clappeth

enwrappeth
flappeth
lappeth
mappeth
nappeth
rappeth
sappeth
slappeth
snappeth
trappeth
wrappeth

ĂP'got
scape-goat

ĂP'gras
scape-grace

ĂP'i
crapy
gapy
red-tapy
scrapy

ĂP'i
chappy
gappy
gapy
happy
knappy
nappy
pappy
sappy
scrappy
snappy

ĂP'id
rapid
sapid
vapid

ĂP'ik
jalapic
Lappic

ĀP'in
rapine

ĀP'ing
aping
draping
escaping
gaping
raping
scraping
shaping

ĂP'ing
capping
clapping
dapping
entrapping
enwrapping
flapping
gaping
handicapping
lapping
mapping
napping
overlapping
rapping
sapping
scrapping
slapping
snapping
strapping
tapping
trapping
understrapping
unwrapping
wrapping
yapping

ĂP'is
apis
lapis
Serapis
tapis

ĂP'is
lapis
tapis

ĂP'ish
apish
papish

ĂP'ish
knappish
snappish

ĀP'ist
lanscapist
papist
redtapist

ĀP'izm
papism
red-tapism

ĀP"l
anti-papal
capel
maple
papal
staple
wool-staple

ĂP"l
ante-chapel
apple
chapel

dapple
grapple
knapple
love-apple
rappel
scapple
scrapple
thrapple

ĀP'les
apeless
capeless
crapeless
escapeless
grapeless
napeless
scrapeless
shapeless
tapeless

ĂP'les
capless
hapless
napless
sapless

ĂP'let
chaplet

ĀP'li
shapely

ĂP'li
haply

ĀP'lin
chaplain
Chaplin

ĀP'ling
dappling

grappling
lapling
sapling

ĀP'l'z
Naples
Staples

ĂP'man
Capman
Chapman
Knapman

ĂP'nel
grapnel
shrapnel

ĀP'on
capon
misshapen
tapen
unshapen

ĀP'ril
April

ĂP'shun
caption
collapsion
contraption
elapsion
recaption

ĂP'shus
captious

ĂP'sing
collapsing
lapsing
relapsing

ĂP'stan
capstan

ĂP'stur
tapster

ĂP'ted
adapted

ĂP'test
adaptest
aptest
inaptest
raptest

ĂP'tin
captain

ĂP'tiv
adaptive
captive

ĂP'tizm
anabaptism
baptism

ĂPT'li
aptly
inaptly
raptly

ĂPT'nes
aptness
inaptness
raptness
unaptness

ĂP'trap
clap-trap

ĂP'tūr
capture

enrapture
rapture
recapture

ĂP'tŭr
adapter
apter
captor
chapter
rapter
recaptor

ĀP'ur
aper
caper
draper
escaper
gaper
landscaper
paper
raper
sapor
scraper
shaper
sky-scraper
taper
tapir
undraper
vapor

ĂP'ur
capper
clapper
dapper
entrapper
enwrapper
flapper
fly-flapper
gaper
handicapper
lapper

mapper
napper
overlapper
rapper
sapper
slapper
snapper
snippersnapper
strapper
tapper
trapper
understrapper
unwrapper
whipper-
   snapper
wrapper
yapper

ĀP'urz
walking-papers
capers, etc.

ĂP'us
pappus
trappous

ĂP'wing
lapwing

Ā'ra
cordillera
dulcamara
Marah
Sara
Sarah

ÂR'a
Sahara
tiara

Ă'ra
Bara
Clara

Ă'ra
caracara
Ferrara
Gemara
Sahara
solfatara
tiara

ĂR'ab
Arab
scarab

ĂR'ak
arrack
barrack
carrack

Â'rans
abearance
forbearance
(cf. apparence)

Â'rant
declarant
forbearant
(cf. parent,
   etc.)

ĂR'ant
arrant

ĂR'ant
warrant
(see ŎR'ent)

ĂR'as
arras

debarrass
disembarrass
embarrass
harass

ÄR'bel
harebell
prayer-bell

ÄR'bi
Darby
Derby

ÄR'bij
garbage

ÄR'b'l
barbel
emmarble
garbel
garble
marble

ÄR'blur
garbler
marbler

ÄR'bling
garbling
marbling

ÄR'bord
larboard
starboard

ÄR'boil
parboil

ÄR'bon
carbon
charbon

ÄR'bur
arbor
barber
Barbour
enharbor
harbor
unharbor

ÄR'chest
archest
enarchest
marchest
parchest
starchest

ÄR'cheth
archeth
enarcheth
marcheth
parcheth
starcheth

ÄR'chez
arches
counter-
    marches
larches
marches
outmarches
overarches
parches
starches

ÄR'chi
archy
larchy
starchy

ÄR'ching
arching
counter-
    marching

marching
outmarching
overarching
overmarching
parching
starching

ÄRCH'ment
archment
emparchment
parchment

ÄRCH'nes
archness

ÄR'chur
archer
clear-starcher
Larcher
marcher
starcher

ÄRCH'wa
archway

ÄR'dant
gardant
regardant
(cf. ardent)

ÄRD'arm
yard-arm

ÄR'ded
bombarded
carded
discarded
disregarded
guarded
larded
regarded

retarded
sharded
unguarded
unregarded
unretarded

ÄR'del
fardel

ÄR'den,
    ÄR'don
beergarden
bombardon
caseharden
enharden
garden
harden
pardon

ÄR'dend,
    ÄR'dond
case-hardened
hardened
pardoned
weather-
    hardened

ÄR'dent
ardent
(cf., ÄR'dant)

ÄR'dest
bombardest
discardest
disregardest
guardest
hardest
lardest
regardest
retardest

ÄR'deth
discardeth
disregardeth
guardeth
lardeth
regardeth
retardeth

ÄRD'ful
disregardful
guardful
regardful

ÄR'di
foolhardy
hardy
tardy

ÄRD'ik
anacardic
bardic
bezoardic
Lombardic
pericardic

ÄR'din
nardine
sardine

ÄR'ding
bombarding
carding
discarding
disregarding
guarding
Harding
larding
placarding
regarding
retarding

unguarding
wool-carding

ÄR'd'l
Bardle
McArdle

ÄRD'les
cardless
guardless
regardless

ÄRD'li
hardly

ÄRD'ment
bombardment
retardment

ÄRD'nes
hardness

ÄRD'ning
gardening
hardening
pardoning

ÄRD'nur
gardener
hardener
pardner
pardoner

ÄR'do
bocardo
bombardo

ÂR'dom
backstairdom
heirdom

ÄRD'ship
guardship
hardship

ÄRDZ'man
guardsman

ÄR'dur
ardor
bombarder
carder
discarder
disregarder
guarder
harder
larder
regarder
retarder

ÄR'e
shikaree
(cf. ÄR'i)

ÄR'el
apparel
barrel
carol
Carroll
disapparel
Farrell
Harrell
parrel
pork barrel

ÄR'eld
apparelled
carolled
double-
    barrelled

ÂR'em
harem

ÄR'en
Karen
McLaren

ÄR'ens
apparence
Clarence
transparence
(cf. forbear-
    ance)

ÄR'ent
apparent
celarent
parent
transparent
(cf. declarant,
    etc.)

ÂR'es
heiress

ÂR'est
airest
barest
bearest
carest
comparest
darest
declarest
despairest
ensnarest
fairest
farest
forbearest
glarest
impairest
outdarest
pairest
parest
preparest

āle,   câre,   ădd,   ärm,   åsk;   mē,   hẹre,   ĕnd;   īce,   ĭll;

rarest
repairest
sharest
snarest
sparest
squarest
starest
swearest
tearest
unfairest
wearest

ĂR′est

barrest
debarrest
jarrest
marrest
scarrest
sparrest
starrest
tarrest

ĂR′et

carat
carrot
claret
garret
Garrett
parrot

ÂR′eth

aireth
bareth
beareth
careth
compareth
dareth
declareth
despaireth
ensnareth

fareth
flareth
forbeareth
forsweareth
glareth
impaireth
outdareth
paireth
pareth
prepareth
repaireth
shareth
snareth
spareth
squareth
stareth
sweareth
teareth
wearth

ĂR′eth

barreth
debarreth
marreth
scarreth
sparreth
starreth
tarreth

ÂR′ez

Benares
Buenos Ayres

ÂR′fasd

barefaced
fair-faced

ĂR′fish

garfish
starfish

ÂR′for

wherefore
(cf. therefore,
ÛR′for).

ÂR′ful

careful
prayerful
uncareful

ĂR′gan

Dargan

ĂR′gēt

target

ĂR′gin

bargain

ĂR′g′l

argle-bargle
gargle

ĂR′go

Argo
argot
botargo
cargo
Dargo
embargo
Fargo
largo
Spargo
supercargo

ĂR′gon

argon
jargon

ĂR′gu

argue

ÂR′i

ablutionary
accessary
accidentiary
accustomary
actuary
additionary
adminculary
adversary
airy
ancillary
antiquary
apothecary
arbitrary
Ave Mary
beneficiary
bicentenary
canary
capillary
Carey
cassowary
cautionary
centenary
chary
commentary
commissary
confectionary
constabulary
contemporary
contrary
contributary
corollary
culinary
customary
dairy
depositary
dictionary
dietary
dignitary
disciplinary
discretionary

dromedary
eleemosynary
elocutionary
epistolary
estuary
evolutionary
extraordinary
fairy
February
fiduciary
formulary
fragmentary
functionary
ganglionary
glairy
hairy
hebdomadary
hereditary
honorary
imaginary
incendiary
insurrectionary
intermediary
janissary
January
legendary
legionary
literary
luminary
Mary
maxillary
mercenary
military
millenary
missionary
momentary
monetary
mortuary
necessary
obituary
ordinary

passionary
pecuniary
pensionary
petitionary
planetary
prairie
prebendary
processionary
prolegomenary
proprietary
prothonotary
provisionary
pulmonary
quandary
questionary
questuary
reactionary
reliquary
residuary
reversionary
revolutionary
rosemary
salivary
salutary
sanctuary
sanguinary
sanitary
scapulary
scary
secondary
secretary
sedentary
seditionary
seminary
snary
solitary
stationary
statuary
stipendiary
sublunary
subsidiary

sumptuary
supernumerary
temporary
tertiary
Tipperary
titulary
traditionary
tributary
tuitionary
tumulary
tumultuary
tutelary
ubiquitary
unchary
unwary
vagary
valetudinary
vairy
vary
veterinary
vicissitudinary
visionary
vocabulary
voluntary
voluptuary
vulnerary
wary
(cf. ĘR′i)

ĂR′i

Barrie
Carrie
carry
charivari
harri-karri
harry
intermarry
Larry
marry
miscarry

parry
tarry

ĂR′i

araçari
barry
carbonari
charry
scarry
sparry
starry
tarry
(cf. shikaree)

ĂR′id

varied

ĂR′id

arid
carried
harried
intermarried
married
miscarried
parried
tarried

ĂR′if, ĂR′if

hairif

ĂR′if

harif
tariff

ĂR′ij

carriage
disparage
intermarriage
marriage
miscarriage

railway-
  carriage
water-carriage

ĂR'ik

agaric
Amharic
Balearic
barbaric
baric
Bulgaric
cinnabaric
Garrick
isobaric
Megaric
pimaric
Pindaric
polaric
saccharic
stearic
tartaric

ĂR'ik

Amharic

ÂR'ing

airing
baring
bearing
blaring
caring
chairing
charing
cheese-paring
comparing
daring
declaring
despairing
ensnaring
fairing
faring

flaring
forbearing
forswearing
glaring
impairing
outdaring
outstaring
outswearing
outwearing
overbearing
pairing
paring
preparing
repairing
scaring
sea-faring
sharing
snaring
sparing
squaring
staring
swearing
tale-bearing
tearing
unbearing
underbearing
unsparing
upbearing
upstaring
uptearing
wayfaring
wearing

ĂR'ing

barring
charring
debarring
disbarring
jarring
marring
scarring

sparring
starring
tarring
unbarring

ĂR'ingks

larynx
pharynx

ĂR'is

Farris
Harris
Paris
phalaris
polaris

ÂR'ish

bearish
debonairish
fairish
garish
marish
squarish
tarish

ĂR'ish

marish
parish

ÂR'izm

proletairism
Voltairism

ĂR'jent

argent
sergeant

ĂR'jest

chargest
dischargest

enlargest
largest
overchargest

ĂR'jet

garget
parget

ĂR'jeth

chargeth
dischargeth
enlargeth
overchargeth

ĂR'jez

barges
charges
discharges
enlarges
marges
targes

ĂR'jik

lethargic

ĂR'jin

margin

ĂR'jing

barging
charging
discharging
enlarging
overcharging

ĂRJ'li

largely

ĂRJ'ment

enlargement

ÄRJ'ur
barger
charger
discharger
enlarger
larger
sparger
surcharger
undercharger

ÄR'kal
anarchal
hierarchal
monarchal
oligarchal
patriarchal
squirearchal

ÄR'kazm
sarcasm

ÄR'ken
bedarken
darken
endarken
hearken

ÄR'kest
barkest
darkest
embarkest
markest
remarkest
starkest

ÄR'ket
market

ÄR'keth
barketh
embarketh

marketh
remarketh

ÄR'ki
barky
darky
heterarchy
hierarchy
larky
oligarchy
patriarchy

ÄR'kik
anarchic
antianarchic
climatarchic
heptarchic
hierarchic
monarchic
oligarchic
patriarchic

ÄR'kin
Larkin

ÄR'king
barking
carking
disembarking
embarking
harking
larking
marking
parking
remarking
sky-larking

ÄR'kish
darkish
larkish
sparkish

ÄR'kist
heptarchist
oligarchist, etc.

ÄR'kivs
archives

ÄR'k'l
darkle
sparkle

ÄRK'let
parklet
sparklet

ÄRK'li
clarkly
darkly
starkly

ÄRK'ling
darkling
sparkling

ÄRK'nes
darkness

ÄRK'nur
darkener
hearkener

ÄR'kol
charcoal

ÄRK'som
darksome

ÄRK'spur
larkspur

ÄRK'tik
Antarctic
Arctic

ÄR'kur
barker
darker
embarker
harker
larker
marcor
marker
parker
sharker
sparker
starker

ÄRK'wis
marquis

ÄR'land
engarland
Farland
garland

ÂR'les
airless
careless
hairless
heirless
pairless
prayerless
snareless
tareless

ÄR'les
scarless
starless, etc.

ÄR'let
carlet
scarlet
starlet
varlet
(cf. harlot)

303

ÄR'li — ÄR'nal

ĂR'li
barely
fairly
rarely
unfairly
yarely

ÄR'li
Arleigh
barley
Charley
Farley
gnarly
Harley
marli
McCarley
parley

ÄR'lĭk
starlike, etc.

ÄR'lĭk
garlic
pilgarlick
sarlyk

ÂR'lin
air-line
hair-line

ÂR'lind
carelined
hair-lined

ÄR'ling
darling
Harling
snarling
sparling
starling

ÄR'lĭt
starlight

ÄR'lĭt
far-lit
starlit

ÄR'lok
charlock
harlock
(cf. Harlech)

ÄR'lot
Charlotte
harlot
(cf. scarlet)

ÂR'lum
heirloom

ÄR'lur
gnarler
parlor
snarler

ÄR'lus
parlous

ÄR'mad
barmaid

ÂR'man
chairman

ÄR'men
carmen

ÄR'ment
debarment
disbarment
garment
sarment

ÄR'mest
alarmest
armest
charmest
disarmest
farmest
harmest

ÄR'met
armet

ÄR'meth
alarmeth
armeth
charmeth
disarmeth
farmeth
harmeth

ÄRM'ful
armful
charmful
harmful
unharmful

ÄR'mi
army
barmy

ÄR'mik
alexipharmic
lexipharmic
ptarmic

ÄR'min
carmine
harmine

ÄR'ming
alarming
arming

baby-farming
charming
disarming
farming
forearming
harming
unalarming
unarming
uncharming
unharming

ÄRM'les
armless
charmless
harmless

ÄRM'let
armlet
charmlet

ÄR'mot
carmot
marmot

ÄR'mur
alarmer
armor
baby-farmer
charmer
disarmer
farmer
harmer
plate-armor
serpent-
    charmer

ÄR'nal
carnal
carnel
charnel
darnel
uncharnel

old, ôr, ŏdd, oil, fŏŏt, out; ūse, ûrn, ŭp; THis, thin

ÄR'nard
Barnard

ÄR'nat
incarnate

ÂR'nes
bareness
debonairness
fairness
rareness
spareness
squareness
threadbare-
ness
unfairness
whereness

ÄR'nes
farness
harness

ÄRN'ham
Farnham
(cf. Farnum,
Barnum)

ÄR'ni
blarney
carney
Killarney

ÄR'nij
carnage

ÄR'nish
garnish
tarnish
varnish

ÄR'nisht
garnished

tarnished
ungarnished
untarnished
unvarnished
varnished

ÄR'nold
Arnold

ÄRN'li
Darnley

ÄR'nur
darner
garner
yarner

ÄR'o
pharaoh
Rio de Janeiro

ÂR'o
bolero
caballero
faro
llanero
sombrero
vaquero

ÄR'o
arrow
barrow
farrow
harrow
marrow
narrow
sparrow
yarrow

ÄR'o
carbonaro

claro
taro

ÂR'on
Aaron
Charon

ÄR'old
Harold
carolled, etc.

ÄR'on
baron
barren

ÄR'pest
carpest
harpest
sharpest

ÄR'pet
carpet

ÄR'peth
carpeth
harpeth

ÄR'pi
carpy
harpy

ÄR'ping
carping
harping
sharping

ÄR'pist
harpist

ÄRP'nes
sharpness

ÄR'pur
carper
harper
sharper

ÄR'sal
metatarsal
tarsal
varsal

ÄR'sel
parcel
sarcel

ÄR'sez
farces
parses
sarses

ÄR'shal
earl-marshal
field-marshal
immartial
impartial
marshal
Marshall
martial
partial
unmartial

ÂRS'li
scarcely

ÂRS'ness
scarceness

ÄR'son
arson
Carson
Larsen

Larson	leaden-hearted	**ÄR'test**	**ÄR'ti**
parson	light-hearted	*cartest*	Astarte
	lion-hearted	*dartest*	charter-party
ÄR'sur	marble-hearted	*departest*	ex parte
parser	open-hearted	*impartest*	hearty
sparser	pale-hearted	*partest*	McCarty
	parted	smartest	party
ÄR'tan	pigeon-hearted	*startest*	
Spartan	proud-hearted	*upstartest*	**ÄR'tin**
tartan	public-hearted		martin
(cf. marten)	right-hearted	**ÄR'teth**	
	sad-hearted	*carteth*	**ÄR'ting**
ÄR'ted	shallow-hearted	*darteth*	carting
broken-hearted	simple-hearted	*departeth*	darting
carted	single-hearted	*imparteth*	departing
charted	smarted	*parteth*	hearting
chicken-hearted	soft-hearted	*smarteth*	imparting
cold-hearted	started	*starteth*	smarting
darted	stony-hearted	*upstarteth*	starting
departed	stout-hearted		sweet-hearting
double-hearted	tender-hearted	**ÄRT'ful**	uncarting
down-hearted	traitor-hearted	artful	upstarting
faint-hearted	triparted		
false-hearted	truehearted	**ÄR'tha**	**ÄR'tist**
flint-hearted	unhearted	Martha	artist
frank-hearted	unimparted		Chartist
free-hearted	upstarted	**ÄR'thest**	
full-hearted	warm-hearted	farthest	**ÄR'tit**
gentle-hearted	weak-hearted		bipartite
great-hearted	wise-hearted	**ÄR'thi**	
half-hearted		McCarthy	**ÄR't'l**
hard-hearted	**ÄR'ten, Är'ton**		dartle
hare-hearted	barton	**ÄR'thing**	startle
hearted	carton	farthing	
hen-hearted	dishearten		**ÄRT'les**
high-hearted	enhearten	**ÄR'THur**	artless
imparted	hearten	farther	chartless
iron-hearted	kindergarten		heartless
kind-hearted	marten	**ÄR'thur**	**ÄRT'let**
large-hearted	smarten	Arthur	heartlet

ōld, ôr, ŏdd, oil, fŏŏt, out; ūse, ûrn, ŭp; THis, thin

martlet
tartlet

ÄRT'li
partly
smartly
tartly

ÄRT'ling
startling

ÄRT'ment
apartment
compartment
department
impartment

ÄRT'nes
smartness
tartness

ÄRT'rij
cartridge
partridge

ÄRT'wa
cartway
part-way

ÄR'tur
barter
bemartyr
carter
charter
darter
departer
garter
imparter
martyr
parter
protomartyr

smarter
starter
tartar
tarter
unmartyr
upstarter

ÄR'um
arum
carrom
harum-scarum
larum
marum

ÄR'um
alarum

ÄR'ur
airer
armor-bearer
barer
bearer
blarer
comparer
darer
declarer
despairer
ensnarer
fairer
flarer
forbearer
forswearer
glarer
impairer
mace-bearer
outdarer
outstarer
overbearer
parer
preparer

rarer
repairer
sea-farer
sharer
snarer
sparer
squarer
standard-
  bearer
starer
swearer
sword-bearer
tale-bearer
tankard-bearer
tearer
train-bearer
upbearer
way-farer
wearer

ÄR'ur
barrer
bizarrer
debarrer
marrer
sparrer
tarrer

ÄR'val
larval

ÄR'vel
carvel
marvel

ÄR'veld
marvelled

ÄR'ven
carven

ÄR'vest
harvest
starvest

ÄR'vi
Garvey
Harvey

ÄR'ving
carving
starving

ÄRV'ling
marvelling
starveling

ÄR'vur
carver
marver
starver

ÄR'wavs
air-waves

ÄR'wel
farewell

ÄR'whil
erewhile

ÄR'worn
careworn
prayerworn

ÄS'a
Amasa
Asa

ÄS'a
Hadasseh
Manasseh

ālc,   câre,   ădd,   ärm,   åsk;   mē,   hĕre,   ĕnd;   īce,   ĭll;

Ā'sal
basal
casal

ĂS'at
cassate
incrassate

Ā'sens, Ā'sans
abaisance
adjacence
complacence
connascence
interjacence
obeisance
renascence

Ā'sent, Ā'sant
adjacent
circumjacent
complacent
connascent
"daycent"
enascent
indurascent
interjacent
jacent
naissant
nascent
renaissant
renascent
"raycent"
subjacent
superjacent

ĀS'est
abasest
basest
begracest
belacest

bracest
chasest
debasest
defacest
disgracest
displacest
effacest
embracest
enlacest
erasest
facest
gracest
interlacest
lacest
outpacest
pacest
placest
racest
replacest
retracest
spacest
tracest
unlacest

ĂS'est
amassest
classest
crassest
massest
passest
surpassest

ĂS'et
asset
basset
brasset
facet
fascet
placet
(cf. tacit)

ĀS'eth
abaseth
baseth
begraceth
belaceth
braceth
chaseth
debaseth
defaceth
disgraceth
displaceth
effaceth
embraceth
enlaceth
eraseth
faceth
graceth
interlaceth
laceth
outpaceth
paceth
placeth
raceth
replaceth
retraceth
spaceth
traceth
unlaceth

ĂS'eth
amasseth
classeth
masseth
passeth
surpasseth

ĀS'ez
aces
bases
begraces
belaces

braces
breathing-
  spaces
cases
chariot-traces
chases
commonplaces
debases
defaces
disgraces
displaces
effaces
embraces
enlaces
faces
footpaces
footraces
graces
grimaces
hiding-places
horse-races
interlaces
interspaces
laces
maces
misplaces
outfaces
outpaces
paces
places
races
replaces
resting-places
retraces
spaces
steeple-chases
traces
trysting-places
ukases
uncases

ōld, ôr, ŏdd, oil, fŏŏt, out; ūse, ûrn, ŭp; THis, thin

unlaces
vases

ĀS'ez

amasses
asses
brasses
classes
gases
glasses
grasses
lasses
masses
molasses
morasses
passes
surpasses

ĀS'ful

disgraceful
graceful
ungraceful

ĂSH'a

attaché
cachet
sachet

Ā'shal

abbatial
craniofacial
facial
glacial
palatial
prelatial
racial
spatial
unifacial
(cf. basial)

Ā'shan
(cf. Ā'shun)

ĂSH'bord

dashboard
splashboard

Ā'shens

patience

Ā'shent

impatient
patient

ĂSH'est

cashest
clashest
crashest
dashest
flashest
gashest
gnashest
lashest
mashest
slashest
smashest
splashest
thrashest

ĂSH'eth

casheth
clasheth
crasheth
dasheth
flasheth
gasheth
gnasheth
lasheth
masheth
slasheth
smasheth
splasheth
thrasheth

ĂSH'ez

abashes
ashes
caches
cashes
clashes
crashes
dashes
flashes
gashes
gnashes
hashes
lashes
mashes
mustaches
rashes
rehashes
sashes
slashes
smashes
splashes
unlashes

ĂSH'ful

bashful
gashful
rashful
unbashful

ĂSH'i

ashy
flashy
hashy
mashie
mashy
plashy
slashy
splashy
trashy

ĂSH'ing

abashing

balderdashing
cashing
clashing
crashing
dashing
fashing
flashing
gashing
gnashing
hashing
lashing
mashing
plashing
slashing
smashing
splashing
thrashing
unlashing

ĂSH'li

Ashley
flashly
gashly

ĂSH'man

ashman
"flashman"

Ā'sho

Horatio

Ā'shun

abalienation
abacination
abbreviation
abdication
aberration
abjudication
abjuration
ablactation
ablation

abnegation
abomination
abrogation
absentation
acceleration
acceptation
acclamation
acclimatation
acclimation
acclimatization
accommodation
accreditation
accrimination
accubation
accumulation
accusation
acervation
acidification
activation
actualization
actuation
acumination
acupunctuation
adaptation
adequation
adhortation
adjudication
adjuration
administration
admiration
adoration
adornation
adulation
adulteration
adumbration
adversation
advocation
aëration
aërostation
affectation
affiliation

affirmation
afflation
afforestation
aggeration
agglomeration
agglutination
aggrandization
aggravation
aggregation
agitation
agnation
agnomination
alcoholization
alienation
alimentation
alkalization
allegation
allegorization
alleviation
alligation
alliteration
allocation
alteration
altercation
alternation
amalgamation
ambulation
amelioration
Americaniza-
    tion
ampliation
amplification
amputation
analysation
anathematiza-
    tion
anglicization
Anglification
angulation
animalization
animation

annexation
annihilation
annomination
annotation
annulation
annumeration
annunciation
anticipation
antilibration
appellation
application
appreciation
approbation
appropriation
approximation
aration
arbitration
arcuation
argentation
argumentation
aromatization
arrestation
arrogation
articulation
Asian
asphyxiation
aspiration
assassination
assentation
asseveration
assignation
assimilation
assimulation
association
atomization
attenuation
attestation
attrectation
augmentation
auguration
auscultation

authentication
authorization
averruncation
aviation
avocation
backwardation
basification
beatification
beautification
bifurcation
blood-relation
blus'teration
bombilation
botheration
brutalization
brutification
cachinnation
calcification
calcination
calculation
calorification
calumniation
cameration
canalization
cancellation
canonization
cantillation
capitalization
capitation
capitulation
caprification
captivation
carbonization
carbunculation
carnation
cassation
castellation
castigation
castrametation
catechization
causation

cauterization
celebration
cementation
centralisation
cerebration
certification
cessation
cetacean
chain station
characteriza-
tion
chrismation
Christian-
ization
cineration
circulation
circumgyration
circumnaviga-
tion
circumnutation
circumvallation
circumvolation
citation
civilization
clarification
classification
coagulation
coaxation
codification
cogitation
cognation
cohabitation
collation
colligation
collocation
colonization
coloration
columniation
combination
commemora-
tion

commendation
commensura-
tion
communication
commination
commiseration
communication
commutation
compellation
compensation
compilation
complication
compotation
compurgation
computation
concentration
concertation
conciliation
condemnation
condensation
condonation
confabulation
confederation
configuration
confirmation
confiscation
conflagration
conformation
confrontation
confutation
congelation
conglomeration
congratulation
congregation
conjugation
conjuration
connotation
consecration
conservation
consideration
consolation

consolidation
constellation
consternation
consubstantia-
tion
consultation
consummation
contamination
contemplation
continuation
contravallation
conversation
convocation
co-operation
co-optation
co-ordination
copulation
cornification
coronation
corporation
correlation
corroboration
corrugation
coruscation
creation
cremation
crenellation
crepitation
crimination
crustacean
crustation
crystallization
cubation
culmination
cultivation
cupellation
curvation
Dalmatian
damnation
damnification
debarkation

debilitation
decalcification
decantation
decapitation
decentraliza-
tion
decimation
declamation
declaration
declination
decollation
deconsecration
decoration
decortication
decrepitation
decubation
decussation
dedication
defalcation
defamation
defecation
deflagration
defloration
deformation
defraudation
degeneration
degradation
degustation
dehortation
deification
delation
delectation
delegation
deliberation
delimitation
delineation
deliration
deltafication
demarcation
dementation
demonetization

demonstration
demoralization
denationaliza-
   tion
denization
denomination
denotation
dentation
denticulation
dentilation
denudation
denunciation
deodorization
deoppilation
deosculation
deoxidation
deoxygenation
depilation
deploration
depopulation
deportation
depositation
depravation
deprecation
depreciation
depredation
deprivation
depuration
deputation
derivation
derogation
desecration
desiccation
desideration
designation
desolation
desperation
despoliation
desquamation
destination
deterioration

determination
deterration
detestation
detonization
detruncation
devastation
deviation
devirgination
dictation
diffarreation
differentiation
digitation
dilapidation
dilatation
dilation
dimidiation
disapprobation
discoloration
discontinuation
discrimination
disculpation
disfiguration
disinclination
disintegration
dislocation
dispensation
disputation
disqualification
dissemination
dissentation
dissertation
disseveration
dissimulation
dissipation
dissociation
distillation
divagation
divarication
diversification
divination
divulgation

documentation
domestication
domiciliation
domination
donation
dotation
dulcification
duplication
duration
economization
edification
education
edulcoration
effectuation
effemination
effeminization
efflation
effoliation
ejaculation
ejulation
elaboration
elation
electrification
electrization
electrolyzation
elevation
elimination
elixation
elucidation
emaciation
emanation
emancipation
emasculation
embrocation
emendation
emigration
emulation
endenization
enervation
enthronization
enucleation

enumeration
enunciation
equalization
equation
equilibration
equitation
equivocation
eradication
eructation
estimation
estivation
eternization
etherealization
etiolation
evacuation
evangelization
evaporation
eventuation
evisceration
evocation
evolation
exacerbation
exaggeration
exaltation
examination
exasperation
excavation
excitation
exclamation
excogitation
excommuni-
   cation
excoriation
excruciation
exculpation
execration
exemplification
exercitation
exfoliation
exhalation
exhilaration

exhortation
exhumation
exoneration
expatiation
expatriation
expectation
expectoration
experimen-
tation
expiation
expiration
explanation
explication
exploitation
exploration
expoliation
exportation
expostulation
expropriation
expugnation
expurgation
exsiccation
exsufflation
extemporiza-
tion
extenuation
extermination
externalization
extirpation
extravasation
extrication
exudation
exultation
fabrication
facilitation
falcation
falsification
familiarization
fasciation
fascination
fecundation

federation
felicitation
feneration
fenestration
fermentation
ferrumination
fertilization
feudalization
fibrination
figuration
filiation
filtration
fissiparation
fixation
flagellation
flagitation
flirtation
floccillation
florification
flossification
flotation
fluctuation
flusteration
fluxation
foliation
fomentation
forcipation
foreordination
formation
formulization
fortification
fossilification
fossilization
foundation
fraternation
fraternization
frequentation
friation
frication
frondation
fructification

frumentation
frustration
fulguration
fulmination
fumigation
furcation
furfuration
galvanization
gasification
gelatination
gelatinization
gemination
gemmation
generalisation
generation
generification
geniculation
germination
gestation
gesticulation
glaciation
glandulation
glomeration
gloriation
glorification
glutination
gradation
graduation
granitification
granulation
graticulation
gratification
gratulation
gravidation
gravitation
gunation
gustation
gyration
habilitation
habitation
habituation

hallucination
hariolation
harmonization
hebetation
hellenization
hepatization
hesitation
hibernation
Hibernization
homologation
horrification
hortation
humanization
humectation
humiliation
hybridization
hydration
hypothecation
idealization
ideation
identification
illaqueation
illation
illustration
imagination
imbrication
imitation
immaculation
immanation
immigration
immoderation
immolation
immortalization
impanation
impersonation
implication
imploration
importation
imprecation
impregnation
improvisation

313

Ā'shun

impugnation
imputation
inadequation
inaffectation
inanimation
inapplication
inappreciation
inarticulation
inauguration
inauration
incameration
incantation
incapacitation
incarceration
incarnation
incarnification
inchoation
incineration
incitation
incivilization
inclination
incommodation
inconsideration
incorporation
incrassation
incremation
incrustation
incubation
inculcation
inculpation
incultivation
incurvation
indemnification
indentation
indetermination
indication
indigitation
indignation
indiscrimina-
tion

individualiza-
tion
individuation
indoctrination
induration
inebriation
inequation
infatuation
infestation
infeudation
infiltration
inflammation
inflation
information
ingemination
ingratiation
ingravidation
ingurgitation
inhabitation
inhalation
inhumation
initiation
innervation
innovation
inoculation
inordination
inosculation
insinuation
inspiration
inspissation
installation
instauration
instigation
instillation
instrumentation
insubordination
insufflation
insulation
insultation
integration

integumenta-
tion
inteneration
intensation
intensification
intercalation
intercolumni-
ation
intercommu-
nication
interdigitation
interlineation
interlocation
intermediation
intermigration
intermutation
interpellation
interpenetra-
tion
interpolation
interpretation
interrelation
interrogation
interstratifi-
cation
intimation
intimidation
intoleration
intonation
intoxication
intrication
inundation
invalidation
investigation
invigoration
invitation
invocation
irradiation
irrigation
irritation
isolation

iteration
jactitation
jaculation
jobation
jollification
jubilation
Judaization
justification
laceration
lachrymation
lactation
lallation
lamentation
lamination
lancination
laniation
lapidation
lapidification
Latinization
laudation
laureation
lavation
laxation
legalization
legation
legislation
legitimation
levation
levigation
levitation
libation
liberation
libration
licentiation
lignification
limitation
lineation
liquation
liquidation
literalization
litigation

ōld, ôr, ŏdd, oil, fŏŏt, out; ūse, ûrn, ŭp; THis, thin

lixiviation
localization
location
lubrication
lucubration
lunation
lustration
luxation
luxuriation
macadam-
  ization
maceration
machicolation
machination
maculation
magnetization
magnification
maladmin-
  istration
maleficiation
malformation
malleation
malversation
manifestation
manipulation
marmoration
martyrization
mastication
materialization
materiation
matriculation
maturation
maximization
mediation
mediatization
medication
meditation
melioration
mellification
mendication
mensuration

mesmerization
metallization
methodization
migration
ministration
miscegenation
mitigation
mobilization
moderation
modernization
modification
modulation
molestation
mollification
monetization
monstration
moralization
mortification
multiplication
mummification
mundification
murmuration
mutation
mutilation
mutuation
mystification
narration
nasalization
natation
nation
naturalization
navigation
necessitation
negation
negotiation
neologization
nervation
neutralization
nictation
nictitation
nidification

nidulation
nigrification
nitrification
nobilitation
noctambulation
noctivagation
nodation
nomination
normalization
notation
notification
Novatian
novation
nudation
nudification
nugation
nullification
numeration
obfuscation
objurgation
oblation
oblatration
obligation
obliteration
obnubilation
obscuration
obsecration
observation
obstination
obviation
occultation
occupation
oneration
operation
oppugnation
oration
orbiculation
orchestration
ordination
organization
orientation

origination
ornamentation
oscillation
oscitation
osculation
ossification
ostentation
otiation
ovation
oxidation
oxygenation
ozonation
ozonification
ozonization
pacation
pacification
pagination
palification
palliation
palpation
palpitation
pandiculation
panification
paralysation
participation
patronization
pauperization
pausation
pectination
peculation
penetration
perambulation
percolation
peregrination
perfectation
perfectionation
perforation
perlustration
permeation
permutation
pernoctation

āle, câre, ădd, ärm, åsk; mē, hẹre, ĕnd; īce, ĭll;

315 Ā'shun

peroration
perpetration
perpetuation
perscrutation
personation
personification
perspiration
perturbation
pestillation
petrification
philosophation
phonation
phonetization
piscation
placation
plantation
plebification
plication
pluralization
polarization
police-station
pollicitation
pollination
polling-station
population
porphyrization
postillation
postulation
potation
precipitation
predacean
predation
predestination
predication
predomination
premeditation
pre-occupation
preparation
preponderation
presensation
presentation

preservation
prestidigitation
prevarication
privation
probation
proclamation
procrastination
procreation
procuration
profanation
profligation
prognosticion
prolation
prolification
prolongation
promulgation
pronation
pronunciation
propagation
propination
propitiation
propugnation
prorogation
prostration
protestation
protuberation
provocation
publication
pullulation
pulsation
pulverization
punctuation
purgation
purification
quadruplica-
  tion
qualification
quantification
quartation
quassation
quotation

racemation
radiation
radication
ramification
ratification
ratiocination
ration
realization
recalcitration
recantation
recapitulation
recidivation
reciprocation
recitation
reclamation
recognization
recommenda-
  tion
reconciliation
recordation
recreation
recrimination
rectification
recubation
recuperation
recurvation
recusation
redintegration
reformation
refrigeration
refutation
regelation
regeneration
registration
regulation
rehabilitation
reiteration
rejuvenation
relation
relaxation
relegation

relocation
remanation
remonetization
remonstration
remuneration
renegation
renovation
renunciation
reparation
repatriation
replication
representatio(
reprobation
reptation
repudiation
reputation
reservation
resignation
resinification
respiration
restoration
resupination
resuscitation
retaliation
retardation
reticulation
retractation
retrogradation
revelation
reverberation
revibration
revivification
revocation
rhetorication
roboration
rogation
rose-carnation
rotation
rubification
ruination
rumination

ōld, ôr, ŏdd, oil, fŏŏt, out; ūse, ûrn, ŭp; THis, thin

rustication
saburration
sacrification
salification
salination
salivation
saltation
salutation
salvation
sanctification
sanguification
sanitation
saponification
satiation
sation
saturation
scarification
scintillation
sciscitation
scorification
scrutation
secularization
secundation
sedimentation
segmentation
segregation
self-centration
self-
  preservation
self-
  renunciation
semination
sensation
sensualization
separation
sequestration
serration
serrulation
sibilation
siccation
sideration

signation
signification
silicification
simplification
simulation
sinuation
situation
solarization
solemnization
solicitation
solidification
somnambula-
  tion
sophistication
specialization
specification
speculation
speechification
spiflication
spiritualization
spoliation
sputation
stagnation
starvation
station
stellation
sternutation
stigmatization
stimulation
stipulation
strangulation
stratification
striation
stridulation
stultification
stupration
subarrhation
subjugation
sublation
sublevation
subligation

sublimation
sublimification
sublimitation
sublineation
subordination
subornation
subrogation
substantiation
subtilization
succussation
sudation
sufflation
suffocation
suggilation
sulcation
sulphuration
summation
superannuation
supererogation
supination
supplantation
supplementa-
  tion
supplication
supportation
suppuration
surrogation
suspensation
suspiration
sustentation
susurration
syllabication
syllogization
symbolization
synchroniza-
  tion
syncopation
systematiza-
  tion
tabularization
tabulation

tantalization
tarnation
tartarization
taxation
temeration
temporization
temptation
terebration
tergiversation
termination
tessellation
testacean
testamentation
testation
testification
theorization
Thracian
thurification
tintinnabula-
  tion
titillation
titration
titteration
titubation
toleration
trabeation
tractation
tractoration
tralation
tranquillization
transanimation
transcolation
transfiguration
transformation
translation
transliteration
translocation
transmigration
transmogrifica-
  tion
transmutation

---

transpiration
transplantation
transportation
transubstantia-
    tion
transudation
tremulation
trepidation
triangulation
tribulation
triplication
tripudiation
trituration
trucidation
trullization
truncation
tubulation
tumultuation
turbination
typification
ulceration
ultimation
ululation
undulation
unification
ustulation
usurpation
utilization
vacation
vaccination
vacillation
vacuolation
validation
valuation
vaporation
vaporization
vapulation
variation
variegation
vaticination
vegetation

vellication
venation
venenation
veneration
ventilation
verbalization
verberation
verification
vermiculation
vernation
versification
vesication
vexation
vexillation
vibration
vigesimation
vilification
vindemiation
vindication
violation
visitation
vitalization
vitiation
vitrification
vitriolation
vitriolization
vituperation
vivification
vocalization
vocation
vociferation
volatilization
volcanization
vulcanization
(cf. ĀSH'i-an)
    words

ĂSH'en,
ĂSH'un
ashen
compassion

fashion
impassion
master-passion
passion
(cf. Circassian,
    and ĂSH'i-
    an words)

ĂSH'und
dispassioned
fashioned
impassioned
old-fashioned
passioned
unfashioned
unimpassioned
unpassioned

ĂSH'ur
Asher
baggage-
    smasher
Brasher
casher
clasher
crasher
dasher
flasher
gasher
haberdasher
lasher
masher
rasher
slasher
smasher
splasher
thrasher
unlasher

Ā'shus
audacious

bibacious
capacious
contumacious
disgracious
disputatious
edacious
efficacious
execratious
fallacious
feracious
flirtatious
fugacious
fumacious
gracious
incapacious
inefficacious
linguacious
loquacious
mendacious
minacious
misgracious
mordacious
ostentatious
palacious
perspicacious
pertinacious
pervicacious
predacious
procacious
pugnacious
rampacious
rapacious
sagacious
salacious
sequacious
spacious
tenacious
ungracious
veracious
vexatious

ōld, ôr, ŏdd, oil, fŏŏt, out; ūse, ûrn, ŭp; THis, thin

vivacious
voracious

acanaceous
acanthaceous
alliaceous
amylaceous
arenaceous
bulbaceous
cactaceous
camphoraceous
capillaceous
carbonaceous
cetaceous
corallaceous
coriaceous
cretaceous
crustaceous
cylindraceous
erinaceous
fabaceous
farinaceous
ferulaceous
filaceous
foliaceous
frumentaceous
fungaceous
furfuraceous
gallinaceous
gemmaceous
herbaceous
lappaceous
lardaceous
liliaceous
marlaceous
micaceous
olivaceous
orchidaceous
palmaceous
pectinaceous
perdaceous

perlaceous
piperaceous
pomaceous
porraceous
psittaceous
pulveraceous
ranunculaceous
resinaceous
rosaceous
rutaceous
sabaceous
salicaceous
saponaceous
sarmentaceous
saxifragaceous
schorlaceous
scoriaceous
sebaceous
setaceous
stercoraceous
testaceous
tophaceous
torfaceous
truttaceous
turbinaceous
vinaceous
violaceous

ĂSH'vil

Ashville
Nashville

ĀS'ĭ

Gracie
Lacey
lacy
précis
racy

ĂS'ĭ

brassie

brassy
classy
gassy
glassy
grassy
lassie
Malagasy
massy
morassy
sassy
Tallahassee

Ā'sĭd

bayside
braeside
wayside

ĂS'ĭd

acid
placid

ĂS'ĭj

brassage
passage

ĂS'ĭk

aphasic
basic
bibasic
dibasic
quadribasic
tribasic

ĂS'ĭk

boracic
classic
Jurassic
Liassic
potassic
sebacic

thoracic
Triassic

ĂS'il

facile
gracile

ĀS'in

basin
(cf. ĀS'n)

ĀS'ĭn

assassin

ĂS'in

spadassin

ĀS'ing

abasing
basing
begracing
belacing
bracing
casing
chasing
debasing
defacing
disgracing
displacing
effacing
embracing
enlacing
erasing
facing
foot-racing
gracing
horse-racing
interlacing
interspacing
lacing
misplacing

āle, câre, ădd, ärm, ȧsk; mē, hẹre, ĕnd; īce, ĭll;

outfacing
outpacing
pacing
placing
racing
replacing
retracing
self-abasing
spacing
steeple-chasing
tight-lacing
tracing
uncasing
underbracing
unlacing

ĂS'ing

amassing
classing
gassing
massing
overpassing
passing
surpassing
underclassing

ĀS'is

basis
crasis
glacis
oasis
phasis

ĂS'is

chassis

ĂS'it

tacit
(cf. ĂS'et)

ĀS'iv

assuasive

dissuasive
evasive
invasive
persuasive
pervasive
suasive

ĂS'iv

impassive
massive
passive

ĂS'ka

Alaska
Athabaska
Nebraska

ĂS'kal

mascle
paschal
rascal
(cf. Haskell,
etc.)

ĂS'kar

Lascar
Madagascar

ĂS'kest

askest
baskest
bemaskest
maskest
taskest
unmaskest

ĂS'ket

basket
bread-basket
casket
flasket

gasket
lasket

ĂS'keth

asketh
basketh
bemasketh
masketh
tasketh
unmasketh

ĂS'king

asking
basking
bemasking
masking
overtasking
tasking
unmasking

ĂS'ko

Belasco
fiasco
tabasco
tasco

ĂS'kur

asker
basker
casquer
masker

ĂS'kus

Damascus

ĂSK'with

Asquith

ĂS' 'l

castle
entassel

envassal
tassel
vassal
wrastle

ĀS'les

aceless
baseless
caseless
faceless
graceless
laceless
maceless
paceless
placeless
raceless
spaceless
traceless

ĀS'let

bracelet

ĂS'let

haslet
taslet

ĀS'li

basely
commonplacely

ĀS'man

baseman
first baseman
laceman
paceman
placeman
raceman
second baseman
third baseman

ĂS'man

classman

ōld, ôr, ŏdd, oil, fŏŏt, out; ūse, ûrn, ŭp; THis. th̷

gasman
glassman

ĀS'ment
abasement
basement
begracement
belacement
casement
debasement
defacement
displacement
effacement
embracement
encasement
enlacement
erasement
interlacement
misplacement
placement
replacement
retracement
self-abasement

ĂS'ment
amassment

**ĂS'min or
ĂZ'min**
jasmine

ĀS' 'n
chasten
enchasten
hasten
(cf. ĀS'in,
Ās'on)

ĀS' 'n
fasten
(cf. casson)

ĀS'nur
chastener
hastener

ĂS'nes
crassness

ĀS'o
say-so

ĀS'o, ĂS'o
basso
lasso
Sargasso
Tasso

ĂS'ok
cassock
hassock

ĀS'on
caisson
Grayson
Jason
mason
(cf. ĀS'n)

ĂS'on
casson
(cf. fasten)

ĂS'pen
aspen

ĂS'pest
claspest
enclaspest
gaspest
graspest
raspest
unclaspest

ĂS'peth
claspeth
enclaspeth
gaspeth
graspeth
raspeth
unclaspeth

ĂS'pik
aspic

ĂS'ping
clasping
enclasping
engrasping
gasping
grasping
rasping
unclasping

ĂS'pur
asper
Caspar
Casper
clasper
gasper
grasper
jasper
rasper

ĀS'ta
Shasta

Ā'star
day-star

ĀS'ted
basted
hasted
long-waisted
pasted

short-waisted
tasted
untasted
unwasted
war-wasted
wasted

ĂS'ted
blasted
contrasted
fasted
flabbergasted
lasted
masted
outlasted
unblasted
undermasted

ĂS'tel
pastel

ĀST'est
bastest
chastest
foretastest
hastest
pastest
tastest
wastest
wastest

ĂST'est
castest
contrastest
fastest
lastest
outlastest
vastest

ĀST'eth
basteth

foretasteth
hasteth
pasteth
tasteth
wasteth

ĂST'eth
casteth
contrasteth
fasteth
lasteth
outlasteth

ĂST'ful
distasteful
tasteful
wasteful

ĂS'ti
hasty
pasty
tasty

ĂS'ti
blasty
epinasty
genioplasty
masty
nasty
vasty

ĂS'tif
mastiff

ĂS'tij
wastage

ĂS'tik
amphiblastic
anaclastic
antiphrastic

antonomastic
bioplastic
bombastic
ceroplastic
chiliastic
clastic
deutoplastic
dichastic
docimastic
drastic
dynastic
ecclesiastic
elastic
emplastic
encomiastic
enthusiastic
esemplastic
fantastic
galvanoplastic
gelastic
gymnastic
Hudibrastic
iconoclastic
inelastic
mastic
metaphrastic
monastic
neoplastic
onomastic
orgiastic
paraphrastic
parasceuastic
paronomastic
peirastic
periphrastic
phelloplastic
plagioclastic
plastic
pleonastic
proplastic
protoplastic

sarcastic
scholastic
scholiastic
spastic
tetrastich

ĂS'tiks
ecclesiastics
elastics
fantastics
gymnastics
phelloplastics

ĂS'tim
pastime

ĂST'ing
basting
foretasting
hasting
pasting
tasting
unwasting
wasting

ĂST'ing
blasting
casting
contrasting
everlasting
fasting
flabbergasting
forecasting
lasting
recasting

ĂS'tingz
Hastings
bastings, etc.

ĂST'les
basteless

hasteless
pasteless
tasteless
waistless
wasteless

ĂST'li
ghastly
lastly
steadfastly
vastly

ĂST'ment
blastment
contrastment

ĂST'nes
fastness
vastness

ĂST'ning
fastening

ĂS'ton
Aston
Gaston

ĂS'tral
astral
cadastral
subastral

ĂS'tri
pastry

ĂS'trik
cacogastric
digastric
gastric
hypogastric
perigastric

ĂS'tron	grammaticaster	**ĀS'ur**	passer
apastron	grand-master	abaser	placer
plastron	interpilaster	ambulance-	surpasser
	Latinitaster	chaser	
ĂS'trus	master	baser	**ÄS'ur**
disastrous	medicaster	begracer	kirsh-wasser
	oleaster	belacer	
ĂS'tur	overmaster	bracer	**Ā'ta**
baster	pastor	chaser	albata
chaster	piaster	debaser	data
foretaster	pilaster	defacer	dentata
paster	plaster	disgracer	errata
taster	poetaster	displacer	Invertebrata
waster	postmaster	effacer	postulata
	quarter-master	embracer	pro rata
ĂS'tūr	schoolmaster	encaser	strata
pasture	shĭn-plaster	eraser	ultimata
	sticking-plaster	facer	Vertebrata
ĂS'tŭr, ĂS'tur	taskmaster	footracer	
alabaster	vaster	gracer	**ĂT'a**
aster		grimacer	matamata
Astor	**ÄS'tur**	horse-racer	regatta
band-master	shaster	interlacer	strata
barrack-master		lacer	(cf. yerba-
beplaster	**ĂS'turd,**	macer	mata)
blaster	**ÅS'turd**	misplacer	
burgomaster	bastard	outpacer	**Ä'ta**
bushmaster	beplastered	pacer	a ballata
cadastre	dastard	placer	batata
canaster	mastered	racer	cantata
caster	overmastered	replacer	data
castor	pilastered	retracer	imbrocata
china-aster	plastered	spacer	inamorata
contraster	unmastered	steeple-chaser	Mahratta
courtplaster		tracer	pro rata
criticaster	**ĂS'tus**	unlacer	reata
disaster	Erastus		serenata
faster	Rastus	**ĂS'ur**	sonata
flabbergaster		amasser	(cf. yerba-
forecaster	**ĂS'tyun**	antimacassar	mata)
Goniaster	bastion	masser	
	(cf. Erastian)		

323   ĀT'al — ĀT'ed

ĀT'al
fatal
natal
prenatal
post-natal
Statal

ĀT'an
Satan
(cf. ĀT'on)

ĀT'ant
blatant
latent
natant
patent
statant

ĀT'ed
abated
abbreviated
abdicated
ablocated
abnegated
abominated
abrogated
accelerated
accentuated
accommodated
accumulated
acidulated
actuated
addle-pated
adjudicated
adulterated
advocated
aërated
affiliated
agglomerated
aggravated
aggregated

agitated
alienated
alleviated
allocated
alternated
amalgamated
ameliorated
ampliated
amputated
annihilated
annotated
annulated
annumerated
annunciated
antedated
anticipated
antiquated
appreciated
approbated
appropriated
approximated
arbitrated
armillated
armor-plated
arrogated
articulated
asphyxiated
aspirated
assassinated
asseverated
assimilated
assimulated
associated
asteriated
attenuated
augurated
aurated
authenticated
awaited
baited
bated

belated
berated
bifurcated
calculated
calumniated
camphorated
capacitated
capitulated
captivated
carbonated
castellated
castigated
celebrated
certificated
circulated
circumstanti-
    ated
coagulated
cogitated
collated
collocated
commemo-
    rated
comminated
commiserated
communicated
compensated
complicated
concentrated
conciliated
confabulated
confederated
confiscated
conglomerated
congratulated
congregated
conjugated
consecrated
consolidated
consummated
contaminated

contemplated
co-operated
co-ordinated
copper-plated
copulated
coronated
correlated
corroborated
corrugated
created
cremated
crenellated
crepitated
culminated
cultivated
dated
debated
debilitated
decapitated
decimated
decorated
dedicated
degenerated
delegated
deliberated
delineated
demonstrated
denominated
depopulated
deprecated
depreciated
derogated
desecrated
desiderated
designated
desolated
deteriorated
detonated
devastated
deviated
dictated

_____
ōld, ôr, ŏdd, oil, fŏŏt, out; ūse, ûrn, ŭp; THis, thin

differentiated
dilapidated
dilated
discriminated
disintegrated
dislocated
disseminated
dissimulated
dissipated
dissociated
domesticated
dominated
dunder-pated
duplicated
educated
effectuated
efflated
ejaculated
elaborated
elated
electro-plated
elevated
eliminated
elucidated
emaciated
emanated
emancipated
emasculated
emigrated
emulated
enumerated
enunciated
equivocated
eradicated
estimated
evacuated
evaporated
eventuated
exaggerated
exasperated
excavated

excommuni-
    cated
excoriated
execrated
exhilarated
exonerated
exorbitated
expatiated
expatriated
expectorated
expiated
expostulated
extenuated
exterminated
extricated
fabricated
facilitated
fascinated
fated
federated
felicitated
fêted
flagellated
fluctuated
foreordinated
formulated
freighted
frustrated
fulminated
fumigated
gaited
gated
generated
germinated
gesticulated
graduated
granulated
grated
gratulated
gravitated
habituated

hated
heavy-gaited
heavy-
    weighted
hesitated
humiliated
idle-pated
ill-fated
illuminated
illustrated
imitated
immigrated
immolated
impersonated
implicated
imprecated
impropriated
inaugurated
incapacitated
incarcerated
incastellated
incinerated
incorporated
incriminated
incubated
indicated
indoctrinated
indurated
inebriated
infatuated
inflated
infuriated
ingratiated
initiated
innovated
inoculated
insinuated
instated
instigated
insulated
interpolated

interrogated
intimated
intimidated
intoxicated
inundated
invalidated
investigated
invigorated
invocated
irradiated
irrigated
irritated
isolated
iterated
jasperated
legislated
levigated
liberated
liquidated
located
lubricated
luxuriated
macerated
manipulated
marinated
masticated
mated
matriculated
medicated
meditated
methylated
migrated
militated
mitigated
moderated
modulated
mutilated
narrated
navigated
necessitated
negotiated

nickle-plated
nominated
nucleolated
obligated
obliterated
obviated
officiated
operated
opinionated
originated
oscillated
osculated
overrated
overstated
palliated
palpitated
participated
penetrated
perambulated
percolated
peregrinated
perforated
permeated
perpetrated
perpetuated
personated
placated
plaited
plated
plicated
populated
postulated
prated
precipitated
predestinated
predicated
predominated
premeditated
prevaricated
procrastinated
prognosticated

propagated
propitiated
punctuated
radiated
rated
rattle-pated
recapitulated
reciprocated
recreated
recriminated
recuperated
refrigerated
regenerated
regulated
rehabilitated
reinstated
reiterated
rejuvenated
related
relegated
remunerated
renovated
Reno-vated
repatriated
repudiated
resuscitated
retaliated
reverberated
ruminated
rusticated
salivated
sated
satiated
saturated
scintillated
segregated
separated
shallow-pated
sibilated
silicated
silver-plated

simulated
situated
skated
slated
sophisticated
speculated
spifflicated
stated
stimulated
stipulated
subjugated
sublimated
subordinated
substantiated
suffocated
superannuated
supplicated
syncopated
syndicated
tabulated
tergiversated
terminated
tessellated
titillated
tittivated
tolerated
translated
triangulated
triturated
ululated
unabated
unappropri-
　ated
unauthenti-
　cated
uncreated
undecorated
underrated
understated
undulated
unilluminated

unmitigated
unpremedi-
　tated
unrelated
unsophisti-
　cated
unstated
vacated
vaccinated
vacillated
validated
variated
variegated
vegetated
venerated
ventilated
vindicated
violated
vitiated
vituperated
vociferated
waited
weighted

ĂT′ed

batted
chatted
dratted
fatted
hatted
matted
patted
plaited
platted
(cf. caryatid)

ĂT′en

batten
fatten
flatten

paten
ratten

ĂT'ent or
   ĂT'ent

patent

ĂT'est

abatest
abdicatest
accommodatest
accumulatest
adulteratest
advocatest
aggravatest
agitatest
alleviatest
animatest
annihilatest
anticipatest
appreciatest
articulatest
assimilatest
associatest
awaitest
baitest
beratest
calculatest
captivatest
celebratest
cogitatest
commemoratest
communicatest
conjugatest
consecratest
contaminatest
contemplatest
createst
cultivatest
debatest

decoratest
deprecatest
devastatest
dictatest
dilatest
ejaculatest
elevatest
emulatest
exaggeratest
fascinatest
frustratest
graduatest
greatest
hatest
hesitatest
imitatest
indicatest
irritatest
latest
liberatest
matest
narratest
necessitatest
overratest
plaitest
pratest
radiatest
ratest
regulatest
relatest
repudiatest
skatest
slatest
statest
toleratest
translatest
underratest
vacatest
violatest
waitest

ĂT'est

battest
chattest
fattest
flattest
pattest

ĂT'eth

abateth
abdicateth
accelerateth
accommodateth
accumulateth
adulterateth
advocateth
agitateth
alleviateth
ameliorateth
animateth
annihilateth
anticipateth
appropriateth
arbitrateth
articulateth
associateth
awaiteth
baiteth
calculateth
cancellateth
captivateth
celebrateth
circulateth
conciliateth
confiscateth
congratulateth
consecrateth
contaminateth
contemplateth
createth
cremateth
cultivateth

debateth
decorateth
dedicateth
depopulateth
devastateth
dictateth
dilateth
dissipateth
dominateth
educateth
ejaculateth
elevateth
emulateth
estimateth
exaggerateth
excavateth
excommuni-
   cateth
exhilarateth
expiateth
extenuateth
extricateth
fabricateth
fascinateth
frustrateth
hateth
hesitateth
imitateth
indicateth
irritateth
liberateth
locateth
luxuriateth
mateth
meditateth
narrateth
operateth
overrateth
prateth
rateth
regulateth

relateth
separateth
skateth
stateth
suffocateth
underrateth
vaccinateth
violateth
waiteth

ĂT′eth
batteth
chatteth
fatteth
patteth

ĂT′ez
penates

ĂT′foot
flatfoot

ĂT′form
platform

ĂT′ful
fateful
grateful
hateful
ungrateful

ĂT′ha
Jagannatha
(cf. marana-
    tha)

Ăth′an
Elnathan
Nathan

ĂT′hed
fathead
flathead

Ăth′en
lathen

Ăth′ful
faithful

Ăth′ful, Ăth′ful
wrathful

Ăth′ik
allopathic
antipathic
chrestomathic
electropathic
felspathic
heteropathic
homeopathic
hydropathic
idiopathic
kinemato-
    graphic
neuropathic
orthognathic
osteopathic
philomathic
polymathic
prognathic
psycopathic
spathic
telepathic
theopathic

ĂTH′ing
bathing
swathing
unswathing

Ā′thing
plaything
(cf. scathing)

Ăth′ing
bathing
lathing

Ăth′les
faithless
scatheless

Ăth′les
bathless
pathless
wrathless

ĂTH′om
fathom

ĂTH′omd
unfathomed

Ăth′os
bathos
pathos

Ăth′u
Matthew

ĂTH′ur
bather
swather

ĂTH′ur
blather
forgather
gather
lather
ungather
upgather

ĂTH′ur,
ĀTH′ur
father

rather
(cf. bother,
    etc.)

ĂTH′urz
slathers
gathers, etc.

ĂT′i
Ate
eighty
ex necessitate
Haiti
Jubilate
maty
platy
slaty
weighty

ĂT′ī
antenati
illuminati
literati

ĂT′i
batty
catty
chatty
Cincinnati
fatty
Hattie
Mattie
matty
natty
patty
Pattie
ratty

ĂT′ĭd
bat-eyed
cat-eyed

ĂT′ĭd
caryatid
(cf. batted, etc.)

ĀT′if
caitiff

ĂT′ik
achromatic
acousmatic
acroatic
acrobatic
acromono-
  grammatic
adiabatic
Adriatic
aerostatic
agnatic
anagram-
  matic
anastatic
aphorismatic
aplanatic
apophtheg-
  matic
aquatic
aristocratic
arithmocratic
aromatic
Asiatic
astatic
asthmatic
attic
autocratic
automatic
axiomatic
bureaucratic
caryatic
categorematic
chromatic
climatic

commatic
dalmatic
democratic
diagrammatic
diaphragmatic
dichromatic
dilemmatic
diplomatic
dogmatic
dramatic
ecbatic
ecstatic
Eleatic
emblematic
emphatic
endermatic
enigmatic
epigrammatic
erratic
fanatic
fluviatic
geostatic
grammatic
hallelujatic
Hanseatic
hepatic
hieratic
hierogram-
  matic
hydrostatic
hyperbatic
hypostatic
idiocratic
idiomatic
idiosyncratic
isochromatic
isodiabatic
kinematic
lavatic
lipogrammatic
lymphatic

magistratic
majestatic
mathematic
melodramatic
miasmatic
mobocratic
monochro-
  matic
monogram-
  matic
morganatic
muriatic
noematic
numismatic
ochlocratic
operatic
palatic
pancratic
pancreatic
pantisocratic
paradigmatic
parallelo-
  grammatic
pathematic
phantomatic
phlegmatic
phosphatic
piratic
platic
pleochromatic
plutocratic
pneumatic
poematic
polychromatic
pragmatic
prelatic
prismatic
problematic
proceleus-
  matic
prostatic

protatic
quadratic
rhematic
rheumatic
sabbatic
Sarmatic
schematic
schismatic
sciatic
smegmatic
Socratic
somatic
static
stigmatic
stromatic
subaquatic
sulphatic
sylvatic
symptomatic
systematic
thematic
theocratic
theorematic
thermostatic
timocratic
traumatic
trigrammatic
truismatic
vatic
viatic
villatic
zeugmatic
zygomatic

ĂT′ik
aquatic
(see chaotic,
  etc.)

ĂT′iks
aerostatics

āle, câre, ădd, ärm, åsk; mē, hẹre, ĕnd; īce, ĭll;

electro-statics
hydrostatics
hygrostatics
mathematics
pneumatics
statics
attics, etc.

Ā′tim
daytime
playtime

ĀT′im
literatim
seriatim
verbatim

ĀT′in
Latin
matin
patine
platen
satin

ĀT′ing
abating
abbreviating
abdicating
abnegating
abominating
accelerating
accentuating
accommodating
accumulating
adulterating
advocating
aërating
aggravating
aggregating
agitating
alienating

alleviating
alternating
amalgamating
ameliorating
amputating
animating
annihilating
annumerating
anticipating
appreciating
appropriating
approximating
arbitrating
armor-plating
articulating
assassinating
assimilating
associating
attenuating
augurating
authenticating
awaiting
baiting
bating
berating
calculating
calumniating
capitulating
castigating
celebrating
circulating
coagulating
cogitating
collocating
commemorat-
    ing
commiserating
communicating
compensating
complicating
concentrating

conciliating
confabulating
confederating
confiscating
congratulating
congregating
conjugating
consecrating
consolidating
consummating
contaminating
contemplating
co-operating
corroborating
corrugating
creating
cremating
criminating
culminating
cultivating
dating
debating
debilitating
decapitating
decimating
decorating
dedicating
degenerating
delegating
deliberating
delineating
demonstrating
denominating
depopulating
deprecating
depreciating
derivating
derogating
desecrating
designating
deteriorating

determinating
detonating
devastating
deviating
dictating
differentiating
dilapidating
dilating
discriminating
disintegrating
dislocating
disseminating
dissimulating
dissipating
dissociating
dominating
duplicating
educating
ejaculating
elaborating
electro-plating
elevating
eliminating
elucidating
emaciating
emanating
emancipating
emigrating
emulating
enumerating
equivocating
eradicating
estimating
evacuating
evaporating
exaggerating
exasperating
excavating
excommunica-
    ting
excruciating

___

ōld, ôr, ŏdd, oil, fŏŏt, out; ūse, ûrn, ŭp; THis, thin

execrating
exhilarating
exonerating
expatiating
expectorating
expiating
expostulating
extenuating
extricating
fabricating
facilitating
fascinating
federating
felicitating
fêting
flagellating
fluctuating
formulating
fornicating
freighting
frustrating
fulminating
fumigating
generating
germinating
gesticulating
graduating
granulating
grating
gratulating
gravitating
hating
hesitating
humiliating
illuminating
illustrating
imitating
immigrating
immolating
impersonating
implicating

imprecating
inaugurating
incapacitating
incarcerating
incriminating
incubating
indicating
indiscrimi-
    nating
inebriating
infanticipating
infatuating
inflating
infuriating
ingratiating
initiating
innovating
inoculating
insinuating
instigating
insulating
interpolating
interrogating
intimating
intimidating
intoxicating
inundating
invalidating
investigating
invigorating
invocating
irradiating
irrigating
irritating
isolating
iterating
legislating
liberating
liquidating
locating
lubricating

luxuriating
manipulating
masticating
mating
matriculating
mediating
meditating
migrating
militating
mitigating
moderating
modulating
mutilating
narrating
navigating
necessitating
negotiating
nickle-plating
nominating
obliterating
obviating
operating
originating
oscillating
osculating
overrating
overstating
palliating
palpitating
participating
penetrating
perambulating
percolating
peregrinating
perforating
permeating
perpetrating
perpetuating
personating
plaiting
plating

populating
postulating
prating
precipitating
predominating
premeditating
prevaricating
prognosticat-
    ing
promulgating
propagating
propitiating
punctuating
quadrupli-
    cating
radiating
rating
rebating
recapitulating
reciprocating
recreating
recriminating
recuperating
refrigerating
regulating
reinstating
reiterating
rejuvenating
relating
relegating
remunerating
renovating
repudiating
resuscitating
retaliating
reverberating
ruminating
rusticating
satiating
saturating
scintillating

separating
simulating
skating
slating
sophisticating
speculating
stating
stimulating
stipulating
subjugating
suffocating
supplicating
syncopating
tabulating
terminating
titillating
tittivating
tolerating
translating
unabating
unaccommo-
   dating
underrating
understating
undeviating
undiscrimi-
   nating
undulating
vacating
vaccinating
vacillating
validating
variegating
vegetating
venerating
ventilating
verberating
vindicating
violating
vitiating
vituperating

vociferating
waiting
weighting

ĂT'ing

batting
chatting
fatting
matting
patting
platting
ratting
tatting
vatting

ĀT'ir

satire

ĀT'is

gratis

ĂT'is

brattice
lattice

ĂT'ish

cattish
fattish
flattish

ĀT'iv

abrogative
accelerative
accumulative
administrative
agglomerative
agglutinative
aggregative
agitative
alleviative
alliterative

alterative
ameliorative
animative
anticipative
annunciative
appreciative
approbative
appropriative
approximative
assimilative
associative
authoritative
coagulative
cogitative
collative
commemora-
   tive
commiserative
communica-
   tive
confederative
consolidative
contaminative
continuative
co-operative
co-ordinative
copulative
corroborative
creative
criminative
cumulative
dative
decorative
degenerative
deliberative
denominative
denunciative
deprecative
depreciative
desiderative
designative

determinative
dilative
discriminative
disseminative
dominative
duplicative
edulcorative
elaborative
elucidative
emanative
emulative
enumerative
enunciative
eradicative
estimative
evaporative
exaggerative
execrative
exonerative
explicative
federative
generative
germinative
glutinative
gravitative
hesitative
illuminative
imaginative
imbricative
imitative
implicative
incogitative
incommunica-
   tive
incorporative
incriminative
incubative
indiscrimina-
   tive
initiative
innovative

ōld, ôr, ŏdd, oil, fŏŏt, out; ūse, ûrn, ŭp; THis, thin

inoperative
insinuative
interpenetra-
  tive
interpretative
investigative
irritative
iterative
justificative
lacerative
legislative
manipulative
meditative
ministrative
mitigative
modificative
native
operative
opinionative
originative
oscillative
palliative
participative
penetrative
perforative
predestinative
procreative
prognostica-
  tive
pronunciative
propagative
purificative
qualificative
qualitative
quantitative
radiative
ratiocinative
recreative
recriminative
recuperative
refrigerative

regenerative
reiterative
remunerative
replicative
reprobative
resuscitative
retaliative
reverberative
sative
separative
significative
speculative
stative
stimulative
subordinative
suffocative
supplicative
suppurative
terminative
translative
undulative
vegetative
velicative
ventilative
verificative
vindicative
violative
vituperative
vivificative

ĂT'kins
Atkins
Batkins
(cf. Watkins)

ĂT' 'l
battel
battle
cattle
chattel
death-rattle ·

embattle
prattle
rattle
Seattle
tattle
tittle-tattle

ĂT'las, ĂT'les
atlas
cravatless
hatless
(see ĀT + less)

ĀT'les
baitless
dateless
estateless
freightless
gaitless
gateless
grateless
hateless
mateless
rateless
stateless
weightless

ĀT'li (ĬT'li)
accurately
adequately
affectionately
alternately
appropriately
approximately
compassion-
  ately
consummately
delicately
desolately
desperately
disconsolately

effeminately
elaborately
extortionately
fortunately
greatly
illiterately
immaculately
immoderately
inarticulately
inconsider-
  ately
intemperately
intimately
irately
lately
legitimately
moderately
sedately
stately
straitly
ultimately

ĂT'li
fatly
flatly
patly
rattly

ĂT'ling
battling
catling
fatling
gatling
prattling
rattling
tattling

ĂT'lur
battler
prattler
rattler

Statler	Ä'to	ĂT'res	ĂT'u
tattler	annatto	mattress	statue
	chateau	mulattress	
ĀT'ment	enamorato		**ĀT'um**
abatement	legato	**ĂT'rik**	datum
affreightment	obbligato	hippiatric	desideratum
instatement	pizzicato	iatric	erratum
overstatement	pomato	kinesiatric	pomatum
reinstatement	staccato	matric	postulatum
statement	tomato	Patrick	stratum
understate-		theatric	substratum
ment	**ĂT'om**		superstratum
	atom	**ĀT'riks**	ultimatum
ĀT'nes		administratrix	
appropriate-	**ĀT'on**	aviatrix	**ĂT'um**
ness	Clayton	cicatrix	stratum
considerate-	Dayton	generatrix	
ness	Leighton	imitatrix	**ĂT'um**
greatness	peyton	impropriatrix	datum
innateness	Satan	matrix	pomatum
lateness		mediatrix	
ornateness	**ĂT'on**	spectatrix	
sedateness	baton	testatrix	**ĀT'ūr**
straightness	Hatton		good-nature
		ĀT'ris, ĂT'ris	ill-nature
ĂT'nes	**ĂT'ra**	matrice	legislature
fatness	Cleopatra		nature
flatness		**ĀT'ron**	nomenclature
patness	**Ā'tre**	matron	plicature
	baytree	natron	unnature
ĀT'o	maytree	patron	
literato			**ĀT'ŭr**
Plato	**ĀT'red**	**ĀTS'man**	abator
pomato	hatred	statesman	abbreviator
potato			abdicator
tomato	**ĀT'res**	**ĂTS'man**	abnegator
	dictatress	batsman	abrogater
ĂT'o	imitatress		accelerator
chateau	spectatress	**ĂT'son**	accumulator
mulatto	traitress	Batson	adjudicator
plateau	waitress	Matson	administrator

---

adulator
affreighter
aggravator
agitator
alienator
alleviator
alligator
alma mater
amalgamator
ameliorator
annihilator
annotator
annunciator
appropriator
arbitrator
arch-traitor
aspirater
asseverator
assimilator
authenticator
aviator
awaiter
baiter
berater
calculator
calumniator
captivator
castigator
cater
cogitator
collaborator
commemo-
    rator
commentator
comminator
commiserator
compotator
compurgator
computator
concentrator
conciliator

confiscator
conjugator
consecrator
conservator
consolidator
contaminator
contemplator
co-operator
corroborator
crater
creator
cremator
criminator
cultivator
dater
debater
decapitator
decorator
dedicator
deliberator
delineator
demonstrator
denominator
denunciator
depopulator
depreciator
depredator
designator
devastator
deviator
dictater
dictator
disintegrator
disseminator
dissimulator
duplicator
dura mater
educater
ejaculator
elaborator
elevator

eliminator
elucidator
emanator
emancipator
emendator
emulator
enumerator
enunciator
equator
equivocator
eradicator
evaporator
exaggerator
excavator
execrator
exhilarator
exonerator
expatiator
expectorator
expiator
extenuator
exterminator
extricator
fabricator
facilitator
fascinator
federator
felicitator
first-rater
flagellator
formulator
fornicator
frater
freighter
frustrator
fumigator
gaiter
generator
germinator
gesticulator
gladiator

grater
greater
hater
hesitater
humilater
hypothecator
illuminator
illustrator
imitator
imperator
impersonator
imprimatur
incarcerator
incorporator
incriminator
incubator
indicator
inflater
initiator
innovator
inoculator
insinuator
instigator
insulator
interpolator
interrogator
intimidator
investigator
invigorator
invocator
irrigator
irritator
later
laudator
legislator
liberator
liquidator
litigator
locater
lubricator
manipulator

---

masticator	promulgator	supplicator	patter
mater	propagator	tabulator	platter
mediator	propitiator	"tater"	ratter
meditator	radiator	tergiversator	satyr
migrater	rater	testator	scatter
mitigator	reciprocator	third-rater	shatter
moderator	refrigerator	titillator	smatter
modulator	regenerator	tittivator	spatter
mutilator	regrater	traitor	splatter
narrator	regulator	translator	subject-matter
navigator	reinstater	vaccinator	tatter
negotiator	reiterator	vacillator	
nominator	relater	vaticinator	**ĂT´ur**
obliterator	remonstrator	venerator	alma mater
officiator	renovator	ventilator	mater
operator	repudiator	versificator	pater
originator	respirator	vindicator	Stabat Mater
oscillator	resuscitator	violator	
pacificator	retaliator	vituperator	**ĂT´urn**
palliator	ruminator	vociferator	pattern
palpitator	rusticator	waiter	Saturn
pater	satyr		slattern
perambulator	scintillator	**ĂT´ūr**	willow-pattern
percolator	scrutator	stature	
peregrinator	second-rater		**ĀT´us**
perforator	sedater	**ĂT´ŭr**	afflatus
permeator	separator	attar	apparatus
perpetrator	simulator	batter	hiatus
personator	skater	beflatter	literatus
pia mater	slater	bepatter	saleratus
piscator	sophisticator	bescatter	senatus
plaiter	spectator	bespatter	status
plater	speculator	blatter	stratous
prater	Stabat Mater	chatter	stratus
precipitator	stater	clatter	
predominator	stimulator	clitter-clatter	**ĂT´us**
prestidigitator	stipulator	fatter	apparatus
prevaricator	straighter	flatter	
procrastinator	straiter	hatter	**ĂT´ut**
procurator	subjugator	latter	statute
prognosticator	supererogator	matter	

ĀT'wa
gateway
straitway

Ā'ur
affrayer
allayer
arrayer
assayer
belayer
betrayer
brayer
conveyer
defrayer
delayer
disarrayer
dismayer
disobeyer
displayer
essayer
flayer
gainsayer
gayer
grayer
greyer
hoorayer
inlayer
interlayer
inveigher
layer
matineer
mayor
mislayer
missayer
neigher
obeyer
outlayer
outstayer
outweigher
overlayer
payer

player
portrayer
prayer
preyer
prepayer
purveyor
relayer
repayer
slayer
soothsayer
sprayer
stayer
strayer
surveyer
swayer
underpayer
underplayer
viséer
waylayer
weigher

Ă'va
brava
cassava
guava
Java
lava

ĂV'al
travail

ĀV'e
agave
ave

Ă've
ave

ĀV'el
gavel
naval
navel

ĂV'el
gavel
gravel
ravel
travel
unravel
(cf. cavil)

ĂV'eld
gravelled
ravelled
travelled
untravelled

ĂV'en
craven
engraven
graven
haven
shaven

ĀV'est
behavest
beslavest
bravest
cravest
depravest
engravest
enslavest
forgavest
gavest
gravest
lavest
pavest
ravest
savest
shavest
slavest
suavest
waivest
wavest

ĀV'eth
behaveth
beslaveth
braveth
craveth
depraveth
engraveth
enslaveth
forgaveth
gaveth
laveth
paveth
raveth
saveth
shaveth
slaveth
waiveth
waveth

ĀV'ez
Davies

ĀV'i
affidavy
cavy
Davie
Davy
gravy
navy
peccavi
ravy
slavey
wavy

ĀV'id
David
engraved, etc.

ĂV'id
avid
gravid

impavid	waving	staveless	cadaver
pavid	wood-engrav-	waveless	claver
	ing		craver
ĂVʹij		**ĀVʹli**	demiquaver
ravage	**ĂVʹing**	bravely	depraver
savage	having	gravely	disfavor
scavage	salving	knavely	engraver
		suavely	enslaver
ĂVʹik	**ĂVʹing**		favor
gravic	calving	**ĂVʹlin**	flavor
Pan-Slavic	halving	javelin	graver
Slavic	salving	ravelin	laver
			marriage-
ĂVʹin	**ĀVʹis**	**ĂVʹling**	favor
savin	clavis	shaveling	Papaver
spavin	Davis		paver
	mavis	**ĂVʹment**	quaver
ĀVʹing	rara avis	depravement	raver
behaving		engravement	saver
belaving	**ĀVʹish**	enslavement	savor
beslaving	bravish	lavement	semiquaver
braving	knavish	pavement	shaver
caving	slavish		slaver
craving		**ĀVʹnes**	suaver
depraving	**ĂVʹish**	braveness	waiver
engraving	enravish	graveness	waver
enslaving	lavish	suaveness	wood-engraver
graving	McTavish		
labor-saving	ravish	**ĀVʹo**	**ĂVʹur**
laving		bravo	beslaver
misbehaving	**ĀVʹit**	octavo	cadaver
outbraving	affidavit		palaver
paving	indicavit	**ĂVʹo**	haver
raving		bravo	
saving	**ĂVʹit**	octavo	**ĂVʹur**
shaving	davit		palaver
slaving		**ĂVʹok**	suaver
staving	**ĀVʹles**	havoc	
steel-engrav-	caveless		**ĀVʹurd**
ing	graveless	**ĀVʹur**	favored
waiving	slaveless	braver	flavored

ōld, ôr, ŏdd, oil, fŏŏt, out; ūse, ûrn, ŭp; THis, thin

ill-favored
quavered
savored
wavered
well-favored

ĂV′urn
cavern
tavern

ĂV′us
Gustavus

ĀV′yur
behavior
havior
misbehavior
Pavier
pavior
savior
Xavier

Ā′ward
wayward

Ă′ward
vaward

Ā′wir
haywire

Ā′worn
sprayworn
wayworn

Ā′ya
Aglaia
ayah
calisaya
Isaiah
naia

Ā′yan
Altaian
Cataian
Himalayan
Malayan

Ă′yan
Himalayan

Ā′yard
Bayard

Ā′yo
K.O.
kayo
Mayo

Ā′yu
gay-you
Vayu

ĀZ′a
Gaza

ĂZ′a
cazazza
piazza
plaza

ĀZ′al
appraisal
hazel
nasal
witch-hazel

ĂZ′ard
haphazard
hazard
mazard
mazzard

ĀZ′est
amazest
braisest
bepraisest
blazest
dazest
gazest
hazest
glazest
paraphrasest
phrasest
praisest
raisest
razest
upraisest

ĀZ′eth
amazeth
bepraiseth
blazeth
braiseth
dazeth
gazeth
glazeth
hazeth
paraphraseth
phraseth
praiseth
raiseth
razeth
upraiseth

ĀZ′ez
amazes
bemazes
blazes
braises
brazes
chaises
crazes
daisies

dazes
gazes
glazes
grazes
hazes
mayonnaises
mazes
paraphrases
phases
phrases
praises
raises
razes

Ā′zhun
abrasion
dissuasion
erasion
evasion
invasion
occasion
persuasion
suasion
(cf. Caucasian,
    and Ā′zhi-an
    words)

Ā′zhur
azure
brazier
embrasure
erasure
Frazier
glazier
grazier
razure

ĂZH′ur
åzure

ĀZ′i
blazy

crazy
daisy
hazy
jasey
lackadaisy
lazy
mazy
phrasey
paraphrasey

ĂZ'i
ghawazi
ghazi

ĂZ'il
Basil
(cf. ĂZ"l)

ĂZ'in
raisin

ĀZ'ing
ablazing
amazing
bemazing
bepraising
blazing
braising

brazing
dazing
gazing
glazing
grazing
hazing
lazing
outblazing
outgazing
paraphrasing
phrasing
praising
raising
self-praising
star-gazing
upblazing
upraising

ĂZ"l
Basil
bedazzle
dazzle
frazzle
razzle-dazzle

ĀZ'les
praiseless

ĂZ'ling
dazzling
frazzling

ĂZ'ma
asthma
miasma
phantasma
Phasma
plasma
protoplasma

ĂZ'mal
miasmal
phantasmal
protoplasmal

ĂZ'ment
amazement
appraisement
praisement

ĂZ'mi
chasmy

ĂZ'mik
bioplasmic
miasmic
protoplasmic

ĂZ'mus
Erasmus

ĀZ'on
blazon
brazen
diapason
emblazon
glazen
scazon

ĀZ'ur
appraiser
blazer
dispraiser
Eleazer
Fraser
gazer
geyser
lazar
paraphraser
phraser
praiser
raiser
razer
razor
self-praiser
star-gazer
upgazer
upraiser

E

For a discussion of words included under the accented vowels following, see the beginning of E rhymes in Section I.

Ē'a
Althæa
Astræa
Ave Maria
Cassiopea

cavalleria
Crimea
Cypræa
dahabeah
Dorothea

dyspnea
Hosea
Hygeia
idea
Latakia

Lucia
Maria
Medea
melopœia
obeah

ōld, ôr, ŏdd, oil, fŏŏt, out; ūse. ûrn, ŭp; THis, thin

onomatopœia

panacea

pathopœia

pharmacopœia

ratafia

Rhea

spiræa

Zea

Ē'al

Arctogaeal

beau ideal

empyreal

hymeneal

ideal

laryngeal

real

unideal

unreal

Ē'an

Achean

adamantean

Adonean

Ægean

amœbean

amphigean

Andean

Anomoean

antipodean

apogean

Archimedean

Argean

Assidean

astraean

Atlantean

Augean

Berean

Cadmean

Caribbean

Chaldean

Circean

colossean

Crimean

cyclopean

Cytherean

ditrochean

empyrean

epicurean

Etnean

European

Galilean

gigantean

Hasmonaean

Hyblæan

hymenean

Indo-European

Judean

Laodicean

laryngean

lethean

Linnaean

lyncean

Maccabean

Manichaean

mausolean

Medicean

Melibean

Nemean

Niobean

nymphean

Orphean

pæan

Palæogæan

pampean

Pandean

perigean

phalangean

Pharisean

plebeian

protean

Pyrenean

Pythagorean

Sabæan

Sadducean

Sisyphean

terpsichorean

theodicean

Vendean

Zoilean

Ē'as

Aeneas

Zaccheus

Ē'ba

amœba

Reba

Seba

Sheba

zareba

Ē'be

Hebe

Phoebe

T.B.

ĔB'en

Eben

ĔB'ing

ebbing

unebbing

webbing

ĔB"l

enfeeble

feeble

ĔB"l

arch-rebel

djebel

pebble

rebel

treble

Ē'bo

gazeebo

Nebo

placebo

ĔB'on

ebon

Ē'bord

free-board

key-board

seaboard

Ē'born

free-born

sea-born

ĔB'ra

zebra

ĔB'rok

pibroch

ĒB'ru

Hebrew

ĒB'ur

Gheber

ĔB'ur

ebber

webber

Weber

Ē'bus

glebous

Phoebus

rebus

ĔCH′ed
wretched
(see ĔCH+ed)

ĔCH′est
beseechest
bleachest
foreachest
impeachest
overreachest
preachest
reachest
screechest
sea-chest
tea-chest
teachest

ĔCH′eth
beseecheth
bleacheth
forereacheth
impeacheth
overreacheth
preacheth
reacheth
screecheth
teacheth

ĔCH′ez
beaches
beeches
beseeches
bleaches
breaches
breeches
forereaches
impeaches
leeches
overreaches
peaches
preaches

reaches
screeches
sea-reaches
speeches
teaches

ĔCH′i
beachy
Beatrice
beechy
bleachy
breachy
campeachy
peachy
preachy
reachy
queachy
reechy
screechy
speechy

ĔCH′i
fetchy
sketchy
stretchy
tetchy
vetchy

ĔCH′ing
beaching
beseeching
bleaching
breaching
breeching
forereaching
foreteaching
impeaching
leaching
leeching
overreaching
peaching

preaching
reaching
screeching
teaching

ĔCH′ing
etching
fetching
sketching
stretching

ĔCH′les
beachless
beechless
breachless
peachless
reachless
speechless
teachless

ĔCH′ment
beseechment
impeachment
preachment

ĔCH′up
catchup
ketchup

ĔCH′ur
Beecher
beseecher
bleacher
breacher
breecher
forereacher
impeacher
leacher
leecher
overreacher
peacher

preacher
reacher
screecher
teacher
(cf. Ē′tūr)

ĔCH′ur
etcher
fetcher
fletcher
lecher
retcher
sketcher
stretcher
treacher

Ē′da
Leda
olla podrida
Theda
Veda
Vida

ĔD′a
Edda
Nedda

ĔD′ant
pedant

ĔD′bed
reedbed
seedbed
weedbed

ĔD′bet
deadbeat

ĔD′breast
redbreast

ōld, ôr, ŏdd, oil, fŏŏt, out; ūse, ûrn, ŭp; THis, thin

ĔD′bug
bedbug
redbug

ĒD′ed
acceded
anteceded
beaded
ceded
conceded
deeded
exceeded
heeded
impeded
interceded
kneaded
needed
pleaded
preceded
proceeded
receded
reeded
retroceded
seceded
seeded
stampeded
succeeded
superseded
unheeded
unweeded
weeded

ĔD′ed
addle-headed
arrow-headed
bare-headed
bedded
beetle-headed
beheaded
blunderheaded
bullheaded

chuckle-
  headed
clear-headed
dreaded
dunder-headed
embedded
fat-headed
feather-headed
fiddle-headed
flat-headed
giddy-headed
gross-headed
headed
heavy-headed
hoary-headed
hot-headed
hydra-headed
idle-headed
Janus-headed
leaded
light-headed
longheaded
many-headed
muddle-
  headed
pig-headed
pudding-
  headed
puzzle-headed
rattle-headed
shock-headed
shredded
sleek-headed
soft-headed
thick-headed
threaded
trundle-
  headed
unbedded
undreaded
unthreaded

unwedded
warm-headed
weak-headed
wedded
wrong-headed

ĒD′en
Eden
reeden
Sweden

ĔD′en
deaden
leaden
redden
threaden

ĔD′ens
antecedence
credence
intercedence
precedence
(cf. antece-
  dents)

ĔD′ent
antecedent
credent
decedent
intercedent
needn't
precedent
retrocedent
sedent

Ē′dep
knee-deep
sea-deep
three-deep

ĒD′est
accedest

bleedest
breedest
cedest
concedest
exceedest
feedest
heedest
impedest
intercedest
kneadest
leadest
misleadest
needest
overfeedest
pleadest
precedest
proceedest
readest
recedest
secedest
seedest
speedest
stampedest
succeedest
supersedest
weedest

ĔD′est
beheadest
dreadest
outspreadest
reddest
sheddest
spreadest
threadest
treadest
weddest

ĒD′eth
accedeth
bleedeth

āle, câre, ădd, ärm, ăsk; mē, hĕre, ĕnd; īce, ĭll;

breedeth	**ĒD′ful**	**ĔD′ĭ**	interceding
cedeth	deedful	already	interpleading
concedeth	heedful	Eddie	kneading
exceedeth	meedful	eddy	leading
feedeth	needful	Freddie	love-lies-
heedeth	speedful	heady	bleeding
impedeth	unheedful	leady	misleading
intercedeth	unneedful	ready	misreading
kneadeth		reddy	needing
leadeth	**ĔD′ful**	shreddy	outspeeding
misleadeth	dreadful	steady	over-feeding
needeth		thready	pleading
overfeedeth	**ĒD′gron**	unready	preceding
pleadeth	reed-grown	unsteady	proceeding
precedeth	seed-grown		reading
proceedeth	weed-grown	**ĒD′ik**	receding
readeth		comedic	reeding
recedeth	**ĔD′hed**	cyclopædic	retroceding
secedeth	deadhead	encyclopædic	seceding
seedeth	redhead	Vedic	seeding
speedeth			speeding
stampedeth	**ĔD′het**	**ĔD′ik**	stampeding
succeedeth	dead-heat	Eddic	succeeding
supersedeth	red-heat	Samoyedic	superseding
weedeth			unbleeding
	ĒD′ĭ	**ĒD′ĭkt**	underfeeding
ĔD′eth	beady	edict	unheeding
beheadeth	creedy		weeding
dreadeth	deedy	**ĒD′ing**	
headeth	encyclopedy	acceding	**ĔD′ing**
outspreadeth	greedy	beading	bedding
overspreadeth	heedy	bleeding	beheading
sheddeth	indeedy	breeding	bespreading
shreddeth	Leedy	ceding	dreading
spreadeth	needy	conceding	embedding
threadeth	*predy*	exceeding	heading
treadeth	reedy	feeding	leading
weddeth	seedy	God-speeding	outspreading
	speedy	heeding	overspreading
ĔD′fast	unheedy	impeding	redding
steadfast	weedy	interbreeding	shedding

ōld, ôr, ŏdd, oil, fŏŏt, out; ūse, ûrn, ŭp; THis, thin

shredding
sledding
spreading
steading
tedding
threading
treading
wedding

ĔD'ish
deadish
eddish
reddish

ĔD'it
accredit
credit
discredit
edit
miscredit
subedit
you said it

ĔD'ith
Edith
(cf. needeth,
etc.)

ĔD'iz
teddies
(see ĔD'i+s)

ĔD″l
beadle
bi-pedal
centipedal
dædal
needle
pedal
semipedal
tweedle
wheeled

ĔD″l
bi-pedal
heddle
intermeddle
medal
meddle
pedal
peddle
reddle
treadle
tripedal

ĔD'lam
Bedlam

ĔD'land
headland

ĒD'les
breedless
creedless
deedless
heedless
needless
seedless
speedless
steedless
weedless

ĔD'les
bedless
breadless
dreadless
headless
leadless

ĔD'li
chance-medley
deadly
medley
redly

ĔD'lin
breadline
dead-line
head-line

ĒD'ling
needling
reedling
seedling
wheedling

ĔD'ling
intermeddling
meddling
peddling

ĔD'lit
dead-light
red-light

ĔD'lok
deadlock
wedlock

ĒD'lur
needler
wheedler

ĔD'lur
intermeddler
meddler
medlar
peddler
treadler

ĔD'man
Friedman

ĔD'man
dead-man
Edman

headman
red-man

ĔD'na
Edna

ĔD'nes
deadness
redness

Ē'do
credo
Lido
stampedo
teredo
Toledo
torpedo

ĔD'o
meadow

ĒD'ra
ex cathedra
exedra

ĒD'ral
cathedral
decahedral
didecahedral
diedral
dihedral
pro-cathedral

ĔD'rest
bed-rest
head-rest

ĔD'ston
headstone

ĒD'tim
feed-time
seed-time

Ē'dum
freedom
(cf. sedum)

ĒD'ūr
procedure
supersedure

ĒD ŭr
acceder
anteceder
breeder
cedar
ceder
conceder
exceeder
feeder
heeder
impeder
impleader
interceder
interpleader
kneader
leader
misleader
needer
overfeeder
pleader
preceder
proceeder
reader
receder
retroceder
ring-leader
scripture-
 reader
seceder
seeder
speeder
stampeder

succeeder
superseder
weeder

ĔD'ur
bedder
beheader
bespreader
Cheddar
deader
double-header
dreader
edder
embedder
header
leader
redder
shedder
shredder
spreader
tedder
threader
treader
unthreader

ĔD'wa
headway

ĔD'ward
bedward
Edward

ĔD'wood
dead-wood
redwood

ĒDZ'man
beadsman
bedesman
seedsman

ĔDZ'man
headsman
leadsman

ĔD'zo
intermezzo
mezzo

Ē'est
agreest
feest
fleest
foreseest
freest
overseest
refereest
seest
weest

Ē'eth
agreeth
feeth
fleeth
foreseeth
freeth
overseeth
seeth

ĒF'as
Cephas
(cf. Josephus)

ĒF'dom
chiefdom

ĔF'en
deafen
(cf. Strephon)

ĒF'i
beefy

leafy
reefy
sheafy

ĒF'ij
leafage

ĔF'ik
malefic
peristrephic

ĒF'les
briefless
chiefless
griefless
leafless
sheafless

ĔF'nes
deafness

Ē'fom
sea-foam

Ē'foul
pea-fowl
sea-fowl

ĔFT'nes
deftness

ĔF'ri
Geoffrey
Jeffrey

ĒF'stak
beefsteak

ĒF'tin
chieftain

ōld, ôr, ŏdd, oil, fŏŏt, out; ūse, ûrn, ŭp; THis, thin

ĔF'uj
refuge

Ē'ful
gleeful

ĔF'ur
beefer
briefer
chiefer
liefer
reefer

ĔF'ur
deafer
feoffor
heifer
zephyr

Ē'ga
omega
Riga
Talladega
Vega

ĔG'i
dreggy
eggy
leggy
Peggy

ĒG'ing
fatiguing
intriguing
leaguing

ĔG'ing
begging
egging
legging
pegging
unpegging

ĒG' 'l
bald eagle
beagle
eagle
gregal
illegal
inveigle
kleagle
legal
regal
vice-regal
(cf. sea-gull)

ĒG'lur
beagler
inveigler

ĔG'ment
segment

ĔG'nant
impregnant
pregnant
queen-regnant
regnant

Ē'go
ego
Oswego
Otsego

Ē'gren
pea-green
sea-green

ĒG'res
egress
negress
regress

ĒG'ro
negro

ĒG'ur
beleaguer
eager
eagre
fatiguer
intriguer
leaguer
meagre
overeager

ĔG'ur
beggar
booklegger
bootlegger
egger
legger
pegger
seggar

Ē'gurt
sea-girt

Ē'ik
caffeic
mythopœic
rheic
xanthoproteic

Ē'in
caffeine
codeine
zein

Ē'ing
agreeing
being
clear-seeing
decreeing
disagreeing
feeing
fleeing

foreseeing
freeing
guaranteeing
inbeing
overseeing
refereeing
seeing
spreeing
teeing
unforeseeing
unseeing
well-being

Ē'ist
antitheist
deist
hylotheist
manicheist
monotheist
polytheist
theist

Ē'it
albeit
sobeit

Ē'izm
absenteeism
antitheism
autotheism
cosmotheism
deism
henotheism
hylotheism
manicheism
monotheism
Parseeism
Phariseeism
polytheism
Sadduceeism
sciotheism

āle,   câre,   ădd,   ärm,   åsk;   mē,   hęre,   ĕnd;   īce,   ĭll;

Sutteeism
theism
weism

Ē′jance
allegiance

ĔJ′burd
hedge-bird
sedge-bird

ĔJ′end
legend

ĔJ′ent
regent

ĔJ′est
allegest
dredgest
fledgest
hedgest
impledgest
pledgest
wedgest

ĔJ′eth
allegeth
dredgeth
fledgeth
hedgeth
impledgeth
pledgeth
wedgeth

ĔJ′ez
alleges
dredges
edges
hedges
kedges

ledges
pledges
sledges
wedges

ĔJ′i
cledgy
edgy
hedgy
ledgy
sedgy
wedgy

ĔJ′ing
alleging
dredging
edging
enhedging
fledging
hedging
kedging
impledging
interpledging
pledging
sledging
wedging

ĔJ′ling
fledgeling

ĔJ′man
liegeman

ĔJ′ment
besiegement

ĔJ′un
legion
region
under-region
(cf. collegian

and Ē′ji-an
words)

ĔJ′ur
alleger
dredger
edger
hedger
ledger
leger
pledger
sledger

ĒJ′us
egregious
sacrilegious

ĔJ′wood
Edgewood
Wedgewood

Ē′ka
bibliotheca
chica
Costa Rica
Dominica
eureka
Frederica
Fredrika
glyptotheca
Meeka
Tanganyika
Topeka
Ulrica
zotheca

ĔK′a
Rebecca
Mecca

ĔK′ad
decade

ĔK′al
bibliothecal
cæcal
fæcal
thecal
treacle

ĔK′ant
piquant
precant
secant

ĔK′ant
impeccant
peccant

ĔK′en
weaken
(see ĔK′on)

ĔK′est
bespeakest
bleakest
meekest
leakest
reekest
seekest
shriekest
sneakest
speakest
squeakest
streakest
uniquest
weakest
wreakest

ĔK′est
bedeckest
checkest
deckest
reckest
wreckest

ĒK′eth
bespeaketh
leaketh
reeketh
seeketh
shrieketh
sneaketh
speaketh
squeaketh
streaketh
wreaketh

ĔK′eth
bedecketh
checketh
decketh
recketh
wrecketh

ĒK′i
bleaky
Bolsheviki
cheeky
cliquey
cockaleekie
creaky
leaky
Mensheviki
peeky
reeky
sheiky
sleeky
sneaky
squeaky
streaky

ĒK′id
meek-eyed
oblique-eyed
weak-eyed

ĒK′ing
bespeaking
cheeking
creaking
eking
forespeaking
leaking
reeking
seeking
self-seeking
sheiking
shrieking
sneaking
speaking
squeaking
tweaking
wreaking

ĔK′ing
bedecking
bewrecking
checking
decking
flecking
henpecking
pecking
recking
trekking
wrecking

ĒK′ish
bleakish
cliquish
freakish
Greekish
meekish
peakish
sneakish
weakish

ĔK′ish
peckish

ĒK″l
treacle
(see ĒK′al)

ĔK″l
befreckle
bespeckle
deckle
freckle
heckle
Jeckyll
keckle
Seckel
shekel
speckle

ĔK′les
feckless
fleckless
necklace
reckless
speckless

ĒK′li
bleakly
meekly
obliquely
sleekly
treacly
uniquely
weakly
weekly

ĔK′li
freckly
speckly

ĒK′ling
weakling

ĔK′ling
freckling

heckling
keckling
speckling

ĔK′lur
heckler
freckler, etc.

ĔK′mat
checkmate
deck-mate

ĒK′nes
antiqueness
bleakness
meekness
obliqueness
sleekness
uniqueness
weakness

ĔK′nik
philotechnic
polytechnic
pyrotechnic
technic
theotechnic

ĔK′ning
beckoning
reckoning
unreckoning

Ē′ko
beccafico
fico

ĔK′o
echo
gecko
re-echo
secco

Ē′kok
Leacock
meacock
peacock

ĔK′on
archdeacon
beacon
deacon
meeken
weaken

ĔK′on
beckon
reckon

ĔK′ond
second
unreckoned,
  etc.

Ē′krab
pea-crab
sea-crab
tree-crab

ĔK′ret
secret

ĔK′sas
Texas

ĔK′sest
annexest
flexest
perplexest
unsexest
vexest

ĔK′seth
annexeth

flexeth
perplexeth
unsexeth
vexeth

ĔK′shun
abjection
adjection
affection
bisection
by-election
circumspection
circumvection
collection
complexion
confection
connection
convection
correction
defection
deflection
dejection
detection
dilection
direction
disaffection
disinfection
dissection
effection
ejection
election
erection
evection
flection
genuflexion
imperfection
incorrection
indirection
infection
inflection
injection

insection
inspection
insubjection
insurrection
intellection
interjection
intersection
introspection
irreflection
lection
misdirection
objection
perfection
predilection
prelection
projection
prospection
protection
provection
recollection
rection
re-election
reflection
rejection
resurrection
retrospection
section
selection
subjection
trajection
trisection
venesection
vivisection

ĔK′shus
infectious

ĔK′si
apoplexy
kexy
kyriolexy

prexy
pyrexy

ĔK′sil
exile
flexile

ĔK′sing
annexing
flexing
inflexing
perplexing
unsexing
vexing

ĔK′sis
Alexis

ĔK′sit
exit

ĔK′stant
extant
sextant

ĔK′stil
bissextile
sextile
textile

ĔK′ston
sexton

ĔK′strin
dextrin
textrine

ĔK′strus
ambidextrous
ambisextrous
dextrous

ōld, ôr, ŏdd, oil, fŏŏt, out; ūse, ûrn, ŭp; THis, thin

ĔK'stūr	bisected	resurrected	*subjectest*
intertexture	collected	selected	*suspectest*
texture	complected	subjected	
	confected	suspected	**ĔK'teth**
ĔK'stŭr	connected	unaffected	*affecteth*
ambidexter	corrected	unconnected	*bisecteth*
dexter	defected	unexpected	*collecteth*
	deflected	unprotected	*connecteth*
ĔK'sūr	dejected	unsuspected	*detecteth*
deflexure	detected		*directeth*
flexure	directed	**ĔK'test**	*disinfecteth*
inflexure	disaffected	abjectest	*dissecteth*
plexure	disconnected	*affectest*	*effecteth*
	disinfected	*bisectest*	*ejecteth*
ĔK'sŭr	dissected	*collectest*	*electeth*
annexer	effected	*connectest*	*erecteth*
flexor	ejected	*detectest*	*expecteth*
perplexer	elected	directest	*infecteth*
unsexer	erected	*disinfectest*	*injecteth*
vexer	expected	*dissectest*	*inspecteth*
	flected	*effectest*	*interjecteth*
ĔK'sus	ill-affected	*ejectest*	*misdirecteth*
nexus	infected	*electest*	*neglecteth*
plexus	inflected	*erectest*	*objecteth*
(cf. Texas)	injected	*expectest*	*projecteth*
	inspected	*infectest*	*protecteth*
ĔK'tant	interjected	*injectest*	*recollecteth*
amplectant	intersected	*inspectest*	*reflecteth*
annectent	invected	*interjectest*	*rejecteth*
aspectant	misdirected	*neglectest*	*respecteth*
disinfectant	neglected	*objectest*	*resurrecteth*
expectant	objected	*projectest*	*selecteth*
humectant	obtected	*protectest*	*subjecteth*
inexpectant	perfected	*recollectest*	*suspecteth*
reflectant	prelected	*reflectest*	*trisecteth*
respectant	projected	*rejectest*	
suspectant	protected	*respectest*	**ĔKT'ful**
unexpectant	recollected	*resurrectest*	disrespectful
	reflected	*resurrectest*	neglectful
ĔK'ted	rejected	selectest	respectful
affected	respected		

ĔK′tik
acatalectic
analectic
apoplectic
brachycatalec-
  tic
cachectic
catalectic
dialectic
eclectic
hectic
hypercatalectic
pectic

ĔK′tiks
dialectics

ĔK′til
insectile
projectile
sectile

ĔK′ting
affecting
bisecting
collecting
connecting
deflecting
detecting
directing
disconnecting
disinfecting
dissecting
effecting
ejecting
electing
erecting
expecting
infecting
injecting
inspecting

interjecting
misdirecting
neglecting
objecting
projecting
protecting
recollecting
reflecting
rejecting
respecting
resurrecting
selecting
self-respecting
subjecting
suspecting
trisecting
unsuspecting

ĔK′tiv
affective
circumspective
collective
connective
corrective
defective
deflective
detective
directive
effective
elective
erective
humective
ineffective
infective
inflective
injective
inspective
introspective
invective
irreflective
irrespective

neglective
objective
perfective
perspective
prospective
protective
recollective
refective
reflective
rejective
respective
retrospective
sective
selective
subjective

ĔK′tizm
eclectism
sectism

ĔKT′ment
ejectment
projectment
rejectment

ĔKT′nes
abjectness
correctness
directness
erectness
incorrectness
indirectness
selectness

ĔK′tor
Hector
nectar
rector
sector
vector

vivisector
(cf. ĔK′tur)

ĔK′tord
hectored
nectared
rectored

ĔK′tral
spectral

ĔK′tres
directress
electress
inspectress
protectress
rectress

ĔK′tric
anelectric
dielectric
electric
idioelectric

ĔK′tron
electron

ĔK′trum
electrum
plectrum
spectrum

ĔK′tūr
architecture
belecture
confecture
conjecture
lecture
projecture

ĔK′tur
bisecter
collector

ōld, ôr, ŏdd, oil, fŏŏt, out; ūse, ûrn, ŭp; THis, thin

connector
corrector
deflector
detector
director
disrespector
dissector
ejector
elector
erecter
expecter
flector
hector
infecter
injecter
inspector
interjecter
lector
misdirecter
nectar
neglecter
objector
prelector
projector
prospector
protector
recollecter
rector
reflector
rejecter
respecter
resurrecter
sector
selector
spectre
subjecter
suspecter
trisecter

ĔK'tus

conspectus

pectous
prospectus

ĒK'um

cæcum
vade-mecum

ĒK'und

fecund
infecund

ĒK'ur

beaker
bespeaker
bleaker
Bleecker
cheeker
creaker
meeker
peeker
reeker
seeker
self-seeker
shrieker
sleeker
sneaker
speaker
squeaker
stump-speaker
tweaker
weaker

ĔK'ur

bedecker
brekker
checker
chequer
decker
exchequer
flecker
henpecker

pecker
three-decker
trekker
woodpecker
wrecker

ĒK'urz

sneakers
beakers, etc.

ĔK'urz

checkers
henpeckers, etc.

ĒK'wal

coequal
equal
inequal
sequel

ĒK'wence

frequence
infrequence
sequence

ĒK'went

frequent
infrequent
sequent

Ē'la

gila
philomela
sequela
stele
seguidilla
Venezuela

ĔL'a

a capella
Adela

Bella
capella
Della
Ella
fellah
fenestella
gentianella
Isabella
lamella
lirella
Littorella
Marcella
patella
Pimpinella
prunella
Rosabella
scutella
stella
tarantella
umbella
umbrella

ĔL'an

Atellan
Magellan
McClellan

ĔL'ant

appellant
divellent
impellent
interpellant
propellent
repellent
revellent

ĔL'arz

Sellars
(cf. Sellers)

ĔL'at

appellate

constellate
debellate
flabellate
interpellate
ocellate
prelate
stellate

ĔL'ba
Elba
Melba

ĔL'born
hell-born
well-born

ĔL'bound
hell-bound
spell-bound

ĔL'burt
Elbert

ĔL'chest
belchest, etc.

ĔL'cheth
belcheth, etc.

ĔL'ching
belching
squelching
welching

ĔL'chur
belcher
squelcher
welsher

ĔL'da
Griselda

Nelda
Zelda

ĒL'dans
yieldance

ĒL'ded
fielded
shielded
unshielded
wielded
yielded

ĔL'dest
eldest
heldest
weldest

ĔL'dur
elder
Gelder
Melder
Van Gelder
welder

ĒLD'far
fieldfare

ĒL'di
unwieldy

ĒL'ding
enshielding
fielding
shielding
unshielding
unyielding
wielding
yielding

ĔL'ding
gelding
welding

ĔL'dom
seldom
swelldom

ĔL'en
Ellen
Helen
Llewellyn
Mellen
(cf. Mellon)

ĔL'est
annealest
appealest
concealest
congealest
dealest
feelest
genteelest
healest
kneelest
lealest
pealest
peelest
reelest
repealest
revealest
sealest
squealest
stealest
steelest
wheelest

ĔL'est
compellest
dispellest
dwellest
excellest
expellest
fellest
foretellest

impellest
knellest
propellest
quellest
rebellest
repellest
sellest
shellest
smellest
spellest
swellest
tellest
undersellest
yellest

ĔL'eth
annealeth
appealeth
concealeth
congealeth
dealeth
feeleth
healeth
kneeleth
pealeth
peeleth
reeleth
repealeth
revealeth
sealeth
squealeth
stealeth
steeleth
wheeleth

ĔL'eth
compelleth
dispelleth
dwelleth
excelleth
expelleth

ōld, ôr, ŏdd, oil, fŏŏt, out; ūse, ûrn, ŭp; THis, thin

felleth
foretelleth
impelleth
knelleth
propelleth
quelleth
rebelleth
repelleth
selleth
shelleth
smelleth
spelleth
swelleth
telleth
underselleth
yelleth

ĔL'far
welfare

ĔL'fik
Delphic
Guelphic

ĔL'fin
delphin
delphine
elfin

ĔL'fir
hellfire

ĔL'fish
elfish
pelfish
selfish
shellfish
unselfish

ĔL'fri
belfry
pelfry

ĔL'ful
seelful
wealful
zealful

Ē'lī
Eli

Ĕl'ī
Ealey
freely
Healey
Keeley
mealy
seely
steely
wheely
(cf. genteelly)

Ĕ'li
belly
cancelli
Donatelli
felly
helly
jelly
Kelly
O'Delly
rakehelly
Shelley
shelly
Skelly
smelly
vermicelli

ĔL'id
bellied
gelid
jellied

ĔL'ij
keelage
wheelage

ĔL'ij
pellage

ĔL'ik
parhelic

ĔL'ik
angelic
archangelic
Aristotelic
bellic
evangelic
melic
nickelic
parhelic
Pentelic
pimelic
relic
superangelic
telic

ĔL'iks
Felix
helix

Ē'lin
bee-line
feline
sea-line

ĔL'ing
annealing
appealing
automobiling
ceiling
concealing
congealing
dealing
double-dealing
feeling
fellow-feeling

healing
heeling
interdealing
keeling
kneeling
misdealing
pealing
peeling
reeling
repealing
revealing
sealing
self-healing
shealing
squealing
stealing
steeling
uncongealing
underdealing
unfeeling
unsealing
wheeling

ĔL'ing
belling
cloud-
    compelling
compelling
dispelling
dwelling
excelling
expelling
felling
foretelling
fortune-telling
impelling
knelling
misspelling
paralleling
propelling
quelling

āle,   câre,   ădd,   ärm,   åsk;   mē,   hẹre,   ĕnd;   īce,   ĭll;

355

rebelling
repelling
selling
sentinelling
shelling
smelling
spelling
swelling
telling
underselling
welling
yelling

ĔL'is
Ellis
trellis

ĔL'ish
disrelish
embellish
hellish
relish
swellish

ĔL'kom
welcome

ĔL'ma
Elma
Selma
Thelma
Velma

ĔL'man
bellman
Elman
Wellman

ĔL'ment
concealment
congealment

repealment
revealment

ĔL'met
helmet

ĔL'ming
dishelming
helming
overwhelming
unhelming
whelming

ĔL'mur
Elmer

ĔL'nes
genteelness
lealness

ĔL'nes
fellness
wellness

ĔL'o
bellow
brocatello
cobra-de-
  capello
cello
duello
felloe
fellow
good-fellow
mellow
morello
niello
play-fellow
prunello
punchinello
saltarello

scrivello
violoncello
yellow

ĔL'od
unmellowed
bellowed, etc.

ĔL'on
enfelon
felon
melon
water-melon

ĔL'op
develop
envelop

ĔL'ot
helot
zealot

ĔL'oz
bellows
fellows, etc.

ĔLP'ful
helpful
self-helpful
unhelpful

ĔL'pi
kelpie

ĔL'ping
helping
yelping

ĔLP'les
helpless
whelpless
yelpless

ĔL'pur
helper
self-helper
yelper

ĔL'sa
Elsa

ĔL'skin
eel-skin
seal-skin

ĔL'son
kelson
Nelson

ĔL'ta
delta
pelta

ĔL'ted
belted
felted
melted
pelted
smelted
unbelted
welted

ĔL'test
beltest, etc.

ĔL'teth
belteth, etc.

ĔL'thi
healthy
stealthy
wealthy

ĔL'tik
Celtic
Keltic

ĔL'ting
belting
felting
melting
pelting
smelting
unbelting
welting

ĔLT'les
beltless
Celtless
feltless
peltless
weltless

ĔL'tri
peltry
sweltry

ĔL'tur
belter
felter
helter-skelter
inshelter
kelter
melter
pelter
shelter
smelter
spelter
swelter
welter

ĔL'turd
unsheltered
sheltered, etc.

ĔL'ud
prelude

ĔL'ug
deluge

ĔL'um
cerebellum
flabellum
flagellum
vellum

ĔL'ur
annealer
appealer
concealer
congealer
dealer
double-dealer
feeler
four-wheeler
healer
heeler
interdealer
keeler
kneeler
misdealer
pealer
peeler
reeler
repealer
revealer
sealer
squealer
stealer
steeler
ward heeler
wheeler

ĔL'ur
appellor
cave-dweller
cellar

cloud-com-
  peller
compeller
dispeller
dweller
exceller
expeller
feller
foreteller
fortune-teller
Geller
impeller
interstellar
Keller
lamellar
"meller"
propeller
queller
rebeller
repeller
screw propeller
Sellar
seller
sheller
smeller
speller
stellar
sweller
tale-teller
teller
twin propeller
underseller
Weller
wine-cellar
yeller

ĔL'us
apellous
entellus
jealous
overzealous

procellous
vitellus
zealous

ĔL'vet
velvet

ĔL'ving
delving
helving
shelving

ĔL'vish
elvish

ĔL'vur
delver
helver
shelver

ĔL'ya
Amelia
Aurelia
Bedelia
camellia
Cecelia
Celia
Cordelia
Cornelia
Delia
Lelia
lobelia

ĔL'yal
Belial

ĔL'yon
chameleon
(see Ē'li+on)

ĔL'yon
rebellion

(cf. rhymes on
  ĔL'+on)

ĔL'yus
rebellious

ĔL'za
Elsa

ĒM'a
bema
blastema
eczema
edema
empyema
erythema
Fatima
Lima
myxedema
schema
seriema
terza-rima

ĔM'a
analemma
dilemma
Emma
gemma
lemma
maremma
neurilemma
stemma
trilemma

Ē'māl
female
she-male

ĔM'ăl
blastemal
hemal

Ē'man
able-seaman
beeman
freeman
G-man
gleeman
he-man
leman
merchant-sea-
  man
seaman
teaman
(cf. Bremen)

ĔM'b'l
assemble
dissemble
resemble
semble
tremble

ĔM'blans
assemblance
dissemblance
resemblance
semblance

ĔM'blant
resemblant
semblant

ĔM'b'ld
undissembled
assembled, etc.

ĔM'blem
emblem

ĔM'bli
assembly
trembly

ĔM'blij
assemblage

ĔM'bling
assembling
dissembling
resembling
trembling

ĔM'blur
assembler
dissembler
resembler
trembler

ĔM'bral
bimembral
trimembral

ĔM'brans
remembrance

ĔM'bur
December
dismember
disremember
ember
member
November
remember
September

ĔM'burd
dismembered
unremembered,
  etc.

ĔM'ens
Clemens

Ē'meat
agreement

decreement
disagreement

ĔM'ent
clement
inclement

ĒM'est
beamest
blasphemest
deemest
dreamest
esteemest
extremest
gleamest
misdeemest
reedemest
schemest
screamest
seemest
steamest
streamest
supremest

ĔM'est
begemmest
condemnest
hemmest
stemmest

ĔM'et
Emmett

ĒM'eth
beameth
blasphemeth
deemeth
dreameth
esteemeth
gleameth
redeemeth

ōld, ôr, ŏdd, oil, fŏŏt, out; ūse, ûrn, ŭp; THis, thin

schemeth
screameth
seemeth
steameth
streameth

ĔM′eth
begemmeth
condemneth
contemneth
hemmeth
stemmeth

ĒM′ful
beamful
dreamful
schemeful
teemful

ĒM′i
beamy
creamy
daydreamy
dreamy
gleamy
screamy
seamy
steamy
streamy
teemy
(cf. Mimi)

ĔM′i
demi
gemmy
jemmy
semi

ĒM′ik
anemic
racemic
systemic

ĔM′ik
academic
alchemic
chemic
endemic
epidemic
pandemic
polemic
stratagemic
systemic
theoremic
totemic

ĒM′ing
beaming
beseeming
blaspheming
creaming
daydreaming
deeming
dreaming
esteeming
gleaming
overstreaming
redeeming
scheming
screaming
seeming
steaming
streaming
summer-
    seeming
teeming
unbeseeming

ĔM′ing
begemming
condemning
contemning
Fleming
gemming

hemming
leming
self-condemn-
    ing
stemming

ĔM′ish
blemish
Flemish
unblemish

ĔM′isht
blemished
unblemished

ĒM′ist
extremist
schemist

ĔM′ist
chemist

ĔM′it, ĒM′it
Semite

ĒM′land
dreamland

ĒM′less
beamless
creamless
dreamless
schemeless
seamless
streamless

ĒM′let
streamlet

ĒM′li
extremely

seemly
supremely
unseemly

ĔM′non
Agamemnon
Memnon

ĒM′o
a tempo primo
Cremo
primo

ĔM′o
memo

ĒM′on
agathodæmon
cacodemon
demon
eudæmon

ĔM′on
lemon
(cf. "gem-
    man")

ĔM′pest
tempest

ĔM′pir
empire

ĔM′p'l
Semple
stemple
temple

ĔM′plar
exemplar
templar

āle, câre, ădd, ärm, åsk; mē, hẹre, ĕnd; īce, ĭll;

ĔM'plat
contemplate
template

ĔMP'shun
ademption
coemption
diremption
emption
exemption
pre-emption
redemption

ĔMP'stur
dempster
sempster

ĔMP'ted
attempted
exempted
pre-empted
tempted
unattempted
untempted

ĔMP'test
attemptest
exemptest
temptest

ĔMP'teth
attempteth
exempteth
tempteth

ĔMP'ti
empty

ĔMP'ting
attempting
exempting

pre-empting
tempting

ĔMP'tiv
pre-emptive
redemptive

ĔMP'tres
temptress

ĔMP'tur
attempter
exempter
pre-emptor
tempter
unkempter

ĔM'pur
attemper
distemper
Semper
temper
untemper

ĔM'purd
ill-tempered
tempered
untempered

ĔM'son
Clemson
Empson

ĔM'song
theme-song

ĔM'stur
deemster
seamster
teamster

ĔM'ur
beamer
blasphemer
daydreamer
dreamer
femur
lemur
reamer
redeemer
schemer
screamer
seamer
seemer
steamer
streamer
teemer

ĔM'ur
begemmer
condemner
contemner
hemmer
stemmer

ĔM'us
Nicodemus
Remus

ĔM'yer
premier

ĒN'a
arena
Alexandrina
Argentina
Athena
catena
cavatina
Celestina
Christina
Clementina

concertina
Czarina
farina
Faustina
galena
gena
Georgina
Helena
hyena
Justina
Lena
Magdalena
maizena
Medina
Messina
Modena
Paulina
philopena
scarlatina
scena
Selena
semolina
Serena
signorina
subpœna
Tsarina
verbena
Wilhelmina

ĔN'a
antenna
duenna
Gehenna
henna
Ravenna
senna
Sienna
Vienna

ĒN'al
machinal

penal
plenal
renal
venal
weanel

ĔN'al
antennal

ĔN'ant
lieutenant
pennant
sub-lieutenant
tenant

ĔN'ard
Leonard

Ē'nas
Enas
Zenas

ĔN'as
menace
tenace
(cf. tennis)

ĔN'at
brevipennate
impennate
longipennate
pennate
tripennate

ĔN'chant
trenchant

ĔN'chest
bedrenchest
blenchest
clenchest

drenchest
flenchest
intrenchest
quenchest
retrenchest
trenchest
unclenchest
wrenchest

ĔN'cheth
bedrencheth
blencheth
clencheth
drencheth
flencheth
intrencheth
quencheth
retrencheth
trencheth
unclencheth
wrencheth

ĔN'ching
bedrenching
benching
blenching
clenching
drenching
flenching
intrenching
quenching
retrenching
trenching
unclenching
unquenching
wrenching

ĔNCH'les
quenchless
(see ĔNCH +
  less)

ĔNCH'man
Frenchman
henchman

ĔNCH'ment
intrenchment
retrenchment

ĔN'chur
bedrencher
bencher
blencher
clencher
drencher
intrencher
quencher
retrencher
trencher
unclencher
wrencher

ĔN'da
agenda
Benda
Brenda
corrigenda
delenda
hacienda
Zenda

ĔN'dal
prebendal
sendal
trendle

ĔN'dans
ascendance
attendance
condescendence
dependence
descendance

impendence
independence
interdepend-
  ence
pendence
resplendence
superintend-
  ence
tendance
transcendence
(cf. attendant
  + s)

ĔN'dant,
  ĔN'dent
appendant
ascendant
attendant
contendant
defendant
dependant
dependent
descendant
descendent
equipendent
impendent
independent
intendant
interdependent
pendant
pendent
resplendent
splendent
superintendent
transcendent
transplendent

ĔN'ded
amended
appended
apprehended

ascended	undefended	*tendest*	*subtendeth*
attended	unextended	*unbendest*	*suspendeth*
befriended	unfriended	*vendest*	*tendeth*
bended	wended	*wendest*	*transcendeth*
blended	(cf. splendid)		*vendeth*
commended		**ĔN′deth**	*wendeth*
comprehended	**ĔN′dest**	*amendeth*	
condescended	*amendest*	*appendeth*	**ĔN′di**
contended	*appendest*	*apprehendeth*	bendy
defended	*apprehendest*	*ascendeth*	Effendi
depended	*ascendest*	*attendeth*	
descended	*attendest*	*befriendeth*	**ĔN′dik**
distended	*befriendest*	*bendeth*	Wendic
emended	*bendest*	*blendeth*	zendik
ended	*blendest*	*commendeth*	
expended	*commendest*	*comprehendeth*	**ĔN′ding**
extended	*comprehendest*	*condescendeth*	amending
fended	*condescendest*	*contendeth*	appending
friended	*contendest*	*defendeth*	apprehending
impended	*defendest*	*dependeth*	ascending
inextended	*dependest*	*descendeth*	attending
intended	*descendest*	*emendeth*	befriending
interblended	*emendest*	*endeth*	bending
mended	*endest*	*expendeth*	blending
misappre-	*expendest*	*extendeth*	commending
hended	*extendest*	*fendeth*	comprehending
offended	*fendest*	*impendeth*	condescending
portended	*intendest*	*intendeth*	contending
pretended	*interblendest*	*interblendeth*	defending
reascended	*lendest*	*lendeth*	depending
recommended	*mendest*	*mendeth*	descending
reprehended	*offendest*	*misapprehendeth*	distending
subtended	*pretendest*	*offendeth*	emending
superintended	*recommendest*	*portendeth*	ending
suspended	*rendest*	*pretendeth*	expending
tended	*reprehendest*	*reascendeth*	extending
transcended	*sendest*	*recommendeth*	*forfending*
trended	*spendest*	*rendeth*	*forelending*
unattended	*subtendest*	*reprehendeth*	*forespending*
unbefriended	*superintendest*	*sendeth*	heart-rending
unblended	*suspendest*	*spendeth*	impending

ōld, ôr, ŏdd, oil, fŏŏt, out; ūse, ûrn, ŭp; THis, thin

intending
interblending
lending
mending
misspending
offending
pending
perpending
portending
pretending
recommending
rending
reprehending
sending
spending
subtending
superintending
suspending
tending
transcending
trending
unattending
unbending
unending
unfriending
unoffending
unpretending
vending
wending

ĒN'dish
fiendish

ĔND'les
endless
friendless

ĔND'li
friendly
unfriendly

ĔND'ment
amendment
befriendment
intendment

ĔN'do
cresendo
decrescendo
diminuendo
innuendo

ĔN'dron
liriodendron
lithodendron
rhododendron

ĔND'ship
friendship

ĔN'dum
addendum
agendum
corrigendum
credendum
referendum

ĔN'dur
amender
apprehender
ascender
attender
befriender
bender
blender
commender
comprehender
contender
defender
depender
descender
emender

ender
engender
entender
expender
extender
fender
gender
intender
interblender
lender
mender
money-lender
offender
perpender
pretender
recommender
render
reprehender
sender
slender
spender
splendor
surrender
suspender
tailender
tender
vendor
week-ender
wender

ĔN'durd
unsurrendered
tendered, etc.

**ĔN'dus, not
ĔN'jus**
stupendous
tremendous

ĔND'waz
endways

ĔN'el
fennel
Fennell
kennel
unkennel

ĔN'elm
Kenelm

ĒN'est
bescreenest
cleanest
contravenest
convenest
demeanest
gleanest
greenest
intervenest
keenest
leanest
meanest
screenest
serenest
supervenest
weanest
weenest

ĔN'et
Bennett
jennet
rennet
senate
tenet

ĒN'eth
bescreeneth
cleaneth
contraveneth
conveneth
demeaneth
gleaneth

interveneth
keeneth
leaneth
meaneth
screeneth
superveneth
weaneth
weeneth

ĔN'eth
Kenneth
penneth, etc.

ĔNG'then
lengthen
strengthen

ĔNG'thi
lengthy

ĒN'horn
greenhorn

ĒN'i
Cheney
Cheyney
fantoccini
genie
greeny
Hippocrene
meany
Selene
sheeny
spleeny
Sweeney
teeny
visne
weeny

ĔN'i
any

Benny
fenny
Jenny
Kilkenny
Penney
many
penny
Rennie
spinning-jenny
tenney
true-penny
wenny

ĒN'id
green-eyed
keen-eyed

ĒN'ij
careenage
greenage
teenage

ĒN'ik
phenic
scenic

ĔN'ik
alphenic
anthropogenic
asthenic
callisthenic
chromogenic
crystallogenic
Demosthenic
deuterogenic
Diogenic
diplogenic
ecumenic
Edenic
embryogenic
eugenic

galenic
geoselenic
glycogenic
Hellenic
hygienic
hysterogenic
irenic
lichenic
metagenic
neurasthenic
nitrogenic
organogenic
oxygenic
Panhellenic
paragenic
parthenic
parthenogenic
pathogenic
phenic
Philhellenic
phosphorogenic
photogenic
phrenic
protogenic
Prutenic
pyrogenic
pythogenic
Saracenic
scenic
selenic
splenic
sthenic
thermogenic
tungstenic
zoogenic

ĔN'im
denim

ĔN'in
Lenin

ĒN'ing
advening
bemeaning
cleaning
contravening
convening
demeaning
double-mean-
  ing
eaning
gleaning
greening
intervening
keening
leaning
machining
meaning
overweening
preening
queening
screening
shebeening
subvening
supervening
unmeaning
upleaning
weaning
weening
well-meaning
yeaning

ĒN'ingz
screenings
cleanings, etc.

ĔN'ingz
Jennings
pennings, etc.

ĔN'is
Dennis

tennis
(cf. menace,
  tenace)

ĒN'ish
cleanish
greenish
keenish
leanish
meanish
queenish
spleenish

ĔN'ish
plenish
replenish
Rhenish
wennish

ĒN'ist
machinist
magazinist
plenist
routinist

ĔN'iz
bennies
pennies
spinning-jen-
  nies

ĔN'jans
vengeance

ĔN'jin
engine

ĔN'jing
avenging
revenging
venging

ĔN'jur
avenger

ĒN'li
cleanly
greenly
keenly
leanly
meanly
obscenely
queenly
serenely

ĔN'li
cleanly
Henley
Schenley
Senley
uncleanly

ĒN'ling
weanling
yeanling

ĔN'man
fenman
penman

ĒN'nes
cleanness
greenness
keenness
leanness
meanness
obsceneness
sereneness
uncleanness

ĒN'o
andantino
baldachino

bambino
casino
festino
Filipino
keno
maraschino
merino
peacherino
peperino
pianino
Reno
San Marino
Sereno
tondino
Valentino
vetturino

ĒN'ok
Enoch

ĒN'old
Reynold

ĔN'olz
Reynolds

ĔN'om
envenom
venom

ĔN'on
pennon
tenon

ĒN'os
Enos

ĔN'ri
Denry
Henry

ĔN'sal
bimensal
commensal
forensal
mensal

ĔN'sat
compensate
condensate
insensate
intensate

ĔN'sest
commencest
condensest
densest
dispensest
fencest
incensest
intensest
recompensest

ĔN'seth
commenceth
condenseth
dispenseth
fenceth
incenseth
recompenseth

ĔN'sez
Albigenses
amanuenses
menses

ĔNS'forth
henceforth
thenceforth
whenceforth

ĔN'shal
agential

bigential
coessential
conferential
confidential
consequential
credential
deferential
differential
equipotential
essential
evidential
existential
expediential
experiential
exponential
inconsequential
indulgential
inessential
inferential
influential
intelligential
irreverential
jurisprudential
nonessential
obediential
omnipresential
penitential
pestilential
potential
precedential
preferential
presidential
Provencial
providential
prudential
querulential
quintessential
referential
reminiscential
residential
reverential

rodential
sapiential
sciential
sentential
sequential
superessential
tangential
torrential
transferential
unessential

ĒN'ship

deanship
queenship

ĔN'shun

abstention
accension
apprehension
ascension
attention
circumvention
coextension
comprehension
condescension
contention
contravention
convention
declension
deprehension
descension
detention
dimension
dissension
distention
extension
inapprehension
inattention
incomprehen-
    sion
inextension

intension
intention
intervention
invention
mention
misapprehen-
    sion
obtention
obvention
ostension
pension
portention
preapprehen-
    sion
prehension
presention
pretension
prevention
propension
recension
reprehension
retention
subvention
supervention
suspension
tension
thermo-tension

ĔN'shund

unmentioned
unpensioned
well-inten-
    tioned

ĔN'shus

conscientious
contentious
dissentious
licentious
pestilentious
pretentious

sententious
silentious

ĔN'sil

extensile
pencil
pensile
prehensile
stencil
tensile
utensil

ĔN'sild

pencilled
stencilled

ĔN'sing

commencing
condensing
dispensing
fencing
incensing
recompensing

ĔN'siv

apprehensive
ascensive
comprehensive
condensive
condescensive
defensive
descensive
distensive
expensive
extensive
inapprehensive
incensive
incomprehen-
    sive
indefensive
inexpensive

influencive
inoffensive
intensive
offensive
ostensive
pensive
protensive
recompensive
reprehensive
self-defensive
suspensive
tensive
unapprehen-
  sive

ĔNS′les
defenceless
expenseless
fenceless
offenceless
senseless

ĔNS′ment
commencement
incensement

ĔNS′nes
denseness
immenseness
intenseness
propenseness
tenseness

ĔN′son
Benson
Henson

ĔN′sūr
censure

ĔN′sŭr
censer

censor
commencer
condenser
denser
dispenser
extensor
fencer
incensor
intenser
prehensor
recompenser
spencer
Spenser
tensor

ĔN′sus
census

ĔN′ta
magenta
Pimenta
polenta

ĔN′tal
accidental
alimental
antecedental
argental
argumental
atramental
bidental
cental
coincidental
complemental
complimental
continental
dental
dentil
dentile
departmental
detrimental

developmental
documental
elemental
experimental
falcon-gentle
firmamental
fragmental
fundamental
gentle
governmental
impedimental
incidental
instrumental
intercontin-
  ental
kentle
labiodental
Lental
ligamental
linguadental
medicamental
mental
monumental
nutrimental
occidental
oriental
ornamental
parental
parliamental
pedimental
pigmental
placental
predicamental
recremental
regimental
rental
rudimental
sacramental
segmental
sentimental
supplemental

temperamental
tenemental
testamental
transcendental
trental
tridental
ungentle
(cf. ĔN′til)

ĔN′tans
repentance
sentence
unrepentance

ĔN′tant
repentant
representant
unrepentant

ĔN′tat
bidentate
commentate
dementate
dentate
edentate
quadridentate
tridentate

ĔN′te
aguardiente
cognoscente
diapente

ĔN′ted
absented
accented
assented
augmented
battlemented
cemented
circumvented

commented
complimented
consented
contented
demented
dented
discontented
dissented
fermented
frequented
fomented
ill-contented
indented
invented
lamented
misrepresented
ornamented
presented
prevented
relented
rented
repented
represented
resented
scented
supplemented
sweet-scented
tented
tormented
unlamented
unornamented
unprecedented
unprevented
unrepented
untented
untormented
vented
well-contented

ĔN'test
absentest

accentest
assentest
augmentest
cementest
circumventest
commentest
complimentest
consentest
contentest
dissentest
fermentest
fomentest
frequentest
indentest
inventest
lamentest
misrepresentest
ornamentest
presentest
preventest
relentest
rentest
repentest
representest
resentest
sentest
scentest
supplementest
tormentest
ventest

ĔN'teth

absenteth
accenteth
assenteth
augmenteth
cementeth
circumventeth
commenteth
complimenteth
consenteth

contenteth
dissenteth
fermenteth
fomenteth
frequenteth
indenteth
inventeth
lamenteth
misrepreseneth
ornamenteth
presenteth
preventeth
relenteth
renteth
repenteth
representeth
resenteth
scenteth
supplementeth
tormenteth
venteth

ĔNT'ful

eventful
resentful
uneventful

ĔNT'hous

penthouse

ĔN'ti

dolce far niente
Henty
plenty
presidente
tormenty
twenty

ĔN'tij

percentage
ventage

ĔN'tik

argentic
authentic
identic

ĔN'tīl

Gentile

ĔN'tĭl

lentil
(cf. ĔN'tal)

ĔN'tin

dentine
Quentin
San Quentin
torrentine
tridentine

ĔN'ting

absenting
accenting
assenting
augmenting
cementing
circumventing
commenting
complimenting
consenting
contenting
denting
dementing
dissenting
fermenting
fomenting
frequenting
indenting
inventing
lamenting
misrepresent-
ing

ornamenting
presenting
preventing
relenting
renting
repenting
representing
resenting
scenting
self-tormenting
suppplement-
  ing
tenting
tormenting
unconsenting
unrelenting
unrepenting
venting

ĔN'tis
appentice
apprentice
non compos
  mentis
pentice
prentice

ĔN'tist
apprenticed
dentist
preventist

ĔN'tiv
adventive
assentive
attentive
circumventive
inattentive
incentive
inventive
irretentive

pendentive
presentive
preventive
resentive
retentive

ĔNT'les
cementless
centless
dentless
lamentless
relentless
rentless
scentless
tentless, etc.

ĔNT'li
eminently
evidently
gently
impotently
innocently
insolently
intently
(see ĔNT+ly)

ĔNT'ment
contentment
discontentment
presentment
relentment
representment
resentment

ĔNT'nes
intentness

ĔN'to
cento
cinque-cento
divertimento

lento
memento
pimento
polento
portamento
pronuncia-
  mento
quattrocento
rifacimento
Sacramento

ĔN'ton
Benton
Denton
Fenton
Trenton

ĔN'tor
bucentaur
centaur
mentor
stentor
succentor
(cf. ĔN'tur)

ĔN'tral
central
ventral

ĔN'trans
entrance

ĔN'trat
concentrate

ĔNT'res
inventress
tormentress

ĔN'tri
entry

gentry
sentry

ĔN'trik
acentric
anthropocen-
  tric
barycentric
centric
concentric
eccentric
geocentric
gynecocentric
heliocentric
paracentric
selenocentric

ĔN'tum
momentum
sarmentum

ĔN'tūr
adventure
debenture
indenture
misadventure
peradventure
tenture
venture

ĔN'tŭr
assenter
augmenter
cementer
center
circumventor
commenter
concenter
consenter
contenter
dead-center

denter
dissenter
enter
experimenter
fermenter
fomenter
frequenter
indenter
inventor
lamenter
lentor
misrepresenter
ornamenter
precentor
presenter
preventer
re-enter
relenter
renter
repenter
representer
resenter
supplementer
tenter
tormenter
venter
(cf. centaur,
  etc.)

ĔN′turd
entered
self-centered
centered, etc.

ĔN′tus
immomentous
ligamentous
momentous
pedetentous
pigmentous
portentous

sarmentous
unguentous

ĔN′um
frenum
plenum

ĔN′ur
cleaner
contravener
convener
demeanor
gleaner
greener
intervener
keener
leaner
machiner
magaziner
meaner
misdemeanor
obscener
screener
seiner
serener
shebeener
supervener
weaner
wiener

ĔN′ur
Fenner
penner
tenner
tenor
Venner

ĔN′us
genus
Silenus

venous
Venus

ĔN′vi
envy

ĔN′vil
Bienville
Glenville
Grenville

ĔN′yal
congenial
(see ĒN′i-al)

ĔN′yan
Armenian
(see ĒN′i-an)

ĔN′yens
lenience
(see ĒN′i-ens)

ĔN′yent
convenient
(see ĒN′i-ent)

ĔN′yor
monsignor
seignior
senior
signor

ĔN′yus
genius
(see ĒN′i-us)

ĔN′za
cadenza
influenza

ĔNZ′da
Wednesday

ĔN′zes
cleanses
lenses

ĔN′zi
frenzy
McKenzie

ĔN′zo
Lorenzo

ĔN′zon
tenzon
venison

Ē′o
Cleo
Leo
Theo
trio

Ē′on
æon
Creon
Leon
neon
odeon
pæon
pantheon
peon
pheon

ĔP′ard
jeopard
leopard
peppered
shepherd

ĒP'en
cheapen
deepen
steepen

ĒP'est
cheapest
cheepest
creepest
deepest
heapest
keepest
leapest
outsleepest
overleapest
oversleepest
peepest
reapest
sleepest
steepest
sweepest
weepest

ĒP'eth
cheepeth
creepeth
heapeth
keepeth
leapeth
outsleepeth
overleapeth
oversleepeth
peepeth
reapeth
sleepeth
sweepeth
weepeth

ĒP'i
cheepy
creepy

heapy
kepi
seepy
sleepy
steepy
sweepy
tepee
weepy

ĔP'i
tepee

ĔP'id
intrepid
lepid
tepid
trepid

ĒP'ij
seepage
sweepage

ĔP'ik
epic
orthoepic

ĒP'ing
cheeping
creeping
heaping
house-keeping
keeping
leaping
outsleeping
overleaping
oversleeping
peeping
reaping
safe-keeping
sleeping
steeping

sweeping
unsleeping
unweeping
weeping

ĒP'ish
deepish
sheepish
steepish

ĒP' 'l
empeople
people
steeple
unpeople

ĒP'les
sleepless
weepless

ĒP'nes
cheapness
deepness
sleepness

ĔP'on
weapon

ĔP'shun
abreption
apperception
arreption
conception
contraception
deception
ereption
exception
imperception
inception
interception
introsusception

intussusception
misconception
obreption
perception
preconception
preperception
reception
self-deception
subreption
surreption

ĔP'si
apepsy
catalepsy
dyspepsy
epilepsy
eupepsy

ĔP'sis
asepsis
analepsis
epanalepsis
metalepsis
paralepsis
prolepsis
scepsis
syllepsis

ĒP'skin
sheepskin

ĔP'tans
acceptance

ĔP'tant
acceptant
exceptant
reptant

ĔP'ted
accepted

excepted
intercepted

ĔP′test

acceptest
adeptest
exceptest
interceptest

ĔP′teth

accepteth
excepteth
intercepteth

ĔP′tik

acataleptic
analeptic
antiseptic
aseptic
bradypeptic
cataleptic
dyspeptic
epileptic
eupeptic
metaleptic
nympholeptic
organoleptic
peptic
proleptic
sceptic
septic
sylleptic

ĔP′ting

accepting
excepting
incepting
intercepting

ĔP′tiv

acceptive

conceptive
deceptive
exceptive
imperceptive
inceptive
insusceptive
interceptive
intussusceptive
irreceptive
perceptive
preceptive
receptive
susceptive

ĔPT′nes

ineptness

ĔP′tun

Neptune

ĔP′tur

accepter
adepter
excepter
inceptor
intercepter
preceptor
sceptre
susceptor

Ē̆P′ur

cheaper
cheeper
creeper
deeper
heaper
hedge-keeper
housekeeper
keeper
leaper
peeper

reaper
shopkeeper
sleeper
steeper
sweeper
wall-creeper
weeper
wicket-keeper

ĔP′ur

hepper
high-stepper
leper
overstepper
pepper
stepper

ĔP′wôk

sheep-walk
sleep-walk

Ē′ra

Ça ira
chimera
era
gerah
Hera
lira
Madeira
Vera

ĔR′af

seraph
teraph

Ę̄R′al

feral
spheral

ĔR′ald

Gerald

herald
Herrold

ĔR′ans

aberrance

ĔR′ant

aberrant

ĔR′as

terrace
(cf. ĔR′is)

ĔR′at

serrate

Ē̆R′ded

bearded

Ē̆RD′li

weirdly

Ē̆R′ens

adherence
appearance
arrearance
clearance
coherence
disappearance
incoherence
inherence
interference
perseverance
reappearance

Ē̆R′ent

adherent
coherent
inadherent
incoherent
inherent
perseverant

querent
vicegerent

ĘR'est
adherest
appearest
austerest
besmearest
careerest
cheerest
clearest
coherest
dearest
disappearest
drearest
endearest
fearest
gearest
hearest
insincerest
interferest
jeerest
leerest
merest
nearest
overhearest
peerest
perseverest
queerest
reappearest
rearest
reverest
searest
serest
severest
uprearest
shearest
sheerest
sincerest
smearest
sneerest

spearest
steerest
unrearest
veerest

ĔR'et
ferret
terret

ĘR'eth
adhereth
appeareth
besmeareth
careereth
cheereth
cleareth
disappeareth
endeareth
feareth
geareth
heareth
interfereth
jeereth
leereth
overheareth
peereth
persevereth
reappeareth
reareth
revereth
seareth
sheareth
smeareth
sneereth
speareth
steereth
upreareth
veereth

ĘR'fon
earphone

ĘR'ful
cheerful
earful
fearful
sneerful
tearful
uncheerful
unfearful

Ę'ri, Ē'ri
ærie
aweary
beery
bleary
cheery
deary
dreary
eerie
Erie
forweary
hara-kiri
jeery
leary
life-weary
miserere
overweary
peri
quære
query
smeary
sneery
sphery
teary
uncheery
veery
weary

ĔR'i
beriberi
berry
bury

cemetery
cherry
Derry
ferry
Gerry
Kerry
lamasery
merry
millinery
monastery
perry
Pondicherry
presbytery
sherry
skerry
stationery
very
wherry
(cf. ÂR'i)

ĘR'īd
blear-eyed
clear-eyed
tear-eyed

ĘR'ĭd
queried
unwearied
war-wearied
wearied
world-wearied
(cf. virid)

ĔR'id
berried
buried
cherried
ferried
serried
unburied

āle,   câre,   ădd,   ärm,   åsk;   mē,   hĕre,   ĕnd;   īce,   ĭll;

ĔR'if
sheriff
(cf. ĔR'af)

ḖR'ij
arrearage
clearage
peerage
pierage
steerage

ĔR'ik
alexiteric
amphoteric
anisomeric
atmospheric
chimeric
chromospheric
cleric
climacteric
derrick
enteric
Eric
esoteric
exoteric
ferric
generic
helispheric
hemispheric
Herrick
Homeric
hysteric
icteric
isomeric
masseteric
mesmeric
neoteric
numeric
peripheric
perispheric
phylacteric

piperic
spheric
suberic
valeric

ĔR'iks
esoterics
hysterics
clerics, etc.

ĔR'il
beryl
chrysoberyl
peril
sterile

ḖR'in
Erin

ḖR'ing
adhering
appearing
auctioneering
Bering
besmearing
blearing
cannoneering
careering
cashiering
cheering
clearing
cohering
Dearing
disappearing
domineering
earing
electioneering
endearing
engineering
fearing
gearing

gondoliering
hearing
interfering
jeering
leering
mountaineering
nearing
overhearing
peering
persevering
pioneering
privateering
queering
reappearing
rearing
rehearing
revering
searing
shearing
skeering
sneering
spearing
steering
ungearing
upcheering
uprearing
veering
venecring
volunteering
(cf. earring)

ĔR'is
ferris
terrace
Terris

ĔR'ish
cherish
perish

ĔR'it
demerit

disherit
disinherit
immerit
inherit
merit

ḖR'iz
dearies
overwearies
queries
series
wearies

ĔR'iz
berries
buries
cherries
ferries
sherries
wherries

ḖR'les
cheerless
earless
fearless
gearless
peerless
spearless
tearless
yearless

ḖR'li
austerely
cavalierly
cheerly
clearly
dearly
merely
nearly
queerly
severely

ōld, ȯr, ŏdd, oil, fŏŏt, out; ūse, ûrn, ŭp; THis, thin

sincerely
yearly

ĒR'ling
shearling
steerling
yearling

ĒR'ment
cerement
endearment

ĒR'nes
austereness
clearness
dearness
nearness
queerness
severeness
sincereness

ĒR'o, Ē'ro
hero
lillibullero
zero

ĔR'on
heron

Ē'room
sea-room
tea-room

ĔR'or
error
terror

ĒR'os, ĔR'os
Eros

ĒRS'nes
fierceness

ĒR'sur
fiercer
piercer

ĒR'sing
ear-piercing
piercing
transpiercing

ĒR'son
Grierson
Pearson

ĔR'ub
cherub

ĔR'ul
ferrule
ferule
perule
spherule

ĒR'ur
adherer
appearer
austerer
besmearer
cheerer
clearer
dearer
disappearer
electioneerer
endearer
fearer
fleerer
hearer
interferer
jeerer
leerer
nearer
overhearer

peerer
perseverer
queerer
rearer
reverer
severer
shearer
sneerer
spearer
steerer
teerer
ungearer
veerer
(cf. mirror)

ĒR'us
sclerous
serous

ĔR'us
ferrous

ĒRZ'man
privateersman
steersman

Ē'sa
Felica
mesa
Theresa

Ē'saj
presage

ĔS'chun
congestion
digestion
indigestion
ingestion
question
suggestion

ĔS'chund
questioned
unquestioned

ĔS'ed
blessed
(see ĔS+ed)

ĒS'el
Diesel

ĔS'en
lessen

ĒS'ens
indecence

ĔS'ens
accrescence
acquiescence
adolescence
arborescence
calescence
calorescence
candescence
coalescence
concrescence
contabescence
convalescence
defervescence
deliquescence
delitescence
effervescence
efflorescence
emollescence
erubescence
essence
evanescence
exacerbescence
excrescence
florescence

fluorescence
fremescence
frondescence
fructescence
frutescence
glaucescence
hyalescence
incalescence
incandescence
incoalescence
ineffervescence
inflorescence
intumescence
iridescence
juvenescence
lactescence
lapidescence
latescence
obsolescence
opalescence
petrescence
phosphor-
  escence
pubescence
putrescence
quiescence
quintessence
recrudescence
reflorescence
rejuvenescence
revalescence
revirescence
rubescence
senescence
spumescence
supercrescence
torpescence
tumescence
turgescence
viridescence

virilescence
vitrescence

ĔS'ent

decent
indecent
recent

ĔS'ent

accrescent
acquiescent
adolescent
albescent
alkalescent
arborescent
cessant
coalescent
convalescent
crescent
decrescent
deliquescent
delitescent
depressant
effervescent
efflorescent
erubescent
evanescent
excrescent
fervescent
flavescent
florescent
fluorescent
fremescent
fructescent
frutescent
gangrenescent
glaucescent
herbescent
ignescent
incalescent
incandescent

incessant
increscent
ineffervescent
iridescent
jessant
juvenescent
lactescent
languescent
lapidescent
latescent
liquescent
lutescent
marcescent
maturescent
nigrescent
obsolescent
opalescent
petrescent
phosphorescent
pubescent
putrescent
quiescent
rancescent
recrudescent
rejuvenescent
revalescent
rubescent
rufescent
senescent
spinescent
spinulescent
spumescent
suffrutescent
sugescent
supercrescent
torpescent
turgescent
violescent
virescent
viridescent
vitrescent

ĔS'ept

precept

ĔS'est

ceasest
creasest
decreasest
fleecest
greasest
increasest
leasest
releasest

ĔS'est

acquiescest
addressest
assessest
blessest
caressest
compressest
confessest
depressest
digressest
distressest
dressest
expressest
guessest
impressest
oppressest
possessest
pressest
professest
progressest
redressest
repressest
suppressest
trangressest
undressest

ĔS'eth

ceaseth

creaseth
decreaseth
fleeceth
greaseth
increaseth
leaseth
releaseth

ĔS'eth

acquiesceth
addresseth
assesseth
blesseth
caresseth
compresseth
confesseth
depresseth
digresseth
distresseth
dresseth
expresseth
guesseth
impresseth
oppresseth
possesseth
presseth
professeth
progresseth
redresseth
represseth
suppresseth
transgresseth
undresseth

ĔS'ez

battlepieces
caprices
ceases
creases
decreases
fleeces

greases
increases
leases
mantel-pieces
master-pieces
nieces
peaces
pelisses
pieces
releases

ĔS'ez

dresses
presses, etc.

ĔS'ful

capriceful
peaceful
unpeaceful

ĔS'ful

successful
(see ĔS+ful)

ĔSH'al

especial
special

ĔSH'an

Grecian
(see ĔSH'un)

ĔSH'est

enmeshest
freshest
immeshest
refreshest
threshest

ĔSH'eth

enmesheth

immesheth
mesheth
refresheth
thresheth

ĔSH'ez

species

ĔSH'i

fleshy
meshy

ĔSH'ing

meshing
refreshing
threshing

ĔSH'ingz

fleshings
meshings, etc.

ĔSH'les

fleshless
meshless

ĔSH'li

fleshly
freshly
unfleshly

ĔSH'man

freshman

ĔSH'ment

refreshment

ĔSH'nes

freshness

Ē'shor

sea-shore

Ē'shun

accretion
completion
concretion
deletion
depletion
Grecian
impletion
incompletion
internecion
repletion
secretion
(cf. Ē'shi-an,
    etc.)

ĔSH'un

accession
aggression
cession
compression
concession
confession
depression
digression
discretion
dispossession
egression
expression
freshen
impression
indiscretion
ingression
insession
intercession
introgression
intropression
obsession
oppression
possession
precession
prepossession

procession
profession
progression
recession
regression
repossession
reimpression
repossession
repression
retrocession
retrogression
secession
self-possession
session
succession
supersession
suppression
transgression
(cf. Hessian,
  etc.)

ĔSH'unz
quarter-ses-
  sions, acces-
  sions, etc.

ĔSH'ur
flesher
fresher
mesher
pressure
refresher
thresher
tressure

Ē'shus
facetious
specious

ĔSH'us
precious

ĔS'i
creasy
fleecy

ĔS'i
Bessie
Cressy
dressy
Jesse
Jessie
messy
Tessie
tressy
(cf. in esse)

Ē'sid
lee-side
sea-side

ĔS'ij
expressage
message
pesage
presage

ĔS'ik
eugenesic
geodesic

**Ē'sil, ĔS'il or
  ĬS'il**
Cecil

ĔS'ing
ceasing
creasing
decreasing
fleecing
greasing
increasing
leasing

piecing
policing
releasing
surceasing
unceasing

ĔS'ing
acquiescing
addressing
assessing
blessing
caressing
coalescing
compressing
confessing
convalescing
depressing
digressing
dispossessing
distressing
dressing
excessing
expressing
guessing
impressing
messing
oppressing
possessing
prepossessing
pressing
professing
progressing
redressing
repressing
retrogressing
suppressing
undressing
unprepos-
  sessing
water-dressing

ĔS'is
anamnesis
anesthesis
anthesis
aposiopesis
catachresis
deesis
diaphoresis
diesis
erotesis
exegesis
hyperesthesis
mathesis
mimesis
ochlesis
paracentesis
perichoresis
schesis
synteresis
thesis
tmesis

ĔS'iv
adhesive
cohesive

ĔS'iv
accessive
aggressive
compressive
concessive
concrescive
congressive
crescive
depressive
digressive
excessive
expressive
impressive
inexpressive
oppressive

possessive
progressive
recessive
redressive
regressive
repressive
retrogressive
successive
suppressive
transgressive
unexpressive

ĔS'ki
de Reszke
pesky

ĔSK'nes
grotesqueness
picturesqueness
statuesqueness

ĔS'ko
al fresco
fresco
tedesco

ĔS'ku
fescue
rescue

Ē'skwar
T-square

ĔS"l
Cecil
chessel
nestle
pestle
redressal
trestle
unnestle

vessel
wrestle

ĔS'les
capriceless
ceaseless
creaseless
fleeceless
leaseless
peaceless

ĔS'ling
nestling
pestling
wrestling

ĔS'lur
nestler
wrestler

ĔS'man
policeman

ĔS'man
pressman
yes man

ĔS'mat
mess-mate

ĔS'mel
piecemeal

ĔS'ment
assessment
impressment
redressment

ĔS'nes
obeseness

ĔS'on
Gleason
Leisen

ĔS'on
lessen
lesson

ĔS'pit
respite

ĔS'pur
Hesper
vesper

ĔS'ta
podesta
siesta
Vesta
Zend-Avesta

ĔS'tal
festal
vestal

ĔS'tan
Avestan
sebesten

ĔS'tant
contestant
gestant

ĔS'tat
intestate
testate

ĔS'ted
arrested
attested
bested

breasted
castle-crested
chested
chicken-
  breasted
congested
contested
crested
detested
digested
disinterested
divested
double-breasted
foam-crested
indigested
infested
ingested
interested
invested
jested
manifested
marble-
  breasted
molested
nested
pigeon-
  breasted
predigested
protested
redigested
requested
rested
sable-vested
single-breasted
suggested
tested
unbreasted
undigested
unmolested
unrested

vested
wrested

ĔS'test
arrestest
attestest
bestest
breastest
contestest
crestest
detestest
digestest
divestest
infestest
interestest
investest
jestest
manifestest
molestest
protestest
requestest
restest
suggestest
testest
wrestest

ĔS'teth
arresteth
attesteth
breasteth
contesteth
cresteth
detesteth
digesteth
divesteth
infesteth
interesteth
investeth
jesteth
manifesteth
molesteth

nesteth
protesteth
requesteth
resteth
suggesteth
testeth
wresteth

ĔS'tez
Estes

ĔST'ful
blestful
jestful
restful
unrestful

ĔS'ti
beastie
bheesty
yeasty

ĔS'ti
chesty
cresty
resty
testy
yesty

ĔS'tij
prestige
vestige

ĔS'tik
agrestic
alkahestic
anamnestic
anapestic
aposiopestic
asbestic
catachrestic

domestic
gestic
majestic
telestic
telestich

ĔS'tin
asbestine
clandestine
destine
intestine
predestine
sestine

ĔS'tind
destined
predestined
undestined

ĔS'ting
easting
feasting
unpriesting
yeasting

ĔS'ting
arresting
attesting
besting
breasting
congesting
contesting
cresting
detesting
digesting
disinteresting
divesting
infesting
ingesting
interesting
investing
jesting

manifesting
molesting
nesting
protesting
questing
reinvesting
requesting
resting
suggesting
testing
uninteresting
unresting
vesting
westing
wresting

ĔS'tiv
attestive
congestive
digestive
festive
infestive
restive
suggestive
tempestive

ĔST'les
breastless
crestless
guestless
jestless
questless
restless

ĔST'li
beastly
priestly

ĔST'ling
nestling
westling

ĔST'ment
arrestment
divestment
investment
vestment

ĔS'to
manifesto
presto

Ē'ston
freestone
keystone

ĔS'ton
Weston

ĔS'tral
ancestral
campestral
fenestral
kestrel
orchestral
trimestral

ĔS'trat
fenestrate
sequestrate

ĔS'trik
orchestric
palaestric

ĔS'tur
divesture
gesture
investure
purpresture
revesture
vesture

ĔS'tus
asbestus
cestus

ĒST'ward
eastward

ĔST'ward
westward

ĒS'ter
Dniester
down-easter
Easter
feaster
north-easter
south-easter

ĔS'tur
arrester
attester
Bester
Bestor
breaster
Chester
contester
digester
divester
Dnestr
Esther
fester
Hester
infester
investor
jester
Leicester
Lester
mid-sementer
molester
nester

nor'-wester
pester
prester
protester
requester
rester
semester
sequester
sou'-wester
suggester
Sylvester
tester
trimester
vester
wrester
yester

ĔS'turd
sequestered
unsequestered
festered, etc.

ĒS'turn
eastern

ĔS'turn
hestern
north-western
south-western
western
yestern

ĒS'ur
creaser
decreaser
fleecer
greaser
increaser
leaser

piecer
releaser

ĔS'ŭr
acquiescer
addresser
aggressor
antecessor
assessor
blesser
caresser
cesser
compressor
confessor
depressor
digresser
distresser
dresser
excesser
guesser
impresser
intercessor
lesser
messer
oppressor
possessor
predecessor
presser
professor
progressor
redresser
represser
successor
suppressor
transgressor

ĒT'a
cheetah
Chiquita
Juanita

Rita
zeta

ĔT′a

animetta
arietta
biretta
burletta
codetta
comedietta
Etta
Henrietta
lametta
mozetta
operetta
Retta
Rosetta
vendetta
Yetta

ĒT′ed

accreted
bleated
cheated
competed
completed
conceited
defeated
deleted
depleted
entreated
escheated
evil-treated
excreted
greeted
heated
ill-treated
incompleted
maltreated
meted
receipted

reheated
repeated
retreated
seated
secreted
self-conceited
sheeted
sleeted
treated
unmeeted
unseated
wine-heated
(cf. fetid)

ĔT′ed

abetted
benetted
betted
brevetted
coquetted
coroneted
curvetted
fretted
gazetted
indebted
interfretted
jetted
netted
petted
pirouetted
regretted
sweated
unfretted
unnetted
wetted
whetted
(cf. fetid)

ĒT′en

beaten
Cretan

eaten
moth-eaten
overeaten
storm-beaten
sweeten
tempest-beaten
unbeaten
weather-beaten
wheaten
worm-eaten
(cf. ĒT′on)

ĔT′en

fretten
threaten
(cf. Bretton)

ĒT′est

beatest
bleatest
cheatest
competest
completest
defeatest
deletest
depletest
discreetest
eatest
effetest
elitest
entreatest
fleetest
greetest
heatest
ill-treatest
incompletest
maltreatest
meetest
neatest
overeatest
pleatest

receiptest
repeatest
repletest
retreatest
seatest
sweetest
treatest
(cf. defeatist,
    etc.)

ĔT′est

abettest
backsettest
bayonettest
begettest
benettest
besettest
bettest
coquettest
forgettest
frettest
gettest
lettest
nettest
oversettest
pettest
regrettest
settest
upsettest
wettest
whettest

ĒT′eth

beateth
bleateth
cheateth
competeth
completeth
defeateth
deleteth
depleteth

eateth
entreateth
greeteth
heateth
maltreateth
meeteth
overeateth
pleateth
receipteth
repeateth
retreateth
seateth
treateth

ĔT'eth
abetteth
begetteth
benetteth
betteth
bewetteth
coquetteth
forgetteth
fretteth
getteth
letteth
netteth
petteth
regretteth
setteth
whetteth

ĒT'ful
deceitful

ĔT'ful
forgetful
fretful
regretful

ĒTH'al
bequeathal

Ēth'al
ethal
lethal

Ēth'an
Ethan

Ēth'el
Bethel
ethal
Ethel
(cf. Ĕth'il)

ĒTH'en
heathen
wreathen

Ēth'i
heathy
Lethe
lethy

Ēth'i
deathy

Ĕth'il
ethyl
methyl

ĒTH'ing
bequeathing
breathing
ensheathing
enwreathing
inbreathing
incense-
   breathing
interwreathing
inwreathing
seething
sheathing

teething
terror-
   breathing
unsheathing
wreathing

Ēth'les
sheathless
wreathless

Ĕth'les
breathless
deathless

Ĕth'li
deathly

ĒTH'ment
bequeathment
ensheathment
enwreathment

Ĕth'nik
ethnic
holethnic

Ĕth'od
method

ĔTH'ren
brethren

ĒTH'ur
bequeather
breather
either
enwreather
neither
seether
sheather
wreather

Ēth'ur
ether

ĔTH'ur
altogether
aweather
blether
feather
heather
leather
nether
patent-leather
pinfeather
tether
together
weather
wether
white-feather
whitleather
whether

ĔTH'urd
unfeathered
weathered
feathered, etc.

ĒT'i
entreaty
meaty
peaty
sleety
spermaceti
sweetie
sweety
treaty

ĔT'i
Alligretti
Bettie
betty
confetti

fretty
Hettie
Hetty
Irish confetti
jetty
Lettie
Letty
libretti
netty
Nettie
petit
petty
Rossetti
spaghetti
spermaceti
Vanizetti
sweaty

ĔT'id, ĔT'id
fetid
(cf. ĒT'ed,
  ĒT'ed)

ĔT'ij
cheatage
cleatage
eatage
escheatage
metage

ĔT'ik
acetic
cetic
Cretic
Rhætic

ĔT'ik
abietic
abiogenetic
æsthetic
agamogenetic

alexipyretic
allopathetic
aloetic
alphabetic
amuletic
anesthetic
anchoretic
antipathetic
antithetic
apathetic
apologetic
arithmetic
ascetic
athletic
auletic
Baphometic
bathetic
biogenetic
biomagnetic
catechetic
colletic
cometic
cosmetic
diamagnetic
dianoetic
diaphoretic
dietetic
docetic
electro-
  magnetic
emetic
emporetic
energetic
epigenetic
epithetic
erotetic
eugenetic
exegetic
frenetic
galactopoietic
Gangetic

genetic
geodetic
Helvetic
hermetic
histogenetic
homiletic
homogenetic
hypothetic
idiopathetic
inergetic
Japhetic
kinetic
Lettic
logarithmetic
magnetic
Masoretic
metic
mimetic
mythopoetic
noetic
nomothetic
ochletic
onomatopoetic
ontogenetic
palingenetic
pangenetic
parathetic
parenthetic
paretic
partheno-
  genetic
pathetic
pathogenetic
peripatetic
phonetic
phrenetic
phylogenetic
plethoretic
poetic
polygenetic
polysynthetic

prophetic
quercetic
quodlibetic
splenetic
strategetic
sympathetic
syncretic
synthetic
tabetic
theopathetic
theoretic
threnetic
zetetic

ĔT'iks
apologetics
dietetics
exegetics
homiletics
poetics
aesthetics, etc.

ĒT'ing
beating
bitter-
  sweeting
bleating
cheating
competing
completing
concreting
defeating
eating
entreating
fleeting
flesh-eating
greeting
heating
ill-treating
maltreating
meeting

ōld, ôr, ŏdd, oil, fŏŏt, out; ūse, ûrn, ŭp; THis. thin

meting
overeating
receipting
repeating
retreating
seating
secreting
sheeting
sweeting
toad-eating
treating
unseating

ĔT'ing
abetting
backsetting
begetting
benetting
besetting
betting
brevetting
coquetting
curvetting
forgetting
fretting
gazetting
getting
intersetting
jetting
letting
minuetting
netting
oversetting
petting
regretting
retting
setting
somersetting
sweating
undersetting
upsetting

wetting
whetting

ĔT'is
Thetis

ĔT'is
lettuce

ĔT'ish
coquettish
fetish
Lettish
pettish
wettish

ĔT'ist
defeatist, etc.

ĔT'it
beat it

ĔT'iv
accretive
completive
concretive
decretive
depletive
discretive
repletive
secretive

ĔT'iz
entreaties
sweeties
treaties
treatise

ĔT"l
beetle
betel

decretal
fetal

ĔT"l
abettal
Babbitt metal
Chettle
fettle
kettle
metal
mettle
Monel metal
nettle
petal
Popocatapetl
resettle
settle
type-metal
white-metal

ĔT"ld
high-mettled
nettled
petalled
unsettled
mettled, etc.

ĔT'les
debtless
threatless

ĔT'li
completely
concretely
discreetly
featly
fleetly
indiscreetly
meetly
neatly
obsoletely

sweetly
unmeetly

ĔT'ling
nettling
settling
unsettling

ĔT'ment
entreatment
ill-treatment
maltreatment
treatment

ĔT'ment
abetment
besetment
indebtment
revetment

ĔT'nes
completeness
concreteness
discreetness
effeteness
featness
fleetness
incompleteness
meetness
neatness
obsoleteness
repleteness
sweetness

ĔT'nes
setness
wetness

ĔT'o
bonito
mosquito

āle, câre, ădd, ärm, ȧsk; mē, hẹre, ĕnd; īce, ĭll;

385   ĒT′o — ĔT′ur

san-benito
veto

ĔT′o

allegreto
amoretto
falsetto
ghetto
lazaretto
libretto
palmetto
stiletto
terzetto
zucchetto

ĒT′on

Beaton
Eaton
Eton
Keaton
Keyton
Seaton
Seyton
Zyzzogeton
(cf. ĒT′en)

ĔT′on

Bretton

ĒT′ral, ĒT′rel

diametral
petrel

ĒT′ri

Petrie

ĔT′rik

actinometric
alkalimetric
anemometric
anisometric

audiometric
barometric
bathymetric
calorimetric
clinometric
chlorometric
chronometric
diametric
dimetric
electrometric
endosmometric
eudiometric
gasometric
geometric
goniometric
gravimetric
hexametric
hydrometric
hygrometric
hypsometric
isobarometric
isometric
logometric
magnetometric
metric
micrometric
monometric
obstetric
ozonometric
pedometric
photometric
stereometric
symmetric
tasimetric
thermometric
trigonometric
trimetric
volumetric

ĒT′rok

sheetrock

ĒT′rus, ĔT′rus
petrous
saltpetrous
triquetrous

ĒT′um

arboretum
fretum
pinetum
zibetum

ĒT′ūr

creature
feature
(cf. ĒCH′ur)

ĒT′ur

beater
beefeater
bleater
cake-eater
cheater
centimeter
competer
completer
decaliter
defeater
Demeter
depleter
eater
entreater
escheator
fire-eater
fleeter
frog-eater
gas-meter
goldbeater
greeter
heater
hectoliter
ill-treater

kilometer
liter
lotus-eater
meeter
meter
metre
neater
overeater
Peter
prætor
receipter
repeater
retreater
saltpeter
seater
secreter
skeeter
smoke-eater
superheater
sweeter
teeter
toad-eater
treater
unseater
water-meter

ĔT′ur

abettor
begetter
besetter
better
carburetor
coquetter
curvetter
dead-letter
debtor
enfetter
fetter
forgetter
fretter
getter

ōld, ôr, ŏdd, oil, fŏŏt, out; ūse, ûrn, ŭp; THis, thin

go-getter
jetter
letter
netter
petter
red-letter
regretter
resetter
setter
somersetter
sweater
type-setter
wetter
whetter

ĔT'urd
featured

ĔT'urd
fettered
unfettered
unlettered
bettered, etc.

ĔT'urz
Peters

ĔT'us
acetous
Cetus
fetus
quietus

ĔT'wurk
fretwork
network

Ē'um
amœbæum
athenæum
bronteum

colosseum
lyceum
mausoleum
museum
peritoneum
prytaneum
Te Deum

Ē'ur
agreer
feer
fleer
freer
over-seer
seer
sight-seer

Ē'us
choreus
corypheus
gluteus
onomatopœous
plumbeous
scarabæus

Ē'va
diva
Eva
Geneva
Kamadeva
Kivah
Mahadeva
viva

ĒV'al
coeval
longeval
medieval
primeval
retrieval
shrieval

upheaval
(cf. weevil)

ĔV'an
Evan
Devon
(cf. Ĕv'en)

ĒV'ans
achievance
grievance
perceivance
retrievance

ĔV'el, ĔV'l
bedevil
bevel
devil
dishevel
Greville
kevel
level
Neville
revel
sea-level
spirit-level
water-level

ĔV'en
even
good-even
Hallow-even
Stephen
Steven
unbereaven
uneven
yester-even

ĔV'en
eleven
heaven

leaven
seven

ĔV'end
leavened
unleavened

ĔV'enth
eleventh
seventh

ĒV'enz
Stevens

ĒV'est
achievest
believest
bereavest
cleavest
conceivest
deceivest
disbelievest
grievest
heavest
inweavest
leavest
perceivest
receivest
relievest
reprievest
retrievest
thievest
upheavest
weavest

ĒV'eth
achieveth
believeth
bereaveth
cleaveth
conceiveth

deceiveth
disbelieveth
grieveth
heaveth
inweaveth
leaveth
perceiveth
receiveth
relieveth
reprieveth
retrieveth
thieveth
upheaveth
weaveth

Ē′vī
Levi

Ē′vĭ
Levy

ĔV′i
bevy
chevy
clevy
heart-heavy
heavy
levee
levy
nevvy
top-heavy

ĒV′ij
cleavage
leavage

ĔV′il
evil
king's-evil
weevil

ĔV′il
devil
Neville
(see ĔV′el)

ĔV′ilz
blue-devils
devils, etc.

ĔV′in
levin
replevin

ĒV′ing
achieving
aggrieving
believing
bereaving
cleaving
conceiving
deceiving
disbelieving
grieving
heaving
interweaving
inweaving
leaving
misconceiving
perceiving
preconceiving
receiving
relieving
reprieving
retrieving
sheaving
steeving
thieving
unbelieving
undeceiving
unweaving

upheaving
weaving

ĒV′ingz
leavings, etc.

ĒV′ish
peevish
thievish

ĒV′les
leaveless
sheaveless
sleeveless

ĒV′ment
achievement
bereavement
retrievement

ĒV′ning
evening

ĔV′ri
every

ĒV′ur
achiever
aggriever
ballast-heaver
beaver
believer
bereaver
brever
cantilever
cleaver
coal heaver
conceiver
deceiver
Deever
disbeliever

enfever
fever
griever
Guadalquivir
heaver
interleaver
interweaver
jungle-fever
keever
leaver
lever
liever
livre
makebeliever
misconceiver
naïver
perceiver
preconceiver
reaver
reever
receiver
reiver
reliever
repriever
retriever
sheaver
unbeliever
undeceiver
upheaver
weaver
weever
yellow-fever

ĔV′ur
assever
cantilever
clever
dissever
endeavor
ever
forever

howstever
howsoever
lever
never
sever
unsever
whatever
whatsoever
whencesoever
whenever
whensoever
wheresoever
wherever
whichever
whichsoever
whithersoever
whoever
whomsoever
whosesoever
whosoever

ĔV'urd
unsevered
dissevered, etc.

ĔV'us
grievous
longevous
primevous

Ē'wa
leeway
seaway

Ē'ward
leeward
seaward

Ē'wit
peewit

Ē'ya
Cassiopeia
(cf. Ē'a)

Ē'yan
Tarpeian
(cf. Ē'an)

ĒZ'a
Liza
Louisa
Pisa

ĒZ'ans
defeasance
easance
malfeasance
misfeasance

ĔZ'ans, ĔZ'ens
omnipresence
pleasance
presence
peasants, etc.

ĔZ'ant, ĔZ'ent
displeasant
omnipresent
peasant
pheasant
pleasant
present
unpleasant

ĒZ'dal
Teasdale

ĔZ'dal
Esdale

ĒZ'el
easel

teasel
Teazle
weasel

ĔZ'el
bezel
(cf. ĔZ''l)

ĒZ'els
easels
measles, etc.

Ē'zha
magnesia
(see Ēz'i-a)

Ē'zhan
Milesian
(see ĒZ'i-an)

Ē'zhun
adhesion
cohesion
inadhesion
inhesion
lesion
Silesian
trapezian
(cf. ĒZ'i-on)

Ē'zhur
leisure
seizure

ĔZH'ur
admeasure
displeasure
entreasure
leisure
measure
outmeasure

pleasure
treasure

Ē'zhurd
unleisured

Ē'zhurd
immeasured
unleisured
unmeasured
untreasured
measured, etc.

ĒZ'i
breezy
cheesy
easy
free-and-easy
freezy
greasy
queasy
sleazy
sneezy
speakeasy
uneasy
wheezy
Zambezi

ĒZ'iks
skeeziks

ĒZ'in
seizin

ĒZ'ing
appeasing
breezing
displeasing
easing
foreseizing
freezing
greasing

pleasing
seizing
self-pleasing
sneezing
squeezing
teasing
unpleasing
wheezing

ĒZ'it
cheese it

ĔZ"l
embezzle
(cf. ĔZ'el)

ĔZ'lur
embezzler

ĒZ'ment
appeasement
easement

ĒZ'on
reason
season
treason
unreason
unseason

ĔZ'ra
Ezra

ĒZ'ur
appeaser
Cæsar
easer
Ebenezer
freezer
friezer
geezer
greaser
leaser
pleaser

sneezer
squeezer
teaser
tweezer
wheezer

ĔZ'urt
desert

ĒZ'urz
tweezers, etc.

ĒZ'us
Jesus

I

For a discussion of words included under the accented vowels
following, see the beginning of I rhymes in Section I.

Ī'a
Amariah
asthenia
Ave Maria
Azariah
Beniah
Beriah
Black Maria
gorgoneia
Hezekiah
Isaiah
Jedediah
Jeremiah
Josiah
Keziah
latria
Maria
messiah
Obadiah

Sophia
stria
Thalia
Tobiah
Uriah
via
Zachariah
Zebediah
Zedekiah
Zephaniah

Ī'ad
dryad
dyad
hamadryad
Jeremiad
Pleiad
triad

Ī'adz
Hyads
dryads, etc.

Ī'ak
elegiac
guiac
kayak
phrenesiac

Ī'al, Ī'ol
basihyal
bass-viol
decrial
denial
dial
espial
genial
phial

retrial
rial
self-denial
supplial
trial
vial
viol

Ī'am
Priam
Siam

Ī'amb
iamb

Ī'an
Altaian
Brian
Bryan

Chian
genian
Orion
O'Ryan
Ryan
styan
thalian
(cf. Ī'on)

Ī'and
viand

Ī'andz
viands

Ī'ans
affiance
alliance
appliance
compliance
defiance
incompliance
misalliance
reliance
science
self-reliance
suppliance
(cf. giants,
    etc.)

Ī'ant
affiant
alliant
calorifient
client
compliant
defiant
giant
pliant
reliant

scient
self-reliant

Ī'as
Ananias
bias
Elias
eyas
Jeremias
Josias
Lias
Matthias
Messias
Tobias, etc.
unbias
(see Ī'us)

Ī'at
fiat

Ī'azm
miasm

Ī'ba
capaiba
Ziba

ĬB'ald
ribald
Theobald

ĬB'dis
Charybdis

ĬB'est
ascribest
bribest
circumscribest
describest
gibest
imbibest

inscribest
prescribest
proscribest
subscribest
superscribest
transcribest

ĬB'est
fibbest
glibbest
jibbest

ĬB'et
flibbertigibbet
gibbet
Tibbett
zibet
(cf. ĬB'it)

ĬB'eth
ascribeth
bribeth
circumscribeth
describeth
gibeth
imbibeth
inscribeth
prescribeth
proscribeth
subscribeth
superscribeth
transcribeth

ĬB'eth
fibbeth
jibbeth

ĬB'i
Kibbee
Libbey

Libby
Tibbie

ĪB'ing
ascribing
bribing
circumscribing
describing
gibing
imbibing
inscribing
prescribing
proscribing
subscribing
transcribing

ĬB'ing
fibbing
jibbing
ribbing
squibbing

ĬB'it
adhibit
cohibit
exhibit
inhibit
prohibit

Ī'b'l
Bible
libel
tribal

ĬB″l
cribble
dibble
dribble
fribble
gribble
ish ka bibble

---

kibble
nibble
quibble
scribble
sibyl
thribble

ĬB″ld

cribbled
ribald
dibbled, etc.

ĬB′lest

dribblest
scribblest, etc.

ĬB′let

driblet
giblet
triblet

ĬB′leth

dribbleth
scribbleth, etc.

ĬB′li

dribbly
glibly
nibbly
quibbly
scribbly
thribbly
tribbly

ĬB′lik

niblick

ĬB′ling

cribbling
dibbling
dribbling

fribbling
kibbling
nibbling
quibbling
scribbling
tribbling

Ī′blo

by-blow
fly-blow

ĬB′lur

cribbler
dibbler
dribbler
fribbler
kibbler
nibbler
quibbler
scribbler
transcribbler

Ī′bôl

eye-ball
high-ball
sky-ball

Ī′bôld

piebald

ĬB′on

gibbon
ribbon

ĬB′onz

Gibbons
ribbons, etc.

Ī′born

high-born
sky-born

ĬB′rant

vibrant

ĬB′rat

equilibrate
librate
vibrate

Ī′brou

eyebrow
high-brow

ĬB′sen

Ibsen

ĬB′son

Ibson
Gibson

ĬB′un

tribune

ĬB′ur

ascriber
briber
circumscriber
describer
fiber
giber
imbiber
inscriber
Leiber
liber
prescriber
proscriber
scriber
subscriber
Tiber
transcriber

ĬB′ur

bibber

cribber
dibber
fibber
flibbergibber
gibber
glibber
jibber
nibber
quibber
squibber
wine-bibber

ĬB′ut

attribute
contribute
distribute
redistribute
retribute
tribute

ĬCH′ard

Pritchard
Richard

ĬCH′el

Kitchell
Mitchell
Turchell
switchel

ĬCH′en

kitchen
lichen

ĬCH′est

bewitchest
enrichest
hitchest
pitchest
ṛichest
stitchest

ōld,   ôr,   ŏdd,   oil,   fŏŏt,   out;   ūse,   ûrn,   ŭp;   THis,   thin

switchest
twitchest

ĬCH′et
fitchet
Fitchett
Pritchett
Twichett
witchet

ĬCH′eth
bewitcheth
enricheth
hitcheth
pitcheth
stitcheth
switcheth
twitcheth

ĬCH′ez
bewitches
bitches
breeches
ditches
enriches
flitches
hitches
itches
niches
pitches
riches
scritches
stitches
switches
twitches
witches

ĬCH′i
fitchy
itchy
pitchy

Richie
stitchy
witchy

ĬCH′ing
bewitching
ditching
enriching
hitching
itching
miching
pitching
stitching
switching
twitching
witching

ĬCH′les
hitchless
itchless
stitchless
switchless
witchless

ĬCH′ment
bewitchment
enrichment

ĬCH′nes
richness

ĬCH′ur
bewitcher
ditcher
enricher
hitcher
itcher
pitcher
richer
stitcher
switcher
twitcher

ĬCH′us
righteous

Ī′da
Ida
Lida
Oneida

ĪD′ans
abidance
guidance
misguidance
subsidence

ĬD′ans
forbiddance
riddance

ĪD′ant
dividant
guidant

ĪD′ed
backslided
betided
bided
chided
coincided
collided
confided
decided
derided
divided
elided
glided
guided
lopsided
many-sided
misguided
one-sided
presided

prided
provided
resided
sided
slab-sided
subdivided
subsided
tided
undecided
undivided
unguided
unprovided
(cf. tidied)

ĬD′ed
kidded
lidded, etc.

ĪD′en
Dryden
widen
(cf. ĪD′on)

ĬD′en
bidden
chidden
forbidden
hag-ridden
hidden
kitchen-midden
midden
overridden
priest-ridden
ridden
slidden
stridden
unbidden
unforbidden
wife-ridden

ĪD′ent
bident

rident
strident
trident

ĪD'est
abidest
backslidest
bidest
chidest
coincidest
collidest
confidest
decidest
deridest
dividest
elidest
glidest
guidest
hidest
overridest
presidest
pridest
providest
residest
ridest
sidest
slidest
stridest
subdividest
subsidest
tidest
widest

ĬD'est
biddest
forbiddest, etc.

ĬD'eth
abideth
betideth
bideth

chideth
coincideth
collideth
confideth
decideth
derideth
divideth
elideth
glideth
guideth
hideth
overrideth
presideth
prideth
provideth
resideth
rideth
sideth
slideth
strideth
subdivideth
subsideth
tideth

ĬD'eth
biddeth
forbiddeth, etc.

ĪD'i
bonafide
Friday
sidy
tidy
untidy
vide

ĬD'i
biddy
chickabiddy
giddy
kiddy

middy
stiddy
"widdy"

ĬD'id
tidied
(cf. ĪD'ed)

ĬD'ij
guidage
hidage

ĬD'ik
druidic
fatidic
juridic
pyramidic

ĪD'il or ĬD'il
idyll

ĪD'ing
abiding
backsliding
bestriding
betiding
biding
chiding
coinciding
colliding
confiding
deciding
deriding
dividing
eliding
gliding
guiding
hiding
law-abiding
misguiding
niding

outriding
outstriding
overriding
presiding
priding
providing
residing
riding
siding
sliding
striding
subsiding

ĬD'ing
bidding
forbidding
kidding
lidding
outbidding
overbidding
ridding
skidding
unforbidding

ĪD'ingz
tidings
backslidings,
    etc.

ĪD″l
bridal
bridle
fratricidal
homicidal
idle
idol
infanticidal
matricidal
parricidal
patricidal
regicidal

ōld, ôr, ŏdd, oil, fŏŏt, out; ūse, ûrn, ŭp; THis, thin

sidle
suicidal
tidal
tyrannicidal

ĪD″l

Biddle
fiddle
diddle
flumadiddle
griddle
Liddle
middle
quiddle
riddle
rum-tum-tiddle
tiddle
twiddle
unriddle

ĪD″ld

unbridled
bridled, etc.

ĬD′ld

fiddled, etc.

ĪD′lest
idlest, etc.

ĬD′lest
fiddlest, etc.

ĪD′leth
idleth, etc.

ĬD′leth
fiddleth, etc.

ĪD′li

bridely
widely

ĪD′ling

bridling
idling
sidling

ĬD′ling

diddling
fiddling
kidling
middling
riddling
twiddling

ĬD′lings

middlings
kidlings, etc.

ĪD′lit

guide-light
side-light

ĪD′lur

bridler
idler

ĬD′lur

fiddler
quiddler
riddler
tiddler
twiddler

ĪD′nes

piedness
wideness

ĬD′ni

kidney
Sidney
Sydney

ĪD′o

Dido
Fido

ĬD′o

kiddo
widow

ĪD′on

guidon
Poseidon
Sidon
(cf. widen)

ĪD′or

nidor
stridor
(cf. ĪD′ur)

ĪD′rule

slide rule

ĪD′ur

backslider
bestrider
chider
cider
coincider
collider
confider
decider
derider
divider
eider
elider
Fulenwider
glider
guider
hider
insider
misguider

one-sider
outrider
outsider
presider
provider
resider
rider
rough-rider
Schneider
sider
slider
Snider
Snyder
spider
strider
subdivider
subsider
wider

ĬD′ur

bidder
consider
forbidder
kidder
outbidder
overbidder
ridder
skidder

ĬD′urd

considered
ill-considered
unconsidered

Ī′ens

science
(see Ī′ans)

Ī′ent

calorifient
client

āle,   câre,   ădd,   ärm,   åsk;   mē,   hẹre,   ĕnd;   īce,   ĭll;

395

Ī'ent — Ī'eth

inscient
scient
(see affiant,
 etc.)

Ī'est

alliest
amplifiest
appliest
awryest
beautifiest
bedyest
beliest
bespyest
brutifiest
buyest
certifiest
clarifiest
classifiest
compliest
criest
crucifiest
decriest
defiest
deifiest
deniest
descriest
diest
dignifiest
diversifiest
driest
dyest
edifiest
electrifiest
espiest
eyest
falsifiest
fliest
fortifiest
friest
glorifiest

gratifiest
hiest
highest
horrifiest
identifiest
impliest
justifiest
liest
liquefiest
magnifiest
modifiest
mollifiest
mortifiest
multipliest
mystifiest
nighest
notifiest
nullifiest
occupiest
ossifiest
outviest
pacifiest
personifiest
pliest
prophesiest
pryest
purifiest
qualifiest
ratifiest
rectifiest
reliest
repliest
sanctifiest
satisfiest
shyest
sighest
signifiest
simplifiest
slyest
specifiest
spryest

spyest
stupefiest
suppliest
terrifiest
testifiest
tiest
tryest
typifiest
untiest
verifiest
versifiest
viest
vilifiest
vitrifiest
wryest

Ī'et

diet
inquiet
piet
quiet
(cf. riot)

Ī'eth

allieth
amplifieth
applieth
bedyeth
belieth
bespyeth
buyeth
certifieth
clarifieth
classifieth
complieth
crieth
crucifieth
decrieth
defieth
deifeth
denieth

descrieth
dieth
dignifieth
diversifieth
drieth
dyeth
edifieth
electrifieth
espieth
eyeth
falsifieth
flieth
fortifieth
frieth
glorifieth
gratifieth
hieth
horrifieth
identifieth
implieth
justifieth
lieth
liquefieth
magnifieth
modifieth
mollifieth
mortifieth
multiplieth
mystifieth
notifieth
nullifieth
occupieth
outvieth
pacifieth
personifieth
plieth
prophesieth
purifieth
qualifieth
ratifieth
rectifieth

ōld, ôr, ŏdd, oil, fŏŏt, out; ūse, ûrn, ŭp; THis, thin

relieth
replieth
sanctifieth
satisfieth
sigheth
signifieth
simplifieth
specifieth
spyeth
stupefieth
supplieth
terrifieth
testifieth
tieth
trieth
typifieth
untieth
verifieth
versifieth
vieth
vilifieth
vitrifieth
vivifieth

ĪF'en, ĪF'on

hyphen
siphon
Typhon

ĪF'en, ĪF'on

griffon
stiffen

ĬF'est

sniffest
stiffest
whiffest

ĬF'et

whiffet

ĬF'eth

sniffeth, etc.

ĬF'i

cliffy
jiffy
sniffy
spiffy
squiffy

ĬF'ik

acidific
algific
anaglyphic
aurific
beatific
calorific
classific
colorific
cornific
damnific
deific
diaglyphic
dolorific
finific
frigorific
glyphic
grandific
hieroglyphic
honorific
horrific
humorific
incoherentific
lactific
lapidific
lithoglyphic
lucific
magnific
mellific
mirific
morbific

mucific
omnific
ossific
pacific
petrific
petroglyphic
photoglyphic
phytoglyphic
pontific
prolific
pulsific
rubific
sacrific
salvific
saporific
scientific
sensific
siccific
somnific
sonorific
soporific
specific
sudorific
tabific
tenebrific
terrific
torporific
triglyphic
vaporific
vivific
vulnific

ĬF'in

biffin
griffin
tiffin
(cf. stiffen,
etc.)

ĬF'ing

sniffing

tiffing
whiffing

ĬF'ish

miffish
sniffish
stiffish
tiffish

Ī'f'l

Eiffel
rifle
stifle
trifle

ĬF''l

piffle
riffle
sniffle
whiffle

ĪF'les

fifeless
knifeless
lifeless
strifeless
wifeless

ĪF'li

rifely
wifely

ĪF'lik

lifelike
wifelike

ĪF'ling

rifling
stifling
trifling

ĬF'ling
piffling
riffling
sniffling
whiffling

ĬF'lur
rifler, etc.

ĬF'lur
piffler
riffler
sniffler
whiffler

ĬF'on, ĬF'en
hyphen
siphon
Typhon

ĬF'ted
drifted
gifted
lifted
rifted
shifted
sifted
ungifted
uplifted

ĬF'test
driftest
liftest
riftest
shiftest
siftest
swiftest
upliftest

ĬF'teth
drifteth

lifteth
rifteth
shifteth
sifteth
uplifteth

ĬF'ti
clifty
drifty
fifty
fifty-fifty
nifty
rifty
shifty
thrifty

ĬF'ting
drifting
lifting
rifting
shifting
shop-lifting
sifting
uplifting

ĬFT'les
driftless
riftless
shiftless
thriftless

ĬFT'nes
swiftness

ĬF'ton
Clifton

ĬF'thong
diphthong
triphthong

ĬFT'ur
drifter
lifter
scene-shifter
shifter
shop-lifter
sifter
swifter
uplifter

ĬF'ur
cipher
decipher
fifer
lifer
knifer
rifer

ĬF'ur
differ
sniffer
stiffer

Ī'ga
saiga

ĬG'and
brigand

ĬG'at
frigate
(cf. bigot)

ĬG'bi
Digby

ĬG'est
biggest
diggest
riggest
triggest

ĬG'eth
diggeth, etc.

ĬG'i
biggy
piggy
piggy-wiggy
spriggy
twiggy

ĬG'ing
digging
gigging
jigging
rigging
sprigging
swigging
thimblerigging
trigging
twigging
unrigging
wigging

ĬG'inz
Dwiggins
Higgins
Wiggins

ĬG'ish
piggish
priggish
whiggish

ĬG"l
giggle
higgle
jiggle
niggle
sniggle
squiggle
wiggle
wriggle

ōld, ôr, ŏdd, oil, fŏŏt, out; ūse, ûrn, ŭp; THis, thin

Ī'glas
eye-glass
spy-glass

ĬG''ld
giggled, etc.

ĬG'lest
gigglest, etc.

ĬG'leth
giggleth, etc.

ĬG'li
Piggly-Wiggly
giggly, etc.

ĬG'lif
diglyph
monotriglyph
triglyph

ĬG'ling
giggling
higgling, etc.

ĬG'lur
giggler
higgler, etc.

ĬG'ma
enigma
sigma
stigma

ĬG'ment
figment
pigment

ĬG'mi
pygmy

ĬG'nal
signal

ĬG'nans
malignance

ĬG'nant
benignant
indignant
malignant

ĬG'net
cygnet
signet

ĬG'nit
lignite

ĬG'num
ecce signum
lignum

Ī'go
caligo
fuligo
impetigo
Loligo
vertigo

Ī'gon
bygone
trigone

ĬG'on
big 'un
Ligon

Ī'gor
rigor
vigor
(cf. ĬG'ur)

Ī'got
bigot
gigot
spigot
(cf. frigate)

ĪG'res
tigress

Ī'gur
Niger
tiger

ĬG'ūr
configure
disfigure
figure
ligure
prefigure
transfigure

ĬG'ur
bigger
chigger
digger
"figger"
gold-digger
grave-digger
gigger
jigger
ligger
market-rigger
nigger
outrigger
prigger
rigger
snigger
sprigger
swigger
thimblerigger
trigger
twigger

(cf. rigor
and vigor)

ĬG'urd
"figgered"
jiggered
niggard
sniggered
unniggard

Ī'ing
acidifying
adrying
alibing
allying
amplifying
applying
beatifying
beautifying
bedying
belying
bespying
brutifying
butterflying
buying
candifying
certifying
clarifying
classifying
codifying
complying
countrifying
crucifying
crying
damnifying
dandifying
decrying
defying
deifying
denying
descrying

āle,   câre,   ădd,   ärm,   åsk;   mē,   hẹre,   ĕnd;   īce,   ĭll;

dignifying
disqualifying
dissatisfying
diversifying
drying
dulcifying
dyeing
dying
edifying
electrifying
emulsifying
espying
exemplifying
eyeing
falsifying
fying
fortifying
Frenchifying
fructifying
frying
glorifying
gratifying
guying
hieing
horrifying
humanifying
hushabying
identifying
implying
indemnifying
intensifying
justifying
kite-flying
labifying
liquefying
lying
magnifying
modifying
mollifying
mortifying
multiplying

mystifying
notifying
nullifying
occupying
ossifying
outcrying
outflying
outlying
outvying
pacifying
personifying
petrifying
piing
plying
preachifying
preoccupying
prophesying
prying
purifying
putrefying
qualifying
ramifying
rarefying
ratifying
rectifying
relying
replying
revivifying
sanctifying
satisfying
scarifying
scorifying
self-denying
self-relying
self-satisfying
shying
sighing
signifying
simplifying
skying
solidifying

specifying
spying
stultifying
stupefying
supplying
terrifying
testifying
torpifying
torrefying
trying
typifying
uncomplying
under-buying
underlying
undying
unifying
unsatisfying
untying
verifying
versifying
vieing
vilifying
vitrifying
vivifying

Ī'ja

Abijah
Elijah

Ī'jak

highjack

ĬJ'est

digest
disobligest
obligest

ĬJ'id

frigid
rigid

ĬJ'il

sigil
strigil
vigil

ĬJ'ing

disobliging
obliging

ĬJ'ing

abridging
bridging
ridging

ĬJ'it

Bridget
Brigit
digit
fidget
"ijjit"
midget

ĬJ'on

irreligion
pigeon
religion
widgeon

ĬJ'ur

abridger
bridger

ĬJ'us

irreligious
litigious
prodigious
religious
sacrilegious

ĪK'a

balalaika

lorica
mica
Micah
pica
pika

Ī′kal
Michael

ĬK′ard
Pickard
Rickard

ĬK′at
exsiccate
siccate

Ĭk′ed
wicked
(see ĬK+ed)

ĪK′en
lichen
liken
unliken

ĬK′en
chicken
horror-stricken
quicken
sicken
stricken
terror-stricken
thicken
wicken
wonder-
   stricken

ĬK′enz
chickens
slickens
the dickens

ĪK′est
dislikest
likest
obliquest
spikest
strikest

ĬK′est
clickest
flickest
kickest
lickest
pickest
prickest
slickest
stickest
thickest
tickest
trickest

Ĭk′et
clicket
cricket
midwicket
picket
Pickett
pricket
Prickett
Rickett
thicket
ticket
walking-ticket
wicket

ĬK′eth
disliketh
liketh
spiketh
striketh

ĬK′eth
clicketh

flicketh
kicketh
licketh
picketh
pricketh
sticketh
ticketh
tricketh

ĬK′ets
rickets
crickets, etc.

ĪK′i
spiky
(cf. Psyche)

ĬK′i
bricky
dickey
do-hickey
Ficke
gin-rickey
quickie
rickey
sticky
tricky

ĪK′ik
psychic

ĪK′iks
psychics

ĪK′ing
biking
disliking
dyking
misliking
piking
spiking

striking
viking
well-liking

ĬK′ing
besticking
bricking
clicking
cricking
flicking
kicking
licking
picking
pocket-picking
pricking
snicking
sticking
thicking
ticking
tricking
wicking

ĬK′ish
brickish
sickish
slickish
thickish

ĪK″l
cycle
epyicycle
psychal

ĬK″l
fickle
mickle
nickel
pickle
prickle
sickle
stickle

strickle
tickle
trickle

ĬK′lest
ficklest
picklest
ticklest
tricklest

ĬK′leth
pickleth
prickleth
tickleth
trickleth

ĬK′li
belikely
likely
obliquely
unlikely

ĬK′li
prickly
quickly
sickly
slickly
stickly
thickly
trickly

ĬK′lik
bicyclic
cyclic
encyclic
epicyclic
geocyclic

ĬK′ling
cycling

ĬK′ling
chickling
pickling
prickling
tickling
trickling

ĬK′lish
pricklish
ticklish

ĬK′list
cyclist

ĬK′lon
cyclone

ĬK′lur
fickler
prickler
stickler
strickler
tickler

ĬK′nes
likeness
obliqueness
unlikeness

ĬK′nes
love-sickness
quickness
sickness
slickness
thickness

ĬK′nik
picnic
strychnic

ĬK′nin
strychnine

ĬK′ning
quickening
sickening
thickening

ĬK′on
icon

ĬK′or
ichor

Ī′kount
viscount

ĬK′sen
mixen
vixen

ĬK′sest
affixest
fixest
intermixest
mixest
prefixest
transfixest

ĬK′set
quickset
thick-set

ĬK′seth
affixeth
fixeth
intermixeth
mixeth
prefixeth
transfixeth

ĬK′shun
abstriction
addiction

affixion
affliction
affriction
benediction
confliction
constriction
contradiction
conviction
crucifixion
depiction
dereliction
diction
eviction
fiction
friction
indiction
infliction
interdiction
jurisdiction
malediction
obstriction
prediction
prefixion
reliction
restriction
suffixion
transfixion
valediction

ĬK′shus
contradictious
fictious

ĬK′si
Dixey
Dixie
nixie
pixie
tricksy
Trixie
water-nixie

ōld, ôr, ŏdd, oil, fŏŏt, out; ūse, ûrn, ŭp; THis, thin

ĬK'sing
admixing
affixing
fixing
intermixing
mixing
prefixing
transfixing

ĬK'son
Dickson
Dixon
Hickson
Hixon

ĬK'sti
sixty

ĬK'stūr
admixture
affixture
fixture
immixture
incommixture
intermixture
mixture

ĬK'stŭr
trickster

ĬK'sur
affixer
elixir
fixer
intermixer
mixer
prefixer
transfixer

ĬK'tat
dictate
nictate

ĬK'ted
addicted
afflicted
conflicted
constricted
contradicted
convicted
depicted
evicted
inflicted
interdicted
predicted
relicted
restricted
self-inflicted
unrestricted

ĬK'test
addictest
afflictest
conflictest
contradictest
convictest
depictest
evictest
inflictest
predictest
restrictest
strictest

ĬK'teth
addicteth
afflicteth
conflicteth
contradicteth
convicteth
depicteth
evicteth
inflicteth
predicteth
restricteth

ĬK'tik
apodictic
deictic
endeictic
epideictic
ictic

ĬK'tim
victim

ĬK'ting
addicting
afflicting
conflicting
constricting
contradicting
convicting
depicting
evicting
inflicting
interdicting
predicting
restricting

ĬK'tiv
addictive
afflictive
benedictive
conflictive
constrictive
contradictive
convictive
depictive
fictive
indictive
inflictive
interdictive
jurisdictive
predictive
restrictive
vindictive

ĬKT'li
derelictly
strictly

ĬKT'nes
strictness

ĬK'tor
(see ĬK'tur)

ĬK'tum
dictum

ĬK'tūr
depicture
impicture
picture
stricture
word-picture

ĬK'tŭr
afflicter
boa-constrictor
conflicter
constrictor
contradicter
depicter
fictor
inflicter
lictor
Pictor
predicter
restricter
stricter
victor

ĬK'tus
acronyctous
Benedictus
ictus

ĬK'ur
biker

āle, câre, ădd, ärm, ăsk; mē, hẹre, ĕnd; īce, ĭll;

Diker	**ĪL′a**	**ĬL′an**	**ĪL′dest**
hiker	Hyla	arch-villain	mildest
liker	Lila	villain	wildest
obliquer		villein	
piker	**ĬL′a**		**ĬL′dest**
Riker	anilla	**Ī′land**	*begildest*
spiker	armilla	highland	*buildest*
striker	barilla	island	*gildest*
	bismillah	Rhode Island	
ĬK′ur	camarilla		**ĪL′deth**
bicker	Camilla	**Ī′lark**	*begildeth*
clicker	cascarilla	phylarch	*buildeth*
dicker	cedilla	sky-lark	*gildeth*
flicker	chinchilla		
kicker	codilla	**ĬL′as**	**ĪLD′hood**
knicker	Drusilla	Silas	childhood
licker	flotilla	Vilas	
liquor	gorilla		**ĪL′ding**
nicker	granadilla	**Ī′lash**	childing
picker	granilla	eyelash	wilding
pricker	guerrilla		
quicker	Lilla	**ĬL′at**	**ĬL′ding**
sicker	Manila	distillate	begilding
slicker	manilla	penicillate	building
snicker	mantilla		castle-building
sticker	maxilla	**ĬL′burt**	gilding
thicker	Priscilla	filbert	rebuilding
ticker	sabadilla	Gilbert	unbuilding
tricker	sapodilla	Wilbert	ungilding
vicar	sarsaparilla		
wicker	seguidilla	**ĬL′da**	**ĪL′dish**
	Sybilla	Hilda	childish
ĬK′urz	vanilla	Mathilda	mildish
knickers	villa	Matilda	wildish
bickers, etc.			
	ĪL′ak	**ĬL′ded**	**ĪLD′les**
ĪK′us	lilac	begilded	childless
Picus		builded	mildless
spicous	**ĪL′aks**	gilded	
	lilacs	ungilded	**ĪLD′li**
ĬK′wid	smilax		childly
liquid			

---

mildly	ĪL'est	pilot	*tilleth*
wildly	*beguilest*	sky-pilot	*trilleth*
	compilest	stylet	*willeth*
ĪLD'lik	*defilest*		
childlike	*filest*	**ĪL'et**	**ĪL'ful**
	pilest	billet	guileful
ĪLD'nes	*reconcilest*	fillet	smileful
mildness	*revilest*	millet	wileful
riledness	*rilest*	rillet	
unmildness	*smilest*	skillet	**ĪL'ful**
wildness	*stylest*	willet	skilful
	vilest		wilful
ĪL'dred	*whilest*	**ĪL'eth**	unskilful
Mildred	*wilest*	*beguileth*	
		compileth	**ĪL'fur**
ĪLD'ren	**ĪL'est**	*defileth*	pilfer
children	*befrillest*	*fileth*	
	chillest	*pileth*	**ĪL'grim**
ĪL'dur	*distillest*	*reconcileth*	pilgrim
milder	*drillest*	*revileth*	
wilder	*enthrillest*	*rileth*	**Ī'li**
	fillest	*smileth*	ancile
ĪL'dur	*frillest*	*styleth*	drily
begilder	*fulfillest*	*tileth*	highly
bewilder	*grillest*	*up-pileth*	O'Reilly
builder	illest	*whileth*	Reilly
castle-builder	*instillest*	*wileth*	Riley
gilder	*killest*		shyly
guilder	*millest*	**ĪL'eth**	slily
rebuilder	shrillest	*chilleth*	wily
wilder	*spillest*	*distilleth*	wryly
	stillest	*drilleth*	
ĪLD'wood	*swillest*	*enthrilleth*	**ĪL'i**
wildwood	*thrillest*	*filleth*	Billee
	tillest	*fulfilleth*	Billie
ĪL'ens	*trillest*	*instilleth*	billy
silence	*willest*	*killeth*	Chile
		milleth	chili
ĪL'ent	**Ī'let, Ī'lot**	*spilleth*	chilly
silent	eyelet	*stilleth*	daffy-down-
si'lent	islet	*thrilleth*	dilly

filly
frilly
gillie
grilly
hilly
illy
lily
Millie
Milly
Piccadilly
piccalilli
silly
shrilly
skilly
stilly
tiger-lily
Tillie
Tilly
water-lily
Willie
Willy
willy-nilly

Ī'lid
eyelid

ĬL'id
lilied

ĬL'ij
grillage
pillage
tillage
village
thrillage, etc.

ĬL'ik
amylic
basilic
Cyrillic
dactylic

idyllic
macrodactylic
methylic
odylic
salicylic
zygodactylic

Ī'lin
sky-line
styline

ĬL'in
MacMillin
McQuillin
(cf. McMillan,
  Dillon, etc.)

ĬL'ing
beguiling
compiling
defiling
filing
piling
reconciling
reviling
riling
smiling
styling
tiling
time-beguiling
up-piling
whiling
wiling

ĬL'ing
befrilling
billing
chilling
distilling
drilling
enthrilling

filling
frilling
fulfilling
grilling
instilling
killing
milling
shilling
shrilling
skilling
spilling
stilling
swilling
thrilling
tilling
trilling
unwilling
upfilling
willing

ĬL'ingz
Billings
drillings, etc.

ĬL'ip
Philip

ĬL'ips
Philips

ĬL'is
Amaryllis
Myrtillis
Phyllis
Willis
Wyllis

ĬL'ish
stylish

Ī'lit
dry-light

high-light
skylight
stylite
twilight
xylite

ĬL'iz
chilies
fillies
gillies
lilies
sillies
the Willies

ĬL'izm
Carlylism
hylism

ĬL'joy
killjoy

ĬL'ken
milken
silken

ĬL'ki
milky
silky

ĬL'king
bilking
milking

ĬL'koks
Philcox
Silcox
Wilcox

ĬL'les
guileless
smileless
wileless

ĬL'man
billman
Gilman
grillman
hill-man
mill-man
Stillman

ĬL'ment
beguilment
defilement
exilement
irreconcilement
reconcilement
revilement

ĬL'ment
distilment
fulfilment
instilment

ĬL'mi
filmy

ĬL'mor
Filmore
Gilmore

ĪL'nes
juvenileness
vileness

ĬL'nes
chillness
illness
shrillness
stillness

ĬL'nur
Milner

ĪL'o
high-low
milo
silo

ĬL'o
armadillo
billow
embillow
grenadillo
killow
kilo
negrillo
peccadillo
pillow
pulvillo
weeping-
  willow
willow

ĬL'od
unpillowed
billowed, etc.

ĬL'oid
styloid
xyloid

Ī'lok
Shylock

ĬL'ok
hillock

ĪL'om
whilom

ĬL'on
Dillon

ĬL'ot
pilot

sky-pilot
(cf. islet)

ĬL'pin
Gilpin

ĬL'room
grill-room
still-room

ĬL'sid
hillside
rill-side

ĬL'son
Gilson
Stillson
Wilson

ĬL'ted
hilted
jilted
kilted
lilted
overtilted
quilted
silted
stilted
tilted
tip-tilted
wilted

ĬL'test
jiltest
kiltest
liltest
quiltest
tiltest
wiltest

ĬL'teth
jilteth

kilteth
lilteth
quilteth
tilteth
wilteth

ĬL'thi
filthy

ĬL'ti
guilty
silty
stilty

ĬL'ting
jilting
kilting
lilting
quilting
silting
tilting
wilting

ĬL'ton
Chilton
Hilton
Milton
Stilton
Tilton

ĬL'tur
filter
infilter
jilter
kilter
philter
quilter
tilter
wilter

ĬL'um
asylum

phylum
Wylam

ĬL'ur
beguiler
bifilar
compiler
defiler
filar
filer
Huyler
piler
reconciler
reviler
riler
Schuyler
smiler
stylar
tiler
Tyler
up-piler
viler
wiler
Zuyler

ĬL'ur
befriller
biller
caterpillar
chiller
distiller
driller
filler
friller
fulfiller
griller
iller
ill-willer
instiller
Joe-Miller
killer

lady-killer
man-killer
maxillar
miller
pillar
Schiller
shriller
siller
spiller
stiller
swiller
thiller
thriller
tiller
willer

ĬL'us
aspergillus
bacillus
favillous
fibrillous
orgillous
villus

ĬL'van
sylvan

ĬL'vur
silver

ĬL'yam
Gilliam
William

ĬL'yans
brilliance
(cf. ĬL'i-ans,
 ĬL'i-ens)

ĬL'yant
brilliant

(cf. ĬL'i-ant,
 ĬL'i-ent)

ĬL'yar
atrabiliar
auxiliar
conciliar
domiciliar
familiar
(cf. ĬL'i-ur)

ĬL'yardz
billiards
milliards

ĬL'yun
billion
carillon
cotillion
decillion
mandillon
million
modillion
nonillion
octillion
pavilion
pillion
postillion
quadrillion
quintillion
sextillion
stillion
trillion
tourbillion
vermilion
(cf. ĬL'i-an)

ĬL'yunth
billionth
millionth
trillionth, etc.

ĬM'a
cyma
Jemima
Lima

ĬM'aks
anti-climax
climax

ĬM'al
isocheimal
isocrymal
primal

Ī'man
Hymen
pieman
Simon
Wyman

ĬM'at
acclimate
climate
primate

ĬM'bal
cymbal
fimble
gimbal
nimble
symbol
thimble
tymbal
wimble

ĬM'bo
akimbo
bimbo
kimbo
limbo

ĬM'brel
timbrel
whimbrel

ĬM'bur
imber
limber
timber
timbre
unlimber

ĬM'burd
untimbered
limbered, etc.

ĬM'bus
limbus
nimbus

ĬM'el
Friml
gimmal
Grimmell
Himmel
kümmel

Ī'men
Hymen
(see Ī'man)

ĬM'en
women
(cf. persim-
mon)

ĬM'est
begrimest
berhymest
beslimest
chimest
climbest

primest
rhymest
sublimest

ĬM'est
brimmest
dimmest
grimmest
primmest
skimmest
slimmest
swimmest
trimmest

ĪM'eth
begrimeth
berhymeth
beslimeth
chimeth
climbeth
rhymeth

ĬM'eth
brimmeth
dimmeth
skimmeth
swimmeth
trimmeth

ĬM'flam
flimflam

ĪM'i
beslimy
blimy
grimy
limy
rimy
rhymy
slimy

stymie
thymy

ĬM'i
gimme
jimmy
shimmy
whimmy

ĬM'id
timid

ĬM'ij
image
scrimmage

ĬM'ik
alchimic
cacochymic
cherubimic
eponymic
etymic
homonymic
lipothymic
metonymic
metronymic
mìmic
pantomimic
patronymic
synonymic
zymic (also
    ĪM'ik)

ĪM'ing
begriming
beliming
berhyming
besliming
chiming
climbing
griming

liming
priming
rhyming
sliming
timing

ĬM'ing
bedimming
betrimming
brimming
dimming
grimming
skimming
slimming
swimming
trimming

ĬM'ist
rhymist
timist

ĬM'it
limit

ĬM'jams
jimjams

ĬM'krak
gimcrack

ĬM'les
chimeless
crimeless
grimeless
limeless
rhymeless
rimeless
slimeless
thymeless
timeless
overtimeless

ĬM'les
brimless
hymnless
limbless
rimless
swimless
vimless
whimless

ĪM'li
primely
sublimely
timely
untimely

ĬM'li
dimly
grimly
primly
slimly
trimly

ĬM'nal, ĬM'nel
hymnal
simnel

ĪM'nes
primeness
sublimeness

ĬM'nes
dimness
grimness
primness
slimness
trimness

ĬM'ni
chimney

Ī'mon
Simon

Timon
(see Ī'man)

ĬM'on
persimmon
Rimmon
(cf. women)

ĬM'onz
Simmons
persimmons

ĬM'pet
limpet

ĬM'pi
crimpy
impi
impy
skimpy

ĬM'ping
blimping
crimping
imping
limping
primping
scrimping
shrimping
skimping

ĬM'pish
impish

ĬM'pit
lime-pit
slime-pit

ĬM'p'l
bewimple
crimple
dimple

pimple
rimple
simple
wimple

ĬM'plest
crimplest
dimplest
pimplest
rimplest
simplest
wimplest

ĬM'pleth
crimpleth, etc.

ĬM'pli
crimply
dimply
limply
pimply
simply

ĬM'pling
crimpling
dimpling
impling
pimpling
rimpling
shrimpling
wimpling

ĬM'plur
crimpler
dimpler
rimpler
simpler
wimpler

ĬM'pur
crimper

limper
scrimper
shrimper
simper
skimper
whimper

ĬM'ros
primrose

ĬM'shi
imshi

ĬM'son
jimson

ĬM'stur
rhymester

ĪM'ur
begrimer
chimer
climber
Hergesheimer
old-timer
primer
rhymer
timer
sublimer

ĬM'ur
brimmer
dimmer
gimmer
glimmer
grimmer
primer
primmer
shimmer
simmer
skimmer

ōld, ôr, ŏdd, oil, fŏŏt, out; ūse, ûrn, ŭp; THis, thin

slimmer
swimmer
trimmer
Zimmer

ĬM'us
primus
rimous
simous
timeous
untimeous

ĬM'zi
flimsy
slimsy
whimsey

ĬM'zon
crimson
encrimson

Ī'na
Adelina
Angelina
Carolina
Catalina
China
Dinah
Evelina
farina
Jaina
Lucina
Meleagrina
Messalina
Platyrhina
Regina
Sabina
Sabrina
salina
semolina

Shekinah
trichina

Ĭn'a
Corinna
Erinna
Minna

ĬN'al
acclinal
anticlinal
binal
caninal
cerebro-spinal
crinal
declinal
endocrinal
equinal
final
isoclinal
matutinal
officinal
periclinal
piscinal
rhinal
spinal
synclinal
trinal
Vinal

ĬN'as
pinnace

ĬN'at
binate
quinate

ĬN'chest
clinchest
flinchest

lynchest
pinchest

ĬN'cheth
clincheth
flincheth
lyncheth
pincheth

ĬN'ching
clinching
flinching
lynching
pinching
unflinching

ĬN'chur
clincher
flincher
lyncher
pincher

ĬN'churz
pinchers, etc.

ĬN'da
Belinda
Chlorinda
Dorinda
Ethelinda
Lucinda

ĬN'ded
alike-minded
blinded
bloody-minded
carnal-minded
double-minded
even-minded
earthly-minded
evil-minded

fair-minded
feeble-minded
fleshly-minded
free-minded
high-minded
light-minded
like-minded
low-minded
minded
narrow-minded
public-minded
reminded
rinded
self-blinded
simple-minded
single-minded
snow-blinded
soberminded
strongminded
winded
worldly-minded

ĬN'ded
abscinded
brinded
broken-winded
exscinded
interscinded
long-winded
rescinded
short-winded
winded

ĬN'den
linden
Lindon
Minden

ĬN'dest
bindest
blindest

āie,   câre,   ădd,   ärm,   ăsk;   mē,   hẹre,   ĕnd;   īce,   ĭll;

411 IN'dest — IN'est

findest
grindest
kindest
remindest
windest

ĪN'deth
bindeth
blindeth
findeth
grindeth
mindeth
remindeth
windeth

ĪND'ful
mindful
remindful
unmindful

ĬN'di
Lindy
Lucindy
shindy
windy

ĬN'dig
shindig

ĬN'dik
indic
syndic

ĬN'ding
binding
blinding
finding
grinding
inbinding
minding
reminding

unbinding
unwinding
upbinding
upwinding
winding

ĬN'd'l
brindle
dwindle
enkindle
kindle
rekindle
spindle
swindle

ĬN'd'ld
brindled, etc.

ĬN'dlest
brindlest, etc.

ĬN'dleth
brindleth, etc.

ĪND'li
blindly
kindly
unkindly

ĬND'li
Hindley
spindly

ĬND'ling
brindling
dwindling
enkindling
kindling
rekindling
swindling

ĬND'lur
dwindler

kindler
swindler, etc.

ĪND'nes
blindness
color-blindness
kindness
loving-kindness

ĬN'do
window

ĬN'drans
hindrance

ĬN'dred
kindred

ĬN'dur
binder
blinder
faultfinder
finder
grinder
hinder
kinder
minder
pathfinder
reminder
spellbinder
stem-winder
water-finder
winder

ĬN'dur
cinder
flinder
hinder
pinder
rescinder
tinder

ĬN'en
linen

Ī'nes
dryness
highness
nighness
shyness
slyness
spryness
wryness

ĬN'es
Inness
Guinness
(cf. pinnace)

ĬN'est
assignest
benignest
combinest
condignest
confinest
consignest
countersignest
declinest
definest
designest
dinest
divinest
enshrinest
entwinest
finest
inclinest
intertwinest
malignest
minest
outlinest
outshinest
overtwinest
pinest

reassignest
reclinest
refinest
resignest
shinest
signest
superfinest
supinest
twinest
underlinest
underminest
undersignest
untwinest
whinest
winest

ĬN'est
beginnest
dinnest
grinnest
pinnesi
sinnest
skinnest
spinnest
thinnest
winnest

ĬN'et
linnet
minute
spinet

ĬN'eth
assigneth
combineth
confineth
consigneth
countersigneth
declineth
defineth
designeth

dineth
divineth
cnshrineth
entwineth
inclineth
intertwineth
maligneth
mineth
outlineth
outshineth
overtwineth
pineth
reassigneth
reclineth
refineth
resigneth
shineth
signeth
twineth
underlineth
undermineth
undersigneth
untwineth
whineth
wineth

ĬN'eth
beginneth
dinneth
ginneth
grinneth
pinneth
sinneth
skinneth
spinneth
winneth

ĬN'fant
infant

ĬN'ful
sinful

ĬNG'am
Bingham

ĬNG'bolt
king-bolt
ring-bolt
wring-bolt

ĬNG'dom
kingdom

ĬNG'duv
ring-dove

ĬNG'ed
winged
(see ĭng + ed)

ĬNG'est
bringest
clingest
flingest
outwingest
ringest
singest
slingest
springest
stingest
stringest
swingest
wingest
wringest

ĬNG'eth
bringeth
clingeth
flingeth
outwingeth
ringeth
singeth
slingeth

springeth
stingeth
stringeth
swingeth
unslingeth
wingeth
wringeth

ĬNG'ga
anhinga

ĬNG'gi
dinghy
(cf. Feringhee)

ĬNG'g'l
commingle
cringle
dingle
immingle
intermingle
jingal
jingle
Kriss Kringle
mingle
shingle
single
springal
surcingle
swingle
tingle
tringle

ĬNG'g'ld
unmingled
commingled,
etc.

ĬNG'glest
jinglest
minglest
tinglest

ĬNG'gleth
jingleth
mingleth
tingleth

ĬNG'gli
jingly
mingly
shingly
singly
tingly

ĬNG'gling
intermingling
jingling
kingling
mingling
singling
tingling
wingling

ĬNG'glish
English
tinglish

ĬNG'glur
intermingler
jingler
mingler
shingler
tingler

ĬNG'go
dingo
flamingo
gringo
jingo
lingo
stingo

ĬNG'gur
finger

forefinger
index-finger
linger
malinger

ĬNG'gurd
light-fingered
rosy-fingered
web-fingered
fingered, etc.

ĬNG'gus
dingus

ĬNG'gwal
bilingual
lingual

ĬNG'gwish
contradistin-
  guish
distinguish
extinguish

ĬNG'i
clingy
springy
stingy
stringy
swingy
wingy

ĬNG'ing
bringing
clinging
dinging
enringing
flinging
outwinging
plainsinging
ringing

singing
slinging
springing
stinging
stringing
swinging
unslinging
unstringing
upbringing
upstringing
winging
wringing

ĬNGK'est
bethinkest
blinkest
chinkest
clinkest
drinkest
hoodwinkest
inkest
linkest
pinkest
shrinkest
sinkest
slinkest
stinkest
thinkest
winkest

ĬNGK'et
trinket

ĬNGK'eth
bethinketh
blinketh
chinketh
clinketh
drinketh
hoodwinketh
inketh

linketh
pinketh
shrinketh
sinketh
slinketh
stinketh
thinketh
winketh

ĬNGK'go
ginkgo

ĬNGK'i
blinky
inky
kinky
pinky
zincky

ĬNGK'id
blink-eyed
pink-eyed

ĬNGK'ing
bethinking
blinking
chinking
clinking
drinking
enlinking
free-thinking
hoodwinking
inking
interlinking
linking
pinking
rinking
shrinking
sinking
slinking
stinking

thinking
unblinking
unlinking
unshrinking
unthinking
unwinking
winking

ĬNGK"l
besprinkle
crinkle
inkle
periwinkle
sprinkle
tinkle
twinkle
winkle
wrinkle

ĬNGK"ld
unwrinkled
besprinkled,
　etc.

ĬNGK'lest
crinklest
sprinklest
tinklest
twinklest
wrinklest

ĬNGK'leth
crinkleth
sprinkleth
tinkleth
twinkleth
wrinkleth

ĬNGK'li
crinkly
pinkly

tinkly
twinkly
wrinkly

ĬNGK'ling
besprinkling
crinkling
inkling
sprinkling
tinkling
twinkling
wrinkling

ĬNGK'lur
sprinkler
tinkler
twinkler
wrinkler

ĬNGK'o
stinko

ĬNGK'on
Lincoln
pink 'un

ĬNGK'shun
contradistinc-
　tion
distinction
extinction
indistinction
intinction

ĬNGK'tiv
contradistinc-
tive
distinctive
instinctive

ĬNGK'tnes
distinctness

indistinctness
succinctness

ĬNGK'tur
cincture
encincture
tincture

ĬNGK'turd
cinctured
encinctured
uncinctured
untinctured

ĬNGK'ur
bethinker
blinker
clinker
drinker
enlinker
free-thinker
hoodwinker
inker
linker
pinker
prinker
rinker
shrinker
sinker
slinker
stinker
thinker
tiddledewinker
tinker
winker

ĬNGK'us
ornithorhyn-
chus
oxyrhynchus
scincus
zincous

ĬNG'les
kingless
ringless
springless
stingless
wingless

ĬNG'let
kinglet
ringlet
springlet
winglet

ĬNG'lik
kinglike
springlike
winglike

ĬN'gram
Ingram

ĬNG'song
singsong
spring-song

ĬNG'tim
ring-time
spring-time

ĬNG'ur
ballad-singer
bringer
clinger
dinger
flinger
humdinger
master-singer
Meistersinger
minnesinger
ringer
singer

āle, câre, ădd, ärm, åsk; mē, hẹre, ĕnd; īce, ĭll;

slinger
springer
stinger
stringer
swinger
unslinger
unstringer
whinger
winger
wringer

ĪN′i
briny
Heine
liney
miny
moonshiny
outliney
piney
shiny
spiny
sunshiny
tiny
twiney
viny
whiney
winy

ĬN′i
finny
guinea
hinny
ignominy
jinny
Minnie
ninny
pickaninny
pinny
Pliny
shinney
skinny

spinney
squinny
tinny
vinny
whinny

ĬN′ik
kinic
pinic
vinic

ĬN′ik
aclinic
actinic
adiactinic
Brahminic
clinic
cynic
delphinic
diactinic
finic
Franklinic
fulminic
isoclinic
Jacobinic
mandarinic
monoclinic
narcotinic
Odinic
pinic
platinic
polygynic
quinic
rabbinic
vinic

ĬN′im
minim
(cf.
  houyhnhmn)

ĪN′ing
aligning
assigning
beshining
combining
confining
consigning
countermining
countersigning
declining
defining
designing
dining
divining
enshrining
entwining
fining
inclining
interlining
intermining
intertwining
lining
maligning
mining
moonshining
opining
outlining
outshining
overtwining
pining
reclining
refining
repining
resigning
shining
signing
subsigning
trephining
twining
underlining
undermining

untwining
whining
wining

ĬN′ing
beginning
chinning
dinning
grinning
inning
pinning
shinning
sinning
skinning
spinning
thinning
tinning
underpinning
unpinning
unsinning
winning

ĬN′ingz
innings
beginnings, etc.

ĬN′ish
diminish
finish
Finnish
thinnish
tinnish

ĬN′ist
violinist

ĬN′it
crinite
finite

ĬN′jens
contingence

(cf. astringents, etc.)

ĬN'jent

astringent
constringent
contingent
fingent
impingent
refringent
restringent
ringent
stringent
tingent

ĬN'jest

befringest
cringest
fringest
hingest
imfringest
infringest
singest
swingest
tingest
twingest
unhingest

ĬN'jeth

befringeth
cringeth
fringeth
hingeth
impingeth
infringeth
singeth
swingeth
tingeth
twingeth
unhingeth

ĬN'jez

befringes
constringes
cringes
fringes
hinges
impinges
infringes
perstringes
scringes
singes
springes
swinges
tinges
twinges
unhinges

ĬN'ji

cringy
dingy
fringy
stingy
swingy
twingy

ĬN'jing

cringing
fringing
hinging
infringing
singeing
swingeing
tingeing
twingeing

ĬNJ'les

fringeless
hingeless
swingeless
tingeless
twingeless

ĬNJ'ment

impingement
infringement
unhingement

ĬNJ'ur

cringer
fringer
ginger
hinger
infringer
injure
singer
swinger
twinger

ĬN'ka

Inca
Katinka

ĬN'klad

pine-clad
vine-clad

ĬN'kom

income

ĬN'kres

increase

ĬN'kround

pine-crowned
vine-crowned

ĬN'kwent

delinquent
relinquent

ĬN'kwish

relinquish
vinquish

ĬN'les

dinless
finless
ginless
kinless
pinless
sinless
skinless
tinless
winless

ĬN'li

aquilinely
benignly
caninely
condignly
divinely
finely
malignly
saturninely
superfinely
supinely

ĬN'li

Finley
inly
McGinley
McKinley
thinly

ĬN'ment

alignment
assignment
confinement
consignment
designment
entwinement
inclinement
interlinement
refinement
resignment

ĪN'nes
condignness
divineness
fineness
salineness
superfineness
supineness

ĬN'nes
thinness
(cf. ĬN'es)

ĪN'o
Aino
albino
jure divino
rhino

ĬN'o
minnow
winnow

ĬN'of
sign-off

ĬN'sel
tinsel
(cf. Insull)

ĬN'sens
incense

ĬN'sent
St. Vincent
vincent

ĬN'ses
princess

ĬN'sest
convincest

evincest
mincest
rinsest
wincest
(cf. incest)

ĬN'ceth
convinceth
evinceth
minceth
rinseth
winceth

ĬN'shal
provincial

ĬN'si
Quincy
rinsey

ĬN'sing
convincing
evincing
mincing
rinsing
unconvincing
wincing

ĬN'siv
evincive

ĬNS'li
princely

ĬNS'ment
convincement
evincement

ĬN'som
winsome

ĬN'strel
minstrel

ĬN'stur
minster
spinster

ĬN'sur
convincer
mincer
rinser
wincer

ĬN'surz
pincers
convincers, etc.

ĬN'ted
dinted
glinted
hinted
imprinted
minted
misprinted
printed
rainbow-tinted
rosy-tinted
sprinted
squinted
stinted
tinted
vinted

ĬN'test
glintest
hintest
imprintest
mintest
printest
sprintest
squintest
stintest
tintest

ĬN'teth
glinteth
hinteth
imprinteth
minteth
printeth
sprinteth
squinteth
stinteth
tinteth

ĬN'ti
ninety

ĬN'ti
Dinty
flinty
glinty
linty
McGinty
squinty

ĬNT'id
flint-eyed
squint-eyed

ĬN'tij
mintage
vintage

ĬN'thick
absinthic
labyrinthic

ĬN'thin
hyacinthine
labyrinthine
terebinthine

ĬN'ting
aquatinting

dinting
glinting
hinting
imprinting
minting
misprinting
printing
sprinting
squinting
stinting
tinting

ĬN't'l
lintel
pintle
quintal

ĬN'to
mezzotinto
Shinto

ĬN'trest
interest
self-interest
winterest

ĬN'tri
splintry
vintry
wintry

ĬN'tur
aquatinter
dinter
hinter
imprinter
minter
printer
splinter
sprinter
squinter

stinter
tinter
winter

ĬN'u
continue
discontinue
retinue
sinew
unsinew

ĬN'ud
continued
discontinued
sinewed
unsinewed

ĬN'ur
arch-designer
assigner
benigner
calciner
combiner
confiner
consigner
decliner
definer
designer
diner
diviner
enshriner
entwiner
finer
incliner
intertwiner
liner
maligner
miner
minor
penny-a-liner
decliner

refiner
repiner
shiner
signer
Steiner
supiner
twiner
underliner
underminer
whiner

ĬN'ur
beginner
bread-winner
Bynner
dinner
finner
grinnēr
inner
pinner
shinner
sinner
skinner
spinner
thinner
tinner
twinner
winner

ĪN'us
binous
echinus
linous
Linus
Lupinus
minus
Pinus
salinous
sinus
spinous
vinous

ĬN'ward
inward

ĬN'yon
dominion
minion
opinion
pinion
(cf. ĬN'i-an)

ĬN'yond
dominioned
opinioned
pinioned
self-opinioned

ĬN'zi
Lindsay
Lindsey
linsey
quinsey
thinsey

ĬN'zik
extrinsic
intrinsic

ĬN'zman
kinsman

ĬN'zor
Windsor

Ī'o
Clio
Io
trio

Ī'ol
bass-viol
(see Ī'al)

Ī'on
dandelion
ion
Ixion
lion
Orion
scion
sea-lion
Zion

Ī'or
prior
(see Ī'ur)

Ī'ot
eyot
piot
riot
Sciot
(cf. quiet)

ĬP'a
Philippa

Ī'pal, Ī'p'l
disciple
ectypal

ĬP'ant
flippant
trippant

ĪP'en
enripen
ripen

ĪP'end
ripened
stipend

ĪP'est
pipest

ripest
typest
wipest
(cf. typist)

ĬP'est
chippest
clippest
dippest
drippest
equippest
flippest
grippest
gyppest
horsewhippest
nippest
outstrippest
rippest
shippest
sippest
skippest
slippest
snippest
strippest
tippest
trippest
whippest

ĬP'et
sippet
skippet
snippet
tippet
(cf. skip it)

ĪP'eth
gripeth
pipeth
typeth
wipeth

ĬP'eth
chippeth
clippeth
dippeth
drippeth
equippeth
flippeth
grippeth
gyppeth
horsewhippeth
nippeth
outstrippeth
rippeth
shippeth
sippeth
skippeth
slippeth
snippeth
strippeth
tippeth
trippeth
whippeth

ĪP'i
pipy
swipey
(cf. I.P.)

ĬP'i
chippy
dippy
grippy
Lippo Lippi
lippy
Mississippi
nippy
shippy
snippy
zippy

ĬP'id
insipid

ĬP'ij
kippage
scrippage
strippage

ĬP'ik
daguerreotypic
electrotypic
hippic
homotypic
idiotypic
monotypic
philippic
phonotypic
stereotypic
typic

ĬP'in
pippin

ĪP'ing
griping
Peiping
piping
stereotyping
striping
swiping
typing
wiping

ĬP'ing
atripping
chipping
clipping
dipping
dripping
equipping
flipping
gripping
nipping
outstripping

overtripping
quipping
ripping
shipping
sipping
skipping
slipping
snipping
stripping
tipping
transhipping
tripping
whipping

ĬP'ish

grippish
hippish
hyppish
snippish

ĬP''l

becripple
cripple
grippal
nipple
ripple
sipple
stipple
swiple
tipple
triple

ĬP'let

liplet
ripplet
siplet
triplet

ĬP'li

cripply
ripply

stipply
triply

ĬP'ling

crippling
Kipling
rippling
stippling
stripling
tippling

ĬP'lur

crippler
tippler

ĬP'ment

equipment
shipment
transhipment

ĬP'nes

dead-ripeness
overripeness
ripeness

ĬP'o

hippo
gippo

ĬP'res

cypress

ĬP'shun

ascription
circumscription
conniption
conscription
description
Egyptian
inscription
prescription

proscription
rescription
subscription
superscription
transcription

ĬP'si

gypsy
Poughkeepsie
Skipsey
tipsy

ĬP'sis

ellipsis
tripsis

ĬP'tik

anaglyptic
apocalyptic
cryptic
diptych
ecliptic
elliptic
glyptic
holocryptic
iatraliptic
styptic
triptych

ĬP'tiv

adscriptive
ascriptive
circumscriptive
descriptive
indescriptive
inscriptive
prescriptive
proscriptive
rescriptive
transcriptive

ĬP'tur

scripture

ĬP'ur

bag-piper
daguerreotyper
electrotyper
griper
linotyper
monotyper
piper
riper
stereotyper
sniper
striper
swiper
typer
viper
wiper

ĬP'ur

chipper
clipper
dipper
dripper
flipper
fripper
gallinipper
gripper
kipper
lady's-slipper
nipper
outstripper
ripper
shipper
sipper
skipper
slipper
snipper
stripper
swipper

tipper
tripper
whipper

ĬP'urd
kippered
skippered
slippered

Ī'ra
Almira
Elmira
Elvira
Ira
Lyra
Myra
Palmyra
Thyra

ĬR'ah
sirrah

ĬR'al
gyral
retiral
spiral

ĬR'am
Hiram

ĬR'ant
arch-tyrant
aspirant
conspirant
expirant
gyrant
spirant
tyrant
(cf. inquirent,
   etc.)

ĪR'āt
circumgyrate
dextro-gyrate
gyrate
irate
lyrate

ĬR'ăt
pirate

ĪR'e
Dies Irae
præmunire
(cf. ĬR'i)

ĬR'el
squirrel

Ī'rem
bireme
trireme

Ī'rēn
pyrene
squireen

Ī'rĕn
lepidosiren
siren

ĪR'ent
inquirent
sempervirent
virent
(cf. tyrant, etc.)

ĪR'est
acquirest
admirest
aspirest
attirest

bemirest
conspirest
desirest
direst
enquirest
expirest
firest
hirest
inquirest
inspirest
mirest
perspirest
requirest
respirest
retirest
suspirest
tirest
transpirest
umpirest
wirest

ĪR'eth
acquireth
admireth
aspireth
attireth
bemireth
conspireth
desireth
enquireth
expireth
fireth
hireth
inquireth
inspireth
mireth
perspireth
requireth
respireth
retireth
suspireth

tireth
transpireth
umpireth
wireth

ĬR'fli
firefly

ĬR'ful
direful
ireful

ĬR'i
acquiry
dairi
enquiry
inquiry
miry
spiry
squiry
wiry
(cf. ĬR'e)

ĬR'i
eyrie

ĬR'id
irid

ĬR'ik
butyric
empiric
lyric
panegyric
Pyrrhic
satiric
satyric

ĬR'il
Cyril
virile

ĪR'ing
acquiring
admiring
aspiring
attiring
bemiring
conspiring
desiring
enquiring
expiring
firing
hiring
inquiring
inspiring
miring
perspiring
requiring
respiring
retiring
squiring
suspiring
tiring
transpiring
unaspiring
undesiring
untiring
wiring

ĪR'is
iris
Osiris

ĪR'ish
Irish

ĪR'ist
irised
lyrist

ĪR'ist
lyrist
panegyrist

ĪR'it
dispirit
inspirit
master-spirit
party-spirit
spirit

ĪR'ling
hireling
squireling

ĪR'man
fireman

ĪR'ment
acquirement
aspirement
bemirement
requirement
retirement

ĪR'nes
direness
entireness

ĪR'o
Cairo
tyro

Ī'rod
byroad
highroad

ĪR'on
Byron
Chiron
environ
gyron

ĪR'os
gyrose
virose

ĪR'sid
fireside

ĪR'som
iresome
tiresome

ĬR'up
chirrup
stirrup
syrup

ĪR'ur
acquirer
admirer
aspirer
attirer
bemirer
conspirer
desirer
direr
enquirer
expirer
firer
hirer
inquirer
inspirer
mirer
perspirer
requirer
respirer
retirer
suspirer
tirer
wirer

ĪR'us
apyrous
Cyrus
desirous
Epirus

papyrus
virus

ĪR'wurks
fire-works
wire-works

ĬS'a
Clarissa
Lissa
Melissa
Nerissa

Ī'sal
sky-sail
try-sail

ĬS'al
paradisal

ĬS'chif
mischief

ĬS'chan
anti-Christian
Christian

ĪS'ens
license

ĬS'ens
dehiscence
fatiscence
indehiscence
reminiscence
resipiscence
reviviscence

ĬS'ent
dehiscent
indehiscent

reminiscent
reviviscent

ĪS'est
bespicest
concisest
enticest
nicest
precisest
pricest
sacrificest
slicest
spicest
splicest
sufficest

ĬS'est
dismissest
hissest
kissest
missest

ĪS'eth
bespiceth
enticeth
priceth
sacrificeth
sliceth
spiceth
spliceth
sufficeth

ĬS'eth
dismisseth
hisseth
kisseth
misseth

ĬS'ēz
Ulysses

ĬS'ĕz
abysses
artifices
benefices
blisses
cockatrices
dismisses
edifices
hisses
kisses
misses
precipices
prejudices
Swisses

ĬS'ful
blissful
remissful
unblissful

ĬSH'a
Elisha

ĬSH'a
Delicia
Letitia

ĬSH'al
accrementitial
artificial
beneficial
comitial
edificial
exitial
extrajudicial
gentilitial
inartificial
initial
interstitial
judicial
natalitial

official
policial
prejudicial
recrementitial
rusticial
sacrificial
solstitial
superficial
tribunitial
veneficial

ĬSH'an
academician
logician
magician
optician, etc.
(see ĬSH'un)

ĬSH'ens
deficience
efficience
insufficience
maleficience
omniscience
perspicience
proficience
prospicience
self-sufficience

ĬSH'ent
beneficient
calorificient
co-efficient
deficient
efficient
indeficient
inefficient
insufficient
maleficient
objicient
omniscient

perficient
proficient
self-sufficient
sufficient
volitient

ĬSH'est
dishest
fishest
swishest
wishest

ĬSH'eth
dishetk
fisheth
swisheth
wisheth

ĬSH'ful
dishful
wishful

ĬSH'i
fishy
swishy

ĬSH'ing
dishing
fishing
ill-wishing
swishing
well-wishing
wishing

ĬSH'op
bishop

ĬSH'un
abannition
abligurition
abolition

academician
accrementition
acoustician
acquisition
addition
adhibition
admission
admonition
affinition
aglutition
ambition
ammunition
Apician
apparition
apposition
arithmetician
atomician
attrition
audition
bipartition
circuition
coalition
cognition
commission
competition
composition
condition
contraposition
contrition
decomposition
definition
deglutition
demission
demolition
dentition
departition
deperdition
deposition
detrition
dialectician
dismission

disposition
disquisition
ebullition
edition
electrician
emission
epinician
erudition
exhibition
expedition
exposition
extradition
fission
fruition
futurition
Galician
geometrician
Hebrician
hydrostatician
ignition
illinition
imbibition
immission
imposition
inanition
indisposition
inhibition
inition
inquisition
insition
insubmission
intermission
interposition
intromission
intuition
irremission
juxtaposition
logician
magician
magnetician
manumission

mathematician
mechanician
metaphysician
metrician
mission
monition
munition
musician
Neoplatonician
nolition
nutrition
obdormition
obstetrician
omission
opposition
optician
partition
parturition
patrician
Paulician
perdition
permission
perquisition
petition
Phenician
physician
politician
position
practician
precognition
precondition
predisposition
premonition
preposition
presupposition
preterition
prohibition
proposition
punition
pyrotechnician
readmission

recognition
recomposition
reddition
redition
remission
rendition
repetition
reposition
requisition
resilition
reunition
rhetorician
rubrician
sedition
simplician
sortition
statistician
submission
submonition
superaddition
superposition
superstition
supposition
suspicion
tactician
tradition
tralatition
transition
transmission
transposition
tribunitian
tripartition
tuition
vendition
volition
vomition

ĬSH'und
ill-conditioned
uncommis-
   sioned

āle,   câre,   ădd,   ärm,   åsk;   mē,   hĕre,   ĕnd;   ïce,   ïll;

conditioned,
  etc.

ĬSH'ur
disher
Fischer
fisher
fissure
ill-wisher
kingfisher
swisher
well-wisher
wisher

ĬSH'us
addititious
adjectitious
adscititious
advectitious
adventitious
ambitious
arreptitious
ascititious
ascriptitious
auspicious
avaricious
capricious
cilicious
deglutitious
delicious
exitious
expeditious
factitious
fictitious
flagitious
gentilitious
inauspicious
injudicious
inofficious
judicious
lateritious

malicious
meretricious
multiplicious
natalitious
nutritious
obreptitious
obstetricious
officious
pernicious
piceous
profectitious
propitious
pumiceous
puniceous
satellitious
secretitious
seditious
sericeous
silicious
stillatitious
superstitious
supposititious
surreptitious
suspicious
tralatitious
veneficious
vermicious
vicious

ĪS'i
Datisi
icy
nisi
spicy

ĬS'i
missy
sissy

ĬS'ik
masticic
silicic

ĬS'il
fissile
missile
scissile
(cf. abyssal,
  scissel, etc.)

ĬS'id
viscid

ĬS'in
datiscin
viscin

ĪS'ing
bespicing
dicing
enticing
icing
pricing
sacrificing
self-sacrificing
self-sufficing
slicing
spicing
splicing
sufficing

ĬS'ing
dehiscing
dismissing
hissing
kissing
missing

ĪS'is
crisis
Isis
phthisis

ĬS'ish
missish

ĬS'it
elicit
explicit
illicit
implicit
licit
solicit

ĪS'iv
cicatrisive
collisive
decisive
derisive
divisive
incisive
indecisive
precisive

ĬS'iv
admissive
commissive
demissive
emissive
intermissive
irremissive
missive
nonsubmissive
omissive
permissive
promissive
remissive
submissive
transmissive

ĬS'ka
Mariska

ĬS'kal
discal
fiscal
obeliscal

ĬS'kat
confiscate
inviscate

ĬS'kest
briskest
friskest
riskest
whiskest

ĬS'ket
brisket
frisket

ĬS'keth
frisketh
risketh
whisketh

ĬSK'ful
friskful
riskful

ĬS'ki
frisky
risky
whiskey

ĬS'kin
griskin
siskin

ĬS'king
brisking
frisking
risking
whisking

ĬS'kit
biscuit

ĬS'ko
Crisco
Francisco
San Francisco

ĬS'kur
bewhisker
brisker
frisker
risker
whisker

ĬS'kus
abaciscus
discous
discus
hibiscus
lemniscus
lentiscus
meniscus
trochiscus
viscous

ĬS"l
abyssal
bristle
dismissal
epistle
gristle
missal
scissel
thistle
whistle
(cf. missile,
etc.)

ĪS'les
adviceless
diceless
iceless
miceless

priceless
spiceless
spliceless
viceless, etc.

ĪS'li
Cicely
concisely
nicely
precisely

ĬS'li
bristly
gristly
thistly

ĬS'ling
bristling
whistling

ĪS'ment
enticement
sufficement

ĬS'mus
isthmus
(see Christmas)

ĬS"n
christen
glisten
listen
relisten

ĪS'nes
conciseness
niceness
overniceness
preciseness

ĬS'nes
remissness
thisness

ĬS'ning
Christening
glistening
listening

ĬS'om
lissome

ĪS'on
bison
Dyson
grison
hyson
Tyson
vison

ĬS'pest
crispest
lispest

ĬS'peth
crispeth
lispeth

ĬS'pi
crispy

ĬS'pin
Crispin
St. Crispin

ĬS'ping
crisping
lisping

ĬS'pur
crisper
lisper
stage-whisper
whisper

ĬS'ta
ballista
genista
vista

ĬS'tal, ĬS't'l
crystal
listel
pistol
pocket-pistol

ĬS'tan
Tristan

ĬS'tans
assistance
coexistence
consistence
desistance
distance
equidistance
existence
inconsistence
inexistence
insistence
nonexistence
persistence
pre-existence
resistance
subsistence
(cf. assitants,
    etc.)

ĬS'tant, ĬS'tent
assistant
coexistent
consistent
distant
equidistant
existent
inconsistent

inexistent
insistent
nonexistent
nonresistant
persistent
pre-existent
resistant
subsistent

ĪST'dom
Christdom

ĬS'ted
assisted
black-listed
close-fisted
consisted
cysted
desisted
encysted
enlisted
entwisted
existed
fisted
hard-fisted
insisted
intertwisted
iron-fisted
listed
misted
persisted
resisted
subsisted
twisted
unassisted
unresisted
untwisted
white-listed

ĬS'tem
system

ĬS'test
assistest
consistest
desistest
enlistest
existest
insistest
listest
persistest
resistest
subsistest
twistest

ĬS'teth
assisteth
consisteth
desisteth
enlisteth
existeth
insisteth
listeth
misteth
persisteth
resisteth
resisteth
subsisteth
twisteth

ĪST'ful
mistful
wistful

ĬS'tik
absolutistic
adiaphoristic
agonistic
alchemistic
altruistic
anabaptistic
anachronistic
animistic

annalistic
anomalistic
antagonistic
anarchistic
aoristic
aphlogistic
aphoristic
artistic
atheistic
ballistic
baptistic
belletristic
bibliopegistic
bibliopolistic
Buddhistic
cabalistic
Calvinistic
cameralistic
canonistic
casuistic
catechistic
characteristic
Chauvinistic
communalistic
communistic
curialistic
cystic
deistic
dialogistic
dualistic
egoistic
egotistic
eleetro-
    ballistic
Elohistic
epilogistic
eristic
Eucharistic
eudemonistic
euhemeristic
eulogistic

euphemistic
euphuistic
evangelistic
familistic
fatalistic
fetichistic
fistic
formularistic
Hebraistic
Hellenistic
humanistic
humoristic
idealistic
illuministic
individualistic
interimistic
Jehovistic
journalistic
Judaistic
juristic
Latinistic
liberalistic
linguistic
logistic
materialistic
methodistic
monistic
monotheistic
mystic
naturalistic
neologistic
nihilistic
nominalistic
optimistic
palæocrystic
pantheistic
papistic
parallelistic
patristic
pessimistic

philanthropis-
tic
philosophistic
phlogistic
pietistic
polaristic
polytheistic
pugilistic
puristic
quietistic
rationalistic
realistic
ritualistic
schistic
sciolistic
sensualistic
simplistic
socialistic
solecistic
somnambu-
listic
sophistic
spiritualistic
stylistic
syllogistic
synchronistic
talmudistic
theistic
touristic
tritheistic
unionistic
universalistic

ĬS'tiks

agonistics
mystics
sphragistics
statistics

ĬS'til

pistil

ĬS'tin

amethystine
Philistine
pristine
Sistine

ĬS'ting

assisting
consisting
desisting
enlisting
entwisting
existing
insisting
intertwisting
listing
misting
pre-existing
persisting
resisting
subsisting
twisting
unresisting
untwisting

ĬS'tiv

persistive
resistive

ĬST'les

listless
resistless
twistless

ĬST'mus

Christmas
cf. isthmus

ĬST'ment

agistment
enlistment

ĬS'tral

mistral

ĬS'tram

Tristram

ĬS'tres

mistress

ĬS'tur

agistor
assister
bister
blister
enlister
exister
foster-sister
glister
insister
intertwister
lister
magister
mister
passive-resister
persister
resister
sister
subsister
twister

ĬS'turn

cistern

ĬS'tus

acathistus
schistous

ĬS'u

issue
tissue

ĪS'ur
conciser
dicer
enticer
geyser
nicer
preciser
sacrificer
slicer
spicer
splicer

ĬS'ŭr
dehiscer
dismisser
hisser
kisser
misser
remisser

ĬS'us
byssus
Issus
"missus"
narcissus

ĪT'al
cital
detrital
entitle
parasital
recital
requital
title
vital

ĪT'alz
vitals
recitals, etc.

ĪT'an
Titan

ĬT'an, ĬT'en
Britain
Britten
(cf. Briton)

ĬT'ans
acquittance
admittance
omittance
permittance
pittance
quittance
remittance
transmittance

ĪT'e
Amphitrite
Aphrodite
arbor-vitæ
lignum-vitæ
(cf. ĪT'i)

ĪT'ed
affrighted
alighted
attrited
bedighted
beknighted
benighted
blighted
cited
clear-sighted
delighted
despited
detrited
dighted
cagle-flighted
eagle-sighted
excited
far-sighted
foresighted

frighted
ignited
incited
indicted
indited
invited
knighted
lighted
long-sighted
near-sighted
nighted
oversighted
plighted
quick-sighted
recited
requited
reunited
righted
second-sighted
sharp-sighted
short-sighted
sighted
sited
slighted
spited
troth-plighted
unaffrighted
unbenighted
undighted
unfrighted
united
unplighted
unrequited
unrighted
unsighted

ĬT'ed
acquitted
admitted
after-witted
befitted

benefited
bitted
blunt-witted
committed
counterfeited
emitted
fat-witted
fitted
flitted
gritted
half-witted
interknitted
intermitted
knitted
lean-witted
manumitted
nimble-witted
omitted
outwitted
permitted
pitted
quick-witted
quitted
ready-witted
recommitted
refitted
remitted
sharp-witted
short-witted
slitted
spitted
submitted
subtle-witted
transmitted
twitted
unbenefited
unbitted
underwitted
unfitted
unremitted
witted

writted
(cf. pitied, etc.)

ĪT'em
item

ĪT'en
brighten
enlighten
frighten
heighten
lighten
tighten
Titan
whiten
(cf. Ī'ton)

ĬT'en
bitten
Briton
conscience-
  smitten
flea-bitten
fly-bitten
hunger-bitten
kitten
mitten
smitten
sun-smitten
terror-smitten
underwritten
unsmitten
unwritten
weather-bitten
written

ĬT'ent
emittent
intermittent
intromittent
remittent

ĪT'est
affrightest
alightest
beknightest
bitest
blightest
brightest
citest
delightest
excitest
fightest
impolitest
incitest
inditest
invitest
knightest
lightest
mightest
plightest
politest
recitest
requitest
reunitest
rightest
sightest
sleightest
slightest
smitest
spitest
tightest
tritest
unitest
uprightest
whitest
writest

ĬT'est
acquittest
admittest
benefitest

committest
fittest
flittest
hittest
knittest
omittest
outwittest
permittest
pittest
quittest
refittest
remittest
sittest
slittest
spittest
splittest
submittest
twittest

ĪT'eth
affrighteth
alighteth
beknighteth
biteth
blighteth
citeth
delighteth
exciteth
fighteth
igniteth
inciteth
inditeth
inviteth
plighteth
reciteth
requiteth
righteth
sighteth
sleighteth
smiteth

spiteth
uniteth
writeth

ĬT'eth
acquitteth
admitteth
befitteth
benefiteth
committeth
fitteth
flitteth
hitteth
knitteth
omitteth
out-witteth
permitteth
pitteth
quitteth
refitteth
remitteth
sitteth
slitteth
spitteth
splitteth
submitteth
twitteth

ĪT'ez
pyrites
sorites

ĪT'ful
delightful
despiteful
frightful
mightful
rightful
spiteful
sprightful

ĬT′ful
fitful
witful

ĬTH′ee
prithee

ĪTH′en
battle-writhen
writhen

ĪTH′est
blithest
lithest
writhest

ĪTH′eth
writheth

ĪTH′ful
blitheful
litheful

ĪTH′i
blithy
lithy

Ĭth′i
pithy
smithy
stithy
withy

Ĭth′ik
eolithic
lithic
megalithic
microlithic
monolithic
mythic
neolithic
ornithic

palæolithic
trilithic

ĪTH′ing
nithing
scything
tithing
trithing
writhing

ĬTH″m
rhythm

ĬTH′mik
logarithmic
polyrhythmic
rhythmic

ĪTH′nes
blitheness
litheness

Ī′thon
python

ĪTH′som
blithesome
lithesome

ĪTH′ur
blither
either
neither
tither
writher

ĬTH′ur
anywhither
behither
blither
dither

hither
nowhither
slither
somewhither
swither
thither
whither
wither

ĬTH′urd
withered
unwithered

ĬTH′urz
withers

ĪT′i
almighty
blighty
flighty
highty-tighty
mighty
mity
whity
(cf. Aphrodite,
    etc.)

ĬT′i
banditti
city
committee
ditty
flitty
Giovanitti
gritty
kitty
pity
pretty
self-pity
witty

ĬT′id
cities
pitied
unpitied
(cf. acquitted,
    etc.)

ĬT′ik
aconitic
actinolitic
Adamitic
aerolitic
analytic
anthracitic
anthropomor-
    phitic
arthritic
biolytic
Cabiritic
catalytic
cenobitic
conchitic
critic
dendritic
diacritic
dialytic
diphtheritic
dolomitic
electrolytic
enclitic
eophytic
epiphytic
eremitic
gingitic
granitic
Hamitic
hematitic
hermaphro-
    ditic
heteroclitic
hypercritic

hypocritic
Islamitic
Israelitic
Jacobitic
Jesuitic
Levitic
lignitic
margaritic
mephitic
Nazaritic
nummulitic
oneirocritic
oolitic
palmitic
paralytic
parasitic
phosphoritic
pleuritic
porphyritic
preadamitic
proclitic
rachitic
sagenitic
selenitic
Semitic
Shemitic
Sinaitic
stalactitic
stalagmitic
steatitic
strontitic
sybaritic
syenitic
theodolitic
Titanitic
tonsilitic
toxophilitic
trilobitic
trogodytic
tympanitic
uranitic

variolitic
zeolitic
zoophytic

ĬT'iks

analytics
critics, etc.

ĪT'in

chitin
(cf. ĬT'en,
    ĪT'on)

ĪT'ing

affrighting
alighting
back-biting
beknighting
biting
blighting
citing
copyrighting
delighting
disuniting
dynamiting
exciting
expediting
fighting
frighting
hand-writing
igniting
inciting
indicting
inditing
inviting
kiting
knighting
lighting
plighting
reciting
requiting

reuniting
righting
sighting
slighting
smiting
spiting
underwriting
uniting
whiting
writing

ĬT'ing

acquitting
admitting
befitting
benefiting
bitting
committing
counterfeiting
emitting
fitting
flitting
gritting
hair-splitting
hitting
knitting
manumitting
misfitting
omitting
outsitting
outwitting
permitting
pitting
pretermitting
quitting
recommitting
refitting
remitting
sitting
skitting

slitting
spitting
splitting
submitting
transmitting
twitting
unbefitting
unfitting
unremitting
unsubmitting
unwitting
witting

ĬT'is

appendicitis
arthritis
bronchitis
carditis
colitis
endocarditis
gastritis
hyalitis
laryngitis
meningitis
neuritis
pericarditis
pharyngitis
rachitis
tonsillitis
trachitis

ĬT'ish

anchoritish
Canaanitish
eremitish
Ishmaelitish
Israelitish
lightish
tightish
whitish

āle,   câre,   ădd,   ärm,   åsk;   mē,   hẹre,   ĕnd;   īce,   ĭll;

ĬT'ish
British
skittish

ĬT'iv
appetitive
expeditive

ĬT"l
entitle
title
(cf. ĪT'al)

ĬT"l
acquittal
belittle
brittle
committal
knittle
lickspittle
little
non-committal
remittal
skittle
spital
spittle
tittle
transmittal
victual
whittle

ĬT'les
delightless
fightless
frightless
heightless
knightless
lightless
nightless
riteless
sightless

spiteless
sprightless

ĬT'les
witless
(see ĬT+less)

ĬT'lest
brittlest
littlest
belittlest, etc.

ĬT'leth
belittleth, etc.

ĬT'li
brightly
impolitely
Kneightly
knightly
lightly
nightly
politely
rightly
sightly
slightly
sprightly
tightly
tritely
unknightly
unsightly
uprightly
whiteley
whitely

ĬT'li
fitly
unfitly

ĬT'ling
entitling
titling

ĬT'ling
kitling
titling
witling
whittling

ĬT'lur
brittler
littler
victualler
whittler

ĬT"lz
skittles
victuals
belittles, etc.

ĬT'ment
affrightment
excitement
frightment
incitement
indictment
invitement

ĬT'ment
acquitment
commitment
fitment
refitment
remitment

ĪT'nes
brightness
impoliteness
lightness
politeness
rightness
slightness

tightness
triteness
uprightness
whiteness

ĬT'nes
eye-witness
fitness
unfitness
witness

ĬT'ni
jitney
Mt. Whitney
Whitney

ĪT'ning
brightening
frightening
heightening
lightening
lightning
sheet-lightning
tightening
whitening

ĪT'nur
brightener
frightener
heightener
lightener
whitener

ĪT'on
chiton
triton
(cf. whiten, chitin, etc.)

ĪT'rat
nitrate
titrate

ĬT′ri
mitry
nitry

ĬT′rik
nitric

ĬT′rik
citric
vitric

ĬT′ur
alighter
arbeiter
back-biter
bemitre
biter
blighter
brighter
citer
delighter
dynamiter
exciter
fighter
flighter
igniter
impoliter
inciter
indicter
inditer
inviter
lamplighter
lighter
miter
moonlighter
niter
plighter
politer
reciter
requiter
righter

sighter
slighter
smiter
tighter
triter
typewriter
underwriter
uniter
unmiter
whiter
writer

ĬT′ur
acquitter
admitter
befitter
benefitter
bitter
committer
counterfeiter
critter
embitter
emitter
fitter
flitter
fritter
glitter
gritter
hitter
intermitter
intromitter
knitter
litter
manumitter
misfitter
omitter
outsitter
outwitter
permitter
pitter
pretermitter

quitter
recommitter
refitter
remitter
sitter
slitter
spitter
splitter
submitter
titter
transmitter
twitter
unfitter
Witter

ĬT′urd
unembittered
frittered, etc.

ĬT′urn
bittern
flittern
gittern

ĬT′urz
bitters
glitters, etc.

ĪT′us
St. Vitus
Titus
Vitus

ĪT′wat
lightweight

ĪT′wit
nitwit

ĪT′zi
Fritzy

itsy-bitsy
Ritzy

Ī′umf
triumph

Ī′un
triune

Ī′ur
amplifier
applier
Bayer
beautifier
Biedermeier
briar
brier
buyer
certifier
clarifier
classifier
codifier
complier
crier
crucifier
cryer
decryer
defier
defyer
deifier
denier
descrier
dignifier
disqualifier
diversifier
drier
dyer
edifier
electrifier
exemplifier
eyer

---

falsifier
flier
fortifier
friar
frier
fructifier
glorifier
gratifier
hier
higher
horrifier
identifier
implier
indemnifier
intensifier
justifier
kite-flier
lammergeier
liar
lier
liquefier
magnifier
Mayer
Meier
Meyer
modifier
mollifier
mortifier
multiplier
Myer
mystifier
nigher
notifier
nullifier
occupier
pacifier
personifier
petrifier
plyer
prior
prophesier

pryer
purifier
putrifier
qualifier
ramifier
ratifier
rectifier
relier
replier
revivifier
sanctifier
satisfier
scarifier
scorifier
shyer
sigher
signifier
simplifier
skyer
slyer
specifier
speechifier
spryer
spyer
stultifier
stupefier
supplier
sweet-briar
terrifier
testifier
tier
town-crier
trier
trior
tyer
typifier
Untermyer
untier
verifier
versifier
vier

vilifier
vivifier
white-friar
wryer
(cf. tiar)
(cf. fire, etc.)

Ī'urn

grappling-iron
iron
lofting-iron

Ī'urz

Meyers
Myers
pliers
briers, etc.

Ī'us

bacchius
Darius
nisi prius
pious
Pius
(see Ī'as)

ĪV'a

Saiva
saliva
Siva

ĪV'al

adjectival
archival
arrival
conjunctival
estival
imperatival
nominatival
outrival
revival

rival
salival
survival

ĪV'an

Ivan
(cf. ĪV'en)

ĪV'ans

arrivance
connivance
contrivance
survivance

ĪV'ant

trivant

ĪV'at

private

ĪV'en

enliven

ĪV'en

driven
forgiven
given
overdriven
riven
scriven
shriven
stormdriven
thriven
undriven
unforgiven
unshriven
weather-
  driven

ĪV'ent

connivent

ĪV'est
arrivest
connivest
contrivest
deprivest
derivest
divest
drivest
livest
revivest
rivest
shrivest
strivest
survivest
thrivest

ĬV'est
forgivest
givest
livest
misgivest
outlivest

ĬV'et
civet
grivet
privet
rivet
trivet
unrivet

ĪV'eth
arriveth
conniveth
contriveth
depriveth
deriveth
diveth
driveth
reviveth
shriveth

striveth
surviveth
thriveth

ĬV'eth
forgiveth
giveth
liveth
misgiveth
outliveth

ĬV'i
ivy

ĬV'i
chivvy
divi-divi
divvy
Livy
privy
tantivy
tivy

ĪV'id
ivied

ĬV'id
livid
vivid

ĬV'ik
civic

ĬV'il, ĬV'el
civil
drivel
rivel
shrivel
snivel
swivel
uncivil

ĪV'ing
arriving
conniving
contriving
depriving
deriving
diving
driving
hiving
reviving
shriving
striving
surviving
thriving
uncontriving
wiving

ĬV'ing
ever-living
forgiving
giving
lawgiving
life-giving
living
misgiving
outliving
thanksgiving
unforgiving

ĪV'li
lively

ĬV'li
absotively
positively

ĬV'ling
shrivelling
snivelling

ĪV'ment
deprivement
revivement

ĬV'nes
forgiveness

ĬV'ot
divot
pivot

ĬV'ring
delivering
quivering
shivering
slivering

ĪV'ur
arriver
conniver
contriver
depriver
deriver
diver
driver
fiver
hiver
liver
pearl-diver
reviver
river
shriver
skiver
slave-driver
sliver
stiver
striver
surviver
thriver

ĬV'ur
cantaliver

deliver
flivver
forgiver
freeliver
giver
Indian giver
liver
misgiver
outliver
quiver
river
shiver
skiver
sliver
Spoon River
stiver
tiver

ĬV'urd
delivered
lily-livered
pigeon-livered
quivered
shivered
slivered
unshivered
white-livered

ĪV'us
acclivous
declivous
proclivous
salivous

ĬV'yal
trivial
(see ĬV'i-al)

Ī'wa
byway

highway
skyway

Ī'za
Eliza
Isa

ĬZ'ak
Isaac

ĬZ'al
comprisal
revisal
surprisal

ĬZ'ard
blizzard
gizzard
izzard
lizard
lounge-lizard
scissored
visored
vizard
wizard

ĬZ'dal
Grisdale

ĬZ'dom
wisdom

ĪZ'en
bedizen
dizen

ĬZ'en, ĬZ'on
arisen
bedizen
dizen
imprison

mizzen
prison
risen
ptisan
wizen

ĪZ'est
advertisest
advisest
agonizest
apologizest
arisest
baptizest
catechizest
chastisest
civilizest
comprisest
compromisest
criticizest
despisest
devisest
disguisest
dramatizest
emphasizest
eulogizest
excisest
exercisest
exorcisest
improvisest
merchandisest
mobilizest
monopolizest
organizest
patronizest
premisest
prizest
realizest
recognizest
revisest
risest
sizest

solemnizest
supervisest
surmisest
surprisest
sympathizest
theorizest
tyrannizest
uprisest
wisest

ĬZ'est
fizzest, etc.

ĪZ'eth
advertiseth
adviseth
agonizeth
apologizeth
ariseth
baptizeth
catechizeth
chastiseth
civilizeth
compriseth
compromiseth
criticizeth
despiseth
deviseth
disguiseth
dramatizeth
emphasizeth
eulogizeth
exerciseth
exorciseth
improviseth
merchandiseth
mobilizeth
monopolizeth
organizeth
patronizeth
premiseth

ōld, ôr, ŏdd, oil, fŏŏt, out; ūse, ûrn, ŭp; THis, thin

prizeth
realizeth
recognizeth
reviseth
riseth
sizeth
solemnizeth
superviseth
surmiseth
surpriseth
sympathizeth
theorizeth
tyrannizeth
upriseth

ĪZ'eth
fizzeth, etc.

ĬZH'un
abscission
allision
collision
concision
decision
derision
division
elision
envision
excision
illision
imprecision
incision
indecision
irrision
misprision
precision
prevision
provision
recision
rescission
revision

scission
subdivision
supervision
television
transition
vision
(cf. ĪZ'i-an)

ĬZH'und
provisioned
visioned

ĬZH'ur
scissure

ĪZ'i
sizy

ĬZ'i
busy
dizzy
frizzy
jizzy
Lizzy
tin-lizzie
tizzy

ĬZ'id
busied
dizzied
unbusied

ĬZ'ij
visage

ĬZ'ik
metaphysic
paradisic
phthisic
physic

ĬZ'iks
physics

ĪZ'ing
advertising
advising
aggrandizing
agonizing
analyzing
anglicizing
antagonizing
apologizing
apostatizing
appetizing
apprising
arising
authorizing
baptizing
brutalizing
canonizing
capitalizing
capsizing
catechizing
Catholicizing
cauterizing
centralizing
characterizing
chastising
civilizing
colonizing
comprising
compromising
criticizing
crystallizing
demising
demoralizing
deodorizing
despising
devising
disguising
disorganizing

dramatizing
economizing
emphasizing
enterprising
equalizing
eternalizing
eulogizing
evangelizing
exercising
exorcising
familiarizing
fertilizing
galvanizing
generalizing
gormandizing
harmonizing
Hebraizing
humanizing
hybridizing
hypnotizing
idealizing
idolizing
immortalizing
improvising
italicizing
jeopardizing
journalizing
localizing
macadamizing
magnetizing
materializing
mesmerizing
methodizing
minimizing
mobilizing
modernizing
monopolizing
moralizing
neutralizing
organizing
paralyzing

patronizing
pauperizing
plagiarizing
premising
prizing
pulverizing
rationalizing
realizing
recognizing
revising
revolution-
  izing
rising
ruralizing
scandalizing
scrutinizing
secularizing
sermonizing
signalizing
sizing
solemnizing
soliloquizing
specializing
standardizing
sterilizing
stigmatizing
subsidizing
summarizing
supervising
surmising
surprising
symbolizing
sympathizing
systematizing
tantalizing
temporizing
terrorizing
theorizing
totalizing
tranquillizing
tyrannizing

uncompromis-
  ing
underprizing
uprising
utilizing
vaporizing
visualizing
vitalizing
vocalizing
volatilizing
vulgarizing

ĬZ'ing
befrizzing
fizzing
frizzing
phizzing
quizzing
whizzing

ĬZ'it
visit
what-is-it

ĪZ'krak
wisecrack

ĬZ"l
drizzle
chisel
crizzle
enchisel
fizzle
frizzle
grizzle
mizzle
sizzle
swizzle
twizzle

ĬZ"ld
grizzled
drizzled, etc.

ĬZ'li
chiselly
drizzly
frizzly
grisly
grizzly

ĬZ'ling
chiseling
drizzling
fizzling
frizzling
grizzling
mizzling
sizzling
swizzling

ĬZ"m
izzum-wizzum

ĬZ'mal
abysmal
aneurismal
baptismal
cataclysmal
catechismal
chrismal
dismal
embolismal
paroxysmal
rheumatismal

ĪZ'man
exciseman
prizeman

ĪZ'ment
aggrandize-
  ment

apprizement
assizement
baptizement

ĬZ'met
kismet

ĬZ'mi
prismy

ĬZ'mik
aphorismic
cataclysmic
clysmic
embolismic
paroxysmic

ĬZ'mus
accismus
strabismus
tarantismus
trismus

ĪZ'nes
wiseness

ĬZ'nes
business

ĬZ'om
chrisom
(cf. schism)

ĪZ'on
horizon
Kyrie eleison

ĪZ'ord
visored

ĬZ'ord
(see ĬZ'ard)

ĬZ'ur
advertiser
adviser
aggrandizer
agonizer
analyzer
apologizer
appetizer
apprizer
assizer
atomizer
authorizer
baptizer
canonizer
capsizer
catechizer
cauterizer
chastiser
civilizer
colonizer
deodorizer
despiser
deviser
devisor
dialyser

disguiser
disorganizer
divisor
dogmatizer
economizer
elisor
epitomizer
equalizer
eulogizer
exerciser
exorciser
extemporizer
fertilizer
galvanizer
generalizer
geyser
gormandizer
guiser
harmonizer
humanizer
hybridizer
idolizer
improviser
incisor
itemizer
Kaiser

Keyser
Kyser
lionizer
magnetizer
miser
moralizer
organizer
pauperizer
polarizer
prizer
proselytizer
pulverizer
realizer
reviser
riser
scandalizer
scrutinizer
sermonizer
sizer
solemnizer
sterilizer
stigmatizer
supervisor
surmiser
surpriser
sympathizer

synchronizer
tantalizer
temporizer
terrorizer
theorizer
tranquillizer
tyrannizer
upriser
vaporizer
victimizer
vitalizer
vocalizer
vulgarizer
vulcanizer
wiser

ĬZ'ur
befrizzer
frizzer
quizzer
scissor
vizor

ĬZ'urz
scissors, etc.

O

For a discussion of words included under the accented vowels
following, see the beginning of O rhymes in Section I.

Ō'a
boa
entozoa
epizoa
Genoa
Gilboa
jerboa
metazoa

moa
Noah
proa
protozoa
quinoa
Samoa
spermatazoa
(cf. aloha)

Ō'ab
Joab
Moab

Ō'al
bestowal

Ô'al
withdrawal

Ō'ba
arroba
bona-roba
dagoba

Ŏ'ba
Cahaba
Catawba

āle,   câre,   ădd,   ārm,   ăsk;   mē,   hẹre,   ĕnd;   īce,   ĭll;

Ō'ball
no-ball
snow-ball

Ō'bat
globate
lobate
probate

ŌB'est
disrobest
enrobest
probest
robest
unrobest

ÔB'est
daubest, etc.

ŎB'est
robbest
sobbest
throbbest

ŌB'eth
disrobeth
enrobeth
probeth
robeth
unrobeth

ŎB'et
Cobbett

ÔB'eth
daubeth, etc.

ŎB'eth
robbeth
sobbeth
throbbeth

Ō'bī
go-by

ŌB'ĭ, ŌB'e
adobe
globy
Gobi
hydrophoby
Kobe
obi

ŎB'ĭ
bobby
cobby
hobby
knobby
lobby
mobby
nobby
scobby
snobby
squabby

ŌB'il, ŌB'ēl
automobile
immobile
mobile

ŎB'in
bobbin
dobbin
ragged-robin
robbin
robin
round robin

ŌB'ing
disrobing
enrobing
globing
probing

robing
unrobing

ŎB'ing
blobbing
bobbing
cobbing
hobnobbing
jobbing
knobbing
lobbing
mobbing
robbing
snobbing
sobbing
swabbing
throbbing

ŎB'inz
Jobbins
Robbins
bobbins, etc.

ŎB'ish
bobbish
mobbish
nobbish
snobbish
squabbish

ŎB'jekt
object

ŌB''l
ennoble
ignoble
noble
unnoble

ÔB''l
bauble

ŎB''l
cobble
coble
gobble
hobble
nobble
squabble
wabble

ŎB'li
cobbly
squabbly
wabbly
Wobbly

ŎB'lin
goblin

ŎB'ling
cobbling
gobbling
hobbling
nobbling
snobling
squabbling
wabbling

ŎB'lur
cobbler
gobbler
hobbler
knobbler
nobbler
sherry-cobbler
squabbler
wabbler

ŌB'o
hobo
lobo
zobo

Ō'boi
doughboy

Ō'bonz
jawbones
sawbones

ŌB'ra
cobra

Ō'brou
lowbrow

ŌB'son
Jobson
Robeson
Robson

ŎB'son
dobson
Jobson
Robson

ŎB'stur
lobster

ŎB'ul
globule
lobule

ŌB'ur
disrober
enrober
October
prober
rober
sober

ŎB'ur
bedauber
dauber

ŎB'ur
beslobber
blobber
clobber
cobber
jobber
knobber
lobber
robber
slobber
snobber
sobber
swabber
throbber

ŎB'urn
auburn

ŌB'us
globus
jacobus
obus

ŎB'web
cobweb

ŌCH'est
approachest
broachest
encroachest
poachest
reproachest

ŎCH'est
blotchest, etc.

ŎCH'et
crotchet
rotchet

ŌCH'eth
approacheth

broacheth
encroacheth
poacheth
reproacheth

ŎCH'eth
blotcheth, etc.

ŌCH'ez
approaches
broaches
brooches
coaches
encroaches
loaches
poaches
reproaches
roaches
self-reproaches

ŌCH'ful
reproachful

ŎCH'i
blotchy
botchy
notchy
splotchy

ŌCH'ing
approaching
broaching
coaching
encroaching
poaching
reproaching

ŎCH'ing
blotching
botching
notching

scotching
splotching
watching

ŎCH'man
Scotchman
watchman

ŌCH'ment
approachment
encroachment

ŌCH'ur
approacher
broacher
encroacher
poacher
reproacher
self-reproacher

ŎCH'ur
blotcher
botcher
notcher
splotcher
watcher

ŎCH'wurd
watchword

ŌD'a
coda
pagoda
Rhoda
soda
trinoda

ŌD'al
internodal
modal
nodal

trinodal
yodel

ŌD'al

bicaudal
caudal
caudle
dawdle

ŏD'ard

Goddard
Stoddard
(cf. foddered)

ŌD'ed

boded
coded
corroded
eroded
exploded
foreboded
goaded
loaded
outmoded
overloaded
unloaded
woaded

ŏD'ed

nodded
plodded
podded
prodded
sodded
wadded
(cf. bodied,
    etc.)

ŌD'el

yodel
(cf. ŌD'al)

ŌD'en

foreboden
Woden

ôD'en

broaden

ŏD'en

hodden
sodden
trodden
untrodden
water-sodden
(cf. ÄD'en)

ŌD'ent

corrodent
erodent
explodent
rodent

ŏD'es

goddess
(cf. bodice)

ŌD'est

bodest
corrodest
explodest
forebodest
goadest
loadest
unloadest

ôD'est

applaudest
belaudest
broadest
defraudest
laudest
maraudest

ŏD'est

immodest
modest
noddest
oddest
ploddest
proddest

ŌD'eth

bodeth
corrodeth
explodeth
forebodeth
goadeth
loadeth
unloadeth

ôD'eth

applaudeth
belaudeth
defraudeth
laudeth
maraudeth

ŏD'eth

noddeth, etc.

ŌD'i

toady

ôD'i

bawdy
dawdy
gaudy

ŏD'i

body
busy-body
cloddy
embody
hoddy

noddy
roddy
shoddy
soddy
somebody
squaddy
toddy
waddy
(cf. ÄD'i)

ŏD'id

ablebodied
bodied
disembodied
unbodied
unembodied
(cf. ŏD'ed)

ŏD'ik

odic

ŏD'ik

anodic
episodic
exodic
hellanodic
hydriodic
iodic
kinesodic
melodic
methodic
odic
parodic
periodic
rhapsodic
sarcodic
spasmodic
synodic

ŌD'in

Odin
Wodin

ŌD'ing
boding
corroding
exploding
foreboding
goading
loading
outmoding
overloading
unloading

ÔD'ing
applauding
belauding
defrauding
lauding
marauding

ŎD'ing
codding
nodding
plodding
podding
prodding
wadding

ŎD'is
bodice
(cf. goddess)

ŎD'ish
cloddish
goddish

ŌD'ist
codist
modist
palinodist

ÔD'it
audit
plaudit

ŎD'kast
broadcast

ŎD''l
coddle
model
mollycoddle
noddle
remodel
swaddle
toddle
twaddle
waddle

ŎD'li
godly
twaddly
ungodly
waddly

ÔD'lin
maudlin

ŎD'ling
coddling
codling
godling
modelling
remodelling
swaddling
toddling
twaddling
waddling

ŎD'lur
coddler
modeller
mollycoddler
swaddler
toddler

twaddler
waddler

ŎD'nes
oddness

Ō'do
dodo
quasimodo

ŎD'om
Sodom

ÔD'ri
bawdry
tawdry

ŎD'ron
squadron

ŎD'son
Dodson
Hodson

ŌD'ston
loadstone
lodestone
toad-stone

ŌD'stur
goadster
roadster

ŎD'ukt
product

ŎD'ul
module
nodule

ŌD'ur
corroder

exploder
foreboder
goader
loader
malodor
muzzle-loader
Oder
odor
unloader

ÔD'ur
applauder
belauder
broader
defrauder
lauder
marauder
sawder
soft-sawder

ŎD'ur
codder
dodder
fodder
nodder
odder
plodder
podder
prodder
solder

ŎD'urn
modern

ŌD'us
modus
nodous

Ō'ed
coed

Ō'el
Crowell
Joel
Lowell
Noel

Ō'em
poem
proem

Ō'en
Bowen
Cohen
Owen

Ō'est
bestowest
blowest
crowest
flowest
foregoest
foreknowest
foreshowest
glowest
goest
growest
hoest
knowest
lowest
mowest
outgoest
overflowest
overgrowest
overthrowest
owest
rowest
sewest
showest
slowest
snowest
sowest

stowest
throwest
towest
undergoest
undertowest
upthrowest

Ô'est
awest
drawest
overawest
rawest
withdrawest

Ō'et
poet

Ō'eth
bestoweth
bloweth
croweth
floweth
foregoeth
foreknoweth
foreshoweth
gloweth
goeth
groweth
hoeth
knoweth
loweth
moweth
outgoeth
overfloweth
overgroweth
overthroweth
oweth
roweth
seweth
showeth
snoweth

soweth
stoweth
throweth
toweth
undergoeth

Ô'eth
aweth, etc.

Ō'fa
sofa

Ō'fet
Tophet

ŎF'et, ŎF'it
archprophet
profit
prophet
soffit
weather-
   prophet

ŌF'i
Sóphie
strophe
trophy

ŎF'i
coffee
spoffy
toffy

ŎF'ik
antistrophic
apostrophic
catastrophic
hypertrophic
philosophic
theosophic
theophilosophic

ŌF'il
profile

ŎF'in
coffin
encoffin

ŎF'ing
coughing
doffing
golfing
offing
scoffing

ŎF'is
office

ÔF'ish
crawfish
standoffish

ŎF'ish
offish
spoffish

ŎF'l
offal
waffle

ŎF'n
often
soften

ŎF'ted
lofted

ŎF'test
softest

ŎF'ti
lofty
softy

ŎFT′li
softly

ŎF′tur
crofter
lofter
softer

Ō′ful
woeful

Ô′ful
awful
lawful
unlawful

ŌF′ur
chauffeur
gopher
loafer
Ophir

ŎF′er
coffer
cougher
doffer
goffer
golfer
offer
proffer
scoffer

ŌG′a
Saratoga
snoga
Ticonderoga
toga
yoga

ÔG′a
Chicamauga
Sylacauga

ŌG′al
dogal

ŎG′al
synagogal

ŌG′an
brogan
Hogan
slogan

ŎG′an
toboggan

ŌG′i
bogey
bogie
dogie
fogey
stogie
yogi

ŎG′i
boggy
cloggy
doggy
foggy
froggy
groggy
joggy
soggy

ŎG′in
noggin

ŎG′ing
befogging
bogging
clogging
cogging
dogging

flogging
fogging
jogging
nogging
slogging
togging
unclogging

ŎG′ish
doggish
hoggish

ŌG′ish
roguish

ŌG″l
bogle
fogle
ogle

ŎG″l
boondoggle
boggle
coggle
goggle
joggle
toggle

ŎG′ling
boondoggling
boggling
goggling
joggling

ŌG′lur
ogler

ŎG′lur
boondoggler
boggler
goggler
joggler

ŎG′mir
quagmire

ŌG′ram
programme

ŌG′res
ogress
progress

ŎG′res
progress

ŎG′trot
dog-trot
jog-trot

ŌG′ur
ogre

ÔG′ur
auger
augur
inaugur
mauger

ŎG′ur
befogger
clogger
cogger
dogger
flogger
hogger
jogger
logger
pettifogger
slogger
togger
wholehogger

ŌG′us
bogus

ÔG'ust
August

ŏG'wood
bog-wood
dog-wood
logwood

Ō'hen
Cohen

Ō'hunk
Bohunk

Ō'i
blowy
Bowie
Chloe
doughy
Floey
glowy
Joey
showy
snowy
towy
Zoe

Ŏ'i
flawy
jawy
strawy
thawy
(cf. Ä'i)

OI'al
chapel-royal
disloyal
loyal
pennyroyal
royal
sur-royal

OI'ans
annoyance
buoyance
clairvoyance
joyance

OI'ant
annoyant
buoyant
chatoyant
clairvoyant
flamboyant
prevoyant

OI'b'l
foible

OID'al
asteroidal
colloidal
conchoidal
conoidal
coralloidal
crinoidal
cycloidal
dendroidal
discoidal
elephantoidal
ellipsoidal
ethnoidal
ganoidal
hemispheroidal
lithoidal
metalloidal
negroidal
ooidal
ovoidal
paraboloidal
planetoidal
prismatoidal
prismoidal

rhomboidal
saccharoidal
sigmoidal
spheroidal
trochoidal
typhoidal

OID'ans
avoidance

OID'ed
avoided
voided

OID'en
hoyden

OID'ur
avoider
broider
embroider
moider
voider

OI'e
employee

OI'est
annoyest
buoyest
cloyest
convoyest
coyest
decoyest
deployest
destroyest
employest
enjoyest
joyest
toyest

OI'eth
annoyeth
buoyeth
cloyeth
convoyeth
decoyeth
destroyeth
employeth
enjoyeth
joyeth
toyeth

OI'ful
joyful

OI'ij
alloyage
buoyage
voyage

OI'ing
annoying
buoying
cloying
convoying
decoying
deploying
destroying
employing
enjoying
joying
toying

OI'ish
boyish
coyish
toyish

Ō'ij
flowage
stowage
towage

Ō'ik
azoic
benzoic
Cenozoic
dichroic
dyspnoic
Eozoic
heroic
hylozoic
hypozoic
melanochroic
Mesozoic
mock-heroic
Neozoic
Palæozoic
pleochroic
protozoic
Stoic
Troic
xanthochroic

OIL'est
boilest
broilest
coilest
despoilest
embroilest
foilest
recoilest
roilest
soilest
spoilest
toilest
uncoilest

OIL'et
oillet
toilet

OIL'eth
boileth

broileth
coileth
despoileth
embroileth
foileth
recoileth
roileth
soileth
spoileth
toileth
uncoileth

OIL'i
coyly
doily
oily
roily

OIL'ing
assoiling
boiling
broiling
coiling
despoiling
embroiling
foiling
moiling
oiling
recoiling
soiling
spoiling
toiling
uncoiling

OIL'ment
despoilment
embroilment
recoilment

OIL'ur
boiler

broiler
coiler
despoiler
embroiler
foiler
oiler
recoiler
soiler
spoiler
toiler
uncoiler

OI'man
decoy-man
hoyman
toyman

OI'ment
deployment
employment
enjoyment

OIN'dur
rejoinder

OI'nes
coyness

Ō'ing
bestowing
blowing
bowing
cock-crowing
crowing
easy-going
flowing
foregoing
foreknowing
foreshowing
glass-blowing
glowing

going
growing
helloing
hoeing
inflowing
knowing
lowing
mowing
oboeing
outflowing
outgoing
outgrowing
overcrowing
overflowing
overgrowing
overthrowing
owing
rowing
sea-going
self-knowing
sewing
showing
slowing
snowing
sowing
stowing
strowing
thorough-going
throwing
toeing
towing
undergoing
undertowing
unknowing
unflowing
upgrowing

Ô'ing
awing
begnawing
cawing

chawing
clawing
drawing
gnawing
guffawing
heehawing
jawing
lawing
outlawing
overawing
overdrawing
pawing
pshawing
sawing
thawing
wiredrawing
withdrawing
yawing

OIN'ij
coinage

OIN'ing
adjoining
coining
conjoining
disjoining
enjoining
groining
joining
purloining
rejoining
subjoining

OIN'ted
anointed
appointed
conjointed
disappointed
disjointed
jointed

pointed
unanointed
unpointed
unjointed

OIN'ting
anointing
appointing
disappointing
disjointing
jointing
pointing

OINT'les
jointless
pointless

OINT'ment
anointment
appointment
disappointment
disjointment
ointment

OIN'tur
anointer
appointer
disappointer
disjointer
jointer
pointer

OIN'ur
coiner
conjoiner
enjoiner
joiner
purloiner
rejoiner

OI'ride
joyride

Ō'is
Lois

Ō'ish
showish
snowish

OIS'ing
rejoicing
voicing
unrejoicing

OIS'les
choiceless
voiceless

OI'som
noisome
toysome

OIS'ti
foisty
moisty

OI'stik
joystick

OIS'ting
foisting
hoisting
joisting

OIS'tral
cloistral
coystrel

OIS'tur
cloister
encloister
foister
hoister

moister
oyster
pearl-oyster
royster
uncloister

OIT'ed
doited
exploited

OIT'i
dacoity
hoity-toity

OIT'ring
loitering
reconnoitring

OIT'ūr
exploiture
voiture

OIT'ŭr
adroiter
exploiter
goiter
loiter
reconnoiter

OI'ur
annoyer
Boyar
Boyer
coyer
decoyer
deployer
destroyer
employer
enjoyer
self-destroyer
toyer

OI'us
joyous

OIZ'ez
boyses
noises
poises

OIZ'ï
noisy

OIZ'ing
noising
poising

OIZ'on
empoison
foison
poison
toison

OIZ'onz
foisons
poisons, etc.

Ō'jan
Trojan

ŎJ'ez
Hodges
dodges, etc.

ŌJ'e
anagoge
apagoge
èpagoge
paragoge

ŎJ'i
pedagogy
podgy
stodgy

ŎJ'ik
aerologic
anagogic
anthropologic
archæologic
astrologic
biologic
chronologic
curiologic
demagogic
demonologic
dialogic
entomologic
epagogic
epilogic
ethnologic
ethologic
etymologic
eulogic
geologic
gnomologic
hierologic
histologic
horologic
ichthyologic
idealogic
isagogic
lithologic
logic
martyrologic
meteorologic
mineralogic
morphologic
mycologic
myologic
mystagogic
mythologic
necrologic
neologic
ontologic
ophiologic

paragogic
pathologic
pedagogic
philologic
phonologic
photologic
phraseologic
physiologic
psychologic
sarcologic
sociologic
tautologic
theologic
tropologic
zymologic

ŎJ'iks
pedagogics

ŎJ'ing
dislodging
dodging
lodging

ŎJ'ur
codger
dislodger
dodger
lodger
Roger

ŌJ'urn
sojourn

Ō'kā
croquet
roquet

ŌK'ă
coca
tapioca

ŌK'al
bocal
focal
local
phocal
socle
vocal
yokel

ŌK'e
troche
trochee
(cf. choky, etc.)

ŌK'en
bespoken
betoken
broken
fair-spoken
fine-spoken
forespoken
foretoken
freespoken
heart-broken
Hoboken
oaken
outspoken
soft-spoken
spoken
token
unbroken
unspoken

ŎK'en
Brocken

ŌK'est
chokest
cloakest
convokest
croakest

evokest
invokest
jokest
provokest
revokest
smokest
soakest
spokest
unyokest
yokest

ÔK'est

balkest
stalkest
talkest
walkest

ŎK'est

bemockest
blockest
dockest
flockest
knockest
lockest
mockest
rockest
sockest
shockest
smockest
stockest
unfrockest
unlockest

ŎK'et

air-pocket
brocket
cocket
crocket
Crockett
docket
impocket

locket
Lockett
pickpocket
pocket
rocket
sky-rocket
socket
sprocket

ŌK'eth

choketh
cloaketh
convoketh
croaketh
evoketh
invoketh
joketh
poketh
provoketh
revoketh
smoketh
soaketh
spoketh
unyoketh
yoketh

ÔK'eth

balketh
stalketh
talketh
walketh

ŎK'eth

bemocketh
blocketh
docketh
flocketh
knocketh
locketh
mocketh
rocketh

shocketh
smocketh
stocketh
unlocketh

ŎK'hed

blockhead
shock-head

ŌK'i

choky
cokey
croaky
hokey
joky
Loki
moky
oaky
okey-dokey
poky
roky
slow-poky
smoky
soaky
yoky
(cf. troche and
trochee)

ÔK'i

balky
chalky
gawky
Milwaukee
pawky
squawky
stalky
talkie
talky
walkie

ŎK'i

cocky

crocky
flocky
hockey
jockey
locky
rocky
stocky

ŎK'id

cockeyed

ŌK'ij

brokage
cloakage
soakage

ŎK'ij

dockage
lockage
soccage

ŌK'ing

besmoking
choking
cloaking
convoking
croaking
evoking
invoking
joking
poking
provoking
revoking
smoking
soaking
stoking
stroking
troching
uncloaking
yoking

ÔK'ing
balking
calking
hawking
jaywalking
squawking
stalking
talking
walking

ŎK'ing
bemocking
blocking
clocking
cocking
docking
flocking
hocking
interlocking
knocking
locking
mocking
rocking
shocking
smocking
stocking
unlocking

ÔK'inz
Dawkins
Hawkins

ÔK'ish
hawkish
mawkish

ŎK'ish
blockish
cockish
mockish
stockish

ŎK"l
cockle
hockle
socle
strockle

ŌK'les
cloakless
jokeless
smokeless
yokeless
yolkless

ŎK'ling
cockling
flockling
rockling

ŌK'lor
folklore

ŎK'man
Brockman
lockman
socman

ŌK'ment
invokement
provokement
revokement

ŎK'ni
cockney

Ō'ko
baroco
coco
cocoa
koko
loco
locofoco

rococo
troco

ŎK'o
Morocco
sirocco

ŎK'port
Brockport
Lockport
Stockport

ŌK'ra
okra

ŎK'sen, ŎK's'n
cockswain
oxen

ŎK'shal
equinoctial
trinoctial

ÔK'shun
auction

ŎK'shun
concoction
decoction

ŎK'shus
innoxious
noxious
obnoxious

ŎK'si
cacodoxy
Coxey
doxy
foxy
heterodoxy

orthodoxy
paradoxy
proxy

ŎK'sid
fox-eyed
ox-eyed
oxide

ŎK'sin
tocsin

ŌK'sing
coaxing
hoaxing

ŎK'sing
boxing
foxing

ŌKS'man
spokesman
strokesman

ŌK'smith
jokesmith

ŌK'sur
coaxer
hoaxer

ŎK'sur
boxer
oxer

ŎK'til
coctile
trioctile

ŎK'tiv
concoctive
decoctive

ŎK'ton
Blockton
Brockton
Stockton

ŎK'trin
doctrine

ŎK'tur
concocter
doctor
proctor

ŎK'turn
nocturne

Ō'kum
hokum
oakum

Ō'kund
jocund

ŌK'ur
broker
choker
cloaker
convoker
croaker
evoker
invoker
joker
mediocre
ocher
poker
provoker
revoker
smoker
soaker
stoker
stroker

uncloaker
yoker

ŎK'ur
balker
calker
deer-stalker
gawker
hawker
jaywalker
shop-walker
sleep-walker
squawker
stalker
street-walker
talker
tomahawker
walker

ŎK'ur
blocker
cocker
docker
Fokker
hougher
Knickerbocker
knocker
locker
mocker
rocker
shocker
soccer
socker
stocker

ŎK'urz
knickerbockers
dockers, etc.

Ō'kus
crocus

focus
hocus
hocus-pocus
Hohokus
locus

ÔK'us
caucus
Daucus
glaucous
raucous

Ō'kust
locust
focussed, etc.

ÔK'ward
awkward

Ō'la
Angola
Appalachicola
carambola
coca-cola
gola
gondola
Gorgonzola
kola
Leola
Maizola
Pensacola
Ramola
scagliola
stola
Viola
Zola

ÔL'a
Eufaula
Guatamala
Paula

ŎL'a
corolla
holla
mollah

ŌL'ak
Polack

ŌL'an
Dolan
Nolan

Ō'land
Boland
Bowland
lowland
Noland
Roland
Rowland

ŌL'ar
(see ŌL'ur)

ŎL'ard
bollard
collard
collared
dollared
Lollard
pollard
scollard

ŎL'as
solace

ÔL'chun
falchion

ÔL'da
Alda

ŌL'ded
blindfolded

enfolded
infolded
manifolded
molded
refolded
scolded
unfolded

ŌL'den
beholden
embolden
golden
holden
misbeholden
olden
withholden

ÔL'den
Alden

ŌL'dest
beholdest
boldest
coldest
enfoldest
foldest
holdest
infoldest
interfoldest
moldest
oldest
refoldest
scoldest
unfoldest
upholdest
withholdest

ÔL'dest
baldest
scaldest

ŌL'deth
beholdeth
enfoldeth
foldeth
holdeth
infoldeth
interfoldeth
moldeth
refoldeth
scoldeth
unfoldeth
upholdeth
withholdeth

ÔL'deth
scaldeth

ŌLD'ham
Oldham

ŌL'di
foldy
moldy

ŌL'ding
beholding
enfolding
folding
holding
infolding
interfolding
molding
refolding
scolding
slave-holding
unfolding
upholding
weather-
　molding
withholding

ÔL'ding
Balding
Paulding
scalding
Spaulding

ŌL'dish
coldish
oldish

ŌLD'li
boldly
coldly
manifoldly

ŌLD'man
Goldman
Oldman

ŌLD'ment
enfoldment
withholdment

ŌLD'nes
boldness
coldness
oldness

ÔLD'ron
caldron
pauldron

ŌL'drumz
doldrums

ŌLD'smith
Goldsmith

ŌL'dur
beholder
bolder
bottleholder

boulder
colder
enfolder
freeholder
holder
householder
infolder
interfolder
landholder
leaseholder
molder
older
pattern-
　molder
polder
refolder
scolder
shareholder
shoulder
slave-holder
smolder
unfolder
upholder
withholder

ÔL'dur
alder
balder
Baldur
scalder

ŌL'durd
bouldered
broad-
　shouldered
moldered
shouldered
smoldered

ÔLD'win
Baldwin

ŏL'eg
colleague

ŏL'ej
acknowledge
college
foreknowledge
knowledge
self-knowledge

ŏL'ejd
acknowledged
unacknowl-
    edged

ŏL'em, ŏL'um
column
solemn

ōL'en
stolen
swollen

ŏL'en
chop-fallen
fallen
wind-fallen

ŏL'ent
equipollent
prepollent

ōL'er
(see ŌL'ur)

Ô'les
clawless
flawless
jawless
lawless
mawless
sawless

ŌL'est
bowlest
cajolest
condolest
consolest
controllest
dolest
drollest
enrollest
patrollest
pollest
rollest
strollest
tollest
trollest
unrollest
uprollest

ŏL'est
bawlest
bemawlest
brawlest
callest
crawlest
drawlest
enthrallest
forestallest
maulest
scrawlest
smallest
sprawlest
squallest
tallest

ŏL'et
collet
La Follette
wallet

ŏL'eth
bowleth

cajoleth
condoleth
consoleth
controlleth
doleth
enrolleth
patrolleth
polleth
rolleth
strolleth
tolleth
trolleth
unrolleth
uprolleth

ŏL'eth
bawleth
bemawleth
brawleth
calleth
crawleth
drawleth
enthralleth
forestalleth
mauleth
scrawleth
sprawleth
squalleth

ŏL'fin
dolphin

ōL'fing
golfiing

ŏL'ful
bowlful
doleful
soulful

ŏL'fur
golfer

ŏL'fus
Adolphus
Rodolphus
Rudolphus

ōL'hous
poll-house
toll-house

ŌL'i
coaly
holy
lowly
moly
roly-poly
shoaly
slowly
unholy
(cf. ŌL'li)

ŏL'i
Macaulay
Macauley
sprawly
squally
whally

ŏL'i
Bali
collie
dolly
folly
golly
Holley
holly
jolly
loblolly
melancholy
Molly
Polly
rolley

Tolley
trolley
volley

ŎL'id

jollied
olid
solid
squalid
stolid
volleyed

Ō'lif

lowlife

ÔL'ij

hallage
haulage
stallage

ÔL'ik

aulic
Gallic
hydraulic
interaulic

ŎL'ik

Aeolic
alcoholic
apostolic
bibliopolic
bucolic
carbolic
colic
diabolic
diastolic
embolic
epipolic
epistolic
frolic
hyperbolic

melancholic
metabolic
parabolic
petrolic
rollick
symbolic
systolic
variolic
vicar-apostolic
vitriolic

ÔL'in

tarpaulin

ŌL'ing

bolling
bowling
cajoling
caracoling
coaling
condoling
consoling
controlling
doling
drolling
enrolling
extolling
foaling
holing
inscrolling
parolling
patrolling
poling
rolling
shoaling
strolling
tolling
trolling
unrolling
uprolling

ÔL'ing

appalling
balling
bawling
befalling
bemawling
blackballing
brawling
calling
caterwauling
crawling
drawling
enthralling
falling
footballing
forestalling
galling
hauling
installing
mauling
miscalling
overhauling
palling
Pawling
recalling
scrawling
snow-balling
sprawling
squalling
thralling
trawling
walling

ŎL'ing

caracolling
extolling
lolling

ŎL'inz

Collins

Hollins
Rollins

ŏL'is

Collis
Cornwallis
Hollis
Wallace
Wallis

ŏL'ish

drollish
Polish

ÔL'ish

Gaulish
smallish
squallish
tallish

ŏL'ish

abolish
demolish
polish

ŏL'isht

abolished
demolished
polished
unpolished

ŏL'iv

olive

ōL'jur

soldier

ŌL'ka

polka

ÔL'kon

falcon

457   ÔL'kon — ÔL 'ti

gerfalcon
soar-falcon
sorefalcon

ÔLK'nur
falconer

ŌL'li
drolly
solely
wholly
(cf. ŌL'i)

ŌL'man
coal-man
Coleman
Colman
Holman
toll-man

ŌL'ment
cajolement
condolement
controlment
enrollment

ÔL'ment
appallment
disenthrallment
enthrallment
epaulement
instalment
installment

ÔL'most
almost

ŌL'nes
drollness
soleness
wholeness

ÔL'nes
allness
smallness
tallness

Ō'lo
polo
solo

ŏL'o
Apollo
follow
hollo
hollow
swallow
wallow

Ō'lok
Moloch
rowlock

ŌL'on
colon
eidolon
semicolon
Solon
stolon
(cf. ŌL'an,
  ŌL'en)

ŏL'op
collop
dollop
escalop
lollop
scallop
trollop
wallop

ŌL'or
dolor

ÔLS'hood
falsehood

ÔL'sid
palsied

ÔLS'nes
falseness

ÔL'so
also

ÔL'som
dolesome
wholesome

ŌL'son
Jolson
Olsen
Olson
Tolson
Toulson

ŌL'star
pole-star

ŌL'ston
gallstone

ÔL'ston
Alston
Balston
Ralston

ŌL'stur
bolster
holster
upholster

ŌL'ted
bolted

jolted
molted
revolted
unbolted

ÔL'ted
assaulted
defaulted
exalted
faulted
halted
malted
salted
vaulted

ŌL'ten
molten

ŌL'test
boltest, etc

ÔL'test
*assaultest
defaultest
exaltest
haltest
vaultest*

ŌL'teth
bolteth, etc.

ÔL'teth
*assaulteth
defaulteth
exalteth
halteth
vaulteth*

ÔL'ti
faulty
malty

ōld, ôr, ŏdd, oil, fŏŏt, out; ūse, ûrn, ŭp; THis, thin

salty
vaulty

ŌL'tij
voltage

ŌL'tij
maltage
vaultage

ŌL'tik
asphaltic
Baltic
basaltic
cobaltic
peristaltic

ŌL'ting
bolting
jolting
molting
revolting
unbolting

ŌL'ting
assaulting
defaulting
exalting
faulting
halting
malting
salting
vaulting

ŌL'tish
coltish
doltish

ŌLT'les
faultless
maltless
saltless

ŌL'ton
Bolton
Colton
Moulton

ŌL'ton
Dalton
Walton

ŌL'tri
poultry

ŌL'tur
bolter
colter
jolter
revolter
unbolter

ŌL'tur
altar
alter
assaulter
defaulter
exalter
falter
Gibraltar
halter
malter
McWalter
palter
psalter
Salter
unalter
vaulter
Walter

ŌL'turn
saltern
subaltern

ŌLT'sur
waltzer
(cf. falser)

ŌL'ūm
colyum
volume

ŌL'um
column
solemn

ŌL'ur
bowler
cajoler
circumpolar
coaler
condoler
consoler
controller
doler
dolor
droller
enroller
molar
patroller
polar
poler
poller
roller
scroller
shoaler
solar
stroller
toller
troller
unipolar
unroller
uproller

ŌL'ur
bawler

bemawler
brawler
caller
crawler
drawler
enthraller
faller
footballer
forestaller
hauler
mauler
scrawler
smaller
sprawler
squaller
taller
trawler

ŎL'ur
choler
collar
dollar
extoller
loller
scholar
sollar
squalor

ŌL'us
bolus
holus-bolus
solus

ŎL'usk
mollusk

ŎL'vent
dissolvent
evolvent
insolvent
resolvent
solvent

āle,   câre,   ădd,   ärm,   åsk;   mē,   hẹre,   ĕnd;   īce,   ĭll;

ŎL'vest
absolvest
devolvest
dissolvest
evolvest
involvest
resolvest
revolvest
solvest

ŎL'veth
absolveth
devolveth
dissolveth
evolveth
involveth
resolveth
revolveth
solveth

ŎL'ving
absolving
devolving
dissolving
evolving
involving
resolving
revolving
solving

ŎLV'ment
devolvement
evolvement
involvement

ŎL'vur
absolver
dissolver
evolver
involver
resolver

revolver
solver

ŎL'wart
stalwart

ŎL'waz
always

Ō'ma
aboma
aroma
coma
diploma
Natoma
sarcoma
Roma
Sonoma
Tacoma
theobroma
zygoma

ŎM'a
comma
momma

Ō'mad
nomad
ohmad

Ō'man
bowman
foeman
Roman
showman
yeoman

ŎM'as
Thomas

ŎM'bat
combat
wombat

ŎM'bi
Abercrombie
Dombey
zombie

ŎM'brus
sombrous

ŎM'bur
hombre
omber
Scomber
somber

ŎM'en, Ō'men
abdomen
agnomen
bowmen
cognomen
foemen
omen
prænomen
yeomen
(cf. gnomon)

ŎM'end
ill-omened
omened

Ō'ment
bestowment
moment

ŎM'et
comet
domett
grommet

ŌM'i
foamy

homy
loamy

ŎM'i
mommy
Tommie

ŎM'ij
homage

ŌM'ik
bromic
chromic
gnomic
hydrobromic
polychromic

ŎM'ik
agronomic
anatomic
astronomic
atomic
autonomic
cinnamomic
comic
diatomic
dystomic
economic
entomic
gastronomic
heliochromic
isonomic
metronomic
microtomic
monatomic
nomic
orthodromic
palindromic
phantomic
physiognomic
serio-comic

stereochromic
stereotomic
taxonomic
tragi-comic
triatomic
vomic

ŎM'iks
economics
phoronomics

ŌM'in
bromine
theobromine

ŌM'ing
befoaming
coaming
combing
foaming
gloaming
homing
roaming

ŎM'is
promise

ŎM'ish
Romish

ŌM'les
foamless
combless
homeless

ŌM'let
homelet
tomelet

ŎM'let
omelet

ŌM'li
homely

Ō'mo
chromo
Como
Ecce Homo
major-domo

ŎM'on
common

ŎM'pi
Pompey

ŎMP'ish
rompish
swampish

ŎM'plish
accomplish

ŎMP'ted
prompted
unprompted

ŎMP'ton
Brompton
Compton
Lecompton

ŎMP'us
pompous

ŌM'spun
homespun

ŌM'sted
homestead

ŌM'ur
beachcomber

comber
gomer
homer
Homer
misnomer
omer
roamer
vomer
wool-comber

ŎM'ur
bomber

ŎM'urs
commerce

ŎM'ward
homeward

Ō'na
annona
Arizona
Barcelona
Bellona
Bologna
cinchona
corona
Cremona
Desdemona
Iona
Jonah
mona
Nona
Pomona
Ramona
Zona

ŎN'a
Mauna

ŎN'a
belladonna

donna
Madonna
prima donna

ŌN'al
coronal
subumbonal
tonal
zonal

ŌN'ald
Donald
McDonald
Ronald

ŌN'ant
intersonant
sonant
(cf. deponent,
etc.)

ŎN'ark
monarch

ŌN'as
Jonas

ŌN'at
donate
zonate

ŎN'da
anaconda

ŎN'de
arrondi

ŎN'de
dispondee
spondee

ŎN'ded
absconded
bonded
corresponded
desponded
responded

ŌN'def
stone-deaf
tone-deaf

ŎN'del
rondel

ŎN'dens
correspondence
despondence
respondence

ŎN'dent
co-respondent
correspondent
despondent
frondent
respondent

ŎN'dest
abscondest
bondest
correspondest
fondest
respondest

ŎN'deth
abscondeth
bondeth
correspondeth
respondeth

ŎN'dij
bondage

frondage
vagabondage

ŎN'ding
absconding
corresponding
desponding
responding

ŎN'd'l
fondle
rondle

ŎND'li
fondly

ŎND'ling
bondling
fondling

ŎND'nes
blondness
fondness

ŎN'dur
absconder
bonder
corresponder
desponder
fonder
hypochonder
ponder
responder
squander
wander
yonder
(cf. condor)

ÔN'durz
Saunders

ÔN'e
Pawnee
Punxatawnee
Sewanee
Shawnee
Swanee
(cf. ÔN'i)

ŌN'ent
component
deponent
exponent
interponent
opponent
proponent
(cf. sonant)

Ō'nes
lowness
slowness

ŌN'est
atonest
bemoanest
condonest
dethronest
disownest
dronest
enthronest
groanest
intonest
honest
loanest
lonest
moanest
ownest
postponest
stonest
thronest
tonest

ŎN'est
connest
dishonest
donnest
honest
non-est
wannest

ŎN'et
bonnet
sonnet
unbonnet

ŎN'eth
atoneth
begroaneth
bemoaneth
condoneth
dethroneth
disowneth
droneth
enthroneth
groaneth
honeth
intoneth
loaneth
moaneth
owneth
postponeth
stoneth
throneth
toneth

ŎNG'est
longest
strongest

ŎNG'ful
songful
throngful
wrongful

ŎNG'go
Bongo
Congo

ŎNG'gur
conger
longer

ŎNG'ing
belonging
longing
prolonging
thronging
wronging

ŎNG'ish
longish
prongish
songish
strongish

ŎNG'ki
donkey

ŎNG'kur
conker
conquer

ŎNG'kurz
conquers
Yonkers

ŎNG'li
longly
wrongly

ŎNG'nes
longness
wrongness

ŎNG'stur
songster

ŎNG'ur
prolonger
wronger

ŎNG'wav
long-wave

ŌN'hed
bonehead

Ō'ni
alimony
aloney
antimony
baloney
bologney
bony
Coney
cony
crony
drony
lazzaroni
macaroni
Mahoney
Maloney
matrimony
parsimony
patrimony
phony
pony
sanctimony
stony
testimony
tony
(cf. cicerone)

ŌN'i
brawny
lawny
mulligatawny
orange-tawny

sawney
scrawny
tawny
yawny

ŎN'i
bonnie
bonny
Connie
Lonnie
Renee
Ronnie

ŌN'ik
phonic
zonic

ŎN'ik
Aaronic
acronyc
Adonic
agonic
Amphictyonic
anharmonic
antiphonic
architectonic
atonic
Babylonic
cacophonic
canonic
carbonic
cataphonic
Chalcedonic
chronic
colophonic
conic
crotonic
cyclonic
dæmonic
demonic
diaphonic

diatonic
draconic
embryonic
euphonic
ganglionic
geogonic
geoponic
gnominic
harmonic
hedonic
hegemonic
histrionic
homophonic
Housatonic
intergan-
    glionic
Ionic
ironic
isotonic
jargonic
laconic
macaronic
masonic
Metonic
Miltonic
mnemonic
monochronic
monophonic
monotonic
neoplatonic
Olympionic
paratonic
parsonic
pathogno-
    monic
Pharaonic
philharmonic
phonic
photophonic
Platonic
Plutonic

pneumonic
polyphonic
pulmonic
Pyrrhonic
pythonic
sardonic
semitonic
sermonic
siphonic
Slavonic
Solomonic
stentoronic
stratonic
symphonic
tectonic
telephonic
Teutonic
theogonic
tonic
Tychonic
zoonic

ŎN'iks

geoponics
hedonics
histrionics
Megalonyx
mnemonics
onyx

ŌN'ing

atoning
bemoaning
boning
dethroning
disowning
droning
enthroning
groaning
intoning
moaning

owning
postponing
stoning
throning
toning

ÔN'ing

awning
dawning
fawning
pawning
spawning
undawning
yawning

ŎN'ing

conning
donning

ŌN'is

Adonis
Coronis

ŌN'ish

Babylonish
dronish

ŎN'ish

admonish
astonish
tonnish
wannish

ŎN'je

congee
pongee

ŌN'les

boneless
throneless
toneless
zoneless

ŌN'li

lonely
only

ŌN'ment

atonement
condonement
dethronement
disownment
enthronement
postponement

ŌN'nes

loneness
proneness
unknownness

ŌN'or

donor
(cf. ŌN'ur)

ŎN'rad

Conrad

ŎN'shens

conscience

ŎN'shus

conscious
self-conscious
sub-conscious

ŎN'siv

corresponsive
irresponsive
responsive

ŌN'som

lonesome

ŎN'son

Johnson

Jonson
(cf. Wiscon-
    sin)

ŎN'sor

sponsor
tonsor

ŎN'stant

constant
inconstant

ŎN'ston

Johnston

ŎN'strans

monstrance
remonstrance

ŎN'strat

demonstrate
remonstrate

ŎN'strous

monstrous

ŎN'stur

monster

ŎN'tal

fontal
frontal
horizontal
peridontal

ŎN'tan

cismontane
tramontane
ultramontane

ŎN'ted

daunted

ōld, ôr, ŏdd, oil, fŏŏt, out; ūse, ûrn, ŭp; THis, thin

flaunted
haunted
taunted
undaunted
vaunted
wanted

ŎN'ted
wanted

ÔN'test
dauntest
flauntest
hauntest
tauntest
vauntest
wantest

ÔN'teth
daunteth
flaunteth
haunteth
taunteth
vaunteth
wanteth

ÔN'ti
flaunty
jaunty

ŎN'tif
pontiff

ÔN'tij
wantage

ŎN'tij
pontage
wantage

ŎN'tik
Anacreontic

archontic
mastodontic
pontic
quantic

ŎN'tin
dracontine
Hellespontine
pontine
(cf. tontine)

ÔN'ting
daunting
flaunting
haunting
jaunting
taunting
vaunting
wanting

ŎN'ting
wanting

ÔNT'les
dauntless
tauntless
vauntless

ÔNT'let
gantlet
gauntlet

ŎN'ton
wanton
(cf. fronton)

ÔN'trit
contrite
uncontrite

ŎN'tum
quantum

ÔN'tur
daunter
flaunter
gaunter
haunter
saunter
taunter
vaunter

ŌN'ur
atoner
bemoaner
boner
condoner
dethroner
droner
groaner
honer
intoner
moaner
owner
phoner
postponer
telephoner
stoner
(cf. donor)

ÔN'ur
awner
barley-awner
brawner
fawner
pawner
spawner
yawner

ŎN'ur
Bonner
conner
Connor
dishonor

goner
honor
O'Conner
O'Connor
wanner

ŎN'urd
dishonored
honored
timehonored
unhonored

ŎN'urz
Conners
Connors
O'Connors
honors, etc.

Ō'nus
bonus
onus
tonous

ŎN'yard
poniard

ŎN'zo
Alonzo
Alphonso
Alphonzo

Ō'on
entozoon
epizoon
phytozoon
zoon

ŎOD'ed
hooded
wooded

O͞OD'en
wooden

O͞OD'i
goody
goody-goody
woody

O͞OD'ing
gooding
hooding
pudding

O͞OD'ish
goodish

O͞OD'li
goodly

O͞OD'man
goodman
hoodman
woodman

O͞OD'nes
goodness

O͞OG'ur
sugar

O͞OK'ed
crooked
(see O͞OK +
   ed)

O͞OK'i
bookie
cooky
hookey

hooky
rooky

O͞OK'ing
booking
brooking
cooking
crooking
hooking
ill-looking
looking
over-looking
rooking
unhooking
well-looking

O͞OK'let
booklet
brooklet

O͞OK'up
hook-up

O͞OK'ur
cooker
hooker
looker
overlooker
stooker

O͞OL'bul
bulbul

O͞OL'en
woollen

O͞OL'et
bullet
pullet

O͞OL'i
bully
fully
pulley
woolly

O͞OL'id
bullied, etc.

O͞OL'ing
bulling
pulling

O͞OL'ish
bullish
fullish

O͞OL'man
Pullman
Woolman

O͞OL'nes
fullness

O͞OL'ur
buller
fuller
puller
wire-puller

O͞OM'an
woman

O͞O'si
pussy

O͞OT'ed
footed
nimble-footed

O͞OT'ing
footing
putting

O͞OT'ur
footer
putter

ō'pa
Europa

ō'pal, ō'p'l
Adrianople
Bhopal
Constantinople
nopal
opal

ō'paz
topaz

ō'pen
open

ōP'est
copest
elopest
gropest
hopest
interlopest
mopest
ropest
soapest

ŏP'est
choppest
droppest
hoppest
loppest
moppest

ōld, ôr, ŏdd, oil, fo͞ot, out; ūse, ûrn, ŭp; THis, thin

overtoppest
poppest
proppest
shoppest
stoppest
toppest

ŎP'et

moppet
poppet

ŎP'eth

copeth
elopeth
gropeth
hopeth
interlopeth
mopeth
ropeth
soapeth

ŎP'eth

choppeth
droppeth
hoppeth
loppeth
moppeth
poppeth
proppeth
shoppeth
stoppeth
toppeth

ŎP'ful

hopeful
unhopeful

ŎP'hed

hophead

ŌP'i

dopey

mopy
ropy
slopy
soapy

ŌP'ī

Pop-eye

ŎP'ĭ

choppy
copy
croppy
droppy
floppy
hoppy
loppy
moppy
poppy
shoppy
sloppy
soppy

ŎP'ij

proppage
stoppage

ŎP'ik

acopic
allotropic
anthropic
canopic
Cyclopic
dichroscopic
eletroscopic
Ethiopic
galvanoscopic
geotropic
helioscopic
heliotropic
horoscopic
hydroscopic

hygroscopic
isotropic
kaleidoscopic
laryngoscopic
metopic
metoscopic
microscopic
misanthropic
myopic
necroscopic
pantascopic
periscopic
philanthropic
presbyopic
psilanthropic
spectroscopic
stereoscopic
stethoscopic
telescopic
theanthropic
theophilan-
   thropic
topic
tropic

ŎP'iks

topics
tropics

ŌP'ing

coping
doping
eloping
groping
hoping
interloping
loping
moping
roping
sloping
soaping

stoping
toping

ŎP'ing

bedropping
chopping
clip-clopping
copping
cropping
dropping
eavesdropping
flopping
hopping
lopping
mopping
overtopping
plopping
popping
propping
shopping
slopping
sopping
stopping
stropping
swapping
topping
Wapping
whopping

ŌP'ish

mopish
popish

ŎP'ish

foppish
shoppish

ŎP"l

estoppel
hopple
popple

āle,   câre,   ădd,   ärm,   åsk: mē,   hĕre,   ĕnd;   īce,   ĭll;

stopple
topple

ŌP′les
hopeless
popeless
soapless

ŎP′ling
fopling
toppling

ŌP′ment
elopement

Ō′pô
pawpaw

Ō′pok
slowpoke

ŎP′shun
adoption
option

ŎP′si
copsy
dropsy
Mopsy
Topsy

ŎP′sis
ampelopsis
lycopsis
synopsis
thanatopsis

ŌP′stur
dopester

ŎP′ted
adopted
co-opted

ŎP′tik
autoptic
Coptic
optic
synoptic

ŎP′trik
catadioptric
catoptric
dioptric

ŌP′ur
coper
doper
eloper
groper
interloper
moper
roper
sloper
soaper
toper

ŎP′ur
pauper
scauper

ŎP′ur
chopper
clodhopper
copper
cropper
dropper
eaves-dropper
finale-hopper
grasshopper
hopper
improper
lopper
mopper
overtopper

plopper
popper
proper
propper
shopper
sopper
stopper
swapper
tiptopper
topper
whopper

Ō′pus
Canopus
lagopous
Lagopus
opus

Ō′ra
Angora
aurora
Cora
Dora
dumb Dora
Eldora
Endora
flora
Floradora
Leonora
Marmora
Masora
Nora
Pandora
passiflora
signora
Theodora
Torah

ŎR′a
aura
Chamæsaura

Laura
Maura

ŎR′ā
foray

ŎR′ă
Andorra
Gomorrah

Ō′raks
borax
corax
storax
thorax

Ō′ral
auroral
chloral
choral
floral
horal
oral
sororal
thoral
trifloral

ŎR′al
aural
binaural
(cf. laurel)

ŎR′al
coral
immoral
moral
quarrel
sorrel
(cf. laurel)

ŎR′anj
orange

ŌR'ant
soarant
vorant

Ō'rat
chlorate
deflorate
perchlorate

ŎR'at
inaurate
instaurate

ŎR'bi
corbie
orby

ŎR'bid
morbid

ŎR'bing
absorbing
orbing
resorbing

ŎR'b'l
corbel
warble

ŎR'blur
warbler

**ŎR'chard, ŎR'-
churd**
orchard
tortured

ŎR'chur
scorcher
torcher

ŎR'dan
Jordan
(cf. ŎR'don)

ŎR'dans
accordance
concordance
discordance

ŎR'dant
accordant
concordant
disaccordant
discordant
inaccordant
mordant

ŌR'ded
afforded
boarded
forded
hoarded
sworded
unforded
unhoarded
uphoarded

ŎR'ded
accorded
awarded
belorded
chorded
corded
lorded
recorded
rewarded
swarded
unlorded
unrecorded
unrewarded
warded
(cf. sordid)

ŎR'den
warden
way-warden

ŌR'dest
boardest
fordest
hoardest

ŎR'dest
accordest
awardest
belordest
lordest
recordest
rewardest
wardest

ŌR'deth
boardeth
fordeth
hoardeth

ŎR'deth
accordeth
awardeth
belordeth
cordeth
lordeth
recordeth
rewardeth
wardeth

ŎRD'ful
discordful
rewardful

ŎR'did
sordid
(cf. accorded,
etc.)

ŌR'dij
boardage
bordage

ŌR'dij
cordage

ŌR'ding
affording
boarding
fording
hoarding
unhoarding
uphoarding
weather-board-
ing

ŎR'ding
according
awarding
belording
cording
lording
recording
rewarding
unrecording
unrewarding
warding

ŎRD'li
lordly
unlordly

ŎR'don
cordon
Gordon

ŎRD'ship
lordship
wardship

ŌR'dur
boarder
forder
hoarder

parlor-
    boarder

ŌR'dur
accorder
awarder
border
corder
disorder
emborder
money-order
order
recorder
reorder
rewarder
unorder
warder

ÔR'durd
bordered
disordered
ordered
reordered
well-ordered

ŌRDZ'man
swordsman

ŎR'ed
forehead

ÔR'el, ŎR'el
laurel
(cf. ÔR'al,
    ŎR'al)

ÔR'en, ÔR'an
sporran
warren

ÔR'ens
abhorrence

Lawrence
St. Lawrence

ŎR'ens
Dorrance
Florence
(cf. torrents,
    etc.)

ŎR'ent, ŎR'ant
death-warrant
horrent
torrent
warrant
(cf. abhôrrent)

ŌR'est
adorest
borest
deplorest
encorest
explorest
floorest
gorest
hoarest
ignorest
implorest
outsoarest
porest
pourest
restorest
roarest
scorest
snorest
soarest
sorest
storest

ÔR'est
abhorrest
warrest

ŎR'est
afforest
disafforest
enforest
forest

ŌR'eth
adoreth
boreth
deploreth
encoreth
exploreth
flooreth
goreth
ignoreth
imploreth
outsoareth
poreth
poureth
restoreth
roareth
scoreth
snoreth
soareth
storeth

ÔR'eth
abhorreth
warreth

ÔR'fan
orphan

ÔR'fik
allomorphic
anthropo-
    morphic
automorphic
dimorphic
endomorphic
heteromorphic

ichthyomor-
    phic
idiomorphic
isomorphic
metamorphic
morphic
ophiomorphic
Orphic
pantamorphic
polymorphic
protomorphic
pseudomor-
    phic
theormorphic
trimorphic
zoomorphic

ÔR'fing
dwarfing
wharfing

ÔR'fist
anthropomor-
    phist
metamorphist
wharfist

ÔR'fit
forfeit

ÔR'fizm
allomorphism
amorphism
anamorphism
anthropomor-
    phism
automorphism
dimorphism
isodimorphism
isomeromor-
    phism

isomorphism
isotrimor-
　phism
metamorphism
monomor-
　phism
pleomorphism
polymorphism
trimorphism
zoomorphism

ŎR'fūs
Morpheus
Orpheus

ŎR'fŭs
amorphous
anthropomor-
　phous
dimorphous
isodimor-
　phous
isomorphous
isotrimorphous
ophiomorphous
paramor-
　phous
polymor-
　phous
trimorphous

ŎR'gan
barrel-organ
Dorgan
Morgan
morgen
organ

ŌR'hand
aforehand
beforehand
forehand

ŎR'hous
storehouse
whorehouse

Ō'ri
abbreviatory
abjuratory
absolutory
acceleratory
acclamatory
accusatory
additory
adhortatory
adjuratory
admonitory
adulatory
a fortiori
allegory
amatory
ambagitory
ambulatory
amendatory
annotatory
annunciatory
a posteriori
appellatory
applicatory
appreciatory
approbatory
a priori
aratory
aspiratory
asseveratory
assimilatory
auditory
auxiliatory
basement-story
bibitory
cachinnatory
calculatory
calumniatory

castigatory
category
circulatory
commandatory
commemora-
　tory
commendatory
comminatory
communicatory
compellatory
compensatory
conciliatory
condemnatory
confabulatory
confirmatory
confiscatory
congratulatory
conservatory
consolatory
contributory
corroboratory
crematory
criminatory
damnatory
declamatory
declaratory
dedicatory
defamatory
delineatory
demonstratory
denunciatory
depilatory
depository
deprecatory
depreciatory
depredatory
derogatory
designatory
desultory
dictatory
dilatory

disapprobatory
discriminatory
dispensatory
dormitory
dory
edificatory
ejaculatory
emendatory
emulatory
exaggeratory
exclamatory
exculpatory
execratory
executory
exhortatory
expiatory
expiratory
explanatory
expostulatory
expurgatory
extenuatory
exterminatory
extirpatory
feudatory
flory
frigeratory
funambulatory
gesticulatory
gladiatory
glory
gory
gradatory
grallatory
gratulatory
gustatory
gyratory
habilatory
hallucinatory
hoary
hortatory
hunky-dory

āle, câre, ădd, ärm, ȧsk; mē, hẹre, ĕnd; īce, ĭll;

imperatory
imprecatory
improvisatory
incantatory
incriminatory
incubatory
inculpatory
indicatory
inflammatory
initiatory
inspiratory
interlocutory
interrogatory
inventory
investigatory
invitatory
invocatory
jaculatory
judicatory
laboratory
laudatory
libatory
liberatory
lory
Maggiore
mandatory
masticatory
migratory
monitory
narratory
natatory
negatory
negotiatory
nugatory
oary
objurgatory
obligatory
observatory
offertory
oratory
oscillatory

osculatory
pacificatory
palliatory
peremptory
perfumatory
perspiratory
piscatory
plauditory
postulatory
potatory
predatory
predicatory
prefatory
premonitory
preparatory
probatory
procrastinatory
procuratory
profanatory
prohibitory
promissory
promontory
pronunciatory
propitiatory
punitory
purgatory
purificatory
recommenda-
 tory
recriminatory
reformatory
refrigeratory
refutatory
regeneratory
remuneratory
repertory
repository
reprobatory
reptatory
requisitory
respiratory

restoratory
retaliatory
retardatory
retributory
reverberatory
revocatory
rogatory
rotatory
sacrificatory
saltatory
salutatory
sanatory
sanitory
shory
sibilatory
signatory
significatory
simulatory
snory
speculatory
sternutatory
stillatory
story
stridulatory
sublimatory
sudatory
supplicatory
terminatory
territory
tory
transitory
transpiratory
undulatory
usurpatory
vacillatory
vain-glory
vehiculatory
vibratory
vindicatory
vomitory
whory

ŎR′i

Laurie
Maury

ŎR′i

Corrie
Florrie
lorry
quarry
sorry
(cf. ÄR′ĭ)

ŌR′id

gloried
storied

ŎR′id

florid
horrid
torrid

ŌR′ij

shorage
storage

ŎR′ij

borage
forage

Ō′rik

chloric
choric
euchloric
hydrochloric
perchloric
roric

ŎR′ik

allegoric
amphigoric
amphoric

armoric
caloric
camphoric
Doric
elydoric
historic
lithophosphoric
metaphoric
meteoric
paregoric
peloric
phantasmagoric
phosphoric
pictoric
plethoric
prehistoric
prophoric
pyloric
Pythagoric
semaphoric
sophomoric
theoric
zoophoric
zoosporic

Ō'rin

florin

ŌR'ing

adoring
boring
choring
deploring
encoring
exploring
flooring
goring
ignoring
imploring
Loring
outsoaring

poring
pouring
restoring
roaring
scoring
shoring
snoring
soaring
storing
upsoaring

ŎR'ing

abhorring
warring

ŌR'is

Doris
loris

ŎR'is

Doris

ŎR'is

doch-an-dorris
Doris
Horace
loris
morris
orris

ŎR'ja

Borgia
Georgia

**ŎR'jal,
ŎRD'yal**

cordial

ŎR'ji

orgy

porgy
storge

ŎR'jing

forging

ŎR'jiz

Georges
George's
orgies, etc.

ŎR'jur

forger

ŎR'jus

gorgeous

ŎR'kas

Dorcas

ŎR'ki

corky
forky

ŎR'kid

orchid

ŎR'king

corking
Dorking
forking
uncorking

ŎR'les

coreless
oarless
oreless
shoreless

ŎR'li

schorly
warly

ŌR'ling

shoreling

ŌR'lok

forelock
oarlock

ŎR'lok

warlock

ŎR'mal

abnormal
anormal
cormal
formal
informal
normal
uniformal
(cf. cormel)

ŌR'man

doorman
floorman
foreman
longshoreman
shoreman

**ŎR'man,
ŎR'mon**

Gorman
Mormon
Norman
O'Gorman

ŎR'mans

conformance
dormance
performance

ŎR'mant

conformant
dormant
informant

ŌR'ment
adorement
deplorement
explorement
ignorement
implorement
restorement

ÔR'ment
torment

ÔR'mest
conformest
deformest
formest
informest
performest
reformest
stormest
swarmest
transformest
warmest

ÔR'meth
conformeth
deformeth
formeth
informeth
performeth
reformeth
stormeth
swarmeth
transformeth
warmeth

ÔR'mi
dormy
stormy
swarmy

ÔR'ming
bestorming

conforming
deforming
forming
informing
nonconforming
performing
reforming
storming
swarming
transforming
warming

ÔR'mist
conformist
nonconformist
reformist

ÔRM'les
formless
stormless

ÔRM'li
warmly
uniformly

ŌR'most
foremost
head-foremost

ÔR'mur
barn-stormer
conformer
deformer
dormer
foot-warmer
former
informer
performer
reformer
stormer
swarmer

transformer
warmer

ÔR'mus
abnormous
cormous
cormus
enormous
multiformous

ÔR'na
cromorna
Lorna
Norna

ÔR'nat
ornate

ŌR'nes
soreness

ÔR'nest
adornest
bescornest
forewarnest
scornest
subornest
warnest

ÔR'net
cornet
hornet

ÔR'neth
adorneth
bescorneth
forewarneth
scorneth
suborneth
warneth

ÔRN'ful
mournful

ÔRN'ful
scornful

ÔR'ni
corny
Hornie
horny
thorny

ŌR'ning
mourning

ÔR'ning
adorning
bescorning
dehorning
dishorning
forewarning
good-morning
horning
morning
scorning
suborning
yester-morning
warning

ÔR'nis
Aepyornis
cornice
Dinornis
Gastornis
Heliornis
Ichthyornis

ÔR'nish
Cornish
hornish

ÔRN'les
hornless

scornless
thornless

ŌRN'ment
adornment

ŌR'nun
forenoon

ŌR'nur
mourner

ŌR'nur
adorner
bescorner
chimney-corner
corner
forewarner
horner
scorner
suborner
warner

Ō'ro
Moro
toro

ŌR'o
amorrow
borrow
good-morrow
morrow
sorrow
to-morrow

ŌR'od
borrowed
sorrowed
unsorrowed

ŌR'old
Thorold
(cf. quarrelled)

ŏR'or
horror

ŏR'pid
torpid

ŏR'por
torpor

ŏR'sal
dextrorsal
dorsal
dorsel
morsel
torsel

ŏR'sen
coarsen
hoarsen

ŏR'sest
coarsest
coursest
discoursest
divorcest
enforcest
forcest
hoarsest
reinforcest

ŏR'sest
endorsest, etc.

ŌR'seth
courseth
discourseth
divorceth
enforceth
forceth
reinforceth

ŏR'seth
endorseth, etc.

ŌRS'ful
forceful
resourceful

ŏRS'ful
remorseful

ŌR'shun
apportion
disproportion
portion
proportion

ŌR'shun
abortion
consortion
contortion
detortion
distortion
extorsion
intorsion
retortion
torsion

ŌR'shund
apportioned
disproportioned
portioned
proportioned
unportioned

ŌR'si
gorsy
horsy

ŌR'sing
coursing
discoursing
divorcing
enforcing
forcing
reinforcing

ŌR'siv
discoursive
divorcive
enforcive

ŌRS'les
forceless
resourceless
sourceless

ŏRS'les
horseless
remorseless

ŌRS'man
horseman
lighthorseman
Norseman

ŌRS'ment
deforcement
divorcement
enforcement
forcement
reinforcement

ŏRS'ment
endorsement

ŌRS'nes
coarseness
hoarseness

ŌR'som
foursomē

ŏR'son
Orson

ŏR'song
warsong

ŌR'sur
coarser
courser
discourser
divorcer
enforcer
forcer
hoarser
reinforcer

ÔR'sur
endorser

ŌR'tal
portal
transportal

ÔR'tal
aortal
immortal
mortal
(cf. ÔRT"l)

ŌR'tans
supportance
transportance

ÔR'tans
importance

ÔR'tant
important

ŌR'ted
courted
disported
exported
imported
reported
sported
supported
transported

ÔR'ted
aborted
assorted
consorted
contorted
detorted
distorted
escorted
exhorted
extorted
resorted
retorted
snorted
sorted
thwarted
unsorted

ÔR'teks
cortex
vortex

ÔR'tem
post-mortem

ÔR'ten
shorten

ŌR'tent
portent

ŌR'test
courtest
disportest
exportest
importest
reportest
sportest
supportest
transportest

ÔR'test
assortest
consortest
contortest
detortest
distortest
escortest
exhortest
extortest
resortest
retortest
shortest
snortest
sortest
swartest
thwartest

ŌR'teth
courteth
disporteth
exporteth
importeth
reporteth
sporteth
supporteth
transporteth

ÔR'teth
assorteth
consorteth
contorteth
detorteth
distorteth
escorteth
exhorteth
extorteth
resorteth
retorteth
snorteth
sorteth
thwarteth

ŌRT'gid
court-guide
port-guide

ÔR'thi
swarthy

ÔR'ti
forty
pianoforte
snorty
sortie
swarty
warty

ÔR'tij
shortage

ŌR'tim
aforetime
beforetime

ŌR'ting
courting
deporting
disporting
exporting
importing
reporting
sporting
supporting
transporting

ÔR'ting
aborting
assorting
consorting
contorting
detorting
distorting
escorting

exhorting
extorting
resorting
retorting
snorting
sorting
thwarting

ŌR'tiv

sportive
transportive

ÔR'tiv

abortive
contortive
distortive
ortive
retortive
tortive

ÔRT"l

chortle
whortle
(cf. ÔR'tal)

ŌRT'land

Courtland
Portland

ŌRT'li

courtly
portly
uncourtly

ÔRT'li

shortly

ŌRT'ment

comportment
deportment

disportment
transportment

ÔRT'ment

assortment

ÔRT'nes

swartness
thwartness

ÔRT'nit

fortnight

ÔR'ton

Horton
Morton
Norton

ÔR'trat

portrait

ÔR'tres

fortress

ŌRT'ship

courtship

ŌRTS'man

sportsman

ÔR'tun

befortune
enfortune
fortune
importune
misfortune

ŌR'tur

courter
disporter
exporter
importer

porter
reporter
sporter
supporter
transporter

ÔR'tūr

torture

ÔR'tŭr

assorter
consorter
contorter
detorter
distorter
escorter
exhorter
extorter
mortar
quarter
resorter
retorter
shorter
snorter
sorter
thwarter
weather-
  quarter
woolsorter

**ÔR'turd,
  ÔR'chard**

orchard
tortured

ÔR'turz

winter-quarters
assorters, etc.

ÔRT'wav

short-wave

Ō'rum

decorum
forum
indecorum
jorum
quorum
variorum
cf. ad valorem

ŌR'ur

adorer
borer
corer
decorer
deplorer
encorer
explorer
floorer
gorer
ignorer
implorer
outpourer
outsoarer
porer
pourer
restorer
roarer
scorer
snorer
soarer
sorer
storer

Ō'rus

canorous
chorus
decorous
Horus
imporous
indecorous
porous

---

pylorus
sonorous
torous
torus

ŎR′us

brontosaurus
dolichosaurus
hadrosaurus
ichthyosaurus
megalosaurus
mososaurus
nanosaurus
pleiosaurus
plesiosaurus
protosaurus
regnosaurus
Taurus
teleosaurus
thesaurus
tyranosaurus

ŌR′ward

foreward
shoreward

ŎR′ward

forward
henceforward
norward
straightforward
thenceforward

ŎR′worn

war-worn

ŌRZ′man

oarsman

Ō′sa

amorosa

Formosa
mimosa

ŎS′chun

exhaustion

ŎS′est

closest, etc.
grossest
dosest, etc.

ŎS′est

crossest
embossest
glossest
tossest

ŎS′et

faucet

ŎS′et

bosset
cosset
posset
sack-posset

ŎS′eth

crosseth
embosseth
glosseth
tosseth

Ō′shal

antisocial
intersocial
social

ŎSH′i

boshy
sloshy
squashy

swashy
toshy
washy
wishy-washy

ŎSH′ing

sloshing
squashing
swashing
washing

ŌSH′ur

gaucher
kosher

ŎSH′ur

cosher
josher
squasher
swasher
washer

Ō′shun

Bœotian
commotion
devotion
emotion
groschen
indevotion
locomotion
lotion
motion
nicotian
notion
ocean
potion
prenotion
promotion
remotion
self-devotion

ŎSH′un

caution
incaution
precaution

ŌSH′us

atrocious
ferocious
nepotious
precocious

ŎSH′us

cautious
incautious
precautious

ŎS′i

saucy

ŎS′i

bossy
drossy
Flossie
flossy
glossy
mossy
posse
tossy

ŎS′ij

sausage

ŎS′ik

fossick
glossic

ŌS′il

docile
indocile

ŎS′il

docile

dossil
fossil
(see ŎS''l)

ŌS'ing
dosing
engrossing

ŎS'ing
bossing
crossing
dossing
embossing
glossing
railway-
  crossing
tossing

ŎS'ip
gossip

Ō'sis
anadiplosis
anamorphosis
ankylosis
apotheosis
carcinosis
chlorosis
cirrhosis
diagnosis
enantiosis
endosmosis
epanadiplosis
epanorthosis
exosmosis
geognosis
heliosis
heterosis
hypnosis
hypotyposis
ichthyosis

meiosis
metasomatosis
metem-
  psychosis
metemptosis
metensomatosis
morosis
morphosis
narcosis
necrosis
neurosis
osmosis
proemptosis
prognosis
psychosis
ptosis
pyrosis
sarcosis
scirrhosis
sorosis
tuberculosis
zygosis
zymosis

ŎS'is
proboscis

ŌS'iv
corrosive
erosive
explosive
inexplosive

ŎS'kar
Oscar

ŎS'ki
bosky

ŎS''l
apostle

colossal
dosel
dossil
fossil
hypoglossal
jostle
throstle
tossel
wassail

ŎS'lur
hostler
jostler
Rossler

ŎS'li
crossly

ŎS'nes
closeness
grossness
jocoseness
moroseness
verboseness

Ō'so
amoroso
arioso
doloroso
gracioso
so-so
virtuoso

ŎS'om
blossom
odontoglossum
opossum
orangeblossom
possum

ŎS'on
Dawson

Lawson
Rawson

ŎS'pel
gospel

ŎS'pish
waspish

ŎS'pur
prosper

ŌS'tal
coastal
postal

ŎS'tal
costal
infracostal
intercostal
Pentecostal
supra-costal

ŎS'tat
apostate
laticostate
quadricostate

ŌS'ted
boasted
coasted
posted
roasted
toasted
unposted

ŎS'ted
exhausted

ŎS'ted
accosted
frosted

ŎS'tel, ŎS"l
hostel

ŎS'ten
Austen

ŌS'tes
hostess

ŌS'test
boastest
coastest
postest
roastest
toastest

ŌS'teth
boasteth
coasteth
posteth
roasteth
toasteth

ŌST'hous
oasthouse
post-house

ŎS'ti
frosty

ŌS'tij
postage

ŎS'tij
hostage

ŎS'tik
catacaustic
caustic
diacaustic
encaustic

ŎS'tik
acrostic
agnostic
diagnostic
eteostic
geognostic
gnostic
paracrostic
pentacostic
prognostic

ŎS'til
hostile

ŎS'tin
Austin

ŎS'ting
boasting
coasting
posting
roasting
toasting

ŎS'ting
exhausting

ŎS'ting
accosting
costing
frosting

ŎS'tiv
exhaustive
inexhaustive

ŎS'tiv
costive

ŌST'li
ghostly
mostly

ŎST'li
costly

ŌST'man
postman

ŌST'mark
postmark

ŎS'ton
Boston

Ō'storm
snow-storm

ŎS'tral
austral
claustral

ŎS'tral, ŎS'trel
costrel
lamellirostral
longirostral
rostral
(cf. nostril)

ŎS'trat
prostrate
rostrate

ŎS'trich
ostrich

ŎS'trum
nostrum
rostrum

ŎS'tum
costume

ŌS'tur
boaster

coaster
four-poster
poster
roaster
throwster
toaster

ŎS'tur
auster
exhauster

ŎS'tūr
imposture
posture

ŎS'tŭr
accoster
coster
foster
Gloucester
imposter
Paternoster
pentecoster
roster

ŎS'turn
postern

ŎS'tus
Faustus

ŌS'ur
closer
doser
engrosser
grocer
grosser
jocoser
moroser

ŎS'ur
Chaucer

Naw sir | ŌT'at | jotted | *denotest*

saucer | *denotate* | knotted | *devotest*
| notate | lotted | *dotest*
ŎS'ur | rotate | plotted | *floatest*
bosser | | potted | *gloatest*
crosser | **ŎT'ash** | rotted | *misquotest*
dosser | potash | shotted | *notest*
embosser | | slotted | *promotest*
glosser | **ŌT'ed** | sotted | *quotest*
josser | bloated | spotted | *votest*
tosser | boated | squatted |
| coated | totted | **ŎT'est**
ŎS'us | demoted | trotted | *clottest, etc.*
colossus | denoted | unblotted |
molossus | devoted | underplotted | **ŌT'eth**
| doted | unknotted | *demoteth*
Ō'ta | floated | unspotted | *denoteth*
Dakota | gloated | wainscotted | *devoteth*
flota | misquoted | (cf. carotid | *doteth*
iota | moated | and parotid) | *floateth*
Minnesota | noted | | *gloateth*
quota | parti-coated | **ŌT'en** | *noteth*
rota | petticoated | oaten | *misquoteth*
| promoted | | *promoteth*
ŌT'al | quoted | **ŎT'en, ŎT'on** | *quoteth*
anecdotal | refloated | begotten | *voteth*
antidotal | self-devoted | cotton |
dotal | throated | first-begotten | **ŎT'eth**
extradotal | unnoted | forgotten | *clotteth, etc.*
notal | voted | gotten |
rotal | | hard-gotten | **ŌT'ful**
sacerdotal | **ŎT'ed** | ill-gotten | thoughtful
sclerotal | allotted | misbegotten |
teetotal | besotted | misgotten | **Ōth'a**
total | bespotted | rotten | quotha
| blood-bespotted | unbegotten |
ŌT'ant, ŌT'ent | blotted | unforgotten | **Ōth'al**
flotant | cheviotted | ungotten | betrothal
potent | clotted | |
prepotent | dotted | **ŌT'est** | **Ōth'am**
| garotted | *demotest* | Gotham
| | | Jotham

ŎTH'am
Gotham

ŌTH'est
clothest
loathest

ŌTH'eth
clotheth
loatheth

ŌTH'ful
loathful

Ōth'ful
slothful

Ôth'ful
wrathful

Ŏth'ĭ
frothy
mothy

Ŏth'ik
Gothic
Mœso-gothic
Ostrogothic
Visigothic

ŌTH'ing
clothing
loathing

Ōth'ment
betrothment

ŌT'hook
boathook
coathook

Ô'thorn
Cawthorn
hawthorn

ŌTH'som
loathsome

Ôth'ur
author

ŎTH'ur
bother
fother
pother
(cf. father,
rather)

ŌT'i
bloaty
coyote
dhoty
Doty
Doughty
floaty
goaty
throaty

Ôt'i
haughty
naughty

Ŏt'ĭ
clotty
dotty
knotty
spotty
totty

ŎT'id
carotid

parotid
(cf. ŎT+ed)

ŌT'ij
anecdotage
dotage
floatage
flotage

Ŏt'ij
cottage
pottage
wattage

ŌT'ik
otic

Ôt'ik
aeronautic
argonautic
nautic

Ŏt'ik
acrotic
agrypnotic
anaptotic
anecdotic
ankylotic
anti-patriotic
aptotic
aquatic
carotic
chaotic
chlorotic
cirrhotic
culottic
demotic
despotic
endosmotic
epiglottic
epizootic

erotic
escharotic
exotic
glottic
henotic
hidrotic
hypnotic
idiotic
macrobiotic
narcotic
nepotic
neurotic
Nilotic
osmotic
otic
patriotic
pyrotic
quixotic
san-culottic
sarcotic
sclerotic
semeiotic
zootic
zymotic

ŌT'ing
bloating
boating
coating
demoting
denoting
devoting
doting
floating
gloating
misquoting
noting
promoting
quoting
throating
voting

ŎT'ing
allotting
besotting
blotting
clotting
dotting
garotting
jotting
knotting
plotting
potting
rotting
sotting
spotting
squatting
totting
trotting
underplotting
unknotting
yatching

ŎT'is
epiglottis
glottis

ŎT'ish
dotish
goatish

ŎT'ish
Scottish
sottish

ŌT'ist
anecdotist
noticed
Scotist
unnoticed

ŎT'ist
sans-culottist

ŎT'iv
emotive
locomotive
motive
promotive
votive

ŎT'kinz
Otkins
Watkins

ŎT''l
bottle
dottle
glottal
mottle
pottle
throttle
tottle
twattle
wattle

ŎT'les
thoughtless

ŎT'les
blotless
clotless
cotless
dotless
jotless
knotless
lotless
potless
rotless
sotless
spotless
totless
trotless

ŎT'li
hotly
motley

ŎT'ling
bottling, etc.

ŌT'man
boatman

ŎT'man
Cotman
Ottman

ŎT'ment
demotement
denotement
devotement

ŎT'ment
allotment
besotment

ŎT'nes
hotness
whatness

Ō'to
De Soto
divoto
ex voto
fagotto
in toto
Kioto
photo

ŎT'o
blotto
grotto
lotto
motto

otto
ridotto
risotto
(cf. staccato)

ŎT'om
bottom

Ō'ton
Croton
proton
(cf. oaten)

Ō'ton
Lawton

ŎT'on
cotton
Groton
(see ŎT'en)

ŎT'rel
Cottrell
dottrel

ŎT'si
hotsy-totsy

ŎTS'man
Scotsman
yachtsman

ŎT'son
Watson

Ō'tum
quotum
tee-totum

ŎT'um
autumn

ŌT'ur
bloater
boater
demoter
denoter
devoter
doter
fagot-voter
floater
gloater
locomotor
magnetomotor
motor
noter
promoter
quoter
rotomotor
rotor
scoter
toter
vaso-motor
voter

ÔT'ur
backwater
daughter
fire-water
fizz-water
giggle-water
milk-and-
    water
slaughter
soda-water
water

ŎT'ur
blotter
bogtrotter
clotter
complotter
cotter

dotter
garotter
globe-trotter
hotter
jotter
knotter
ottar
otter
plotter
potter
rotter
spotter
squatter
totter
trotter
underplotter
unknotter
yachter

Ō'tus
Gymnotus
lotus
macrotous

OU'al
avowal
disavowal
(cf. OU''el)

OU'an
gowan
McGowan
rowan
rowen

OU'ans
allowance
avowance
disallowance
disavowance

OU'ard
coward
Howard
(cf. OU'urd)

OUCH'est
avouchest, etc.

OUCH'eth
avoucheth, etc.

OUCH'ing
avouching
couching
crouching
grouching
pouching
slouching
vouching

OUCH'ur
avoucher
coucher
croucher
Goucher
groucher
poucher
sloucher
voucher

OU'da
howdah

OUD'ed
beclouded
clouded
crowded
enshrouded
overclouded
overcrowded
shrouded

unbeclouded
unclouded
unshrouded

OUD'est
becloudest
beshroudest
cloudest
crowdest
enshroudest
loudest
overcloudest
overcrowdest
proudest
shroudest

OUD'eth
becloudeth
beshroudeth
cloudeth
crowdeth
enshroudeth
overcloudeth
overcrowdeth
shroudeth

OUD'i
cloudy
crowdy
dowdy
Gowdy
howdie
howdy
pandowdy
proudy
rowdy
shroudy
uncloudy
(cf. summa
    cum laude)

OUD'ing
beclouding
beshrouding
clouding
crowding
enshrouding
overclouding
overcrowding
shrouding
unshrouding

OUD'ish
loudish
proudish

OUD'li
loudly
proudly

OUD'nes
loudness
proudness

OUD'ur
baking powder
clam chowder
bepowder
chowder
crowder
louder
powder
prouder
seidlitz-powder

OU'el
bowel
dowel
embowel
Howell
Powell
Prowell

rowel
towel
trowel
vowel
(cf. OU'al)

OU'es
prowess

OU'est
allowest
avowest
bowest
cowest
disallowest
endowest
ploughest
vowest

OU'et
Howett
Jowett

OU'eth
alloweth
avoweth
boweth
coweth
disalloweth
endoweth
plougheth
voweth

OU'i
Dowie
zowie

OU'ing
allowing
avowing
bowing

cowing
disallowing
endowing
ploughing
plowing
rowing
vowing

OUL'est
foulest
growlest
howlest
prowlest
scowlest

OUL'et
owlet

OUL'eth
growleth
howleth
prowleth
scowleth

OU'li
Cowley
Powley
Rowley

OUL'ing
fouling
fowling
growling
howling
prowling
scowling

OUL'ish
foulish
owlish

OUL'ur
fouler
fowler
growler
howler
prowler
scowler
yowler

OU'ment
avowment
endowment

OUN'ded
abounded
astounded
bounded
compounded
confounded
dumfounded
expounded
founded
grounded
hounded
impounded
mounded
pounded
propounded
rebounded
redounded
resounded
rounded
sounded
superabound-
ed
surrounded
unbounded
unfounded
ungrounded
unsounded

āle, câre, ădd, ärm, åsk; mē, hęre, ĕnd; īce, ĭll;

well-founded
wounded

OUN'del
roundel

OUN'den
bounden

OUN'dest
aboundest
astoundest
boundest
compoundest
confoundest
expoundest
foundest
groundest
houndest
impoundest
poundest
profoundest
propoundest
reboundest
resoundest
roundest
soundest
*superabound-
    est*
surroundest

OUN'deth
aboundeth
astoundeth
boundeth
compoundeth
confoundeth
dumfoundeth
expoundeth
foundeth
groundeth

houndeth
impoundeth
poundeth
propoundeth
reboundeth
redoundeth
resoundeth
roundeth
soundeth
surroundeth

OUN'dij
groundage
poundage
soundage

OUN'ding
abounding
astounding
big-sounding
bounding
compounding
confounding
dumfounding
expounding
founding
grounding
high-sounding
hounding
impounding
pounding
propounding
rebounding
redounding
resounding
rounding
sounding
superabound-
    ing
surrounding

unbounding
wounding

OUND'les
boundless
groundless
soundless

OUND'li
profoundly
roundly
soundly
unsoundly

OUND'ling
foundling
groundling

OUND'nes
profoundness
roundness
soundness
unsoundness

OUN'drel
scoundrel

OUN'dri
foundry

OUN'dur
bounder
compounder
confounder
dumfounder
expounder
flounder
founder
four-pounder
impounder
iron-founder

pounder
profounder
propounder
rebounder
resounder
rounder
sounder
surrounder
type-founder

OUN'est
brownest
crownest
drownest
frownest

OUN'eth
browneth
crowneth
drowneth
frowneth

OUN'i
brownie
browny
downy
frowny
towny

OUN'ing
browning
clowning
crowning
discrowning
downing
drowning
frowning
gowning
intowning
uncrowning

ōld, ôr, ŏdd, oil, fŏŏt, out; ūse, ûrn, ŭp; THis, thin

OUN'ish
brownish
clownish
frownish

OUN'jing
lounging

OUN'les
crownless
frownless
gownless

OUN'sest
announcest, etc.

OUN'seth
announceth, etc.

OUN'sez
announces
bounces
denounces
flounces
ounces
pounces
pronounces
renounces
trounces

OUN'sing
announcing
bouncing
denouncing
flouncing
pouncing
pronouncing
renouncing
trouncing

OUNS'ment
announcement

denouncement
pronounce-
ment
renouncement

OUN'sur
announcer
bouncer
denouncer
flouncer
pouncer
pronouncer
renouncer
trouncer

OUN'ted
accounted
amounted
counted
discounted
dismounted
miscounted
mounted
recounted
remounted
surmounted
uncounted
unmounted
unrecounted

OUN'tes
countess

OUN'test
accountest
amountest
countest
discountest
dismountest
miscountest
mountest

recountest
remountest
surmountest

OUN'teth
accounteth
amounteth
counteth
discounteth
dismounteth
miscounteth
mounteth
recounteth
remounteth
surmounteth

OUN'ti
bounty
county
mounty
viscounty

OUN'tin
catamountain
fountain
mountain

OUN'ting
accounting
amounting
counting
discounting
dismounting
miscounting
mounting
recounting
remounting
surmounting

OUN'tur
accounter

counter
discounter
encounter
mounter
recounter
remounter
reencounter
surmounter

OUN'ur
browner
crowner
drowner
frowner

OUN'ward
downward
townward

OUN'zman
gownsman
townsman

Ō'ur
bestower
blower
flower
foregoer
foreknower
foreshower
glass-blower
goer
glower
grower
hoer
knower
lower
mower
outgoer
overthrower
ower

āle, câre, ădd, ärm, åsk; mē. hĕre, ĕnd; īce, ĭll;

rower
sewer
shower
slower
sower
stower
thrower
tower
undergoer
wine-grower

Ō'ur
cawer
clawer
drawer
gnawer
guffawer
"jawer"
overawer
pawer
rawer
sawer
tawer
wiredrawer
withdrawer

Ō'urd, Ō'ard
lowered
toward
untoward

OUR'est
bescourest
deflowerest
devourest
scourest
sourest

OUR'eth
bescoureth
deflowereth

devoureth
scoureth
soureth

OUR'i
avowry
cowrie
dowry
floury
houri
(cf. OU'ur-i)

OUR'ing
bescouring
deflowering
devouring
flouring
off-scouring
scouring
souring
(cf. OU'ur-
    ing)

OUR'li
hourly
sourly

OUR'nes
sourness

OUR'ur
deflowerer
devourer
scourer
sourer

OU'son
Dowson

OUT'ed
clouted

doubted
flouted
gouted
grouted
misdoubted
pouted
redoubted
routed
scouted
shouted
spouted
sprouted
undoubted

OUT'est
cloutest
devoutest
doubtest
floutest
poutest
scoutest
shoutest
spoutest
sproutest
stoutest

OUT'eth
clouteth
doubteth
flouteth
pouteth
scouteth
shouteth
spouteth
sprouteth

OUT'i
doughty
droughty
gouty
grouty

louty
moughty
pouty
snouty
touty

OUT'ing
beshouting
bespouting
besprouting
clouting
doubting
flouting
grouting
louting
outing
pouting
routing
scouting
shouting
spouting
sprouting
touting
undoubting

OUT'let
outlet
troutlet

OUT'li
devoutly
stoutly

OUT'nes
devoutness
stoutness

OUT'ur
devouter
doubter

down-and-
   outer
flouter
jowter
out-and-outer
pouter
router
scouter
shouter
spouter
sprouter
stouter
touter

OU'ur

allower
avower
beacon-tower
beflower
bower
Brower
candle-power
cauliflower
cower
deflower
dower
embower
empower
endower
enflower
flower
glower
horse-power
imbower
lower
overpower
overtower
passion-flower
plougher
plower
power

rower
shower
thunder-show-
   er
tower
vower
water-power
(cf. OUR)

OU'urd

unshowered
untowered
bowered, **etc.**
(cf. OU'ard)

OU'urz

Powers
avowers, **etc.**

OU'wou

bow-wow
pow-wow
wow-wow

OU'zal

arousal
carousal
espousal
housel
ousel
spousal
tousle

OU'zand

thousand

OUZ'est

arousest, **etc.**

OUZ'eth

arouseth, **etc.**

OUZ'ez

arouses
blouses
browses
carouses
espouses
houses
rouses
spouses

OUZ'i

bowsie
drowzy
frowzy
lousy
mousy

OUZ'ij

espousage
housage
spousage

OUZ'ing

arousing
blowzing
browzing
carousing
housing
rousing

OUZ'ur

arouser
browser
carouser
espouser
mouser
rouser
Towser
trouser

OUZ'urz

trousers
carousers, **etc.**

Ō'va

Jehovah

Ō'val

oval

ŎV'el

grovel
hovel
novel

ŌV'en

cloven
hoven
interwoven
inwoven
uncloven
woven

ŌV'i

anchovy
covy
grovy

ŌV'in

bovine
ovine

ŌV'ing

roving
shroving

ŌV'o

ab ovo
de novo

ŌV'ur

clover

Dover

drover

flopover

half-seas-over

moreover

over

plover

pushover

rover

sea-rover

stover

trover

walkover

ŏV′urb

proverb

ŌV′urz

estovers

drovers, etc.

Ō′ward

froward

Ō′whar

nowhere

Ō′yez

oyez

Ō′yur

bowyer

oyer

Ô′yur

lawyer

sawyer

topsawyer

ŌZ′a

Rosa

Spinoza

ŌZ′al

desposal

disposal

interposal

opposal

presupposal

proposal

reposal

rosal

supposal

transposal

ŌZ′bud

rosebud

ŌZ′div

nose-dive

ŌZ′en

chosen

forechosen

frozen

hosen

Posen

rosen

squozen

ŏZ′enj

lozenge

ŌZ′est

closest

composest

decomposest

deposest

disclosest

discomposest

disposest

dozest

enclosest

exposest

imposest

inclosest

interposest

juxtaposest

opposest

posest

presupposest

proposest

recomposest

reimposest

reposest

superimposest

supposest

transposest

ŌZ′eth

closeth

composeth

decomposeth

deposeth

discloseth

discomposeth

disposeth

dozeth

encloseth

exposeth

imposeth

incloseth

intercloseth

interposeth

juxtaposeth

opposeth

poseth

presupposeth

proposeth

recomposeth

reimposeth

reposeth

superimposeth

supposeth

transposeth

ŌZ′ez

Moses

roses, etc.

ÔZ′ez

causes

clauses

gauzes

pauses

vases

ŌZ′ga

nosegay

Ō′zhan

ambrosian

(cf. Ō′zi-an,

Ō′zi-on)

Ō′zhun

corrosion

erosion

explosion

implosion

(cf. Ō′zi-an,

etc.)

Ō′zhur

crosier

Dozier

hosier

osier

ŌZ′i

cozy

dozy

nosy

posy

prosy

rosy

ŌZ'ĭ
gauzy
causey

ŌZ'ĭd
posied
rosied

ŌZ'ĭng
closing
composing
decomposing
deposing
disclosing
discomposing
disposing
dozing
enclosing
exposing
imposing
inclosing
interposing
juxtaposing
nosing
opposing
posing
predisposing
presupposing
proposing

prosing
recomposing
reposing
supposing
transposing
unclosing
unimposing

ŎZ'ĭng
causing
pausing

ŎZ'ĭt
closet
deposit
interposit
juxtaposit
posit
reposit

ŎZ'ĭv
applausive
plausive
unapplausive

ŎZ"l
nozzle
schnozzle
sozzle

ŎZ'mĭk
cosmic
endosmic
microcosmic

ŌZ'o
bozo

ŌZ'on
ozone

ŌZ'ūr
closure
composure
disclosure
discomposure
disposure
exposure
foreclosure
inclosure
reposure

ŌZ'ŭr
bulldozer
closer
composer
deposer
discloser

disposer
dozer
encloser
exposer
forecloser
glozer
imposer
incloser
interposer
juxtaposer
opposer
poser
predisposer
presupposer
proposer
roser
reimposer
reposer
superimposer
supposer
transposer
uncloser

ŎZ'ur
causer
hawser
pauser

U

For a discussion of words included under the accented vowels following, see the beginning of U rhymes in Section I.

Ū'al
dual
eschewal
pursual
renewal
reviewal
subdual
(cf. Ū'el)

Ū'an
Chouan
duan
Peguan

Ū'ans
eschewance
pursuance
renewance

Ū'ant
pursuant
truant

Ū'ard
leeward
steward
(see Ū'urd)

Ū'ba
Cuba
juba
tuba

Ū'ben
Reuben

Steuben
(cf. Lubin)

ŬB'i
booby
looby
ruby

ŬB'i
bubby
chubby
cubby
fubby
grubby
hubby
nubby
rabi
rubby
scrubby
shrubby
stubby
tubby

ŬB'id
rubied

ŬB'ik
cherubic
cubic
pubic

ŪB'ing
cubing
tubing

ŬB'ing
blubbing
clubbing
drubbing
dubbing
grubbing
nubbing
rubbing
scrubbing
snubbing
stubbing
subbing
tubbing

ŬB'ish
clubbish
cubbish
grubbish
rubbish
tubbish

ŪB'it
cubit

ŬB'jekt
subject

Ū'b'l
ruble

ŬB''l
bubble
double
grubble
Hubbell

hubble-bubble
nubble
redouble
rubble
stubble
trouble

ŬB''ld
bubbled
doubled
redoubled
stubbled
troubled
untroubled

ŬB'lest
bubblest, etc.

ŬB'let
doublet

ŬB'leth
bubbleth, etc.

ŬB'li
bubbly
doubly
knubbly
nubbly
rubbly
stubbly

ŬB'lik
public
republic

ŬB'ling
bubbling
doubling
troubling

ŬB'lish
publish

ŬB'lur
bubbler
doubler
troubler

ŬB'lus
troublous

ŬB'orn
stubborn

ŬB'rik
lubric
rubric

ŬB'stak
grubstake

ŬB'stans
substance

ŪB'ur
goober
Huber
tuber

ŬB'ur
blubber
clubber
drubber
dubber
grubber
india-rubber

landlubber
lubber
money-grub-
  ber
rubber
scrubber
slubber
snubber
stubber
tubber
tub-drubber

ŬB'urd
blubbered
cupboard
Hubbard
mother hub-
  bard
rubbered

ŬB'urt
Hubert

ŬCH'es
archduchess
duchess
Dutchess

ŬCH'est
clutchest, etc.

ŬCH'eth
clutcheth, etc.

ŬCH'ez
clutches
crutches
hutches
retouches
scutches
smutches
touches

ŬCH'i
coochy
hoochy-**coochy**

ŬCH'i
archduchy
clutchy
duchy
smutchy
touchy

ŬCH'ing
clutching
retouching
scutching
smutching
touching

ŬCH'on
escutcheon

ŬCH'ur
retoucher
scutcher
smutcher
toucher

Ū'da
Barbuda
barracuda
Bermuda
Buddha
Ishkooda
Judah

Ū'dad
doodad

ŪD'al
feudal

paludal
udal

ŪD'ed
alluded
brooded
colluded
concluded
deluded
denuded
detruded
duded
eluded
excluded
extruded
exuded
illuded
included
interluded
intruded
obtruded
occluded
precluded
preluded
protruded
recluded
retruded
secluded
snooded
subtruded
transuded
undeluded

ŬD'ed
bestudded
blooded
budded
flooded
scudded
spudded
studded

thudded
(cf. muddied,
etc.)

ŬD′en
sudden

ŬD′ens
jurisprudence
prudence

ŬD′ent
concludent
imprudent
jurisprudent
occludent
prudent
student

ŬD′est
alludest
broodest
concludest
crudest
deludest
denudest
detrudest
eludest
excludest
extrudest
exudest
illudest
includest
intrudest
nudest
obtrudest
precludest
preludest
protrudest
recludest
retrudest

rudest
secludest
shrewdest
subtrudest

ŬD′eth
alludeth
broodeth
colludeth
concludeth
deludeth
denudeth
detrudeth
eludeth
excludeth
extrudeth
exudeth
illudeth
includeth
intrudeth
obtrudeth
occludeth
preludeth
protrudeth
retrudeth
recludeth
secludeth
subtrudeth
transudeth

ŬD′i
broody
moody
scudi

ŬD′i
bloody
buddy
cuddy
muddy
puddy

ruddy
studdy
study

ŬD′id
bloodied
muddied
ruddied
studied
unstudied
(cf. studded,
etc.)

ŬD′ing
abrooding
alluding
brooding
concluding
deluding
denuding
detruding
eluding
excluding
extruding
exuding
illuding
including
intruding
obtruding
occluding
precluding
preluding
protruding
recluding
retruding
secluding
snooding
subtruding
transuding

ŬD′ing
bestudding

budding
flooding
scudding
spudding
studding

ŬD′ish
prudish
rudish
shrewdish

ŬD′ith
Judith

ŬD″l
boodle
caboodle
canoodle
flapdoodle
kiyoodle
noodle
poodle
Yankee-doodle

ŬD″l
bemuddle
buddle
cuddle
fuddle
huddle
muddle
nuddle
puddle
ruddle
scuddle

ŬD′lest
bemuddlest, etc.

ŬD′leth
bemuddleth, etc.

ŬD′li

crudely
lewdly
nudely
rudely
shrewdly

ŬD′li

Dudley

ŬD′ling

bemuddling
cuddling
fuddling
huddling
muddling
puddling
scuddling

ŬD′lum

hoodlum

ŬD′lur

cuddler
fuddler
huddler
muddler
puddler

ŬD′nes

lewdness
nudeness
crudeness
rudeness
shrewdness

ŬD′ok

puddock
ruddock

ŬD′os

kudos

ŬD′son

Hudson
Judson

ŬD′ur

alluder
brooder
concluder
cruder
deluder
denuder
detruder
eluder
excluder
extruder
exuder
illuder
includer
intruder
obtruder
occluder
precluder
preluder
protruder
recluder
retruder
ruder
secluder
shrewder
subtruder
transuder
Tudor

ŬD′ur

dudder
flooder
mudder
pudder
rudder
scudder

shudder
udder

ŬD′zi

sudsy

Ū′e

cooee
(see Ū′i)

Ū′el

bejewel
crewel
cruel
duel
fuel
gruel
Hewell
jewel
newel
Reuel
Sewell
tewel
(cf. Ū′al)

Ū′es

Jewess

Ū′est

accruest
bedewest
beshrewest
bluest
brewest
chewest
cooest
doest
drewest
enduest
ensuest

eschewest
fewest
flewest
gluest
grewest
hallooest
hewest
imbrewest
imbuest
interviewest
knewest
mewest
newest
pursuest
renewest
reviewest
ruest
screwest
shampooest
shoest
shooest
spuest
stewest
strewest
subduest
suest
tattooest
threwest
truest
undoest
unscrewest
untruest
ungluest
viewest
withdrewest
wooest

Ū′et

cruet
suet

āle, câre, ădd, ärm, ăsk; mē, hĕre, ĕnd; īce, ĭll;

Ū'eth
accrueth
bedeweth
beshreweth
breweth
cheweth
cooeth
doeth
dreweth
endueth
ensueth
escheweth
glueth
greweth
hallooeth
heweth
imbreweth
imbueth
intervieweth
kneweth
meweth
pursueth
reneweth
revieweth
rueth
screweth
shampooeth
shoeth
shooeth
speweth
steweth
subdueth
sueth
streweth
tabooeth
tattooeth
threweth
undoeth
unglueth
unscreweth
vieweth

withdreweth
wooeth

Ū'fa
chufa
stufa
tufa
Ufa

Ū'feld
Bluefield
Newfield

ŬF'en
roughen
toughen

ŬF'est
bepuffest
bluffest
cuffest
gruffest
luffest
muffest
puffest
rebuffest
roughest
sloughest
snuffest
stuffest
toughest

ŬF'et
buffet

ŬF'eth
bluffeth, etc.

ŬF'hous
roughhouse

ŬF'i
goofy
roofy
spoofy
woofy

ŬF'i
bluffy
buffy
chuffy
fluffy
huffy
pluffy
puffy
sloughy
snuffy
stuffy

ŬF'in
muffin
puffin
ragamuffin

ŬF'ing
roofing
waterproofing
woofing

ŬF'ing
bluffing
cuffing
fluffing
huffing
luffing
puffing
roughing
sloughing
stuffing

ŬF'ish
gruffish

huffish
roughish
toughish

ŬF"l
bemuffle
buffle
double- shuffle
duffel
muffle
ruffle
scuffle
shuffle
snuffle
truffle
unmuffle
unruffle

ŬF"ld
bemuffled, etc.

ŬF'lest
bemufflest, etc.

ŬF'leth
bemuffleth, etc.

ŬF'li
bluffly
gruffly
muffly
roughly
ruffly
scuffly
sluffly
snuffly
toughly
truffly

ŬF'ling
bemuffling

---

muffling
ruffling
scuffling
shuffling
snuffling
unmuffling
unruffling

ŬF'lur

muffler
ruffler
scuffler
shuffler
snuffler
unmuffler

ŬF'nes

bluffness
gruffness
roughness
toughness

ŬF'ted

tufted

ŬF'ti

mufti
tufty

ŬF'ur

aloofer
hoofer
roofer
spoofer

ŬF'ur

bluffer
buffer
cuffer
duffer
gruffer

huffer
luffer
puffer
rougher
snuffer
stuffer
suffer
tougher

Ŭ'fus

goofus
rufous
Rufus

ŬG'a

meshuggah

Ŭ'gar

cougar

ŬG'ard

sluggard

ŬG'ed

rugged
(see ŬG + ed)

ŬG'est

druggest
huggest
juggest
luggest
muggest
pluggest
shruggest
sluggest
smuggest
snuggest
tuggest
(cf. druggist)

ŬG'et

drugget
nugget

ŬG'eth

druggeth
huggeth
juggeth
luggeth
muggeth
pluggeth
shruggeth
sluggeth
tuggeth

ŬG'hous

bughouse

ŬG'i

buggy
muggy
puggi
puggy
sluggy

ŬG'ij

luggage

ŬG'ing

drugging
hugging
jugging
lugging
mugging
plugging
shrugging
slugging
tugging

ŬG'ish

muggish

sluggish
smugish
snuggish

ŬG'ist

druggist

ŬG'l

bugle
febrifugal
frugal
fugal
infrugal
jugal
McDougall
vermifugal

ŬG'l

death-struggle
guggle
juggle
smuggle
snuggle
struggle

ŬG'lest

jugglest, etc.

ŬG'leth

juggleth, etc.

ŬG'li

guggly
juggly
plug-ugly
smugly
snuggly
struggly
ugly

ŬG'ling

guggling

juggling
smuggling
struggling

ŬG'lur
bugler
fugler

ŬG'lur
juggler
smuggler
snuggler
struggler

ŬG'nes
smugness
snugness

Ū'go
Hugo

ŬG'ur
drugger
hugger
hugger-
  mugger
lugger
mugger
plugger
rugger
shrugger
snugger
tugger

ŬG'wump
mugwump

Ū'i
bedewy
bluey
Bowie

buoy
chop suey
coo-ee
coue
dewy
fluey
gluey
Louis
screwy
thewy
viewy

Ū'īd
blue-eyed
true-eyed

Ū'ĭd
druid
fluid

Ū'ij
brewage
sewage

Ū'ik
catechuic
toluic

Ū'in
blue-ruin
bruin
ruin
sewen

Ū'ing
accruing
barbecuing
bedewing
bestrewing
blueing
brewing
canoeing

chewing
clewing
cooing
cueing
doing
enduing
ensuing
eschewing
eweing
gluing
hallooing
hewing
imbruing
imbuing
interviewing
mewing
mildewing
misconstruing
misdoing
mooing
outdoing
overdoing
poohpoohing
pursuing
renewing
reviewing
screwing
shampooing
shoeing
spewing
stewing
strewing
subduing
suing
tattooing
undoing
unscrewing
viewing
well-doing
wooing
wrong-doing

Ū'ingz
doings
misdoings, etc.

Ū'is
Lewis
Louis
(cf. Jewess)

Ū'ish
blueish
glueish
Jewish
newish
shrewish
truish

ŬJ'el
cudgel

ŬJ'est
begrudgest, etc.

ŬJ'et
budget

ŬJ'eth
begrudgeth, etc.

ŬJ'ez
adjudges
begrudges
budges
drudges
forejudges
fudges
grudges
judges
misjudges
nudges
prejudges

rejudges
sludges
smudges
trudges

Ŭ J'i
pudgy
sludgy
smudgy

Ŭ J'ing
adjudging
begrudging
budging
drudging
forejudging
fudging
grudging
judging
misjudging
nudging
prejudging
rejudging
sludging
smudging
trudging
ungrudging

Ŭ J'ment
judgment

Ŭ J'on
bludgeon
curmudgeon
dudgeon
gudgeon

Ŭ J'ur
adjudger
begrudger
budger

drudger
forejudger
fudger
grudger
judger
misjudger
nudger
prejudger
rejudger
sludger
smudger
trudger

Ū'ka
bucca
felucca
festuca
fistuca
garookuh
palooka
sambouka
yucca

Ū'kal
archducal
ducal
noctilucal
nuchal
Pentateuchal

Ū'kan
antelucan
toucan

Ū'kas
ukase

Ū K'ăs
Clucas
Lucas

Ŭ K'est
rebukest, etc.

Ŭ K'est
pluckest, etc.

Ŭ K'et
bucket
Luckett
Nantucket
Pawtucket
Puckett
sucket
tucket

Ŭ K'eth
rebuketh, etc.

Ŭ K'eth
plucketh, etc.

Ū K'i
fluky
snooky
spooky

Ŭ K'i
ducky
Kentucky
lucky
mucky
plucky
unlucky

Ŭ K'ing
puking
rebuking

Ŭ K'ing
bucking
chucking

clucking
ducking
mucking
plucking
shucking
sucking
trucking
tucking

Ŭ K'ish
buckish
muckish
puckish

Ŭ K'l
bruckle
buckle
chuckle
honeysuckle
huckle
knuckle
muckle
parbuckle
suckle
truckle
unbuckle

Ŭ K''ld
buckled
chuckled
knuckled
suckled
truckled
unbuckled
(cf. cuckold)

Ŭ K'les
luckless

Ŭ K'lest
bucklest, etc.

ŬK′leth
buckleth, etc.

ŬK′ling
buckling
chuckling
duckling
knuckling
suckling
truckling
unbuckling

ŬK′lur
buckler
chuckler
knuckler
swash-buckler
truckler

Ū′ko
Duco
Pernambuco

ŬK′old
cuckold
(cf. ŬK″ld)

ŬK′rak
muckrake

ŬK′shot
buck-shot
duck-shot

ŬK′siv
influxive

ŬK′som
buxom
lucksome

ŬK′stur
huckster

ŬK′shun
abduction
adduction
affluxion
conduction
construction
deduction
defluxion
destruction
diduction
duction
eduction
effluxion
fluxion
induction
influxion
instruction
introduction
manuduction
misconstruc-
    tion
non-conduc-
    tion
obduction
obstruction
over-produc-
    tion
production
reduction
reproduction
ruction
seduction
self-destruction
subduction
substruction
suction
superinduction

superstruction
traduction

ŬK′tans
reluctance

ŬK′tant
reluctant

ŬK′ted
abducted
conducted
constructed
deducted
fructed
inducted
instructed
miconstructed
obstructed
superstructed
unobstructed

ŬK′test
abductest
conductest
constructest
deductest
inductest
instructest
misconstructest
obstructest

ŬK′teth
abducteth
conducteth
constructeth
deducteth
inducteth
instructeth
misconstructeth
obstructeth

ŬK′til
ductile
inductile
productile

ŬK′ting
abducting
conducting
constructing
deducting
inducting
instructing
misconducting
non-conducting
non-obstruct-
    ing
obstructing

ŬK′tiv
adductive
conductive
constructive
deductive
destructive
inductive
instructive
introductive
obstructive
productive
reconductive
reconstructive
reductive
reproductive
seductive
self-destructive
superinductive
superstructive
traductive

ŬK′tres
conductress

instructress
introductress
seductress

ŬK'tūr
structure
substructure
superstructure

ŬK'tŭr
abductor
adductor
conductor
constructor
destructor
ductor
eductor
inductor
instructor
introductor
manuductor
non-conductor
obstructor

ŬK'u, ŌŌ'ku
cuckoo

Ū'kur
euchre
fluker
lucre
puker
rebuker

ŬK'ur
bucker
chucker
chukker
clucker
ducker
mucker

pucker
sap-sucker
seer-sucker
shucker
succor
sucker
trucker
tucker

Ū'kus
caducous
fucus
leucous
mucous
noctilucous
rukus

Ū'la
Ashtabula
Beulah
Boola Boola
Eula
hula-hula
Loula
Missoula
Wallula

ŬL'a
ampulla
medulla
mullah
nullah

ŬL'da
Hulda

ŬL'en
Cullen
sullen
(cf. ŬL'in)

Ū'lep
julep
(cf. tulip)

Ū'les
clueless
cueless
dewless
Jewless
mewless
pewless
screwless
viewless

ŪL'est
befoolest
coolest
foolest
pulest
rulest

ŬL'est
annullest
cullest
dullest
lullest
scullest

ŬL'et
cullet
gullet
mullet

ŪL'eth
befooleth, etc.

ŬL'eth
annulleth
gulleth
lulleth
sculleth

ŬL'fur
sulphur
(cf. Gulfer)

ŬL'gar
vulgar

ŬL'gat
promulgate
vulgate

Ū'li
bluely
Cooley
coolie
coolly
Dooley
duly
Gilhooley
Gillooley
Gilluley
guly
newly
patchouli
Thule
truly
tule
Ultima Thule
unduly
unruly

ŬL'i
cully
dully
gully
hully
sully

ŬL'id
gullied
sullied
unsullied

ŬL'ij
Coolidge

ŬL'ij
gullage
sullage
ullage

ŬL'in
McMullin
mullein

ŬL'ing
befooling
cooling
drooling
fooling
mewling
misruling
overruling
puling
ruling
schooling
spooling
tooling

ŬL'ing
annulling
culling
dulling
gulling
hulling
lulling
mulling
sculling

ŬL'inz
Mullins

Ū'lip
tulip
(cf. julep)

ŬL'is
portcullis

ŬL'ish
coolish
foolish
mulish
pound-foolish
tom-foolish

ŬL'ish
dullish
gullish

Ū'liks
spondulix

ŬL'jens
effulgence
indulgence
refulgence
self-indulgence

ŬL'jent
circumfulgent
effulgent
emulgent
fulgent
indulgent
interfulgent
profulgent
refulgent
self-indulgent

ŬL'jest
indulgest, etc.

ŬL'jeth
indulgeth, etc.

ŬL'jez
bulges

divulges
effulges
indulges

ŬL'jing
bulging
divulging
effulging
indulging
promulging

ŬLJ'ment
divulgement
indulgement

ŬL'jur
divulger
indulger
promulger

ŬL'kat
inculcate
sulcate
trisulcate

ŬLK'ing
bulking
hulking
skulking
sulking

ŬLK'i
bulky
hulky
sulky

ŬLK'ur
bulker
skulker
sulker

ŬL'man
Ullman

ŬL'nes
coolness

ŬL'nes
dullness

ŬL'ok
hullock
rowlock

ŬL'pat
disculpate
exculpate
inculpate

ŬL'pest
gulpest, etc.

ŬL'peth
gulpeth, etc.

ŬL'pi
gulpy
pulpy

ŬL'pin
vulpine

ŬL'prit
culprit

ŬLP'tor
sculptor

ŬLP'tur
sculpture

ŬL'sest
repulsest, etc.

ŬL'set
dulcet

ŬL'seth
repulseth, etc.

ŬL'shun
appulsion
avulsion
compulsion
convulsion
demulsion
divulsion
emulsion
evulsion
expulsion
impulsion
propulsion
pulsion
repulsion
revulsion

ŬL'sing
convulsing
pulsing
repulsing

ŬL'siv
appulsive
compulsive
convulsive
divulsive
emulsive
expulsive
impulsive
propulsive
pulsive
repulsive
revulsive

ŬL'sur
repulser
ulcer

ŬL'tan
sultan

ŬL'tans
exultance
resultance

ŬL'tant
exultant
resultant

ŬL'ted
consulted
exulted
insulted
occulted
resulted

ŬL'test
consultest, etc.

ŬL'teth
consulteth, etc.

ŬL'ting
consulting
exulting
insulting
occulting
resulting

ŬL'tiv
consultive
resultive

ŬLT'nes
adultness
occultness

ŬL'tri
sultry

ŬL'tūr
agriculture
apiculture
arboriculture
aviculture
culture
floriculture
horticulture
inculture
multure
pisciculture
self-culture
sylviculture
terra-culture
viticulture
vulture

ŬL'tur
consulter
exulter
insulter
resulter

Ū'lu
Honolulu
Lulu
Zulu

Ū'lur
cooler
drooler
mewler
puler
ridiculer
ruler
spooler
wine-cooler

ŬL'ur
annuller
color

cruller
culler
discolor
duller
guller
huller
luller
medullar
miscolor
Muller
multicolor
rose-color
sculler
technicolor
tricolor
water-color

ŬL'urd
colored
discolored
dullard
high-colored
over-colored
party-colored
peach-colored
rosy-colored
sky-colored
wine-colored

Ū'lus
screw-loose

ŬL'yar
peculiar

ŬL'yun
cullion
mullion
scullion

Ū'ma
duma

mazuma
Montezuma
puma
Yuma

Ū′man
human
inhuman
Newman
superhuman
Truman

ŬM′at
despumate
exhumate
inhumate

ŬM′at
consummate

ŬM′ba, ŪM′ba
rumba

ŬM′bat
combat
(cf. wombat)

ŬM′bel
dumbbell

ŬM′bent
accumbent
decumbent
incumbent
procumbent
recumbent
superincum-
  bent

ŬM′bik
columbic
plumbic

ŬM′b′l
bejumble
bumble
crumble
fumble
grumble
humble
jumble
mumble
rumble
scumble
stumble
tumble
umbel

ŬM′b′ld
unhumbled
crumbled, etc.

ŬM′blest
crumblest
fumblest
grumblest
humblest
jumblest
mumblest
rumblest
stumblest
tumblest

ŬM′bleth
crumbleth
fumbleth
grumbleth
humbleth
jumbleth
mumbleth
rumbleth
stumbleth
tumbleth

ŬM′bli
crumbly
humbly
stumbly
tumbly

ŬM′bling
crumbling
fumbling
grumbling
humbling
jumbling
mumbling
rumbling
stumbling
tumbling

ŬM′blur
crumbler
drumbler
fumbler
grumbler
humbler
jumbler
mumbler
rumbler
stumbler
tumbler

ŬM′bo
gumbo
Jumbo
Mumbo-Jumbo

ŬM′brat
adumbrate
inumbrate
obumbrate

ŬM′brij
umbrage

ŬM′bril
tumbril

ŬM′brus
cumbrous
penumbrous
slumbrous
unslumbrous

ŬM′bug
humbug

ŬM′bul
Trumbull

ŬM′bur
cumber
disencumber
encumber
Humber
lumbar
lumber
number
outnumber
slumber
number

ŬM′burd
unnumbered
cumbered, etc.

ŬM′drum
humdrum

ŬM′el
bepummel
hummel
pommel

Ū′men
acumen

ōld, ôr, ŏdd, oil, fŏŏt, out; ūse, ûrn, ŭp; THis, thin

albumen
bitumen
catechumen
legumen
rumen
(cf. illumine,
   etc.)

Ū'ment
accrument
eschewment
imbruement
imbuement
induement
subduement

ŬM'est
assumest
bloomest
boomest
consumest
costumest
doomest
entombest
exhumest
fumest
groomest
illumest
perfumest
plumest
presumest
resumest

ŬM'est
becomest
comest
drummest
dumbest
glummest
gummest
hummest

numbest
rummest
strummest
succumbest

ŬM'et
grummet
plummet
(cf. summit)

ŪM'eth
assumeth
bloometh
boometh
consumeth
costumeth
doometh
entombeth
exhumeth
fumeth
groometh
illumeth
perfumeth
plumeth
presumeth
resumeth

ŬM'eth
becometh
cometh
drummeth
gummeth
hummeth
strummeth
succumbeth

ŬM'fal
triumphal

ŬM'fant
triumphant

ŬM'fit
comfit

ŬM'fort
comfort

ŬM'fri
Humphrey

ŬM'friz
Humphreys

ŬM'ful
bloomful
doomful

ŪM'i
bloomy
broomy
Fiume
fumy
gloomy
plumy
rheumy
roomy
spumy

ŬM'i
crumby
crummie
dummy
gummy
lummy
mummy
plummy
rummy
scrummy
scummy
thrummy
tummy
yummy

ŬM'id
humid
tumid

ŪM'ij
fumage
plumage

ŬM'ij
chummage
rummage
scrummage

ŬM'in
illumine
relumine
(cf. acumen,
   etc.)

ŬM'ing
assuming
blooming
booming
consuming
disentombing
dooming
entombing
exhuming
fuming
glooming
grooming
illuming
looming
perfuming
pluming
predooming
presuming
resuming
unassuming
unpresuming

ŬM′ing

becoming
benumbing
chumming
coming
drumming
forthcoming
gumming
humming
mumming
numbing
overcoming
plumbing
plumming
scrumming
shortcoming
slumming
strumming
succumbing
summing
thumbing
unbecoming

ŬM′is

pumice

ŬM′it

summit
(cf. grummet,
   etc.)

ŬM′les

bloomless
broomless
doomless
fumeless
groomless
loomless
plumeless
roomless
tombless

ŬM′let

boomlet
groomlet
plumelet

ŬM′li

Cholmondesley
Chumley
comely
cumbersomely
dumbly
frolicsomely
glumly
humorsomely
numbly
rumly
troublesomely,
   etc.

ŬM′nal

autumnal
columnal

ŬM′nes

dumbness
glumness
numbness

ŬM′nur

Sumner

ŬM′ok

hummock
stomach

ŬM′oks

lummox
(cf. stomachs)

ŬM′on

come-on
summon

ŬM′ond

Drummond

ŬM′pas

compass
encompass
rumpus

ŬM′pest

bethumpest
bumpest
dumpest
humpest
jumpest
lumpest
plumpest
pumpest
stumpest
thumpest
trumpest

ŬM′pet

crumpet
strumpet
trumpet

ŬM′peth

bethumpeth
bumpeth
dumpeth
humpeth
jumpeth
lumpeth
pumpeth
stumpeth
thumpeth
trumpeth

ŬM′pi

bumpy
chumpy

clumpy
crumpy
dumpy
frumpy
grumpy
humpy
jumpy
lumpy
mumpy
plumpy
slumpy
stumpy
thumpy

ŬMP′ing

bethumping
bumping
dumping
bumping
jumping
lumping
mumping
plumping
pumping
slumping
stumping
thumping
trumping

ŬMP′ir

umpire

ŬMP′ish

bumpish
dumpish
frumpish
grumpish
humpish
jumpish
lumpish
mumpish

plumpish
slumpish

ŬMP'kin
bumpkin
pumpkin
(cf. Lumkin)

ŬM'p'l
crumple
rumple
unrumple

ŬM'plest
crumplest, etc.

ŬM'pleth
crumpleth, etc.

ŬM'pling
crumpling
dumpling
rumpling

ŬMP'nes
plumpness

ŬM'po
Bumpo

ŬMP'shun
assumption
consumption
gumption
presumption
resumption
subsumption

ŬMP'shus
bumptious
scrumptious

ŬMP'tiv
assumptive
consumptive
presumptive
resumptive
subsumptive

ŬM'pur
bethumper
bumper
counter-jumper
dumper
jumper
lumper
mumper
plumper
pumper
stumper
thumper
trumper
tub-thumper

ŬM'pus
rumpus
(see ŬM'pas)

ŬM'ston
tombstone

ŬM'tur
Sumter

ŬM'ur
assumer
bloomer
boomer
consumer
doomer
entomber
fumer
humor

ill-humor
illumer
perfumer
plumer
presumer
resumer
roomer
rumor
tumor

ŬM'ur
comer
Cummer
drummer
dumber
glummer
grummer
gummer
hummer
incomer
midsummer
mummer
newcomer
number
plumber
rummer
scrummer
scummer
strummer
summer

ŬM'urd
good-humored
humored
ill-humored
rumored

ŬM'urz
bloomers
rumors, etc.

ŬM'urz
Somers

ŬM'us
brumous
dumous
fumous
grumous
humous
humus
implumous
plumous
spumous

ŬMZ'da
doomsday

ŬM'zi
clumsy
mumsie

ŬMZ'man
doomsman
groomsman

Ū'na
Acuna
fortuna
lacuna
luna
Peruna
Una
vicuna

Ū'nal
lacunal
tribunal

ŬN'chest
bunchest, etc.

ŬN'cheth
buncheth, etc.

ŬN'chez
brunches
bunches
crunches
hunches
lunches
munches
punches
scrunches

ŬN'chi
bunchy
crunchy
hunchy
punchy

ŬN'ching
bunching
crunching
hunching
lunching
munching
punching
scrunching

ŬN'chun
bruncheon
luncheon
nuncheon
puncheon
scuncheon
truncheon

ŬN'chur
bruncher
buncher
cruncher
huncher

luncher
muncher
puncher
scruncher

ŬN'dan
antemundane
extramundane
infra-mundane
intermundane
intramundane
mundane
supermundane
supramundane
ultramundane

ŬN'dans
abundance
redundance
sun dance
superabun-
    dance

ŬN'dant
abundant
redundant
superabundant

ŬN'dat
fecundate
secundate

ŬN'ded
unwounded
wounded

ŬN'ded
funded
refunded
retunded

ŬN'dest
woundest, etc.

ŬN'dest
fundest, etc.

ŬN'deth
woundeth, etc.

ŬN'deth
fundeth, etc.

ŬN'di
Bundy
fundi
Fundy
Grundy
Lundy
Monday
salmagundi
Sunday

ŬN'din
hirundine

ŬN'ding
funding
refunding

ŬN'dit
conduit
pundit

ŬN'd'l
bundle
trundle
unbundle

ŬN'dlest
bundlest, etc.

ŬN'dleth
bundleth, etc.

ŬN'dling
bundling
trundling, etc.

ŬN'don
London
(cf. undone)

ŬN'dred
hundred

ŬN'dri
sundry
thund'ry

ŬN'drus
wondrous

ŬN'dur
asunder
blunder
dissunder
dunder
down-under
enthunder
Gunder
plunder
refunder
rotunder
sunder
thereunder
thunder
under
wonder

ŬN'el
funnel
gunwale

ōld, ôr, ŏdd, oil, fŏŏt, out; ūse, ûrn, ŭp; THis, thin

runnel
trunnel
tunnel

ŬN'et
punnet
runnet

Ŭ'nes
blueness
fewnesss
newness
trueness

ŬN'est
attunest
communest
croonest
entunest
harpoonest
importunest
impugnest
moonest
oppugnest
prunest
soonest
spoonest
swoonest
tunest

ŬN'est
runnest, etc.

ŬN'eth
attuneth
communeth
crooneth
entuneth
harpooneth
impugneth
mooneth

oppugneth
pruneth
spooneth
swooneth
tuneth

ŬN'eth
runneth, etc.

ŬN'ful
tuneful
runeful
spoonful

UNG'g'l
bungle
jungle

ŬNG'gling
bungling

ŬNG'gur
ballad-monger
borough-
    monger
costermonger
enhunger
fishmonger
hunger
ironmonger
monger
Munger
younger

ŬNGK'al
carbuncle
caruncle
peduncle
truncal
uncle

ŬNGK'at
averruncate
detruncate
truncate

ŬNGK'en
drunken
shrunken
sunken

ŬNGK'et
junket
Plunkett

ŬNGK'i
chunky
flunkey
funky
hunky
monkey
powder-
    monkey
punkie
spunky

ŬNG'kin
punkin
(cf. ŬN'kan)

ŬNGK'ish
funkish
monkish
skunkish

ŬNGK'o
bunco
junco

ŬNGK'shun
adjunction
compunction

conjunction
defunction
disjunction
expunction
function
injunction
interjunction
interpunction
inunction
junction
punction
sejunction
subjunction
unction

ŬNGK'shus
compunctious
rambunctious
unctious

ŬNGK'tiv
abjunctive
adjunctive
compunctive
conjunctive
disjunctive
subjunctive

ŬNGK'tur
acupuncture
conjuncture
juncture
puncture

ŬNGK'um
Buncombe
bunkum

ŬNGK'ur
bunker
drunker

āle,   câre,   ădd,   ärm,   åsk;   mē,   hẹre,   ĕnd;   īce,   ĭll;

dunker
flunker
funker
hunker
junker
punker
tunker

ŬNGK'urd
bunkered
drunkard
Dunkard

ŬNGK'us
aduncous
dohunkus
juncous

ŬNG'ling
youngling

ŬN'gri
hungry

ŬNG'stur
tonguester
youngster

ŬNG'ur
lunger

ŪN'i
Dooney
loony
Mooney
moony
Mulrooney
Muni
puisne
puny
spoony

ŬN'i
acrimony
agrimony
alimony
antimony
bunny
funny
gunny
honey
matrimony
money
parsimony
patrimony
sanctimony
sonny
sunny
Tunney
tunny
unsunny

ŬN'ij
dunnage
gunnage
tonnage

ŪN'ik
Munich
Punic
runic
tunic

ŬN'in
run-in

ŪN'ing
ballooning
communing
crooning
expugning
harpooning
impugning

mooning
nooning
oppugning
pruning
spooning
swooning
tuning

ŬN'ing
cunning
dunning
funning
gunning
outrunning
overrunning
punning
running
shunning
stunning
sunning

Ū'nis
Eunice
Tunis

ŪN'ish
buffoonish
poltroonish

ŬN'ish
punish
Hunnish

ŪN'ist
balloonist
bassoonist
harpoonist
opportunist

Ū'nit
unit

ŬN'izm
buffoonism
opportunism
poltroonism

ŬN'jent
pungent

ŬN'jest
expungest, etc.

ŬN'jeth
expungeth, etc.

ŬN'jez
expunges
lunges
plunges
sponges

ŬN'ji
plungy
spongy

ŬN'jing
expunging
lunging
plunging
sponging

ŬN'jun
dungeon
plungeon

ŬN'jur
blunger
expunger
lunger
plunger
sponger

ŬN'kan
Duncan
(cf. ŬNG'kin)

ŬN'les
moonless
runeless
tuneless

ŬN'les
runless
sonless
sunless

ŬN'lit
moonlight
noon-light

ŬN'man
gunman

ŪN'nes
inopportune-
   ness
jejuneness
opportuneness

Ū'no
Bruno
Juno

ŪN'riz
moonrise

ŬN'si
Munsey

ŬN'stan,
  ŬN'ston
Dunstan
Funston

ŬN'stur
gunster
punster

ŬN'tal
contrapuntal
frontal
gruntle

ŬN'ted
affronted
blunted
bunted
confronted
fronted
grunted
hunted
punted
shunted
stunted
unblunted
unwonted
wonted

ŬN'test
affrontest
bluntest
buntest
confrontest
gruntest
huntest
puntest
shuntest
stuntest

ŬN'teth
affronteth
blunteth
bunteth
confronteth
grunteth

hunteth
punteth
shunteth
stunteth

ŬN'ti
punty
runty
stunty

ŬN'ting
affronting
bunting
confronting
fronting
grunting
head-hunting
hunting
punting
reed-bunting
shunting
stunting
yellow-bunting

ŬNT'les
frontless
wontless

ŬNT'nes
bluntness
stuntness

ŬN'to
junto

ŬN'tri
country

ŬN'tu
unto

ŬN'tur
affronter
blunter
bunter
confronter
fortune-hunter
grunter
Gunter
head-hunter
hunter
legacy-hunter
punter
shunter
stunter

ŬNTS'vil
Blountsville
Huntsville

Ū'nuk
eunuch

ŪN'ur
attuner
ballooner
communer
crooner
dragooner
harpooner
importuner
impugner
interlunar
lacunar
lampooner
lunar
mooner
novilunar
oppugner
piano-tuner
plenilunar
pruner

---

schooner

ŬP'ans

come-uppance
thruppence

ŪP'e

whoopee
(cf. ŪP'i)

ŪP'est

coopest
droopest
dupest
groupest
loopest
recoupest
scoopest
stoopest
swoopest
troopest
whoopest

ŬP'est

suppest, etc.

ŬP'et

puppet

ŪP'eth

coopeth
droopeth
dupeth
groupeth
loopeth
recoupeth
scoopeth
stoopeth
swoopeth
troopeth
whoopeth

ŬP'eth

suppeth, etc.

ŬP'i

croupy
droopy
soupy
(cf. whoopee)

ŬP'i

cuppy
guppy
puppy

Ū'pid

Cupid
stupid

Ū'pil

pupil
(cf. Ū'p'l)

ŬP'ing

cooping
drooping
duping
grouping
hooping
looping
recouping
scooping
stooping
swooping
trooping
whooping

ŬP'ing

cupping
supping
tupping

ŬP'ish

puppish
uppish

ŪP''l

octuple
quadruple
quintuple
septuple
sextuple
scruple
subduple
(cf. pupil)

ŬP''l

couple
supple

ŪP'lest

scruplest, etc.

ŬP'lest

couplest, etc.

ŪP'let

octuplet
quintuplet, etc.

ŪP'leth

scrupleth, etc

ŬP'leth

coupleth, etc.

ŬP'lur

coupler
suppler

ŬP'ment

aggroupment
recoupment

Ū'pon

coupon
jupon

semilunar
sooner
spooner
sublunar
swooner
translunar
tuner

ŬN'ur

dunner
forerunner
gunner
overrunner
punner
runner
stunner

ŪN'yon

communion
disunion
excommunion
intercom-
    munion
reunion
trades-union
union

ŬN'yon

bunion
munnion
onion
ronyon
trunnion

ŪN'yor

junior

Ū'pa

pupa
supa

ŬP'or

stupor
(see ŬP'ur)

ŬP'shal

antenuptial
nuptial
post-nuptial

ŬP'shun

abruption
corruption
disruption
eruption
incorruption
interruption
irruption
ruption

ŬP'ted

abrupted
corrupted
disrupted
interrupted
irrupted

ŬP'test

abruptest
corruptest
interruptest

ŬP'teth

corrupteth, etc.

ŬP'ting

corrupting
erupting
interrupting

ŬP'tiv

corruptive

disruptive
eruptive
incorruptive
interruptive
irruptive

ŬPT'li

abruptly
corruptly, etc.

ŬPT'nes

abruptness
corruptness
incorruptness

ŬP'ur

cooper
drooper
duper
grouper
hooper
looper
recouper
scooper
snooper
stooper
stupor
super
swooper
trooper
whooper

ŬP'ur

crupper
cupper
scupper
supper
upper

ŬP'urt

Rupert
(cf. Newport)

ŬP'ward

upward

Ū'ra

Angostura
appoggiatura
bravura
caesura
coloratura
Cuticura
datura
fissura
flexura
Keturah
pietra-dura
pleura
purpura
sura
velatura
vettura

Ū'ral

antemural
caesural
commissural
crural
extramural
intermural
interneural
intramural
jural
mural
neural
pleural
plural
rural
sinecural
sural
tellural
Ural

ÛR'ans

allurance
assurance
durance
endurance
insurance
perdurance
reassurance

ÛR'āt

curate

ÛR'ăt

jurat

ÛR'bal

herbal
verbal

ÛR'ban

suburban
turban
urban

ÛR'bans

disturbance

ÛR'bar

durbar

ÛR'bat

acerbate
perturbate

ÛR'best

blurbest
curbest
disturbest
perturbest

ÛR'bet

sherbet

āle,   câre,   ădd,   ärm,   ăsk;   mē,   hĕre,   ĕnd;   īce,   ĭll:

ÛR'beth
blurbeth
curbeth
disturbeth
perturbeth

ÛR'bi
Derby
herby
Iturbi
Kirby

ÛR'bid
herbid
turbid

ÛR'bin
turbine

ÛR'bing
curbing
disturbing
perturbing

ÛR'bot
burbot
turbot

ÛR'bur
Berber
blurber
curber
disturber
Ferber
Gerber
perturber
superber

ÛR'burt
Herbert

ÛR'chant
merchant
perchant

ÛR'chas
purchase

ÛR'chast
purchased

ÛR'chen
birchen
(cf. urchin)

ÛR'chest
birchest
lurchest
perchest
searchest
smirchest
(cf. purchased)

ÛR'cheth
bircheth
lurcheth
percheth
searcheth
smircheth

ÛR'chez
besmirches
birches
churches
lurches
perches
researches
searches
smirches

ÛR'chif
kerchief

ÛR'ching
besmirching
birching
churching
lurching
perching
searching
smirching

ÛRCH'les
churchless
smirchless

ÛR'chur
besmircher
bircher
lurcher
percher
researcher
searcher
smircher
(cf. nurture)

ÛRD'book
herdbook
word-book

ÛR'ded
begirded
curded
engirded
girded
herded
sherded
worded

ÛR'den
burden
disburden
overburden

unburden
(cf. ÛR'don)

ÛR'dest
absurdest
begirdest
engirdest
girdest
heardest

ÛR'deth
begirdeth, etc.

ÛR'di
birdie
curdy
hurdy-gurdy
sturdy
wordy

ÛR'dikt
verdict

ÛR'ding
begirding
engirding
girding
herding
ungirding
wording

ÛR'd'l
begirdle
curdle
engirdle
girdle
hurdle

ÛR'don
Burdon
guerdon
(cf. ÛR'den)

ōld, ôr, ŏdd, oil, fŏŏt, out; ūse, ûrn, ŭp; THis, thin

ŬR'dŭr
verdure
(cf. perjure)

ŬR'dŭr
absurder
Burder
engirder
girder
herder
murder
self-murder
thirder

ŬRDZ'man
herdsman
wordsman

ŬR'el
squirrel
Burrell

ŬR'ens
concurrence
deterrence
incurrence
intercurrence
occurrence
recurrence
transference

ŬR'ent, ŬR'ant
concurrent
currant
current
decurrent
deterrent
intercurrent
recurrent
susurrant
undercurrent

ŬR'est
abjurest
adjurest
allurest
assurest
conjurest
curest
demurest
endurest
ensurest
immurest
impurest
insurest
lurest
maturest
moorest
obscurest
poorest
procurest
purest
reassurest
securest
surest
tourest
unmoorest

ŬR'est
bestirrest
blurrest
concurrest
conferrest
deferrest
demurrest
errest
incurrest
inferrest
interrest
preferrest
purrest
referrest
spurrest

stirrest
transferrest

ŬR'et
turret

ŬR'eth
abjureth
adjureth
allureth
conjureth
cureth
endureth
immureth
lureth
matureth
obscureth
procureth
secureth
assureth
ensureth
insureth
mooreth
reassureth
toureth
unmooreth

ŬR'eth
bestirreth
blurreth
concurreth
conferreth
deferreth
erreth
demurreth
incurreth
inferreth
interreth
occurreth
preferreth
purreth

recurreth
referreth
spurreth
stirreth
transferreth

ŬR'fas
surface

ŬR'fekt
perfect

ŬR'fi
Durfey
Murphy
scurfy
surfy
turfy

ŬR'fit
surfeit

ŬR'for
therefore
(cf. wherefore)

ŬR'fum
perfume

ŬR'gat
expurgate
objurgate
virgate

ŬR'g'l
burgle
gurgle

ŬR'glar
burglar
gurgler

ÛR′go
a tergo
ergo
Virgo

ÛR′gur
burgher
jerguer

ÛR′gus
demiurgus
Mergus
thaumaturgus

ÛR′i
de jure
Drury
ewry
fury
houri
Jewry
jury
Missouri

ÛR′i
burry
curry
firry
flurry
furry
hurry
hurry-scurry
lurry
Murray
scurry
Surrey
slurry
whirry
worry

ÛR′id
lurid

ÛR′id
curried
flurried
hurried
scurried
worried

ÛR′ij
moorage
murage

ÛR′ij
courage
demurrage
discourage
encourage

ÛR′ik
hydrosulphuric
hydrotelluric
purpuric
sulphuric
telluric

ÛR′ik
myrrhic

ÛR′im
purim
urim

ÛR′in
burin
daturin
neurin
neurine

ÛR′ing
abjuring
adjuring
alluring

assuring
conjuring
curing
during
enduring
ensuring
everduring
immuring
insuring
inuring
juring
luring
manuring
maturing
mooring
non-juring
obscuring
procuring
reassuring
securing
touring
unmooring

ÛR′ing
astirring
bestirring
blurring
concurring
conferring
deferring
demurring
erring
incurring
inferring
interring
non-concurring
occurring
preferring
purring
recurring
referring

shirring
slurring
spurring
stirring
transferring
unerring
whirring
(cf. herring)

ÛR′ish
amateurish
boorish
Moorish
poorish

ÛR′ish
burrish
currish
flourish
nourish

ÛR′ist
caricaturist
jurist
purist
tourist

ÛR′iz
curries
flurries
hurries
scurries
worries

ÛR′izm
purism
tourism

ÛR′jens
convergence
deturgence

divergence
emergence
resurgence
submergence

ŬR'jent
abstergent
assurgent
convergent
detergent
divergent
emergent
insurgent
resurgent
splurgent
turgent
urgent
vergent

ŬR'jest
convergest
dirgest
divergest
emergest
mergest
purgest
scourgest
splurgest
submergest
surgest
urgest

ŬR'jeth
convergeth
dirgeth
divergeth
emergeth
mergeth
purgeth
scourgeth
splurgeth

submergeth
surgeth
urgeth

ŬR'jez
asperges
Boanerges
converges
dirges
diverges
emerges
merges
purges
scourges
serges
submerges
surges
urges
verges

ŬR'ji
aciurgy
clergy
dirgie
dramaturgy
metallurgy
periergy
surgy
thaumaturgy

ŬR'jid
turgid

ŬR'jik
chirurgic
demiurgic
dramaturgic
energic
liturgic
metallurgic

thaumaturgic
theurgic

ŬR'jin
virgin

ŬR'jing
converging
dirging
diverging
emerging
immerging
merging
purging
scourging
splurging
submerging
surging
urging
verging

ŬR'jist
dramaturgist
metallurgist
thaumaturgist

ŬR'jun
burgeon
Spurgeon
sturgeon
surgeon

ŬR'jūr
perjure
(cf. verdure)

ŬR'jŭr
converger
dirger
diverger
emerger

merger
purger
scourger
submerger
urger
verger

ŬR'jus
verjuice

ŬR'kal
Lupercal
novercal
(cf. circle)

ŬR'kest
clerkest, etc.

ŬR'keth
clerketh, etc.

ŬR'ki
jerky
lurky
mirky
murky
perky
quirky
shirky
smirky
talk turkey
turkey

ŬR'kin
firkin
gherkin
jerkin
merkin

ŬR'kins
Firkins

āle, câre, ădd, ärm, åsk; mē, hĕre, ĕnd; īce, ĭll:

Perkins
gherkins, etc.

ÛR'king
aworking
clerking
hard-working
jerking
lurking
perking
shirking
smirking
working

ÛR'kish
quirkish
Turkish

ÛR'kit
circuit

ÛR'k'l
circle
encircle
Merkle
semicircle
turkle

ÛR'klet
circlet

ÛR'kli
circly
clerkly

ÛR'kling
circling

ÛRK'man
Turkman
workman

ÛRK'som
irksome
mirksome

ÛR'kur
burker
jerker
jerquer
lurker
shirker
smirker
wonder-worker
worker

ÛR'kus
bifurcous
circus
Quercus
(cf. work-
house)

ÛR'kwoiz
turquoise

ÛRLD'li
worldly

ÛRLD'ling
worldling

ÛR'lest
curlest
furlest
hurlest
swirlest
twirlest
unfurlest
whirlest

ÛR'leth
curleth

furleth
hurleth
purleth
swirleth
twirleth
unfurleth
whirleth

ÛRL'hood
girlhood

ÛR'li
demurely
maturely
obscurely
poorly
purely
securely

ÛR'li
burly
churly
curly
early
girlie
girly
hurly-burly
knurly
pearly
Shirley
surly
swirly
whirly

ÛR'lin
merlin
pearlin

ÛR'ling
curling
furling
herling

hurling
pearling
purling
Sperling
sterling
Stirling
swirling
twirling
uncurling
unfurling
upcurling
upwhirling

ÛR'lish
churlish
girlish
pearlish

ÛR'loin
purloin
sirloin

ÛR'lu
curlew
purlieu

ÛR'lur
burler
curler
furler
hurler
pearler
purler
skirler
twirler
whirler

ÛR'ma
Burma
derma
Irma
syrma

ÛR'mad
mermaid

ÛR'mal
dermal
diathermal
epidermal
geothermal
hydrothermal
hypodermal
isogeothermal
isothermal
pachydermal
synthermal
taxidermal
thermal

ÛR'man
cousin-german
firman
German
merman
(cf. sermon)

ÛR'mans
affirmance
confirmance
disaffirmance

ÛR'ment
abjurement
allurement
conjurement
immurement
obscurement
procurement

ÛR'ment,
ÛR'mant
affirmant

averment
deferment
determent
disinterment
ferment
interment
preferment
referment

ÛR'mest
confirmest
firmest
infirmest
squirmest
termest
wormest

ÛR'meth
confirmeth, etc.

ÛR'mez
Hermes
kermes

ÛR'mi
germy
taxidermy
wormy

ÛR'mik
adiathermic
dermic
diathermic
endermic
epidermic
geothermic
hydrodermic
hypodermic
isogeothermic
pachydermic
sclerodermic

taxidermic
thermic

ÛR'min
determine
ermine
vermin

ÛR'mind
determined
ermined
undetermined

ÛR'ming
affirming
confirming
squirming
worming

ÛR'mis
dermis
epidermis

ÛR'mish
skirmish

ÛR'mīt
termite

ÛR'mĭt
hermit
permit

ÛRM'li
firmly
termly

ÛR'moil
turmoil

ÛR'mur
affirmer

bemurmur
confirmer
firmer
infirmer
murmur
squirmer
termer
termoı
wormer

ÛR'na
Myrna
Verna

ÛR'nal
cavernal
coeternal
colonel
diurnal
diuternal
eternal
external
fraternal
hesternal
hibernal
hodiernal
infernal
internal
journal
kernel
lucernal
maternal
nocturnal
paraphernal
paternal
semi-diurnal
sempiternal
sternal
supernal
urnal
vernal

**ÛR′nant,
 ÛR′nent**
alternant
secernent
vernant

ÛR′nard
Bernard

ÛR′nas
furnace

ÛR′nat
alternate
cothurnate
subalternate
ternate

ÛR′ned
learned
(see ÛRN +
ed)

ÛR′nes
demureness
immatureness
impureness
insecureness
matureness
obscureness
poorness
pureness
secureness
sureness

ÛR′nes
Furness
(cf. furnace)

ÛR′nest
adjournest

burnest
churnest
concernest
discernest
earnest
Ernest
learnest
over-earnest
overturnest
returnest
sojournest
spurnest
sternest
turnest
yearnest

ÛR′neth
adjourneth
burneth
churneth
concerneth
discerneth
learneth
overturneth
returneth
sojourneth
spurneth
turneth
yearneth

ÛR′ni
attorney
Berney
Birney
burny-burny
ferny
Gurney
journey
Turney
tourney

ÛR′ning
adjourning
booklearning
burning
churning
concerning
discerning
earning
heart-burning
learning
overburning
overturning
returning
sojourning
spurning
table-turning
turning
undiscerning
unlearning
upturning
urning
yearning

ÛR′nish
burnish
furnish

ÛR′nisht
burnished
furnished
unburnished
unfurnished

ÛRN′ment
adjournment
attornment
concernment
discernment
secernment
sojournment

ÛRN′nes
sternness

ÛR′no
inferno
Sterno

ÛR′num
laburnum

ÛR′nur
adjourner
burner
discerner
earner
learner
overturner
returner
sojourner
spurner
sterner
turner
yearner

ÛR′nus
cothurnus

ÛR′o
bureau
chiaroscuro
maduro

ÛR′o
borough
burrow
furrow
thorough

ÛR′od
burrowed
furrowed
unfurrowed

ŬR'or
furor
juror
(cf. ŬR'ur)

ŬR'pent
serpent

ŬR'pest
chirpest, etc.

ŬR'peth
chirpeth
turpeth
usurpeth

ŬR'ping
burping
chirping
usurping

ŬR'p'l
empurple
purple

ŬR'pos
purpose

ŬR'pur
burper
chirper
usurper

ŬR'sa
ursa
vice versa

ŬR'sal
controversal
rehearsal
reversal

tercel
transversal
universal
ursal
versal

ŬR'sant
aversant
recursant
versant

ŬR'sed
accursed
(see ŬRS+ed)

ŬR'sest
accursest
becursest
coercest
conversest
cursest
disbursest
dispersest
immersest
interspersest
nursest
rehearsest
reimbursest
reversest
traversest

ŬR'set
tercet

ŬR'seth
accurseth
becurseth
coerceth
converseth
curseth
disburseth

disperseth
immerseth
intersperseth
nurseth
rehearseth
reimburseth
reverseth
traverseth

ŬR'sez
accurses
amerces
becurses
coerces
converses
curses
disburses
disperses
hearses
immerses
intersperses
nurses
purses
rehearses
reimburses
reverses
submerses
traverses
verses

ŬR'shal
commercial
controversial
tertial
uncommercial

ŬR'ship
worship

ŬR'shum
nasturtium

ŬR'shun
abstersion
animadversion
apertion
aspersion
assertion
aversion
circumversion
coercion
concertion
contraversion
controversion
conversion
demersion
desertion
disconcertion
discursion
dispersion
diversion
emersion
eversion
excursion
exertion
extersion
immersion
incursion
insertion
inspersion
intersertion
interspersion
introversion
inversion
mersion
nasturtion
obversion
perversion
recursion
retroversion
reversion
self-assertion
submersion

subversion
tertian
version
(cf. ŬR'si-an)

ŬR'si
Circe
controversy
gramercy
mercy
Mersey
Percy
pursy
Searcy

ŬR'sing
accursing
becursing
coercing
conversing
cursing
disbursing
dispersing
immersing
nursing
rehearsing
reimbursing
reversing
transversing
traversing
versing

ŬR'siv
abstersive
animadversive
aspersive
aversive
coercive
conversive
cursive
decursive

detersive
discursive
dispersive
eversive
excursive
incursive
perversive
precursive
subversive

ŬRS'ment
amercement
disbursement
imbursement
reimburse-
    ment

ŬRS'nes
adverseness
averseness
perverseness
terseness

ŬR'son
Gerson
McPherson
person

ŬR'sted
bursted
thirsted
worsted

ŬR'stest
burstest, etc.

ŬR'steth
bursteth, etc.

ŬR'sti
thirsty

ŬR'sting
bursting
thirsting
worsting

ŬR'stur
burster
thirster

ŬR'sur
accurser
amercer
ante-cursor
bursar
coercer
commercer
converser
curser
cursor
disburser
disperser
hearser
immerser
mercer
nurser
perverser
precursor
purser
rehearser
reimburser
reverser
traverser
verser
worser

ŬR'sus
excursus
thyrsus
ursus
versus

ŬR'ta
Alberta
Elberta

ŬR'tan
certain
curtain
encurtain
incertain
uncertain

ŬR'ted
adverted
asserted
averted
blurted
concerted
converted
deserted
disconcerted
diverted
exerted
flirted
inserted
interserted
inverted
perverted
preconcerted
reverted
spurted
squirted
subverted
undiverted
unperverted

ŬR'ten
thirteen

ŬR'tens
advertence
inadvertence
misadvertence

ōld, ȯr, ŏdd, oil, fŏŏt, out; ūse, ûrn, ŭp; THis, thin

ÛR'test
advertest
assertest
avertest
blurtest
concertest
controvertest
convertest
curtest
disconcertest
divertest
exertest
hurtest
insertest
invertest
pertest
pervertest
revertest
skirtest
spurtest
subvertest

ÛR'teth
averteth
asserteth
averteth
blurteth
concerteth
controverteth
converteth
disconcerteth
diverteth
exerteth
hurteth
inserteth
inverteth
perverteth
reverteth
skirteth
spurteth
subverteth

ÛR'tha
Bertha
Hertha

ÛR'THen
burthen
disburthen
unburthen

ÛR'then
earthen

ÛR'THur
further

ÛR'THest
furthest

ÛRth'ful
mirthful
worthful

ÛRth'les
birthless
mirthless
worthless

ÛR'THi
noteworthy
sea-worthy
trust-worthy
worthy
unworthy

ÛR'thi
earthy

ÛR'ti
cherty
dirty

flirty
Gertie
thirty

ÛR'ting
adverting
asserting
averting
blurting
concerting
controverting
converting
deserting
disconcerting
diverting
exerting
flirting
hurting
inserting
interserting
interverting
inverting
perverting
preconcerting
retroverting
reverting
self-asserting
shirting
skirting
spurting
squirting
subverting

ÛR'tiv
assertive
divertive
exertive
furtive
revertive
self-assertive

ÛR'tis
Curtis

ÛR't'l
fertile
hurtle
kirtle
myrtle
spurtle
turtle
whortle

ÛRT'les
shirtless
skirtless

ÛRT'li
alertly
curtly
expertly
inertly
inexpertly
pertly

ÛRT'nes
alertness
curtness
expertness
inertness
inexpertness
pertness

ÛR'ton
Berton
(cf. ÛR'tan)

ÛR'trud
Gertrude

ÛRT'si
curtsey

āle, câre, ădd, ärm, åsk; mē, hęre, ĕnd; īce, ĭll;

ŪR'tu
virtue

ŪR'tūr
nurture
(cf. ŪR'chur)

ŪR'tŭr
adverter
animadverter
asserter
averter
converter
curter
disconcerter
diverter
exerter
hurter
inserter
inverter
perter
perverter
preconcerter
spurter
squirter
subverter

ŪR'up
stirrup
(cf. ĬR'up)

ŪR'ur
abjurer
adjurer
allurer
assurer
conjurer
curer
demurer
endurer
ensurer

immurer
impurer
insurer
inurer
juror
lurer
manurer
maturer
moorer
nonjuror
obscurer
poorer
procurer
purer
reassurer
securer
surer
tourer
unmoorer
(cf. ŪR'or)

ŪR'ur
averrer
bestirrer
blurrer
concurrer
conferrer
deferrer
demurrer
incurrer
inferrer
interrer
preferrer
spurrer
stirrer
transferrer

ŪR'us
anurous
Arcturus
dolichurus

Eurus
urus

ŪR'us
susurrous
wurrus

ŪR'uz
Burroughs
Burrows
(cf. ŪR'o + s)

ŪR'va
Minerva

ŪR'val
acerval
curval

ŪR'vans,
　　ŪR'vens
fervence
inobservance
observance
unobservance

ŪR'vant,
　　ŪR'vent
conservant
curvant
fervent
inobservant
observant
recurvant
servant
unobservant

ŪR'vat
acervate
curvate
enervate

incurvate
recurvate
trinervate

ŪR'ven
nervine

ŪR'vest
conservest
curvest
deservest
observest
preservest
reservest
servest
swervest
unnervest

ŪR'veth
conserveth
curveth
deserveth
observeth
preserveth
reserveth
serveth
swerveth
unnerveth

ŪR'vi
nervy
scurvy
topsy-turvy

ŪR'vid
fervid
perfervid
topsy-turvied

ŪR'vĭl
servile

ÛR'vĭl
chervil
servile

ÛR'vĭm
cervine
nervine

ÛR'vĭng
conserving
curving
deserving
Irving
nerving
observing
preserving
reserving
serving
swerving
time-serving
undeserving
unnerving
unobserving
unswerving

ÛR'vĭs
lip-service
merchant-serv-
   ice
Purvis
sea-service
service
unservice

ÛRV'les
nerveless

ÛR'vur
conserver
deserver
fervor

game-preserver
life-preserver
nerver
observer
preserver
reserver
server
swerver
time-server
unnerver

ÛR'vus
nervous
recurvous

ÛR'win
Erwin
Irwin
Merwin

ÛRZ'da
Thursday

ÛR'zha
Persia

ÛR'zhun
animadver-
   sion
aspersion
aversion
conversion
demersion
discursion
dispersion
diversion
excursion
incursion
introversion
inversion
perversion

reversion
subversion
version

ÛR'zi
furzy
jersey
kersey

Ū'sa
Arethusa
Coosa
Medusa
Sousa
Susa
Tallapoosa
Tuscaloosa

ŪS'al
hypotenusal

ŬS'chun
adustion
combustion
fustian

ŪS'ed
deuced
(see ŪS+ed)

ŪS'en
loosen
unloosen

ŪS'ens
translucence

ŪS'ent
abducent
adducent
conducent

interlucent
lucent
producent
reducent
relucent
traducent
tralucent
translucent
unlucent

ŪS'est
abstrusest
adducest
conducest
deducest
inducest
introducest
loosest
producest
profusest
reducest
reproducest
seducest
sprucest
traducest
unloosest

ŬS'est
fussest, etc.

ŬS'et
gusset
russet

ŪS'eth
adduceth
conduceth
deduceth
educeth
induceth
introduceth

looseth
produceth
reduceth
reproduceth
seduceth
spruceth
traduceth
unlooseth

ŬS'eth
fusseth, etc.

ŬS'ez
abuses
adduces
burnooses
cabooses
conduces
deduces
Druses
excuses
induces
introduces
juices
looses
nooses
produces
reduces
reproduces
seduces
sluices
spruces
traduces
truces
unlooses
uses

ŬS'ez
buses
busses
cusses

discusses
fusses
Gus's
musses
trusses

ŬS'ful
juiceful
useful

ŪSH'a
Jerusha

ŬSH'a
Prussia
Russia

ŬSH'al
crucial
fiducial

ŬSH'an
Prussian
Russian

ŬSH'est
blushest
brushest
crushest
flushest
gushest
hushest
rushest

ŬSH'eth
blusheth
brusheth
crusheth
flusheth
gusheth
husheth
rusheth

ŬSH'ez
blushes
brushes
crushes
flushes
gushes
hushes
lushes
mushes
onrushes
plushes
rushes
thrushes
tushes
uprushes

ŬSH'i
blushy
brushy
gushy
lushy
rushy
slushy

ŪSH'ing
douching
ruching

ŬSH'ing
blushing
brushing
crushing
flushing
gushing
hushing
lushing
rushing
unblushing

Ū'shun
ablution

absolution
allocution
attribution
circumlocution
circumvolu-
    tion
collocution
comminution
constitution
contribution
convolution
destitution
devolution
dilution
diminution
dissolution
distribution
electrocution
elocution
evolution
execution
imminution
insecution
institution
interlocution
involution
irresolution
Lilliputian
locution
obvolution
persecution
pollution
prosecution
prostitution
redargution
resolution
restitution
retribution
revolution
solution
substitution

ventrilocution
volution

ŬSH'un
concussion
discussion
incussion
percussion
Prussian
recussion
repercussion
Russian
succussion

ŬSH'ur
blusher
brusher
crusher
flusher
gusher
husher
plusher
rusher
usher

ŪSH'us
Lucius

ŬSH'us
luscious

ŪS'i
goosy
juicy
Lucy
sluicy

ŬS'ĭ
fussy
hussy
mussy

ŪS'id
lucid
mucid
pellucid
translucid

ŪS'ij
abusage
usage

ŪS'il
protrusile

ŪS'ing
adducing
conducing
deducing
educing
inducing
introducing
loosing
producing
reducing
reproducing
seducing
sprucing
traducing
unloosing

ŬS'ing
bussing
cussing
discussing
fussing
mussing
trussing

ŪS'iv
abusive
allusive
collusive

conclusive
conducive
confusive
contusive
deducive
delusive
diffusive
effusive
elusive
exclusive
illusive
inclusive
inconclusive
infusive
inobtrusive
intrusive
obtrusive
perfusive
reclusive
seclusive
seducive
transfusive

ŬS'iv
concussive
discussive
percussive
repercussive
successive

ŬS'kan
Della-Cruscan
dusken
Etruscan
molluscan
Tuscan

ŬS'kat
coruscate
infuscate
obfuscate

ŬS'kest
duskest, etc.

ŬS'ket
busket
musket

ŬS'keth
dusketh, etc.

ŬSki
dusky
husky
musky
tusky

ŬS'kin
buskin
Ruskin

ŬS'king
dusking
husking
tusking

ŬS'kul
crepuscule
majuscule
minuscule
opuscule

ŬS'kur
husker
tusker

ŬS'l
bustle
corpuscle
hustle
justle
muscle

mussel
opuscle
rustle
tussle

ŬS'les
juiceless
useless

ŬS'lest
bustlest, etc.

ŬS'leth
bustleth, etc.

ŬS'ling
bustling
hustling
muscling
rustling
tussling

ŬS'lur
bustler
hustler
rustler
tussler

ŬS"lz
Brussels
bustles, etc.

ŬS'ment
conducement
deducement
inducement
reducement
seducement
superinduce-
    ment
traducement

ŬS'nes
abstruseness
diffuseness
looseness
obtuseness
profuseness
recluseness
spruceness

Ū'so
Crusoe
trousseau
whoso

Ū'som
gruesome
twosome

ŬS'ta
Augusta

ŬS'tas
Eustace

ŬS'tat
incrustate

ŬS'ted
adjusted
bedusted
betrusted
busted
combusted
crusted
disgusted
distrusted
dusted
encrusted
entrusted
fusted
lusted

mistrusted
rusted
trusted

ŬS'test
adjustest
disgustest
distrustest
dustest
encrustest
entrustest
justest
lustest
mistrustest
robustest
rustest
thrustest
trustest

ŬS'teth
adjusteth
disgusteth
distrusteth
dusteth
encrusteth
entrusteth
lusteth
mistrusteth
thrusteth
trusteth

ŬST'ful
distrustful
lustful
mistrustful
overtrustful
trustful
untrustful

ŬS'ti
crusty

dusty
fustie
fusty
gusty
lusty
musty
rusty
trusty

ŬS'tik
fustic
rustic

ŬS'tin
Dustin
Justin

ŬS'ting
adjusting
bedusting
betrusting
busting
coadjusting
crusting
disgusting
distrusting
dusting
encrusting
entrusting
lusting
mistrusting
overtrusting
rusting
self-adjusting
thrusting
trusting
unmistrusting

ŬS'tingz
dustings
hustings
thrustings

ŬS'tis
Custis
justice

ŬS'tiv
adjustive
combustive

ŬST'li
augustly
justly
robustly

ŬST'ment
adjustment
encrustment
maladjustment

ŬST'nes
augustness
justness
robustness

ŬS'to
gusto

ŬS'tom
custom
(cf. Rustum)

ŬS'tral
lacustral
lustral
palustral

ŬS'trat
frustrate
illustrate

ŬS'trin
lacustrine
palustrine

ŬS'trum
flustrum
lustrum

ŬS'trus
blustrous
lustrous

ŬS'tur
booster
brewster
Fewster
jouster
rooster
Worcester

ŬS'tur
adjuster
bluster
buster
coadjuster
cluster
Custer
distruster
duster
filibuster
fluster
juster
knuckle-duster
lack-lustre
luster
lustre
muster
robuster
thruster
trust-buster
truster

ŬS'turd
blustered
bustard

clustered
custard
flustered
lustered
mustard
mustered

ŬS'tus
Augustus
Justus

ŬS'ur
abstruser
adducer
conducer
deducer
inducer
introducer
looser
producer
reducer
reproducer
seducer
sprucer
traducer

ŬS'ur
cusser
discusser
fusser
musser
trusser

ŪT'al
brutal
footle
tootle
(cf. ŪT'il)

ŪT'at
circumnutate

immutate
scutate

ŪT'ed
allocuted
bebooted
booted
bruited
comminuted
commuted
computed
confuted
constituted
convoluted
deputed
diluted
disputed
elocuted
electrocuted
executed
fluted
fruited
hooted
immuted
imputed
instituted
involuted
looted
mooted
persecuted
polluted
prosecuted
prostituted
recruited
refuted
reputed
rooted
saluted
self-constituted
substituted
suited

tooted
transmuted
unbooted
unconfuted
undisputed
unpersecuted
unpolluted
unrooted
unsuited
uprooted
voluted
(cf. bootied,
   putid)

ŪT′ed
butted
rutted, etc.

ŪT′est
acutest
astutest
commutest
confutest
constitutest
cutest
deputest
dilutest
disputest
executest
hootest
imputest
institutest
lootest
minutest
mutest
persecutest
recruitest
refutest
resolutest
salutest
shootest

substitutest
suitest
transmutest
uprootest

ŬT′est
buttest
ruttest, etc.

ŪT′eth
commuteth
confuteth
constituteth
deputeth
diluteth
disputeth
executeth
hooteth
imputeth
instituteth
looteth
overshooteth
persecuteth
polluteth
prosecuteth
recruiteth
refuteth
rooteth
saluteth
shooteth
suiteth
transmuteth
unbooteth
uprooteth

ŬT′eth
butteth
rutteth, etc.

ŪT′ful
fruitful

ŪTH′est
smoothest
soothest

Ūth′ful
ruthful
toothful
truthful
untruthful
youthful

ŪTH′ing
smoothing
soothing

Ūth′ing
toothing

Ŭth′ing
doth-ing
nothing

Ūth′les
ruthless
toothless
truthless

ŪTH′nes
smoothness

Ūth′nes
uncouthness

Ūth′som
toothsome
youthsome

ŪTH′ur
smoother
soother

Ūth′ur
Luther
uncouther

Ŭth′ur
another
brother
Charter
   brother
foremother
foster-brother
foster-mother
half-brother
mother
other
smother
t′other

ŬTH′urn
Sothern
southern

ŪT′i
agouti
booty
beauty
cootie
cutie
Djibouti
duty
fluty
freebooty
fruity
Jibuti
looty
rooty
snooty
sooty
tutti-frutti

ōld, ôr, ŏdd, oil, fŏŏt, out; ūse, ûrn, ŭp; THis, thin

ŬT'i
butty
gutty
jutty
nutty
putty
rutty
smutty
tutty

ŬT'ij
fruitage
mutage
scutage

ŬT'ik
diazeutic
emphyteutic
hermeneutic
maieutic
pharmaceutic
propædeutic
scorbutic
therapeutic
toreutic

ŬT'il
futile
inutile
rutile
sutile
(cf. ŪT'al)

ŬT'ing
booting
comminuting
commuting
computing
confuting
constituting
darned tooting

deputing
diluting
disputing
executing
fluting
fruiting
high-faluting
hooting
imputing
instituting
looting
mooting
offshooting
outshooting
overshooting
permuting
persecuting
polluting
prosecuting
prostituting
reconstituting
recruiting
refuting
rooting
saluting
scooting
shooting
substituting
suiting
tooting
transmuting
unbooting
unrooting
uprooting

ŬT'ing
abutting
butting
crosscutting
cutting
glass-cutting

glutting
gutting
jutting
nutting
putting
rebutting
rutting
shutting
strutting

ŬT'ish
brutish
sootish

ŬT'ish
ruttish
sluttish

ŬT'ist
flutist
hermeneutist
lutist
pharmaceutist
therapeutist

ŬT'iv
coadjutive
constitutive
indutive
persecutive
resolutive

ŬT'izm
brutism
mutism

ŬT''l
abuttal
cuttle
guttle
rebuttal

ruttle
scuttle
shuttle
subtle
suttle
Tuttle

ŬT'las
cutlass

ŬT'les
bootless
fruitless

ŬT'lest
scuttlest, etc.

ŬT'let
cutlet

ŬT'leth
scuttleth, etc.

ŬT'li
absolutely
posilutely

ŬT'ling
footling
tootling

ŬT'ling
gutling
scuttling
sutling

ŬT'lur
butler
cutler
scuttler
subtler
sutler

ŪT'ment
confutement
imbrutement
recruitment

ŪT'nes
absoluteness
acuteness
astuteness
cuteness
hirsuteness
minuteness
muteness

Ū'to
Pluto

Ū'ton
Brewton
Newton
Teuton

ŬT'on
bachelor-
    button
button
Dutton
glutton
Hutton
mutton
Sutton

ŬT'or
suitor
tutor, etc.
(see ŪT'ur)

ŪT'ral
neutral

ŬT'res
buttress

ŪT'rid
putrid

ŪT'riks
persecutrix
tutrix

ŪT'ron
neutron

ŪT'si
tootsie-wootsie

ŪT'ūr
future
puture
suture

ŪT'ŭr
accoutre
acuter
astuter
booter
chuter
coadjutor
commuter
computer
confuter
constitutor
cuter
deputer
diluter
disputer
executor
fluter
fouter
freebooter
hooter
imputer
institutor
looter

luter
minuter
mooter
muter
neuter
parachuter
pea-shooter
permuter
persecutor
pewter
polluter
prosecutor
prostitutor
recruiter
refuter
restitutor
ringtailed
    tooter
rooter
saluter
sharp-shooter
shooter
substitutor
suitor
tooter
transmuter
tutor
uprooter

ŬT'ur
abutter
bread-and-
    butter
butter
clutter
cutter
flutter
glutter
gutter
mutter
nutter

pilot-cutter
putter
rebutter
scutter
shutter
splutter
sputter
strutter
stutter
utter
wood-cutter

ŬT'urd
unuttered
fluttered, etc.

Ū'ur
bedewer
bestrewer
bluer
brewer
canoer
chewer
cooer
derring-doer
doer
enduer
eschewer
evildoer
ewer
fewer
gluer
hallooer
hewer
imbuer
interviewer
mewer
misconstruer
misdoer
newer
outdoer

overdoer
pursuer
renewer
reviewer
ruer
sewer
screwer
shampooer
shoer
skewer
stewer
subduer
tattooer
truer
undoer
unscrewer
viewer
well-doer
wooer
wrong-doer

Ū'urd

leeward
sewered
skewered
steward

ŬV'al

approval
disapproval
disproval
removal
reproval

ŬV'ed

beloved

ŬL'el

scovel
shovel

ŪV'en

hooven
proven

ŬV'en

coven
oven
sloven

ŪV'est

approvest
disapprovest
disprovest
improvest
movest
provest
removest
reprovest

ŪV'eth

approveth
disapproveth
disproveth
improveth
moveth
proveth
removeth
reproveth

ŪV'i

movie

ŬV'i

covey
dovey
lovey

ŪV'ing

approving
disapproving
disproving
grooving

improving
moving
proving
removing
reproving
unmoving

ŬV'ing

gloving
loving
self-loving
shoving
ungloving
unloving

ŬV'les

gloveless
loveless

ŪV'ment

approvement
improvement
movement

ŪV'ur

approver
disapprover
disprover
groover
Hoover
improver
maneuver
mover
prover
remover
reprover
Vancouver
(cf. Louvre)

ŬV'ur

cover
discover

glover
lover
plover
recover
rediscover
shover
table-cover
uncover

ŬV'urn

govern

Ū'ya

alleluia

Ū'yans

buoyance

Ū'yant

buoyant

ŪZ'a

lallapalooza

ŪZ'al

musal
refusal
(cf. fusil)

ŪZ'an

Susan

ŪZ'ard

buzzard

ŪZ'band

husband

ŪZ'di

Tuesday

ŪZ'est

abusest

accusest
amusest
boozest
bruisest
choosest
confusest
cruisest
diffusest
excusest
fusest
infusest
losest
musest
oozest
perusest
refusest
snoozest
suffusest
transfusest
usest

ŬZ'est

buzzest, etc.

ŪZ'eth

abuseth
accuseth
amuseth
boozeth
bruiseth
chooseth
confuseth
cruiseth
diffuseth
excuseth
fuseth
infuseth
loseth
museth
oozeth

peruseth
refuseth
snoozeth
suffuseth
transfuseth
useth

ŬZ'eth

buzzeth, etc.

ŪZ'ez

abuses
accuses
amuses
bemuses
bruises
chooses
circumfuses
confuses
contuses
cruises
diffuses
disabuses
disuses
druses
excuses
fuses
infuses
interfuses
loses
misuses
muses
nooses
oozes
peruses
refuses
snoozes
suffuses
transfuses
uses

ŬZ'ez

buzzes
fuzzes

Ū'zhun

abstrusion
abusion
affusion
allusion
circumfusion
collusion
conclusion
confusion
contusion
delusion
detrusion
diffusion
dissillusion
effusion
elusion
exclusion
extrusion
fusion
illusion
inclusion
infusion
interclusion
interfusion
intrusion
Malthusian
obtrusion
occlusion
perfusion
pertusion
preclusion
profusion
prolusion
protrusion
reclusion
refusion
retrusion

seclusion
self-delusion
suffusion
transfusion
trusion
(cf. ŪZ'i-an)

ŪZ'i

boozy
fluzie
oozy
woozy

ŬZ'i

fuzzy
hussy

ŪZ'ik

music

ŬZ'in

cousin
cozen
dozen

ŪZ'ing

abusing
accusing
amusing
boozing
bruising
choosing
confusing
contusing
cruising
diffusing
disusing
excusing
fusing
infusing
interfusing

losing
musing
oozing
perusing
refusing
self-accusing
snoozing
suffusing
transfusing
using

ŬZ'ing
buzzing
fuzzing

ŬZ'inz
cousins
cozens
couzens
dozens

ŪZ'iv
amusive
unamusive

ŬZ"l, ŬZ'al
bamboozle

foozle
gumfoozle
perusal
refusal

ŬZ"l
bemuzzle
fuzzle
guzzle
muzzle
nuzzle
puzzle
unmuzzle

ŬZ'lest
bemuzzlest, etc.

ŬZ'leth
bemuzzleth, etc.

ŬZ'lin
muslin

ŬZ'ling
bemuzzling
guzzling
muzzling

nuzzling
puzzling

ŪZ'lur
bamboozler
foozler

ŬZ'lur
guzzler
muzzler
puzzler

ŬZ'm
izzum-wuzzum

ŪZ'man
newsman
trewsman

ŪZ'ment
amusement

ŬZ'om
bosom

Ūz'rel
newsreel

ŪZ'ur
abuser
accuser
amuser
boozer
bruiser
chooser
confuser
cruiser
diffuser
excuser
fuser
infuser
interfuser
lallapaloozer
loser
muser
non-user
oozer
peruser
refuser
snoozer
suffuser
transfuser
user

āle, câre, ădd, ärm, åsk; mē, hęre, ĕnd; īce, ĭll;

WORDS ACCENTED ON THE THIRD SYLLABLE FROM THE END: ANTEPENULTS; TRIPLE RHYMES

A

For a discussion of words included under the accented vowels following, see the beginning of A rhymes in Section I.

(Note on Archaic Verb-forms among Triple Rhymes.—The archaic verb forms ending in-*est* and -*eth* have not as a rule been listed among the triple rhymes, to avoid needlessly expanding the book. When desired, they can be found by locating the present participles of triple-rhymed verbs, the -*ing* form: such forms as *laboring, bracketing, fracturing, dallying, hampering, clamoring, meandering,* and the rest. These can be turned without difficulty into the desired archaic forms: as, *laborest, laboreth; bracketest, bracketeth;* and so with all of them.)

Ā′a-b'l
conveyable
defrayable
impayable
payable
portrayable
repayable
unpayable
unprayable
unswayable

ĂB′a-sis
anabasis
catabasis
metabasis

ĀB′el-ur
gabeler
labeller

ĀB′i-a
Arabia
labia
Suabia

ĀB′i-an
Arabian
Fabian
Sabian
Sorabian
Suabian

ĂB′id-nes
rabidness
tabidness

ĂB′i-est
flabbiest
shabbiest

ĀB′i-ez
rabies
scabies

ĂB′i-fi
dissyllabify
labefy
syllabify
tabefy

ĂB′i-kal
Arabical
monosyllabical
polysyllabical

ĂB′i-li
flabbily
shabbily

ĂB′i-nes
flabbiness
scabbiness
shabbiness
slabbiness

ĂB′i-net
cabinet
tabinet

ĂB′i-tud
habitude
tabitude

ĂB′i-ur
flabbier
gabbier
shabbier

ĂB'la-tiv
ablative
bablative

ĂB''1-ment
babblement
brabblement
dabblement
gabblement
rabblement

ĀB''1-nes
sableness
stableness
unstableness

ĂB'o-la
Metabola
parabola

ĂB'ri-el
Gabriel

ĂB'u-lar
confabular
pabular
tabular
tintinnabular

ĂB'u-lat
confabulate
tabulate

ĂB'u-list
fabulist
vocabulist

ĂB'u-lum
acetabulum
pabulum
tintinnabulum

ĂB'u-lus
fabulous
pabulous
sabulous
tintinnabulous

ĀB'ur-ing
belaboring
laboring
neighboring
unlaboring

ĀB'ur-ur
laborer
taborer

ĂCH'a-b'l
attachable
catchable
detachable
immatchable
matchable
scratchable
unmatchable

ĀD'a-b'l,
  ĀD'i-b'l
evadible
persuadable
shadable
tradable
wadable

ĀD'ed-nes
bejadedness
degradedness
fadedness
jadedness
persuadedness
shadedness

ĀD'e-us
Amadeus

ĂD'e-us
Thaddeus

ĀD'i-an
Acadian
Arcadian
Barbadian
Canadian
nomadian
Orcadian
Palladian

ĀD'i-ant
irradiant
radiant

ĀD'i-ent
gradient

ĂD'i-tiv
additive
traditive

ĀD'i-um
palladium
radium
stadium
vanadium

ĂD'o-ing
foreshadowing
overshadowing
shadowing

ĂF'a-nus
diaphanous

ĂF'i-kal
autobiographi-
  cal

autographical
bibliographical
biographical
calligraphical
cartographical
cosmographical
diagraphical
ethnographical
geographical
glossographical
graphical
lexicographical
lexigraphical
orthographical
palæonto-
  graphical
photographical
physiograph-
  ical
phytographical
pterylograph-
  ical
seraphical
topographical
typographical

ĂF'ti-li
craftily
draughtily

ĂG'ed-li
jaggedly
raggedly

ĂG'ed-nes
craggedness
jaggedness
raggedness

ĂG'i-nes
bagginess

cragginess
knagginess
scragginess
shagginess

ĂG'on-ist
agonist
antagonist
protagonist

ĂG'on-iz
agonize
antagonize

ĂG'on-izm
agonism
antagonism

ĂG'ran-si
flagrancy
fragrancy
vagrancy

ĂG'ur-i
faggery
jaggery
raggery
waggery
zigzaggery

ĂG'ur-ing
staggering
swaggering

ĂG'ur-ur
staggerer
swaggerer

Ā'ik-al
algebraical
archaical
Hebraical

laical
paradisaical
pharisaical

Ā'it-i
gaiety
laity

ĀJ'a-b'l
assuageable
gaugeable

ĀJ'i-an
Brobdignagian
magian
pelagian
(cf. contagion)

ĀJ'i-kal
magical
tragical

ĀJ'il-nes
agileness
fragileness

ĀJ'in-al
imaginal
paginal
vaginal

ĀJ'in-us
cartilaginous
farraginous
lumbaginous
mucilaginous
oleaginous
voraginous

ĀJ'us-nes
advantageous-
   ness

courageous-
   ness
disadvan-
   tageousness
outrageous-
   ness
rampageous-
   ness
umbrageous-
   ness

ĀK'a-b'l
breakable
impacable
implacable
mistakable
pacable
placable
undertakable
unshakable

ĂK'et-ed
bracketed
jacketed
racketed

ĂK'et-ing
bracketing
jacketing
racketing

ĂK'i-an
batrachian
eustachian
Noachian

ĂK'i-nes
flakiness
quakiness
shakiness
snakiness

ĂK'ish-nes
brackishness
knackishnes
slackishness

ĂK'ri-ti
acrity
alacrity

ĂK'ron-izm
anachronism
metachronism

ĂK'sa-b'l
relaxable
taxable

ĂK'shun-al
factional
fractional
pactional

ĂK'shus-nes
factiousness
fractiousness

ĂK'ta-b'l,
  ĂK'ti-b'l
attractable
compactible
contractible
detractible
distractible
extractible
infractible
intactable
intractable
refractable
retractable
tactable
tractable

ōld, ôr, ŏdd, oil, fŏŏt, out; ūse, ûrn, ŭp; THis, thin

ĂK'ted-nes
abstractedness
contractedness
distractedness
protractedness

ĂK'tĭ-kal
didactical
practical

ĂK'tĭ-lus
didactylous
hexadactylous
leptodactylous
pachydacty-
  lous
pterodacty-
  lous

ĂK'tiv-nes
abstractive-
  ness
activeness
attractiveness
contractive-
  ness
detractiveness
distractiveness
protractiveness
putrefactive-
  ness
refractiveness

ĂK'to-ri
detractory
dissatisfactory
factory
lactary
manufactory
olfactory
phylactery

refractory
satisfactory
tractory

ĂK'tu-al
actual
factual
tactual

ĂK'tur-ing
fracturing
manufacturing

ĂK'u-lar
oracular
piacular
spectacular
supernacular
tabernacular
tentacular
vernacular

ĂK'u-lat
bimaculate
ejaculate
immaculate
jaculate
maculate

ĂK'u-lus
abaculus
miraculous
oraculous
piaculous
vernaculous

ĀK'ur-i
bakery
fakery
fakiry
rakery

ĂK'ur-i
hackery
hijackery
knick-knackery
quackery
Thackeray
Zachary

ĀK'ur-izm
fakirism
Quakerism
Shakerism

ĀK'we-us
aqueous
subaqueous
terraqueous

ĀL'a-b'l
assailable
available
bailable
exhalable
mailable
retailable
sailable
saleable
unassailable
unavailable
unsailable

ĀL'e-a
azalea
(cf. regalia)

ĀL'e-at, ĂL'ĭ-at
malleate
palliate

ĂL'en-tin
Ballantine
Valentine

Ā'li-a
Adalia
Attalia
Australia
Centralia
echolalia
Eulalia
Fidelia
regalia
Rosalia
Sedalia
Thalia
(cf. azalea, and
  ĀL'ya)

ĂL'ĭ-bur
caliber
Excalibur

ĂL'id-nes
impallidness
invalidness
pallidness
validness

ĂL'ĭ-fi
alkaify
calefy
salify

ĂL'ĭ-ing
dallying
rallying
sallying
tallying

ĀL'ĭ-nes
dailiness
scaliness

ĂL'ĭ-sis
analysis

catalysis | *curiality* | inimicality | personality
dialysis | dextrality | instrumen- | plurality
paralysis | duality | tality | potentiality
 | egality | integrality | practicality
ĂL′i-son | elementality | intellectuality | preternatur-
Alison | ephemerality | intentionality | ality
Callison | essentiality | intrinsicality | principality
 | ethereality | irrationality | prodigality
ĂL′i-ti | eventuality | joviality | proportion-
abnormality | externality | laicality | ality
accidentality | exterritorial- | laterality | provinciality
actuality | ity | legality | prudentiality
alamodality | fantasticality | liberality | punctuality
animality | fatality | lineality | radicality
artificiality | feminality | literality | rascality
banality | feudality | locality | rationality
bestiality | finality | logicality | reality
Biblicality | finicality | magistrality | reciprocality
brutality | formality | materiality | regality
carnality | frugality | mentality | rivality
causality | fundamen- | meridionality | rurality
centrality | tality | mesnality | sectionality
circumstan- | generality | modality | sensuality
tiality | geniality | morality | sentimentality
classicality | graduality | mortality | septentrion-
comicality | gutturality | municipality | ality
confidentiality | horozontality | mutuality | seriality
congeniality | hospitality | nasality | sesquiped-
conjecturality | ideality | nationality | ality
conjugality | illegality | naturality | severality
connubiality | immateriality | neutrality | sexuality
constitution- | immorality | notionality | signality
ality | immortality | occidentality | sociality
consubstan- | impartiality | officiality | sodality
tiality | imperiality | orientality | speciality
conventionality | impersonality | originality | spectrality
conviviality | inconsequen- | orthodoxality | spirality
cordiality | tialty | parochiality | spirituality
corporality | individuality | partiality | substantiality
corporeality | ineffectuality | pedality | superficiality
criminality | informality | *penality* | supernaturality

ōld, ôr, ŏdd, oil, fŏŏt, out; ūse, ûrn, ŭp; THis, thin

technicality
temporality
theatricality
tonality
totality
traditionality
transcenden-
   tality
triality
triviality
universality
unusuality
vegetality
venality
veniality
verbality
verticality
visuality
vitality
vocality
whimsicality

ĂL'i-um
pallium
thallium

ĂL'i-ur
dallier
rallier
sallier
tallier

ĂL'ji-a
neuralgia
nostalgia

ĂL'o-est
callowest
hallowest
sallowest
shallowest

ĂL'o-gi
analogy
crustalogy
genealogy
genethlialogy
mammalogy
mineralogy
paralogy
petralogy
pyroballogy
tetralogy

ĂL'o-gist
analogist
decalogist
dialogist
genealogist
mammalogist
mineralogist
penalogist

ĂL'o-giz
analogize
dialogize
genealogize
paralogize

ĂL'o-gizm
analogism
dialogism
paralogism

ĂL'o-ish
sallowish
shallowish
tallowish

ĂL'o-nes
callowness
fallownes

sallowness
shallowness

ĂL'o-ur
callower
hallower
sallower
shallower
tallower

ĂL'ur-i
nailery
raillery

ĂL'ur-i
gallery
raillery
salary

**ĀL'yen-izm,
   ĀL'yan-izm**
alienism
bacchanalian-
   ism
episcopalian-
   ism
saturnalianism
sesquipeda-
   lianism
universalian-
   ism

ĀM'a-b'l
blamable
claimable
framable
irreclaimable
namable
reclaimable
tamable
unblamable
untamable

ĂM'a-ri
gramarye
mammary

ĂM'a-tist
dramatist
epigrammatist
grammatist
hierogram-
   matist
lipogrammatist
melodramatist

ĂM'a-tiv
amative
exclamative

ĂM'a-tiz
anagramma-
   tize
diagramma-
   tize
dramatize
epigramma-
   tize

ĂM'bu-lat
ambulate
deambulate
funambulate
perambulate
somnambu-
   late

ĂM'bu-list
funambulist
noctambulist
somnambulist

ĂM'bu-lizm
funambulism

noctambulism
somnambulism

ĂM'et-er
diameter
dynameter
hexameter
octameter
parameter
pentameter
peirameter
pluviameter
tetrameter
viameter
voltameter

ĂM'ful-nes
blamefulness
shamefulness

Ā'mi-a
lamia
Mesoptomania

ĂM'i-kal
amical
balsamical
dynamical

ĂM'in-a
lamina
stamina

ĂM'i-nat
contaminate
laminate

ĂM'is-tri
palmistry
psalmistry

ĂM'i-ti
amity
calamity

ĂM'les-nes
aimlessness
blamelessness
damelessness
famelessness
namelessness
shamelessness
tamelessness

ĂM'on-it
Ammonite
Mammonite

ĂM'on-izm
Mammonism
Shamanism

ĂM'or-us
amorous
clamorous
glamorous

ĂM'pi-on
campion
champion
tampion

ĂM'pur-ing
hampering
pampering
scampering
tampering

ĂM'pur-ur
hamperer
pamperer
scamperer
tamperer

ĂM'ul-us
famulus
hamulus
ramulous

ĂM'ur-ing
clamoring
hammering
stammering
yammering

ĂM'ur-on
Decameron
Heptameron

ĂM'ur-ur
clamorer
hammerer
stammerer

ĂN'a-b'l
ascertainable
attainable
chainable
constrainable
containable
detainable
distrainable
drainable
explainable
gainable
maintainable
obtainable
ordainable
overstrainable
restrainable
retainable
sprainable
strainable
sustainable

trainable
unattainable

ĂN'a-b'l
insanable
sanable
tannable
(cf. cannibal)

ĂN'ar-i
chicanery
lanary
planary

ĂN'a-ri
granary
panary
(see ĂN'ur-i)

ĂN'ches-tur
Granchester
Manchester

ĂND'a-b'l
commandable
countermand-
    able
demandable
reprimandable
sandable
understandable

ĂN'di-fi
candify
dandify

ĂN'di-nes
dandiness
handiness
sandiness

ōld, ôr, ŏdd, oil, fŏŏt, out; ūse, ûrn, ŭp; THis, thin

ĂN′dri-an
Alexandrian
meandrian
Menandrian

ĂN′dur-ing
meandering
pandering
philandering
slandering

ĂN′dur-ing
wandering
(see ŎN-dur-
ing)

ĂN′dur-son
Anderson
Sanderson

ĂN′dur-ur
meanderer
panderer
philanderer
slanderer

ĂN′dur-ur
launderer
wanderer
(see ŎN′dur-
ur)

ĂN′dur-us
panderous
slanderous

ĂN′el-ing
channelling
panelling

ĀN′e-us
antecedaneous

araneous
circumforane-
ous
coëtaneous
contemporane-
ous
cutaneous
dissentaneous
extemporane-
ous
exterraneous
extraneous
instantaneous
*mediterra-
neous*
membraneous
miscellaneous
momentaneous
porcelaneous
simultaneous
spontaneous
subcutaneous
subterraneous
succedaneous
temporaneous
terraneous

ĀN′ful′i
banefully
disdainfully
painfully

ĀN′ful-nes
disdainfulness
gainfulness
painfulness

**ĂNGK′ur-ing,
ĂNGK′or-ing**
anchoring
cankering

encankering
hankering

ĂNGKur-us
cankerous
cantankerous

ĂNG″lsom
anglesome
tanglesome
wranglesome

ĂNG′u-lar
angular
octangular
pentangular
quadrangular
rectangular
slangular
triangular

Ā-ni-a
Albania
Anglo-mania
Aquitania
bibliomania
decalcomania
demonomania
dipsomania
eleuthero-
mania
erotomania
Gallomania
kleptomania
Lithuania
logomania
Lusitania
mania
Mauretania
megalomania
metromania

miscellanea
monomania
nymphomania
Pennsylvania
pyromania
Rumania
succedanea
Tasmania
Titania
Transylvania
Tripolitania
Ukrainia
Urania

Ā′ni-ak
bibliomaniac
dipsomaniac
eleutheroman-
iac
kleptomaniac
maniac
megalomaniac
monomaniac
nymphomaniac

Ā′ni-al
çranial
domanial
subterraneal

Ā-ni-an
Albanian
Alcmanian
Aquitanian
circumforanean
cyanean
extemporanean
Iranian
Lithuanian
Mauretanian
Mediterranean

Pennsylvani-
an
Rumanian
Sandemanian
subterranean
Tasmanian
Transylvanian
Tripolitanian
Turanian
Ukrainian
Uranian
volcanian

ĂN'i-bal
cannibal
Hannibal
(cf. sanable)

ĂN'i-el
Daniel
Nathaniel
(cf. spaniel)

ĂN'i-gan
Brannigan
Flannigan
Mullanigan

ĂN'i-kal
botanical
Brahmanical
charlatanical
galvanical
mechanical
panicle
tyrannical

ĂN'i-fi
humanify
insanify
sanify

ĂN'i-mus
animus
magnanimous
multanimous
pusillanimous
unanimous

ĂN'i-shing
banishing
planishing
vanishing

ĂN'ish-ment
banishment
evanishment
vanishment

ĂN'is-tur
banister
canister
ganister

ĂN'i-ti
aldermanity
Christianity
gigmanity
humanity
immanity
inanity
inhumanity
inorganity
insanity
inurbanity
mundanity
paganity
profanity
sanity
subterranity
urbanity
vanity
volcanity

Ā'ni-um
cranium
geranium
pericranium
succedaneum
titanium
uranium

ĂN'jen-si
plangency
tangency

ĂN'ji-b'l
frangible
infrangible
intangible
refrangible
tangible

ĂN'i-kin
manikin
pannikin

ĂN'o-graf
galvanograph
pianograph

ĂN'o-skop
diaphanoscope
galvanoscope

ĂN'shi-an
Byzantian
(cf. ĂN'shun)

ĂN'shi-at
circumstantiate
substantiate
transubstanti-
ate

ĂN'siv-nes
advanciveness
expansiveness

ĂN'som-est
handsomest
ransomest

ĂN'som-ur
handsomer
ransomer

ĂNT'a-b'l
grantable
plantable

ĂN'tur-ing
bantering
cantering

ĂNT'ur-ur
banterer
canterer

ĂN'thro-pi
apanthropy
aphilanthropy
lycanthropy
misanthropy
philanthropy
physianthropy
psilanthropy
theanthropy
theophilan-
thropy
zoanthropy

ĂN'thro-pist
misanthropist
philanthropist

ōld, ôr, ŏdd, oil, fŏŏt, out; ūse, ûrn, ŭp; THis, thin

psilanthropist
theophilan-
    thropist

ĂN'thro-pizm
psilanthropism
theanthropism
theophilanthro-
    pism

ĂN'ti-sid
giganticide
infanticide

ĂN'tik-nes
franticness
giganticness
romanticness

ĂN'u-al
annual
manual

ĂN'u-la
cannula
granula

ĂN'u-lar
annular
cannular
penannular

ĂN'u-lat
annulate
campanulate
granulate

ĂN'ur-et
banneret
lanneret

ĂN'ur-i
cannery

charlatanery
granary
panary
stannary
tannery

ĀP'a-b'l
capable
drapable
escapable
incapable
inescapable
papable
shapeable

ĂP'id-li
rapidly
sapidly
vapidly

ĂP'id-nes
rapidness
sapidness
vapidness

ĂP'i-est
happiest
sappiest
snappiest

ĂP'i-li
happily
snappily

ĂP'i-nes
happiness
sappiness
snappiness

ĂP'i-ur
happier

sappier
snappier

ĂP'o-lis
Annapolis
Indianapolis
Minneapolis

ĀP'ur-i
apery
drapery
grapery
napery
papery
vapory

ĀP'ur-ing
capering
papering
tapering
vaporing

ĀP'ur-ur
caperer
paperer
vaporer

ÂR'a-b'l
airable
bearable
dareable
declarable
pairable
repairable
swearable
tearable
unbearable
unwearable
wearable

ĂR'a-b'l
arable
parable

ĂR'a-dis
imparadise
paradise

ĂR'as-ing
embarrassing
harassing

ĂR'as-ment
embarrassment
harassment

ĂR'a-tiv
comparative
declarative
narrative
preparative
reparative

ĂR'bur-ing
barbering
harboring

ĂR'di-an
guardian
pericardian

ĂR'di-nes
fool-hardiness
hardiness
tardiness

Â're-a
area
(see Â'ri-a)

ÂR'ful-i
carefully
prayerfully
uncarefully

ÂR'ful-nes
carefulness
prayerfulness
sparefulness
uncarefulness
warefulness

Ā'ri-a
adversaria
area
Bulgaria
caballeria
Calceolaria
Cineraria
dataria
digitaria
Hilaria
malaria
wistaria
(cf. pariah)

ĂR'i-al
actuarial
areal
calendarial
commissarial
diarial
glossarial
malarial
nectarial
notarial
ovarial
puparial
secretarial
vicarial

ÂR'i-an
abecedarian
Adessenarian
agrarian
alphabetarian

altitudinarian
anecdotarian
antiquarian
antisabbatarian
antitrinitarian
apiarian
Apollinarian
aquarian
Arian
Aryan
atrabilarian
attitudinarian
barbarian
Bavarian
Briarean
Bulgarian
Cæsarian
centenarian
diarian
dietarian
disciplinarian
doctrinarian
equalitarian
estuarian
experimenta-
   rian
futilitarian
grammarian
humanitarian
Hungarian
Icarian
Janizarian
lapidarian
latitudinarian
libertarian
librarian
limitarian
lunarian
Megarian
millenarian
miscellanarian

necessarian
necessitarian
nectarian
nonagenarian
octagenarian
ovarian
Parian
parliamenta-
   rian
platitudinarian
plenitudinarian
predestinarian
proletarian
riparian
sabbatarian
sacramentarian
sanitarian
sectarian
sententiarian
septuagenarian
sexagenarian
societarian
stipendarian
sublapsarian
supralapsarian
Tartarean
tractarian
trinitarian
ubiquarian
ubiquitarian
unitarian
utilitarian
valetudinarian
vegetarian
veterinarian
vulgarian

ÂR'i-ant
contrariant
omniparient
variant

ÂR'i-at
variate
vicariate

ĂR'i-at
commissariat
lariat
proletariat
prothonotariat
secretariat

ÂR'i-est
chariest
variest
wariest

ĂR'i-et, ĂR'i-ot
Harriet
Iscariot
Marryatt
Marriott

Ā'ri-ez
Aries
caries

ĂR'i-fi
clarify
saccharify
scarify

ÂR'i-form
peariform
scalariform

ĂR'i-gan
Garrigan
Harrigan

ĂR'i-ing
carrying
harrying

marrying
tarrying

ÄR'i-nes
airiness
arbitrariness
chariness
contrariness
glariness
hairiness
salutariness
sanguinariness
sedentariness
solitariness
temporariness
tumultuariness
ubiquitariness
voluntariness
wariness

ÄR'i-nes
starriness
tarriness

ÂR'ing-li
blaringly
daringly
flaringly
glaringly
sparingly
tearingly

ÄR'ing-ton
Barrington
Carrington
Farrington
Harrington

ÄR'i-o
impresario
(cf. Lothario)

ÄR'i-on
clarion
Marion
(cf. Marian)

ÄR'i-son
garrison
Harrison

ÂR'i-ti
debonairity
rarity

ÄR'i-ti
angularity
barbarity
charity
circularity
clarity
disparity
dissimilarity
exemplarity
familiarity
fissiparity
gemmiparity
globularity
hilarity
imparity
insularity
irregularity
jocularity
molecularity
muscularity
omniparity
parity
particularity
peculiarity
perpendicu-
    larity
piacularity
polarity

popularity
pupilarity
rectangularity
rectilinearity
regularity
secularity
similarity
singularity
solidarity
titularity
triangularity
uncharity
vascularity
viviparity
vulgarity

ÄR'i-tud
amaritude
claritude

ÂR'i-um
aquarium
aqua-vivarium
barium
columbarium
glaciarium
honorarium
sacrarium
sanitarium
tepidarium
termitarium
vivarium

ÂR'i-ur
charier
warier

ÄR'i-ur
barrier
carrier

farrier
harrier
marrier
tarrier

ÂR'i-us
arbitrarious
arenarious
Aquarius
atrabilarious
calcareous
contrarious
denarius
frumentarious
gregarious
hilarious
horarious
malarious
multifarious
nectareous
nefarious
omnifarious
precarious
quadragena-
    rious
Sagittarius
tartareous
temerarious
testudinarious
vagarious
valetudinarious
various
vicarious
viparious

ÄR'ki-kal
archical
hierarchical
hylarchical
monarchical
tetrarchical

ÄR′la-tan
charlatan
tarlatan

ÄR′ming-li
alarmingly
charmingly
farmingly
harmingly

ÄR′nish-ing
garnishing
tarnishing
varnishing

ÄR′nish-ur
garnisher
tarnisher
varnisher

ÄR′o-est
harrowest
narrowest

ÄR′o-i
arrowy
marrowy
sparrowy
yarrowy

ÄR′o-ing
harrowing
narrowing

Ä′ron-it
Aaronite
Maronite

ĂR′o-ur
harrower
narrower

ÄR′sen-i
coparceny
larceny

ÄR′sen-ur
coparcener
larcener
parcener

ÄR′shal-izm
martialism
partialism

ĂR′ted-nes
departedness
false-
   heartedness
frank-
   heartedness
free-
   heartedness
hard-
   heartedness
kind-
   heartedness
light-
   heartedness
open-
   heartedness
soft-
   heartedness
tender-
   heartedness
true-
   heartedness
warm-
   heartedness

ÄR′ti-k′l
article
particle

ÄR′ti-zan
artizan
bartizan
partisan

ÄRT′les-li
artlessly
heartlessly

ÄRT′les-nes
artlessness
heartlessness

ÄRT′ur-ing
bartering
chartering
martyring

ÄRT′ur-ur
barterer
charterer

ĀS′a-b′l
chasable
effaceable
erasible
evasible
ineffaceable
retraceable
traceable

ĀS′en-si
adjacency
complacency
interjacency

ĀS′ful-nes
disgracefulness

gracefulness
ungracefulness

A′shi-a
acacia
Asia
Aspasia
(cf. Ā′zhi-a,
  Ā′zi-a, Ā′sha,
  Ā′zha. So in
  all similar
  cases)

ĂSH′i-a
cassia
Parnassia
quassia

Ā′shi-al
basial
(cf. spatial)

Ā′shi-an
Alsatian
Asian
Athanasian
Australasian
Galatian
Haytian
Hieracian
Horatian
Latian
Pancratian
Thracian
(cf. Ā′shun,
  Ā′zhun)

ĂSH′i-an
Circassian
Parnassian
(cf. ĂSH′un)

Ā′shi-at
emaciate
expatiate
glaciate
ingratiate
insatiate
satiate

Ā′shi-ent
calefacient
delirefacient
facient
liquefacient
parturifacient
rubefacient
sensifacient
sorbefacient
stupefacient
tumefacient
(cf. Ā′shent)

ĂSH′i-nes
ashiness
flashiness
trashiness

Ā′shun-al
associational
congregational
conservational
conversational
creational
denominational
derivational
dissertational
educational
emigrational
gradational
gyrational
ideational
imitational

inspirational
observational
probational
relational
representational
respirational
rotational
sensational
stational
terminational

ĂSH′un-al
international
irrational
national
rational

ĂSH′un-at
compassionate
dispassionate
impassionate
incompassion-
ate
passionate

ĂSH′un-ing
compassioning
fashioning
passioning

Ā′shun-ist
annexationist
annihilationist
annotationist
causationist
conversationist
convocationist
cremationist
degenerationist
educationist
emancipationist

emigrationist
imitationist
inflationist
innovationist
inspirationist
repudiationist
restorationist
transmutation-
ist

Ā′shun-les
conversation-
less
educationless
emigrationless
foundationless
immigration-
less
imitationless
inspirationless
temptationless

Ā′shun-ur
foundationer
oblationer
probationer
reprobationer
restorationer
stationer

ĂSH′ur-i
fashery
haberdashery
sashery

Ā′shus-nes
audaciousness
capaciousness
contumacious-
ness

disputatious-
ness
edaciousness
efficaciousness
fallaciousness
fugaciousness
graciousness
incapacious-
ness
ineffacious-
ness
loquaciousness
mendaciousness
ostentatious-
ness
perspicacious-
ness
pertinacious-
ness
pugnaciousness
rapaciousness
sagaciousness
salaciousness
sequaciousness
spaciousness
tenaciousness
ungraciousness
veraciousness
vexatiousness
vivaciousness
voraciousness

ĂS′i-b'l
impassible
irascible
passable
passible
renascible
surpassable

ĂS′i-nat
abbacinate

assassinate
deracinate
exacinate
fascinate

ĂS'i-nes
laciness
raciness

ĂS'i-nes
brassiness
classiness
glassiness
grassiness
massiness
sassiness

ĂS'i-ti
audacity
bellacity
bibacity
capacity
contumacity
dicacity
edacity
feracity
fugacity
incapacity
loquacity
mendacity
minacity
mordacity
opacity
perspicacity
pertinacity
pervicacity
procacity
pugnacity
rapacity
sagacity
salacity

saponacity
sequacity
tenacity
veracity
vivacity
voracity

ĂS'iv-li
impassively
massively
passively

Ā'siv'nes
dissuasiveness
evasiveness
persuasiveness
pervasiveness
suasiveness

ĂS'iv-nes
impassiveness
massiveness
passiveness

ĂSP'ing-li
gaspingly
raspingly

ĂS'tar-di
bastardy
dastardy

ĀST'ful-i
tastefully
wastefully
distastefully

ĂS'ti-kal
ecclesiastical
elastical
encomiastical

enthusiastical
fantastical
gymnastical

ĂS'ti-li
hastily
pastily
tastily

ĂS'ti-sizm
ecclesiasticism
fantasticism
monasticism
scholasticism

ĂS'tri-an
alabastrian
Lancastrian
Zoroastrian

ĂS'tro-fe
catastrophe
epanastrophe

ĂS'tur-ship
mastership
pastorship

ĂS'tur-i
dicastery
mastery
plastery
self-mastery

ĂS'tur-ing
beplastering
mastering
overmastering
plastering

ĂS'ur-at
emacerate

lacerate
macerate

ĂS'ur-i
bracery
embracery
tracery

ĀT'a-b'l
abatable
beratable
collatable
creatable
debatable
dilatable
gratable
hatable
matable
ratable
regulatable
statable
translatable
untranslatable

ĂT'a-b'l
combatable
(see ĂT'i-b'l)

ĂT'e-lit
patellite
satellite

Ā'ten-si
latency
patency

ĀT'ful-i
fatefully
gratefully
hatefully

ĀT'ful-nes
fatefulness

ōld, ôr, ŏdd, oil, fŏŏt, out; ūse. ûrn. ŭp; THis, thin

gratefulness
hatefulness

Ā′thi-an
Carpathian
Sabbathian

Ăth′e-sis
diathesis
parathesis

Ăth′i-kal
anthropopath-
  ical
chrestomath-
  ical

ĂTH′ur-ing
blathering
foregathering
gathering
lathering
upgathering
wool-gathering

ĂTH′ur-ur
foregatherer
gatherer
latherer
tax-gatherer
toll-gatherer
upgatherer

ĂT′i-b'l
combatable
come-atable
compatible
impatible
incompatible
patible

ĂT′i-fi
beatify
gratify
ratify
stratify

ĂT′ik-a
Attica
dalmatica
hepatica
sciatica

ĂT′ik-al
abbatical
acroamatical
aerostatical
anathematical
anidiomatical
apophthegmat-
  ical
apostatical
aristocratical
asthmatical
autocratical
automatical
axiomatical
bureaucratical
climatical
democratical
diplomatical
dogmatical
dramatical
ecstatical
emblematical
emphatical
enigmatical
epigrammat-
  ical
fanatical
grammatical
hebdomatical

idiomatical
leviratical
mathematical
phantasmatical
piratical
pragmatical
primatical
sabbatical
schismatical
separatical
Socratical
spasmatical
statical
vatical

ĂT′in-at
gelatinate
Palatinate

ĀT′i-nes
slatiness
weightiness

ĂT′i-nes
chattiness
fattiness
nattiness

ĂT′in-iz
gelatinize
Latinize
platinize

ĂT′i-nus
gelatinous
platinous

ĂT′i-siz
emblematicize
fanaticize
grammaticize

ĂT′i-sizm
Asiaticism

fanaticism
grammaticism

ĂT′i-tud
attitude
beatitude
gratitude
ingratitude
latitude
platitude

Ā′tiv-nes
alliterativeness
imitativeness
nativeness
penetrative-
  ness

ĂT″l-ment
battlement
embattlement
prattlement
tattlement

ĂT′om-i
anatomy
atomy

ĂT′om-ist
anatomist
atomist

ĂT′om-iz
anatomize
atomize

ĂT′om-izm
anatomism
atomism

ĂT′om-us
diatomous
paratomous

ĀT′or-i
obsecratory
ratiocinatory
recapitulatory

ĂT′ri-kal
idolatrical
theatrical

ĂT′ri-sid
fratricide
matricide
patricide

Ā′tron-al
matronal
patronal

Ā′tron-ij
matronage
patronage

Ā′tron-iz
matronize
patronize

ĂT′u-lat
congratulate
gratulate
spatulate

ĂT′ūr-al
natural
preternatural
supernatural

ĂT′ŭr-al
bilateral
collateral
equilateral
lateral

quadrilateral
unilateral

ĂT′ur-an
cateran
Lateran

ĂT′ur-at
maturate
saturate
supersaturate

ĂT′ur-i
battery
flattery
shattery
slattery
tattery

ĂT′ur-ing
battering
beflattering
bepattering
bescattering
bespattering
blattering
chattering
clattering
flattering
pattering
scattering
shattering
smattering
spattering
splattering

ĂT′ur-ur
batterer
blatterer
chatterer
clatterer

flatterer
patterer
scatterer
shatterer
smatterer
splatterer

Ā′ur-i
aëry
faërie

ĂV′an-ez
Havanese
Javanese

ĂV′el-ing
gravelling
ravelling
travelling
unravelling

ĂV′el-ur
raveller
traveller
unraveller

ĂV′en-dur
chavender
lavender

Ā′vi-a
Batavia
Belgravia
Jugo-slavia
Moravia
Octavia
Pavia
Scandinavia

Ā′vi-an
avian

Batavian
Belgravian
Moravian
Scandinavian
Shavian

ĂV′ij-ing
ravaging
scavaging

ĂV′ij-ur
ravager
savager
scavager

ĂV′ish-ing
enravishing
lavishing
ravishing

ĂV′ish-ment
enravishment
lavishment
ravishment

ĂV′ish-nes
knavishness
slavishness

ĂV′ish-ur
lavisher
ravisher

ĂV′i-ti
cavity
concavity
depravity
gravity
pravity
suavity

ĀV′ur-i
bravery

gravery
savory
slavery
unsavory

ĀV'ur-ing
favoring
flavoring
quavering
savoring
unwavering
wavering

ĀV'ur-ur
favorer
flavorer
quaverer
waverer

ĀV'ur-us
flavorous
savorous

ĂV'ur-us
cadaverous
papaverous

Ā'zi-a
Aspasia
athanasia
aphasia
euthanasia
paronomasia

A'zi-an
Asian
Athanasian
Australasian
Caucasian
Eurasian

Rabelaisian
(cf. Ā'zhun)

ĀZ'i-b'l
persuasible
praisable
raisable
suasible

ĀZ'i-nes
craziness
haziness
laziness
maziness

E

For a discussion of words included under the accented vowels following, see the beginning of E rhymes in Section I.

Ē'a-b'l
agreeable
creable
decreeable
disagreeable
feeable
irremeable

Ē'al'ist
idealist
realist

Ē'al-iz
idealise
realise

Ē'al-izm
idealism
realism

Ē'al-ti
fealty
realty

Ē'an-izm
epicureanism
Laodiceanism
peanism
plebeianism
Pythagorean-
  ism
Sabæanism

ĒB'ri-us
ebrious
funebrious
inebrious
tenebrious

ĒCH'a-b'l
bleachable

impeachable
reachable
teachable
unimpeachable
unteachable

ĔCH'i-nes
sketchiness
tetchiness

ĔCH'ur-i
lechery
treachery

ĔCH'ur-us
lecherous
treacherous

ĒD'a-b'l
exceedable

impedible
obedible
pleadable
readable

ĔD'a-b'l
dreadable
(see ĔD'i-b'l)

ĒD'ful-nes
heedfulness
needfulness
unheedfulness
unneedfulness

Ē'di-al
bimedial
intermedial
medial
pedial
remedial

Ē'di-an
comedian
encyclopedian
median
tragedian

Ē'di-at
immediate
intermediate
mediate

ĔD'i-b'l
credible
dreadable
edible
incredible

Ē'di-ens
disobedience
expedience
inexpedience
obedience

Ē'di-ent
disobedient
expedient
inexpedient
ingredient
obedient

ĔD'i-est
beadiest
greediest
neediest
reediest
seediest
speediest
weediest

ĔD'i-est
headiest

readiest
steadiest
unsteadiest

ĔD'i-kal
medical
pedicle

ĔD'i-kant
medicant
predicant

ĔD'i-kat
dedicate
medicate
predicate

ĒD'i-li
greedily
needily
speedily

ĔD'i-li
headily
readily
steadily
unsteadily

ĔD'i-ment
impediment
pediment
sediment

ĒD'i-nes
greediness
neediness
seediness
speediness
weediness

ĔD'i-nes
headiness

readiness
steadiness
threadiness
unreadiness
unsteadiness

ĔD'i-nus
mucedinous
putredinous
rubedinous

ĔD'i-ted
accredited
credited
discredited
edited
miscredited
unaccredited

ĔD'i-ting
accrediting
crediting
discrediting
editing
miscrediting

ĔD'i-tiv
redditive
sedative

ĔD'i-tor
creditor
editor

Ē'di-um
medium
tedium

ĔD'i-ur
beadier
greedier

needier
reedier
seedier
speedier
weedier

ĔD'i-ur
headier
readier
steadier
unsteadier

Ē'di-us
intermedious
tedious

ĔD'les-li
heedlessly
needlessly

ĔD'les-nes
heedlessness
needlessness

ĔD'u-lus
credulous
incredulous
sedulous

ĔD'ur-al
federal
hederal

ĔD'ur-ship
leadership
readership

ĒF'i-nes
beefiness
leafiness

ōld, ôr, ŏdd, oil, fŏŏt, out; ūse, ûrn, ŭp; THis, thin

ĔF′i-sens
beneficence
maleficence

ĔF′i-sent
beneficent
maleficent

ĔF′ur-ens
cross-reference
deference
preference
reference

ĔF′ur-ent
deferent
efferent

ĔG′a-b'l
beggable
legable

Ē′gal-izm
legalism
regalism

Ē′gal-nes
illegalness
legalness
regalness

ĔG′i-nes
dregginess
legginess

ĔG′nan-si
pregnancy
regnancy

ĔG′ur-i
beggary

eggery
(cf. Gregory)

Ē′gur-li
eagerly
meagrely
overeagerly

Ē′gur-nes
eagerness
meagreness
overeagerness

Ē′i-ti
aseity
contempora-
　neity
corporeity
deity
diathermaneity
extraneity
femineity
gaseity
hæcceity
hermaphro-
　deity
heterogeneity
homogeneity
incorporeity
instantaneity
multeity
omneity
personeity
plebeity
seity
simultaneity
spontaneity
terreity
velleity

Ē′ji-an
collegian

Fuegian
Norwegian
(cf. ĒJ′un)

ĔJ′i-b'l
allegeable
illegible
legible

Ē′jus-nes
egregiousness
sacrilegious-
　ness

ĔK′a-b'l
speakable
unspeakable

ĔK′a-b'l
impeccable
insecable
peccable

ĒK′i-li
cheekily
creakily
leakily
sleekily
sneakily
squeakily

ĒK′i-nes
cheekiness
creakiness
leakiness
sneakiness
squeakiness

ĒK′ish-nes
cliquishness
freakishness
sneakishness

ĔK′on-ing
beckoning
dead-reckoning
reckoning

ĔK′re-ment
decrement
recrement

ĔK′shun-al
affectional
complexional
correctional
inflectional
insurrectional
interjectional
intersectional
protectional
sectional

ĔK′shun-ist
insurrectionist
perfectionist
protectionist
resurrectionist

ĔK′shun-iz
resurrectionize
sectionize

ĔK′si-b'l
flexible
inflexible
nexible
reflexible

ĔK′si-ti
complexity
convexity
intercom-
　plexity

perplexity
reflexity

ĔK'siv-nes
perplexiveness
reflexiveness

ĔK'ta-b'l
respectable
(see ĔK'ti-b'l)

ĔK'tar-i
nectary
(see ĔK'to-ri)

ĔK'ted-nes
abjectedness
affectedness
dejectedness
disaffectedness
infectedness
suspectedness
unsuspected-
    ness

ĔK'ti-b'l
affectible
collectible
correctible
defectible
delectable
detectible
dissectible
effectible
erectable
expectable
indefectible
indelectable
objectable
prefectible
reflectible

rejectable
respectable
suspectable

ĔK'ti-fi
objectify
rectify

ĔK'ti-kal
apoplectical
dialectical

ĔK'ti-tud
rectitude
senectitude

ĔK'tiv-li
collectively
defectively
effectively, etc.

ĔK'tiv-nes
collectiveness
defectiveness
effectiveness
ineffectiveness
objectiveness
prospectiveness
protectiveness
reflectiveness
subjectiveness

ĔK'to-ral
electoral
pectoral
protectoral
rectoral
sectoral

ĔK'to-rat
directorate

electorate
expectorate
protectorate
rectorate

ĔK'to-ri
correctory
directory
nectary
rectory
refectory
sectary

ĔK'tu-al
effectual
ineffectual
intellectual
lectual

ĔK'tur-al
architectural
conjectural

ĔK'tur-ur
conjecturer
lecturer

ĔK'u-lar
molecular
secular
specular

ĔK'u-lat
peculate
speculate

ĔK'u-tiv
consecutive
executive
subsecutive

ĒL'a-b'l
concealable
congealable
healable
inconcealable
repealable
revealable

ĒL'a-tiv
compellative
correlative
relative

ĒL'e-gat
delegate
relegate

ĒL'fish-nes
elfishness
selfishness

Ē'li-a
Amelia
Aurelia
Bedelia
Cecelia
Celia
Cordelia
Cornelia
Fidelia
Lelia
Ophelia
(also ĒL'ya)

Ē'li-an
Aristotelian
carnelian
Delian
Hegelian
Ismaelian
Machiavelian

ōld, ôr, ŏdd, oil, fŏŏt, out; ūse, ûrn, ŭp; THis, thin

Mephisto-
  phelian
Mingrelian
(also ĒL'yan)

ĔL'i-an
Boswellian
Cromwellian
evangelian
selion
(also ĔL'yan,
  ĔL'yun,
  which see)

ĔL'i-b'l,
  ĔL'a-b'l
compellable
delible
expellable
fellable
gelable
indelible
ingelable
spellable
tellable

ĔL'i-kal
angelical
bellical
evangelical
helical
pellicle

Ē'li-on
anthelion
aphelion
chameleon

ĔL'ish-ing
embellishing
relishing

ĔL'ish-ment
embellishment
relishment

Ē'li-us
Aurelius
Cornelius
(also ĒL'yus)

ĔL'o-est
bellowest
mellowest
yellowest

ĔL'o-ing
bellowing
mellowing
yellowing

ĔL'on-i
felony
melony

ĔL'o-ur
bellower
mellower
yellower

ĔL'thi-est
healthiest
stealthiest
wealthiest

ĔL'thi-li
healthily
stealthily
wealthily

ĔL'thi-ur
healthier
stealthier
wealthier

ĔL'tur-i
sheltery
smeltery

ĔL'tur-ing
sheltering
weltering

ĔL'tur-ur
shelterer
welterer

ĔL'u-lar
cellular
intercellular
stellular
unicellular

ĔL'ur-i
celery
stellary

ĔL'us-li
jealously
overzealously
zealously

ĒM'a-b'l
esteemable
redeemable

Ē'ma-tist
schematist
thematist

ĔM'a-tist
emblematist
theorematist

ĔM'bur-ing
Decembering

dismembering
membering
Novembering
remembering
unremembering

Ē'mi-a
Bohemia
Euphemia

Ē'mi-al
academial
endemial
gremial
vindemial

Ē'mi-an
academian
Bohemian

ĔM'i-kal
academical
alchemical
chemical
electro-chem-
  ical
endemical
epidemical
polemical

ĒM'i-li
beamily
creamily
dreamily
steamily

ĔM'i-nal
feminal
geminal
seminal

ĔM'i-nat
effeminate

geminate
ingeminate

ĔM′i-nes
creaminess
dreaminess
steaminess

Ē′mi-on
anthemion
procœmion

ĔM′i-ur
beamier
creamier
dreamier
premier

ĔM′ni-ti
indemnity
solemnity

ĔM′on-e
Agapemone
anemone
(cf. Gethsem-
ane)

ĔM′or-al
femoral
nemoral
(cf. ephemeral)

ĔM′o-ri
Emery
Emory
memory

**ĔM′por-ur,
ĔM′pur-ur**
emperor
temperer

ĔM′u-lent
temulent
tremulent

ĔM′u-lus
emulous
tremulous

Ĕm′ur-ald
emerald
ephemeralled

ĔM′ur-i
creamery
dreamery

ĔM′ur-i
gemmery
(cf. ĔM′o-ri)

ĔM′ur-ist
ephemerist
euhemerist

Ē′na-b'l
amenable
convenable

ĔN′a-ri
centenary
denary
decennary
hennery

ĔN′a-tor
senator
progenitor

ĔND′i-b'l
accendible

amendable
commendable
comprehendible
defendable
dependable
descendable
endable
extendible
invendible
lendable
mendable
recommendable
rendible
unascendable
vendible

ĔN′den-si
ascendancy
attendancy
dependency
equipendency
impendency
independency
intendancy
interdepend-
ency
resplendency
superintend-
ency
tendency
transcendency
transplendency

ĔN′di-us
compendious
incendious

ĔND′les-li
endlessly
friendlessly

ĔND′les-nes
endlessness
friendlessness

ĔN′dur-est
engenderest
renderest
slenderest
surrenderest
tenderest

ĔN′dur-ing
engendering
gendering
rendering
surrendering
tendering

ĔN′dur-li
slenderly
tenderly

ĔN′dur-nes
slenderness
tenderness

ĔN′dur-ur
engenderer
renderer
slenderer
surrendered
tenderer

ĔN′dus-li
(not ĔN′jus-li)
stupendously
tremendously

ĔN′e-sis
abiogenesis
biogenesis

ōld, ôr, ŏdd, oil, fŏŏt, out; ūse, ûrn, ŭp; ᴛʜis, thin

ectogenesis
eugenesis
genesis
heterogenesis
homogenesis
ontogenesis
organogenesis
palingenesis
pangenesis
paragenesis
parenesis
partheno-
    genesis
phylogenesis
phytogenesis
polygenesis
psychogenesis
xenogenesis

ĔN'et-ing
jenneting
renneting

Ē'ni-a
Armenia
Eugenia
gardenia
neurosthenia
Parthenia
Xenia

Ē'ni-al
congenial
demesnial
genial
menial
primigenial
uncongenial
venial
(cf. ĒN'yal)

ĔN'i-al
biennial
centennial
decennial
duodecennial
millennial
novennial
octennial
perennial
quadrennial
quinquennial
septennial
triennial
vicennial

Ē'ni-an
Armenian
Athenian
Cyrenian
Estremenian
Fenian
Hellenian
Madrilenian
Ruthenian

Ē'ni-ens
convenience
inconvenience
lenience
(cf. ĒN'yens)

Ē'ni-ent
advenient
convenient
inconvenient
intervenient
introvenient
lenient
supervenient
(cf. ĒN'yent)

ĔN'i-form
antenniform
penniform

ĔN'i-kal
arsenical
cathechumen-
    ical
ecumenical
scenical
sirenical

ĔN'i-ti
amenity
lenity
obscenity
serenity
terrenity

ĔN'i-tiv
genitive
lenitive
primogenitive
splenitive

ĔN'i-tud
lenitude
plenitude
serenitude

Ē'ni-um
proscenium
selenium
xenium

Ē'ni-us
arsenious
extrageneous
genius
heterogeneous
homogeneous

ingenious
nitrogeneous
pergameneous
primigenious
selenious

ĔN'i-zon
benison
denizen
endenizen
venison

ĔN'sa-b'l
condensable
(see ĔN'si-b'l)

ĔN'sa-ri
dispensary
(see ĔN'so-ri)

ĔN'sa-tiv
compensative
condensative
defensative
dispensative
insensitive
intensitive
pensative
sensitive

ĔN'sha-ri
penitentiary
residentiary

ĔN'shi-at
essentiate
licentiate
potentiate

ĔN'shi-ent
assentient

āle,   câre,   ădd,   ärm,   åsk;   mē,   hĕre,   ĕnd;   īce,   ĭll;

consentient
dissentient
insentient
presentient
sentient

ĔN′shun-al
ascensional
conventional
descensional
extensional
intentional
preventional

ĔN′shun-ist
ascentionist
extensionist
recensionist

ĔN′shus-nes
conscientious-
  ness
contentiousness
licentiousness
pretentious-
  ness

ĔN′si-b'l
comprehensible
condensable
defensible
deprehensible
dispensable
distensible
extensible
incomprehen-
  sible
incondensable
indefensible
indispensable
insensible

ostensible
reprehensible
sensible
subsensible
suspensible
tensible

ĔN′si-kal
forensical
nonsensical

ĔN′si-ti
condensity
density
immensity
intensity
propensity
tensity

ĔN′siv-nes
comprehensive-
  ness
expensiveness
extensiveness
inoffensive-
  ness
intensiveness
offensiveness
pensiveness

ĔNS′les-li
defencelessly
senselessly

ĔNS′les-nes
defencelessness
senselessness

ĔN′so-ri
defensory
dispensary

incensory
ostensory
prehensory
reprehensory
sensory
suspensory

ĔN′ta-b'l
fermentable
frequentable
inventible
presentable
preventable
rentable
representable

ĔN′ta-k'l
pentacle
tentacle

ĔN′tal-i
accidentally
experimentally
fundamentally
incidentally
instrumentally
sentimentally
transcendent-
  ally

ĔN′tal-ist
experimentalist
fundamentalist
instrumentalist
Orientalist
sentimentalist
transcendenta-
  list

ĔN′tal-iz
experimental-
  ize

Orientalize
sentimentalize

ĔN′tal-izm
accidentalism
elementalism
Orientalism
sentimentalism
transcendental-
  ism

ĔN′tal-nes
accidentalness
fundamental-
  ness
gentleness
incidentalness
instrumental-
  ness
sentimental-
  ness
ungentleness

ĔN′ta-ri
accidentary
alimentary
complementary
complimentary
dentary
elementary
filamentary
instrumentary
integumentary
parliamentary
pigmentary
placentary
rudimentary
sacramentary
sedimentary
tegumentary
tenementary

testamentary
unparliamen-
tary

ĔN′ta-tiv
argumentative
augmentative
commentative
complimenta-
tive
alimentative
experimenta-
tive
fermentative
frequentative
misrepresenta-
tive
presentative
pretentative
preventative
representative
tentative

ĔN′ti-kal
authentical
conventical
conventicle
denticle
identical

ĔN′ti-kul
denticule
lenticule

ĔN′ti-ment
presentiment
sentiment

ĔN′ti-nal
dentinal
sentinel

ĔN′ti-ti
entity
identity
nonentity

ĔN′tiv-nes
alimentiveness
attentiveness
inattentiveness
inventiveness
retentiveness

ĔN′tu-al
accentual
adventual
conventual
eventual

ĔN′tu-at
accentuate
eventuate

ĔN′tus-li
momentously
portentously

ĔN′tus-nes
momentous-
ness
portentousness

ĔN′u-ant
attenuant
genuant

ĔN′u-at
attenuate
extenuate
tenuate

ĔN′ur-at
degenerate

generate
ingenerate
intenerate
progenerate
regenerate
venerate

ĒN′ur-i
deanery
greenery
machinery
plenary
scenery

ĔN′ū-ri
penury

ĔN′ŭr-i
denary
decennary
hennery
senary
venery

ĔN′u-us
disingenuous
ingenuous
strenuous
tenuous

ĒN′yen-si
conveniency
inconveniency
leniency

ĒP′i-li
creepily
sleepily

ĒP′i-nes
creepiness

sleepiness
steepiness
weepiness

ĔP′ta-b'l
acceptable
deceptible
imperceptible
insusceptible
perceptible
receptible
susceptible

ĔP′ti-kal
antiseptical
protreptical
receptacle
sceptical

ĔP′tiv-nes
deceptiveness
receptiveness
susceptiveness

ĔP′ur-us
leperous
obstreperous
perstreperous
streperous

ĔR′an-si
aberrancy
errancy
inerrancy

ĔR′a-pi
balneotherapy
hydrotherapy
kinesitherapy
phototherapy
radiotherapy

ĒR'ful-i
cheerfully
fearfully
tearfully

ĒR'ful-nes
cheerfulness
fearfulness
tearfulness

ĒR'i-a, Ē'ri-a
Algeria
diphtheria
Egeria
eleutheria
Etheria
hesperia
hysteria
icteria
Liberia
Nigeria
Valkyria

ĒR'i-al, Ē'ri-al
aerial
arterial
cereal
ethereal
ferial
funereal
immaterial
imperial
magisterial
managerial
manerial
material
ministerial
monasterial
presbyterial
rhinocerial
serial

siderial
vizierial

ĒR'i-an
Abderian
aerian
Algerian
Celtiberian
Cimmerian
Hanoverian
Hesperian
Iberian
Keplerian
Luciferian
phalansterian
Pierian
Presbyterian
Shakespearean
Shakesperian
Siberian
Spenserian
Valerian
Valkyrian
Wertherian
(cf. ĒR'i-on
and ĬR'i-an)

ĔR'i-dez
Anterides
Hesperides
Pierides

ĒR'i-est
beeriest
bleariest
cheeriest
dreariest
eeriest
weariest

ĔR'i-est
buriest

ferriest, etc.
merriest

ĒR'i-ez
congeries
series

ĔR'-ing
berrying
burying
ferrying
wherrying

ĔR'i-kal
alexiterical
atmospherical
chimerical
clerical
climacterical
esoterical
exoterical
heliospherical
helispherical
hysterical
numerical
phylacterical
rhinocerical
spherical
sphericle

ĒR'i-li
cheerily
drearily
eerily
wearily

ĔR'i-li
merrily
verily

ĔR'i-man
ferryman

Merriman
wherryman

ĔR'i-ment
merriment
(cf. ŪR'i-ment)

ĒR'i-nes
beeriness
bleariness
cheeriness
dreariness
eeriness
weariness

ĒR'i-on
allerion
criterion
Hyperion
(cf. ĒR'i-an)

ĒR'i-or
anterior
exterior
inferior
interior
posterior
superior
ulterior
(cf. ĒR'i-ur)

ĔR'ish-ing
cherishing
perishing
unperishing

ĔR'i-ted
disherited
disinherited
emerited
ferreted

inherited
merited
(cf. turreted)

ĔR′i-ti
ambidexterity
asperity
austerity
celerity
dexterity
indexterity
insincerity
legerity
posterity
procerity
prosperity
severity
sincerity
temerity
verity

ĔR′it-ing
ferreting
inheriting
meriting

Ē′ri-um
acroterium
apodyterium
dinotherium
megatherium
palæotherium
titanotherium

ẸR′i-ur
beerier
blearier
bleerier
cheerier
drearier
eerier

wearier
(cf. ẸR′i-or)

ĔR′i-ur
burier
merrier
terrier

Ē′ri-us, ẸR′i-us
cereous
cereus
deleterious
ethereous
imperious
mysterious
serious
sidereous

ẸR′les-nes
cheerlessness
fearlessness
peerlessness

ĔR′o-gat
interrogate
(cf. ŬR′o-gat)

ẸR′yal-ist
immaterialist
imperialist
materialist

ẸR′yal-izm
immaterialism
imperialism
materialism

ĒS′a-b'l
creasable
releasable

ĔS′a-ri
confessary

intercessory
pessary
professory
successary

Ē′sen-si
decency
indecency
recency

ĔS′en-si
acescency
acquiescency
adolescency
alkalescency
convalescency
defervescency
delitescency
effervescency
efflorescency
erubescency
excrescency
incalescency
incandescency
liquescency
pubescency
quiescency
recrudescency
rejuvenescency
turgescency

Ē′sent-li
decently
indecently
recently

Ē′shi-an
Capetian
Epictetian
Grecian
Venetian

geodesian
gynæcian
Megalesian
Melanesian
Peloponnesian
Silesian
(cf. ĒSH′an,
ĒSH′un)

ĔSH′i-ens
nescience
prescience

ĔSH′i-nes
fleshiness
meshiness

ĔSH′li-nes
fleshliness
freshliness
unfleshliness

ĔSH′un-al
accessional
confessional
congressional
digressional
discretional
expressional
intercessional
possessional
processional
professional
progressional
recessional
retrocessional
sessional
successional
transgressional

ĔSH′un-ist
impressionist

progressionist
secessionist
successionist

ĔSH′un-ur
possessioner
processioner
secessioner

Ē′shus-nes
facetiousness
speciousness

ĔS′i-b'l
accessible
compressible
concessible
concrescible
effervescible
expressible
fermentescible
impressible
imputrescible
inaccessible
incessable
incompressible
ineffervescible
inexpressible
insuppressible
irrepressible
marcescible
putrescible
redressible
repressible
suppressible
transgressible
vitrescible

ĔS′i-mal
centesimal
decimal

infinitesimal
millesimal
nonagesimal
quadragesimal
septuagesimal
sexagesimal

ĔS′i-ti
obesity

ĔS′i-ti
necessity
obesity

ĔS′iv-nes
aggressiveness
depressiveness
excessiveness
expressiveness
impressiveness
inexpressive-
    ness
oppressiveness
progressiveness

ĔS′ti-al
agrestial
bestial
celestial
supercelestial

ĔS′ti-b'l
comestible
congestible
contestable
detestable
digestible
divestible
incontestable
indigestible

intestable
testable

ĔS′tin-al
destinal
intestinal

ĔS′tin-at
destinate
festinate
predestinate

ĔS′ti-nes
reastiness
yeastiness

ĔS′ti-nes
restiness
testiness

ĔS′tiv-nes
festiveness
restiveness
suggestiveness

ĔST′li-nes
beastliness
priestliness

ĔS′tri-al
pedestrial
superterrestrial
terrestrial
trimestrial

ĔS′tri-an
campestrian
equestrian
palestrian
pedestrian
sylvestrian

ĔS′tri-us
pedestrious
terestrious

ĔS′tu-ral
gestural
vestural

ĔS′tur-ing
festering
pestering
westering

ĔS′tu-us
incestuous
tempestuous

ĔT′a-b'l
cheatable
eatable
entreatable
escheatable
uneatable

ĔT′a-b'l
forgetable
getable
regretable
setable
unforgetable

ĔT′al-en
acetylene

ĔT′a-lin
metalline
petaline

ĔT′al-izm
bimetallism

monometallism
petalism

ĔT′ful-i
forgetfully
fretfully
regretfully

ĔT′ful-nes
forgetfulness
fretfulness
regretfulness

Ĕth′les-li
breathlessly
deathlessly

Ĕth′les-nes
breathlessness
deathlessness

ĔTH′ur-i
feathery
heathery
leathery
weathery

ĔTH′ur-ing
feathering
leathering
tethering
weathering

ĔT′i-kal
æsthetical
aloetical
alphabetical
anchoretical
antipathetical
antithetical
apathetical

apologetical
arithmetical
catechetical
cosmetical
dietetical
emporetical
energetical
epithetical
exegetical
heretical
hermetical
homiletical
hypothetical
noetical
planetical
poetical
theoretical

ĔT′i-kul
poeticule
reticule

ĔT′i-nes
meatiness
peatiness
sleetiness

ĔT′i-nes
jettiness
pettiness
sweatiness

ĔT′in-u
detinue
retinue

ĔT′ish-li
coquettishly
pettishly

ĔT′ish′nes
coquettishness
pettishness

ĔT′i-sizm
æstheticism
asceticism
athleticism
peripateticism

ĔT′o-ri
completory
depletory
repletory
secretory

ĔT′ri-kal
alkalimetrical
asymmetrical
barometrical
craniometrical
diametrical
geometrical
gnomiometrical
graphometrical
horometrical
isoperimetrical
metrical
obstetrical
perimetrical
planimetrical
pluviometrical
stichometrical
symmetrical
trigonometrical

ĔT′ri-ment
detriment
retriment

ĔT′ur-ing
bettering
fettering
lettering

ĔV′a-b′l
achievable
believable
cleavable
conceivable
deceivable
grievable
imperceivable
inconceivable
irretrievable
perceivable
receivable
relievable
retrievable
unbelievable
undeceivable

ĔV′el-est
bevellest
dishevellest
levellest
revellest

ĔV′el-ing
bedevilling
bevelling
dishevelling
levelling
revelling

ĔV′el-izm
devilism
levelism

ĔV′el-ur
beveller
bedeviller
disheveller
leveller
reveller

āle,   câre,   ădd,   ärm,   åsk;   mē,   hẹre,   ĕnd;   īce,   ĭll;

Ē'vi-at
abbreviate
alleviate
deviate

ĔV'il-ment
bedevilment
devilment
revelment

ĔV'il-ry
devilry
revelry

Ē'vish-li
peevishly
thievishly

Ē'vish-nes
peevishness
thievishness

ĔV'i-ti
brevity
levity
longevity

Ē'vi-us
devious
previous

ĔV'ol-ens
benevolence
malevolence

ĔV'ol-ent
benevolent
malevolent

ĔV'ol-us
benevolous
malevolous

ĔV'ol-ut
evolute
revolute

ĔV'ur-est
cleverest
endeavourest
Everest
severest

ĔV'ur-mor
evermore
nevermore

ĔV'ur-ur
cleverer
endeavorer
severer

Ē'za-b'l
appeasable
cohesible
defeasible
feasible
freezable
inappeasable
indefeasible
infeasible

seizable
squeezable
unappeasable

ĔZ'an-tri
peasantry
pheasantry
pleasantry

Ē'zhi-a, Ē'zi-a
amnesia
anæsthesia
ecclesia
esthesia
magnesia
parrhesia
Rhodesia
Silesia
Zambesia

Ē'zi-an
artesian
cartesian
ecclesian
Ephesian
etesian
magnesian
Milesian
Polynesian
trapezian
(cf. ĒZH'yan)

ĔZ'i-dent
president
resident

ĒZ'i-li
breezily
easily
greasily
uneasily
wheezily

ĒZ'i-nes
breeziness
cheesiness
easiness
greasiness
queasiness
sleaziness
uneasiness
wheeziness

ĒZ'ing-li
appeasingly
freezingly
pleasingly
teasingly
wheezingly

Ē'zon-ing
reasoning
seasoning
unreasoning

ĔZ'ur-ing
measuring
pleasuring
treasuring

ĔZ'ur-ur
measurer
pleasurer
treasurer

ōld, ôr, ŏdd, oil, fŏŏt, out; ūse, ûrn, ŭp; THis, thin

I

For a discussion of words included under the accented vowels following, see the beginning of I rhymes in Section I.

Ī′a-b′l
acidifiable
appliable
classifiable
compliable
deniable
diversifiable
electrifiable
exemplifiable
falsifiable
fortifiable
friable
impliable
justifiable
liable
liquefiable
magnifiable
modifiable
pacifiable
petrifiable
pliable
qualifiable
rarefiable
rectifiable
reliable
saponifiable
satisfiable
solidifiable
triable
undeniable
verifiable
viable
vitrifiable

Ī′a-bli
deniably

justifiably
reliably
undeniably, etc.

Ī′a-dez
hamadryades
Hyades
Pleiades

Ī′a-kal
bibliomaniacal
cardiacal
demoniacal
elegiacal
encyclopediacal
heliacal
hypochondria-
cal
maniacal
monomaniacal
paradisiacal
prosodiacal
simoniacal
zodiacal

Ī′an-si, Ī′en-si
cliency
compliancy
pliancy
riancy

Ī′ant-li
compliantly
defiantly
pliantly
reliantly

Ī′ar-i
friary
(see Ī′ur-i)

Ī′ar-ist
diarist
Piarist

Ī′ar-ki
diarchy
triarchy

Ī′a-sis
elephantiasis
hypochondria-
sis

Ī′a-sizm
demoniacism
hypochondriac-
ism

Ī′a-tur
psychiater
(cf. archiater)

ĪB′a-b′l
bribable
describable
indescribable
inscribable
scribable
subscribable
undescribable

ĬB′i-a
amphibia

Libya
tibia

ĬB′i-al
amphibial
stibial
tibial

ĬB′i-an
amphibian
Libyan

ĬB′i-tiv
exhibitive
prohibitive

ĬB′i-us
amphibious
bathybius
stibious

ĬB′u-lar
fibular
infundibular
mandibular
vestibular

ĬCH′i-nes
itchiness
pitchiness

ĬCH′ur-i
bewitchery
michery
stitchery
witchery

ĬD′a-b′l
decidable
dividable
ridable
bestridable, etc.

ĬD′en-nes
forbiddenness
hiddenness

ĬD′e-us
hideous
(see ĬD′i-us)

ĬD′i-al
noctidial
presidial

ĬD′i-an
antemeridian
Gideon
Lydian
meridian
Midian
nullifidian
Numidian
obsidian
ophidian
Ovidian
postmeridian
quotidian
rachidian

ĬD′i-at
dimidiate
insidate

ĬD′i-fi
acidify
lapidify
solidify

ĬD′i-kal
druidical
juridical
pyramidical
veridical

ĬD′i-nus
libidinous
(cf. pingue-
   dinous)

ĬD′i-ti
acidity
acridity
aridity
avidity
cupidity
frigidity
insipidity
insolidity
intrepidity
invalidity
gelidity
gravidity
hispidity
humidity
hybridity
limpidity
liquidity
lividity
lucidity
marcidity
morbidity
pallidity
pavidity
pellucidity
putidity
putridity
quiddity
rabidity

rancidity
rapidity
rigidity
sapidity
solidity
squalidity
stolidity
stupidity
timidity
torpidity
torridity
trepidity
tumidity
turbidity
turgidity
validity
vapidity
viridity
viscidity
vividity

**ĬD′i-om,
  ĬD′i-um**
idiom
iridium
peridium

ĬD′i-us
avidious
fastidious
hideous
insidious
invidious
lapideous
ophidious
parricidious
perfidious
Phidias
splendidious
stillicidious

ĬD′u-al
individual
residual

ĬD′u-at
assiduate
individuate

ĬD′u-lat
acidulate
stridulate

ĬD′u-lus
acidulous
stridulous

ĬD′u-us
assiduous
deciduous
prociduous
residuous
succiduous
viduous

Ī′en-si
cliency
(see Ī′an-si)

Ī′et-al
dietal
hyetal
parietal
varietal

Ī′et-ed
dieted
disquieted
quieted
rioted

Ī′et-est
dietest

quietest
riotest

Ī'et-i

anxiety
contrariety
dubiety
ebriety
filiety
impiety
impropriety
inebriety
insobriety
luxuriety
mediety
nimiety
notoriety
nullibiety
omniety
piety
propriety
satiety
sobriety
society
ubiety
variety

Ī'et-ing

dieting
disquieting
quieting
rioting

Ī'et-ist

anxietist
dietist
pietist
proprietist
quietist
varietiest

Ī'et-izm

pietism
quietism
varietism

Ī'et-ur, Ī'et-or

dieter
proprietor
quieter
rioter

ĬF'i-kal

beatifical
dolorifical
lanifical
pontifical
specifical

ĬF'i-kant

insignificant
mundificant
sacrificant
significant

ĬF'i-kat

certificate
pontificate
significate

ĬF'i-sens

magnificence
munificence

ĬF'i-sent

magnificent
mirificent
munificent

ĬF'i-sur

artificer
opificer

ĬF'lu-us

dulcifluous
fellifluous
ignifluous
mellifluous
sanguifluous

ĬF'on-i

antiphony
oxyphony
polyphony

ĬF'ra-gus

fedrifragous
ossifragous
saxifragous

ĬF'ta-b'l

liftable
shiftable

ĬF'ti-li

shiftily
thriftily

ĬF'ti-nes

shiftiness
thriftiness

ĬFT'les-nes

shiftlessness
thriftlessness

ĬF'u-gal

centrifugal
febrifugal
vermifugal

ĬF'ur-us

acidiferous
aliferous

aluminiferous
ammonitiferous
antenniferous
argentiferous
armiferous
astriferous
auriferous
balaniferous
balsamiferous
bulbiferous
calcariferous
calciferous
carboniferous
cheliferous
cirriferous
conchiferous
coniferous
coralliferous
cruciferous
diamantiferous
diamondiferous
doloriferous
ensiferous
fatiferous
ferriferous
filiferous
flammiferous
floriferous
fluctiferous
foliferous
foraminiferous
fossiliferous
frondiferous
frugiferous
fumiferous
furciferous
gemmiferous
geodiferous
glandiferous
glanduliferous

graniferous
granuliferous
guttiferous
gypsiferous
hederiferous
herbiferous
igniferous
lactiferous
lamelliferous
laminiferous
lanciferous
laniferous
laticiferous
lauriferous
lethiferous
ligniferous
lignitiferous
luciferous
lucriferous
luminiferous
magnetiferous
maliferous
mammaliferous
mammiferous
margaritiferous
melliferous
membrani-
  ferous
metalliferous
monstriferous
mortiferous
multiferous
nectariferous
nickeliferous
nimbiferous
nitriferous
noctiferous
nubiferous
nuciferous
odoriferous
oleiferous

omniferous
oolitiferous
ossiferous
ostriferous
ozoniferous
palmiferous
pestiferous
pistilliferous
platiniferous
plumbiferous
polypiferous
proliferous
pruniferous
pulmoniferous
quartiziferous
racemiferous
resiniferous
roriferous
sacchariferous
sacciferous
saliferous
saliniferous
salutiferous
sanguiferous
scopiferous
scutiferous
sebiferous
sensiferous
setiferous
siliciferous
somniferous
soniferous
soporiferous
spiciferous
spiniferous
spumiferous
stameniferous
stanniferous
stelliferous
stoloniferous
succiferous

sudoriferous
tentaculiferous
tergiferous
thuriferous
tuberiferous
umbelliferous
umbraculifer-
  ous
umbriferous
vaporiferous
vasculiferous
vociferous
zinciferous

ĬG′am-i

bigamy
digamy
polygamy
trigamy

ĬG′am-ist

bigamist
polygamist
trigamist

ĬG′am-us

bigamous
digamous
polygamous
trigamous

ĬG′ma-tist

enigmatist
stigmatist

ĬG′ma-tiz

enigmatize
paradigmatize
stigmatize

ĬG′nan-si

indignancy
malignancy

ĬG′ne-us

igneous
ligneous

ĬG′ni-fi

dignify
ignify
lignify
malignify
signify
undignify

ĬG′ni-ti

benignity
dignity
indignity
malignity

ĬG′or-us

rigorous
vigorous

ĬG′ra-fi

calligraphy
epigraphy
lexigraphy
pasigraphy
poligraphy
pseudepigrahy
stratigraphy
tachygraphy

ĬG′u-lat

figulate
ligulate

ĬG′ur-i

piggery
Whiggery
wiggery

ōld, ôr, ŏdd, oil, fŏŏt out; ūse, ûrn, ŭp; THis, thin

ĬG′u-us
ambiguous
contiguous
exiguous
irriguous

ĬJ′en-us
alkaligenous
coralligenous
epigenous
fuliginous
gelatigenous
ignigenous
indigenous
marigenous
melligenous
montigenous
nubigenous
omnigenous
oxygenous
polygenous
pruriginous
sanguigenous
terrigenous
uliginous
unigenous
vertiginous
vortiginous

ĬJ′i-an
Cantabrigian
Phrygian
Stygian

ĬJ′id-li
frigidly
rigidly

ĬJ′id-nes
frigidness
rigidness

ĬJ′i-ti
digity
fidgety

ĬJ′ur-at
belligerate
frigerate
refrigerate

ĬJ′ur-ent
belligerent
refrigerant

ĬJ′ur-us
aligerous
armigerous
belligerous
cirrigerous
coralligerous
cornigerous
crucigerous
dentigerous
immorigerous
lanigerous
linigerous
morigerous
navigerous
ovigerous
palpigerous
pedigerous
pennigerous
piligerous
plumigerous
proligerous
setigerous
spinigerous

ĬJ′us-nes
litigiousness
prodigiousness
religiousness

ĬK′a-ment
medicament
predicament

ĬK′a-tiv
abdicative
desiccative
exsiccative
fricative
indicative
predicative
siccative

ĬK′en-ing
quickening
sickening
thickening

ĬK′et-i
pernicketty
rickety
thicketty

ĬK′et-ing
cricketing
picketing
ticketing

ĬK′et-ur
cricketer
picketer

ĬK′i-li
stickily
trickily

ĬK′i-nes
stickiness
trickiness

ĬK′li-nes
prickliness
sickliness

ĬK′o-list
agricolist
ignicolist
plebicolist

ĬK′o-lus
agricolous
sepicolous
terricolous

ĬK′o-mus
auricomous
flavicomous

ĬK′sa-b'l
fixable
mixable

ĬK′shun-al
contradictional
fictional
frictional
jurisdictional

ĬK′si-ti
fixity
prolixity
siccity

ĬK′tiv-li
restrictively
vindictively

ĬK′tiv-nes
restrictiveness
vindictiveness

ĬK′to-ri
benedictory
contradictory
interdictory

valedictory
victory

ĬK'u-la
Canicula
fidicula
zeticula

ĬK'u-lar
acicular
adminicular
articular
auricular
calycular
canicular
clavicular
cubicular
cuticular
fascicular
follicular
funicular
lenticular
navicular
orbicular
ovicular
particular
pellicular
perpendicular
quinquarticular
radicular
reticular
spicular
subcuticular
vehicular
ventricular
vermicular
versicular
vesicular

ĬK'u-lat
articulate

canaliculate
denticulate
fasciculate
funiculate
geniculate
gesticulate
matriculate
monticulate
paniculate
particulate
reticulate
spiculate
vehiculate
vermiculate
vesiculate

ĬK'u-lum
curriculum
geniculum

ĬK'u-lus
dendiculus
denticulus
fasciculus
folliculous
meticulous
ridiculous
urbiculous
ventriculous
vermiculous
vesiculous

ĬK'wi-ti
antiquity
iniquity
obliquity
ubiquity

ĬK'wi-tus
iniquitous
ubiquitous

ĬL'a-b'l
distillable
fillable
refillable
syllable
tillable
unrefillable

Ĭ'lan-dur
highlander
islander

ĬL'a-ri
Hilary
(see ĬL'ur-i)

ĬL'et-ed
billeted
filleted
unfilleted

ĬL'et-ing
billeting
filleting

ĬL'ful-i
guilefully
wilefully

ĬL'ful-i
skilfully
wilfully
unskilfully

ĬL'ful-nes
guilefulness
wilefulness

ĬL'ful-nes
skilfulness

wilfulness
unskilfulness

ĬL'i-a
memorabilia
notabilia
sedilia

ĬL'i-ad
chiliad
Iliad
(cf. Gilead)

ĬL'i-an
Brazilian
Castilian
Cecilian
crocodilian
Kurilian
lacertilian
Lilian
Maximilian
perfectibilian
reptilian
Virgilian
(cf. ĬL'yun)

ĬL'i-ar
atrabiliar
auxiliar
conciliar
domiciliar
(see ĬL'yar)

ĬL'i-at
affiliate
conciliate
domiciliate
filiate
humiliate

ōld, ôr, ŏdd, oil, fŏŏt, out; ūse, ûrn, ŭp; THis, thin

ĬL'i-ens
consilience
dissilience
resilience
transilience
(cf. brilliance)

ĬL'i-ent
dissilient
resilient
transilient
(cf. brilliant)

ĬL'i-est
chilliest
hilliest
silliest
stilliest

ĬL'i-fi
fossilify
nobilify
stabilify
vilify

ĬL'i-form
filiform
plumiliform

ĬL'i-gan
Gilligan
McMilligan

ĬL'ij-ur
pillager
villager

ĬL'i-ka
basilica
silica

ĬL'i-kal
basilical

filical
silicle
umbilical

ĬL'i-nes
chilliness
hilliness
silliness

ĬL'ing-li
killingly
thrillingly
trillingly
willingly

ĬL'i-o
pulvillio
punctilio

ĬL'i-tat
abilitate
debilitate
facilitate
habilitate
impossibilitate
militate
nobilitate
rehabilitate
stabilitate

ĬL'i-ti
ability
absorbability
accendibility
acceptability
accessibility
accountability
acquirability
adaptability
addibility
admirability

admissibility
adoptability
adorability
advisability
affability
affectibility
agility
agreeability
alienability
alterability
amenability
amiability
amicability
amissibility
anility
appetibility
applicability
assimilability
associability
attainability
attemptability
attractability
audibility
availability
capability
changeability
civility
cognoscibility
cohesibility
combustibility
communicabil-
    ity
commutability
compatibility
comprehensibil-
    ity
compressibility
computability
conceivability
condensability
conducibility

conductability
conformability
confusability
contemptibility
contractibility
contractility
convertibility
corrigibility
corrodibility
corrosibility
credibility
creditability
crocodility
culpability
curability
damnability
debility
deceptibility
deducibility
defectibility
demisability
demonstrabil-
    ity
deplorability
descendibility
desirability
despicability
destructibility
determinability
detestability
diffusibility
digestibility
dilatability
disability
dissolubility
dissolvability
distensibility
divisibility
docibility
docility
ductility

durability
edibility
educability
eligibility
equability
exchangeability
excitability
exhaustibility
expansibility
extensibility
facility
fallibility
feasibility
fermentability
fertility
fictility
flexibility
fluctuability
fluxibility
formidability
fossility
fragility
frangibility
friability
fusibility
futility
generability
gentility
gracility
gullibility
habitability
hostility
humility
ignobility
illability
imbecility
imitability
immeability
immeasura-
  bility
immiscibility

immovability
immutability
impalpability
impartibility
impassibility
impeccability
impenetrability
impercepti-
  bility
imperdibility
impermeability
imperturba-
  bility
imperviability
implacability
impossibility
impregnability
imprescripti-
  bility
impressibility
impressiona-
  bility
improbability
imputability
inability
inaccessibility
incivility
incogitability
incognoscibility
incombusti-
  bility
incommensura-
  bility
incommunica-
  bility
incommuta-
  bility
incompatibility
incomprehensi-
  bility

incompressi-
  bility
inconceiva-
  bility
incondensa-
  bility
incontroverti-
  bility
inconvertibility
incorrigibility
incorruptibility
incredibility
incurability
indefatigability
indefeasibility
indefectibility
indelibility
indemonstra-
  bility
indestructi-
  bility
indigestibility
indiscernibility
indiscerpti-
  bility
indispensability
indisputability
indissolubility
indivisibility
indocibility
indocility
inductility
ineffability
ineffervesci-
  bility
ineligibility
inevitability
inexhaustibility
inexorability
inexplicability
infallibility

infeasibility
infertility
inflammability
inflexibility
infrangibility
infusibility
inhability
inhabitability
inheritability
inimitability
innumbera-
  bility
insanability
insatiability
insensibility
inseparability
insociability
insolubility
instability
insuperability
insurmounta-
  bility
insusceptibility
intangibility
intelligibility
interchange-
  ability
intractability
inutility
invendibility
invincibility
inviolability
invisibility
invulnerability
irascibility
irreconcilability
irreductibility
irremovability
irreparability
irresistibility
irresponsibility

ōld, êr, ŏdd, oil, fŏŏt, out; ūse, ûrn, ŭp; THis, thin

irritability
juvenility
lability
laminability
laudability
legibility
liability
malleability
manageability
memorability
mensurability
miscibility
mobility
modifiability
modificability
motility
movability
mutability
navigability
negotiability
neurility
nihility
nobility
notability
opposability
organizability
ostensibility
palpability
partibility
passibility
peccability
penetrability
pensility
perceptibility
perdurability
perfectibility
permissibility
persuasibility
perturbability
placability
plausibility

pliability
ponderability
portability
possibility
practicability
precipitability
preferability
prescriptibility
preventability
probability
producibility
puerility
quotability
ratability
readability
receivability
receptibility
redeemability
reductibility
reflexibility
refragability
refrangibility
refutability
reliability
remissibility
removability
remunerability
renewability
reparability
repealability
resistibility
resolvability
respectability
responsibility
reversibility
revocability
risibility
saleability
salvability
sanability
satiability

scurrility
senility
sensibility
separability
servility
sociability
solubility
solvability
sportability
squeezability
stability
sterility
suability
subtility
suitability
susceptibility
suspensibility
tactility
tamability
tangibility
taxability
temptability
tenability
tensibility
tensility
tolerability
torsibility
tortility
tractability
tractility
tranquillity
transferability
transmissibility
transmutability
transportability
unaccount-
   ability
unbelievability
unutterability
utility
vaporability

variability
vegetability
vendibility
venerability
verisimility
vernility
versability
versatility
viability
vibratility
vindicability
virility
visibility
volatility
volubility
vulnerability
writability

ĬL'ĭ-us

atrabilious
bilious
punctilious
supercilious
(cf. as ĬL'yus)

ĬL'ki-est

milkiest
silkiest

ĬL'ki-ur

milkier
silkier

Ī'lo-bat

stylobate
trilobate

ĬL'o-i

billowy
pillowy
willowy

ĬL'o-ing
billowing
pillowing

ĬL'o-ji
antilogy
brachylogy
dilogy
fossilogy
palilogy
trilogy

ĬL'o-jiz
epilogize
syllogize

ĬL'o-jizm
epilogism
episyllogism
syllogism

ĬL'o-ri
pillory
(see ĬL'ur-i)

ĬL'o-kwens
blandiloquence
breviloquence
grandiloquence
magniloquence
somniloquence
stultiloquence

ĬL'o-kwent
flexiloquent
grandiloquent
magniloquent
melliloquent
pauciloquent
sanctiloquent
stultiloquent

suaviloquent
veriloquent

ĬL'o-kwi
dentiloquy
gastriloquy
pauciloquy
pectoriloquy
soliloquy
somniloquy
stultiloquy
suaviloquy
ventriloquy

ĬL'o-kwist
dentiloquist
gastriloquist
somniloquist
ventriloquist

ĬL'o-kwiz
soliloquize
ventriloquize

ĬL'o-kwizm
gastriloquism
pectoriloquism
somniloquism
ventriloquism

ĬL'o-kwus
grandiloquous
magniloquous
pectoriloquous
somniloquous
ventriloquous

ĬL'ur-i
artillery
capillary
cilery

codicillary
distillery
Hilary
phyllary
pillory
Sillery

ĬL'yan-si
brilliancy
resiliency
transiliency

ĬL'yar-i
atrabiliary
auxiliary

ĬM'a-nus
longimanous
pedimanous

ĬM'a-tur
climature
limature

ĬM'bri-kat
fimbricate
imbricate

Ī'mer-i
primary
rhymery

ĬM'et-ri
alkalimetry
asymmetry
bathymetry
calorimetry
isoperimetry
longimetry
planimetry
polarimetry

saccharimetry
symmetry

ĬM'et-ur
alkalimeter
altimeter
calorimeter
dasymeter
dimeter
focimeter
gravimeter
limiter
lucimeter
pelvimeter
perimeter
planimeter
polarimeter
pulsimeter
rhysimeter
saccharimeter
salimeter
scimiter
tasimeter
trimeter
velocimeter
zymosimeter
(cf. scimitar)

**ĬM'i-an,
ĬM'i-on**
Endymion
simian
Simeon

ĬM'i-kal
alchymical
homonymical
inimical
metonymical
mimical

ĬM'i-nal
criminal
regiminal
subliminal
viminal

ĬM'i-nat
accriminate
criminate
discriminate
eliminate
incriminate
indiscriminate
recriminate

ĪM'i-nes
griminess
sliminess

ĬM'i-ni
Bimini
jiminy
nimini-pimini
postliminy

ĬM'i-nus
criminous
moliminous

ĬM'i-ti
anonymity
dimity
equanimity
magnanimity
parvanimity
proximity
pseudonymity
pusillanimity
sanctanimity
sublimity
unanimity

ĬM'pur-ing
simpering
whimpering

ĬM'pur-ur
simperer
whimperer

ĬM'u-lat
assimulate
dissimulate
simulate
stimulate

ĬM'u-lus
limulus
stimulus

ĬM'ur-us
dimerous
polymerous

ĪN'a-b'l
assignable
combinable
declinable
definable
designable
finable
inclinable
indeclinable
indefinable
signable

ĪN'ar-i
binary
(see ĪN'ur-i)

ĪN'a-tiv
combinative
finative

ĬN'di-kat
indicate
syndicate
vindicate

ĪN'dur-i
bindery
grindery

ĬN'dur-i
cindery
tindery

ĬN'e-al, ĬN'i-al
consanguineal
finial
gramineal
interlineal
lineal
pectineal
pineal
stamineal

ĬN'e-ma
cinema
kinema

ĬN'e-us
cartilagineous
consanguine-
ous
flamineous
fulmineous
gramineous
ignominious
sanguineous
stamineous
stramineous
testudineous
vimineous

ĬNG'gur-ing
fingering
lingering
malingering

ĬNG'gur-ur
fingerer
lingerer
malingerer

ĬNG'i-nes
ringiness
springiness
stringiness

ĬNGK'a-b'l
drinkable
shrinkable
thinkable
undrinkable
unshrinkable
unsinkable
unthinkable

ĬNGK'i-nes
inkiness
kinkiness
pinkiness
slinkiness

ĬNGK'wi-ti
longinquity
propinquity

ĬN'i-al
finial
(see ĪN'e-al)

ĬN'i-a
Abyssinia
Lavinia

Sardinia
Virginia
zinnia

ĬN′i-an
Abyssinian
anthropopha-
  ginian
Arminian
Augustinian
Carolinian
Carthaginian
czarinian
Darwinian
Delphinian
Eleusinian
Hercynian
Justinian
Palestinean
Sardinian
serpentinian
Socinian
viraginian
Virginian
(cf. ĬN′yon)

ĬN′i-at, ĬN′e-at
delineate
laciniate
lineate
miniate

ĬN′i-est
briniest
shiniest
spiniest
tiniest

ĬN′i-form
actiniform

aluminiform
laciniform

ĬN′i-kin
finikin
minikin

ĬN′i-k'l
adminicle
binnacle
binocle
Brahminical
clinical
cynical
dominical
finical
flaminical
pinnacle
Sinical
synclinical

ĬN′i-ment
liniment
miniment

ĬN′ish-ing
diminishing
finishing

ĬN′is-tral
ministral
sinistral

ĬN′is-tur
administer
minister
sinister

ĬN′i-ti
affinity
alkalinity
asininity

consanguinity
divinity
felinity
femininity
infinity
Latinity
masculinity
patavinity
peregrinity
salinity
sanguinity
satinity
trinity
vicinity
viraginity
virginity

ĬN′i-tiv
combinative
finitive
infinitive

ĬN′i-ur
brinier
shinier
spinier
tinier

ĬN′jen-si
astringency
contingency
refringency
stringency

ĬN′ji-an
Carlovingian
Merovingian
Thuringian

ĬN′ji-li
dingily
stingily

ĬN′ji-nes
dinginess
stinginess

ĬN′lan-dur
Finlander
inlander

ĬN′o-lin
crinoline
quinoline

ĬN′thi-an
absinthian
Corinthian
hyacinthian
labyrinthian

ĬN′tur-est
interest
splinterest
winterest

ĬN′tur-i
printery
splintery
wintery

ĬN′ur-i
alpinery
binary
finary
finery
pinery
quinary
refinery
swinery
vinery

ĬN′u-at
continuate

insinuate
sinuate

Ĭn'u-us
continuous
sinuous

Ī'ol-a
variola
viola

Ī'o-let
triolet
violet

Ī'o-list
sciolist
violist

Ī'o-lus
gladiolus
sciolous
variolous

Ī'o-pe
Calliope
myopy
presbyopy

Ī'o-tur
rioter
(see Ī'et-ur)

Ī'o-sen
Miocene
Pliocene
post-Pliocene

Ĭp'ar-us
biparous
criniparous

deiparous
fissiparous
floriparous
foliiparous
frondiparous
fructiparous
gemelliparous
gemmiparous
larviparous
multiparous
omniparous
opiparous
oviparous
ovoviviparous
polyparous
polypiparous
sebiparous
sudoriparous
tomiparous
uniparous
vermiparous
viviparous

Ĭp'a-thi
antipathy
kinesipathy
somnipathy

Ĭp'a-thist
antipathist
somnipathist

Ĭp'ed-al
equipedal
solipedal
(cf. Ēd'al)

Ĭp'li-kat
sesquiplicate
triplicate

Ĭp'o-li
Gallipoli
Tripoli

Ĭp'o-tens
armipotence
ignipotence
omnipotence
plenipotence

Ĭp'o-tent
armipotent
bellipotent
ignipotent
multipotent
omnipotent
plenipotent

Ĭp'ti-kal
apocalyptical
cryptical
elliptical

Ĭp'tur-us
dipterous
peripterous
tripterous

Ĭp'u-lat
astipulate
manipulate
stipulate

Ĭp'ur-i
frippery
slippery

Ĭr'a-b'l
acquirable
desirable
expirable

perspirable
requirable
respirable
transpirable
untirable

Ĭr'as-i
piracy
retiracy

Ĭr'as-i
conspiracy
deliracy

Ĭr'ful-nes
direfulness
irefulness

Ĭr'i-an
Assyrian
Styrian
Syrian
Tyrian
(cf. Ēr'i-an)

Ĭr'i-kal
empirical
lyrical
miracle
panegyrical
satirical

Ĭr'i-sizm
empiricism
lyricism

Ĭr'i-us
delirious
Sirius
(cf. Ēr'i·us)

āle,   câre,   ădd,   ärm,   åsk;   mē,   hēre,   ĕnd;   īce,   ĭll;

ĬR′on-i

gyronny
irony

ĬS′en-ing

christening
glistening
listening
unlistening

ĬS′en-si

reminiscency
reviviscency

ĬS′en-ur

christener
listener

ĬSH′al-i

judicially
officially
prejudicially
superficially

ĬSH′al-izm

judicialism
officialism

ĬSH′en-si

alliciency
beneficiency
deficiency
efficiency
inefficiency
insitiency
insufficiency
proficiency
self-sufficiency
sufficiency

ĬSH′i-a

Alicia

Delicia
Felicia

ĬSH′i-at

initiate
maleficiate
novitiate
officiate
patriciate
propitiate
vitiate

ĬSH′i-ens

omniscience
(cf. ĬSH′ens)

ĬSH′i-ent

omniscient
(cf. ĬSH′ent)

ĬSH′on-al

additional
commissional
conditional
definitional
dispositional
disquisitional
inquisitional
intuitional
positional
prepositional
propositional
repetitional
suppositional
traditional
transitional
transpositional
volitional

ĬSH′on-ist

abolitionist
coalitionist

exhibitionist
expeditionist
oppositionist
prohibitionist
requisitionist
traditionist

ĬSH′on-ur

admonitioner
coalitioner
commissioner
exhibitioner
missioner
practitioner
traditioner

ĬSH′us-nes

adventitious-
  ness
auspiciousness
avariciousness
capriciousness
deliciousness
expeditiousness
fictitiousness
flagitiousness
inauspicious-
  ness
judiciousness
maliciousness
meretricious-
  ness
perniciousness
propitiousness
seditiousness
superstitious-
  ness
supposititious-
  ness
suspiciousness
viciousness

ĬS′i-b′l

admissible
amissible
dismissible
immiscible
incommiscible
irremissable
miscible
omissible
permiscible
permissible
remissible
scissible
transmissible

ĬS′i-est

iciest
spiciest

Ī′si-k′l

bicycle
icicle
tricycle

ĬS′i-li

icily
spicily

ĬS′i-mo

bravissimo
fortissimo
generalissimo
pianissimo
prestissimo

ĬS′i-nal

fidicinal
medicinal
officinal
vaticinal
vicinal

ĬS'i-nes
iciness
spiciness

ĬS'i-ti
accomplicity
achromaticity
authenticity
benedicite
caloricity
canonicity
catholicity
causticity
centricity
clericity
complicity
conicity
domesticity
duplicity
eccentricity
elasticity
electricity
electrotonicity
ellipticity
endemicity
evangelicity
felicity
historicity
hygroscopicity
immundicity
impudicity
inelasticity
infelicity
lubricity
mendicity
multiplicity
pepticity
periodicity
plasticity
publicity
pudicity

rubricity
rusticity
simplicity
spasticity
sphericity
spheroidicity
stoicity
stypticity
tonicity
triplicity
unicity
verticity
volcanicity
vulcanicity

ĬS'it-nes
explicitness
illicitness
implicitness
licitness

ĬS'i-tud
solicitude
spissitude
vicissitude

Ī'si-us
Dionysius
(cf. Lycias)

ĬS'iv-li
decisively
derisively
incisively
indecisively

ĬS'iv-nes
decisiveness
derisiveness
incisiveness
indecisivenes

ĬS'ki-est
friskiest
riskiest

ĬS'on-us
fluctisonous
unisonous

ĬS'or-i, ĬS'ur-i
decisory
derisory
incisory
spicery

ĬS'or-i
admissory
dismissory
emissory
remisory
rescissory

ĬS'ten-si
consistency
distancy
existency
inconsistency
persistency
pre-existency
subsistency

ĬS'ti-kal
agonistical
alchemistical
anarchistical
anomalistical
antagonistical
antarchistical
aoristical
apathistical
aphoristical
artistical

atheistical
cabalistical
Calvanistical
casuistical
cathechistical
characteristical
chemistical
deistical
dialogistical
egostical
egotistical
eucharistical
eulogistical
euphemistical
hemistichal
linguistical
methodistical
mystical
paragraphisti-
   cal
pietistical
puristical
sophistical
statistical
theistical
theosophistical

ĬS'ti-kat
dephlogisticate
sophisticate

ĬST'les-nes
listlessness
resistlessness

ĬS'to-ri
consistory
history
mystery

ĪT'a-b'l
citable

---

excitable
ignitible
incitable
indictable
lightable
requitable
unitable
writable

ĬT'a-b'l
admittable
fittable
irremittable
knittable
quittable
transmittible

ĬT'an-i
dittany
kitteny
litany

ĬT'a-tiv
excitative
incitative
writative

ĬT'ful-i
delightfully
frightfully
rightfully
spitefully

Ĭth'e-sis
antithesis
epithesis

ĬTH'som-li
blithesomely
lithesomely

ĬTH'som-nes
blithesomeness
lithesomeness

ĬTH'ur-ward
hitherward
thitherward
whitherward

ĬT'i-gant
litigant
mitigant

ĬT'i-gat
litigate
mitigate

ĬT'i-kal
Abrahamitical
acritical
analytical
anchoritical
cosmopolitical
critical
diacritical
electrolytical
hermitical
hypercritical
hypocritical
Jesuitical
Levitical
political
pulpitical
soritical
thersitical

ĬT'i-li
grittily
prettily
wittily

ĬT'i-nes
almightiness
flightiness
mightiness

ĬT'i-nes
flittiness
grittiness
prettiness
wittiness

ĬT'i-sizm
Britticism
witticism

ĬT'li-nes
knightliness
spriteliness
unsightliness

ĬT''l-nes
brittleness
littleness

ĬT'u-al
habitual
obitual
ritual

ĬT'u-at
habituate
situate

ĬT'u-lar
capitular
titular

ĬT'ur-at
illiterate
iterate
literate

obliterate
reiterate
transliterate

ĬT'ur-est
bitterest
embitterest
fritterest
glitterest

ĬT'ur-ing
bittering
embittering
frittering
glittering
tittering
twittering

Ĭ'ur-i
briery
fiery
friary
(cf. diary)

ĬV'a-b'l
contrivable
deprivable
derivable
revivable

ĬV'a-b'l
forgivable
givable
livable
unforgivable

ĬV'a-lent
equivalent
multivalent
omnivalent
quinquivalent

trivalent
univalent

ĬV′an-si
connivancy
survivancy

ĬV′a-tiv
derivative
privative

ĬV′el-ur,
  ĬV′il-ur
civiller
driveller
sniveller

ĬV′i-a
Bolivia
Livia
Olivia
trivia

ĬV′i-al
convivial
lixivial
oblivial
quadrivial
trivial

ĬV′i-an
Bolivian
Vivian
(cf. Vivien)

ĬV′id-nes
lividness
vividness

ĬV′i-ti
absorptivity

acclivity
activity
captivity
causativity
cogitativity
collectivity
conductivity
declivity
festivity
impassivity
incogitativity
instinctivity
motivity
nativity
negativity
objectivity
passivity
perceptivity
positivity
privity
proclivity
productivity
receptivity
relativity
sensitivity
subjectivity

ĬV′i-us
bivious
lascivious
lixivious
multivious
oblivious

ĬV′o-kal
equivocal
univocal

ĬV′o-li
Rivoli
Tivoli

ĬV′o-ri, ĬV′ar-i
ivory
vivary

ĬV′or-us
carnivorous
equivorous
frugivorous
fucivorous
graminivorous
granivorous
herbivorous
insectivorous
omnivorous
ossivorous
panivorous
phytivorous
piscivorous
sanguinivorous
vermivorous

ĬV′ur-i
delivery
gaol-delivery
jail-delivery
livery
rivery
shivery

ĬV′ur-ing
delivering
quivering
shivering

ĬV′ur-ur
deliverer
quiverer
shiverer

ĪZ′a-b'l
advisable

analysable
crystallizable
demisable
despisable
devisable
electrolysable
excisable
exercisable
magnetizable
organizable
oxidizable
prizable
realizable
recognizable
sizable
vaporizable

ĬZ′a-b'l
acquisible
divisible
indivisible
invisible
risible
visible

ĬZH′on-al
divisional
provisional
revisional
transitional
visional

ĬZ′i-an
Elysian
Frisian
Paradisean
Parisian
precisian
(cf. ĬZH′un)

ĬZ'i-est
busiest
dizziest

ĬZ'i-kal
metaphysical
paradisical
phthisical

physical
psychophysical

ĬZ'i-li
busily
dizzily

ĬZ'i-tor
acquisitor

inquisitor
requisitor
visitor

ĬZ'i-ur
busier
dizzier
frizzier

ĪZ'or-i
advisory
irrisory
provisory
revisory
supervisory

O

For a discussion of words included under the accented vowels
following, see the beginning of O rhymes in Section I.

Ō'bi-a
hydrophobia,
    etc.
phobia
Zenobia

ŎB'i-net
bobbinet
robinet

ŎB'u-lar
globular
lobular

ŎB'ur-i
daubery
(cf. straw-
    berry)

ŎB'ur-i
bobbery
jobbery
robbery
slobbery

snobbery
stockjobbery

ŎB'ur-ing
clobbering
slobbering

ŌD'i-al
allodial
custodial
episodial
palinodial
prosodial
threnodial

ŌD'i-an
custodian
Herodian
prosodian
Rhodian
(cf. ŌD'i-on)

ŎD'el-ur
modeller
(cf. ŎD'lur)

ŎD'i-fi
codify
modify

ŎD'i-kal
codical
episcodical
methodical
monodical
nodical
periodical
prosodical
rhapsodical
spasmodical
synodical

ŎD'i-nes
bawdiness
gaudiness

ŎD'i-ti
commodity
incommodity
oddity

ŌD'i-um
odium
rhodium
sodium

ŌD'i-us
commodious
incommodious
melodious
odious

ŎD'ri-nes
bawdriness
tawdriness

ŎD'u-lar
modular
nodular

ŎD'ur-ik
Roderick
Theoderic

ŎD'ur-ing
doddering
foddering

ōld, ôr, ŏdd, oil, fŏŏt, out; ūse, ûrn, ŭp; THis, thin

ŎF′a-gan
saprophagan
sarcophagan
theophagan
zoophagan

ŎF′a-gī
androphagi
anthropophagi
cardophagi
heterophagi
hippophagi
lithophagi
Lotophagi
sarcophagi

ŎF′a-gī
anthropophagy
chthonophagy
hippiphagy
ichthyophagy
pantophagy
phytophagy
theophagy
xerophagy

ŎF′a-gist
galactophagist
geophagist
hippophagist
ichthyophagist
pantophagist

ŎF′a-gus
androphagous
batrachopha-
  gous
esophagus
galactophagous
geophagous
hippophagous

hylophagous
lithophagous
necrophagous
ophiophagous
pantophagous
phytophagous
saprophagous
sarcophagus
theophagous
xylophagous
zoophagous

ŎF′i-kal
philosophical
theosophical
trophical

ŎF′i-list
bibliophilist
Russophilist
zoophilist

ŎF′i-lizm
bibliophilism
necrophilism
Russophilism

ŎF′il-us
acidophilus
anemophilous
Theophilus
xylophilous

ŎF′o-ni
cacophony
homophony
laryngophony
microphony
orthophony
photophony
Satanophany

tautophony
theophany

ŎF′on-us
cacophonous
homophonous
hydrophanous
hygrophanous
megalophonous
monophanous
pyrophanous

ŎF′or-us
actinophorous
adenophorous
electrophorus
galactophorous
isophorus
mastigo-
  phorous
phyllophorous
pyrophorous
zoophorous

Ŏ′ful-i
awfully
lawfully
unlawfully

Ŏ′ful-nes
awfulness
lawfulness
unlawfulness

ŎF′ur-ing
coffering
offering
peace-offering
proffering

ŎG′am-i
cœnogamy

deuterogamy
endogamy
exogamy
misogamy
monogamy

ŎG′am-ist
deuterogamist
misogamist
monogamist
neogamist

ŎG′am-us
endogamus
exogamous
heterogamous
monogamous
phænogamous
phanerog-
  amous

ŎG′a-tiv
derogative
interrogative
prerogative

Ŏ′gi-ism
bogeyism
fogeyism

ŎG′no-mi
craniognomy
pathognomy
physiognomy

ŎG′ra-fi
anthography
anthropog-
  raphy
autobiography
autography

āle,   câre,   ădd,   ärm,   åsk;   mē,   hẹre,   ĕnd;   īce,   ĭll;

balneography
bibliography
biography
cacography
calcography
chartography
chirography
chorography
Christianog-
raphy
chromatog-
raphy
chromophotog-
raphy
chromotypog-
raphy
chromoxylog-
raphy
climatography
cosmography
cryptography
crystalography
dactyliography
demography
dendrography
epistolography
ethnography
galvanography
geography
glossography
glyphography
glyptography
gypsography
hagiography
haliography
heliography
heliotypog-
raphy
hematography
heresiography
heterography

hierography
histography
historiography
horography
horologi-
ography
hyalography
hydrography
hyetography
hymnography
ichnography
ichthyography
iconography
ideography
isography
lexicography
lichenography
lithography
logography
mechanog-
raphy
metallography
microcosmog-
raphy
monography
neography
neurography
nomography
nosography
numismatog-
raphy
odontography
ophiography
oreography
organography
orography
orthography
osteography
palæography
palæontog-
raphy

paneiconog-
raphy
pantography
perspectog-
raphy
petrography
phantasma-
tography
pharmacog-
raphy
phonography
photography
phycography
physiography
phytography
plastography
pneumography
pornography
potamography
psalmography
pseudography
psychography
pterylography
rhyparography
scenography
sciography
seismography
selenography
semeiography
siderography
sphenography
steganography
stelography
stenography
stereography
steoreotypog-
raphy
stratography
stylography
symbolæog-
raphy

tacheography
thermography
topography
toreumatog-
raphy
typography
uranography
xylography
xylopyrography
zincograyhy
zoography

ŎG′ra-fist
chirographist
lichenographist
mechano-
graphist
metallo-
graphist
monographist
museographist
organogra-
phist
orthographist
palæographist
phonographist
photographist
psalmographist
selenographist
siderographist
sphenographist
steganogra-
phist
stenographist
topographist
uranographist
zoographist

ŎG′ra-fur
autobiographer
bibliographer

ōld, ôr, ŏdd, oil, fŏŏt, out; ūse, ûrn, ŭp; ·THis, thin

biographer
calcographer
cartographer
chartographer
chorographer
chronographer
cosmographer
cryptographer
crystallogra-
    pher
ethnographer
geographer
glossographer
glyphographer
glyptographer
haliographer
heresiographer
hierographer
historiographer
horologiogra-
    pher
hydrographer
hymnographer
iambographer
lexicographer
lichenographer
lithographer
logographer
mimographer
monographer
mythographer
nomographer
orthographer
osteographer
palæographer
petrographer
phonographer
photographer
psalmographer
selenographer
sphenographer

stenographer
topographer
typographer
xylographer
zincographer
zoographer

OI′a-b'l

employable
enjoyable

OI′al-i

loyally
royally

OI′al-ist

loyalist
royalist

OI′al-izm

loyalism
royalism

OI′al-ti

loyalty
royalty
viceroyalty

Ō′i-kal

egoical
heroical
stoical

OIN′ted-li

disjointedly
pointedly

OIS′tur-ing

cloistering
roistering

ŎJ′en-i

abiogeny
anthropogeny
biogeny
embryogeny
ethnogeny
geogeny
heterogeny
histogeny
homogeny
hymenogeny
misogyny
monogeny
odontogeny
ontogeny
osteogeny
pathogeny
philogyny
photogeny
phylogeny
progeny
protogyny
zoogeny

ŎJ′en-ist

abiogenist
biogenist
heterogenist
misogynist
monogenist
philogynist

ŎJ′en-us

endogenous
exogenous
hydrogenous
hypogynous
lithogenous
nitrogenous
pyrogenous
thermogenous

Ō′ji-an

archæologian
astrologian
gambogian
geologian
mythologian
neologian
philologian
theologian

ŎJ′i-kal

aërological
amphibiological
amphibological
analogical
anthological
anthropological
archæological
astrological
bibliological
biological
bryological
chronological
climatological
conchological
cosmological
craniological
demagogical
demonological
deontological
dialogical
doxological
Egpytological
etiological
etymological
genealogical
geological
glossological
glottological
homological
hydrological

ichnological
ideological
illogical
lithological
logical
mazological
metalogical
meteorological
mythological
necrological
neological
neurological
nosological
odontological
organological
ornithological
orological
osteological
palæontolog-
  ical
pantological
paralogical
penological
perissological
petrological
philological
phraseological
phrenological
physiological
phytological
pneumatologi-
  cal
pomological
psychological
selenological
semeiological
Sinological
sociological
spectrological
symbological
synagogical

tautological
technicological
technological
teleological
teratological
terminological
theological
toxicological
tropological
universological
zoological
zoophytological
zymological

ŎJ'on-i

autogony
cosmogony
geogony
pathogony
physiogony
theogony
zoogony

ŎJ'o-nist

cosmogonist
theogonist

ŌK'a-liz

focalize
localize
vocalize

ŌK'al-izm

localism
vocalism

ŎK'a-tiv

locative
invocative
provocative
vocative

ŌK'en-li

brokenly
outspokenly

ÔK'i-li

chalkily
gawkily
pawkily

ÔK'i-nes

chalkiness
gawkiness
pawkiness
squawkiness
talkiness

ŎK'i-nes

cockiness
rockiness
stockiness

ŎK'ra-si

aristocracy
arithmocracy
autocracy
cottonocracy
democracy
demonocracy
despotocracy
gerontocracy
gynæcocracy
hagiocracy
hierocracy
hypocrisy
idiocrasy
logocracy
mobocracy
monocracy
neocracy
nomocracy
ochlocracy

pantisocracy
pedantocracy
plantocracy
plousiocracy
plutocracy
shopocracy
slavocracy
snobocracy
stratocracy
theocracy
theocrasy
timocracy

ŎK'ra-tizm

democratism
Socratism

ŎK'ro-mi

heliochromy
metallochromy
monochromy
stereochromy

ŎK'ron-us

isochronous
tautochronous

ŎK'si-kal

orthodoxical
paradoxical
toxical

ŎK'tor-ship

doctorship
proctorship

ŎK'u-lar

binocular
jocular
locular
monocular

ocular
vocular

ŎK'ur-i
crockery
mockery
rockery

ŌL'a-b'l
consolable
controllable
rollable
tollable

ŎL'a-b'l
enthrallable
recallable

ŌL'a-ri
bolary
cajolery
polary
solary
volary

ŌL'ar-iz
polarize
solarize

ŎL'a-tri
anthropolatry
astrolatry
bibliolatry
cosmolatry
demonolatry
geolatry
gyneolatry
heliolatry
hierolatry
ichthyolatry
idiolatry

idolatry
litholatry
lordolatry
Mariolatry
necrolatry
ophiolatry
physiolatry
pyrolatry
symbolatry
thaumatolatry
topolatry
zoolatry

ŎL'a-trus
idolatrous
symbolatrous

ŎL'a-tur
bibliolater
heliolater
iconolater
idolater
Mariolater
pyrolater

ŌL'e-um
linoleum
petroleum
(cf. ŌL'i-um)

ŌL'ful-nes
dolefulness
soulfulness

Ō'li-a
Aetolia
magnolia
melancholia
Mongolia

Ō'li-an
Æolian

capitolian
Creolean
melancholian
metabolian
Mongolian
Pactolian
(cf. Napoleon)

ŌL'i-at
foliate
infoliate
spoliate

ŎL'id-li
solidly
squalidly
stolidly

ŎL'id-nes
solidness
squalidness
stolidness

Ō'li-est
holiest
lowliest

ŎL'i-fi
idolify
mollify
qualify

ŎL'i-fid
mollified
qualified
unqualified

ŎL'i-kal
apostolical
bibliopolical
catholical

diabolical
hyperbolical
parabolical
symbolical

ŎL'ik-som
frolicsome
rollicksome

Ō'li-nes
holiness
lowliness
shoaliness
unholiness

Ō'li-o
folio
olio
portfolio
Sapolio

ŎL'ish-ing
abolishing
demolishing
polishing

ŎL'ish-ur
abolisher
demolisher
polisher

ŎL'i-ti
equality
frivolity
inequality
interpolity
isopolity
jollity
polity
quality

ŌL'i-um

scholium
trifolium

Ō'li-ur

Grolier
holier
lowlier
olier
unholier

ŎL'i-vur

Oliver
Taliaferro
Tolliver

ŎL'o-gus

heterologous
homologous
isologous
tautologous

ŎL'o-ing

following
holloing
hollowing
swallowing
wallowing

ŎL'o-ji

actinology
adenochirapsol-
ogy
aerology
æsthematology
æsthesiology
agmatology
agriology
alethiology
amphibiology
amphibology

angelology
anthology
anthropology
aphnology
apology
arachnology
archæology
aretology
aristology
arteriology
asthenology
astrology
astrometeorol-
ogy
astro-theology
atomology
balneology
barology
battology
bibliology
biology
botanology
bromatology
brontology
bryology
bugology
cacology
campanology
cephalology
Christology
chromatology
chronology
climatology
conchology
conchyliology
cosmology
craniology
cryptology
dactyliology
dactylology
demonology

dendrology
deontology
dermatology
desmology
dialectology
dicæology
dittology
dosology
doxology
ecclesiology
eccrinology
Egyptology
electro-biology
electrology
electro-physi-
ology
embryology
emetology
emmenology
endemiology
enteradenology
enterology
entomology
entozoology
epidemiology
epistemology
eschatology
ethnology
ethology
etiology
etymology
filicology
fossilology
fungology
galvanology
gastrology
genesiology
geology
gigantology
glossology
glottology

gnomology
gnomonology
gynæcology
gypsology
hagiology
heterology
hierology
histology
historiology
homology
horology
hydrology
hyetology
hygiology
hygrology
hylology
hymenology
hymnology
hypnology
hysterology
ichnolithnology
ichnology
ichorology
ichthyology
iconology
ideology
insectology
kinology
laryngology
leptology
lexicology
lichenology
lithology
liturgiology
macrology
malacology
mantology
martyrology
mastology
mazology
membranology

ōld, ôr, ŏdd, oil, fŏŏt, out; ūse, ûrn, ŭp; THis, thin

menology
meteorology
methodology
metrology
miasmology
microgeology
micrology
misology
monadology
monology
morphology
muscology
mycology
myology
mythology
necrology
neology
nephrology
neurology
neurypnology
nomology
noölogy
nosology
numismatology
oceanology
odontology
ology
oneirology
onology
onomatology
ontology
oology
ophiology
ophthalmology
orchidology
organology
orismology
*ornithichnol-
ogy*
ornithology
orology

osmonosolgy
osteology
otology
ovology
palæoëthnology
palæology
palæontology
palæophy-
tology
palæozoology
palætiology
pantheology
pantology
paradoxology
parasitology
parisology
paromology
parthenology
pathology
patronomatol-
ogy
penology
periodology
perissology
petrology
pharmacology
pharology
pharyngology
phenomenol-
ogy
philology
phlebology
phonology
photology
phraseolgy
phrenology
phycology
physiology
phytolithology
phytology

phytopathol-
ogy
phyto-
physiology
pneumatology
pneumology
pomology
ponerology
posology
potamology
protophytology
psilology
psychology
psychonosol-
ogy
pteridology
punnology
pyretology
pyritology
pyrology
quinology
runology
sarcology
seismology
selenology
sematology
semeiology
sinology
sitology
skeletology
sociology
somatology
soteriology
spasmology
speciology
spectrology
spermatology
spermology
splanchnology
splenology
statistology

stoichiology
stromatology
symbology
symptomatol-
ogy
synchronology
syndesmology
systematology
tautology
taxology
technology
teleology
teratology
terminology
termonology
testaceology
thanatology
theology
thereology
thermology
therology
threpsology
tidology
topology
toreumatology
toxicology
tropology
typology
universology
uranology
urology
uronology
vulcanology
zoology
zoophytology
zymology

ŎL'o-jist
aërologist
agriologist
anthropologist

apologist
archæologist
Assyriologist
battologist
biologist
campanologist
chronologist
conchologist
cosmologist
craniologist
crustaceologist
demonologist
dendrologist
deontologist
dermatologist
ecclesiologist
Egyptologist
electro-
    biologist
embryologist
entomologist
ethnologist
ethologist
etymologist
galvanologist
geologist
glossologist
glottologist
gypsologist
hagiologist
hierologist
histologist
horologist
hydrologist
hymnologist
hypnologist
ichthyologist
ideologist
lexicologist
lithologist
mantologist

martyrologist
mazologist
meteorologist
monologist
morphologist
mycologist
myologist
mythologist
necrologist
neologist
neurologist
noölogist
nosologist
numismatolo-
    gist
oneirologist
onomatologist
ontologist
oologist
ophiologist
orchidologist
ornithologist
orologist
osteologist
palæoethnolo-
    gist
palæologist
palæontologist
palætiologist
pantheologist
pantologist
pathologist
petrologist
pharmacologist
philologist
phonologist
photologist
phraseologist
phrenologist
physiologist

phytolitholo-
    gist
phytologist
phytopatholo-
    gist
pneumatologist
pomologist
pseudologist
psychologist
pteridologist
pyrologist
quinologist
runologist
saintologist
sarcologist
seismologist
sinologist
sociologist
symbologist
tautologist
technologist
teleologist
teratologist
theologist
thereologist
therologist
toxicologist
universologist
vulcanologist
zoologist
zymologist, etc.

ŎL'o-jiz

apologize
astrologize
battologize
doxologize
entomologize
etymologize
geologize
mythologize

neologize
philologize
sociologize
tautologize
theologize
zoologize, etc.

ŎL'o-jur

acknowledger
astrologer
botanologer
etymologer
geologer
horologer
mythologer
osteologer
philologer
phonologer
phrenologer
physiologer
sockdolager
theologer

ÔL'o-ur

follower
hollower
swallower
wallower

ÔL'ti-est

faultiest
saltiest

ÔL'ti-nes

faultiness
maltiness
saltiness

ÔL'tur-ing

altering
faltering

paltering
unaltering
unfaltering

ÔL'tur-ur
alterer
falterer
palterer

ÔL'u-b'l
insoluble
soluble
voluble

ÔL'u-tiv
solutive
supervolutive
(cf. evolutive,
   revolutive)

ÔL'va-b'l
absolvable
dissolvable
indissolvable
insolvable
resolvable
solvable

ÔL'ven-si
insolvency
revolvency
solvency

ŎM'ak-i
alectryomachy
gigantomachy
iconomachy
logomachy
monomachy
psychomachy

sciomachy
theomachy

ŎM'ath-i
chrestomathy
philomathy

Ŏ'ma-tizm
achromatism
chromatism
diplomatism

ŎM'en-a
antilegomena
paralipomena
phenomena
prolegomena

ŎM'en-on
phenomenon
prolegomenon

ŎM'e-tri
barometry
biometry
chronometry
craniometry
eudiometry
galvanometry
gasometry
geometry
goniometry
helicometry
horometry
hydrometry
hygrometry
hypsometry
Mahometry
micrometry
odometry
orthometry

ozonometry
pathometry
photometry
planometry
pneumometry
polygonometry
pyrometry
rheometry
saccharometry
seismometry
stereometry
stichometry
stoichiometry
trigonometry

ŎM'e-tur
absorptiometer
actinometer
altometer
astrometer
audiometer
barometer
bathometer
cephalometer
chartometer
chromatometer
chronometer
clinometer
craniometer
declinometer
dendrometer
drosometer
dynamometer
echometer
electrometer
endosmometer
eudiometer
galvanometer
geometer
geothermo-
   meter

goniometer
graphometer
heliometer
horometer
hydrometer
hygrometer
hypsometer
lactometer
logometer
macrometer
magnetometer
micrometer
micronometer
monometer
nauropometer
odometer
oleometer
ombrometer
optometer
ozonometer
pantometer
pedometer
phonometer
photometer
piezometer
planometer
platometer
pluviometer
pneumatometer
pulsometer
pyrometer
radiometer
refractometer
rheometer
saccharometer
salinometer
seismometer
sonometer
spectrometer
speedometer
spherometer

stereometer
stethometer
stratometer
tachometer
tannometer
thermometer
tribometer
trochometer
udometer
vinometer
volumenometer
zymometer

ǑM'ik-al
anatomical
agronomical
astronomical
atomical
comical
coxcombical
domical
economical
iconomachal
tragi-comical
zootomical

ǑM'in-al
abdominal
cognominal
nominal
prenominal
surnominal

ǑM'in-ans
dominance
predominance
prominence

ǑM'in-ant
dominant
predominant

prominent
subdominant
superdominant

ǑM'i-nat
abominate
agnominate
comminate
denominate
dominate
nominate
ominate
predominate
prenominate

ǑM'in-i
Chickahomini
dominie
hominy
(cf. Romany)

ǑM'in-us
abdominous
dominus
ominous
prolegomenous

ǑM'ur-us
glomerous
isomerous

ŌN'a-b'l
loanable
tonable
unatonable

ǑN'dur-ing
pondering
squandering
unwandering
wandering

ǑN'dur-ur
ponderer
squanderer
wanderer

ǑN'el-i
Connolly
Donnelly

Ō'ni-a
Adonia
ammonia
Ansonia
Antonia
aphonia
begonia
bryonia
Donia
Fredonia
Ionia
Laconia
Latonia
Patagonia
pneumonia
Slavonia
Sonia
Sophronia
valonia

Ō'ni-ak
demoniac
simoniac

Ō'ni-al
baronial
ceremonial
colonial
demonial
intercolonial
matrimonial
monial

oxygonial
patrimonial
sanctimonial
testimonial

Ō'ni-an
Aberdonian
Amazonian
Ammonian
Aonian
Ausonion
Babylonian
Baconian
bezonian
Caledonian
Cameronian
Catonian
Chelonian
Chthonian
Ciceronian
colophonian
Cottonian
Daltonian
demonian
Devonian
Draconian
Etonian
Favonian
Gorgonean
Grandisonian
halcyonian
Heliconian
Ionian
Johnsonian
Laconian
Lapponian
Livonian
Macedonian
Miltonian
Myrmidonian
Neronian

Newtonian
Oxonian
Patagonian
Plutonian
Pyrrhonian
Sardonian
Serbonian
Simonian
Slavonian
Thessalonian

ŎN'i-est
brawnies
tawniest

ŎN'i-fi
personify
saponify
(cf. ozonify)

ŎN'i-ka
harmonica
veronica

ŎN'i-kal
acronycal
antichronical
antiphonical
architectonical
Babylonical
canonical
chronicle
conical
diaphonical
euphonical
geoponical
harmonical
iconical
ironical
Sorbonical
synchronical

tautophonical
thrasonical
tonical
uncanonical

ŎN'i-kon
chronicon
harmonicon

ŎN'i-mi
homonymy
metonymy
paronymy
polyonymy
synonymy
(cf. ŎN'o-mi)

ŎN'i-mus
anonymous
autonomous
eponymous
heteronymous
homonymous
paronymous
polyonymous
pseudnymous
synonymous

ŎN'ish-ing
admonishing
astonishing
monishing

ŎN'ish-ment
admonishment
astonishment
premonishment

ŎN'i-sizm
histrionicism

laconicism
Teutonicism

Ō'ni-um
harmonium
pandemonium
pelargonium
stramonium
zirconium

Ō'ni-us
acrimonious
alimonious
Antonius
ceremonious
erroneous
euphonious
felonious
harmonious
inharmonious
matrimonious
parsimonious
querimonious
sanctimonious
simonious
symphonious
Trebonius
ultroneous

ŎN'o-graf
chronograph
monograph
(cf. phono-
   graph)

ŎN'o-mi
agronomy
astronomy
autonomy
dactylonomy
Deuteronomy

economy
gastronomy
heteronomy
isonomy
morphonomy
taxonomy

ŎN'o-mist
agronomist
autonomist
economist
eponymist
gastronomist
synonymist

ŎN'o-miz
astronomize
economize
gastronomize

ŎN'o-mur
astronomer
gastronomer

ŎŎD'i-nes
woodiness
(cf. ŪD'i-nes)

ŎŎK'ur-i
bookery
cookery
rookery

Ō'o-lit
oolite
zoolite

ŎŎM'an-li
womanly
(cf. Ū'man-li)

āle, câre, ădd, ärm, åsk; mē, hẹre, ĕnd; īce. ĭll;

ŎP′ath-i
allopathy
enantiopathy
heteropathy
homœopathy
hydropathy
ideopathy
isopathy
neuropathy
psychopathy
somnopathy
theopathy

ŎP′ath-ist
allopathist
homœopathist
hydropathist
hylopathist
osteopathist
somnopathist

Ō′pi-a
Ethiopia
myopia
presbyopia
Utopia

Ō′pi-an,
  Ō′pe-an
Aesopian
Esopian
Ethiopian
Fallopian
Utopian

ŎP′i-kal
allotropical
metoposcopical
microscopical
misanthropical
sub-tropical

topical
tropical

ŎP′i-nes
dopiness
ropiness
slopiness
soapiness

ŎP′i-nes
choppiness
sloppiness
soppiness

ŎP′ish-nes
dopishness
mopishness
popishness

ŎP′o-lis
acropolis
cosmopolis
Heliopolis
metropolis
necropolis

ŎP′o-list
bibliopolist
monopolist
pharmacopolist

ŎP′o-lit
cosmopolite
metropolite

ŎP′si-kal
dropsical
mopsical
Popsicle

ŎP′ti-kal
autoptical
optical

ŎP′tur-us
lepidopterous
macropterous
orthopterous

ŎP′u-lat
copulate
populate

ŎP′ur-i
dopery
popery
ropery

ŎP′ur-i
coppery
foppery

ŌR′a-b'l
adorable
deplorable
explorable
restorable

ŌR′a-tiv
explorative
restorative

ÔR′di-al
cordial
exordial
primordial

ÔR′di-nat
co-ordinate
foreordinate
insubordinate
ordinate
subordinate

ÔR′di-on,
  ÔR′di-an
accordion
Gordian

ÔR′dur-ing
bordering
ordering

ÔR′e-at
aureate
baccalaureate
laureate
poet-laureate

ÔR′e-ol
aureole
laureole

ÔR′gon-iz,
  ÔR′gan-iz
gorgonize
organize

Ō′ri-a
aporia
Astoria
Castoria
dysphoria
euphoria
Gloria
Honoria
infusoria
littoria
Peoria
phantasma-
  goria
Pretoria
scoria
victoria

Ō′ri-al
accessorial
accusatorial
adaptorial
admonitorial

amatorial
ambassadorial
ancestorial
arboreal
armorial
accessorial
auditorial
authorial
boreal
censorial
commentatorial
compromis-
  sorial
compurgatorial
consistorial
corporeal
cursorial
dedicatorial
dictatorial
directorial
disquisitorial
editorial
electorial
emporial
equatoreal
escritorial
executorial
expurgatorial
exterritorial
extraterritorial
factorial
fossorial
gladiatorial
grallatorial
gressorial
gubernatorial
historial
immemorial
imperatorial
improvisatorial
incorporeal

infusorial
inquisitorial
insessorial
intercessorial
inventorial
legislatorial
manorial
marmoreal
mediatorial
memorial
mentorial
monitorial
motorial
oratorial
phantasma-
  gorial
pictorial
piscatorial
preceptorial
prefatorial
proctorial
procuratorial
professorial
proprietorial
protectorial
purgatorial
raptorial
rasorial
rectorial
reportorial
risorial
sartorial
scansorial
sectorial
seigniorial
senatorial
sensorial
spectatorial
speculatorial
sponsorial
suctorial

territorial
textorial
tinctorial
tonsorial
tutorial
uxorial
victorial
visitatorial

Ō′ri-an

amatorian
Bosphorian
censorian
consistorian
dictatorian
Dorian
gladiatorian
Gregorian
Hectorean
historian
hyperborean
marmorean
mid-Victorian
Nestorian
oratorian
prætorian
purgatorian
salutatorian
senatorian
stentorian
valedictorian
Victorian

Ō′ri-at

excoriate
professoriate

ŎR′id-li

floridly
horridly
torridly

Ō′ri-fi

glorify
scorify

ŎR′i-fi

historify
horrify
torrefy

ŎR′i-kal

allegorical
categorical
coracle
historical
metaphorical
oracle
oratorical
pictorical
rhetorical
tautegorical

ŌR′i-nes

desultoriness
dilatoriness
goriness
hoariness
peremptoriness

Ō′ri-ol

gloriole
gloryhole
oriole

ŎR′i-ti

anteriority
authority
deteriority
exteriority
inferiority
interiority
juniority

---

majority
meliority
minority
posteriority
priority
seniority
sorority
superiority

Ō′ri-um
aspersorium
auditorium
ciborium
corium
crematorium
digitorium
emporium
fumatorium
haustorium
inclinatorium
moratorium
prætorium
prospectorium
sanatorium
scriptorium
sensorium
sudatorium
suspensorium
thorium
triforium

Ō′ri-us
amatorious
arboreous
censorious
circulatorious
desultorious
expiatorious
expurgatorious
glorious
hippicanorious

inglorious
inquisitorious
laborious
lusorious
meritorious
notorious
oratorious
purgatorious
raptorious
saltatorious
scorious
senatorious
stentorious
stertorious
suctorious
uproarious
ustorious
uxorious
vainglorious
victorious

ŎR′ma-tiv
afformative
dormitive
formative
informative
reformative
transformative

ŎR′mi-ti
abnormity
conformity
deformity
enormity
inconformity
multiformity
noncomformity
uniformity

ŎR′o-ing
borrowing
sorrowing

ŎR′o-ur
borrower
sorrower

**ŌRS′a-b′l,
   ŌRS′i-b′l**
divorceable
enforceable
forcible

ŎR′ti-fi
fortify
mortify

ŎRT′i-kal
cortical
vortical

ŎRT′i-nes
swartiness
wartiness

ŌRT′li-nes
courtliness
portliness
uncourtliness

ŎR′tu-nat
fortunate
importunate

Ō′rus-li
decorously
porously
sonorously

ŎR′yus-li
gloriously
ingloriously
laboriously
meritoriously

notoriously
stentoriously
uproariously
uxoriously
vaingloriously
victoriously

ŎS′for-us
Bosphorus
phosphorus

Ō′shi-an
Bœotian
Nicotian
(cf. Ō′shun)

Ō′shun-al
devotional
emotional
notional

Ō′shus-nes
atrociousness
ferociousness
precociousness

ŎS′i-nat
patrocinate
ratiocinate

ŎS′i-nes
drossiness
glossiness
mossiness

ŎS′i-ti
paucity
raucity

ŎS′i-ti
actuosity

anfractuosity
angulosity
animosity
anonymosity
aquosity
atrocity
caliginosity
callosity
carnosity
curiosity
docity
dubiosity
ebriosity
fabulosity
ferocity
foliosity
fuliginosity
fumosity
fungosity
furiosity
gemmosity
generosity
gibbosity
glandulosity
glebosity
globosity
glutinosity
grandiosity
gulosity
gummosity
hideosity
impecuniosity
impetuosity
ingeniosity
inunctuosity
libidinosity
litigiosity
lugubriosity
luminosity
monstrosity
muscosity

musculosity
nebulosity
negotiosity
nervosity
nodosity
oleosity
otiosity
pilosity
plumosity
pomposity
ponderosity
porosity
preciosity
precocity
pretiosity
reciprocity
religiosity
ridiculosity
rimosity
rugosity
sabulosity
saporosity
scirrhosity
scrupulosity
sensuosity
serosity
sinuosity
speciosity
spicosity
spinosity
tenebrosity
torosity
tortuosity
tuberosity
tumulosity
unctuosity
varicosity
velocity
verbosity
viciosity
villosity

vinosity
virtuosity
viscosity
vitiosity
vociferosity

Ō'siv-nes

corrosiveness
explosiveness

ŎS'ko-pi

cranioscopy
geloscopy
geoscopy
hieroscopy
horoscopy
meteoroscopy
metoposcopy
omoplatoscopy
oneiroscopy
organoscopy
ornithoscopy
retinoscopy
stereoscopy
stethoscopy
uranoscopy

ŎS'ko-pist

metoposcopist
microscopist
oneiroscopist
ornithoscopist
stereoscopist
stethoscopist

ŎS'of-i

gymnosophy
philosophy
psilosophy
theosophy

ŎS'o-fist

chirosophist
deipnosophist
gymnosophist
philosophist
theosophist

ŎS'o-fiz

philosophize
theosophize

ŎS'o-fur

philosopher
psilosopher
theosopher

Ō'ta-b'l

floatable
notable
potable
quotable
votable

Ō'tal-izm

sacerdotalism
teetotalism

ŎT'an-i

botany
botonee
cottony
monotony

Ō'ta-ri

notary
rotary
votary

Ō'ta-tiv

connotative

denotative
rotative

Ō T′ed-li
bloatedly
devotedly
notedly

ô T′i-est
haughtiest
naughtiest

ŏ T′i-kal
anecdotical
bigotical
despotical
erotical
exotical
zealotical

ô T′i-li
haughtily
naughtily

ô T′i-nes
haughtiness
naughtiness

ŏ T′i-nes
dottiness
knottiness
spottiness

ô T′i-ur
haughtier
naughtier

ŏ T′om-i
apotome
bottomy
bronchotomy

dermotomy
dichotomy
encephalotomy
ichthyotomy
phlebotomy
phytotomy
scotomy
stereotomy
tracheotomy
zootomy

ŏ T′o-mist
ichthyotomist
phlebotomist
phytotomist
zootomist

ô T′ur-i
cautery
watery

ŏ T′ur-i
lottery
pottery
tottery
trottery

ŏ T′ur-ing
slaughtering
watering

ŏ T′ur-ur
slaughterer
waterer

OU′a-b′l
allowable
avowable
endowable

OUD′ed-nes
cloudedness

crowdedness
overcrowded-
  ness
uncloudedness

OUD′i-izm
dowdyism
rowdyism

OUD′i-nes
cloudiness
dowdiness
rowdiness

OUL′ur-i
owlery
prowlery

OUND′a-b′l
compoundable
soundable
unsoundable

OUND′ed-nes
astoundedness
confounded-
  ness
dumfounded-
  ness
unboundedness
ungrounded-
  ness

OUND′les-li
boundlessly
groundlessly
soundlessly

OUND′les-nes
boundlessness

groundlessness
soundlessness

OUNT′a-b′l
countable
discountable
insurmountable
mountable
surmountable
unaccountable

OUT′i-nes
doughtiness
droughtiness
goutiness

OU′ur-i
bowery
dowery
flowery
glowery
lowery
showery
towery
(cf. OUR′i)

OU′ur-ing
cowering
dowering
empowering
flowering
glowering
lowering
overpowering
overtowering
showering
towering
(cf. OUR′ing)

OUZ′i-nes
drowsiness
frowziness

ōld, ôr, ŏdd, oil, fŏŏt, out; ūse, ûrn, ŭp; THis, thin

ŎV′el-ing
grovelling
hovelling

Ō′vi-al
jovial
synovial

Ō′vi-an
Cracovian
Jovian

Ō′zhi-a, Ō′zi-a
ambrosia
symposia
(cf. Theodosia)

Ō′zhi-al, Ō′zi-al
ambrosial
roseal

O′zhi-an,
   Ō′zi-an
ambrosian
(cf. Ō′zhun)

Ō′zi-est
coziest
nosiest
prosiest
rosiest

Ō′zi-li
cozily
nosily
prosily
rosily

Ō′zi-nes
coziness
doziness
nosiness
prosiness
rosiness

Ō′zi-ur
cozier

crosier
Dozier
hosier
nosier
osier
prosier
rosier

Ō′zur-i
composery
dozery
rosary
(not hosiery)

U

For a discussion of words included under the accented vowels
following, see the beginning of U rhymes in Section I.

Ū′a-b'l
doable
pursuable
renewable
reviewable
suable
subduable

Ū′bi-an
Danubian
Nubian
rubian

Ū′bi-kal
cubical
cherubical

Ū′bi-lat
enubilate

jubilate
nubilate
obnubilate
volubilate

ŬB′i-nes
chubbiness
grubbiness
scrubbiness
shrubbiness
stubbiness

Ū′bi-us
dubious
rubious

Ū′bri-kat
lubricate
rubricate

Ū′bri-us
insalubrious
lugubrious
salubrious

Ū′bur-us
protuberous
suberous
tuberous

ŬD′a-b'l
alludable
deludable
includable
protrudable

ŬD′en-si
concludency

pudency
recrudency

ŪD′i-b'l
eludible
includible

ŬD′i-li
bloodily
muddily
ruddily

Ū′di-nal
aptitudinal
attitudinal
consuetudinal
longitudinal
testudinal

ŪD'i-nes
moodiness
(cf. ŌOD'i-nes)

ŬD'i-nes
bloodiness
muddiness
ruddiness

Ū'di-niz
attitudinize
platitudinize

Ū'di-nus
fortitudinous
latitudinous
multitudinous
paludinous
platitudinous
solicitudinous
vicissitudinous

Ū'di-ti
crudity
nudity
rudity

Ū'di-us
preludious
studious

ŬD'ur-i
duddery
shuddery
studdery

Ū'el-ing
bejewelling
duelling
fueling
gruelling

Ū'el-ur
crueller
dueller
fueller
jeweller

ŬF'i-nes
fluffiness
huffiness
puffiness
stuffiness

ŬG'ur-i
pugaree
snuggery
thuggery

Ū'i-nes
dewiness
glueyness

Ū'in-us
pruinous
ruinous

Ū'ish-nes
Jewishness
shrewishness

Ū'i-ti
acuity
ambiguity
annuity
assiduity
circuity
conspicuity
contiguity
continuity
discontinuity
exiguity
fatuity

gratuity
ingenuity
innocuity
perpetuity
perspicuity
promiscuity
strenuity
suety
superfluity
tenuity
vacuity

Ū'i-tus
circuitous
fatuitous
fortuitous
gratuitous
pituitous

ŪJ'i-nus
æruginous
ferruginous
lanuginous
salsuginous

ŬK'i-li
luckily
pluckily

ŬK'shun-al
constructional
fluxional
inductional
instructional

ŬK'shun-ist
constructionist
destructionist
fluxionist

ŬK'ti-b'l
conductible

destructible
indestructible
instructible

ŬK'tiv-li
constructively
destructively
instructively
productively

ŬK'tiv-nes
constructive-
    ness
destructiveness
instructiveness
productiveness

ŬK'to-ri
conductory
introductory
reproductory

Ū'ku-lent
luculent
muculent
(cf. succulent)

ŬK'ur-ing
puckering
succoring

Ū'le-an
cerulean
herculean
Julian

ŪL'ish-nes
foolishness
mulishness

Ū'li-ti
credulity

garrulity
incredulity
sedulity

ŬL'ki-nes
bulkiness
sulkiness

ŬL'mi-nant
culminant
fulminant

ŬL'mi-nat
culminate
fulminate

ŬL'siv-li
convulsively
impulsively
repulsively

ŬL'siv-nes
compulsiveness
convulsiveness
impulsiveness
repulsiveness
revulsiveness

ŬL'tur-i
adultery
consultary

ŬL'tur-ism
agriculturism,
  etc.
vulturism

ŬL'ur-i
gullery
medullary
scullery

ŬL'vur-in
culverin
pulverin

ŪM'a-b'l
assumable
consumable
presumable
resumable

Ū'man-li
humanly
(cf. womanly)

ŬM'bur-i
slumbery
umbery

ŬM'bur-ing
cumbering
encumbering
lumbering
numbering
outnumbering
slumbering
unslumbering

ŬM'bur-ur
cumberer
encumberer
lumberer
numberer
slumberer

Ū'mi-nant
illuminant
luminant
ruminant

Ū'mi-nat
acuminate

catechumenate
ferruminate
illuminate
luminate
ruminate

ŪM'i-nes
gloominess
roominess
spuminess

ŬM'ing-li
becomingly
benumbingly
hummingly
numbingly
unbecomingly

Ū'mi-nus
aluminous
bituminous
fluminous
leguminous
luminous
voluminous

ŬM'pish-nes
dumpishness
frumpishness
grumpishness
lumpishness
mumpishness

ŬMP'shus-li
bumptiously
scrumptiously

ŬMP'tu-us
presumptuous
sumptuous

Ū'mu-lat
accumulate
tumulate

Ū'mu-lus
cumulus
tumulous

Ū'mur-al
humeral
numeral

ŪM'ur-i
perfumery
plumery
rumory
(cf. roomery)

ŬM'ur-i
flummery
mummery
nummary
plumbery
summary
summery

Ū'mur-us
humerus
humorous
numerous
rumorous

ŪN'a-b'l
expugnable
tunable

Ū'na-ri
lunary
(cf. Ū'nur-i)

ŬN'di-ti
fecundity

āle, câre, ădd, ärm, åsk; mē, hẹre, ĕnd; īce, ĭll;

jocundity
jucundity
moribundity
profundity
rotundity
rubicundity

ŬN'dur-ing
blundering
plundering
sundering
thundering
wondering

ŬN'dur-song
undersong
wonder-song

ŬN'dur-ur
blunderer
plunderer
sunderer
thunderer
wonderer

ŬN'dur-us
blunderous
thunderous
wonderous

ŬN'dur-world
under-world
wonder-world

ŬNG'gur-ing
hungering
mongering

ŬNGK'shun-al
conjunctional
functional

ŬNGK'u-lar
avuncular
carbuncular
caruncular
peduncular
uncular

Ū'ni-kat
communicate
excommunicate
tunicate

Ū'ni-form
cuniform
luniform
uniform

ŬN'i-li
funnily
sunnily

Ū'ni-ti
community
immunity
importunity
impunity
inopportunity
intercommu-
nity
jejunity
opportunity
triunity
unity

Ū'ni-tiv
punitive
unitive

ŬNT'ed-li
affrontedly

stuntedly
unwontedly
wontedly

ŬN'ur-i
buffoonery
cocoonery
pantaloonery
poltroonery

ŬN'ur-i
gunnery
nunnery

Ū'pur-at
recuperate
vituperate

Ū'ra-b'l
assurable
curable
durable
endurable
incurable
insurable
procurable
securable

ŬR'a-b'l
conferrable
demurrable
inferable
referable
transferable

Ū'ral-ist
ruralist
(cf. pluralist)

Ū'ral-ism
ruralism
(cf. pluralism)

Ū'ra-tiv
curative
depurative
indurative
maturative

ŬR'bal-ist
herbalist
verbalist

ŬR'bal-izm
herbalism
verbalism

ŬRB'i-al
adverbial
proverbial
suburbial

ŬR'bu-lent
herbulent
turbulent

ŬR'di-li
sturdily
wordily

ŬRD'ur-ur
murderer
verderer

ŬR'en-si
concurrency
currency
recurrency

ŬR'et-ed
turreted
(cf. ĔR'i-ted)

ŬR'flu-us
subterfluous
superfluous

Ū'ri-a
Lemuria
Manchuria

Ū'ri-al
augurial
figurial
mercurial
purpureal
seigneurial

ŪR'i-an
Ū'ri-an
centurian
Etrurian
Missourian
scripturian
Silurian

Ū'ri-ans
luxuriance

Ū'ri-ant
luxuriant

Ū'ri-at
infuriate
luxuriate
muriate
parturiate

Ū'ri-ens
prurience

Ū'ri-ent
esurient
parturient
prurient
scripturient

ŪR'i-est
furriest

hurriest
worriest

Ū'ri-fi
purify
thurify

ŪR'i-ing
currying
flurrying
hurrying
scurrying
worrying

ŪR'i-ment
worriment
(cf. ĔR'i-ment)

ŪR'ish-ing
flourishing
nourishing

Ū'ri-ti
demurity
immaturity
impurity
insecurity
maturity
obscurity
prematurity
purity
security

ŪR'i-ur
currier
flurrier
furrier
hurrier
scurrier
worrier

Ū'ri-us
curious

furious
incurious
injurious
luxurious
penurious
perjurious
spurious
strangurious
sulphureous
usurious

ŪR'jen-si
assurgency
convergency
detergency
divergency
emergency
insurgency
urgency
vergency

ŪR'ji-kal
chirurgical
clergical
demiurgical
energical
liturgical
surgical
thaumaturgical
theurgical

ŪR'jur-i
chirurgery
perjury
purgery
surgery

ŪR'ku-lar
circular
furcular
tubercular

ŪR'ku-lat
circulate
tuberculate

ŪR'ku-lus
surculus
surculous
tuberculous

ŪR'li-est
burliest
churliest
curliest
earliest
pearliest
surliest

ŪR'li-nes
burliness
curliness
earliness
pearliness
surliness

ŪR'lish-li
churlishly
girlishly

ŪR'lish-nes
churlishness
girlishness

ŪR'mi-nal
germinal
terminal

ŪR'mi-nant
determinant
germinant
terminant

ŪR'mi-nat
determinate

exterminate
germinate
indeterminate
interminate
terminate

ŬR′mi-nus
coterminous
terminus
verminous

ŬR′na-b'l
burnable
discernible
indiscernible
learnable
overturnable
returnable

ŬR′nal-ist
eternalist
journalist

ŬR′nal-iz
eternalize
externalize
journalize

ŬR′nal-izm
externalism
infernalism
journalism

ŬR′ni-an
Avernian
Falernian
Hibernian
Saturnian

ŬR′nish-ing
burnishing
furnishing

ŬR′nish-ur
burnisher
furnisher

ŬR′ni-ti
alternity
diuternity
eternity
fraternity
maternity
modernity
paternity
sempiternity
taciturnity

ŬR′nur-i
fernery
turnery

ŬR′o-gat
surrogate
(cf. ĔR′o-gat)

ŬR′pen-tin
serpentine
turpentine

ŬR′sa-ri
anniversary
aspersory
bursary
controversary
cursory
nursery
percursory

ŬR′shi-al
controversial
(cf. ŬR′shal)

ŬR′shi-an
Cistercian

lacertian
Persian
(also as
  ŬR′shan,
  ŬR′zhan)

ŬR′si-b'l,
  ŬR′sa-b'l
amerceable
conversable
conversible
coercible
immersible
incoercible
irreversible
reimbursable
reversible

ŬR′si-form
diversiform
ursiform
versiform

ŬR′siv-nes
coerciveness
detersiveness
discursiveness
excursiveness

ŬRth′les-nes
mirthlessness
worthlessness

ŬR′ti-tud
certitude
incertitude
inertitude

ŬR′van-si
conservancy
fervency

ŬR′va-tiv
conservative
curvative
enervative
observative
preservative
reservative

ŬR′zhun-ist
excursionist
immersionist
versionist

Ū′se-an, Ū′si-an
caducean
Confucian
Rosicrucian

Ū′sed′li
deucedly
lucidly
mucidly
pellucidly

Ū′sen-si
lucency
tralucency
translucency

Ū′shi-al
crucial
fiducial

Ū′shun-al
circumlocu-
  tional
constitutional
elocutional
evolutional
institutional
substitutional

Ū'shun-ist
circumlocution-
   ist
constitutionist
elocutionist
evolutionist
resolutionist
revolutionist

Ū'shun-ur
ablutioner
executioner
resolutioner
revolutioner

Ū'si-b'l
adducible
conducible
crucible
deducible
educible
inducible
irreducible
producible
reducible
seducible
traducible

Ū'siv-nes
abusiveness
allusiveness
conclusiveness
conduciveness
delusiveness
diffusiveness
effusiveness
exclusiveness
illusiveness
inconclusive-
   ness
inobtrusiveness

intrusiveness
obtrusiveness

ŬS'ki-li
duskily
huskily
muskily

ŬS'ku-lar
bimuscular
corpuscular
crepuscular
muscular

ŬS'ku-lus
corpusculous
crepusculous
musculous

Ū'so-ri
collusory
conclusory
delusory
elusory
exclusory
extrusory
illusory
lusory
prelusory
reclusory

ŬST'ful-i
distrustfully
lustfully
mistrustfully
trustfully

ŬST'i-b'l
adjustible
combustible
dustible

incombustible
(cf. bustable,
   etc.)

ŬS'ti-est
crustiest
dustiest
fustiest
gustiest
lustiest
mustiest
rustiest
trustiest

ŬS'ti-li
crustily
dustily
fustily
gustily
lustily
mustily
rustily
thrustily

ŬS'ti-nes
crustiness
dustiness
fustiness
gustiness
lustiness
mustiness
rustiness
trustiness

ŬS'tri-us
illustrious
industrious

ŬS'tur-ing
blustering
clustering

flustering
mustering

Ū'ta-b'l
commutable
computable
confutable
disputable
executable
immutable
imputable
incommutable
inscrutable
mootable
mutable
permutable
refutable
scrutable
suitable
transmutable

Ū'ta-tiv
commutative
confutative
disputative
imputative
putative
sputative
sternutative

Ū'te-us
beauteous
duteous
luteous

Ūth'ful-i
ruthfully
truthfully
youthfully

Ūth'ful-nes
truthfulness
youthfulness

āle,   câre,   ădd,   ärm,   åsk;   mē,   hĕre,   ĕnd;   īce,   ĭll;

Ūth′les-li

ruthlessly
truthlessly
youthlessly

ŬTH′ur-hood

brotherhood
motherhood

ŬTH′ur-i

brothery
mothery
smothery

ŬTH′ur-ing

brothering
mothering
smothering

ŬTH′ur-li

brotherly
motherly
southerly
unbrotherly
unmotherly

ŬTH′ur-lik

brotherlike
motherlike

Ū′ti-fi

beautify
brutify

Ū′ti-ful

beautiful
dutiful

Ū′ti-k′l, Ū′ti-kal

cuticle
latreutical
pharmaceutical
scorbutical
therapeutical

Ū′ti-ner

mutineer
scrutineer

Ū′ti-ni

mutiny
scrutiny

Ū′ti-nus

glutinous
mutinous
velutinous
scrutinous

ŬT′lur-i

cutlery
sutlery

ŬT′on-i

buttony
gluttony
muttony

Ū′tur-i

freebootery
fruitery
pewtery
rootery

ŬT′ur-ing

buttering
fluttering
guttering
muttering
spluttering
sputtering
stuttering
uttering

ŬT′ur-ur

butterer
flutterer
mutterer
splutterer
sputterer
stutterer
utterer

ŪV′a-b′l

approvable
immovable
improvable
irremovable
movable
provable
removable
reprovable

Ū′vi-al

alluvial
antediluvial
diluvial
effluvial
exuvial

fluvial
postdiluvial
pluvial

Ū′vi-an

antediluvian
diluvian
Peruvian
postdiluvian
Vesuvian

Ū′vi-us

Jupiter Pluvius
Vesuvius

Ū′za-b′l

amusable
confusable
diffusible
excusable
fusible
inexcusable
infusible
losable
transfusible
usable

Ū′zi-an

Carthusian
(cf. Ū′zhun)

ŬZ′i-nes

fuzziness
muzziness
wuzziness

ōld, ôr, ŏdd, oil, fŏŏt, out; ūse, ûrn, ŭp; THis, thin